Civic Discourse:
Multiculturalism, Cultural Diversity, and Global Communication

Civic Discourse for the Third Millennium

Michael H. Prosser, Ph.D., Series Editor

Civic Discourse: Multiculturalism, Cultural Diversity, and Global Communication Volume I
    K.S. Sitaram and Michael H. Prosser, editors

Forthcoming:

Civic Discourse: Intercultural, International, and Global Media Volume II
    Michael H. Prosser and K.S. Sitaram, editors

The Double Helix: Technology, Democracy, and Civic Discourse in the American Future
    Edward Wenk, Jr.

CIVIC DISCOURSE: MULTICULTURALISM, CULTURAL DIVERSITY, AND GLOBAL COMMUNICATION

coedited by
K. S. Sitaram, Ph.D.
Southern Illinois University-Carbondale

and

Michael H. Prosser, Ph.D.
Rochester Institute of Technology

Foreword by Tapio Varis, University of Tampere

Ablex Publishing Corporation
Stamford, Connecticut
London, England

Copyright © 1998 by Ablex Publishing Corporation

Printed in the United States of America

Library of Congress Cataloging-in-Publication Data

Civic discourse: multiculturalism, cultural diversity, and global communication / edited by K.S. Sitaram and Michael H. Prosser

    p. cm.—(Civic discourse for the third millenium ; v. 1)
    Includes bibliographical references and index.
    ISBN 1-56750-409-4 (cloth)   ISBN 1-56750-410-8 (paper)
I. Sitaram, K.S. II. Prosser, Michael H., 1936- . III. Series
HM258.C5348   1998
303.48′2—dc21

        98-28929
        CIP

Ablex Publishing Corporation
100 Prospect Street
P.O. Box 811
Stamford, Connecticut 06904-0811

Published in the U.K. and Europe by:
Ablex Publishing Corp. (U.K.)
38 Tavistock Street
Covent Garden
London WC2E 7PB
England

To the faculty of the Speech-Communication Department at the University of Hawaii-Manoa who encouraged me to establish the ICA Intercultural Division; the more than 25 colleagues from the USA and abroad who signed the petition to the ICA Board of Directors to approve the Intercultural Division; the more than 100 ICA members who attended the first organizational meeting at the 1970 ICA Conference at Minneapolis, Minnesota; and to my daughter, Kavitha, who in 1970 constantly reminded me that intercultural communication had become more important to me than my family life (and forgave me!)

K. S. Sitaram

To Michelle Prosser and Stephen Evans; Leo and Hope Prosser; Louis and Bernadette Prosser; Thurston Hanley and Mary Renstrom; Sabrina O'Hanleigh and William Cavins; Desiree Hanley; and Risa Hanley

Michael H. Prosser

Acknowledgments

We are especially grateful for our nearly thirty-year professional and friendly cooperative experiences together and welcome our recently co-chaired conferences which brought together such stimulating groups of authors as are found in this and the next two volumes. We have a particular interest in introducing young professional academic contributors to the study of intercultural, international, and global communication, as well as authors from diverse cultures and societies. We wish to extend our thanks to the authors whose essays appear herein, to Southern Illinois University at Carbondale on behalf of K. S. Sitaram, and to the Rochester Institute of Technology on the part of Michael Prosser, which through his Kern Professorship in Communications, 1994-1998, has been a most creative sponsor for his endeavors. Special thanks are owed to William J. Daniels, Dean of the College of Liberal Arts for his support toward creativity on the part of Michael Prosser. We are grateful to our wives: Vasantha Sitaram and Joan Ann Kirkeby-Prosser for their encouragement.

We wish to thank the independent jury panels who selected the awardees for the three Rochester Institute of Technology conferences: Barbara Kaye and James McOmber from Southern Illinois University at Carbondale, and Tim Engstrom, Paul Grebinger, M. Ann Howard, Peter Lalley, Joan Stone,and Janet Zandy from the Rochester Institute of Technology.-Sitaram's graduate assistant, Charles Kingsley, and Prosser's student assistants from 1994 to 1998; W. John Carl III, Pam Erwin, Heather Fleck, Jeremy Reichman, and Matthew Staub all have made contributions to the Rochester Institute of Technology summer conferences, as well as Yong Koo Bae, and/or to the three books which were initiated through the conferences. Ablex staff: Publisher, Herbert Johnson, Acquisitions Editor, Kim Burgos, and Book Production Manager, Michelle Manafy, all have been most helpful and we extend our thanks.

K. S. Sitaram, *Carbondale, Illinois*
Michael Prosser, *Rochester, New York*

CONTENTS

FOREWORD

Tapio Varis
University of Tampere

In the late 1960s, the world was deeply divided by the Cold War, particularly the war in South-East Asia. Growing student radicalism, increasing conflict between the rich centers of the North, and the developing countries of the South added to the unrest. Political tension rather than cultural understanding characterized world communications. International governmental organizations like UNESCO, which were based on the principle of "the intellectual and moral solidarity of mankind" and the utilization of communication between peoples "for the purposes of mutual understanding and a truer and more perfect knowledge of each other's lives," faced increasing difficulties in fulfilling their constitutional mandates.

Communication researchers were also affected by these developments. Only few understood the deeper structures of cultures and the need to develop intercultural communication skills. In 1966, Edmund Glenn and Edward Stewart began teaching one of the first university courses on intercultural communication at the University of Delaware. Glenn had been a U.S. Department of State interpreter and translator and Stewart had provided intercultural training for Peace Corps volunteers. David Hoopes had initiated a Regional Council at the University of Pittsburgh, which provided training and training materials for persons seeking to understand intercultural dimensions in their own work. Only now, when we are entering a new millennium, there seems to be a more general understanding of the importance of cultural diversities and intercultural communication. Many scholars take the idea of the clash between civilizations as the most serious threat to our future.

In 1969, Professor Sitaram and some of his colleagues initiated discussions about establishing a separate organization for studying intercultural communication. In 1970, more than 25 colleagues submitted a petition to the International Communication Association (ICA) Board of Directors to establish a separate Division for Intercultural Communication. Sitaram submitted a position paper titled: "Intercultural Communication: The What and Why of It." According to the

ICA Board of Directors at their meeting on May 6, 1970, in Minneapolis, Minnesota, the paper was presented to the Board. According to the minutes of the meeting, Darrell Piersol moved and Malcolm MacLean seconded that Division V be established as the Intercultural Communication Division. The motion carried—seven for and zero against. The board's positive response added this new division to its then "Four Basic Divisions" at ICA. Sitaram became the founding chair and 25 years later, he explained that although the "founders" did not have an acceptable definition of intercultural communication, they all knew that there was an important place for it in academic studies.

In 1971, the Speech Communication Association (SCA—now National Communication Association—NCA) selected Professor Michael Prosser as the founding Chair of its Commission on Intercultural and International Communication (later formed as a Division in SCA). With co-sponsorship of the Canadian Speech Communication Association and SCA, and the presidents of these two organizations, Grace Layman of Memorial University in Newfoundland and William Howell of the University of Minnesota present, Prosser chaired the first "consultation" on forming a field of intercultural communication at Indiana University, with 12 academics and 12 Indiana University graduate students meeting in Brown County State Park, Indiana. The group discussed various ingredients for establishing a field of intercultural communication, such as the need for undergraduate and graduate courses; graduate degrees with an emphasis on intercultural communication; the establishment of divisions in regional, national, and international communication organizations; publication of journal articles and texts; the creation of one or more journals or yearbooks; and conferences devoted to the subject. Later in 1973, Prosser chaired the first national conference on intercultural communication, sponsored by the University of Virginia, and then chaired the second national conference in 1994, cosponsored by SCA, ICA, and The Society for Intercultural Education, Training, and Research (SIETAR—which he also helped found). For the latter conference, Edward Stewart's "Outline of Intercultural Communication" was discussed and debated by more than 200 participants. Sitaram was an active participant in that conference.

In these early days, we did not have any text book in intercultural communication. However, several well known scholars, including Ithiel de Sola Pool, Edward T. Hall, Robert T. Oliver, Alfred G. Smith, Dell Hymes, Clifford Geertz, and Albert Mehrabian has already been working broadly in the general area of intercultural communication. ICA appointed George Gerbner as Editor of the *Journal of Communication (JC)*. The SCA *International and Intercultural Communication Annual* was inaugurated in 1974 under the editorship of Fred Casmir. Dan Landis initiated *The International Journal of Intercultural Relations (IJIR)* which became the official journal of SIETAR International until 1998. Various colleagues such as Edward Stewart, Edmund Glenn, Fred Casmir, Molefi Asante, Dennis Ogawa, Fathi Yusef, John C. Condon, William Howell, Beulah Rorlich, Nobleza Asuncion-Lande, K.S. Sitaram, and Michael Prosser were already teaching early courses on intercultural or interracial communication. Prosser taught the first Canadian university-level course on intercultural communication at Memorial University of Newfoundland in 1972. Now, there are hundreds of such courses in various universities and in a variety of countries.

I had my first public presentation on "Images and Stereotypes in Cross Cultural Relations and Problems in Global Broadcasting" at Ohio State University in 1971. I started my paper by saying that "the very first question one has to answer before approaching the field of international communication is what are or what should be the objectives of communication between nations?" I quoted Fred S. Siebert, who had written that the objective is "to make available to the peoples of the world the kind of communications content which will enable them to maintain a peaceful and productive society and which will also provide them with personal satisfaction." My question then was how well is this objective guaranteed in actual crosscultural communication? To my surprise, one of the distinguished listeners of my presentation was the internationally known communications scholar Professor Fred S. Siebert, who thanked me after my presentation and invited me for a luncheon that I will never forget. Peace and international understanding were very much the slogans of intergovernmental organizations, but these concepts attracted independent academic researchers as well. Now years later, Sitaram argues in his introduction to this book that some of us believe seeing a new beauty in the things that are different might bring about unity in this diverse world and, ultimately, lead to world peace.

As Professor Sitaram has noted, in the early days of developing intercultural communication as a field of study, we focused on studies of cultural differences, stereotyping, ethnocentrism, and in general, divergence. Now we are more likely to study cultural similarities, positive imaging, cultural relativism, and generally, convergence. The ideal of world peace has also figured more recently as a goal of intercultural communication.

The first texts containing intercultural, crosscultural, or interracial communication in their titles included, for example: Jon A. Blublaugh and Dorthy L. Pennington, *Crossing Differences: Interracial Communication* (1976); John C. Condon and Fathi Yousef, *An Introduction to Intercultural Communication* (1975); John C. Condon and Mitsuko Saito (eds), *Communicating Across Cultures for What? A Symposium on Humane Responsibility in Intercultural Communication* (1976); Carley H. Dodd, *Perspectives on Cross Cultural Communication* (1977); Heinz Dietrich-Fischer and John C. Merrill (eds.), *International and Intercultural Communication* (1976); L.S. Harms, *Intercultural Communication* (1973); David W. Hoopes (ed.), *Readings in Intercultural Communication* (1971, 1972, 1973, 1974, 1975); Michael H. Prosser, *The Cultural Dialogue: An Introduction to Intercultural Communication* (1978); Andrea Rich, *Interracial Communication* (1974); Sharon Ruhly, *Orientations to Intercultural Communication* (1976); Larry Samovar and Richard E. Porter (eds.), *Intercultural Communica-*

tion: A Reader (1972, 1976); and K.S. Sitaram and Roy T. Cogdell, *Foundations of Intercultural Communication* (1976).

We have indeed traveled a long way from interculturalism to multiculturalism and from intercultural broadcasting to the information superhighway. We have grown mature teaching intercultural related areas, but technology is making the world ever more interconnected and global. The editors of this book, K.S. Sitaram and Michael H. Prosser, themselves major founders in this field, invited other "founders" and other interested scholars to the Rochester Institute of Technology Conference, "Intercultural Communication: The Last 25 Years and the Next," in 1995 to discuss how intercultural teaching and research have changed our lives. Participants asked themselves what such studies have contributed to the lives and cultures around the world? Have our activities in this area had any impact on the efforts to bring about world peace? What directions should we give to studying this area in the next twenty-five years? Two other conferences were held at RIT, "Multiculturalism, Cultural Diversity, and Global Understanding" in 1996, and "Communication, Technology, and Cultural Values" in 1997. These three conferences are the genesis for three books being published by Ablex, this one, and two others: *Civic Discourse: Intercultural, International, and Global Media* and *Civic Discourse: Communication, Technology, and Cultural Values* both, co-edited by Sitaram and Prosser.

The time is now ripe for a new view of intercultural communication in the new media, digital communication, technology, and the cultural environment. The political debates of the 1970s and 1980s about whether a field such as intercultural communication actually exists and what should be the main content of such a field seem to be over and have worked in a therapeutic way. There is now a better understanding on all sides and a willingness to increase the information gap between cultures and nations, as well as a greater need for cooperation. A 1993 UNESCO document in the field of information and communication notes that profound changes are taking place in the political landscape of Europe and the world, as well as changes in UNESCO itself—as the major international communication facilitator. The document argues: "The end of ideological rivalries and divisions put to rest the bitter controversies of the past and made possible a new consensus on a strategy for the development of communication—a consensus of 161 Member States of UNESCO that accepted fully and without equivocation the fundamental principles of freedom of expression, freedom of the press, and the free flow of information by word and image." The new program calls upon UNESCO to work for the development of free, independent, and pluralistic media in both private and public sectors.

A new critical view is needed to analyze how the political and economic changes in the 1990s and early 2000s confirm these ideals of a free, independent, and pluralistic media. The UNESCO Constitution was drafted by an American poet and a British politician. After Germany and its Axis allies in World War II had demonstrated the power of the communication media in controlling society,

UNESCO's founders wrote into the organization's constitution a mandate to create a communication program that would advance the "understanding of peoples."

The philosophy and the Charter of the United Nations are essentially products of European civilization. They were clearly intended to reinvigorate contacts among peoples and nations with their humanistic principles and aspirations. The scholarly views of communication at the time of founding UNESCO were well reflected by the report of an unofficial organ, the commission on Freedom of the Press, generally known as the Hutchins Commission, with the concept of "peoples speaking to peoples." Communication was seen as a link for "all the habitable parts of the globe with abundant, cheap, significant, and true information about the world from day to day, so all men increasingly may have the opportunity to know, and understand each other." The Commission set several objectives concerning international communication. Major tasks would be to improve physical facilities and operating barriers and the lessening of economic restrictions for transmittal of communication internationally. An important objective was the improvement of the accuracy, representative character, and quality of the words and images transmitted through international communication.

The report also noted that the "surest antidote for ignorance and deceit is the widest possible exchange of objectively realistic information—true information, not merely more information." Many scholars have similarly questioned the success of a mere quantitative increase in the flow of words and images across cultural and national borders which might replace ignorance with prejudice and distortion rather than with more cultural understanding. In a world of an exponential growth in the amount of information, there is now more of a need than ever before to study the quality aspects of information flow and communication in an increasingly intercultural world. Consequently, the various founders of an academic field of study such as intercultural communication, and the many younger scholars who have followed and continue to follow these early developments, which have now become truly international in scope, deserve congratulations for their contributions to its study through this and other published books in the field. Thousands of scholars, teachers, students, crosscultural trainers, members of international businesses, and other interested persons in various countries will find many valuable ideas in an important books such as this one, and others to be published by Ablex in the series, *Civic Discourse for the Third Millennium.*

REFERENCES

The Commission on Freedom of the Press (1947). *A Free and Responsible Press: A General Report on Mass Communication: Newspaper, Radio, Motion Pictures, Magazines, and Books.* University of Chicago Press.

UNESCO (1993). *UNESCO Activities in the Matter of Free Flow of Information and Freedom of Expression.* UNESCO Communication Division.

PREFACE

After being professional colleagues in intercultural and international communication for more than twenty-five years, we hosted a conference in 1995 at the Rochester Institute of Technology on "Intercultural Communication: The Last Twenty-Five Years and the Next." Most of the papers included in the current volume or in the forthcoming volumes, *Civic Discourse: Intercultural, International, and Global Media* and *Civic Discourse: Communication, Technology, and Cultural Values* were presented in an earlier format either at this conference, or at the succeeding RIT conferences: "Multiculturalism, Cultural Diversity, and Global Understanding" in 1996 and "Communication, Technology, and Cultural Values" in 1997. Awards were given for outstanding papers at all three conferences: in 1995 to Kathy Brooks, John Bublic, Kenneth Day, and Shashi Nanjundiah; in 1996, to D. Ray Heisey, Elizabeth Lester and Usha Raman, Michael Maynard, and Young-ok Yum; and in 1997 to Sorin Matei, James McOmber, and Chris Stephenson. K.S. Sitaram served as keynoter for the 1995 conference, Nobleza Asuncion-Lande for the 1996 conference, and Tapio Varis for the 1997 conference. Conference Plenary roundtable members and speakers included Njoku Awa, Tom Bruneau, Kenneth Hadwiger, Michael Prosser, Susan Rogers, Tapio Varis, Juhani Wiio, and Vincenne Waxwood in 1995; plenary speakers D. Ray Heisey, Keith Jenkins, Elizabeth Kunimoto, and Tapio Varis in 1996; and Diane Hope, Ray Donahue, K.S. Sitaram, and Maria Larracuente in 1997.

While conversing together at the first conference (Sitaram and Prosser), we learned that we share the same birthday, March 29, and as such are both Aries. Both of us were pleased that part of the "spirit" of Aries suggests that we are "pioneers." We both like this designation, since each of us was influential in the early development of intercultural and international communication as a serious subject for study, as Tapio Varis has kindly noted in the foreword. Another joint connection is that each of us have been Fulbright awardees, Sitaram to India, and Prosser to Swaziland. Our ongoing efforts interculturally and internationally have led us to collaboration on three collections of essays intended for those interested in intercultural communication, multiculturalism, cultural diversity, international, and global communication/media, technology, and cultural values.

In our earlier books, in the infancy of the introduction of intercultural communication into the university curriculum, each of us attempted to set perimeters for the study of intercultural communication. Sitaram has been especially forceful, in both of his books, *Foundations of Intercultural Communication* and *Communication and Culture: A World View,* in leading his readers to understand the cognitive underpinnings of diverse cultural/philosophical/religious systems beyond the Western context, which has an impact on formulating processes for international development. He has long been a proponent of a world view in relation to interculturalists, media experts and participants, and development agents. Several of Prosser's books, *Intercommunication among Nations and Peoples,* *The Cultural Dialogue: An Introduction to Intercultural Communication,* and *Diplomatic Discourse: International Conflict at the United Nations: Addresses and Analysis,* have linked his interests as Asante, Blake, and Newmark suggest in their *Handbook of Intercultural Communication* as an advocate of the perspective of cultural dialogue as a view toward multiculturalism and globalism in contrast to the perspective of cultural criticism which tends to be comparatively cross cultural in nature as a critique of individual cultures and societies.

Civic Discourse: Multiculturalism, Cultural Diversity, and Global Communication is the first book of an entire new Ablex series, "Civic Discourse for the Third Millennium," for which Prosser is the series editor. The concept of the series links the role of civic discourse and communication to their connections to civil society, both domestically, and more broadly on a global basis. The forthcoming books in this series seek to provide authored books in some cases, and in other cases, edited collections of essays by diverse academic authors, demonstrating different methodological, disciplinary, and cultural contributions to the study of communication, individual cultures, international and developmental communication, in an increasingly global framework. The second and third books, both co-edited by Sitaram and Prosser, will be followed by various other books related to issues like cultural rhetorics and cultural logics, geographical communication developments, and topics relating to cultures and societies such as human rights, peace, health and disabilities as they impact civic discourse and civil society.

INTRODUCTION: MULTICULTURAL COMMUNICATION FOR A HIGHER HUMANITY

K. S. Sitaram
Southern Illinois University at Carbondale

The world has become multicultural. Educational institutions and world organizations should give equal importance to individuality as well as responsibility values and strive to develop the "Higher Humanity in the Third Millennium."

Although "intercultural communication" (IC) was offered as an area of academic inquiry in the late 1960s at the University of Hawaii and a few other American universities, not all educators had heard of it. Most of those who had heard of IC did not study this area seriously. The few professors who taught intercultural communication did not enjoy the same prestige bestowed upon those who specialized in such areas as "Communication Theory" and "Rhetoric." In other words, some of the Brahmins of the communication discipline treated interculturalists as untouchable.

We have come a long way. A library search conducted in 1995 showed several thousand entries of papers, reports, and other articles about intercultural communication. In 1995, the data about concepts such as culture, values, and beliefs found on the internet had occupied more than 20 megabytes of space. Recently, some American universities have begun to internationalize their curricula. A few years ago, the Fulbright Commission included intercultural communication in its list of areas for fellowships. The United States National Institute of Health has started a new program to study "Alternative Medicine" including medical systems of ancient African, Chinese, Hindu, Muslim and other cultures. Even predominantly monocultural yet highly advanced countries—such as Finland and Japan—have realized the importance of multicultural communication. Many universities

1

in the United States and other countries have established academic linkages that enable faculty, staff and student exchanges among themselves. Citizens in many countries have now taken the first step in intercultural communication, taking introductory courses in this area. Some of them have now realized the importance of the next step, "multicultural communication" (MC) which is a part of the area of study entitled *multiculturalism.* Multiculturalism can be defined as the modern way of living that requires the ability on the part of any modern person to understand, respect, and interact with members of different cultures, races, ethnic groups, and nationalities. One's education is incomplete unless one learns theories and skills of multicultural communication which is essential for success in business, politics, and social life in general. Accurate, unbiased, and complete information about multicultural communication is needed today more than ever before. Although data banks and the internet have become popular and easily accessible sources of information, they are not always free from ethnocentrism, Eurocentrism, and other biases. Just because multicultural information is derived from the internet, it does not always mean it is accurate and complete.

Multiculturalism is a positive attitude. Ideally, training in this area should begin at one's own home. Certain individuals do have an aptitude for multicultural communication, but others can learn its theories and skills through education. Peoples of many ancient cultures practiced multicultural communication millennia before academicians began studying it in this century. However, they did not call such communication intercultural or multicultural. Let us look at a few examples.

A FINNISH EXAMPLE

The second stanza of the *Kalevala*, the national epic of Finland, begins with the following invitation to experience the Finnish culture.

> Dearest friend, and much loved brother,
> Best loved of all companions,
> Come and let us sing together,
> Let us now begin our converse
> Since at length we meet together....
> Let us clasp our hands together
> Let us interlock our fingers
> Let us use our best endeavors. (Kirby, 1951, p. 1).

The *Kalevala* is the story of legendary heroes of the ancient land of Kaleva and it is told even today in folk songs and other traditional forms of oral communication by Karelians and others in several parts of Finland. These songs were collected, edited, and published in 1835 by Elias Lonrott, a Finnish physician-scholar. The story of Lonrott's journey into Russian Karelia to collect the songs is in itself an epic. He had to travel from Helsinki to Karelia, often by foot, and talk to folks who played kantele and sang the epic. This story was transmitted orally from generation to generation for many centuries in that part of Europe. In oral traditions, no two story tellers or singers "tell" the story the same way. Depending upon the taste of the audience of the day, each singer in his/her performance contributes a special meaning to the story. It is possible that several versions of this ancient story are still sung by the folks or rune singers in different parts of Finland, somewhat similar to the many versions of the *Ramayana* still performed in rural parts of India, Thailand, Cambodia, and Indonesia. An early collection of the Finnish epic (called *The Old Kalevala*) consisted of "some 1,500,000 lines of verse" (Magoun, 1969, p. xiii.). Lonrott, in 1835, adapted the orally transmitted story into the print medium and published it. Although the print version might have lost some of the charm of the oral tradition, it is now available to a large number of literate people. This printed version "appeared in its definitive form (called *The New Kalevala*) comprising of 22,795 lines" (Collinder, 1964, p. 11.).

Along with the *Mahabharata* of India and the *Iliad* of Greece, the *Kalevala* is an epic of all humanity. It is a beautiful example of multicultural communication since variations of this story have been instrumental, for many centuries, in building a cultural bridge among the peoples who lived in a large area from Lithuania and Estonia to Finland and Sweden. One of the presumed origins of the term "Kalevala" is the Lithuanian word "Kalvis" or the Latvian word "Kalejs" which means blacksmith (Magoun, 1969, pp. 295-6.), and a blacksmith is an important character in the legend of the *Kalevala*. It is the story of different people whose common goal was to uphold positive values and suppress negative ones. It is the story of heroes and villains, of the fight between righteousness and evil and the ultimate victory of the former. In other words, these are the people who strive to build a higher humanity and whose cultures integrate the values of individuality and responsibility.(Kirkinen & Silvo, 1984).

EAST-WEST DIVERGENCE

In a lecture, presented in 1957 at McGill University, Montreal, Canada, Barbara Ward cited an incident that occurred in ancient Greece. A group of Hindu philosophers traveled from India to Greece to talk to Socrates. They asked him what the main concern of Greek philosophy was.

Socrates said,

"Why, it has to do with all things human."
"How can you study anything human until you know what is Divine?" asked the Hindus.

Says Ward,

> "This anecdote gives a hint of the later divergence...The Greeks possessed an overwhelming curiosity about all things human, a belief expressed most fully in the philosophy of Aristotle....Intellectual search and scientific achievement—two hallmarks of the West—are implicit in the Greek approach." (Ward, 1957, p. 15.).

Expanding on the idea of an Eastern approach to intellectual search, Ward says:

> "The more I look at the historical record, the more it seems to me that events are irreducible and that some nations simply do not display behavior which can be wholly analyzed in predetermined and explicable terms. They play their part more in the spirit of the genius or the poet. They are uncomfortable subjects for the systematizer and the proponent of general law." (Ward, 1957, p. 18.).

Another difference between Eastern and Western ways of thinking is that the Easterner's thought process is non-linear or circular and the Westerner's is linear. Easterners believe there is no definite beginning or ending to any idea. What began today as a "brand new idea" had its origin in something that ended yesterday, and today's idea will begin a new one tomorrow. Such a circular model represents the integration of opposite forces. These concepts are explained more fully in the Karma philosophy of Hindus and the Yin-Yang philosophy of Chinese. The Chinese model explains the unity of bipolar variables such as light and shadow. Based on this never-ending process of communication, many theories about perception of reality were proposed by ancient Chinese and Hindus. Westerners, on the other hand, believe in communication as a linear process that has a definite beginning and an ending. Such a linear process begins with an information source—an anchor-person in a television station who encodes and transmits his/her message—and ends with the destination—a viewer who receives the message on his/her television set at home and decodes it. This theory is represented in the Shannon and Weaver's model of communication, often called "the mathematical theory of communication." (Shannon & Weaver, 1964). Shannon and Weaver explain how to calculate the ratio of signal and noise at the origin, as well as at the destination.

THE FOUR ENDS OF LIFE

Ward's story also indicates another important difference between eastern and western scholarship. While western philosophers place importance on the author and the originator of an idea, eastern philosophers did not do so. The easterners did not assume their "copyrights," even on the expressions of their ideas. They believed the idea was more important than the originator of the idea itself. We do know that some Hindu philosophers visited Socrates, but we do not know their names. This is one of the reasons why we do not have the names of the eastern originators of many important ideas. For example, ancient Hindus developed a paradigm of human needs and values which they called the Four Ends of Life or *the Four Purusharthas.*

According to this paradigm, the four basic needs of all humans are "Kama," the biological need; "Artha," the economic need; "Dharma," the ethical need; and "Moksha," the self-realization need. There are references to this paradigm in ancient Hindu epics such as the *Mahabharata* (Kitagawa, 1958, pp. 122-23.), but we do not know the one philosopher who originated the paradigm. Although Maharishi Vyasa, the legendary philosopher, first composed the *Mahabharata*, this story was being told in the oral form in many parts of south Asia. Vyasa transformed the epic from the oral form into the written form many centuries before Christ. The concept of the four ends of life that each person should strive to attain was well known to south Asians for many millennia. Eastern theories, such as the Purushartha theory, say the purpose of human interaction is to understand and improve one's own self while the Western theories, such as the Shannon and Weaver's, explain how to understand others and change their behaviors. Shannon and Weaver define communication as the process in which one mechanism affects the behavior of another mechanism (Shannon & Weaver, 1964, p 1). Hindus, on the other hand, define communication as the process of realizing one's own self—*Athma Sakshatkara.* Explaining self-realization as the goal of speech, Shankara of the eighth century says, "The wise should withdraw from speech into mind, from mind into reasoning, from reasoning into self..." (Chan, Faruqi, & Kitagawa, 1969, p. 33.). Clearly, Shankara's explanation had a philosophical, rather than a sociological, connotation.

Barbara Ward's views confirm the point I would like to expand upon here. Warriors such as Alexander the Great viewed cultural and political differences as conquerable. They tried to integrate different cultures and countries and impose their own values on others, but they failed. However, philosophers such as Socrates accepted cultural differences as facts of life and tried to understand and respect those differences. In his "Allegory of the Cave," Plato explains how some persons will never grow above the level of believing in their personal illusions as universal realities. However, others do realize that "the upward journey and the sight of things on the surface of the earth as the mind's ascent to the intelligible realm...is a prerequisite for intelligent conduct either of one's own private affairs or public business." (Waterfield, 1994, p. 244.).

SOME ANCIENT WORKS

Having conquered Persia in 327 BC, Alexander went to the borders of India and sent his spies to find out about the strengths and weaknesses of the Hindu emperor. The spies returned and reported that the Indian emperor, Chandra Gupta Maurya, not only commanded a powerful army, but he also ruled a people of great culture. His chief counselor, named Kautilya, was a formidable politician and author of the famous book about economics, political science and public administration—the *Arthashastra* (Sastry, 1967.). That book was used as a guide by many kings in south Asia. In addition, Alexander's soldiers were tired and wanted to go home. Being a skilled communicator trained under a famous teacher, Aristotle, Alexander acceded to his soldiers' request.

"Alexander had dreamed of building a great Hellenic empire in the East...But his dream never materialized." (Warshaw & Bromwell 1974, p. 12). As a result of Alexander's visit to the Indus valley, "Hellenistic thought and art spread to India." (Warshaw & Bromwell 1974, p. 32.). A new type of art called the Gandhara School, named after the city of Gandhara (situated along the Silk Route between ancient Greece and China), became popular. An example of the Gandhara art can be seen today in the Buddhist temple at Sarnath, as well as in the Ashoka wheel embedded in the Indian Republic's flag.

We know about Greek philosophers such as Socrates, Plato, and Aristotle. Why is it we do not know names such as Jaimini, Kautilya, and Panini? Kautilya was the author of the *Arthashastra*, written before 327 BC. In the sixth century BC, Jaimini wrote a book on linguistics entitled the *Poorva Mimamsa* or *Early Logic* (Sandal, 1980.) which discusses structure and meaning of language. As was common in many ancient cultures, Jaimini emphasizes the sacredness of the "word." Commenting on the *Poorva Mimamsa*, one author says, "It is an exegesis or science of interpretation." (Sandal, 1980, p. iii.). Jaimini's work is in the form of "Sutras," in which each stanza consists of one or two line enunciation of linguistic principles followed by detailed explanations. Those principles are further interpreted by other scholars of ancient India. Says Jaimini, "Word and meaning are eternally connected...knowledge is the instructional part of language." (Sandal, 1980, p. 2.). According to Jaimini, the purpose of language is to transmit knowledge. Modern linguists might not agree with Jaimini's views about language, but they have to admit that he did discuss structure and meaning of language within the context of the philosophy of those days.

Panini in the second century BC, wrote an early grammar called the *Eight Chapters*, (Vasu, 1980). As Max Muller says, "The grammatical system elaborated by native grammarians is, in itself, most perfect, and those who have tested Panini's work will readily admit that there is no grammar in any language that could vie with the wonderful mechanism of his eight books of grammatical rules." (Vasu, 1980, p. 1.).

Eastern philosophers did not make any effort to spread their names and works around the world. They believed that if their works had any value, someday the world would hear about them. Another reason for the lack of awareness of Eastern works on language, communication, perception, credibility, and other aspects of our discipline in the West is the Eurocentric education which we offer at our universities.

UNDERSTANDING SOCIAL REALITY

We must realize that there are several paths to intellectual pursuit. Ancient Hindus and Buddhists believed there are at least six ways to know the so-called "Reality" or what modern communication specialists refer to as "Social Reality." (Datta, 1932, p. 19). There is no one value system that is best suited for the entire world. There are at least three major value systems: individuality, responsibility, and the integrated value systems. Westerners believe in the individuality system. The United States of America is the best example of this system; where some persons violently oppose having too many government controls that deny individual rights. Easterners believe in the responsibility system. Japan is the best example of this system where the Japanese prime minister takes responsibility for the actions of his ancestors in China and apologizes to the Chinese people. Some Asians and Europeans believe in a balanced system that integrates the positive values of the other two systems. We can witness examples of such an integration in some Scandinavian and European countries where parents allow freedom to their children at certain times and take responsibility for their well being at other times. Yet, many of us still believe the individuality value system is the best because it promotes individual rights and democratic governments. The truth is, many responsibility value systems also promote democratic government and, in fact, the largest democracy in the world belongs to the responsibility system. Some politicians believe it is their divine right to impose the individuality system on the rest of the world.

As Alexander the Great's life indicates, the best way to conquer another culture is to understand it, learn to communicate with its people, and then, make them understand our culture. One way to begin such communication is to accept the value of responsibility as being equal to the value of individuality. As it is well known, each of these values has originated its own elaborate value system consisting of values, beliefs, expectations and customs.

THE UNIVERSAL DECLARATION OF HUMAN RESPONSIBILITIES

Even today the United Nations (UN) only supports *The Universal Declaration of Human Rights*. In 1978, for example, the United Nations Educational, Scientific and Cultural Organization (UNESCO) adopted its *Declaration on Fundamental Principles Concerning the Contribution of Mass Media to Strengthening Peace and International Understanding to the Promotion of Human Rights and Countering Racialism.* (UNESCO, 1985, p. 163.). However, neither the UN nor the UNESCO has even recognized the need to support "The Universal Declaration of Human Responsibilities." The fact is, "racialism" cannot be countered by emphasizing human rights only. The government of each country should be asked to assume the responsibility to end racism and other forms of discrimination in that country. Legislation about rights and responsibilities should be enacted simultaneously. I believe responsibility as a universal value system is as noble as the individuality system. A responsibility value system is needed today, especially in the West, more than ever before. Responsibility is a selfless value and individuality is a selfish value. Responsibility is what we give to others of our own free will and individuality is what we grab from others for ourselves. Of course, no one value is without flaw. We have to choose the positive aspects of each value system for the purpose of supporting a higher humanity at the global level and such details have to be worked out by the member nations. While there are several commissions and committees to investigate human rights violations of other societies, not even one international body looks into each society's and each government's record of its responsibility to its children, its elderly, its poor, its women, and other weaker sections of its society. It is time for the United Nations to establish a *Human Responsibilities Commission*. This proposed commission can bring about the much-needed balance between human rights and responsibilities in this troubled world of ours.

FREE FLOW OF IDEAS

Julian Huxley, Director General of UNESCO, said in 1948:

> In the forefront is set UNESCO's collaboration in the work of advancing the mutual knowledge and understanding of peoples, through all means of mass communication and in the obtaining of international agreements necessary to promote the free flow of ideas by word and image.
>
> Next is...giving of fresh impulse to popular education and to spread of culture...the ideal of equality of educational opportunity without regard to race, sex or any distinctions, economic or social...and educational methods best suited to prepare the children of the world for responsibilities of freedom. (Huxley, 1948, p. 2.).

In spite of what philosophers such as Huxley say, why is it that our young people are being educated even today to believing individual rights are divine truths and individual responsibility is just a collective behavior of lesser people whose cultures are different from our own? In our Eurocentric educational system, the youngsters are not taught to appreciate the unique beauty of other cultures. If they are taught to do so, the young minds are capable of seeing a new beauty in the things that are different. Understanding and respecting cultural differences should be a part of one's knowledge. As Plato said:

> The capacity for knowledge is present in everyone's mind. If you can imagine an eye that can turn from darkness to brightness only if the body as a whole turns, then our organ of understanding is like that. Its orientation has to be accompanied by turning

the mind as a whole away from the world of becoming until it becomes capable of bearing the sight of real being and reality at its most bright ....

That's what education should be, the art of orientation. Educators should devise the simplest and most effective methods of turning minds around. (Waterfeld, 1994, pp. 245-46.).

DIVERGENCE VS CONVERGENCE

In the past twenty-five years, there have been several thousand studies of intercultural and multicultural communication in the disciplines of art, broadcasting, communication, film, journalism, linguistics, and other related areas. Some specialists in engineering, science and technology also are involved in communication studies. For example, early theories of communication science such as Shannon and Weaver's *The Mathematical Theory of Communication* and Norbert Wiener's *Cybernetics or Control and Communication in the Animal and the Machine* (Wiener, 1948.) are now being applied to human communication and performing arts. In the 1960s and 1970s, we studied stereotyping, ethnocentrism, and other aspects of cultural differences or divergence. These days we are studying positive imaging, cultural relativism, and other aspects of cultural similarities or convergence. Several decades ago, educational institutions in each country taught their students how to communicate effectively within their own cultures or what we may call "intracultural communication." In the 1970s, those institutions offered courses in communication between two cultures, or "intercultural communication." (Sitaram, 1995). These days, some institutions are offering courses in communicating with members of several cultures at the same time, or what we may call "multicultural communication." These efforts, however, are designed to make the "differing others" understand us, rather than for us to understand and respect the others.

The trend these days is to integrate the diverse areas of communication into a popular effort called "convergence." New academic programs aimed at "convergence" have sprung up in several communication departments. Some experts say, the so-called information superhighway or *Infobahn* is best suited for convergence. Mass media, advanced technology, satellites, and computers are being combined into what are often called multimedia. Multimedia are the most modern ways of sorting, selecting, storing, sending, and seeking of audio-visual and digital information through a combination of radio, television, the film, the print, computers and other media. These convergent technologies have become multi-billion dollar businesses. As one trade magazine puts it, "Many executives and engineers in the telecommunications industry are preoccupied with the accelerating establishment of the Global Information Infrastructure, also known as the information superhighway or *Infobahn*. Much of the credit (or blame) for this obsession should go to Vice President Al Gore, but perhaps far more should go to Hughes Communication and Teledesic." (Purchase, 1995, p. 18).

We should not forget that all media are not suited for all types of interaction in all cultures. While some media are effective in some situations in some cultures, others are effective in other situations in other cultures. For example, in the early days of the Bolshevik revolution in Russia, clandestine radio was an effective tool in the hands of Vladimir Lenin. During the communist revolution in China the so called traditional media of storytelling and folk songs were effective in the hands of Mao-Tse Tung. Later on, during the Iranian revolution, video and audio cassettes were effective tools in the hands of Ayatollah Khomeini in exile. These media activities resulted in the downfall of the old and establishment of the new governments. The media languages used in these revolutions preached hatred of the old governments and its supporters. The televised incident of the Rodney King beating in the United States of America in 1991 triggered racial conflict across the nation. For the fear of more religious unrest, the Indian government in 1992 banned the telecast of the Babri mosque incident. The point is, the same multimedia that can be used to preach hatred and violence can be used to preach love and peace.

HIGHER HUMANITY

We should realize that the so called "Information Superhighway" or the *Infobahn* is just a bunch of channels or the hardware of communication on land and in space. Software and information are still needed to ensure that the highway leads somewhere. Those media conglomerates that would like to promote convergence should nurture old fashioned divergence and still be in lucrative business. However, those who wish to build a higher humanity should use the greatest technological innovations that are now available. The higher humanity—the dream of multicultural communication specialists—is similar to what Julian Huxley has often termed "Evolutionary Humanism" which is "global in extent and evolutionary in background." (Huxley, 1948, p. 6.). Setting the goals for UNESCO, Huxley further explained his concept of humanism as "evolutionary as opposed to a static or ideal humanism." (Huxley, 1948, p. 5.). Such a humanity should believe in a world culture where individuality and responsibility value systems are of equal importance and where diversity rather than uniformity is considered essential to make life interesting and worth living. The two value systems—individuality and responsibility—make our lives happy and content. They complement each other and make our lives complete. Students in such a humanity believe their learning is incomplete without studying the nature of these value systems. They learn the philosophies of Jaimini, Confucius, Lao Tsu, and Shankara with the same enthusiasm as they would of Socrates, Plato, Aristotle, and Kant. They learn the political thoughts of Kautilya with the same eagerness as they would of John Stuart Mill. The goal of media and interpersonal communication in this humanity would be to inform and educate the audience in the new world culture. Learning about rights, as well as responsibilities will be the "New Fairness Doctrine" of media management students. Multicultural communication will be the modern way to interact in such a humanity.

No one person or company created the radio frequencies that fill the space on this earth and beyond; nature created them for all humans so that we can understand, respect, and help each other. Nature also gave us the multitude of channels so that we can appreciate, nourish, and communicate cultural diversity. As humans, we can employ the frequencies to promote cultural divergence, as well as cultural convergence. We can use these frequencies to make money and keep it for ourselves or pursue "objective truth, and free exchange of ideas and knowledge...and to increase the means of communication between peoples...for the purposes of mutual understanding and a truer and more perfect knowledge of each other's lives." (UNESCO, 1985, p. 151.). The new world culture, higher values and objective truth will emerge when the mass media serve the entire humanity rather than only a part of it. The U.S. Congress has passed legislation leading to an information infrastructure and the eventual information superhighway or the so called *Infobahn* which can also pave the way to the world culture and the higher humanity.

The parallel developments of intracultural, intercultural, and multicultural communication on the one hand, and local, national, and international telecommunication on the other hand, are certainly progress toward the betterment of all humans. Telecommunication began more than a century ago as local and terrestrial means of interaction, sometimes called horizontal communication, among the peoples of the world. Now it has extended to space and beyond, or what is known as "vertical" communication, for transmission of signals between space and earth. There are two problems in integrating communication and technology to develop a global culture of higher values. One is the insistence on our own value-centered behavior as a way of life worth preserving while we consider similar behaviors of others as just old fashioned traditions that need to be changed; the second is our belief that innovations in the electronic technology is for the so-called free market only and not for all humanity. These two problems have resulted in the production and use of words and images that signify separation and hatred among peoples and governments. Some interpersonal and media languages include more words and images that symbolize hatred and terror than love and peace.

In 1945, Clement R. Attlee, the British Prime Minister, said, "ignorance of each other's ways and lives has been a common cause, throughout history of mankind, of that suspicion and mistrust between the people of the world through which their differences have all too often broken into war." (Huxley, 1948, p. 1.).

A CHALLENGE TO COMMUNICATION STUDENTS

Today, we have technology such as the internet that can be adapted to educate and train our students to alleviate ignorance and suspicion between peoples of the world. We should develop theories, skills, words and images of effective multicultural communication that include three steps: (1) understanding one's own culture, (2) understanding audience's cultures, and (3) adapting one's communication techniques to those cultures.

This means that students should not only learn, but also help their teachers build general theories and models of multicultural communication, as well as develop specific skills and techniques of multicultural training. Like Elias Lonrott who, more than a century ago, travelled to the coldest parts of Russia to collect the songs of the *Kalevala*, our students and their teachers should collect ideas about multicultural communication from unknown cultures where people may be interacting effectively. Lonrott set another example to students and scholars. He took upon himself the responsibility to collect the ancient story of the heroes and to make it available to all humans. Although the study of communication as an academic discipline began in this century in Western universities, it has been a part of philosophical inquiry for many centuries in ancient cultures of the East. For example, those ancient philosophers considered communication as a three step process which included first of all perception of the world through the five senses; second, cognition and retention of information in the mind; and third, expression of ideas through verbal and nonverbal symbols. However, as I mentioned earlier, those philosophers conceptualized communication as the process of understanding one's own self rather than affecting others' behaviors, and they proposed elaborate theories to explain their concepts. Our students should learn about those cultures and their communication theories. They should take the risk to learn untested foreign theories and techniques of communicating in this culturally diverse world. This is the greatest challenge to our students as well as to our institutions of higher learning. Because we now have access to multimedia, internet, and other facilities to expand our knowledge of other cultures and countries, it should be possible to meet this challenge. Governments, educational institutions, and business organizations around the world are more open now than ever before to using new technologies to improve their effectiveness in the world. Pekka Tarjanne, Secretary General of the International Telecommunications Union, calls such openness "Telestroika." He says, "the ongoing changes in telecommunications have caused *Telestroika* that is evident in the changed nature of telecommunications…" (Tarjanne, 1990, p. 22.).

Openness to understand, respect and even adapt different ways of life and to accept ideas that question our age-old beliefs are parts of the challenge to our students in the communication discipline and to our institutions of higher learning. First of all, the students should demand that their teachers bring about such a Telestroika in the academe. An open-minded search for knowledge needed to define the new concept of *higher values* and to teach new skills of multicultural communication for the new *world culture* is essential for the survival of all humans. This new culture builds upon the structures and contents of the existing cultures of all the countries of the world. In the past, many philosophers have called such a structure "unity in diversity;" I would like to call it *higher humanity*. These higher values of the world culture that I envision are neither leftist nor rightist. These values neither are blurred by any "centrism" nor are they bound by any fad of the decade. It is not an extension of any one culture; rather, it would be the essence of all the cultures of the entire humanity. They do bring about a balance between rights and responsibilities, as well as linearity and non-linearity and help the West meet the East. They are the essential hardware and software of our future world where we must live and communicate in peace. Communication students can make a beginning by defining these basic concepts that explain the process and skills of communication in such a culture.

I realize that these efforts may appear politically incorrect at this time. It may take several centuries for students around the world to realize that the *new world culture* is needed to lay the foundation for the *higher humanity*, but let us make the beginning in this century.

DISCUSSION QUESTIONS

1. Name at least three books about culture, communication, and related areas from cultures other than your own. Write a few lines about the contents of each book.
2. Explain these concepts in your own words: Cultural Values, Individuality, Responsibility, Multiculturalism, Higher Humanity. Give at least one example for each of the concepts.
3. Explain the need for a Human Responsibilities Commission at the United Nations.
4. In your opinion, how would a successful businessperson or a teacher communicate in the world in the next century.
5. Explain the process of Multiculturalism.

REFERENCES

Chan, W., Faruqi, I. R., & Kitagawa, J. M. (1969). *The great Asian religions*. London: Macmillan Company.

Collinder, B. (1964). *The Kalevala and its background*. Stockholm: Almquist & Wiksell.

Datta, D. M. (1932). *The six ways of knowing* (p. 19). London: Allen and Unwin.

Huxley, J. (1948). *UNESCO on the eve of its 40th anniversary*. Paris: UNESCO.

Kirby, W. F. (1951). *Kalevala, the land of the heroes*. London: J. M. Dent and Sons.

Kirkinen, H., & Silvo, H. (1984). *Kalevala, an epic of Finland and all mankind*. Helsinki: Finnish American Cultural Institute.

Kitagawa, J. K. (1958). *Religions of the East*. Philadelphia: The Westminster Press.

Magoun, Jr., F. P. (1969). *The old Kalevala* (foreword). Cambridge: Harvard University Press.

Purchase, J. F. (1995). Establishing the satellite based infobahn in a multicultural world. *Via Satellite*. X (7).

Sastry, S. R. (1967 Eighth Edition, First Edition 1915). *Kautilya's Artha Sastra*. Mysore, India: Mysore Printing and Publishing House.

Sandal, M. L. (Trans.) (1980/1923). *Mimamsa Sutras of Jaimini*. Volumes I and II. Delhi: Motilal Banarsidass.

Shannon, C. E., & Weaver, W. (1964). *The mathematical theory of communication*. Urbana, IL: University of Illinois Press.

Sitaram, K. S. (1995). *Culture and communication: A world view*. Chicago: McGraw-Hill.

Tarajanne, P. J. (1990). Open framework for telecommunications in the 1990s: Access to networks and markets. *Telecommunications, April*.

UNESCO. (1985). *UNESCO on the eve of its 40th anniversary*. Paris: UNESCO.

Vasu, S. C. (1980/1891). *The astadhyayi of Panini, Volume I*. Delhi: Motilal Banarsidass. (Original work by Panini in Sanskrit translated into English, edited and published by Vasu in 1891. Third printing in 1980).

Ward, B. (1957). *The interplay of East and West*. London: Allen and Unwin.

Warshaw, S., & Bromwell, D. C., with Tudisco A. J. (1974). *India emerges*. San Francisco: Canefield Press.

Waterfield, R. (1994). *Plato Republic*. Oxford: Oxford University Press.

Wiener, N. (1948). *Cybernetics or control and communication in the animal and the machine*. New York: John Wiley.

SECTION I OVERVIEW: INTERCULTURAL, MULTICULTURAL, AND GLOBAL COMMUNICATION THEORIES AND ISSUES

Nearly 30 years ago, intercultural communication as an academic area of instruction and research began—mostly in speech-communication departments in the United States, Japan, Finland, and other countries. There were few departments of radio, television and film, and few intercultural communication courses were offered in these departments. Therefore, it is appropriate to begin these volumes that are designed to commemorate more than a quarter century of intercultural communication in the academe with chapters in the area of speech including rhetoric and interpersonal communication.

It is even more appropriate to begin this volume with a discussion of ethics in intercultural communication. As was pointed out in Section I, Jaimini, Kautilya and Aristotle, who lived more than two thousand years ago, discussed ethics in communication. Aristotle, especially, discussed the importance of ethos or character of the communicator as the most important factor in speech and rhetoric, but in those days they did not foresee the need for elaborate discussion of ethics in communicating across cultures. Now every country in the world is fast becoming multicultural and an important concern in the academe of these countries is ethics in intercultural communication.

Having offered intercultural communication courses for more than 25 years, do we now have a code of ethics for all intercultural communicators around the world? In his chapter, "The Problems of Ethics in Intercultural Communication," Day explains the complexity of developing such a code for all communicators. Some of the existing codes do discuss ethics. They emphasize concepts such as cultural relativism, accommodation, and intercultural personhood. Day explains

15

how none of these seem to be acceptable to all intercultural communicators around the world. He offers some alternatives.

Geertz Hofstede of the Netherlands has done major work with international and multinational companies, in which he argues that "no management activity can be culture free." At the societal level, Hofstede describes 50 countries according to their relative emphasis at the societal level on four dimensions: social differentiation by gender, a desire for certainty, an acceptance of unequal power distribution, and interdependence between individuals. In their chapter, Ross and Faulkner further examine his four dimensions, and their implications for intercultural and international communication, as a means of understanding culture.

Should cultural differences be viewed as positive factors in intercultural discourses? In his chapter, "The Ideology of Difference in Current Discourse," Over argues that in terms of such differences, especially in the case of the oppressed and the oppressor, change occurs on both the groups. The different ideologies help each group acquire some values of the other. Therefore, Over observes, absolute ideas about cultural differences may be a hindrance to effective intercultural communication.

Using values of dominant cultures only and ignoring those of non-dominant ones as the bases for cross cultural research may be a mistake, warns Lang in her chapter, "Multicultural Issues in the Study of Cross Cultural Communication." An example that she offers is blindly applying Hall's model of high and low context cultures which is based on the values of dominant cultures. Another example the author offers is the comparison of western and non-western cultures. Many times these comparisons also are of male values rather than female. Even the use of grammar, syntax and other linguistic factors are often different between males and females. The intercultural communicator should take these and other factors of co-culture into consideration, she argues.

In her chapter, "English as Dominant Language for Intercultural Communication: Prospects for the Next Century," Asuncion-Lande explains how language reflects the culture of its speakers. Similar frames of reference and common languages are essential for successful intercultural communication. A common frame of reference may be built in English which has become the language of international business and global diplomacy. Learning English as the second language is increasing among the peoples around the world. Asuncion-Lande says that English has already become the medium of intercultural communication and should continue to be so.

In the chapter, "How Global Is Global? A Critical Look at the Language and Ideology of Globalization," Rodriguez-Rodriguez says that intercultural communication expressions such as globalization and global are being used loosely in intercultural communication. In order for us to become truly global, we all should strive for a global process and the development of the entire humanity. Even the definitions of terms such as progress should include not only material development, but also improvements in intercultural communication. Globalization must bring about universalization.

In his second chapter in this book, Over offers a different view of cultural relativism which is often considered a solution to ethnocentrism. He questions the practicality of applying cultural relativism as a way of overcoming differences. Universal needs of diverse peoples could be a common point of reference in intercultural communication. With some fine examples, Over brings home the need to use techniques other than relativism.

In his chapter, "The Use and Misuse of Questionnaires in Intercultural Training," Bing applies Hofstede's and Thompson's cultural profile to intercultural studies. Questionnaires, cultural maps, and cultural profiles developed by the two researchers are used to measure how employees value orientations such as individualism and collectivism might affect the employee cross cultural job training. The data bases that are now developed using these questionnaires may have the potential of being misused, warns Bing.

THE PROBLEM OF ETHICS IN INTERCULTURAL COMMUNICATION

Kenneth D. Day
University of the Pacific

Few areas of communication studies raise challenges as great as ethics in intercultural communication. Because different cultures hold different values, have different conceptions of the "good" person, and have different means of expressing ethical behaviors such as "respect" and the "truth," members of any culture proposing an ethics of intercultural communication risk unknowingly imposing one that reflects their own culture. This enterprise is made all the more difficult in Western countries by a generally-shared view that such societies have progressed from a more primitive state still occupied by traditional societies. In this view if modern society ethics are different, they are also superior and should overrule those of traditional societies in intercultural encounters.

This chapter begins by providing background on intercultural communication ethics. Kale's universal code of intercultural ethics is discussed and critiqued in some detail in terms of problems in applying this code in intercultural communication. Additionally, suggestions are provided for revising the code to make it more sensitive to problems in intercultural communication. Finally, an alternate proposal is made for an ethical theory based on the principle of dialogue in communication.

ETHICS IN INTERCULTURAL COMMUNICATION

Western theories of ethics in communication are traditionally traced to the ancient Greeks. Andersen (1991) notes that ethical theories tend to reflect the culture in which they were produced. He notes that the ethical theories of Plato and Aristotle reflect the nature of the Greek city states in which a small number of individuals interacted face to face and in formal ways thought to serve the public. He adds that there has been a tendency to focus discussion of ethical concerns on the source of the message and the message itself without concern for the medium, situation, or audience of the message. Only limited attention has been given to ethics of intercultural communication. Much of this work shows little awareness of how cultural differences influence communication.

A number of codes for professionals involved in intercultural communication have been adopted. Within journalism, these include the Bordeaux Declaration of Journalists' Duties (International Federation of Journalists, 1954), the Mass Media Declaration of UNESCO (UNESCO, 1978), the Code of Newspaper Practice (Federation of International Editors of Journals, 1981), and the International Principles of Professional Ethics in Journalism (Fourth Consultative Meeting of International and Regional Organizations or Working Journalists, 1983). Consideration of these codes raises the issue of politics in the ethics of intercultural communication. Two of these, the Bordeaux Declaration of Journalists and the Code of Newspaper Practice, largely are statements of the principles common in Western industrialized country journalism codes. On the other hand, the remaining two codes are seen by many Western journalists as highly ideological. The 1978 UNESCO Declaration led to the heated debates of the New World Information Order (NWICO). The call for licensing of journalists and the demand for balance in coverage of Third World countries was seen by Western journalists as an attempt to turn journalists into propagandists and an attempt by governments to violate the principle of the free flow of information (Sussman, 1990). The subsequent International Principles of Professional Ethics in Journalism which developed out of the UNESCO declaration is seen by Merrill (1989) as stepping outside the bounds of journalism ethics in its statement that journalists should be committed to "the elimination of apartheid, tyrannical regimes, colonialism, disease, or malnutrition" (p. 285). For Merrill these are matters of personal belief which do not belong in a code of journalistic ethics since a journalist is supposed to be involved in the objective reporting of events. This position is very much placed in doubt by critical studies in mass media such as the work of Fiske and Hartley (1978) and Bennett (1988) who have demonstrated that Western journalists present news events in the context of political ideologies. Nordenstreng (1989) observes that all journalistic codes of ethics are political and that journalists will best serve humanity if they adopt an "impartial" code based on the "universal values of the international community" (p. 283).

Merrill (1989) suggests that codes are not likely to be useful in international journalism because of problems of enforcement but does suggest some general principles. First of all, he proposes pursuing "overriding ethical commonalities" such as "empathy, openmindedness, sincerity, and mutual respect" (p. 286). Next, he suggests that the intercultural communicator should consider the person he/she is talking to and ask not only what should be communicated but whether or not he/she should communicate at all. Sometimes, he adds, the most ethical behavior may be to not communicate at all. Merrill is quite vague as to when such situations occur.

Merrill also proposes two maxims:

1. Communicate only to willing others those things and employing only those techniques which you would be willing for others to use in communicating with you. (p. 287)
2. When in Rome use Roman ethics if such ethics do not do mischief to your own ethical standards. (p. 288)

The first of these maxims is somewhat problematic in that as members of different cultures we may hold very different notions of appropriate communication. Examples might include directness, truthfulness, and expected degree of respect. The second maxim can be interpreted as claiming that we should follow the ethics of another culture only when it is one and the same as our own.

Although Merrill offers only an eclectic set of suggestions, his claim that monologic communication is ethically inferior to dialogic communication will be given serious consideration later in this chapter.

At least one code of international ethics has been adopted by practitioners in international public relations. The International Code of Ethics or Code of Athens was adopted by the International Public Relations Association in 1968. Advocating actions which support the Universal Declaration of Human Rights, the code does acknowledge that public relations practitioners must balance the interests of the organization served with the interest of publics. Somewhat unusual is its prohibition of the use of communication techniques to "create unconscious motivations."

Each of the above codes deals with the function of communicators in narrowly-defined roles. Few statements of ethical principles for all intercultural communicators have been offered. Intercultural textbooks—with their emphasis on effective intercultural communication—tend to avoid this topic. Samovar and Porter (1991a) suggest that in intercultural communication we must "send messages that reaffirm a belief in the intrinsic worth of individuals" (p. 299) and that we must be concerned with how our intercultural communication changes not only individuals but cultures. The first principle is quite vague in its potential application. The second seems to advise us not to communicate at all if we assume that producing cultural change itself is unethical.

The best-known discussion of a general ethics for intercultural communication is David Kale's (1991), *Ethics in Intercultural Communication*. This essay first appeared in the sixth edition of Samovar and Porter's (1991b) widely-used reader on intercultural communication and has since been cited and summarized in at least one other intercultural communication text (Lustig & Koester, 1993).

Kale offers a code of ethics in intercultural communication based on the desire for peace which he claims as a universal cultural value. By extension from this value, he proposes a "universal" code of intercultural communication ethics based on four principles. These four principles are:

1. Ethical communicators address people of other cultures with the same respect that they would like to receive themselves.
2. Ethical communicators seek to describe the world as they see it as accurately as possible.
3. Ethical communicators encourage people of other cultures to express themselves in their uniqueness.
4. Ethical communicators strive for identification with people from other cultures. (Kale, 1991, p. 424)

Each principle in Kale's article is also accompanied by a short discussion of the principle. Both the principle and the accompanying discussion will be considered as the code is critiqued.

Kale's first principle deals with respect. His accompanying discussion admonishes intercultural communicators to avoid demeaning or belittling the cultural identity of others through verbal or nonverbal communication. One such example given of unethical behaviors is the ethnic joke. For Kale, respect appears to be the absence of behavior which belittles or demeans members of another culture. The principle emphasizes that we should treat others with the respect that we would also like to receive.

Kale's conception of respect is at variance with that of societies with high power-distance (Hofstede, 1984), a characteristic of cultures in which there are significant power and status differences between individuals and in which differences in power and status are acknowledged in behavior. While the Confucianist principle of shu, not doing to others what you would not want them to do to you, seems to mirror Kale's first ethical principle, scholars of Confucianism (Bahm, 1992) are quick to point out that Eastern societies apply this principle hierarchically. One treats one's father not as an equal but in the manner one would wish to be treated as a father. Lower-status individuals in high power-distance cultures are expected to display respect to those of higher status, often in a specific manner for people with particular status. For example, in Indianized Southeast Asian countries such as Burma, Cambodia, Laos, and Thailand, the members of the laity are expected to display respect to monks in a number of well-defined ways. These respect behaviors include seating the monks at a higher-level (for example, in a chair while the laity sit on the floor or on a platform while the laity sits at a lower level), sitting in a special posture that avoids pointing one's feet at the monks, greeting and taking leave of the monks through a ritualistic greeting of three bows, dressing modestly with arms and legs covered (especially the case for women), removing one's hat while in the presence of a monk, and employing special monk-respecting vocabulary when the language provides the means. In these countries, younger people are expected to behave in prescribed, respectful ways to those older, and common people traditionally display elaborate respect behavior to royalty. Failure to display these behaviors in such societies constitutes disrespect even though no intention of belittling or demeaning is intended.

Kale's principle, on the other hand, is clearly that of a low-power distance society in which, while we may choose to be disrespectful, we have few gradations of respect. As was demonstrated above, in following this principle in some intercultural interactions we are likely to communicate disrespect despite our intentions. Respect here consists of equal treatment of people while avoiding acts of disrespect.

The second principle of Kale's code asserts that individuals should describe the world as they see it as accurately as possible. The accompanying discussion by Kale focuses on avoidance of deceiving knowingly or misrepresenting something. Here and in earlier work (Kale, 1983), Kale acknowledges the social construction of reality and the cultural boundedness of truth. Although our perception of the world will be influenced, even distorted, by our culture, we should not knowingly lie about what we believe to be otherwise.

Aune and Waters (1994) and Koper (1994) present empirical evidence that members of collectivist societies view deception differently. Collectivist cultures are those which emphasize the group membership of an individual while individualistic societies emphasize the autonomy of the individual (Hofstede, 1984). Among the values associated with collective societies, Triandis, Brislin, and Hui (1991) identify harmony, face-saving, and modesty. Yum (1991) describes the manner in which the collectivist values of Confucianism foster a style of communication in East Asia in which the process of communication is more important than the information exchanged. Fostering a relationship through communication is thus more important than what is actually said. Group harmony, avoidance of loss of face to others and oneself, and a modest presentation of oneself are seen as means to foster these relationships. Koper's (1994) finding that individuals of collectivist societies show greater acceptance of deception that benefits others is quite understandable when viewed from this perspective. One does not say what one actually thinks when it might hurt others in the group. Aune and Waters (1994) found that Samoans were more likely than North Americans to attempt to use deception when dealing with group or family concerns. Koper (1994) notes that such behavior from an individualistic perspective is likely over time to generate distrust of individuals who engage in such behavior. It would seem that members of collectivist societies must be aware that individuals do not necessarily say what they think. Such behavior is not only accepted but expected when the expresion of one's point of view would injure group interaction. Although collectivist individuals may at times treat foreigners as people outside their group and thus dismiss some of these principles, when the interaction is seen as an attempt to form and sustain a new "group," one should expect what is said to be modified to promote group harmony. It is clear that, unqualified, Kale's second principle is not a "universal" ethical principle.

The second ethical principle is also likely to lead intercultural communicators astray with its focus on verbal communication. Members of low-context cultures (Hall, 1976), like our own, rely on explicit verbal communication. High-context cultures, such as those in East Asia, place greater emphasis on indirect communication, nonverbal communication, and contextual cues. As individuals from low-context cultures we are likely later to feel betrayed or bewildered when we fail to understand or misunderstand what we were told earlier through indirect verbal or nonverbal means. On the other hand, individuals from high-context societies are likely to view us as low in intelligence, because we do not easily understand what is being communicated.

Collectivist values are often joined with high-context communication patterns. Ishii and Bruneau (1991) and Yum (1991) provide interesting insights into East Asian views of the communication process. Yum (1991) describes East Asian communication as receiver-oriented rather than sender-oriented. This means that greater emphasis is placed on the receiver's abilities to understand the sender rather than emphasizing the responsibility for the sender to communicate clearly in verbal terms what he/she is trying to say. In specifically discussing Japan, Ishii and Bruneau (1991) describe the ideal qualities of message sender and receiver. Senders should demonstrate a quality known as enryo (reserve). Ideas are expressed with great economy and are evaluated for appropriateness before speaking. Greater responsibility is placed on message receivers who should possess a quality called sasshi (intuition). The sender must intuit what is being communicated through attention to verbal, nonverbal, and contextual details. While low-context-culture receivers of the messages of high-context-culture senders may in fact be sent messages which "describe the world" from the vantage point of the high-context-culture senders "as accurately as possible," low-context-culture receivers may perceive this pattern of communication as deceptive.

It should also be acknowledged that presenting the world as we see it is not always appreciated, particularly in Confucianist societies. At an American-Vietnamese university faculty conference in Vietnam several years ago, several American faculty very forcefully expressed their views regarding the status of human rights in Vietnam with the result that most of the Vietnamese faculty left the conference and did not return.

Principle three encourages people from other cultures to present the world from their own point of view. Much of the discussion of this principle focuses on instances in which members of other nations have been denied a chance to present their views because of their political ideologies. The principle itself suggests that we should take a more active role in encouraging those from other cultures to speak from their own point of view. There is a danger here that members of low-context cultures will, in applying this principle, pressure members of high-context societies to be more verbally direct and open when members of these societies see no need for such direct statement and no benefit to publicly expressing their point of view.

Another issue raised here deals with the question of whether or not members of another culture have the right to break cultural norms in requesting that particular members of a culture present their views. At the same Vietnamese-American conference several years ago, American faculty expressed disappointment to their Vietnamese hosts because no female Vietnamese faculty member had been asked to make a presentation. The female Vietnamese faculty showed discomfort at what most American faculty thought had been a positive action on their behalf.

Kale's last principle, striving for identification with members of another culture, relies on a definition of identification as achievement of sharing of principles held in common. Here he advocates emphasizing shared common beliefs and values across cultures while maintaining cultural uniqueness. This position is somewhat surprising since Kale begins his article with a discussion of the difficulty in finding a cultural value, other than the desire to live in peace, shared by all societies. When societies differ over values which they perceive as important, finding significant common values to share may be difficult. Respect for the differing values of other societies would seem to present better prospects for getting on with the business of intercultural interaction.

Kale's principles can be made more acceptable if one abandons universal value claims and restates the code to be sensitive to cultural differences in the pattern of interaction. One possible restatement of this ethical code would be as follows:

1. Ethical communicators not only avoid displays of disrespect but attempt to treat different status individuals in other cultures with the display of respect expected in their culture.
2. Ethical communicators filter what they say by not speaking until they have considered the ethical principle of truthfulness, the desire to speak their own mind, the desire to accomplish a particular goal through interaction, the desire to present themselves in ways acceptable to the members of the other culture, the desire to foster harmony, and the desire to avoid hurting others.
3. Ethical communicators provide opportunities for others to present their own point of view while never forcing anyone into a face-losing situation.
4. Ethical communicators strive to foster communication situations which will allow people to build and maintain relationships.

One might also add a fifth principle stated as:

5.   Ethical communicators will attempt to be as knowledgeable about another
     culture as possible before beginning to interact and will attempt to learn to
     use and understand the contextual, nonverbal, and indirect speech communi-
     cation styles of the cultures with which they interact as well.

This revised code embraces the principle of cultural relativism. What is ethical
behavior depends on the particular situation in a particular culture and involves
choice among a number of competing ethical claims.

If there is a single ethical principle uniting this revised code, it is that we have
an ethical responsibility as intercultural communicators to be knowledgeable
about and sensitive to the patterns of communication in other cultures. Ignorance
through our own choice is unethical.

INTERCULTURAL DIALOGUE THEORY:
AN ALTERNATIVE APPROACH TO THE ETHICS
OF INTERCULTURAL COMMUNICATION

Merrill's (1989) proposal that monologic intercultural communication is ethically inferior to dialogic intercultural communication is worth serious consideration as a basis for an ethics of intercultural communication. An ethical theory
of this sort would be based on the first premise that intercultural communicators
who do not strive for dialogue are unethical. Monologic communication is characterized by presenting a point of view with no desire for interaction while dialogic communication is characterized by interaction for the purpose of
exchanging understanding, perceptions, and opinions. To engage in only monologic communication when one holds greater power can be seen as unethical in
that it is an abuse of power. When two parties each engage in only monologic
communication directed at the other, opportunities are lost to reach understanding, agreement, or at least compromise. Failure to attempt dialogue in such
instances could also be labeled unethical in that opportunities to achieve "the
good" are sacrificed.

Some interest in dialogic models of communication as more ethical has been
shown in the field of public relations. Grunig (1984) has proposed four models to
account for how public relations is practiced and has advocated only one of these,
the two-way symmetric model of public relations, as ethical public relations. In
this model, public relations practitioners attempt to engage in dialogue with the
publics of an organization to reach agreement on issues of concern. Grunig
believes this model to often be the only approach that is successful in situations in
which an organization is in conflict with its publics.

Also of some relevance here is the writing of Habermas (1984) who has described the resolution of disagreement through dialogue under ethical conditions of communication. When disagreement is over a claim of sincerity, Habermas has proposed that further ordinary communicative action should occur. However, when disagreement is over a claim of validity or appropriateness, he advocates that the parties involved move to special interaction called discourse according to the principles of the ideal speech situation. In this situation all participants have the same opportunity to speak, are given an equal chance to gain individual recognition of feelings and motives, have the same rights to issue commands to others, and provide justification of their actions and discourse using mutually agreed upon norms and rules of interaction. Ironically, Habermas assumes that such interaction is not possible in traditional societies making problematic the application of this model to intercultural interaction. Clearly the ideal speech situation also violates rules of interaction in a society with hierarchy. The model nonetheless can make some valuable contributions to an ethics of intercultural communication based on dialogue even in suggesting accommodations that are required in intercultural communication.

For example, Habermas (1984) suggests that participants in discourse must treat the matter of disagreement as an hypothesis so that they may review the evidence presented within their interaction. To the extent that we treat interaction as a chance to disseminate the truth be it our religious beliefs, our political ideology, or even our scientific explanation of a phenomenon, we inhibit any true dialogue. In intercultural encounters we should present these ideas as *what we believe* rather than the *truth* so that members of another culture may present their own views on the same status level as our own. Common agreement may not be achieved but greater understanding will be.

Williams (1985) has criticized Habermas' discourse model for its assumption of "limitless explicitness" (p. 247). As intercultural communicators we must be aware that communication occurs both through verbal and nonverbal language and that some things may be communicated through indirection in speech. Some topics may be seen as inappropriate generally or at least in certain situations or when talking to certain individuals. To insist on imposing our own norms of interaction is unethical. To be ethical we must work within these restraints.

Conducting intercultural discussions ethically also requires that we make accommodations for different styles of thinking and rhetoric. Lieberman's (1994) work on ethnocognitivism and Anderson's (1994) work on differences between American and Arab conceptions of persuasive rhetoric contribute to a greater understanding of these issues.

Treating all participants with the same power in interaction will also prove difficult when dealing with members of hierarchical or high power distance societies. In the presence of higher status individuals from their own culture, we should not expect people to speak as an equal with these other individuals present. We must recognize that total truthfulness and absolute disclosure do not characterize human interaction and that cultures differ in their norms regarding these. Finally, we must acknowledge that human communication is always imperfect and that we will usually achieve only some degree of dialogic communication.

Further development of this ethical theory can best be served by elaboration through relevant research in intercultural communication and through critique derived from dialogue between members of different cultures. A number of potential criticisms, however, are quite obvious. This ethical theory is vague in its prescription of behaviors. However, the complexity and diversity in intercultural communication make it difficult to prescribe behaviors appropriate in interacting with all cultures in all situations. The ethical intercultural communicator will need to change his/her behavior as he or she interacts with people from different cultures. In this sense intercultural dialogue theory yields what has been called situational ethics (Fletcher, 1966). For those who endorse ethics based on absolute values, this ethical theory will be disturbing because it treats commonly-discussed ethical values such as truth other than as absolute values. While this theory might be labelled a universal/humanitarian ethical theory (Arnett, 1991), an attempt has been made to minimize the claims of values which should be universally shared to one that non-dialogic communication is unethical. The theory can also be shown to be political but in ways which do not serve the interests of those who would use their power to control communication. The ethical mandate of this theory calls for those with power over communication to open communication with those over whom they hold power. The theory does, of course, promote the interests of teachers and scholars in intercultural communication who are seen as providing guidance on intercultural communication. A final criticism might be that this theory considers societies in which communication is dialogic to be more ethical than societies that do not. If traditional societies are less dialogic, then it would seem that that this theory would suggest that they are less ethical. Even if we accept this implication, we should be reminded not to present this ethical theory as the *truth* in our dialogue with members of other cultures and should be encouraged to pursue dialogue in culturally-adaptive ways even when our partners do not understand our ethical point of view.

Application of this model would have far-ranging implications in intercultural communication in areas ranging from diplomacy to international journalism, public relations, and advertising to conducting research on other cultures to ordinary one-on-one encounters between people from different cultures. While Kim's (1994) vision of intercultural personhood uniting eastern and western traditions resulting from communication interaction may be overly optimistic, a dialogic approach to intercultural communication will give nations and societies a better chance of achieving understanding and compromise to address mutual interests and concerns. In a world in which nationalistic conflicts have exploded and in an age in which Americans and other countrries are faced with the challenge of integrating culturally diverse nations, dialogue may be our only rational recourse.

DISCUSSION QUESTIONS

1. What would be an example of an intercultural communication situation in which being respectful by North American standards would result in being disrespectful?
2. Is it always ethical to reveal to another person exactly what you think? What is the difference between lying and simply choosing not to disclose everything you think in a particular situation? How do other cultures view this situation differently?
3. Why is it unethical to interact with people from another culture without making an attempt to be knowledgeable about that culture?
4. What does it mean for communication to be dialogic?
5. What implications does the dialogic approach to intercultural ethics have for ministers or clergy, journalists, or diplomats working in another culture?

REFERENCES

Andersen, K. E. (1991). A history of communication ethics. In K. J. Greenberg (Ed.), *Conversations on communication ethics* (pp. 3-19). Norwood, NJ: Ablex.

Anderson, J. W. (1994). A comparison of American and Arab conceptions of "effective" persuasion. In L. A. Samovar & R. E. Porter (Eds.), *Intercultural communication: A reader* (7th ed., pp. 104-113). Belmont, CA: Wadsworth.

Arnett, R. C. (1991). The status of communication ethics scholarship in speech communication journals from 1915 to 1985. In K. J. Greenberg (Ed.), *Conversations on communication ethics* (pp. 55-74). Norwood, NJ: Ablex.

Aune, R. K., & Waters, L. L. (1994). Cultural differences in deception: Motivations to deceive in samoans and North Americans. *International Jounal of International Relations, 18*, 159-172.

Bahm, A. L. (1992). *The heart of Confucius: Interpretation of genuine living and great wisdom*. Berkeley, CA: Asian Humanities Press.

Bennett, W. L. (1988). *News: The politics of illusion* (2nd ed.). White Plains, NY: Longman.

Federation of International Editors of Journals. (1981). *The code of newspaper practice*.

Fiske, J., & Hartley, J. (1978). *Reading television*. New York: Methuen.

Fletcher, J. (1966). *Situation ethics: The new morality*. Philadelphia, PA: Westminster.

Fourth Consultative Meeting of International and Regional Organizations or Working Journalists. (1983). *The international principles of professional ethics in journalism*.

Grunig, J. E. (1984). Organizations, environments, and models of public relations. *Public Relations Research and Education, 1*, 6-29.

Habermas, J. (1984). *The theory of communicative action: Reason and the rationalization of society*. Boston: Beacon.

Hall, E. T. (1976). *Beyond culture*. Garden City, NY: Doubleday.

Hofstede, G. (1984). *Culture's consequences*. Newbury Park, CA: Sage.

International Federation of Journalists. (1954). *Bordeaux declaration of journalists' duties*.

International Public Relations Association. (1968). *Code of the international public relations association.*

Ishii, S., & Bruneau, T. (1991). Silence and silences in cross-cultural perspective: Japan and the United States. In L. A. Samovar & R. E. Porter (Eds.), *Intercultural communication: A reader* (6th ed., pp. 314-319). Belmont, CA: Wadsworth.

Kale, D. (1983). In defense of two ethical universals in intercultural communication. *Religious Communication Today*, 6, 28-33.

Kale, D. (1991). Ethics in intercultural communication. In L. A. Samovar & R. E. Porter (Eds.), *Intercultural communication: A reader* (6th ed., pp. 421-426). Belmont, CA: Wadsworth.

Kim, Y. Y. (1994). Intercultural personhood: An integration of eastern and western perspectives. In L. A. Samovar & R. E. Porter (Eds.), *Intercultural communication: A reader* (7th ed., pp. 415-424). Belmont, CA: Wadsworth.

Koper, R. J. (1994, June). *Cultural differences in the perception of deceptive behavior.* Paper presented at the annual meeting of the International Communication Association, Sydney, Australia.

Lieberman, D. V. (1994). Ethnocognitivism, problem solving, and hemisphericity. In L. A. Samovar & R. E. Porter (Eds.), *Intercultural communication: A reader* (7th ed., pp. 178-193). Belmont, CA: Wadsworth.

Lustig, M. W., & Koester, J. (1993). *Intercultural competence: Interpersonal communication.* New York: Harper Collins.

Merrill, J. C. (1989). Global commonalities for journalistic ethics: Idle dream or realistic goal. In T. W. Cooper (Ed.), *Communication ethics and global change* (pp. 284-290). White Plains, NY: Longman.

Nordenstreng, K. (1989). Professionalism in transition: Journalistic ethics. In T. W. Cooper (Ed.), *Communication ethics and global change* (pp. 277-283). White Plains, NY: Longman.

Samovar, L. A., & Porter, R.E. (1991a). *Communication between cultures.* Belmont, CA: Wadsworth.

Samovar, L. A., & Porter, R. E. (1991b). *Intercultural communication: A reader* (6th ed.). Belmont, CA: Wadsworth.

Sussman, L. R. (1990). For better journalism, not more propaganda. In L. J. Martin & R. E. Hiebert (Eds.), *Current issues in international communication* (pp. 339-342). White Plains, NY: Longman.

Triandis, H. C., Brislin, R., & Hui, C. H. (1991). Cross-cultural training across the individualism divide. In L. A. Samovar & R. E. Porter (Eds.), *Intercultural communication: A reader* (6th ed., pp. 370-382). Belmont, CA: Wadsworth.

Williams, B. (1985). *Ethics and the limits of philosophy.* Cambridge MA: Harvard University.

UNESCO. (1978). *The Mass Media Declaration of UNESCO.*

Yum, K. O. (1991). The impact of Confucianism on interpersonal relationships and communication patterns in east asia. In L. A. Samovar & R. E. Porter (Eds.), *Intercultural communication: A reader* (6th ed., pp. 66-77). Belmont, CA: Wadsworth.

2

HOFSTEDE'S DIMENSIONS: AN EXAMINATION AND CRITICAL ANALYSIS

Roberta Bell Ross
Sandra L. Faulkner
The Pennsylvania State University

INTRODUCTION

Geertz Hofstede sought to discover theories that could be applied universally to people across cultures because of the dearth of such theories in previous intercultural studies. He suggests that human beings carry "mental programs" that are inherited biologically (e.g. individual or universal human programming) or developed and reinforced socially via family, institutions, and culture (Hofstede, 1984). He contends that within these socially learned, or "collective" mental programs, is where the different values among people of different cultures are expressed. Unlike the universal level (biological) which is shared by all, or almost all, the collective level of mental programming encompasses all that is subjective. This level "is shared with some but not with all other people; it is common to people belonging to a certain group or category, but different among people belonging to other groups or categories" (Hofstede, 1984, p. 15). Through his research, Hofstede discovered and developed four value dimensions that exist in varying degrees in all cultures. This chapter examines these dimensions and offers a critical analysis of the usefulness and applicability of the dimensions as a tool for understanding culture.

HOFSTEDE'S FOUR DIMENSIONS

Hofstede took a culture-general, or "etic," approach to studying culture in order to examine the role of values as they influence the decision-making process of people across culture. As opposed to the culture-specific, or "emic" approach, which attempts to examine similarities and differences between or among two or more specific cultures, the culture-general approach seeks "to identify universal patterns of values and behavior that differentiate among cultures generally" (Henning, 1995, p. 1). Therefore, Hofstede's interests resided in information that would provide insight into those specific elements of which culture itself is composed.

In his original study, Hofstede administered, on two occasions (1968 and 1972), over 116,000 questionnaires to employees of a U.S.-based multinational business organization (and its subsidiaries) in 40 countries (which later rose to 53 countries). He identified four main dimensions (or subsystems) that he named Power Distance, Uncertainty Avoidance, Individualism-Collectivism, and Masculinity-Femininity. Hofstede found that all cultures operate in conjunction with the degree of importance they place on each of these dimensions. In the following pages, we examine each of the dimensions and provide specific examples of cultures that represent each dimension.

Power Distance

Hofstede describes power distance as the measure of interpersonal power or influence between a boss and subordinate as perceived by the least powerful of the two—the subordinate. He states that the "power distance between a boss B and a subordinate S in a hierarchy is the difference between the extent to which B can determine the behavior of S and the extent to which S can determine the behavior of B" (1984, p. 99). Hofstede points out that although it is the bosses who wield more power, "differences in the exercise of power in a hierarchy relate to the value systems of both bosses *and* subordinates" and the way in which each responds to the hierarchy reflects the values of both parties (p. 97). According to Hofstede, the unequal distribution of power remains both an inevitable and functional part of organizations *and* cultures, value systems are created and perpetuated inside and outside organizations. His work suggests, therefore, that the way in which power distance is accepted and supported by the members of society is determined to a great extent by their national culture.

Extending his findings within organizations from a variety of cultures, Hofstede generalized the power distance dimension to culture outside an organization. He generalized from the way in which people in organizations deal with inequalities to the way in which people in various cultures deal with inequalities. Thus, power relations does not constitute the only arena in which inequality is an issue. Human inequality exists in differing wealth, prestige, and laws, and composes all relationships including family, friends, colleagues, etc. The boss-subordinate relationship examined by Hofstede bears a significant resemblance to other important relationships (where unequal distribution of power is common) within a person's life, e.g. parent-child, student-teacher.

Hofstede developed a power distance index (PDI) which indicates whether a particular culture is high power-distance or low power-distance. In high PDI cultures, authority, subordination, and little tolerance for individual freedom are emphasized. People in high PDI cultures view power as a fact of society, not to be judged as good or evil and, therefore, uses of coercive or referent power are common. The subordinate in this type of culture may, for example, have a fear of disagreeing with his/her boss. Another similarity Hofstede found among high PDI cultures was that the wealth tends to be held by a small percentage of the population.

In low PDI cultures, there exists much less fear of confrontation and a higher concern for equality. These cultures can be characterized by the de-emphasis of power. People regard "hierarchy" as an inequality of roles primarily for convenience. People of low PDI cultures believe that only legitimate or expert power should be used, and it can be judged as good or evil. Of the 40 countries in Hofstede's original study, the Philippines ranked the highest in PDI with an index of 94, and Austria ranked lowest with an index of 11 (the United States ranked 26th with an index of 40).

Unccertainty Avoidance

Uncertainty reduction research in the field of communication indicates that communication and anxiety are invariably intertwined. The Uncertainty Avoidance dimension (UA) refers to the level of ambiguity a particular culture can tolerate. It is human nature to be uncertain about the future. Hofstede (1984) stresses that the way in which people manage their uncertainty is to a considerable extent culturally determined. Individuals cope with unccrtainty and the concomitant anxiety it produces through technology, law, and religion. In organizations, people contend with uncertainty through shared rituals defined by technology and rules (e.g. using electronic mail for memos). Hofstede claims that this ritual behavior is rarely recognized, but plays an important role in the way an organization or culture manages novel circumstances.

Hofstede developed an Uncertainty Avoidance Index (UAI) during his research that describes how a culture contends with uncertainity along a continuum from low to high structure. Those cultures registering high on the continuum have a tendency to rely on structure and rules to cope with uncertainty. In the organizational setting, loyalty to an employer is not viewed as a virtue, conflict epitomizes organizational life, the hierarchical structure can be by-passed for pragmatic reasons, and employes tend to adhere strictly to the rules or the "norms" of the organization or culture to avoid experiencing anxiety. Employees in the study tended to worry more, have higher job stress, mistrust foreign managers, be less ready to compromise with opponents, view conflict in organizations as undesirable, and be less emotionally resistant to change.

Hofstede (1984) found that employees with high UAI were correlated with countries that have experienced fast economic growth. Wealthy high UAIs tended to allow faster driving speeds, have more accidents, and require citizens to carry identification. Hofstede also reports a connection between UAI and a scientific approach. Employees with high UAI were more theoretical (which is explained by a need for absolute truth), and employees with low UAI were more empirical-pragmatic. Hofstede found religion and uncertainty to be meaningfully related, where individuals involved in religions that stress absolute certainties had higher UAI scores. For example, countries that are predominantly Catholic possess a strong tendency to display higher UAI values than more Protestant countries (again explained by the stress of absolute certainties, e.g. Catholicism stresses certainties such as the infallibility of the Pope and the uniqueness of the Church).

On the other hand, those cultures registering low UAI view uncertainty as a normal feature of life. Individuals in these cultures are more willing to take each day as it comes, feel less stress, show less aggression and emotions, and view difference with curiosity. Students are comfortable with open-ended learning situations, time constitutes a framework for orientation. People in low UAI cultures generally are more tolerant of deviant and innovative ideas and behavior. Hofstede found that nations with low UAI typically were older democracies with low mean age of population leaders. Organizations were smaller and less structured, contained less ritual behavior, and higher labor turnover. Of the 53 countries examined in Hofstede's later study, Greece was registered as having the highest UAI at 112 and Singapore with the lowest at 8 (the United States was ranked 31st at 46).

Individualism

The third dimension identified by Hofstede is Individualism (IDV) but is better conceptualized on an Individualism/Collectivism continuum. Individualism is associated with a loosely knit social network where people are expected to look after only themselves and their immediate families. Collectivism pertains to societies where people are integrated into strong and cohesive social networks from birth which, throughout life, protect them in exchange for their loyalty to the group or groups to which they belong (e.g. family, tribe, work, etc.).

The individualistic/collectivistic dimension "describes the relationship between the individual and the collectivity which prevails in a given society... and is reflected in the way people live together, e.g. in nuclear families, extended families, or tribes," and by societal norms or value systems (Hofstede, 1994, p. 213). Hofstede suggests that it "affects both people's mental programming and the structure and functioning of many other types of institutions besides the family: educational, religious, political, and utilitarian" (p. 214). In turn, a central component of mental programming consists of the self-concept which is directly related to how an individual sees him/herself. In a highly collectivist culture, an individual does not think of him/herself as an individual and this manifests itself in many ways. For instance, the western (individualist) concept of "personality" does not even exist in Chinese (collectivist) tradition.

In individualistic cultures, identity resides in the individual, everyone has a right to a private life and opinion. These value standards apply to all (universalism). On the other hand, collectivistic cultures reflect a norm for identity that is "we" oriented and, therefore, is based on the social system rather than the individual. Private life is invaded by the organization and/or clan to which one belongs, opinions are predetermined, and value standards differ for ingroups and outgroups (particularism). Employees from cultures that are highly individualistic tended to be emotionally independent from the company where individual initiative is encouraged. In individualistic cultures, managers aspire to leadership positions and rate having autonomy as important. In low individualistic countries, employees are emotionally dependent on the organization where individual initiative is socially frowned upon (fatalism). Managers in these cultures aspire to conformity and orderliness and rate security as important.

Hofstede states that issues surrounding individualism vs. collectivism carry strong moral overtones because they are connected to the value systems of the society. Americans, for example, are very proud of their individualist tradition and, in fact, see it as one of the major contributors to the success of the United States. Collectivist cultures, on the other hand, view the individualist approach, the emphasis of taking responsibility for oneself, as a sign of immaturity and have been known to regard individualism as evil and at the root of selfishness. However, they do not deny the needs of the individual. "Collectivism does not mean a negation of the individual's well-being or interest; it is implicitly assumed that maintaining the group's well-being is the best guarantee for the individual" (Hofstede, 1984, p. 216).

Hofstede also observed the connection between Hall's (1976) "high-context" vs. "low-context" dimension and the IDV dimension. A high-context communication style (where little needs to be said because most information is contained in the environment or person) is often found in collectivist cultures. Low-context communication, where most of the information is vested in explicit code, typifies individualist cultures (Hofstede, 1991). This provides explanation for why American business contracts tend to be much longer than Japanese business contracts.

The individualism/collectivism dimension frequently appears in cross-cultural literature (Augsburger, 1992; Borden, 1991; Gudykunst, 1994; Trompenaars, 1993), has been supported by subsequent works (Bochner, 1994), and utilized by researchers interested in intercultural training (Brislin & Yoshida, 1994; Trompenaars, 1993). Moreover, the IDV dimension has serious implications for intercultural communication training. An awareness and understanding of this dimension can help to avoid mishaps such as the one Schnapper (1979) describes below:

> A Venezuelan vice-president of marketing for an American-owned multinational is fired by the president because he refuses a promotion, which would mean abandoning his parents in Caracas and moving to Boston. In Venezuela, where children are expected to take care of their parents, "abandoning them" would be shameful. The American president of the company is angered and confused by the Latin American's "lack of appreciation and loyalty." (p. 448)

In the United States, ranked highest in individualism (Venezuela ranked lowest), our lifestyles are driven by our desires for personal satisfaction and/or advancement rather than by what is good for the society or organization. In a collectivistic culture like Japan, the people work for the good of the organization. When they join a company, they typically join for life because they are so committed to their company. This difference has been a common source of suspicion when Americans apply to Japanese companies in Japan. The American tendency to view a new position as a "stepping stone" to something better is problematic in a collectivistic culture.

Masculinity

The fourth and final dimension, Masculinity/Femininity (MAS), refers to the degree to which a society values stereotypical masculine traits such as dominance, aggression, toughness, competitiveness, and achievement, as opposed to stereotypical feminine traits such as submission, passivity, modesty, nurturance, and affiliation. We know that the biological differences between men and women are universal. However, what is considered feminine or masculine *behavior* differs among societies. This becomes evident when examining the distribution of men and women in certain professions, for example women dominate as doctors in the Soviet Union and men dominate as nurses in the Netherlands (Hofstede, 1991).

Differences in the degree to which masculine traits are valued can be a source of cross-cultural mishaps that occur between mixed-sex or same-sex interlocutors. For example, the way in which Americans and the Dutch compose resumes is much different. It has much to do with their different emphasis of gender-based values rather than on the sex of the applicant. Americans, who value assertiveness, tend to "sell themselves" and often inflate their experience and abilities by presenting the information in an outstanding fashion. American interviewers are aware of this and, therefore, often downplay the information. On the other hand, the Dutch, who value modesty, tend to be much more subdued on their resumes. It is the role of the interviewer to draw out their experiences by asking questions at the interview. Despite that Dutch and American societies register fairly similar on the dimensions of PD and IDV, they differ considerably on the MAS dimension—Americans registering as masculine and the Dutch as feminine. In an actual case, shared by Hofstede, the Dutch applicant's modesty (in resume and behavior), was interpreted by the American interviewer as submissive and the applicant was not offered the position.

In the organizational context, Hofstede considers these as differences in "ego." The "masculine" traits representing the need for challenge, advancement, recognition, and earnings, and "social," and the "feminine" traits representing the need for a good manager, cooperation, desirable area, employment security, and a friendly atmosphere. Closer inspection of these characteristics might suggest a correlation between low IDV and low MAS, i.e. that collectivistic cultures tend to emphasize feminine traits, however both individualistic and collectivistic cultures appear to be evenly distributed across the MAS continuum. Hofstede found that Japan ranked highest on the MAS index while Sweden ranked the lowest. It is worth noting that the MAS dimension was the only one in which men and women participants differed.

DISCUSSION

Hofstede's work tremendously impacted the study of intercultural communication, especially in the area of organizational communication and the decision-making process. Studies of this magnitude contribute to and advance our understanding of culture-general (or etic) aspects of intercultural communication. The discovery of these dimensions provides researchers with a useful perspective for examining and discussing tendencies across culture. In addition to the utility for cross-cultural communication theorists, the dimensions could prove insightful to a number of disciplines. Much like Rokeach, who measured, through writings, the value systems of notorious political figures, such as Hitler and Lenin (Borden, 1991), Hofstede has provided insight into the political, economical, and social similarities of nations and cultures based upon these dimensions. Thus, Hofstede's work suggests important implications for future theory and research in a number of arenas.

Hofstede's work proves useful for the sojourner. Knowing how a culture registers on various dimensions would be useful in order to understand how a particular culture's belief and value system manifests in the behavior of the people within that culture. For example, if an American, from an individualistic and low power distance culture, plans to do business in Panama, a high power distance and collectivistic culture, it would be extremely useful for him or her to begin understanding the host culture and how it differs from his or her own culture.

Although Hofstede's work contributed to the study of intercultural communication, there are several limitations to consider. From a methodological perspective, it is important to remember that Hofstede's study was conducted in an organizational setting and generalized to the respective cultures/countries. The sample is not, therefore, representative of a random cross-section of the people in any of the participating countries or cultures. Rather, it represents the employees of a single multinational organization (IBM) and its subsidiaries. Organizational research tells us that organizations tend to hire those whose values are consistent with the "corporate culture" and the people who run them (Shockley-Zalabak, 1991). Therefore, consistencies may be more representative of the "corporate culture" than the national culture.

In addition, the sample of people employed at IBM at that time were largely well educated, middle-class males. Although Hofstede examined the differences in male and female responses for all dimensions, the vast majority of respondents were men, and thus (admittedly by Hofstede) the values represented in the study were those of men. Moreover, the women respondents tended to cluster around the clerical and unskilled positions in the organization, which means that manager role models were largely male. We know from gender research that individuals often interpret the same behaviors differently depending upon whether the person doing the behaving (e.g. boss) is male or female. Furthermore, on the survey questions about attitudes toward management styles, responses may reflect expectations of *male* managers rather than managers in general. In addition to gender differences, the population of employees at IBM in the United States (and potentially elsewhere) at that time lacked minority representation, hence, the results are representative of white values.

When we consider that subcultures within the various countries and/or cultures that went unaccounted for, the findings become limited further. In a country like the United States, which is very large and diverse, it seems inadequate to lump together all the various subcultures which display characteristics not consistent with the "mainstream" culture. For example, generalizations would be much less useful in Sumatra (a single island in Indonesia) where there are at least six different cultures with radically different traditions. In addition, people who work for multinational organizations tend to congregate around cities. Therefore, the work fails to make the city vs. rural distinction as well.

Another potential area of concern is the possibility that Hofstede's results are dated. Cultures are not static and a great deal can change over the course of 20-25 years. For instance, Hofstede stated that the United States viewed individualism as good and collectivism as bad. However, there exist indications that these attitudes have been changing over the past ten years, as American businesses have been incorporating Japanese approaches to decision-making and vice versa (Lawler, 1990). Another example of changing cultural values can be seen in relation to the MAS findings. Behaviors viewed as "acceptable" for males and females in this country have changed dramatically over the past twenty years, e.g. the "sensitive male" and "assertive female." These changes could conceivably alter responses with regard to this dimension.

From a theoretical perspective, we would hesitate to rely solely on "dimensional" information for understanding a particular culture. Although they serve as excellent guides to *approach* understanding, overgeneralizing or treating them as absolutes would be dangerous. When we use these categories to pigeonhole the individuals of a particular culture, we run the risk of stereotyping and oversimplifying other people. Therefore, it may be most appropriate to use Hofstede's approach in conjunction with culture-specific approaches. To truly understand a culture, it is important to have contextual understanding. Otherwise, we inhibit our ability to be sensitive, and, thus, inhibit our ability to be interculturally competent in host cultures.

Although there may seem to be a number of limitations, they cannot overshadow the valuable contribution Hofstede's work has made to intercultural understanding. Hofstede's work provides insight into what culture is in and of itself. The dimensions provide a useful tool for culture-general components of intercultural training programs as they provide a framework for the experienced or inexperienced trainee to further understand the issue of and surrounding culture.

SUMMARY

This chapter detailed Hofstede's quest to find theories that could be applied universally to people across cultures. Hofstede discovered and developed four value dimensions that exist in varying degrees in all cultures. These include Power Distance, Uncertainty Avoidance, Individualism-Collectivism, and Masculinity-Femininity. Power Distance refers to the measure of interpersonal power or influence between a boss and subordinate as perceived by the subordinate. In high PDI cultures, authority, subordination, and little tolerance for individual freedom are emphasized, whereas in low PDI cultures, there exists much less fear of confrontation and a higher concern for equality. The Uncertainty Avoidance dimension (UA) refers to the level of ambiguity a particular culture can tolerate. Those cultures registering high on the continuum have a tendency to rely on structure and rules to cope with uncertainty, and those registering low tend to view uncertainty as a normal feature of life. Individualism is associated with a loosely knit social network, while collectivism pertains to societies where people are integrated into strong and cohesive social networks from birth. The final dimension, Masculinity/Femininity (MAS), regards the degree to which a society values stereotypical masculine traits such as dominance, aggression, toughness, competitiveness, and achievement, as opposed to stereotypical feminine traits such as submission, passivity, modesty, nurturance, and affiliation. We argued that these dimensions are important for understanding culture-general components.

DISCUSSION QUESTIONS

1.   How does examining culture from an "etic" perspective provide insight into questions of cultural difference?

2. What do the authors mean when they assert that the dimensions can be used as a tool for understanding culture?
3. Which of the four dimensions do you feel is the most important for understading culture in an organizational setting? Why?
4. Do you agree with the critique of Hofstede's research as biased toward white males? Why or why not?
5. How would you suggest an American doing business with someone from another culture approach the situation? What would he/she need to know?

REFERENCES

Augsburger, D. W. (1992). *Conflict mediation across cultures: Pathways and patterns.* Louisville, KY: Westminister/John Knox Press.

Bochner, S. (1994). Cross-cultural differences in the self concept: A test of Hofstede's Individualism/Collectivism Distinction. *Journal of Cross-Cultural Psychology, 25,* 273-283.

Borden, G. A. (1991). *Cultural orientation: An approach to understanding intercultural communication.* Englewood Cliffs, NJ: Prentice Hall.

Brislin, R., & Yoshida, T. (1994). *Intercultural communication training: An introduction.* Thousand Oaks, CA: Sage Publications.

Gudykunst, W. B. (1994). *Bridging differences: Effective intergroup communication,* (2nd ed.). London: Sage Publications.

Hall, E.T. (1959). *The silent language.* Garden City, NY: Doubleday & Company, Inc.

Henning, G. (1995). Intercultural communication: A chapter prepared. (Unpublished document) Penn State University.

Hofstede, G. (1984). *Cultures Consequences: International differences in work-related values.* Beverly Hills: Sage Publications.

Hofstede, G. (1991). *Culture and organizations: Software of the mind.* London: McGraw-Hill Book Company.

Hofstede, G. & Bond, M. H. (1984). Hofstede's culture dimensions: An independent validation using Rokeach's value system. *Journal of Cross-Cultural Psychology, 15,* 417-433.

Lawler, E. E., III. (1990). The new plant revisited. *Organizational Dynamics, 19,* 5-14.

Schnapper, M. (1979). Multinational training for multinational corporations. In Asante, M. K., Newmark, E., and Blake, C. A. (Eds.) *Handbook of intercultural communication* (pp. 447-474). Beverly Hills: Sage Publications.

Shockley-Zalabak, P. (1991). *Fundamentals of Organizational Communication,* (2nd ed.). New York: Longman.

Trompenaars, F. (1993). *Riding the waves of culture: Understanding cultural diversity in business.* London: Nicholas Brealey Publishing.

3

THE IDEOLOGY
OF DIFFERENCE IN
CURRENT DISCOURSE

William Over
St. John's University

The current urge to recover more pragmatic frameworks that confront human issues, problems, and conditions has uncovered the value of certain universal notions only recently discarded by many advocates of diversity, a circumstance not without its unique irony. Postmodern thought, still a dominant directive in contemporary academe, has often sustained notions of difference internationally and domestically, encouraging, on one hand, many agendas of nationalism (such as in the Balkans and the former Soviet Union), and, on the other hand, doctrines of exceptionalism among the world's superpowers. Chief among the exceptionalist powers has been the United States, which has managed to maintain a comfortable self-image of altruism in foreign policy and international economics, in contrast to most previous world colonial powers. Such exceptionalism has generally gone unrecorded in the mainstream media and, therefore, remains an unconscious motivating element within our society.

Inhibiting common understanding, meaningful intercultural discourse, and universal goals like "peace with justice"—radical relativism, as a concomitant of postmodern thinking—continue to hold favor at our universities. Undergirded by a host of self-serving agendas for university turf, academic parochialism and specialization, and by single-issue politics, radical relativism continues to be associated with leftward leaning political paths, in spite of its ability to serve the status quo quite well. In fact, much of postmodern thinking operates as a form of exclusionary relativism, perpetuating the judgment that crosscultural dialogue is futile, superficial, or impossible. What is needed is a greater understanding of how universal notions such as peace, justice, fairness, democracy, inclusiveness, equality, and equal access can sustain the most important human aspirations today: group self-determination (particularly in the Third World), economic and social equality, cultural and sub-cultural integrity, and the maintenance of human values, both religious and secular.

Although both relativism and universalism derive from rationalist notions, they have been reduced to irreconilable polarities by the currents of contemporary debate. In fact, both epistemologies come in various modern forms (Margolis, 1991), some of which may service approaches to social change. As such, both relativism and universalism can help redefine social and political trajectories. Unhappilly, however, most relativist and universalist discourse today remains in opposition, their proponents unable to recognize points of connectedness. Recently, a small but diverse group of advocates has sought to articulate the unique benefits of each camp and to break down the dichotomies that inhibit their social application (Gutmann, 1992; 1994). These voices include social activists (Todd Gitlin) and philosophers, (Charles Taylor). Taylor has found that "Recognizing difference, like self-choosing, requires a horizon of significance, in this case a shared one" (Taylor, 1991, p. 52). I would like to further this effort by uncovering what I feel is today a largely hidden use of social discourse involving cultural relativism. This is the employment of notions of discourse involving cultural relativism. This is the employment of notions of difference to inhibit progressive change and human identity throughout the world. The various ways in which the language of difference can frustrate human authenticity and social development are based upon certain assumptions of exclusionary relativism that I will also explore.

The recent dialogue among scholars initiated by the University Center for Human Values at Princeton (Gutmann, 1992; 1994) recognizes how public discourse that assumes an exclusionary opposition between relativist and universalist ideas has been both tendentious and limiting. Thus far, however, this groundbreaking discussion has focuesed entirely upon the shortcomings of universalist ideas as they have informed relations of power historically. While Taylor and other contributors recognize and advocate the necessity for both universalist and relativist ideas for salutary intercultural communication, they have been occupied with defending universalist ideas against what they rightly perceived as a recurrent use of such notions to advance the repressive interests of power throughout history. Indeed, universalizing concepts during the past five centuries have been employed with fair consistency by European colonialism to advance its hegemony over non-European cultures. The inclination of colonialists and neo-colonialists to use totalizing thought for self-serving ends has dominated the concerns of the Princeton respondents, not without much justification. However, what has been neglected in this and similar recent discussions is the use of relativist notions by established institutions, organizations, and movements to advance self-serving agendas. Contemporary conceptions of cultural difference have been used to inhibit positive social change and to bolster relations of power both domestically—between perceived social groups—and internationally. Radical relativism, although usually perceived as a thought system enlisted to bring about democratic change through the recognition of diversity and pluralistic understanding has, in fact, also been employed frequently to justify retrograde practices and undemocratic conditions. In simple fact, relativism, like universalism, has both positive and negative potentialities, a reality that has gone largely unnoticed—or unacknowledged—by contemporary advocates throughout the political spectrum.

Todd Gitlin has lamented the recent reversal of political opposition in the United States: "the Left, which once stood for universal values, seems to speak today for select identities, while the Right, long associated with privileged interests, claims to defend the common good" (1995, p. 36). Gitlin blames the embrace of "identity politics" by the Left for this detour into counter-productivity, a condition that he finds responsible for the political perplexities of recent decades. Far from enhancing intercultural communication at home and abroad, identitiy politics—the exclusive preoccupation with a citizen's own perceived group—has hindered understanding between interest groups, and thus has prevented effective political alliances. The result has been a "gorgeous mosaic" with no cement. Notions of difference have thus increased rather than reduced social factionalism, and perhaps more importantly, have undermined social alliances for positive change. Gitlin warns that today's cultivation of cultural otherness tends to suppress the kind of majoritarian thinking necessary for human rights progress.

The political shortcomings of what Gitlin terms identity politics need to be examined from the point of view of the language of difference and to include its radical relativist presuppositions. In this search it will be necessary to look for hidden agendas attached to discourses of cultural difference that overtly claim goals of positive social change and human rights. Groups that advocate essentialist views of themselves—the belief in essential group differences, that their group has an exclusive or supersessionist claim to special preferences—have generally turned inward, proclaiming a separatism that eventually defeats communitarian efforts for political change. Thus, instead of inspiring positive forms of pluralism necessary in our shrinking, increasingly interconnected world, identity politics from both the Left and the Right has tended to inspire a form of non-universal essentialism, a political outlook that can shun universal human rights in favor of particularistic and short-term goals. This is "the scandal of the particular" given a late twentieth-century face. Important examples of this tendency include U.S. claims to exceptionalism—that our empire of manifest destiny and "multinational" corporate power is somehow free of the repressive activities exhibited by all other world empires of the past.

The discourse of difference by no means originated in late twentieth-century America. Seeing human difference across lines of human identity has been universal in history, an irony not overlooked in the contemporary debate between communitarians and separatists. Far less common (and certainly more recent) has been the perception that human cultures and races are commensurable. Johann Gottfried Herder, although a disciple of Kant, vigorously attacked the latter's view of distinct, original races. Kant's assumption that black people were inferior humans justified in part his essentialist view that the races were distinct groups. But Herder assumed the connectedness of races, their common humanity, a position that contradicted Kant's language of difference, which proposed degrees of humanity. Although Herder conceded that there were variant renderings of humankind based on the accidents of climate and geography, he nonetheless affirmed the commensurability of culture and race:

> In short, there are neither four or five races, not exclusive varieties, on this Earth. Complexions run into each other: forms follow the genetic character: and upon the whole, all are at last but shades of the same great picture, extending through all ages, and over all parts of the Earth. They belong...to the physico-geographical history of man. (Herder, 1968, p. 7).

Supporting Herder's holistic view of human difference was a biblical universalism derived from his Lutheranism:

> The ancient allegorical tradition says, that Adam was formed out of all the four quarters of the Globe, and animated by the powers and spirits of the whole Earth. Wherever his children have bent their course, and fixed their abode, in the lapse of ages, there they have taken root as trees, and produced leaves and fruit adapted to the climate (p. 10).

Religious arguments have been enlisted by integrative thinkers since at least the European encounter with increasingly diverse cultures during the Age of Discovery. Early deists such as the Jacobean Edward Herbert wrote poems that explicitly envisioned races and cultures in a communion of equality (Herbert, 1923). Herbert's contemporaries criticized these poems not by citing universal values but rather by positing essentialist notions of incommensurable difference between human groups and traditions (Tokson, 1982, pp. 20-35).

Current social critics often misread universal appeals to tolerance as expressions of cultural relativism. For example, Micaela di Leonardo in The Nation interprets Montaigne's essay "Of Cannibals" as an argument for cultural relativism, when in fact Montaigne enlists universal notions of economic and social equality in rebuttal to prevailing stereotypical opinions of Native Americans:

> take care not to cling to common opinions..to judge by the way of reason, and not by common report....there is more barbarity in eating a man alive [by European torture] than in eating him dead. We may, then, well call these people barbarians in respect

to the rules of reason, but not in respect to ourselves, who in all sorts of barbarity, exceed them. (quoted by di Leonardo, 1996, p. 28)

Di Leonardo goes on to quote Montaigne's description of how the Brazilian Indians viewed with wonderment the "injustice" produced by the great disparity of wealth among Europeans: "and they thought it strange that these needy [citizens] were able to suffer such injustice, and that they did not take the others by the throat and fire their houses" (1996, p. 28). Here "cultural relativism" is an incorrect label for Montaigne's argument from universal moral values about social fairness and equality. The current debate in crosscultural relations has been so confused by the rigidities of binary thinking that such glaring substitutions have commonly resulted. By "cultural relativism" di Leonardo seems to mean Montaigne's empathic appreciation of non-European viewpoints and practices. However, Montaigne nowhere assumes cultural incommensurability. As Jurgen Habermas and others have recently perceived, an adequate theory of human rights can by no means be blind to cultural difference (Gutmann, 1994, pp. 112-13). But recognizing and acting upon cultural differences is not the same as assuming cultural incommensurability, which can often lead to a not so benign neglect and usually mutual hostility. The minimalist view of crosscultural communication routinely assumed today, for example in "encounter sessions" between politically self-defined groups, is more likely to foster even less meaningful dialogue between such groups than prevails outside such meetings. Such programs are usually prefaced with assertions such as "you can't know what it's like to be ...." In these circumstances the old adage "ignorance breeds contempt" must be only slightly altered to apply: "assumed ignorance breeds contempt."

The inalterability of difference pervades contemporary thought in the United States and Europe. It is assumed in discussions of gender language, more trivially in academic battles over territoriality, and, perhaps most significantly, in the divisions of thinking between rich nations and poor nations—the old-style categorizing of peoples defined as nationalism, but now benefiting "multinational" corporations more than any particular ethnic category. The idea of the inalterable nature of cultural and racial entities is a form of essentialism used in the service of radical relativism, which assumes each culture is unique and inaccessible. If particular cultures are inalterable, that is, not influenced by other cultures, and thus unmeasurable by them, then they constitute essential absolutes. Similar logic undergirds much of the postmodern preoccupation with the ethic of "do your own thing" and the narcissism that can justify an indifference to those outside one's perceived group. Such cultural self-absorption retreats from the project, begun during the Enlightenment, of crosscultural dialogue to discover areas of commonality. A current instance of this retreat is Benjamin DeMott's "The Trouble with Friendship" (1996), which critiques recent American videodramas and films about interracial friendships. Its thesis attacks what it regards as the naive view of most Americans that differences and divisions will disappear with interracial discussion and shared experience. Instead of offering more efficacious pathways to reform, however, DeMott falls into an attack on "well-intentioned" white Americans such as Studs Terkel and Roger Rosenblatt, who recommend meaningful intercultural dialogue and offer prescriptions for change. While DeMott probably doesn't believe in the absolute differences of races and cultures, his focus nevertheless follows the postmodern agenda of deconstructing universalist initiatives. He suspects integrative intuitions that seek out common ground between perceived groups. Thus the screenwriters of "Driving Miss Daisy" and "The Cosby Show" are attacked for their "naive" attempts to represent shared experiences and overlapping values, while DeMott's own recommendations for recognizing and valuing connectivity remain decidedly underdeveloped. His view that the global socio-economic disparities between races and historical repressions make individual friendships irrelevant ignores the advantages of intimacy, which can foster the most meaningful forms of what Mikhail Bahktin has coined "the dialogic imagination." DeMott's apparent lack of interest in the (still) socially inhibited realm of interracial relationships seems retrogressive. For him the concern of "well-intentioned" whites can only be interpreted as a facile attempt to remove residual guilt, not as an effort to overcome racial barriers, which DeMott seems unwilling to explore.

To assume that cultures are inalterable, that they are somehow internally pure, ignores the twentieth-century attempt to discover how human beings both acquire and modify their cultural experiences, but also ignores the ways in which cultural perceptions of difference are actuated by the historical relationship of one group to another. In this way even an oppressed group can influence its oppressor group's view of itself. Oppressed and oppressor groups can define and even constitute each other. For example, Jews forced by church doctrine and legal proscriptions into money lending in Medieval Europe fueled negative stereotypes that marginalized them further, while their legal prohibition from the military and civil services later justified conceptions of their unsuitability for such professions. On the other side, European Christians viewed themselves as unwilling or unable to practice the work earlier relegated to Jews (Weiss, 1995). The tendency for groups to influence each other's self-definition might be described as an inclusive negativity. If one culture's view of another is often negative, or self-aggrandizing, then universalizing notions of cultures always present a risk—not that they are impossible, but that forming them can easily result from convenient prejudgments the favor the formulators. However, this is not the same thing as saying that universal human values do not exist, or that they cannot be salutary, indeed necessary for progressive transformation.

In the realm of recent world power politics, conceptions that stressed social and political differences supported the kind of binary thinking that prolonged the Cold War at the expense of domestic and third-world issues. For example, an important U.S. foreign policy axiom, set forth by Jeane J. Kirkpatrick, that Communist cultures, unlike right-wing capitalist dictatorships in the Third World, cannot allow for the peaceful evolution to democracy, must now be seriously questioned (Wilentz, 1996). Such observations only gain credibility within an accepted perceptual framework where points of reference are defined in terms of absolute difference. So Reagan's "evil empire" of Communism cannot be influenced by ideas and movements outside the narrow definitions of Eastern Communism as defined by Western powers. Hence the inalterability of cultural groups is upheld, in this case in the service of continued arms buildups and the projection of power throughout the world. If the Communist East can never be changed short of military overthrow, then Western wealth must be put into arms industries, and Western support of counter-revolutionary terrorism must continue to be funded. Universal human rights documents can be ignored, as the U.S. government chose to ignore the World Court's ruling against it in the mining of Nicaragua's Managua harbor. The still inordinate U.S. military budget—larger than all other countries combined—testified to the kind of ongoing essentialism that presupposes fundamentally incorrigible cultural distinctions.

Although the social sciences and humanities today seem more susceptible to the kind of divisive relativism explored thus far, there is a growing appreciation of the kind of universal thinking that seeks connectivity in issues of gender, race, and culture. This new willingness to understanding and recommend integrative rather than separatist models of human identity appears in the emergent fields of family systems psychology and developmental psychology. For example, after completing a second major study of men and women, Daniel J. and Judy D. Levinson (1995), well-known researchers in adult development, have concluded, "We cannot adequately understand men by the study of men alone, nor women by the study of women" (p. vi). Moreover, the need for the genders to integrate qualities traditionally confined to the other sex has become widely accepted by adult development practitioners. In fact, recent integrative thinking is transforming longstanding conceptions of essential sexual differences, conceptions that have often upheld stereotypical patterns of thought and helped perpetuate homophobic attitudes and sexist prejudgments. While differences between the sexes are demonstrable behaviorally and cognitively, a widely known study of which has been Carol Gilligan's research, *In a Different Voice* (1982), evidence of difference, whether culturally or biologically based, does not indicate incommensurability, nor even fundamental differences. Yet many theorists and social activists have unthinkingly responded as though such evidence does.

The self-appraisal of the United States as a world power that is fundamentally different from previous world powers, therefore exceptional, has been used to justify both foreign policy and overseas business expansion. A current instance of this view is clearly expressed by Fareed Zakaria, managing editor of Foreign Affairs, while commenting on criticism of American foreign policy by George Kennan:

> In one respect, though, America has not changed. It remains different from the older nations it derives from, particularly in its foreign relations, and At a Century's Ending [Kennan's book] is testimony to that exceptionalism. What other country, having defeated its adversary and now striding the world unrivaled, would be so reluctant to extend its might, so uninterested in the satisfactions of empire and influence?...most great tracts on foreign policy are obsessed with national power and glory. It is only fitting that one of the most honored intellectuals of American foreign policy should be someone hesitant about the use of American power and uncomfortable with the very idea of an American Century. (Zakaria, 1996, p. 6)

As history Zakaria's observation is inaccurate. Britain, for instance, remained self-critical and self-limiting throughout its most expansive colonial period, even as it invented new pretexts for invading more and more areas of India and Southeast Asia during the eighteenth and nineteenth centuries. Moreover, in the twentieth century most European colonial powers have remained self-critical of their world empires to the point of forcing their governments to reduce or eliminate them. Furthermore, as presuppositions motivating American foreign policy and covert operations, exceptionalist attitudes of moral superiority promote an uncritical posture that encourages apathy and denial of U.S.-inspired terrorist actions in third-world countries. As psychological strategy, exceptionalism works very simply but effectively. Most Americans would tend not to question its government and business interests abroad if they believed that America, unlike every other world power, has been sincerely interested in democracy and improved living standards for the peoples within its economic and military spheres. Believing this makes it easier to ignore the tremendous economic forces that underpay and otherwise exploit workers in underdeveloped countries. Certain other realities, such as the huge Central Intelligence Agency budget—about 30 billion dollars annually—and the not inconsiderable budgets of a cluster of additional covert government agencies, challenge the flattering view of American innocence abroad. So also do the numerous disclosures of U.S. operations and policies abroad. However, if exceptionalist views of American altruism trump all such evidence, these activities will go unnoticed by the public at large.

Exceptionalist attitudes in America congealed during the nineteenth century, aided by relative geographical isolation, but also by evolving ideas of manifest destiny, which developed into national policy with the Mexican War in the 1840s. When America entered the post-World War II era as the dominant military and economic power, notions of national superiority found renewed expression through the exceptionalist belief in the unique moral incomparability of Americans as a people following the unique goal now called "the American way of life." This point of view was articulated at the highest levels of national institutions by distinguished scholars and intellectuals. In 1953, for example, Daniel Boorstin, a renowned historian and the Librarian of Congress, credited what he described as "the genius of American politics" to a divine providence: "It is not surprising that we have no enthusiasm for plans to make society over. We have actually made a new society without a plan. Or, more precisely, why should we make a five-year plan for ourselves when God seems to have had a thousand-year plan ready for us?" (Lazare, 1995, p. 71) Although new constitutions have appeared in the last 50 years in Germany, France, Portugal, the Netherlands, Russia, Japan, Denmark, Sweden, and a host of other countries, the perfectionist postulates driving U.S. society required that its constitution remain unalterable, a kind of trans-historical essence. If American polity was an essential fulfillment, it followed that American society was fulfilled also, not subject to improvement. Thus, today many Americans still view their own social structure as the most democratic in the world, even though all evidence points to the United States having the greatest differential between rich and poor of any developed country, its corporate executives earning substantially more relative to their own workers than their counterparts in Europe and Japan. The theological language usually associated with American exceptionalist ideas—manifest destiny, divine providence, God's country, state and currency slogans and mottoes—sustains the absolutist framework which has often allowed Americans to judge themselves as qualitatively different from all other peoples and cultures.

Throughout colonial history, colonizers worked to established categories of difference for politically threatening groups, a strategy that aimed to rigidify identities in order to perpetuate tension between native factions. This "divide and conquer" stratagem depended upon perpetuating notions of ethnic, religious, and racial difference. Often, such ethnic labels served as convenient mean of preference, elevating some groups for not participating in rebellion, while stigmatizing more politically assertive groups. For example, after the Great Mutiny of 1857-1858, British imperial policy in India eliminated rebellious Bengalis, Biharis, and Marathas as eligibles for army service, but allowed Sikhs, Gurkhas, Pathans, and Rajputs to serve. The British soon developed spurious theories about "martial races" and "non-martial" races based on their experience with "loyal" and "disloyal" troops during the Great Mutiny. Alongside "martial races" the British conceived "martial castes," a categorization that exploited Hindu prejudices. Supposedly, the castes with the least war-like propensities were the Bengali and Maharashtian brahmans, whose leaders had fought so bitterly during the Mutiny (Wolpert, 1977, pp. 241-42). Generally, British colonialists convinced themselves that their presence was necessary to keep Indian groups from fighting each other, while in fact their policies often excited animosities based on religious, cast, and regional differences.

On the other hand, appeals to universal moral values were of central concern to those colonized subjects who saw the injustices of European colonialism. In India, for example, Western educated activists such as Mahadev Govind Ranade (1842-1901) and his disciple Gopal Krishna Gokhale (1866-1915) used arguments for worldwide human rights to seek political justice and economic equality from the British. Also with reference to universal concepts of human rights, the

Ranade-Gokhale form of nationalism demanded the elimination of Indian social and religious practices, including the subjugation of women to men and the inequities of the caste system, practices premised upon essentialist notions of difference (Seal, 1968).

Even as the independence movement in India accelerated with the formation of the Indian National Congress in 1885, the British colonialist community in India sought to perpetuate European control by forming British-born "Anglo-Indian associations that broadcast separatist views upholding essential racial and cultural differences. When the Bill on Criminal Jurisdiction was introduced in 1883, which allowed Indians in the judicial system to try cases involving Europeans, the British community's reaction was to denounce the "horrendous measure" by running newspaper ads arguing that Indians were not "the peers or equals" of Englishmen (Wolpert, p. 257). Similar rebuttals were employed by white communities in the American South during the 1950s and 1960s when civil rights protest threatened the established "Jim Crow" laws of public and private segregation. In these cases presuppositions of unchangeable human difference propelled arguments for the continuation of separatist practices. Single standards of human fairness and equality in the South had been traditionally rejected in favor of double—and even multiple—standards that sought to maintain segregated social structures. The goal of "justice for all" was thus abandoned; in its place were fabricated semblances of black justice and white justice, brown justice and yellow justice, male fairness and female fairness, often presented in a symmetrical way that seemed to imply a benign balance of equality. What in fact developed were retrogressive systems of "separate but equal." The "fairness" of segregationism required a level plane upon which to set the scales of justice when such even surfaces did not actually exist.

Premised upon the assumption of significant cultural difference, the British project of justice in India made one set of judges and laws for Europeans, another for non-Europeans. In practice such trajectories ignored all goals of "separate but equal" in favor of more justice versus less justice. British-born judges would try Indians, but not the reverse; in America, white school systems would be better funded and staffed than black school systems. Underlying conceptions of cultural and class differences prevailed, thinly disguised under a purported symmetrical framework of equality. In these and similar cases the ideology of difference has led to underprivilege, not, as is often assumed in current discourse, to respect and tolerance for the other.

What is needed is the sort of interactive approach Hannah Arendt begins to envision in her study of modern totalitarian societies. For her, the modern world is made up of a plurality of persons who see reality from different perspectives. Most importantly, however, their opinions are not inalterable. For Arendt, opinions are formed between people and are therefore only partially subjective. Her belief in the alterability of cultural opinions implies a shared realm of values and perceptions akin to Charles Taylor's central view of human culture as fundamentally dialogical. According to Arendt (1967), political opinion possesses an interpersonal provenance, "running, as it were, from place to place, from one part of the world to the other through all kinds of conflicting views, until it finally ascends from all these particularities to some impartial generality" (p. 115). Arendt's "impartial generality," as with Kant's assumption of an enlarged mentality predicated in Critique of Judgment, must therefore accept a domain of universal truth. Although Arendt avoids the bugbears of absolute, rational truth by her stress on plurality and freedom of political thought, her theory seems congruent with Habermas (1970), who characterizes all human communication as "a consensus achieved in unrestrained and universal discourse" (p. 372). Some recent critics have been impressed by Arendt's attempts to find common ground for the particular perceptions of individuals and cultures, but they are clearly uneasy about recognizing the efficacy of universal ideas as human standards and values. Richard Bernstein (1983), for example, has discerned a movement "beyond objectivism and relativism" in recent crosscultural discourse. However, although he affirms the kind of "rational wooing that can take place when individuals confront each other as equals and participants," he nonetheless sidesteps from the universal implications of this "rational wooing" by reaffirming the "nonreducible plurality of opinions that is characteristic of politics and action" (p. 223). His attempt to assure a plurality of opinions in political discourse derives from the commonly felt apprehension today that, to use Margaret Canovan's words, "an absolute ideal of truth is at odds with the diverse opinions that constitute the realm of political discourse" (1988, p. 189). Still, such writers continue to take "rational wooing" and "impartial generality" as givens in crosscultural dialogue, begging the question of exactly where the "absolute ideal of truth" fits in. For, in order to woo rationally and to find the impartial generality, some universal ideals must figure in.

As I have attempted to demonstrate in this chapter, absolute ideas of difference can undermine positive goals of intercultural communication just as effectively as can language based upon the absolutizing of truth. However, current critical thought seems only concerned with deconstructing universal language, not the language of difference. Recent political discourse, concerned more with the universalizing strategies of multinational powers, has chosen to ignore the human urge to invalidate otherness through the misuse of relativistic notions of human difference. Instead of denying the usefulness of universal language, to the extent of denying even the universal dimension altogether, current dialogue needs to explore the boundaries of human universality and particularity to establish a more meaningful connectivity. Whether the recovery of the universal dimension in political and social thinking will take a cautionary approach akin to Charles Taylor's, which seeks more meaningful intercultural dialogue "by using resources internal to each" group's cultural horizon (Tully, 1994, p. 247), or whether a theoretically more substantial approach can be articulated that actively encourages common ground are projects yet to be explored in intercultural communication.

Equally important is a new project that critically examines how the discourse of cultural incommensurability has hindered meaningful crosscultural dialogue and encouraged a complacent acceptance of inequality and narrowly defined self-interests. To assume essential difference remains a prescription for the status quo on all levels of human activity, but to search for connectivity remains our only hope.

DISCUSSION QUESTIONS

1. Give an important current example of how assumed notions of difference have inhibited thinking and change in educational settings.
2. What political advantages follow from approaching social problems and conflicts from the point of view of human connectedness rather than difference?
3. To what extent do the prevalent views of American exceptionalism influence how the U.S. government conducts foreign policy and promotes business interests abroad? Are these attitudes positive or negative?
4. In what ways do underlying and often unspoken notions of absolute difference influence ongoing conflict between ethnic and nationalist groups worldwide?
5. Discuss examples of how meaningful crosscultural dialogue has been restricted by assumptions of absolute difference (incommensurability) between perceived groups within the US.

REFERENCES

Arendt, H. (1967). Truth and politics. In P. Laslett and W. G. Runciman (Eds.), *Philosophy, politics and society* (3rd Series, pp. 177-198). Oxford: Oxford U P.

Bernstein, R. (1983). *Beyond objectivism and relativism: Science, hermeneutics and praxis*. Oxford: Oxford U P.

Canovan, M. (1988). Friendship, truth, and politics: Hannah Arendt and toleration. In S. Mendus (Ed.), *Justifying truth: Conceptual and historical perspectives*. Cambridge, Eng.: Cambridge U P.

DeMott, B. (1996). *The trouble with friendship*. Boston: Atlantic Monthly Press.

Gilligan, C. (1982). *In a different voice*. Cambridge, MA: Harvard U.P.

Gitlin, T. (1995). *The twilight of common dreams: Why America is wracked by culture wars*. New York: Metropolitan Books.

Gutmann, A. (Ed.) (1992). *Multiculturalism and "The politics of recognition"*. Princeton: Princeton U.P.

Gutmann, A. (Ed.) (1994). *Multiculturalism: Examining the politics of recognition*. Princeton: Princeton U.P.

Habermas, J. (1970). Towards a theory of communicative competence. *Inquiry, 13,* 368-391.

Herbert, E. (1980/1923). *The poems, English and Latin, of Edward Lord Herbert of Cher-bury*. G. C. Moore Smith (Ed.) New York: AMS Press.

Herder, J. G. (1968/1784-1791). *Reflections on the philosophy of the history of mankind*. F. E. Manuel (Ed.), Chicago: University of Chicago Press.

Lazare, D. (1995) *The frozen republic: How the constitution is paralyzing democracy*. New York: Harcourt, Brace.

Leonardo, M. di (1996, April 8). Patterns of culture wars. *The Nation*, pp. 25-29.

Levinson, D. J. and J. D. (1995). *The seasons of a woman's life*. New York: Alfred A. Knopf.

Margolis, J. (1991). *The truth about relativism*. Oxford: Blackwell.

Seal, A. (1968). *The emergence of Indian nationalism*. Cambridge, UK: COP.

Taylor, C. (1991). *The ethics of authenticity*. Cambridge, MA: Harvard U P.

Tokson, E. H. (1982). *The popular image of the black man in English drama, 1550-1688*. Boston: G. K. Hall.

Tully, J. (Ed.) (1994). *Philosophy in an age of pluralism: The philosophy of Charles Taylor in question*. Cambridge, UK: Cambridge U.P.

Weiss, J. (1995). *Ideology of death: Why the Holocaust happened in Germany*. Chicago: Ivan R. Dee.

Wilentz, S. (1996, January 21). Seeing red, *New York Times Book Review*, pp.15-17.

Wolpert, S. (1977) *A new history of India*. New York: Oxford U P.

Zakaria, F. (1996, April 7). Divining Russia, *New York Times Book Review*, p. 6.

4

MULTICULTURAL ISSUES IN THE STUDY OF CROSSCULTURAL COMMUNICATION

Eveline Lang
Shippensburg University

INTRODUCTION

An abundance of studies in crosscultural communication are based on definitions of culture and assumptions about communication which reveal a number of biases. The inquiries are guided by a worldview which is the foundation of traditional research in the various human sciences in general. This worldview, referred to as Western dualism, revolves around rational thought and the practice of categorizing, compartmentalizing and fragmenting phenomena. Quantitative approaches typically govern the comparisons of cultures: Culture is fragmented into distinct categories, such as linguistic codes, contexts, values, behavioral standards, and so forth, variables within the categories are compared, while the question of where the meanings and norms originate is left untouched. This chapter examines the value biases inherent in conventional definitions of culture and discusses how crosscultural comparisons which the field has accepted as givens break down once a critical perspective is introduced. Specifically, the critical analysis questions the validity of generalizations about communication styles representative of specific cultures by drawing attention to co-cultural differences not only in terms of interaction codes, but also in terms of the cosmological and epistemologial frameworks.

BIASES IN TRADITIONAL CROSSCULTURAL RESEARCH

The limitations of traditional approaches to crosscultural studies exist on various levels. To begin, the critique will focus on the theoretical frameworks within which conventional crosscultural research has been conducted. As is the case with many other theories in the different areas of communication studies, crosscultural studies are grounded in a rational cosmology and its dualistic perspective on the world. The implications of this worldview, which is posited as a given, or natural and thus remains unexamined in inquiries, need to be highlighted before a deconstruction of specific studies can be undertaken. For this purpose, the most crucial building blocks of theories, i.e. definitions of central concepts and taken for granted assumptions about the context the studies address, will be scrutinized in terms of the biases they introduce.

Couched within a dualistic worldview, traditional studies in culture proceed from definitions in which culture is set in opposition to nature, following a set of binary oppositions the rational worldview is based on. This dualistic perspective polarizes order and chaos; culture and nature; light and dark; the rational and the irrational; permanence and flux; the masculine and the feminine, etc., with the orderly, rational and permanent conquering the chaotic, dark, irrational and fluctuating, and the masculine sphere asserting its power over the feminine sphere. This dichotomization of the world and the dualistic value assignment present not only a masculine bias but also a male bias as "male" in the Western tradition is associated with the masculine sphere (mind/culture) while "female" is associated with the feminine sphere (body/nature). Furthermore, the dominant culture's (i.e. the group within a culture which holds the most power) values and interaction codes are used as the model representative of the specific culture as a whole. The model is then employed in crosscultural comparisons. Non-dominant cultures are erased in the comparisons; they become the *other*, a deviation from the norm. (Folb, 1997, pp. 138-146; Madrid, 1995, pp. 10-15).

One of the most prominent scholars whose crosscultural research is the undisputed foundation of a large number of inquiries is Edward Hall. His distinctions between high context and low context cultures and between polychronic and monochronic cultures arise on the basis of comparisons of communication patterns shared among members of the dominant groups within cultures. (Hall, 1997, pp. 45-54; pp. 277- 283). High context cultures, such as Japan and China, are characterized by language systems and language usage in which symbols are vague and ambiguous so that an intuitive understanding of the meaning and a careful reading of nonverbal cues in face-to-face encounters are crucial for successful communication. Vagueness and indirection are central characteristics of high context languages. Furthermore, silence is highly valued. Low context cultures, on the other hand, which, among others, include cultures in the Germanic tradition, according to Hall, exhibit verbosity, clarity, directness and precision in expressions, redundancies and a low tolerance for ambiguity. Silence is cause for embarrassment and thus largely avoided. What this depiction of low context cultures fails to acknowledge is the bias which arises on the basis of Hall's samples of observation. This is particularly obvious in the following observation Hall makes about his findings regarding cultural contexts:

> Although no culture exists exclusively at one end of the scale, some are high while others are low. American culture, while not at the bottom, is toward the lower end of the scale. *We* are still considerably above the German-Swiss, the Germans, and the Scandinavians in the amount of contexting needed in everyday life. (Hall, 1997, p. 47; emphasis added).

The reductionism performed in Hall's research makes cultures appear to be monolithic systems governed by one unified set of interaction codes. Comparisons between cultures become simple as each is placed on a high-low context continuum without internal language and behavioral code differences being taken into account. Yet the entire system of distinctions collapses as soon as non-dominant groups and their language and interaction codes are taken into consideration. Gender research, for example, has shown how women as a non-dominant group inhabit a communication world of their own. Researchers have identified distinct communication styles, distinct interpretations of experiences, distinct interaction goals, and distinct roles taken up in interactions. The studies reveal that females are often placed in the role of listeners when interacting with males; females have a tendency to seek harmony/cooperation and to deemphasize differences in the interactions as far as status, knowledge, social class, etc.; they seek to establish connections; they observe the interactants more closely; they rely more on intuitive judgment. (See for example Tannen, 1990; Wood, 1994; 1997).

In studies which compare different Western cultures to non-Western traditions, these gender differences are typically ignored and one interaction system—namely the communication styles and interaction codes which males in the dominant culture tend to follow,—are taken as the norm and thus as representative of the culture as a whole. The same is the case with other co-cultures, such as racial and ethnic groups that are accorded non-dominant status. Their unique codes and styles are excluded in the comparative analyses as well. However, an ever increasing amount of research in gender and communication, women's studies and ethnic studies (both characterized by interdisciplinary pursuits) alert us to the complexities of social systems, language systems and ways of being in the world. Once we take all co-cultures into account, the generalizations traditional studies have offered can no longer be upheld. It becomes apparent that the conventional frameworks are over-simplifications with a bias toward the dominant groups in the cultures the researchers examined.

Gender research can further be applied to a critique of Hall's research in the area of chronemics and his distinction between monochronic and polychronic cultures. (Hall, 1997, pp. 277-283). When we look at the characteristics of polychronic cultures, as identified in by Hall, we again find that the characteristics coincide with communication patterns exhibited by females, as observed in gender research in the United States. Females attend to many different things at a time; they are interruptable, patient, not ruled by clock time. (See for example Bate, 1988; Tannen; 1990; Wood, 1997). Hall's characterization of monochronic cultures, on the other hand, focused on the communication patterns usually exhibited by males of the dominant group (and anyone who adopts this code system): attending to one activity at a time, following linear sequential routines, adhering to the dictates of clock time. From these observations it once more becomes apparent that Hall only took into account one segment of the cultures he compared when establishing his ideal types. He failed to include differences in the perception of time and interaction codes based on these perceptual differences found among various groups within a given culture.

Studies in individualism and collectivism as well as in proxemics (the use and arrangement of space), kinesics (including gestures, facial expressions, etc.), oculesics (including eye contact and eye behavior) and haptics (touch) can be challenged in a simliar vein as they reveal the same kinds of omissions. The emphasis on individualism and its stress on competition, having power over others, maintaining independence, establishing hierarchical structures, valuing personal property and being self-oriented again is found predominantly in the dominant groups in Western cultures. In various co-cultures in the United States—including women, African Americans, Native Americans, Latinos, Asian Americans—collectivist values prevail. The collectivist traditions embrace the group as the central unit, emphasize sharing and decentralizing power, being interdependent and strive to attain harmony and cooperation.

Traditional research masks co-cultural differences, including gender differences, when describing the value system which is predominant in the United States. The studies distort the complexities of cultures and mute all but the dominant group. High context systems are characterized as embracing the feminine sphere without further explications as to variations within the cultures. The cultures thus appear to be made up of one undifferentiated group and gender differences as well as other co-cultural differences remain invisible. What about women in Japanese culture, for example? If the communication styles and value orientation of Japanese males are feminine in nature, how does the male culture compare to the female culture? What additional co-cultural variations exist in Japanese culture besides gender differences? What power positioning is at work? In Hall's and other traditionalists' research the question of power and whose value orientation, interaction codes and worldview are enforced in the public sphere is left untouched. Thus claims such as the following can be made only at the expense of rendering co-cultures within the United States invisible and making us blind to the fact that the various social institutions are not neutral agents of socialization but teach us gender lessons and cultural lessons which are biased toward the masculine sphere:

The concept of individualism is instilled from an early age in the U.S. by constant encouragement of children to become self-sufficient. Children are taught to make their own decisions, clarify their own opinions, and solve their own problems. (Ferraro, 1990, p. 95).

Likewise, in studies in proxemics, kinesics, oculesics and haptics, the behaviors and norms observed among members of the dominant group are presented as representative of the entire culture. When the public sphere is the researchers' primary target—business settings, public speaking events and other formal contexts—the behaviors upheld as the norm by the dominant group can usually be observed being emulated by members of non-dominant groups so that it may appear as if a homogeneous set of rules was internalized across gender, racial and ethnic groups. However, what an abundance of communication research sensitive to co-cultural differences and the issue of power has shown is that the members of the non-dominant groups are engaged in a process of "cross coding" or "code/style switching" when interacting with the dominant group, particularly in the public sphere. (Hecht, Collier & Ribeau, 1993, pp. 89-92; Ribeau, Baldwin & Hecht, 1997, p. 151). The question of power—who holds the power to name, set linguistic and behavioral standards, impose a certain body politic, etc.—is a central concern in critical studies in culture and communication, while conventional approaches tend to disregard this dimensions. As a result, we are left with a skewed picture of reality as it is experienced by the members of the various groups of which a specific culture is comprised.

SHORTCOMINGS OF DEFINITIONS OF CULTURE IN TRADITIONAL RESEARCH

As I alluded to at the beginning of the chapter, the problem with traditional approaches to studies in culture and communication starts with the definitions the researchers rely on. Even though in some instances the limitations of the studies are laid out, the implications are not thoroughly pursued. Such is the case, for example, in a textbook on intercultural communication by Dodd (1991) in which culture is defined as "the total accumulation of identifiable groups' beliefs, norms, institutions, and communication patterns." (p. 41). The text then cautions that over-generalizations are a problem because they may lead to stereotyping and proceeds to argue for a "middle ground," which is described as "central tendencies among groups of people, a modality tendency." (p. 43). Having qualified the range of applicability of the claims found in the remainder of the text, the issue is not dealt with in any other passage. A framework similar to Dodd's guides a text by Ferraro (1990) on business communication in an intercultural context. After putting the discussion content in perspective at the beginning of each book, the texts from then on remain based on generalizations so that the "middle ground" established by the researchers reflects the standards of the dominant group in the United States as well as in all other cultures included in the comparisons. This tendency is characteristic of mainstream literature in the field of crosscultural communication, especially textbooks, in general. Non-dominant cultures become peripheral (added on at the end of chapters at times), and, importantly, the question of power is not raised. Thus Ferraro (1990), quoting research findings by Morris (1977), is able to include a whole section on "how men in different parts of the world signal their appreciation of a physically attractive female" without pointing to the condescending, derogatory connotations and the process of objectification of females at work in these instances. Some of the nonverbals mentioned include:

- *The breast curve* (found in a wide range of cultures)—hands simulate the curve of the female breast.
- *The waist curve* (common in English speaking countries)—the hands sweep down to make the curvacious outline of the female trunk.
- *The breast cup* (Europe in general)—both hands make a cupping movement in the air, simulating the squeezing of the woman's breast. (p. 76).

Similarly, in the section on eye contact and eye behavior across cultures, the author can quote a passage from a study by Morsbach (1982) without adding a qualifier to the observation that "in Japan, rather than looking a person straight in the eyes, one should focus the gaze somewhat lower, around the region of the Adam's apple." (Ferraro, 1990, p. 80). This reference is followed by a quote from Hall's observations concerning the differences between England and the United States as far as eye contact and other nonverbal cues which signal that one is paying attention. The data Hall obtained when studying a selected group in each culture are presented as universally applicable to England and the United States. (p. 91). In each of these instances, the cultures are represented from a male point of view (specifically, males in the dominant culture), yet the texts, rather than drawing attention to the body politic at work in these cultural practices, disguise the discussion as an objective examination of symbol systems.

Besides the exclusion of communication styles and value systems, reductionism is also evident in that the cultures' cosmologies (worldviews) and epistemologies (ways of defining truth and knowledge) are not explored in depth. Even though the areas of religion and specific cultural rituals which reveal aspects of the underlying cosmology and epistemology are dealt with at times, the topics remain disjointed from other dimensions which constitute culture and prevent us from gaining a holistic understanding of culture and communication. An approach which seeks to avoid reductionistic representations of cultural expressions would clarify how specific practices become meaningful within a given cosmological and epistemological framework. Such differences can not only be observed across cultural traditions but within cultures as well.

CRITICAL PERSPECTIVES ON CULTURE
AND COMMUNICATION

As noted above, one limitation of traditional approaches to the study of culture and communication arises because they are based on definitions of culture which do not immediately reveal its dynamic aspect. Culture defined as a system of values, beliefs, customs, codes, and so forth, is a static concept. Characteristically, the observation that these aspects are in flux is added on—and usually not dealt with. Culture as a static concept makes it difficult to discern interconnectiones between culture and communication. Only when culture is presented as a process—fluctuating and dynamic—will this interconnection become apparent. (Gonzales, Houston, & Chen, 1994, pp. xvi-xvii). It is through communication that meanings are created, shaped, reformed, circulated and that different expressions of culture and power relations are formed. By focusing on the dynamic aspects of culture, feminist approaches to the study of culture, ethnic studies and cultural semiotics (see for example Fiske, 1989), for instance, highlight the competing meanings of codes among co-cultures. These critical perspectives also introduce power as a central point to be explored by looking at ways by which meanings are created and circulated and by whom.

Such approaches enable us to recognize how access to social institutions, including mass media, as well as access to resources is unequally distributed and provide us with insights into the struggle for meanings the disempowered groups are engaged in. They make visible the multitude of value orientations created and re-created in a culture and draw attention to the underlying differences in world-views and epistemological assumptions. Moreover, critical approaches to the study of culture are able to identify struggles marginalized groups across the world share and may become vehicles for empowerment. As far as research methods, a wide variety of qualitative assessments are performed to reconstruct the multiple dimensions cultures manifest. (Gonzales & Rai Peterson, 1993, pp. 249-278). Multi-perspectival inquiries which yield multiple interpretations of cultural practices are favored in these assessments as the researchers' intent is to make all voices in a culture be heard.

Researchers who incorporate the issue of power are potential agents for change since their studies would perhaps reveal that oppressed groups across the world in certain situations show similar responses to their oppression, as well as similarities in the forms of resistance to accepting the labels they are given and standards they are supposed to adhere to, and highlight the institutional constraints marginalized groups are likely to face. Scholars who pursue non-traditional cultural and crosscultural research, moreover, recognize the centrality of language and the need to examine symbol systems critically. The studies reveal how grammar, syntax, usage and vocabulary in a given language reflect value orientations and highlight biases and their implications for non-dominant groups. (See for example Bosmajian, 1992, pp. 341-347, and Moore, 1992, pp. 331-341). Language, in other words, is not treated as an ahistorical, neutral medium but as a system of signs which incorporates a specific worldview and specific value judgments. As such, language affects our perception in crucial ways.

A final concern that deserves attention are crosscultural studies which focus on different ethnic and racial groups. The critical issue which arises in this context is tied to the very concept of race and its varying definitions in different cultures and across time periods. As pointed out by Omi and Winant 1995, pp. 356-364), race is not a genetic given but a socio-historical concept. To illustrate this notion, the authors compare different meanings the term race has had in different historical contexts within one and the same culture. This comparison reveals that cultural definitions of race shape people's racial identities:

> In the United States, the black/white color line has historically been rigidly defined and enforced. White is seen as a "pure" category. Any racial intermixture makes one "nonwhite."
>
> ... By contrast, a striking feature of race relations on the lowlands of Latin America since the abolition of slavery has been the relative absence of sharply defined racial groupings. ...
>
> Consideration of the term "black" illustrates the diversity of racial meanings which can be found among different societies and historically within a given society. In contemporary British politics the term "black" is used to refer to all nonwhites.
>
> ... (I)n political and cultural movements, Asian as well as Afro-Caribbean youth are adopting the term as an expression of self-identity. The wide-ranging meanings of "black" illustrate the manner in which racial categories are shaped politically. (pp. 360-361).

Incorporating the unequal power distribution among different groups into the reflections on race and ethnicity, Marable (1995, pp. 10-15), in an essay on racial identity politics, notices the absence of a distinction between ethnicity and race and how the two concepts are used interchangeably. He clarifies that:

> "race" should not be understood as an entity, within the histories of all human societies, or grounded in some inescapable or permanent biological or genetic differences between human beings. "Race" is, first and foremost, an unequal relationship between social aggregates, characterized by dominant and subordinate forms of social interaction, and reinforced by the intricate patterns of public discourse, power, ownership and privilege within the economic, social and political institutions of society.
>
> ... "Race" only becomes "real" as a social force when individuals or groups behave toward each other in ways which either reflect or perpetuate the hegemonic ideology of subordination and the patterns of inequality in daily life. (p. 364).

Once we recognize the historical-political nature of racial categories, crosscultural comparisons need to incorporate the complex issues laid out in the previous passages. Studies need to trace out the process of racial identity formation (Martin, 1997, 54-63) in each instance rather than apply a biased system of classifications. In doing so, the issues of dominance and non-dominance, privilege, visibility and invisibility will again be in the foreground and the complex and dynamic aspects of culture formation will be apparent.

SUMMARY

The main objective of this chapter was to draw attention to the crucial need for critical approaches to the study of crosscultural communication. So far, critical studies in culture and communication have mostly addressed specific groups within cultures, such as ethnic studies and gender studies which focus on communication patterns among groups which traditional research has ignored. Contemporary scholars in these fields recognize the importance of incorporating race and class when interpreting findings and drawing generalizations. Yet crosscultural communication research has not been systematically reexamined to adjust its claims to accommodate multicultural frameworks. While a large amount of research on gender differences in communication as well as differences among various co-cultures is already available, the ramifications of such shifts from orthodox to critical inquiries have not been widely acknowledged in the area of crosscultural communication. Most importantly, the field needs to recognize that before crosscultural comparisons can be attempted, differences among groups within each culture need to be explored. The subsequent comparisons will be complex, similarities as well as differences will become visible, and simple generalizations will no longer be possible. Rather than uncritically accepting "landmark studies" such as those conducted by Hall, the old paradigms need to be put into perspective by laying out their biases and limitations and clarifying their validity within those paramaeters. Just as scholars are calling for reinterpretations and the inclusion of diverse narratives in the study of the history of the United States, or, in Takaki's words, for "a different mirror" (1996, pp. 16-17), a multicultural perspective is essential in critical approaches to the study of culture and communication.

DISCUSSION QUESTIONS

1. In what ways are landmark studies in crosscultural communication, such as those conducted by Hall, biased? Examine traditional studies for additional biases not discussed in detail in the chapter.
2. How does research in gender and communication challenge the claims found in traditional approaches to crosscultural research?
3. What characterizes multicultural approaches to crosscultural research and how do researchers who pursue such a perspective avoid different forms of reductionism?

4. Why is it important to view race as a historical-political construct in the study of crosscultural communication? What distortions would occur if each cultures' contemporary categories for racial groups were left unexamined in crosscultural comparisons?
5. Why is it important to address the question of power (dominance and non-dominance) when taking a multicultural perspective in the study of culture and communication?

REFERENCES

Bate, B. (1988). *Communication and the sexes.* New York: Harper and Row.

Bosmajian, H. (1992). The language of sexism. In P. S. Rothenberg (Ed.), *Race, class and gender in the United States: An integrated study* (2nd ed., pp. 341-347). New York: St. Martin's Press.

Dodd, C. H. (1991). *Dynamics of intercultural communication* (3rd. ed.). Dubuque, IA:Wm. C. Brown.

Ferraro, G. P. (1990). *The cultural dimension of international business.* Englewood Cliffs, NJ: Prentice Hall.

Folb, E. (1997). Who's got room at the top? Issues of dominance and non-dominance in intercultural communication. In L. A. Samovar & R. E. Porter (Eds.), *Intercultural communication: A reader* (8th ed., pp. 138-146). Belmont, CA: Wadsworth.

Fiske, J. (1989). *Understanding popular culture.* Winchester, MA: Unwin Hyman.

Gonzales, A., Houston, M., & Chen, V. (1994). *Our voices: Essays in culture, ethnicity, and communication. An intercultural anthology.* Los Angeles: Roxbury.

Gonzales, A. & Rai Peterson, T. (1993). Enlarging conceptual boundaries: A critique of research in intercultural communication. In S. Perlmutter Bowen & N. Wyatt (Eds.), *Transforming visions: Feminist critiques in communication studies* (pp. xvi-xvii). Cresskill, NJ: Hampton Press.

Hall, E. T. (1997). Context and meaning. In L. A. Samovar & R. E. Porter (Eds.), *Intercultural communication: A reader* (8th ed., pp. 45-54). Belmont, CA: Wadsworth.

Hall, E. T. (1997). Monochronic and polychronic time. In L. A. Samovar & R. E. Porter (Eds.), *Intercultural Communication: A reader* (8th ed., pp. 227-283). Belmont, CA: Wadsworth.

Hecht, M. L., Collier, M. J., & Ribeau, S. A. (1993). African American communication: Ethnic identity and cultural interpretation. H. Giles (Series Ed.), *Language and language behaviors* (pp. 89-92). Newbury Park, CA: Sage.

Madrid, A. (1995). Missing people and others: Joining to expand the circle. In M. L. Andersen & P. Hill Collins (Eds.), *Race, class, and gender: An anthology* (pp. 10-15). Belmont, CA: Wadsworth.

Marable, M. (1995). Beyond racial identity politics: Toward a liberation theory for multicultural democracy. In M.L. Andersem & P. Hill Collins (Eds.) *Race, class, and gender: An anthology.* Belmont, CA: Wadsworth.

Martin, J. N. (1997). Understanding whiteness in the United States. In L. A. Samovar & R. E. Porter (Eds.), *Intercultural communication: A reader* (8th ed.). Belmont, CA: Wadsworth.

Moore, R. B. (1991). Racism in the English language. In P. S. Rothenberg (Ed.), *Race, class, and gender in the United States: An integrated study* (pp. 331-341). New York: St. Martin's Press.

Morris, D. (1977). *Manwatching: A field guide to human behavior.* New York: Abrams.

Morsbach, H. (1982). Aspects of nonverbal communication in Japan. In L. A. Samovar & R. E. Porter (Eds.), *Intercultural communication: A reader* (3rd ed., p. 76). New York: St. Martin's Press.

Omi, M. & Winant, H. (1992). Racial formation. In G. Colombo, R. Cullen & B. Lisle (Eds.), *Rereading America: Cultural contexts for critical thinking and writing* (3rd ed., pp. 356-364). Boston: Bedford Books.

Ribeau, S. A., Baldwin, J. R., & Hecht, M. L. (1997). An African American communication perspective. In L.A. Samovar & R.E. Porter (Eds.), *Intercultural communication: A reader* (8th ed., 147-154). Belmont, CA: Wadsworth.

Takaki, R. (1993). *A different mirror: A history of multicultural America.* Boston: Little Brown & Company.

Tannen, D. (1990). *You just don't understand: Women and men in conversation.* New York: William Morrow.

Wood, J. T. (1994). *Gendered lives: Communication, gender, and culture.* Belmont, CA: Wadsworth.

Wood, J. T. (1997). *Gendered lives: Communication, gender, and culture* (2nd ed.). Belmont, CA: Wadsworth.

5

ENGLISH AS THE DOMINANT LANGUAGE FOR INTERCULTURAL COMMUNICATION: PROSPECTS FOR THE NEXT CENTURY

Nobleza C. Asuncion-Lande
The University of Kansas

LANGUAGE, CULTURE AND INTERCULTURAL COMMUNICATION

Language and Culture

Language is one of the most visible and significant symbols and instruments of culture. Without culture there can be no language, but a culture cannot exist without a verbal code. Language functions as a cultural marker that distinguishes one culture from other cultures or even subcultures. Consider the case of "Ebonics" or Black English and General American English in the United States. The former has its own distinct semantic and grammatical features that separate it from what is generally termed as "Standard English" as spoken by the dominant majority. Speakers of a language use it to protect their uniqueness as a culture, and to keep intruders in their place. The French speakers of Quebec remind the non-French speakers that they must learn to speak French to become part of the culture. Similarly, the Basques of northern Spain speak Basque to remind Spanish speakers that they are unique.

Language is the vehicle through which a cultural group's collective perspective on life and the world are expressed. According to the Sapir-Whorf hypothesis," We see and hear and otherwise experience very largely as we do because the language habits of our community predispose certain choices of interpretation" (Whorf, 1956). The presence of specialized vocabularies for particular features of the environment reflect the hierarchical ordering of basic life processes in a given culture. Consider the familiar examples of the variations of terms for "snow" among the Eskimos, "camel" for Arabic speakers, "rice" among rice eaters in Asia and the Pacific, bananas among those who grow and sell them, and computer language in highly industrialized technological societies. There are also cultural variations in grammatical structures of languages, signaling differences in how each linguistic group expresses its conceptions of reality. Edward C. Stewart (1971) has suggested that members of a culture have a predisposed orientation to interpreting reality. This is reflected in the culture's linguistic system. Thus, from its syntactic and semantic components, it is possible to characterize cultures as "doing," "being," and "becoming." These terms refer to cultural orientations to human actions and motivations and the way individuals express themselves through their daily activities.

The dominant culture in the United States is characterized as a "doing" culture. Normative behavior expects that individuals are engaged in some form of activity to change and to control events in their life. Expressions such as "How are you doing?" What have you been doing?" "Keeping busy?" are common greetings in interactions. A "being" culture is characterized as more accepting of the status quo and a belief that fate determines the direction of one's life. Some examples are cultures in South Asia, the Middle East and parts of Africa. Expressions such as "Fate has decided," "Inshallah," God willing" are common platitudes. "Becoming" cultures are predisposed to thinking that people and things change or evolve, and that ways can be found to make this happen. A common expression is "God helps those who help themselves."

A culture's history, its values and beliefs, and its dominant cultural patterns can be deduced from its language. English is rich in terms that express individuality, competitiveness, democracy. Chinese and Southeast Asian languages abound in terms expressing collectivity, harmony and kinship. Americans look into the future, whereas the British are more prone to look into their past. One can sense this from listening to or talking with the natives of these countries. The Hopi language has no tense aspect. Everything is in a state of being. English segments time in terms of past, present and future. A culture's linguistic system thus, provides us with a sense of who its people are, and how and what they think.

As a culture develops, so does its linguistic system. New words are added to its vocabulary reflecting societal changes, as well as providing the means for their articulation. Consider the proliferation of "politically correct" terms in the United States, reflecting a society's awareness of the sensitivities of its various sub-cultures. "Cripple" is no longer an acceptable term. Instead, one now uses "physically challenged." One is "ethically challenged" rather than being called a cheat or a fraud. "I mis-spoke," instead of "I lied." The former somehow conveys a sense that the act is merely a case of misconduct and not a lapse of ethical behavior. Negro is out, African-American is in. The aged and infirm are now referred to as senior citizens. And "guys," once meaning men, is a familiar unisex term to refer to men and women of any age group. Some other gender differentiations are also giving way to other unisex terms such as "host, aviator, waiter (server), actor instead of hostess, aviatrix, waitress, actress. Gay and lesbian are no longer taboo words. Instead of "colored," we now use "people of color." Words such as "multiculturalism, culturally diverse workforce, bicultural, transracial relationships are now more commonly used than before. More examples of socially acceptable terms can be found in the *New Oxford Dictionary*. The new lexicon reflects a change in societal perspective from monoculturalism to multiculturalism.

We also find new terms that refer to developments in information technology. Consider words such as cyberspace, microchip, modem, fax, e-mail, on-line, laptop, virtual community, CD ROM, home page, web site, Internet, World Wide Web, cellular phone, cordless phone, roaming charge. These words did not exist barely a decade ago. And the list of computer-related terms gets longer every day.

A study of language choice reflected in government policy and their implementation can shed light on important political processes and political changes. These can be seen in the language and communication policies of many countries especially in the developing world. The push for Bahasa Malaya as the national language of Malaysia is indicative of the determination of the Malayan majority, to place their identity at the core of this multi-ethnic state. By contrast, Singapore's language policy of English as the medium of instruction at all levels of education in what is in fact a predominantly Chinese city reflects the government's efforts to attract foreign firms to invest in the country, and to provide a neutral language for communication between its various ethnic groups. Such efforts have paid off, and help to explain why Singapore is consistently listed in business related magazines as one of the top ten countries for conducting international business. Elsewhere, nationalist movements that continue their struggle well after independence because they perceive that the control of the economy and communication media have important consequences for their survival, have made language policy an issue of public debate. This has been the case in the Philippines and in some other countries of Asia and Africa.

Language can be viewed as a demarcation line between social classes. Many former colonies of Britain, France, Spain, Portugal and the United States have chosen to retain the languages of their colonizers as one of, or the official languages. These have also been adopted as the medium of communication among the elites, and confer to their speakers positions of status as well as mark them as educated and privileged. Ordinary citizens with little or no education, who were not able to learn English in school remain outside of the mainstream. Opportunities for better paying jobs both at home and abroad are therefore denied them. Even in the homeland of a language, there are variants in the native tongue whose speakers can be distinguished as persons of consequence or not. For example, in the United Kingdom, the presence of both a "U" and a "non-U" variety of English usage distinguish speakers as belonging to the privileged or the common class. Varner and Beamer (1995) mention a study of corporate speech in the United States in which an applicant for a position was denied that job because he was thought to speak a variety of English that did not conform to the linguistic standards set by the firm.

Language and Ethnicity

Language is one of the distinguishing symbols of ethnic identity. To people who live in multilingual states, the selection of their own vernacular as the national language is seen as a way of improving their material and political well-being and enhancing their status within the union. Almost half of the voters of the predominantly French-speaking Canadian province of Quebec have repeatedly voted for autonomy or secession from what they see as an Anglophone-dominated country, despite the fact that both languages enjoy equal rights in the eyes of the law. In the implosion of the Soviet Union, various non-Russian cultural and linguistic groups, on gaining their independence, replaced Russian with their native tongues as their national languages. In the United States, bilingual education is offered to the children of immigrants who are non-native speakers of English who may take it on a voluntary basis. However, the students shift to total English instruction when they reach the junior-high or middle school level. This program, now widely under attack, is the result of the efforts of ethnic groups who demanded and obtained the right for their children to be taught in their native tongue and their root culture.

As a symbol of a specific culture, a language evokes an emotional attachment from its native speakers for it forms part of their national identity and patrimony. Thus, when a particular group is denied the use of their mother tongue in favor of a government mandated national language, or a language spoken by a dominant majority, this can lead to a disruption of the civic cohesion such a unilingual policy is intended to reinforce. For example, in some parts of the United States, there are on-going debates on proposed legislation in the U.S. Congress such as the National Language Act and the Declaration of Official Language Act which call for the elimination of bilingual education and multilingual balloting, and promote English as the official language. Such debates have become strident and recriminatory, prompting a Chicana writer, Gloria Anzaldua to lament that if she is denied the validity of her native tongue, it would be tantamount to denying her cultural identity (Moretti, 1996).

A colonial power's imposition of its own language as the vehicle of wider communication enabled the various ethnic groups who each had their own native tongue to communicate with each other within the country. Here, language was used as the bridge across these cultural divides. Examples of such colonial languages were English, French, Spanish and Portuguese. Through these languages, official and interethnic communications within the respective colonies of each power were facilitated.

Yet, language can also draw together disparate cultures and states. The imposition of their languages by Britain and France, in their respective African colonies, has provided vehicles for wider communication among the former dependencies of each power, and led to informal groupings of Anglophone and Francophone countries. This has helped them to pursue what they see as their common interests. In India, the imposition of a common language by the government has helped to bring together several language communities to form a single national entity.

Conversely, in multilingual states, language can strengthen unity among members of the same linguistic group. In the Philippines, for example, political candidates for national office will appeal to the "solidarity" of a linguistic region to vote as a bloc in support of a candidate who speaks their own language. Bickley (1982) quotes writers such as Marshall and Phillips on examples of language being used to strengthen cohesion among the Kung Bushmen of southwest Africa in their use of speech as an aid to peaceful social relations, and among the Thai, for managing conflict when social avoidance is not possible.

Language and Intercultural Communication

The primary purpose of intercultural communication is to facilitate successful interactions between interlocutors who are faced with cultural barriers. These barriers may range from the most obvious to those that remain outside of our awareness. Communication is culture-specific behavior, and in an intercultural context, the interlocutors begin with differing cultural norms and expectations for their conversations. Effective communication between homophilous interactants is a challenge in the most culturally consistent settings. It becomes even more daunting in intercultural encounters. Cultural variations in verbal/nonverbal codes, worldviews, beliefs, cognitive processes, role definitions and motivational orientations serve as impediments to successful interactions. The breaking down of these barriers is an imperative for intercultural competence.

In an increasingly interdependent world, intercultural communication competence is necessary for harmonious co-existence. Dealing with cultural differences will require knowledge of and an understanding of the role of culture in language and communication and vice versa. A first step is through the use of a common language. A common language can mediate a communication relationship which can lead to mutual discoveries of each other's culture. It does not matter whether the verbal code used is not the native tongue of either one of the speakers. It could be a third language which they share in common (having learned it as a second or as a foreign language), and which they use to traverse the cultural barriers that separate them. Consider the case of a Dane and a Chinese at an American university. Since neither one knows the native tongue of the other, they speak English. Both have learned English as a second language in their respective countries. Although they learned English in different contexts, they are able to communicate proficiently enough to discuss a lecture by their American instructor. This communication may lead to more frequent conversations in which they share each other's experiences in the third culture, as well as insights and knowledge of their own as well as each other's cultural idiosyncrasies. Their common knowledge of English has helped them build an intercultural relationship.

Of course, not all communication across cultural boundaries can proceed in this manner. A crosscultural encounter may be a brief and chance occurrence of a superficial nature so that a "commonality of experience" may not be necessary to sustain it. But intercultural interactions are becoming more ordinary events as the world increasingly becomes a "global village," and as nations become more competitive with each other. Hence, the need for a similar frame of reference and a common language for communication. In the arena of global business and international diplomacy in the latter part of the twentieth century, English has filled these roles.

ENGLISH AS MEDIUM OF INTERCULTURAL COMMUNICATION

The Globalization of English

The emergence of English as the world's lingua franca is an unprecedented phenomenon in the history of linguistics. It was only a few centuries ago that English was spoken mainly by a group of people who were occupying an island off the coast of the European continent. Today, it is estimated that more than three hundred million people speak English as their mother tongue, that another five hundred million use it as a second language, and that a further one hundred million use it fluently as a foreign language (*The Straits Times, July 15, 1994*).

The number of English speakers increases daily as more and more people are willing to pay tuition to learn the language. The teaching of English as a second language (ESL) or as a foreign language (EFL) has become one of the world's fastest growing big business enterprises. In China, though English was initially regarded as a "vehicle of capitalist ideology," the government as early as the 1970s initiated intensive English courses and has recruited native speakers to teach it. Today, it is estimated that there are more students learning English in China than there are native speakers of English in the United States (Bryson, 1990). In the former Soviet Union and its erstwhile satellites, the most favored language of study is English. In Sweden it is the "second" language (ESPN broadcast, April 16, 1995). Even France, perhaps the most determinedly non-English speaking western European nation announced in 1989 that its prestigious Pasteur Institute would henceforth publish its famed *International Medical Review* in English because too few people were reading it in French. Similarly, a consortium of European countries with commercial ties to each other chose English as their working language because they believed that this would put them all at an equal disadvantage. Japanese multinationals are also reported to prefer English for communicating with their subsidiaries in foreign countries.

English is one of the major languages of the United Nations and the sole medium of communication of numerous international and regional organizations. These include the Asia Pacific Economic Cooperation (APEC), the Association of Southeast Asian Nations (ASEAN), the European Economic Council (EEC), the North Atlantic Treaty Organization (NATO), the Organization of Petroleum Exporting Countries (OPEC), the Organization of African States (OAS), General Agreement on Tariff and Trade (GATT) and the North American Foreign Trade Agreement (NAFTA). English is also the worldwide operating language of the Air Traffic Controllers Association.

English is the dominant language of cyberspace. Debates, discussions, advertisements and reports, not to mention computer hard and software and data bases are mostly in English. It is reported that approximately three fourths of e-mail messages are written and addressed in English (Stevenson, 1994). A cruise of the Internet indicates that English is the dominant language. Even among a group of non-native speakers of English consisting of Chinese students and professionals established a virtual community in the United States with English as the organizing medium of communication.

The dominance of English speaking media throughout the world is quite evident when one travels in non-English speaking countries. One can buy copies of *The International Herald Tribune, The London Times, The Guardian, The Wall Street Journal, USA Today, Time* and *Newsweek* at major airports or kiosks that sell print media in cities and great urban centers throughout the world. The English speaking media have also influenced mass media elsewhere in their style of investigative journalism and advocacy reporting. One can always spot a placard or a banner with English messages whenever CNN, BBC World News or local stations broadcast critical events such as protests or calamitous happenings in various parts of the world. Clearly, their use of English is designed to attract foreign media, gain credibility and reach foreign audiences abroad.

Once, when I was riding a bus in the highlands of Papua New Guinea, an English language lesson was in session which could be heard from the bus' radio. Fellow passengers who were mostly Papuans were listening intently. It was possible to travel from one point of the country to the other with English as our only contact language. In the Philippines, cassettes of pop and rock music in English are constantly being played in passenger jeeps ridden by ordinary people.

The export of popular culture in English is growing at a fast pace. Movies and video cassettes of English language films, soap operas and TV dramas, comedies and game shows are major export items of the American and British entertainment industries. Their worldwide popularity has spawned industries of "pirated" copies. Recent trade disputes between the United States and China were caused in part by the relentless pirating of video and audio cassettes as well as of other types of copyrighted materials originating in the United States. An earlier pirate of English language books was Taiwan. The larger effects of the pirating of copyrighted properties further increase the worldwide influence of the originators, and also extend the spread and influence of English as an international language. Thus, while American and British businesses lose in the short run, the influence of the English language keeps growing.

In the realm of advertising, English appears to be the dominant language. A product advertised in English has more cachet than one in the local language. An informal check of advertising copy in Singapore and the Philippines, countries in which English is the second language, revealed that prestige goods such as European cars, jewelry, women's beauty products and communication technology were all advertised in English. Things that may appeal to children will have a sprinkling of the local vernacular, but the overall concept is still English. The Coca Cola bottle, the yellow arches of McDonald hamburgers or the picture of a benign and bearded old colonel for Kentucky Fried Chicken are familiar and well known icons throughout the world. They conjure the same associations as in the United States. These American symbols promote familiarity with English. In cyberspace, job advertisements, regardless of work location, are in English.

International conferences attended by people from various linguistic backgrounds prefer English as the dominant language of the proceedings and deliberations. I have attended major academic conferences in cities where English is not the native or second language. Still, about ninety nine percent of presentations and discussions were conducted in English.

A monolingual speaker of English can travel almost anywhere in the world and reasonably expect to find his/her way around; buy Kentucky Fried Chicken and a Coke; find a copy of *USA Today;* or go browsing in the familiar environment of a shopping mall to find T-shirts and baseball caps emblazoned with the familiar logos of American professional and collegiate sports teams and players, or the names of popular American universities. All these help to familiarize and popularize American culture and its language. But it also makes Americans and other native speakers of English less motivated to learn other languages or cultures and, thus, limit their crosscultural outlook and experience.

The preceding discussion dealt with the global expansion of English and its pre-eminence as the language of choice for intercultural communication. It was not an attempt to present a theory of linguistic dispersion but it endeavored to explain the circumstances of its dissemination. The next section will discuss the diverse implications and consequences of the spread of English in terms of some general propositions that may be useful for the development of theory.

Implications of English as Language of Intercultural Communication

The preceding section has made clear the ubiquity of English as language of wider cross cultural and international communication. The acceptance of its dominance by the world at-large suggest the growth of a commonality of values and norms between nations and peoples. Thus English contributes to the building of a *global third culture*. The contexts for this global third culture are the international economic and technological settings in which English is employed. As this global culture continues to grow, and as it appears to have no rivals, one can predict with a high degree of assurance that English will remain the dominant language of international and intercultural communication long into the twenty-first century.

However, there are some negative implications to these seemingly inevitable developments. These will be discussed in terms of the cultural politics of language use, standardization and neutrality of language, mutual incomprehension between interlocutors speaking a common language based on divergent sociocultural realities, and the possibility of losing linguistic diversity, cultural integrity and uniqueness.

Dramatic illustrations of the cultural politics of language use can be found in the educational policies of former colonial powers. British colonial education policies were significant because they were initially responsible for the spread of spoken and written English, as well as the increase in English language instruction. Freed from British colonial control, English continued to be important to these former British colonies even after the achievement of independence in the years after World War II. The leaders and the elites of most of these newly independent nations continue to maintain English as the official language as well as their preferred language of intra-elite communication. Thus, English continues its position as the language of power and prestige in a number of new nations. Two former colonies in Southeast Asia—one of Great Britain, Singapore, and one of the United States, the Philippines—provide interesting examples of the unanticipated social consequences of language policy.

In Singapore, the government's policy of English language instruction in all schools and at all levels has alienated an earlier generation of "Chinese educated" Singaporeans who received their tertiary instruction in the formerly non-governmental Nanyang University. That institution was an alternative to the government's National University, where the language of instruction has always been English. Nanyang was created, with private subscriptions, by the prominent scholar Lin Yutang in order to provide a university that would serve as a center for Chinese language scholarship after the communist victory on the Chinese mainland. Later, as Nanyang became a center of student radicalism, the government took it over and transformed it into a technological university, with full instruction in English. This has embittered the earlier graduates of Nanyang, who still value their Chinese education, but see that it has lost its standing.

In the Philippines, the bilingual policy adopted by the post-Independence government placed English and Filipino, the national language, on an equal footing, both in government and in education. Filipino is used as the language of instruction at the primary and secondary levels, except in science and mathematics which are taught in English. Filipino was adopted as the symbol of national identity and unity and is taught to inculcate pride and loyalty to Philippine culture. But the social reality is that English continues as the prestige language spoken by the wealthy and educated. Thus, at the tertiary level, since colonial times, English has been and remains the language of instruction, because it is believed to be the "bearer" of knowledge, an instrument for social mobility, and as is now recognized, an instrument for "global competitiveness."

An interesting exception has been the University of the Philippines, the nation's premier public institution of higher learning and self-appointed trendsetter for educational innovations. At this institution in the 1980s, the national language replaced English as the language of instruction, except in science and mathematics. Instructors, however, were given the option to choose either Filipino or English in their class discussions. The rationale for the adoption of the national language as the medium of instruction at the U.P. was that Filipino was part of a program to change the distribution of political power and material wealth within the society (Tollefson, 1986).

However, there have been some negative consequences. Graduates of this influential state university have fallen behind those of elite private universities, where the language of instruction is English, in their professional qualifying or licensure examinations. A belated recognition of this has prompted the University of the Philippines to "strengthen and improve" English language teaching. The administration has created the President's Committee on the Improvement of English Teaching to address the "declining English language proficiency of UP students" (*University of the Philippines System, Facts and Figures, 1996*). This partial reversal in University policy may have also been prompted by what are reported to be changes in the social composition of U.P. students. While this heavily subsidized government institution has always been open to the most gifted students of the nation, therefore offering a route to upward mobility for the brightest children of the poor, a decline in the quality of public secondary education has lessened the number of poor students who could meet the University's high admission requirements. As a result, more spaces are available for the children of prosperous parents who could provide them with superior secondary education in private schools. One may speculate that the parents of these children as well as the elite graduates of this university who are in positions of power, are concerned about the decline in influence of their university have insisted that the students be able to maintain their English competence.

As English continues to be the key to better job opportunities, the educational system in the Philippines as presently constituted perpetuates social class division. Private elite institutions of learning—which use English as language of instruction at all levels—continue to attract the elite and wealthy families, with a few scholarships offered to poor though intellectually-exceptional students. Meanwhile, the children of the poor, who have limited schooling and thus no opportunity to master English, are left behind in the race for upward mobility.

A number of writers have pointed to the political and economic consequences of the expansion of English (Pennycook, 1994). These writers believe that, English having achieved the position of dominance in many countries, has acted as a crucial barrier to social and economic progress. Its role as a key to better paying and more prestigious jobs may prevent many from acquiring such positions. They believe that, instead of helping the poor, the expansion of English worldwide is anti-poor. Its status as a world language gives it a role as an international gatekeeper regulating the flow of people and of information.

There is another side to this argument. Governments, such as those of Singapore and Hong Kong who have reversed their policies from bilingual to a monolingual education in favor of English have seen favorable results. The Singaporean government's purpose in imposing English as the sole language of instruction has been to help the country become an international center of trade that can best attract multinational corporations. This has succeeded in raising the standard of living of all Singaporeans, even though the Chinese educated grumble at their loss of status. Another purpose of Singapore's language policy has been to unify its multi-ethnic and multilingual society.

Malaysia, which for a time deleted English from the curriculum, has restored it for purposes of global competitiveness. The objections of Malay nationalists to the return of English to the curriculum, which they see as a threat to the nation's "cultural purity," are countered by the government's reassurance that English is a "neutral language," and it is necessary for Malaysia's success in the global economy.

This reflects a growing belief in applied linguistic circles that, once English has been de-contextualized from its British or American origins, it becomes a neutral and transparent medium of communication (Kachru, 1982). Support for this position comes from the structuralist/positivist view that language as an abstraction can be free of cultural and political influences. Thus, because of its international status, English can be regarded as a more neutral medium of communication than other languages (Pennycook, 1994). That is the case because the globalization of English puts speakers of various Englishes on an equal footing. As Kachru (1982) argues, "English does have one clear advantage, attitudinally and linguistically: it has acquired a neutrality in a linguistic context where native languages, dialects and styles sometimes have acquired undesirable connotations."

Yet, as suggested by the Sapir-Whorf hypothesis, language and culture always go together. Their interconnection lies in the role that language plays in shaping how people think and experience the world. It also suggests that language is the carrier of a culture's perceptions, its attitudes and its goals, for through it, the speakers absorb entrenched attitudes. Thus, to speak English is to assume a culture where global discourses on capitalism, competition, democracy, education, individualism, freedom, and human rights are expressed. If that is the case, then no language can be wholly neutral. But whether or not English is neutral in a world context, the fact remains that English as global language has facilitated economic interdependence and cultural understanding across cultures.

Related to the problem of neutrality is the debate over whether to maintain a "central standard" of English, or whether the different varieties of English, otherwise referred to as "New Englishes" (Platt, Weber & Ho, 1984), or "World Englishes (Smith, 1984) should be acknowledged as having equal status in their own right. A "New English" according to Platt, Weber and Ho (1984) is one which fulfills the following criteria: (1) It has developed through the education system where it has been taught as a subject or as the medium of instruction in a region where languages other than English are the main tongues. (2) It has developed in an area where a native variety of English is not spoken by a majority of the population. (3) It is used for a range of functions among those who speak or write it in the region where English is not native. (4) It has become localized by adopting some vernacular features into its own in phonology, syntax and lexicon.

Some examples of the "New English" include Philippine English, Indian English, Singapore English, and Nigerian English. In all of these cases, English was first introduced by the colonial power for the conduct of official business and as common vehicle for communication in a multilingual society where none of the vernaculars would do. English was adopted as the language of instruction and native speakers from the colonizing country were brought over initially to teach it. These imported teachers were gradually replaced by trained local non-native speakers when enrollments increased and there were not enough native speakers to fill the demand. These local teachers spoke varieties of modified English that included some structural and lexical influences from their own native languages.

These varieties of English soon became standardized and recognized as "educated" speech in their own communities. They were spoken within the country as regular vehicles of communication in some everyday activities. They were also used by the local media which helped the spread of these common varieties. As more of the people used them for communicating with others, the number of speakers exposed to the language soared. This exposure to English at all levels of the educational system and media contributed to an increase in the range and functions of the new varieties of English. The increase in their number of speakers, and the multiplicity of functions of an English far removed from its native contexts made it an impartial and translucent medium of communication. This new view justifies the reintroduction of English in countries which have previously downgraded its position for nationalistic reasons.

A related issue to the problems of English neutrality and standardization that is of particular relevance to intercultural communication is the problem of miscommunication when interlocutors of different cultural backgrounds communicate in their own varieties of English. Because such speakers believe that they are speaking the same language, they create a false sense of comprehension (Garcia & Otheguy,1989). But their "Englishes" are really different because they have learned them in different sociocultural contexts. As interlocutors construct meanings for the messages they send or receive, they rely on their own "social realities" (Sapir, 1921) to compose or interpret them. So as they share a common medium they are playing out the dual character of English as both a facilitator and an impediment to intercultural communication. Differences in contextual referents and in communication behaviors and expectations can create barriers to successful interactions across cultural boundaries. As the possibilities for intercultural communication multiply, with English as the unstoppable medium, so too will there be an increase in intercultural misunderstandings, but this is balanced by the key role English has also played in providing a shared understanding of the different realities of our global village.

Finally, the spread and influence of English as a global language, in part through information technology, has brought contradictory reactions from concerned scholars and practitioners alike. Satellite television, cellular telephones, fax machines, the Internet, and radio telephones have made it possible for disparate peoples from all over the world instantly to communicate with one another. This necessitates the use of a language that many can understand. In most cases, that language is English. Some critics argue that "given the status of English both within and between countries, there is often a reciprocal reinforcement of the position of English and the position of imported forms of culture and knowledge" (Pennycook, 1994).

Despite the existence of different varieties of English, there are enough commonalities to allow for comprehensible communication. Yet, the ease with which people are able to communicate with one another in English through information technology has also alarmed some specialists and Advancement of Science, various participants expressed their fear for the extinction of less widely-spoken languages including the cultures of which they were a part. They believed that "the world is fast heading towards a homogenized culture that is less interesting and less beautiful." Their concerns are also sparking a new debate on linguistic/cultural colonialism. Those opposed to the globalization of English contend that "language cannot be imported without the baggage of culture" (Stevenson, 1994). The ascendance of American English as the world's lingua franca means the dominance of American cultural values that clash with a country's native cultures. In reply, it can be said that there is really no such thing as "cultural purity," except perhaps in the minds of those in search of the "perfect" culture. Live cultures are dynamic entities in contact with each other, exchanging, adopting, absorbing and discarding features that are found to be unproductive or irrelevant to new realities.

As we move forward in the information age, the prospects for English as the dominant language of intercultural communication at least in the early part of the twenty-first century remains undiminished. It has become an international property that no one country can claim as its own. English has developed its own momentum, aided by developments in information technology and growing interactions in world economy. No other language has achieved such a status or is likely to do so in the foreseeable future.

DISCUSSION QUESTIONS

1. In what ways are culture and language impact upon each other? Provide specific examples.
2. Explain how developments in information technology have contributed to the dominance of English as a global language?
3. Debate the statement: "English is a neutral language."
4. What are the implications of English as a global language for intercultural communication?
5. Discuss how a government's policy of "language choice" can impact upon cultural processes?

REFERENCES

Asuncion-Lande, N. C. (1989). Intercultural communication. In G. L. Dahnke (Ed.) *Human Communication: Theory and research*. Belmont, CA: Wadsworth.

Asuncion-Lande, N. C. (1990). Communicating interculturally. In S. S.King (Ed.) *Effective communication: theory into practice*. Dubuque, IA: Kendall-Hunt.

Bickley, V. C. (1982). Language as bridge. In S. Bochner (Ed.), *Cultures in contact: Studies in cross-cultural interactions*. New York: Pergamon.

Bryson, B. (1990). *The mother tongue: English and how it got that way*. New York: Morrow.

Bailey, R. W., Gorlach, M. (Eds.) (1982). *English as a world language*. Ann Arbor: The University of Michigan Press.

Garcia, O., & Otheguy, R. (Eds.) (1989). *English across cultures, Cultures across English: A Reader in Cross-cultural Communication*. New York: Mouton de Gruyter.

Kachru, B. (1982). *The other tongue-English across cultures*. Urbana, IL: The University of Illinois Press.

Moretti, A. (December, 1995). Hold your tongue, http://hcs.harvard.edu/-perspy/dec.95/biling.html

Pennycook, A. (1994). *The cultural politics of English as an international language*. London: Longman.

Platt, J., Weber, H., & Ho, M. L. (Eds.) (1984). *The New Englishes*. London: Routledge and Kegan Paul.

Sapir, E. (1921). *Language: An introduction to the study of speech*. New York: Harcourt,Brace and World.

Smith, L. E. (1984). *Discourse across cultures—Strategies in world Englishes.* New York: Prentice Hall.

Stevenson, R. L. (1994). *Global communication in the twentieth century.* New York: Longman.

Stewart, E. C. (1971). *American cultural patterns: A crosscultural perspective.* Pittsburgh, PA: Regional Council for International Education.

Tollefson, J. W. (1991). *Planning language inequality-Language policy in the community.* New York: Longman.

Varner, I., & Beamer, L. (1995). *Intercultural communication in the global workplace.* Chicago: Irwin.

Whorf, B. L. (1956). *Language, thought and reality.* Cambridge, MA: MIT Press.

6

HOW GLOBAL IS GLOBAL?
A CRITICAL LOOK AT
THE LANGUAGE AND
IDEOLOGY OF
GLOBALIZATION

Aixa L. Rodríguez-Rodríguez
Quinnipiac College

INTRODUCTION

The words "global" and "globalization" are part of a dominant technological discourse that has come to distinguish "information age rhetoric" (Marvin, 1987). This chapter criticizes the uncritical use of these two words in the current public discourse about technology. The dominant theories of technological development assume that technology is either good or neutral. As part of these theories the term global has become a buzzword that represents a positive change towards the betterment (via telecommunications technology) of the entire world. But how global is global?

Global has become one of the buzzwords of what Carolyn Marvin (1987) has called the "information age rhetoric" (p. 61). Along with a plethora of concepts used to describe and define the so-called information society in which the world lives, global and globalization have become key words which are to be found everywhere. It is not unusual to open a newspaper or a popular magazine and read about the "globalization of the economy." The most recent advertising campaigns for IBM and Microsoft emphasize the global reach their hardware and software products provide. Mutual fund companies name their international investment vehicles, Global Equities (TIAA/Cref) or World Values Global Equity (Calvert Group). The use of the words global and globalization has become common place in economic, political and of course, communication circles. One just has to listen to CNN Headlines News' slogan "the whole world in thirty minutes." A common theme emerging from all these sources of information is that the whole world is becoming one "global village" (McLuhan, 1964).

But despite the constant use of global and globalization, very rarely do we hear a concrete definition of these words. It is assumed that we all know what globalization means. It is taken for granted that we all have a common understanding of the concept. In that sense the assumption is that global is world-wide and globalization is the process by which the whole world works as a single unit linked by the powers of modern technology which helps humans overcome the problem of distance.

One look at *The Synonym Finder* (Rodale, 1978) reveals some thirteen synonyms for the word global. Global could be substituted for "world-wide, universal; extensive, broad,vast, far-reaching, wide-ranging; encyclopedic, comprehensive, all-inclusive, exhaustive, complete, thorough" (p. 461). The synonym of course will depend on the context in which we use the word global in the first place. But besides reading global as world-wide, how are we to interpret the use of such a word in the various contexts in which it is being used?

In the context of this chapter, the most interesting synonyms for global are: universal, comprehensive and all-inclusive. When the word global is used these days, it seems that these three synonyms may be implied. Notice that I use the word *implied* here, because I certainly doubt that universal, comprehensive and all-inclusive is what the globalization process in reality is. I will argue that these are the meanings of global which we are expected to construct, but the reality of the globalization process suggests very different meanings.

In this chapter, I will discuss some of the implications of the uses of these two words. My goal is to present several arguments to question the uncritical use of global and globalization in the dominant public discourse. I will argue that the "meanings" of those words within the current information age rhetoric is not accidental. Instead it derives from the dominant ideology which is the backbone of the world's power relations. It is that dominant ideology what helps maintain the status quo with very little changes in the power structures.

This chapter presents some aspects that should be taken into consideration if a truly global process is to take place. Central to this discussion are the possible definitions of the words global and globalization and their ideological weight in the present state of affairs. I want to propose a different definition of global which will take into account the many aspects being ignored by the current use of the word.

HOW GLOBAL IS GLOBAL?

It seems that global carries with it some "valence" (Bush, 1983, p. 155). This concept of "valence" is defined by Corlann Bush as "a bias or 'charge'"(p. 155), that each technology carries with it and makes it "interact in similar situations in identifiable and predictable ways" (p. 155). What I mean by this is that, like technology, words are not neutral; they carry with them a certain bias towards particular interpretations and against some other possible interpretations.

When used within the dominant information age discourse, global is meant to elicit images and symbols of universality and of integration of several practices into a common one. It carries a positive "valence", for global is to be interpreted as inherently good. Together with the concepts of technology and information society, global and globalization do not seem to be questioned by the mainstream media or by the majority of the population. Of course, many academics such as Bush (1983), Ellul (1991), Mattelart (1987), and Schiller (1994, 1996) to name just a few, have devoted extensive efforts to question the ideology, and rhetoric of the globalization processes and the real forces behind the dominant interpretations of global. However, for the vast majority of the people exposed to the globalization discourse the tendency is to assume that if it is global it is for the betterment of the whole world. They also assume that if it is global, it includes those who were previously left out by localized and/or regional efforts which preceded the current era of human development. In other words, if it is global it is for the advancement of humanity and to transform the world into a global village in which we will be connected through electronic media and telecommunications technology.

The dominant theories of technological development assume that technology is either good or neutral. Jennifer Daryl Slack (1984) argues that technological assessment approaches tend to "equate technological development with progress" (p. 16). As for the neutral evaluations there is a tendency to argue that technology is not good or bad in itself, that it all depends on how humans use it. From these two dominant interpretations of technology's impact on society (good or neutral), emerges a pervasive opinion that the more technologically advanced a society is, the better.

There is an ideological bias reflected in that dominant opinion about technology. In the dominant ideology only particular definitions of progress and economic development are favored. Those are the definitions of progress commonly accepted in the United States and other developed nations, in which progress tends to be measured by income level, by the adoption of new technology, by the health of the economy and by the relative stability of the political system. In this world view, progress is measured in material terms and there is very little or no room for other definitions of progress. As a result "technophiles" and "techno neutralists" (Tehranian, 1988, p. 30-31), will either present telecommunications technology as a triumph of humanity or at the very least as neutral tools which if used correctly will facilitate progress. In this myopic perspective, technological development is seen as equivalent to social and political advancement. This optimistic view of technological advances has permeated popular beliefs about technology and the information age and it is the ideological framework in which the globalization rhetoric has been placed.

Then, a positive view of technology becomes a positive view of "globalization." Its advocates praise the wonders of a telecommunications system which makes possible to communicate New York with Japan in a matter of micro-seconds. But who benefits the most from this marvel? Certainly not the common citizen who has no real power over the world's economy and decision making processes. Within the dominant discourse about technology, global is meant to be "all-inclusive" and therefore, democratic. By using words such as global and globalization technocrats and dominant classes pretend to excuse their real economic interests.

The multinational corporations that rule the world's economy today hide behind the positive "valence" of global and "globalization." In fact, they put a humanistic twist to an enterprise which is economic and exploitative in nature. They make us believe that globalization will bring us together as one world, when in reality what they want is to bring their international business interests closer via a sophisticated telecommunications network, and to create new markets for their products and services. The slogan "the world is moving towards globalization" is supposed to appeal to the audience and convince them that indeed the world is moving in such a direction. The question arises: Who is the world? Is the world the multinational corporations from the developed nations that leave their countries of origin, in search of lower labor costs and unorganized labor forces in developing countries? If they are doing this globalization in their own interest, why are we being drawn into it? There are several reasons.

First of all, we are their potential markets, their customers and, as such, they need to give us a sense of participation. They need to create in us a need to be part of the globalization that everybody is taking about. Also, following Gramsci's interpretation of hegemony (1971), they have to win our consent in order to keep the structures of world power intact. They create a scenario for an apparent move towards democracy, equality and freedom for everyone and by presenting that image through the dominant discourse, they manage to remain in control while giving the impression that they are satisfying the general population's demands for a more egalitarian world. By repeating the idea of "globalization," they give the impression that this is an imminent, natural and spontaneous process which we have no control of and one which we better join before it is too late.

Even though this is the dominant discourse, there are dissenting voices calling into question its accuracy. Carolyn Marvin (1987) describes the dominant perspective as "uncritical optimism" (p. 49) which assumes "that in an open society the availability of truthful information is an instrument of long term social progress towards equal justice and prosperity, and a short-term instrument for surmounting individual inequities of social and material status" (p. 49). Along the same lines Armand Mattelart (1987) warns us against a discourse in which "technological moralism passes for humanistic ideology" (p. 261) and argues that "it is necessary to call into question the facile assimilation made between social progress and technological progress" (p. 261). These are some of the dangers of a dominant technological discourse which leads the general population of both the developed and the developing worlds to believe that technological advancement equals social progress and the elimination of injustice throughout the world.

If as these two authors (among many others) one has come to recognize the current discourse about technology as part of the dominant ideology of capitalism and corporate transnationalism, then it is inevitable to ask the following questions. Just how global is global? What does the dominant ideology want us to understand by global and "globalization?" What do those words really mean in the current state of world affairs?

Lets turn to the three synonyms for the word global mentioned in the introduction to this chapter: "universal, comprehensive, and all-inclusive." In my opinion these words reveal what the word global *is not*, when one compares the rhetoric of globalization with the reality of it. However, those who use the discourse of the information age may want us to believe that global certainly means all those things.

For the technophile global is world-wide, but world-wide does not mean the whole world. It means across the distance and to specific points in the globe. Therefore, if countries in every continent seem to be connected to one another, then there is global communication. Global means that you can reach different geographical points with your telecommunications network. What goes unsaid is that those world-wide points are chosen by the multinational corporations with business interests in those countries. The connection is among industrialized countries in different points of the globe and newly industrialized and developing countries which are at the periphery. Global is far-reaching but not all-inclusive. In countries marked by political instability, the former Yugoslavia and Rwanda for example, multinational corporations may not have an interest in extending access to new telecommunications technology. In these countries foreign investment has been discouraged by devastating ethnic wars and genocide. These and other countries may be left out of the globalization process.

There are serious problems with the fact that industrialized nations and their transnational corporations are leading the so-called globalization process. Some authors have called into question what seems to be the central piece of rhetoric of the information society's discourse: the global village. Ellul (1991) argues that "information may be instantaneous and bring about a new mode of thinking, but it has not changed our world into a global village" (p. 351). Ravault (1987) sees a problem in the transformation that Third World countries have to undergo in order to be part of the global village. He states:

Since the ideological ends of the countries having reached the highest level of technological development are essentially materialistic [economic prosperity or material
happiness] countries becoming technologized have to share similar goals and set
aside their traditional ideologies (p. 182).

What these authors are pointing at is the myth that globalization is inherently
good for the developing world because it will bring them social progress. What
those countries may have to sacrifice in terms of their culture and political sover-
eignty is always ignored. But even more interesting is the fact that this myth of
social progress for the Third World assumes that equality and social progress have
already been achieved within industrialized nations.

In the United States, the gap between the haves and the have nots seems to be
widening, not disappearing as the dominant discourse implies. While corporate
profits continue to increase (in 1994 they increased 40 percent) the average
weekly wage has declined 20 percent since 1973 ("Why Today's Big," 1995., p.
1). With new policies created to reduce government spending by the Republican
controlled Congress, many social programs have disappeared leaving already disadvantaged people in an even worse situation. (Among these new policies the so-
called welfare reform is expected to have profound consequences for the poor and
the disabled in the United States). During the 1996 primary season Republican
presidential hopeful Patrick Buchanan (an unlikely foe of capitalism's excesses)
led an attack against corporate greed, and the practice of using layoffs as a measure to increase profits on the part of large corporations in the United States.
Despite these inequalities, the Internet and Information Superhighway continue to
be promoted as the ultimate democratic media not only for the United States but
globally.

Herbert Schiller (1994) is among those who have questioned the corporate
interests that lie behind the development of the Information Superhighway and he
has denounced a serious problem of inequality in access to the Internet and other
technologies in the United States. Some of the questions that have been raised
refer to the costs of the hardware, the cost of service subscription and the issue of
technological illiteracy. Who will pay to provide democratic and equal access to
the highway to each and every citizen of the United States? Will poor people be
left behind because they cannot afford the cost of service, hardware and software?
One solution that is always proposed is to give the poor and economically disadvantaged citizens, public access to the Internet through the public library system
and other community organizations. Nevertheless, the question as to who will
assume the cost of implementing these measures remains unanswered in a social
climate in which government subsidies for the poor are not seen favorably.

The issue of economic access to telecommunications technology becomes even
more complex when we look at the differences between countries that have and
countries that have not. For developing countries to be part of the globalization
process will probably mean to surrender to the dominant ideology of the industri-

alized nations. This poses a threat to the developing world of yet another form of domination, colonization and exploitation of their resources, this time centered around telecommunications technology. The developing world may become dependent on the technological hardware and know how concentrated in the developed world. Their traditional cultures and world views may also be threatened by the drastic transformations that the careless imposition of technology from without usually causes in any society.

CONCLUSIONS

Globalization is nothing but part of the dominant ideology which pretends to disguise traditional capitalist interests. Words like global and globalization try to present the dominant ideology as a set of humanitarian and democratic processes which will bring the developing nations of the world out of their "backwardness." In my opinion, "globalization," as presented by the dominant discourse, is just the same old imperialist, Eurocentric, ethnocentric, and arrogant view which has always characterized the developed world and its world development projects.

With the claim for globalization, business interests seem to be efforts to lift the totality of the human race from previous stages of division and differences. Technology and the information society may eventually give everyone access to the whole world in a matter of seconds, but what does it matter to a homeless family in Detroit? What does it matter to rural communities in Latin America, Africa and Asia? What does it matter to women all over the world, if they do not have access to the power structures and the decision making processes? What does it matter if basic social and human needs have not been satisfied for the majority of people on this planet?

My conclusion is that global is not universal, comprehensive and all-inclusive as it has been implied by the dominant discourse of the information age. With the globalization of the telecommunication systems the vast majority of the world's population is being left out. The primary reason is because of lack of access to such technological devices. A second reason is that the control over the telecommunications networks is in the hands of those who control economic power all over the industrialized world, namely multinational corporations.

However, the issue of access to technology brings up a more pervasive assumption of the dominant ideology, and that is that the inequalities within the industrialized nations have been taken care of. Based on this assumption, the new goal is to do the same with inequalities among nations. The reality is that even within those countries linked by global networks and telecommunications technology, there are problems of access to the new technologies. Only the privileged benefit from the production and in many instances the consumption of telecommunication technologies. In an industrialized nation, like the United States, the control over the production of technology is in very few hands (corporate hands that is). The same is true for the rest of the industrialized world. In that scenario entire groups of people are left out of the decision making processes (i.e. women, minorities, and workers). The only instance in which those groups of people are taken into consideration is as consumers of the technology. Women, minorities, environmentalists do not participate in the process of deciding which technologies to develop and what impact those might have on society or the natural environment. Their access to technology is limited to their role as consumers. But even at the consumption end of the process there are thousands of people who for economic reasons do not have access to particular technologies. They do not count, like it does not count that industrialized societies have increased the gap between the haves and have nots, instead of decreasing it, as the dominant ideology would make us believe. It certainly does not count that, while billions of dollars are being spent to link the world in a telecommunication network, the basic needs of food, shelter, and a decent job are not being satisfied for millions of people throughout the world, including the United States.

TOWARDS A NEW CONCEPTION OF GLOBAL

In this the last section of this chapter I would like to speculate about several aspects which have to be taken into consideration for a truly global process to happen. In order to transform the current globalization process there is a need for radical change in the power structures of the world. There is a need to transform the power relations within and between nations. The most pressing need seems to be to close the gap between the haves and the have nots of the world before we can even begin to visualize a truly global communication network. Unfortunately, I do not foresee this radical change in the near future, but I do see possibilities for transformations in the current dominant discourse of the information society. In those transformations depend the hope for a new conception of global and the globalization process.

Sue Curry Jansen (1989) has argued that the dominant information age discourse favors male ways of knowing and thinking, but the debate over new technology has ignored this crucial fact (p. 196). Jansen's essay focuses on gender politics and the information age but her arguments are right on target in terms of the possibilities for a transformation of the information age discourse along lines other that gender. The same way the dominant technological discourse "exclude(s) female-gendered beings, modes of reasoning and skills" (p. 206), it also excludes non-white, non-Eurocentric, decentralized technologies and world views. Jansen calls for "a renaissance in the ways we conceive, create, code, use and theorize technologies, gender, information, epistemology and communications."(p. 206) The renaissance which Jansen talks about certainly has to include female forms of discourse and I would argue that it also has to include non-Euro-centric discursive practices.

In order to transform the current discourse on technological advances and "globalization," more discursive spaces for women, minorities, environmentalists, Third World cultures, and modes of thinking need to be opened. The current imposition of particular definitions of social progress has to be questioned. The multilingual nature of the world in which we live has to be acknowledged before we begin to celebrate English as the lingua franca for the Internet. Fortunately, there seems to be little that can be done to prevent, for example, Latin American people in the United States to communicate in Spanish with people in Latin America via e-mail. Still, the majority of the Internet is dominated by English—restricting access for those who speak other languages.

The goal of those working within the discipline of communication has to be to reveal the ideological weight of the current information age rhetoric. We have to call into question our own discourses to make them more open, more inclusive, more truly global. The use of words like global and globalization to imply everyone, everywhere, all-inclusive and democratic as if these were real phenomena, is rooted in a more pervasive way of looking at the world. It is rooted in the dominant ideology which sustains the world's power structures. An ideology that equates technological development with progress and that manages to present the interests of multinational corporations as the interests of the entire world. This dominant ideology has remained dominant by adapting itself to and articulating demands coming from the bottom, as long as those demands do not fundamentally change the distribution of power. Those of us studying communication have to give equal consideration to the oppositional and alternative discourses about technology emerging from both the developed and the developing world.

As for the word global it will only acquire the meaning of universal, comprehensive and all-inclusive when we begin to use it as part of a very different and by then, hopefully, dominant discourse of equality among people and nations.

SUMMARY

The discourse of the information age has been dominated by those who believe technology to be either good or neutral. Their influence is manifested in popular beliefs about technology as well as in the rhetoric of the information society. Words such as global and globalization have become buzzwords, but do not refer to real phenomena (Marvin, 1987). Global and globalization elicit images of universality, of a comprehensive and all-inclusive process but instead they mean: limited to a small group who has access to the technology; exclusion of the world's have nots and oppression.

DISCUSSION QUESTIONS

1. What might be some of the social and political implications of leaving certain segments of the United States society out of the telecommunications revolution?
2. How could the United States as a nation ensure equal access to new telecommunications technologies? Who should/could assume the cost of ensuring equal access?
3. Could you think of ways of helping developing countries achieve better standards of living without necessarily imposing on them telecommunications technologies that may disrupt their lives?
4. Some argue that the world's cultural environment is becoming saturated with cultural products (TV programs, films, magazines) produced by large media corporations in the First World and exported to the developing world. Is there a real threat of cultural domination? Do you foresee one world with one culture?
5. How could you contribute to transform the current dominant discourse about "globalization," to create a future of fair global communication among nations?

REFERENCES

Bush C. G. (1983). Women and the assessment of technology: to think, to unthink, to free. In J. Rothschild (Ed.), *Maxhina ex dea: Feminist perspectives on technology* (pp. 151-170). New York: Pergamon.

Ellul, J. (1991). Preconceived ideas about mediated information. In J. Hanson & A. Alexander (Eds.), *Taking sides: Clashing views on controversial issues in mass media and society* (pp. 344-354). Guilford, CT: The Dushkin Publishing Group, Inc.

Gramsci, A. (1971). *Selections from the prison notebooks.* New York: International Publishers.

Jansen, S. C. (1989). Gender and the information society: A socially constructed silence. In M. Siefert, G. Gerbner & J. Fischer (Eds.), *The information gap* (pp. 196-215). New York: Oxford University Press.

Marvin, C. (1987). Information and history. In J.D. Slack & F. Fejes (Eds.), *The ideology of the information age* (pp. 49-62). Norwood, NJ: Ablex.

Mattelart, A. (1987). Informatics and micro-revolutions in the Third World. In J. D. Slack & F. Fejes (Eds.), *The ideology of the information age* (pp. 243-263). Norwood, NJ: Ablex.

McLuhan, M. (1964). *Understanding media: The extensions of man.* New York: New American Library Peguin Books.

Ravault, R. (1987). The ideology of the information age in a senseless world. In J. D. Slack & F. Fejes (Eds.), *The ideology of the information age* (pp. 178-199). Norwood, NJ: Ablex.

Rodale, J. I. (1978). *The synonym finder.* New York: Warner Books, Inc.

Schiller, H. (1994). The information superhighway: paving over the public. In J. Hanson & A, Alexander (Eds.), *Taking sides: Clashing views on controversial issues in mass media and society* (pp. 330-336). Guilford, CT: The Dushkin Publishing Group, Inc.

Schiller, H. (1996). *Information inequality.* New York and London: Routledge.

Slack, J.D. (1984). *Communication technologies and society: conceptions of causality and the politics of technological intervention.* Norwood, NJ: Ablex Publishing Corp.

Tehranian, M. (1988, May). Information technologies and world development. *Intermedia, 16,* 30-38.

7

CONTEMPORARY ADVOCACY AND INTERCULTURAL COMMUNICATION

William Over
St. John's University

Today, crosscultural communication faces the formidable task of overcoming the partial institutionalization of what has been termed "radical relativism," a mode of thought which I will try to clarify and move beyond in this chapter. Justifiably, various forms of relativism have reappeared in the twentieth century as a rhetorical means for overcoming the harmful effects of excessive abstraction and syllogistic patterns of thinking, quite as much as to counter the prejudices of absolutist racial and ethnic codes. Both tendencies, highly abstracted modes of thought and supremacist notions, have helped reproduced the kinds of absolute statements and either/or fallacies in social thinking that have characterize the colonial and neocolonial periods. To this, relativists have posed the inevitable question, is it possible to hold only one truth for the world and its cultures? Even terms such as "neutral" and "objective" seem to become either totally abstract and empty, or burdened with the freight of particular historical, social, political and institutional meanings. The presumed "noncontrovertial" trajectories of most American scholarship in recent decades reflect this urge to be "neutral" and "objective," as if avoiding political stands somehow makes one objective, or is even possible. While recent forms of relativism have attempted to combat or replace such feckless rhetoric, unhappily, relativism itself has also proven susceptible to certain harmful social and political consequences. Chief among these are what I will term separatism and tribalism.

A common form of separatism played out on an everyday basis today can be illustrated by the following example, related to me by a Hindu graduate student in a 1980s seminar on world religions. Once, in his home city of south India, there was a crisis in the local water supply. The community was extremely diverse, made up of Hindus of various castes, Moslems, Christians of various denominations, Sikhs, and a score of smaller groups. These groups had existed side-by-side for centuries, but regarded each other as outside their own traditions. Their city was suddenly faced with a public circumstance that none of the separate groups could avoid. Water was necessary for everyone's health—a universal need that nobody could dispute. Until then, each group believed they had very little in common with any of the other groups. However, when the leaders of these cultural traditions were forced to sit down at a table together to deal with a problem of immediate survival—well contamination—they soon began talking with one another. As they did so, they began to confront not only their differences, which they had assumed were real all along, but also something more. They began to see what they had in common. And what they had in common was a great deal more than they had imagined.

The lesson for this graduate student was very clear. Each culture of his home city had derived its conceptions of reality not only from the complex set of aesthetic, ethical, social, legal, and historical values imbedded in its traditions, but had also inferred that its own traditions were incommensurate with every other tradition. Each culture had constructed its own ideology in such a way as to seal it off hermetically from other belief systems. Moslem doctrine, for the most part, ignored the belief systems of its neighbors. Protestant Christians from the Church of South India excluded religious tenets from the Hindu pantheon, and so on. It wasn't that these traditions were absolutely different from one another; rather, they each had constructed consistencies of thought that ignored all others. Typically, incommensurability was not consciously assumed, it was instead silently implied—a practice perhaps more deleterious than outright denigration of the other. However, as the various leaders began talking, they realized the connectedness of their systems. To be sure, not all was thought, felt and performed in the same way, but patterns of significance were nonetheless apparent. Commenting on this situation, the Hindu graduate student was straightforward: if groups don't contact, they don't see commonality.

Looking at the world of academe in the late 1990s, I wonder to what degree this event is analogous. Do we academics and students also contend over universal needs that reveal our connectedness? Is there not an urge for connectedness, for a global recognition of shared aspirations, among our artists, writers, activists, teachers, and creative people in general? Isn't this need also evident among workers around the world? Put in a more confrontational way, isn't the possibility of unity within diversity, of cultural commensurability, something that the echelons of private power both fear and deny? For this reason alone, shouldn't we question those outlooks in the contemporary academic setting which advocate, however sincerely, notions of radical relativism? We must ask the inevitable question, who profits most from ideologies of absolute difference, or, put in terms of recent American history, who serves to gain from keeping sealed-off from one another the vast majority of Americans who make up the white and blue-collar working class? Divide and conquer is a dictum as new as it is old.

I offer a second example, this one a call for inclusiveness; it typifies the widespread urge today to locate meaningful forms of connectedness. It also illustrates under what social circumstances the need for some form of foundationalist thinking is sensed, perhaps even more keenly by individuals from disenfranchised or denigrated groups. Commenting recently on his years as artistic director of New York's Public Theatre, George Wolfe (1995) disclosed the personal process through which he has sought to understand the variety of drama presented within our heterogeneous American culture. Wolfe said:

> As a person of color, I was trained from very early on to see "Leave it to Beaver," "Gilligan's Island," or "Hamlet," and look beyond the specifics of it—whether it be silly white people on an island, or a family living in Nowheres, or a Danish person— to leap past the specifics and find the human truths that have to do with me (p. 2.35).

Wolfe's hermeneutic, or interpretation then, has relied upon a universal constant—"the human truths," which he has assumed lie behind the videodramas he grew up on, as well as behind the plays which he has considered for inclusion in his repertoire at The Public Theatre. His intentional policy as head of a theatre company, if I may briefly paraphrase, has been to offer plays that speak from a particular cultural group to a much wider audience. As an artistic director, then, he has assumed that there exists a common understanding between diverse groups, a transcendent set of values, perhaps, although such abstractions are usually not discussed among practitioners nowadays, neither inside nor outside the arts. Wolfe's tenure at the Public Theatre is a plea for crosscultural understanding. In order to succeed at his artistic policy, however, he must assume certain universals that characterize human reality, otherwise there would be no point in producing plays for a diverse audience, which wouldn't understand them from the first line of dialogue. More to the point, Wolfe senses the value in crosscultural understanding, that such perceptions are not only possible, but are a worthwhile pursuit on the personal as well as on the social levels.

American academic efforts have been largely unsuccessful at offering a clear social agenda that would incorporate a positive pluralism with a vision of cultural holism. Still, such a goal is necessary to overcome the ethnic and cultural strife that continues to characterize the post-World War II world. The appeal to many current theorists of such abstracted values as world wide freedom and justice contradicts their affirmation of the doctrine that "there is no point of view, no vantage, no perspective available like an Archimedean principle outside history" that can support a disinterested approach to truth (Said, 1987, p. 19). While many postmodern thinkers believe that universal objectivity is impossible, they nevertheless also insist—quite rightly—that political positions should be judged by whether they are "engaged openly on the side of justice and truth," as Edward Said has stated (p. 22). The dominant relativism today sits uneasily alongside such transcendental notions as justice, equality, and democracy.

I would like to suggest a pathway towards a more inclusive understanding of contemporary advocacy. Recognizing the dilemma faced by many advocates of the left—who wish to "call justice justice and truth truth"—as Edward Said urges, Jurgen Habermas has upheld a vision of a holistic lifeworld that would accommodate cultural and racial diversity (Said, 1987, p. 22; McGowan, 1991, pp. 203, 207-10). Along similar lines, Alain Touraine has argued that "there can be no social relation unless the actors are operating in the same cultural field" (1978, p. 32). Constructive conflict between groups can only be effected among actors who share the same "cultural orientation." Thus, for Touraine, the celebration of mere difference is always unproductive, since "difference is nothing but the absence of relation," and only those who are related to one another in a social order produce social life (p. 33). Put another way, fundamental consensus is precisely what allows for productive conflict.

What is needed for America in the late 1990s is a meaningful celebration of what people have in common, together with a positively directed appreciation of what differentiates people—the understanding that difference does not mean oblivious and irresponsible separatism, and that unity does not always lead to the monolithic hegemony of the most powerful. For the most part, current public discourse has failed to moved beyond these by now habitual implications. The American corporate media have established a strong binary opposition between, on the one hand, the negatives of separatism—usually identified by highly caricatured or villainized groups such as the Waco Davidians and, in education, various "Afrocentric" movements—and, on the other hand, the facile kind of wish for world unity wherein all disputes between groups are subverted for the sake of a vague irenic future.

Overcoming this either/or fallacy demands that a preferential option for humankind, for people over things, needs to be recognized and uplifted. In fact, private organizations such as Amnesty International and Oxfam, as well as pan-Asian and pan-African congresses, already assume a host of such universal values in their worldwide dealings. The problem is that recent thought has not been forthright in acknowledging the significance of such norms in practice. Given the widespread loss among individuals in many cultures today of a sense of belonging within the wider world of mutuality, I submit that a common consciousness can be achieved only by the nurturance of a clear sense of cultural linkage. If men and women, different races and creeds, are "equal," it is not by virtue of their differences, but because encompassing the differences are some common properties of significant value, properties both physical and cultural. We cannot hope to understand such desired universal values as equality, fairness, democracy and pluralism unless we acknowledge that we share a significant common thought world with other cultures. In fact, the very act of appreciating difference assumes a shared horizon of significance—otherwise the value of human difference could not even be recognized. The recovery of "essentialist" thought and the rediscovery of universal modes of thinking have been undertaken by recent scholars. Charles Taylor (1985, 1992), for example, has attempted to examine the limitations of current crosscultural discourse among activists, educators, artists, and academics. Such insights can invigorate current political activism if these movements can succeed in distancing themselves from the seductive intellectual tendencies of postmodernism, with its separatist and highly relativistic notions.

The distrust of "metaphysical abstractions," common among advocates throughout the political spectrum today, is in part a response to the perception that such theory is second-hand. In this view, universal notions work against the possibility of recognizing concrete differences between living cultures. Theory, rife with generalizations and preconceptions, gets in the way of the imminent understanding of otherness. However, such thinking overlooks the vitality of essentialist thought, its very necessity for intercultural understanding. The urge to recognize others in their differences itself depends upon an abstraction, a transcendental value, one, as McGowan states, "based on the ethical imperative to grant full humanity to all other members of the species" (1991, p. 169). On the other hand, radical relativism, still a dominant pattern of thought throughout our cultural institutions, can easily be used to deny the humanity of those perceived as different. History teaches that, at times, radical relativist notions can lead to a not-so-benign indifference, and at worst to an aggressive urge to dominate those who are perceived as so different as to be subhuman. Moreover, radical relativism's persistent hold on theoretical thought in America, I suspect, may have derived in part from its consonance with unrestricted capitalism, the "do your own thing" credo of advanced corporate power.

By contrast, the wider acknowledgment of a universal humanism would help clarify the rights of others within the inclusive whole of humankind. To take one timely example, Edward Said has written forcefully about the long-standing rhetorical strategy to deny Palestinians their humanity by asserting their utter difference, their cultural incompatibility with Israelis and Westerners. Here, a form of radical relativism proves self-serving, enlisted to suppress or exclude a certain political group. On the other hand, Said's arguments in defense of Palestinian rights—even his insightful objections to the rhetorical strategies that exclude or distance Palestinians—assume certain universal values and strongly deny the incommensurability of different cultures (Said, 1987).

Many postmodernist critics are deeply skeptical of the promulgation of universal values throughout history because those values often have been belied by the actions of their advocates. Examples abound. The long-lived Spanish Inquisition was carried out by a church that claimed forgiveness, kindness and charity among its highest universal values. Slavery continued for nearly a century in the United States after its founders declared the proposition, "all men are created equal" the cornerstone of governance. Critics are right to point out these long-standing hypocrisies, but would a value-free/value-neutral philosophy have served such power institutions any less efficiently throughout history? Wouldn't the guards at the World War II extermination camps have drawn some comfort going about their jobs believing that they shared no values or basic human qualities with the Other they were gassing? In fact, for many centuries, a form of radical relativism has been enlisted to justify tyranny and segregation of groups—"We don't want to live or go to school with those people, they're too different from us!" Such views have commonly appeared in this country, even as official political campaign positions. The tacit acceptance of notions of radical relativism throughout much of American thought raises the question to what extent contemporary interpreters and scholars have complied with such traditional separatist attitudes.

Common in current social science is the view that human nature is only or primarily a cultural construction. Without denying the relevance of this important orientation, it needs pointing out that general statements about the cultural basis of human actions are themselves universal, transcendental propositions. For instance, the proposition, "cultures are culturally determined" is a universal statement in itself. Of course, universal thinking cannot be denied on either side of the political spectrum. Cultural construct theorists often mislead by assuming a kind of neutral liberalism in thought and practice, a kind of hands-off approach to any crosscultural issue. Such an approach proves extremely feckless, given the ever-widening venue of crosscultural contact in our shrinking world.

To refuse to judge other cultures is quite simply to refuse to think about them, to avoid the issues. In this way, "neutral" liberalism often plays into the hands of hidden concentrations of power, hidden because not readily apparent to the casual observer. These less altruistic forces in our world enlist current crosscultural orientations to exploit economically weaker peoples. For such powerful economic syndicates, "objective" liberalism's avoidance-and-denial syndrome allows for an open field of exploitation. Clearly, the problem lies not in the act of judging other cultures, but rather in how we set about judging them.

Moreover, to assume the incommensurability of cultural worlds ignores the reality of what Kwame Anthony Appiah (in a 1994 lecture) termed "multiple identities." Slavery, for example, belongs as much to white identity as it does to black identity, as does the history of Chinese immigration exclusion, and so on. Especially America has never been a singular culture, but has always incorporated a diversity of cultures, languages, and traditions. Certainly, middle and upper-class individuals are able to choose more comfortably from a marketplace of crosscultural pursuits, the underclass less so. It is important to remember, however, that class differences within society can be perpetuated fully as much by notions of relativism as by universal notions of race, religion, and class—e. g., "the classes (races, sexes) have their unique cultural values," and so on. Further-more, tribalisms of all kinds can and do thrive well under the not-so-benign neglect of relativism. A good way to turn away from the worldwide calamities of poverty or genocide is to claim some form of cultural incommensurability. On the other hand, to justify humanitarian intervention around the world demands a set of universal, transcultural values and judgments—"all people have the right to food, jobs," and so on.

The paradox is true but easily forgotten, that the important ethic of pluralism depends upon certain inescapable universal notions. As Charles Taylor observes, "To come together on a mutual recognition of difference—that is, of the equal value of different identities—requires that we share more than a belief in this prin-ciple; we have to share also some standards of value on which the identities con-cerned check out as equal" (1992, p. 52). Difference alone can't be the ground of equal value. If, say, women and men are equal it is not because they are different, but because overriding the differences are some faculties, common or perhaps in certain areas complementary, which are of value. These faculties might include the ability to reason, love, remember, converse, appreciate, have courage, and so on. To point out the obvious different interpretations of these human activities among cultures is not to nullify their commonality. In fact, not only to appreciate, but even to have the capacity to recognize difference assumes some common hori-zon of significance, if, for example, someone from the planet Zikon and you both recognize the difference between the UN Charter" (Taylor, 1985, p. 193). Perhaps the right to individual and group life, to have freedom, to pursue unhindered indi-vidual convictions, moral and religious beliefs, for the ability to tolerate other views of reality, for the sense of justice and democratic organization, are all char-acteristics of lifestyles worthy of our respect, and basic human urges. Individuals and societies possessing these qualities must have special significance for us, and be granted special moral status. In this way, our ascription of rights to peoples throughout the world is related to our conception of certain significant attributes of being human. Put the other way around, it would be both incoherent and incom-prehensible to ascribe rights to groups and individuals around the world while at the same time denying the special moral status of certain capacities.

The Caribbean scholar Ronald Dathorne (1994) has recently lamented how colonial people "are filtered through the European haze." Indeed, European and especially U.S.-based hegemony remains a worldwide threat to group identity. However, powerful economic forces, European colonialism and neocolonialism, for example, will be overcome only through collective efforts that model inclu-sive, integrative notions, such as democracy and equality. Of course, even con-cepts of democracy continue to be used to finesse quite different ends in recent history—democratic language incorporated in undemocratic agendas on a large scale. For that matter, all human ideas of universality involve some degree of par-ticularity, which often functions as a negative by-product of their idealized rheto-rics. Throughout history, even the most sincere universal standards have served "the scandal of the particular" to various degrees, oftentimes with the most blatant hypocrisy, and at other times with complete psychological and social denial. Nevertheless, universal standards have also served as significant frameworks through which tolerance and understanding prevail in history. Indeed, such criteria are a precondition for social change and positive agendas globally.

If we affirm the special status of particular human qualities, then we must not merely acknowledge their universal status, but must also affirm that it is worthwhile to encourage and develop such capacities, and that we should enhance their development whenever and wherever possible, and, finally, that we ought to realize that such qualities have a long-standing, not to say "transhistorical," importance for problem solving and progressive change.

I would like to present some typical examples of the overreliance on suppositions that assume the incommensurate nature of cultural value systems. Such habits of thinking appear as common pitfalls in American and European academe, serving to thwart integrative impulses and discourage any manner of connectivity between peoples; moreover, they abandon the field to a minimalist kind of epistemology where crosscultural perceptions are required.

One frequently used argument is directly to challenge the validity of what has been called universal moral beliefs. Thus, operative notions such as democracy, freedom, justice, equality, perhaps even more psychologically based ideas such as the right to live without intimidation, are attacked as less than universal ideas, as arbitrary, even willful, readings into the mental and behavioral worlds of other cultures, particularly those that seem quite different from our own Western constructs. This minimalist approach attempts to rebut the presuppositions of individuals, organizations and internationally initiated projects that seek to overcome violations of basic human rights around the world. Typically, such rebuttals will stress the differences between the culture of the government or institution perpetrating the abuses and the culture of the group seeking redress.

To take a current specific example, women's rights organizations that seek to prevent the practice of female circumcision among certain African cultures might be challenged by the minimalists to prove that such surgical practices actually are regarded as harmful or negative within the culture under question. Denied here is the notion of the right of the individual to possess her or his own body, but also, perhaps more profoundly, the notion that sexual feeling for one group of people (in this case women) is a right, not a privilege to be withdrawn by others. Minimalists will downplay the integrity of such rights among non-Western peoples, in effect attempting to establish the incommensurability of crosscultural contact. Often, however, the crosscultural perceptions of such arguers may reveal certain ethnocentric presumptions that inhibit inductive proof. For instance, to use for a main argument the axiom that certain non-Western cultures "do not strive to create environments where self-expression and freedom of speech is tolerated" ignores the comparative basis of such assumptions. Evidence would have to be offered—and seldom is—that the arguer's own culture (i.e., the United States) "strives to create environments where self-expression and freedom of speech is tolerated." When one considers the extremely limited spectrum of political and social views offered by the U.S. corporate media—the major source of news for the overwhelming majority of Americans—and the strikingly tendentious nature of most Hollywood film and video dramas about current affairs, government foreign policy, and domestic problems, it becomes apparent that such minimalists might see the splinter in the other's eye but not the log in their own. The quite narrow spectrum of political expression in America today belies the unstated assumptions of such arguers.

If another country, Japan for example, provides evidence that freedom of speech is not encouraged (at least not in the way we might provide encouragement in the West), then it cannot be assumed that Japan lacks the notion of freedom of speech in its culture. Since in crosscultural debate we are always comparing one culture with another (the arguers against the other culture in question), then America's problem with false spectra of opinion in broadcasting and the print media—the tendency to call two debaters with similar political beliefs "opponents" (both almost always representing the main currents of the current power structure)—makes such transparent judgments extremely problematic. Generally, it is wise to suspect arguers who uplift negative judgments of other countries and cultures while avoiding any reference to their own country. In another instance, arguers who assume notions of inequality as a major cultural and economic difference need to look at their own culture's assumptions about inequality. In such instances, the negative realities of one's own culture are often ignored or denied. Given that the United States has the greatest differential between economic classes among developed countries, our own operative ideas about social equality need to be examined if we are using them to make a comparative judgment with another country or culture. Minimalists will often point to rights violations in other countries to demonstrate their assumptions about unalterable cultural differences, ignoring similar tendencies to violate rights within their own culture.

Although cultural differences can influence political and social issues and problems internationally as well as locally, still, to assume difference for self-serving agendas becomes just as problematic as to assume a monolithic sameness. Both perspectives have been commonly used to justify the suppression or exploitation of particular cultures—cultures that usually concern the operatives as a competitive or under-exploited economic sphere. In fact, twentieth-century aggressor ideologies have not generally played upon universalist or essentialist ideas to motivate wars of international conquest and internal suppression. Rather, Nazism and Italian fascism, to take two prominent examples, quite successfully relied upon conceptions of difference rife among their populations to justify belligerent sacrifice abroad and extermination of perceived groups at home. For the German public under Hitler, the enslavement of Slavic populations was envisioned on the premise of cultural and genetic difference—not similarity—to presumed Aryan standards. By and large, perceptions of difference, rather than visions of common-ality, have motivated the trajectories of power in modern chauvinist movements.

A chief response to the frequently unreflective judgments made by cultural anthropologists and social scientists among third-world populations is that cross-cultural judgments are really impossible. What leads cultural relativists to affirm such reductive statements is an indisputable history of cultural misjudgments, misperceptions, and, in many cases, utter indifference towards the "subjects" of social science. Stories abound of ambitious academics who have blithely distorted or invented evidence to impress endowment boards, doctoral committees, and editors. Still, what impresses radical relativists is the inaccuracy of the cultural constructs that result. Researchers surely need reminding that social science is a difficult field (which science isn't?), and that one day's insightful observation is the next day's unthinking academic dogma. On the other hand, to abandon all attempts at understanding "radically different cultures"—because of the difficulty of the field —seems reductive and feckless. Aside from certain logical problems with this view—how do you know they are "radically different" when you claim you can't know anything about them?—it is apparent that we do in fact operate in social science making correct (i.e. true to reality) assumptions. Universals do exist in social science research. There are the obvious ones—so blatant as perhaps to go unnoticed by polemicists: all social groups need to manage a food and water sup-ply; all humans have (roughly) the same male and female body parts, physiology, and motor mechanisms; all cultures are gendered (made up of female and male in fairly equal numbers, allowing for temporary distortions from weather, wars, and disease); and all cultures need clothing and shelter (at least part of the year). If these universals are readily apparent, why must it be assumed that others, more subtle or simply not readily apparent, must not also exist?

Moreover, if our cultural differences can prevent us from seeing the differences between cultures, wouldn't such differences also hinder our seeing the similarities as well? Surely, significant social and racial prejudices have prevented research-ers from perceiving similarities, not only differences. After all, it can be a disturb-ing find that a culture one doesn't identify with, and perhaps would prefer to distance oneself from, has similar ways of feeling, thinking, perceiving, and behaving. Such intimate perceptions can offend recent researchers quite as much as they have distressed European colonialists over the past five centuries. Also, perceived differences between peoples have impelled political movements quite as much as much or more than have perceived similarities. As I have already observed, age-old cliches still abound today that justify economic and social seg-regation and suppression by invoking perceived differences—"blacks and whites just don't have enough in common to live together," and so on.

Justificatory agendas associated with minimalist views of crosscultural under-standing continue to have their effect in the fashioning of first-world foreign pol-icy, trade agreements, "foreign aid," and social policy in general. Complacent views of the "other"—as that such peoples are somehow so different from "us" that relations with them are free from the stricter moral and professional obligations in place in the home country—remain operative in the institutions of political and economic power in the first world. Conditions that increase corporate profits by maintaining pauper wages, no benefits, little or no occupational safety regulations, and nonexistent ecological restrains can be justified using common mind sets that draw distinctions and set up mental barriers between cultures. Examples of such self-aggrandizing statements are widespread: "their lifestyles are different from ours and they don't need what we do;" "women and children factory workers have different expectations from adult men;" "we have earned our worker lifestyles and security, they are not at the same evolutionary point of industrialization;" "it cannot be assumed that these people share our goals of fairness, just compensation, democracy, equality, the alleviation of suffering." Of course, more blatantly racist or jingoist attitudes can also be enlisted, attitudes often left unspoken but understood, that validate current transnational corporate power. One example will suffice: "They are used to being walked on and their own people do it to them anyway." In all these instances, perceived differences dominate the discourse of economic exploitation in the neocolonial world order. Such governing attitudes are perpetuated in academic institutions as well—often, though not always, cast in more intellectually acceptable language. Universities have usually serviced the economic hegemony throughout history. Here, the tenets of radical relativism allow for policies of noninterference insofar as global and internal business activities are concerned. The U.S. Bill of Rights stops at the front door.

A more conceptually complex problem in the current study of cultures has arisen over attempts to determine more precisely what constitutes difference and similarity in human culture. This dialogue, though at times abstruse, is nevertheless far from merely "academic," since social and economic policy on all levels depends upon our understanding of what it means to be culturally the same or different. Most thoughtful observers dismiss the simplicities of reducing issues of crosscultural meaning either to a position that denies any sort of communication between radically different cultures, or, on the other extreme, to a position that denies any sort of meaningful difference. Rather, most observers will acknowledge the complexities of the problem without falling into the either/or fallacy that seems to have derailed most public discourse on the subject. There is in fact a "unity in diversity," and, to reverse the equation, also a "diversity in unity" so far as human cultures are concerned. To take one illustration, every culture has courtship customs that anticipate heterosexual sex, but the specificities of such practices vary widely among cultures. Still, even the divergent details of such prenuptial practices often reveal parallels with other cultures. Further study in this new area of learning needs to explore the apparent paradoxes in order to clarify relations between peoples.

Crosscultural interlocutors must be circumspect, since the political consequences remain crucial. Perhaps the student of intercultural meaning needs reminding that the clash of cultures today usually involves unequal forces; that is, major cultures (Western capitalism being by far the most significant) easily dominate others. This usually means that non-Western cultures are denied adequate means of expressing their views, and that the unequal nature of intercultural contact distorts and problematizes meaning. One result is that universal values have become imperiled, a condition not overlooked by such informed advocates as Todd Gitlin (1995). Given the fact that cultural pluralism as a conscious goal has only been fully endorsed in the twentieth century, and that systematic study of how crosscultural contact creates meaning is only just beginning, the frontiers of this discipline are yet to be drawn.

DISCUSSION QUESTIONS

1. What other political and social problems inhibit attempts to arrive at meaningful contact between different cultures today?
2. Considering the international pressures to ignore what peoples have in common today, are there similar inhibitions that prevent meaningful dialogue and activism among subcultures, that is, among groups within countries?
3. Besides the goals of fairness, equality, democracy, justice, what other commonly assumed "universal moral values" are evident today? How have the particularities of these goals changed in recent history?
4. What specific international issues today are ignored or fueled by overhasty notions of cultural difference and/or cultural similarity?
5. Intercultural mutuality is often problematized by thinking that fails to account for "diversity in unity." What are some timely political examples of such breakdowns?

REFERENCES

Appiah, K. A. (1994). *The challenge to pluralism: Multiple cultures or multiple identities.* Paper delivered for the W. E. B. Du Bois Distinguished Lecture Series. Graduate Center, CUNY, New York.

Dathorne, R. (1994). *Gender, race, culture: Diversity or adversity.* Paper presented at the annual meeting of the Caribbean Association of Professionals and Scholars, Washington, DC.

Gitlin, T. (1995). *The twilight of common dreams.* New York: Holt.

Margolis, J. (1991). *The truth about relativism.* Oxford: Blackwell.

McGowan, J. (1991). *Postmodernism and its critics.* Ithaca, NY: Cornell University Press.

Said, E. (1987, March). Interpreting Palestine. *Harpers,* p. 19.

Taylor, C. (1992). *The ethics of authenticity.* Cambridge, MA: Harvard University Press.

Taylor, C. (1985). *Philosophy and the human sciences.* New York: Cambridge University Press.

Touraine, A. (1978). *The voice and the eye: An analysis of social movements*. Trans. A
    Duff. Cambridge, U.K..: Cambridge University Press.
Wolfe, G. (1995, April 23). George Wolfe and his theatre of inclusion. *New York Times*, p.
    H35.

8

PROMOTING INTERCULTURAL COMMUNICATION IN THE MULTICULTURAL CLASSROOM: USING DISCOMFORT AS A LEARNING TOOL

Ruth Johnson
Southern Illinois University at Carbondale

INTRODUCTION

A complex issue facing English as a Second Language/ English as a Foreign Language (ESL/EFL) teachers, besides teaching a second language, relates to promoting cultural awareness and intercultural communication in their students. ESL/EFL teachers themselves need to acquire empathy for others' cultural behaviors and beliefs. For teacher-trainers, the challenge is to educate teachers-in-training in methods for teaching culture alongside language learning. Part of the problem in becoming educated in intercultural communication is that not enough is known about what cultural content to teach.

BACKGROUND

Teachers can begin to acquire empathy for others' cultural behaviors and beliefs by gaining awareness of themselves as cultural beings. Lewald (1968) asks, "What has to happen in the mind of a boy from Kansas to make him react like an Italian when facing a teacher, a companion, or a girl?" The question remains valid today in any foreign context with any person.

The one who can accomplish this feat may be said to be an intercultural communicator. ESL/EFL teachers often do not take into account the fact that they themselves are cultural beings whose cultural beliefs influence—positively or negatively—the learning process.

Part of the problem in becoming educated in intercultural communication is that not enough is known about what cultural content to teach. Boski (1988) developed notions of ethnic identity when emotional/interpersonal issues are at stake for an individual versus in-group rivalry when achievement-related performance is the focus. The ESL/EFL teacher would do well to determine the effect such emotional versus achievement behavior has on interaction in a multicultural classroom.

Prejudice has been defined by Brislin (1978) as negative out-group emotional reactions. He notes that "one of the most amazing facts about a culture is that it can socialize its members into believing that their culture has the *one* correct set of behaviors for all situations which a person is likely to encounter" (p. 33). Prejudices are formed through more than cognitive avenues; they may be formed, say, to please one's parents or to express how one feels about herself/himself. Cushner (1988) contends that "an intercultural…perspective does not come automatically with cognitive development or physical maturity; certain experiences at specific times in one's development are critical to attitude and knowledge formation" (p. 161).

Because emotional reactions are so much a part of being cultural, programs that focus only on the cognitive factor will likely fail (Brislin, 1978). Both Brislin and Cushner propose programs in which people "actively participate in realistic simulations of other cultures" (p. 42). Mantle-Bromley (1992) describes an approach to teaching intercultural communication: Teach students how to revise their cultural patterns, including their attitudes, readiness, and self-awareness and let them experience the process of acculturation. A change in attitude includes acceptance by the student that the target cultural event is "an alternative behavior, rather than a 'wrong' behavior" (p. 118). Readiness is achieved by having students participate "in activities that (are) designed to help them accept the frustration and ambiguity that is inherent in acculturation" (p. 119) while self-awareness serves as "the core of a program of attitude readiness" (p. 119).

An intercultural situation does not insure enhanced intercultural understanding (Rash, 1988), but could result instead in discomfort because the assumptions on which one bases one's behavior are challenged. The goal, Rash says, is not change per se but the integration of oneself into a different cultural situation without losing one's own identity; one must strive "to hold two apparently or really inimical viewpoints in mind at the same time, allowing both the right to exist" (p. 215). What is of importance in a course in intercultural communication for teachers-to-be is their exposure to discomforting cultural situations at the emotional level.

INTERCULTURAL ACTIVITIES

This chapter describes activities in a graduate-level intercultural communication class which are designed to help students experience and understand communication across cultures by focusing on culture-specific behaviors that are based on culture-universal functions and that produce discomfort.

The first activity involves students in a greeting simulation that becomes an integral part of the class and lasts over time. Learning to respect each other's turn-taking rules in a classroom discussion is the objective of the second activity. Most of the learning in the third activity occurs outside the classroom. Each student becomes an observer or a participant in a subcultural group and reports to the class his/her experiences. All of these assignments are meant to demand "behavior that is inconsistent with one's attitudes" (Mantle-Bromley, 1992, p. 124).

From the recommendations found in the literature, I designed each of these experiences to include the following components:

1. A simulation in which students *felt* discomfort because this is one of the feelings most often identified by people experiencing culture shock;
2. An environment in which the students were required to participate and to reflect upon the external behavior *and* their internal feelings in the context of themselves as cultural beings; and
3. A setting in which the students could choose not to participate any longer so that, at the point when negative feelings would presumably be highest, each would have the opportunity to "leave" an uncomfortable situation and *cognitively* reflect upon the reasons why s/he wanted to do so and what that decision would mean in a "real" setting.

To achieve the goal of intercultural communication in the ESL/EFL classroom, ESL/EFL teachers must be intercultural communicators themselves, aware of their own cultural experiences, able to learn from another culture, and committed to teaching others how to communicate across cultures (Ernst, 1993). Simulations are effective in intercultural training if they focus on commonalities. Factual information about other cultures as presented in "global studies" classes or intercultural communication classes is not useful because the result often is a creation of distance between the students and the cultures being studied, leading to a view of the foreign culture as "other," strange, exotic, and incomprehensible (Zevin,

1993). The aim is to minimize the differences between cultures to foster dialogue among people of various cultures, to create a sense that there exists a broader perspective of shared values (Rash, 1988).

Clavijo (1984) suggests that the realization of commonalities can be achieved through culture-specific instruction: To present unique behaviors of another culture while at the same time explaining to students where the commonality is. Thus, for example, although eating behaviors vary from culture to culture, the fact that all people eat and have "rules" for eating is common. Culture-specific instruction coupled with culture-universal awareness can raise students' "perception of similarities between one's own culture and the target culture" (p. 90) and enhance intercultural communication.

Let us now examine each of the simulations designed for this course in light of the criteria set forth above.

Greeting activity

The greeting activity I selected met the above-listed criteria in these ways:

1. The form of the greeting chosen was strange to everyone in the class to encourage feelings of discomfort;
2. Students were required to participate daily, with one exception (see 3), and were required to write a weekly journal entry regarding their reactions;
3. Students were free to stop participating in the greeting ritual whenever their discomfort became too great; at that point, they were required to write a reflection paper, in which they outlined *why* they stopped and what this decision would mean if they were in a real situation where such behavior was mandatory.

What follows is a description of the Yoruba (of western Nigeria) greeting as I adapted it to my classroom. First, the students were arranged in "order," based on age and gender. Then the oldest male and I sat together in the center of a circle and each person greeted us in a particular way based upon his/her position in the "culture." "Young" females had to kneel before the two of us; older females had to curtsy; young males had to prostrate (a position loosely resembling a push-up); older males bowed and touched their right foot. Young females curtsied to the older males and females, and the young males bowed to the older males and females. The process was repeated as a closing.

During the three weeks that we "lived" in this culture, I expanded on the behavior patterns: the elder would place his hands on the heads of the younger ones when they said "Good morning;" the younger members were instructed not to look into the eyes of the elders; the elders were given responsibility for instructing the younger ones when the latter did not follow the prescribed behavior.

Thus, the rationale for introducing the greeting ritual was to raise the level of the students' awareness of themselves as cultural beings by causing the discomfort that is felt when we actually do immerse ourselves in a foreign culture and by having them reflect on their feelings in a personal way.

Whenever this activity has been used, the "culture shock" process, including positive feelings toward the novelty of the situation, anger, and then acceptance did take place among the students. Students began reminding each other about the greeting and how to do it correctly. They transformed themselves into members of this culture without instruction beyond the initial "how to" demonstration; acculturation was taking place. There was also a lot of discomfort.

The "strange" becoming the "familiar" is important in intercultural communication education because, as outlined by Mantle-Bromley (1992), it is not the outside activity that changes, but the person's attitude toward it. This attitude change is a large part of becoming aware of oneself as a cultural being. Some students reacted to the contrived nature of the classroom ritual, and they speculated on their reactions if this type of greeting were expected of them in a real culture. They were becoming aware of themselves as cultural beings. As noted by Cushner (1988), the ability to be aware of one's feelings and then analyze them in a classroom situation is what makes learning intercultural communication possible.

Turn-taking Activity

The turn-taking activity I designed met the above-listed criteria in these ways:

1. The form of the activity was imposed on everyone in the class and was unfamiliar to everyone in the class to encourage feelings of discomfort;
2. Students were required to participate in the activity and were required to discuss their feelings towards it both verbally and in writing;
3. Students could not opt out of the turn-taking activity except when the rules were modified to allow them to pass their turn.

This activity follows the greeting activity. Students are seated in a circle or semi-circle and each is given a 3x5 card on which a number, representing the student's position in the order of discussion, has been written. The instructor asks the opening question for discussion, and it is the responsibility of the student who drew card #1 to speak. No one else may speak while this student has the floor. When the first student has finished, the turn passes to the student holding card #2. Turn-taking proceeds until the student who drew the highest number for turn-taking has spoken. The instructor then allows the discussion to begin again with the first student or s/he introduces another topic and the procedure begins again. The instructor allows five minutes at the end of the period to discuss the turn-taking activity itself within the intercultural context.

The instructor may allow a "pass" option, allowing a student to pass when her/his turn comes; more effective is a modified pass option in which a student temporarily passes his/her turn while understanding that the turn will return to her/him when the student with the highest number has spoken. Another version is to include a few cards with "X" on them rather than numbers. Students drawing these cards have the option of interrupting the turn-taking procedure whenever a student with a numbered card has finished, that is, "X" card holders can "jump into" the conversation without waiting a turn. The group can decide to manufacture its own rules after using the imposed ones for about three weeks.

Again, the rationale for the turn-taking activity was to raise the students' level of awareness of themselves as cultural beings. Although deceptively simple in design, this activity proves powerful in exposing students to the feelings others have when cultural rules are not adhered to. Most American students feel the frustration of waiting to speak, then gradually come to appreciate the longer wait times common in many other cultures. International students feel the pressure to contribute, usually without enough time to prepare and with the discomfort of speaking in the presence of a teacher. They come to appreciate the rules of another culture also.

Subculture Involvement

Students in the intercultural communication course were each involved with a subculture in the area. This activity met the above-mentioned criteria in these ways:

1. The subculture each student was assigned to was an unfamiliar one encouraging feelings of discomfort;
2. Students were required to be observers of their subculture over an extended period of time or could become participant-observers; and
3. At the time assignments were made, students were free to refuse to observe/participate in a particular subculture if they felt their discomfort would be too great. With the refusal they were required to write a reflection paper, in which they outlined why they could not observe/participate in the subculture. Once having accepted a particular subculture, however, students were required to complete the assignment over the course of the semester.

This activity is assigned at the opening of the course and extends through its duration. Each student draws from a hat the name of a subculture's place of congregation, including such places as (open) AA, fundamentalist and mainstream churches, mosque, synagogue, topical bars (bikers', strip, singles', etc.), homeless shelters, women's centers. The specifications were that the student could not already be a member of the subcultural group and that participation in the group that was drawn would last for the duration of the semester, with the exception of point #3 above.

Students observe or participate in their subculture groups at least once a week and keep a journal of the behaviors of the group and their reactions to them. At the end of the semester, each student reports to the class her/his experiences.

SUMMARY

One cannot be exposed, even intellectually, to all aspects of another culture prior to living in that culture. Single-topic assignments may not predict how a student would operate if placed within that culture. What is valuable about the exercise outlined in this article is that the particular *behavior* to be performed by the students is not the important element; their reactions are. These exercises can be adapted to include any type of behavior as long as the criteria outlined above are followed.

What does one do when committed to a teaching contract in a culture whose members manifest unfamiliar behaviors, behaviors to which even the foreigner is expected to adhere? It is in this way that one can challenge oneself to be aware of oneself as a cultural being, not to place oneself in situations that are completely intolerable, and to be more accepting of "strange" behavior.

DISCUSSION QUESTIONS

1. Describe the role that discomfort can play in your learning another culture.
2. Why are intercultural communication courses that focus solely on cognitive tors ineffective in helping you become an intercultural communicator?
3. As Mantle-Bromley points out, what is the value in describing a foreign cultural behavior as an "alternative behavior" rather than a "wrong behavior"?
4. In your opinion, which of the three discomforting activities would be most useful to you? Why?
5. Having read this chapter, how would you describe what it means to become aware of yourself as a cultural being?

REFERENCES

Boski, P. (1988). Cross-cultural studies of person perception. *Journal of Cross-cultural Psychology, 19*, 287-328.

Brislin, R. W. (1978). Structured approaches to dealing with prejudice and intercultural understanding. *International Journal of Group Tensions, 8*, 33-47.

Clavijo, F. J. (1984). Effects of teaching culture on attitude change. *Hispania, 67*, 88-91.

Cushner, K. (1988). Achieving intercultural effectiveness: Current knowledge, goals and practices. *Education and Urban Society, 20,* 159-176.

Ernst, G. (1993, April). *Mirrors of difference: Critical perspectives of bilingual/ESL and mainstream teachers on pedagogy, language, and culture* (Report No. CS-580-337). Atlanta, Georgia: The Annual Meeting of the American Educational Research Association. (ERIC Document Reproduction Service No. 361 823)

Lewald, H. E. (1968). A tentative outline in the knowledge, understanding, and teaching of cultures pertaining to the target language. *Modern Language Journal, 52,* 301-309.

Mantle-Bromley, C. (1992). Preparing students for meaningful culture learning. *Foreign Language Annals, 25,* 117-127.

Rash, J. E. (1988). Practical perspectives on intercultural understanding. *Education and Urban Society, 20,* 211-225.

Zevin, J. (1993). World studies in secondary schools and the undermining of ethnocentrism. *The Social Studies, 84,* 82-86.

9

THE USE AND MISUSE OF QUESTIONNAIRES IN INTERCULTURAL TRAINING[*]

John W. Bing
ITAP International

INTRODUCTION

Cross-Cultural[1] Training programs have many purposes, venues, and audiences. In my experience, they have been used to orient Peace Corps volunteers, government aid workers, health workers, students arriving and departing learning institutions, the military, and employees in many business contexts. As of late, they are being utilized in some diversity programs in the United States and Canada.

Questionnaires can be used in many different ways including assessing the needs of participants before program design; in formative or summative evaluations; as a way of determining the knowledge of participants; and as a way for gathering information about the environment into which, or in which, participants are or may be working. There are also cross-cultural questionnaires which are intended to elicit the preferences of respondents without referring to a research-generated database.

In this chapter, I will focus on a specific form of questionnaire used in intercultural training programs: multi-country questionnaires based on quantitative research.

DESCRIPTION OF THE QUESTIONNAIRES

There are only two major databases which compare cross-national data over more than 50 countries gathered through questionnaires. These have been developed by Geert Hofstede, the pioneer in the field of quantitative research in comparative management, and Fons Trompenaars, a consultant and author in the same field. Both are from The Netherlands. The older of the two questionnaire-generated databases was developed by Hofstede. At IBM, he headed a team of six research-ers to develop the first internationally standardized questionnaires and a system for administering them; the results of his 53 country and region surveys were pub-lished in *Culture's Consequences: International Differences in Work-Related Values* (Hofstede, 1980). The more recent of the two questionnaires and associ-ated databases has been developed by Fons Trompenaars and published in *Riding the Waves of Culture: Understanding Cultural Differences in Business* (Trompenaars, 1993). There were 47 countries represented in this survey at the time of publication of *Riding the Waves of Culture*.

The databases generate mental geographies. They are two different geogra-phies, as if created by explorers who have crafted their own maps of the parts of the same new world each explored. Hofstede calls culture "the software of the mind," set against the "hard wiring" of genetic development. In fact, he draws out three levels of what he calls "mental programs":[2]

1. The "*universal* level of mental programming which is shared by all, or almost all, mankind. This is the biological 'operating system' of the human body, but it includes a range of expressive behaviors such as laughing and weeping and associative and aggressive behaviors which are found in higher animals."
2. "The *collective* level of mental programming is shared with some but not with all other people; it is common to people belonging to a certain group or category.... The whole area of subjective human culture... belongs to this level."
3. "The *individual* level of human programming is the truly unique part—no two people are programmed exactly alike, even if they are identical twins raised together."

These three levels of what Hofstede calls "programming" describe the three fountainheads of human behavior: The biological/ genetic basis of universal human traits; culture; and the combination of the two, which produces our person-alities. Both Hofstede and Trompenaars describe what they are exploring as the map of culture. Hofstede's map is divided into four provinces; Trompenaars' into seven. Only one of the provinces has been named the same (the individualism/col-lective dimension).

A rather significant complication, perhaps it might be better called a confu-sion, to both maps is that, although the information from these studies is often interpreted as cultural dimensions which describe the differences between cultures, in fact they both analyze the differences between national groups. In the case of many countries, perhaps most, this means measuring multicultural societies and lumping the results as national scores. For the Japanese scores, this may not be a problem; for Canadian, Belgian and Malaysian scores it may well be. However, it makes pedagogical sense to gather, analyze, and disseminate information by country name; to gather the data by separate cultures would mean problems in other directions: For example, would Flemish and Dutch cultures be labeled the same, or different? Perhaps future researchers will gather data by both cultural and national names. Certainly this would make it easier to deal with the creation or disappearance of countries, a development more common now than in the past.

It should be noted that in chapter 7 of *Culture's Consequences*, Hofstede (1980) presents data by language area for Belgium and Switzerland and discusses at length the difference between Flemish and Dutch. Once again, Hofstede has established the standard for future research.

The two questionnaires which developed the databases (in the above analogy, the "map") changed over time as questions were substituted or rewritten to improve reliability. Hofstede used many versions of the questionnaire over the years he researched and analyzed the IBM data. Trompenaars has also utilized different versions. Hofstede's database is the larger, with 116,000 questionnaires provided to recipients in their own countries and analyzed to provide the basis for his four-dimension map of cultural geographies. The four dimensions were "discovered" from the data; that is to say, they were determined after data were gathered and derived through study of those data. Later, he and Michael Bond added a fifth dimension, valid only for Asian cultures.

Trompenaars' dimensions were generated through a study of the literature and his questionnaire generated from these dimensions. His database is as of now (1995) smaller, consisting perhaps of around 50,000 questionnaires. Trompenaars' questionnaire is often provided to participants outside their countries, unlike Hofstede's approach. However, Trompenaars' data cover much of the active business world of today, including areas Hofstede never covered because IBM had not yet penetrated these areas. They include Eastern Europe, Russia, and China. Trompenaars has also been successful at popularizing the notion of cultures' influence on business, both in Europe and the Americas.

THE FOUR HOFSTEDE DIMENSIONS

The four Hofstede dimensions are as follows (I am using the original terminology, with simplifications in parentheses):

Individualism—Collectivism

The individual-collective dimension describes differences in how respondents view the focus of their work—as a fundamentally solitary, individual activity, in which credit or blame, reward and punishment, falls on the individual; or as a collective or team enterprise, in which the group receives credit, blame, reward or punishment.

For example, in Hofstede's study, the United States is the most individualistic country. Those coming to work in the United States from any other country (discounting individual differences) should therefore feel themselves relatively unsupported upon their arrival. They may feel a bit as if they were dropped into the U.S. work environment to sink or swim on their own. In my experience (having worked with over 500 arriving employees and their families), this is indeed almost always the case.

Low Power Distance—High Power Distance
(Participative—Hierarchical Orientation)

This dimension differentiates participative and hierarchical workplaces. In high-power-distant organizations, the flow of decision-making and responsibility is top-down; in low power-distant organizations, the authority may be expressed in coaching rather than ordering, and responsibility may be devolved.

For example, if a high-power distance subordinate is matched with a lower power-distance supervisor who prefers coaching to providing strong direction, the subordinate may feel a sense of bewilderment or resentment at what is perceived as a lack of direction.

Low Uncertainty Avoidance—High Uncertainty Avoidance
(Risk—Structure Orientation)

This dimension discriminates between those who prefer a highly structured work environment to those who prefer not to be encumbered by rules, regulations, and red tape.

For example, a work environment in which every person has his or her own distinct work, and is provided with clear guidelines, and for which there are predictable long-term rewards and benefits, is preferred by those with a high need for certainty. Government and university offices are typically so structured. In other cultures and workplaces (the software industry in the United States, for example), rules and regulations are perceived as barriers to creative development or to entrepreneurial advances. This end of the scale is inhabited by those with a preference for risk.

Masculinity—Femininity (Task—Relationship Orientation)

This scale, originally conceived by Hofstede to differentiate between country cultures that emphasized "masculine" traits of task and achievement and "feminine" traits of relationship and concern for quality of life, is now focused (in the "Culture in the Workplace" Questionnaire) on the traits themselves, since it is at best a matter of controversy as to whether those specific traits and genders are linked in all cultures.

For example, in some cultures and workplaces people must form relationships before they can work together effectively; often in these workplaces the quality of life issues (family leave, child-care centers, aesthetic factors in the workplace) are also of importance. On the opposite side of the spectrum, deals are often done by complete strangers with nothing but a formal agreement to affirm the arrangement. In such places, task accomplishment can be accomplished without much attention to forming relationships.

THE TROMPENAARS' DIMENSIONS

Turning to the second research area, the Trompenaars' Dimensions are as follows (again, I use Trompenaars' original terminology, with interpretations in parentheses).

Universalism vs. Particularism (Rules vs. Relationships)

The question at the heart of this dimension revolves around whether rules or relationships regulate workplace behaviors.

For example, if you are a universalist, you will follow societal or work rules in your life and work; a particularist is concerned about whether or not the needs of people, particularly those people closest to him or her, are being met.

Individualism vs. Collectivism

So far as I am able to determine, this area is very similar to Hofstede's; in other words, the two maps overlap at this coordinate.

Neutral vs. Affective (Unemotional vs. Emotional)

This dimension relates to the display of emotion at work. Those who are from cultures which do not show much emotion at work (for example, who do not talk about their health or lack of health) are "neutral;" those who do are "affective."

Specific vs. Diffuse (Brief and Numerous vs. Long-term Relationships)

This dimension distinguishes between people who make many friendships, which are normally brief and superficial, and those who make very few but very deep friendships which last for many years.

In those workplaces in which specific relationships are prevalent, friendships may be instrumental, that is to say, they may enable the participants to accomplish goals. In those organizations and societies in which diffuse relationships are more common, there is a clearer divide between acquaintenceships, which are the norm, and friendships, which are exceptional and significant and take long to develop.

Achievement vs. Ascription (Achievement vs. Assigned Attributes)

This dimension describes the difference between those who value achievement as the primary dimension of success, and those who value achievement, but also the background of the colleague, his or her education, other attainments, and even the reputation of the family or extended family itself.

For example, in parts of Europe, there is still a special cachet for those who are considered to be of aristocratic background. In Islamic cultures, those who have been on the Haj or the pilgrimage are often accorded higher status.

Attitudes toward Time (Relative Emphasis on the Importance of the Past, Present, or Future)

In some societies, for example in France, the importance of the past, as represented in literature, architecture, music, and other streams of culture, are significant; in others, for example the United States., the future is perceived to be more important than a past away from which many Americans immigrated.

Attitudes toward the Environment (Harmony vs. Control of the Outside World)

A basic concept of Japanese life is Wei, or harmony. This is reflected in such societal expressions as the Tea Ceremony and the architecture of gardens and religious sites. In other countries, controlling nature is much more important than understanding or recreating its harmonies. These differences are often reflected in the workplace. In Japan, confrontations are not supposed to occur; collaboration, consensus and other techniques have been developed to maintain harmony. In other societies, workplace disagreements and even violence are not unknown.

With this background we will move to the issue of the proper use of questionnaires associated with these databases.

THE USE OF RESEARCH-BASED QUANTITATIVE
QUESTIONNAIRES IN CROSS-CULTURAL TRAINING PROGRAMS

Over the past six years, cross-national research-based quantitative questionnaires in cross-cultural training programs have been developed to achieve two purposes:

1. To aid participants in developing an understanding of their own cultural profile and thus to foster an understand of others' cultural profiles.
2. To help participants compare country culture profiles on the Hofstede or Trompenaars' dimensions, and to understand what bridging might be required for each participant to be more effective in working with people from those cultures.

These techniques were pioneered in the United States at ITAP International (a company which has since 1986 provided training and consulting to global companies and to nonprofit organizations such as the United Nations and the American Management Association), when ITAP International was licensed to offer a version of Hofstede's questionnaire in its training programs as a didactic tool. ITAP International began providing its clients with the Culture in the Workplace^{TM} Questionnaire (CW), as it is now called, in 1989.

Participants answer a 24-item questionnaire; many of these questions were taken from Hofstede's original study. The scores for each respondent are recomputed as bar charts representing his or her culture profile on the four original Hofstede dimensions. Because the list of questions has been drawn from research questions, the relationship between the participants' scores and the country scores is direct and clear. The soundness of the questionnaire is thus related to original research, as are the participants' scores.

Pedagogical inferences can thereby be drawn between individual scores and country scores. For example, consider participant Bill, an American, who has a high score for individualism and he is being transferred to a job requiring team development in a country with a lower average score for individualism, as determined by the Hofstede database. Bill must determine how best to proceed with his new team, tempered with the knowledge that it is likely that his colleagues on the team will prefer a more collective approach to decision-making, reward provision, task allocation, and so on, than his own preferred personal style. Knowing both his own cultural style and the national average for the country in which he will be working gives Bill the tools to analyze and project alternative approaches. Should he adopt a more "collective" style, allowing decisions to be made more by the team than he would have done? Should he insist on his style even if that might cause his team to resist that process? The point here is that such information gives participants the knowledge that different approaches exist. It also provides training designers the opportunity to create skill-building role-plays and other exercises to assist participants in developing competencies to work effectively in different countries.

The Culture in the Workplace Questionnaire can also be utilized as a way of compiling individual scores of members of a team. This information can then be used to help team members understand the diversity of approaches within the team and which team members might be predisposed toward certain kinds of team activities. For example, if one member had an especially high need for structure (i.e., a high score on Hofstede's uncertainty avoidance dimension) compared with other members, that individual might be pressed into service as the team planner. Variations of the Trompenaars' questionnaire have also been used to analyze corporate culture.

THE MISUSE OF RESEARCH-BASED QUANTITATIVE QUESTIONNAIRES IN CROSS-CULTURAL TRAINING PROGRAMS

With so much competitiveness in the cross-cultural training and consulting market today, there have been examples of questionnaires cobbled together with little research and no statistical analysis of reliability or validity. In these cases, they are more marketing than instructional tools, and they may in fact be misleading. There may also be claims made for the use of such questionnaires which exceed the limits of their development. Such sins are many, and are here enumerated:

Venial Sins

There are six less-serious sins. They are:

1. The use of questionnaires, whether research-based or not, whether in the field of cross-cultural training or not, is too often accompanied by claims of miraculous and quick cures to very complex problems. In fact, because questionnaires create data which represent models of reality, they must be seen for what they are: a simplification and reduction of reality. In fact they gain their pedagogical power, as for example do simulation games as well, from this process of simplification and reduction. It is therefore incumbent on practitioners to carefully explain to their participants the limitation of the models they are using.
2. Representing a national database as a cultural database is an easy sin to commit; however it is important to point out that in multicultural societies there maybe be much cultural variation within a country (e.g., Canada, Belgium, China, the United States).
3. Each database is created within a time frame and has specific limitations. Although the Hofstede database is not contemporary, it is now being updated,

and a recent study (Hoppe, 1990) indicates the dimensions are stable over time.

4. It is tempting to claim that the questionnaires and associated databases provide the coordinates for the entire map of culture. We do not yet know the complete map of culture (that is to say, cultures), nor are we likely to in the near future. It is therefore important to point this out, supplementing these databases with other sources of information about cultural aspects of work in different countries.

5. Practitioners can err by leading our participants to assume that cultural differences will account for all the differences in a cross-cultural interaction. However, it is clear that differences in personality and institutional and environmental influences will also play a role in interactions between people no matter whether those interactions take place between people of different cultures or the same culture. Cross-cultural practitioners should take care to take account of these other influences in their seminars.

6. With quantitative databases and associated questionnaires, it is very easy to make the error of directly comparing individual scores to country scores. However, country scores are average scores, and individual scores cannot be directly compared to averages. It is impossible, for example, for someone, even with a very high score on individualism, to be completely individualistic.

Human beings do not operate as walking scales. Practitioners should therefore be careful to use the information didactically rather than engage in mathematical comparisons of scores.

Mortal Sins

There are three flagrant sins. They are:

1. Assuming that country averages in a database relate to individuals in that country. Country averages are typically (but not always) bell-shaped curves, with individuals at the tails of these curves who may behave in some ways more like members of other cultures than members of their own cultures. I was guilty of such a sin early in my career when I gave the Culture in the Workplace questionnaire to a Japanese employee of an American company and, when his score was very high on individualism, accused him of being insufficiently Japanese. In fact, I surmised later, the employee decided to work for an American company specifically because his own preference, for whatever reason, was higher on individualism than many of his fellow Japanese. Practitioners should help participants in their seminars avoid stereotyping people from other countries and cultures by pointing out that those they meet on their travels may be not "typical" at all, but rather examples of exceptions from cultural norms.

2. Taking for granted that sociologically-based questionnaires and databases developed in one culture are sufficient to explain cultural differences to people from other cultures. This is a serious difficulty in the field, because there are few models which address cultural differences available in the West which have their origin in other cultures. I discovered an example of the kind of problem this causes in a class I taught at the United Nations in Vienna. I had just provided Trompenaars' definition of culture as "a way of solving problems." A man (originally from China) declared: "To me, culture is the water that we swim in: It surrounds and defines us." Clearly, the definition of culture itself is culturally-influenced. Practitioners should be careful to elicit definitions of culture from participants themselves in order to avoid the imposition of one set of ideas over another. Researchers should work to develop models which can serve across cultures.

3. The pressure of competition sometimes causes otherwise sane practitioners to create fictional questionnaires. One, developed by a major training organization some years ago, claimed to be tied to the Hofstede database. However, it is not. Because the Hofstede questionnaire is copyrighted but the database is in the public domain, the practitioner devised his own questions unrelated to the database. But the resulting profile appeared to be related to the database. Why is this a sin? It can yield cultural profiles which do not relate to the dimensions which define them and can seriously mislead participants. Such questionnaires are but smoke and mirrors. Practitioners should maintain standards which prevent such debasing of the field and of research standards.

OTHER CONUNDRUMS

There are other conundrums in these areas which are less sins than areas of uncertainty. Clifford Clarke, one of the leaders in the field of Japan/U.S. business-focused cross-cultural research, has questioned the validity of sociological (multiple national questionnaires) versus anthropological approaches (single-culture questionnaires and interviews). He believes that the reliability of such questionnaires is questionable given the translation problem and the fact that for Japanese, for example, the context of the question is as important as its content.[3]

CONCLUSIONS

Questionnaires and their associated databases must be used sensitively and with caution. Sometimes results may be counter-intuitive such as when the Hofstede questionnaire yields a high "masculinity" or task-orientedness score among Japanese in the Hofstede data. This suggests that Japanese have low relationship concerns, which is quite contrary to other research and observations. The answer to this dilemma may be conjectured in the likely response of the Japanese *as members of a group, not as individuals*. Hence, the answers of Americans on such questionnaires tend to be as individuals; of group-oriented peoples, such as the Japanese, as members of a group. High task- and competitive-orientation appears to be a group characteristic in Japan. It is precisely in these counter-intuitive areas that new understanding of cultural differences may be discovered. If practitioners learn to use questionnaires and their associated databases responsibly, they can provide valuable assistance to people learning to work effectively in other countries.

DISCUSSION QUESTIONS

1.   In what ways are the Trompenaars and Hofstede cultural "maps" different?
2.   What is a cultural profile and how are such profiles used?
3.   Why is an understanding of one's own culture profile important to working in countries other than one's own?
4.   Do you think it would be more difficult for an American to work in Japan, or a Japanese to work in the United States, or would it be the same level of difficulty? Why?
5.   How can you distinguish between cultural differences and differences between individuals? Are differences between people from different countries always cultural? If not, what other differences are important?

NOTES

[1] In this chapter, the terms intercultural and cross-cultural are used interchangeably to refer to training which helps participants learn about, adjust to, or develop skills with respect to a culture other than their own.

[2] Hofstede, G. (1994). *Cultures and Organizations: Software of the Mind. Intercultural Cooperation and Its Importance for Survival.* London: McGraw-Hill International, p. 6.

[3] Conversation with Clarke in 1996.

REFERENCES

Hofstede, G. (1980). *Culture's consequences: International differences in work-related values.* Newbury Park, CA: Sage Publications.

Hoppe, M.H. (1990). *A comparative study of country elites: International differences in work-related values and learning and their implications for management training and development.* Unpublished doctoral dissertation, University of North Carolina.

Trompenaars, F. (1993). *Riding the waves of culture: Understanding cultural diversity in business.* London: The Economist Press.

SECTION II OVERVIEW: CULTURAL DIVERSITY— ETHNICITY, RACE, AND GENDER

A perceived impact of the new technologies on our information societies is called convergence. In fact, it has become fashionable for some scholars to emphasize the need to develop entire communication programs based on the concept of convergence. Unfortunately, this concept includes deemphasizing divergence. However, many intercultural communication scholars still believe divergence should be the guiding light for all communication programs in multicultural countries. Cultural divergence includes understanding the communication patterns and values of the different ethnic and racial, as well as gender, groups that make up all societies. The chapters in this section address the need to maintain such diversity in modern societies.

Effective intercultural communication requires not only an understanding of the other persons's culture, but also respect for that culture. With this requirement in mind, in his chapter, "Fostering Respect for Other Cultures in Teaching Intercultural Communication," Day argues that an objective for introductory courses in intercultural communication should be to teach respect for other cultures. Today's lack of respect emanates from attitudes of ethnocentrism, prejudice, and stereotyping. It is necessary to help cognitive development that includes cultural similarities which may lead to respect for other cultures.

In her informative chapter, "Latinos in the United States: Diversity, Cultural Patterns, and Misconceptions," Albert explains the values of the Latino/Latina Americans. If one wishes to interact effectively with the Latinos/Latinas, it is imperative for one to know their demographics, culture, and communication patterns. Applying popular intercultural theories, Albert tries to erase many misconceptions that exist about this culture. Although Latinos/Latinas are American citizens, their value system includes many values and beliefs of the responsibility oriented culture as opposed to the individuality oriented culture of the majority of

Americans. These Latino/Latina values and beliefs include responsibility, modesty, and respect for elders.

In his chapter, "Critical Discourse Analysis: Racism and the Ethos of Equality," Donahue explains the different interpretations of the concept of equality. He says, although we all believe in equality, this value is interpreted in different ways by different racial groups. Using de Toqueville's writings as the basis, he explains the need for a different approach to the perception of racial equality.

In business organizations, developing mentor-protege relationship between different racial and ethnic managers and employees may result in a successful career for the protege. Brooks' chapter, "The Black Professional: An Analysis of the Communicative Strategies in Cross-Race Mentoring," shows how such a relationship may become an effective practice in corporate cultures. This cross racial mentoring may also result in better interracial communication, as well as increased productivity.

Buttny's and Williams' observation that African-American views are not cited in communication studies is the concern of many intercultural Communication scholars. Discourse analysis of intergroup communication shows that race relations can be troublesome and can indicate social distance. In the discourse cited in their chapter, "African-American Discourses on Problematic Relations with Whites," the authors point out the example of how African-Americans have to earn respect from the whites while the whites simply take it as a given from African Americans.

In the chapter, "Turn Taking and the Extended Pause: A Study of Interpersonal Communication Styles across Generations on the Warm Springs Indian Reservation," McLean explains how silence in speech is a unique form of communication in the Native American culture. Codes and channels of interaction in this culture depend upon with whom and when one is interacting. An analysis of a "get together" of a group of Warm Springs, Oregon, Native Americans showed silence, pauses, and turn taking as cultural forms of communication, which depend upon the age and other demographics of the speakers. Because speech is still the most popular method of interaction between the elders and the youngsters, it is important for the former to encourage communication with the latter.

India is a country made up of peoples of several ancient cultures. It is also a modern democracy. Cultural and religious conflicts are problems that have an impact on social life in India. In his chapter, "The Nature and Culture of Conflict-the Indian case: Some Communication Implications," Ramesh explains how the ancient country of India has gone through many conflicts over the millennia. He shows how the conflicts are often inspired by cultural factors such as ethnicity and religion. Yet, India has been famous for its endurance. A recent conflict of the destruction of a mosque which was built over an ancient temple of Rama is a deviation from the traditional endurance of the Indians. How did such a break from the traditional tolerance occur? Ramesh applies well known socio-cultural and psycho-cultural theories to the Indian conflicts.

Generalizing communication patterns for both genders may prove to be errone-ous. In the chapter, "Communicative Parallels That Characterize Intercultural and Cross-gender Relations," Ross and Faulkner point out the importance of under-standing the different communication patterns of the two genders for meaningful intercultural communication. Such gender differences do exist in verbal, as well as nonverbal communication and they also indicate the roles and hierarchies of the communicators.

10

FOSTERING RESPECT FOR OTHER CULTURES IN TEACHING INTERCULTURAL COMMUNICATION

Kenneth D. Day
University of the Pacific

Introductory level undergraduate courses in intercultural communication are presently a well-established component within the communication curriculum. For most of these courses the primary objective is to explain how cultural differences contribute to problems in communication. As reflected in textbooks (Dodd, 1991; Jandt, 1995; Klopf, 1991; Lustig & Koester, 1996; Samovar & Porter, 1991) these courses approach culture with a definition based on the tradition of anthropology, focus on differences in verbal and nonverbal communication behavior across cultures and to a lesser or greater extent on differences in beliefs, values, and world views across different cultures. Most texts are structured around basic communication concepts as well as the application of theory from intercultural and interpersonal communication and related work in the social sciences. Most texts also address the need to be effective in dealing with members of other cultures and some use the concept of intercultural competence.

Although there is some considerable variation in the specific definition of culture used in any particular text, all of these definitions treat culture as what

Bhabha (1994) critically calls "an object of empirical knowledge" (p. 34). For example, Samovar and Porter (1991) define culture as:

> the deposit of knowledge, experience, beliefs, values, attitudes, meanings, hierarchies, religion, notions of time, spatial relations, concepts of the universe, and material objects and possessions acquired by a group of people in the course of generations through individual and group striving. (p. 51)

This anthropological definition of culture and the orientation to interaction set these courses off from other approaches dealing with cultural diversity at a national and international level.

At many colleges and universities, courses in intercultural communication are a choice in the liberal studies or general education curriculum required for a baccalaureate degree. In such cases the course is likely to be a choice in the liberal studies category dealing with international and intercultural/ethnic studies. This liberal studies category may include courses specifically focused on the study of another country or culture, courses dealing with specific ethnic groups in the United States, and courses such as cultural anthropology and intercultural communication which address the issue of culture more generally. In response to the multiculturalism and cultural diversity movement in education, either explicitly or implicitly, the goals of this liberal studies area often include not only the development of increased knowledge of other cultures but the fostering of increased respect for other cultures and the members of those cultures.

This chapter considers the need for addressing respect for other cultures and the members of other cultures in introductory level courses in intercultural communication. For the purposes of the following discussion, people will be said to show respect for another culture and its members when they show consideration for the culture and its members. Consideration for other cultures involves perceptions of worth and the belief that accommodations should be made for cultural difference. Clearly a major contributor to lack of respect for other cultures and their members is lack of knowledge about the cultures themselves, but this is not the primary emphasis of this chapter. Learning the expected expressions of respect in another culture is, of course, a particularly relevant aspect of cultural knowledge. Imparting knowledge about other cultures, including behaviors of respect, is clearly a goal of most intercultural communication classes.

In the discussion that follows emphasis will be placed on the primary factors, besides ignorance about other cultures, which lead people in their behavior to being inconsiderate of other cultures. These factors are ethnocentrism, prejudice, and stereotyping. Ruhly has defined ethnocentrism as "the tendency to interpret or judge all other groups, their environments, and their communication according to the categories and values of our own culture" (1976, p. 22). Individuals who show respect to another culture must be able to see the culture from the vantage point of the values and beliefs of the members of that culture. Lynch has defined prejudice as "the holding of a belief or opinion without adequate rational grounds or in the face of rational evidence to the contrary of that opinion or belief" (1987, p. 22). Although both positive and negative prejudice exist, particular concern should be expressed for negative prejudice. A stereotype will be defined here as a positive or negative overgeneralization about the members of another culture. Nieto (1992) argues that there should be concern for positive as well as negative stereo-typing of groups of people because both limit our perspectives on people. Stereo-typing is a particular problem in intercultural communication because our attempt to make general observations about the communication behavior of the members of another culture is likely to yield stereotypic statements which do not describe the complex differences in behavior of the members of a culture.

Fulfilling the goals of liberal studies or general education course is not the only reason that we should be concerned with fostering respect for other cultures. There are also ethical reasons why fostering respect should be a component of these courses. I have proposed in another essay in this volume (Day, 1998) that ethical intercultural communication be based on the principle of dialogue in which participants understand their own beliefs to be merely beliefs rather than the truth. Ethnocentrism, prejudice, and stereotyping interfere with the ability to engage in dialogue because they impair our ability to understand what a member of another culture is communicating.

The orientation to the study of culture taken by intercultural communication is in some danger of working against the development of respect for other cultures. This is so because of goals set for success in intercultural interaction and because of the focus on intercultural differences. Several intercultural texts (Dodd, 1991; Lustig & Koester, 1996) describe the concept of intercultural effectiveness which refers to achieving desired outcomes in interaction with members of another culture. While most such texts also raise concerns for the cultural appropriateness of some behaviors which may nonetheless be effective, emphasis on effectiveness is accompanied by the danger of promoting behaviors which exploit members of another culture unless effectiveness is tempered by respect for the culture and its members. When individuals engage in interaction with members of another culture with personal goals such as achieving a business deal or religious conversion, respect for the other culture is needed.

At the same time there is evidence that low ethnocentrism and low prejudice may be necessary conditions for intercultural effectiveness. Dodd (1987) has found high ethnocentric individuals to have difficulties in adjustment in another culture and Gudykunst and Kim (1984) argue that prejudice and ethnocentrism result in lower intercultural effectiveness.

But more seriously, the required focus on cultural difference taken by intercul-tural courses may work to serve as fuel for existing ethnocentrism, prejudice, and stereotyping. Indeed, many of the cultural differences most likely to fascinate American students are those aspects of a culture which seem counter to the values of our own culture. Based on Allport's (1954) theory that prejudice is linked to the conceptualization of ingroups and outgroups, the presentation of this material is likely to foster perception of others as members of outgroups and provide perceived negative traits to foster prejudice toward these outgroups. Samovar and Porter (1991) express concerns that their own text tends necessarily to overemphasize cultural difference and encourage readers to seek the similarities between members of other cultures. While intercultural communication courses may discuss the concepts of ethnocentrism, prejudice, and stereotyping, to be effective in fostering respect for other cultures and the members of those cultures, additional attention needs to be given to how this objective might be better accomplished. Before considering strategies and techniques for fostering respect in the teaching of intercultural communication, several related issues will be considered. These include the different experience and role of foreign students, immigrants, and refugees in intercultural communication courses and factors which have been shown to be related to respect for other cultures.

INTERNATIONAL STUDENTS, IMMIGRANTS, AND REFUGEES AND INTERCULTURAL COMMUNICATION

The experience of an intercultural communication class is likely to be quite different for international students, immigrants, and refugees than for other students. These students are engaged first-hand in the experience with functioning in another culture. While they have much to learn from the intercultural communication class, the challenge of coping with another culture is something which they have already experienced. International students, immigrants, and refugees are a valuable resource in the intercultural classroom. They can often corroborate statements by the teacher, serve as invaluable collaborators with other students on joint projects, and serve as an invaluable source of learning about another culture even for the teacher. These students are particularly likely to desire a discussion of their culture which enhances the respect for their culture by other students. Discussion of cultural differences from the instructor may be seen as fostering rejection or prejudice toward the culture of these students. Discussion of similarities or of cultural achievement or existing prejudice toward members of their culture may be useful in satisfying the needs of these students.

THEORY AND RESEARCH ON FOSTERING RESPECT FOR OTHER CULTURES

The following discussion considers those factors which strongly affect respect for other cultures. While ethnocentrism and stereotyping have been little studied, a considerable body of research exists on prejudice, particularly prejudice toward minorities. Consideration of this research is useful in considering teaching strategies which might address prejudice. Some relevant aspects of this literature are considered in the following discussion. Perhaps the best known of relationships with individual difference factors is the relation between the authoritarian personality type and prejudice (Adorno, 1950). Since personality types are seen as difficult to alter, this relationship is of limited usefulness in changing prejudicial attitudes. The functional approach to attitudes by Katz (1960) has been widely discussed by other authors including Brislin (1991). In the application of this approach prejudicial attitudes can be held for different functional reasons: the utilitarian function, the ego-defensive function, the value-expressive function, and the knowledge function. As a result of the different underlying functions behind prejudicial attitudes different approaches are required to change them. This theory suggests that multiple teaching strategies to reduce prejudice need to be used since prejudices serve different underlying functions. Brislin (1991) notes that teaching strategies which rely on the presentation of positive facts about a culture are likely to change prejudicial attitudes in only those who hold such attitudes because of the knowledge function.

Prejudicial attitudes have been shown to be related to a range of other individual characteristics. For example, Pettigrew (1981) has shown an inverse relationship between prejudice and self esteem. Glover (1994) has found prejudicial attitudes toward minorities to be negatively correlated with an humanitarian-egalitarian outlook and the Protestant work ethic. Allport's (1954) notions of ingroups and outgroups, a theoretical perspective which has been continued by a number of scholars (Hamilton & Trolier, 1986; Hogg & Abrams, 1988; Tajfel, 1969; Turner, 1985; Wilder, 1986) suggests that negative prejudice develops towards individuals that are seen as belonging to outgroups. This theory suggests as a strategy attempting to redefine individuals as belonging to the ingroup rather than the outgroup. Glover's (1994) finding that prejudice toward minorities tends to be negatively correlated with education suggests that education may be an effective means of addressing prejudice. Allport (1954) found that direct teaching about prejudice was less effective than indirect methods. Pate (1989) found that when a number of methods were compared a unit directly teaching against prejudice was found to be less effective than other methods and that the most effective method was cooperative learning. The observations by Allport and Pate, however, are based on children in elementary and secondary school and not college students.

Aboud (1988) argues that prejudicial attitudes shift with moral development based on Kohlberg's theory of moral development (Colby & Kohlberg, 1987). As the individual shifts from focus on the self to group to individual, prejudicial attitudes toward others are expected to decrease. Glover (1994) has found moral reasoning to be a statistically significant predictor of prejudice. Aboud (1988) has also suggested that cognitive development contributes to a decline in attitudes toward minorities though a shift away from egocentric focus on the self. Glover (1994) has attempted to apply Perry's (1968) theory of the development of epistemological reasoning in college students. In this theory, reasoning develops in college students with a shift from the perception of absolutely right and wrong answers, to relativism culminating in a commitment to personal positions as a matter of choice. Glover (1994) has found increased relativism to be negatively correlated with prejudicial attitudes. Ben Ari, Kedem, and Levy-Warner (1992) have found higher levels of cognitive complexity, the number of categories employed in making judgments about people, and other things, to be correlated with less positive evaluation of members of ingroups and less negative evaluations of members of outgroups. Cognitive development would also be expected to be related to a decline in ethnocentrism.

This research suggests that prejudice should be addressed by a number of different teaching strategies and that attempts to foster cognitive and moral development may contribute to a decrease in prejudice. Direct contact between students from different cultural backgrounds may, however, be the most effective way in dealing with prejudice.

STRATEGIES AND TECHNIQUES FOR FOSTERING RESPECT IN INTERCULTURAL COMMUNICATION

Having established fostering respect for other cultures and the members of those cultures as a course objective for intercultural communication and having considered some relevant concerns in how this might be done, teaching strategies and techniques to accomplish this objective need to be considered. Albert and Triandis (1991) identify three approaches to the teaching of intercultural communication: experiential, behavioral, and informational. They, however, suggest that the behavioral approach, reinforcing the accepted behaviors in another culture and discouraging those which are not accepted, has limited usefulness in classrooms in which people from several cultures interact.

The link between self-esteem and prejudice offers another approach which does not clearly fall into either the experiential or informational frame. Pettigrew (1981) has shown an inverse relationship between prejudice and self esteem. Application of this approach to the undergraduate curriculum may be more difficult than for early childhood education. To the extent that the classroom environment can foster higher self-esteem, prejudice may be lowered.

The experiential approach ideally involves emersing students in another culture. Albert and Triandis (1991) suggest that within a single course, more limited use of this approach can be made through food tasting and visits to ethnic neighborhoods. This approach relates to notions presented by Allport (1954) regarding the role that contact with the members of another cultural or racial group potentially play on prejudice. While noting that contact did not always result in reduced prejudice, Allport observed that it held potential for prejudice reduction. Cushner, McClelland, and Safford (1992) suggest that reduction in prejudice against members of another group is most likely to happen when individuals from different groups have contact in which they perceive that they have equal status, are required to work on a common task, do so in a school in which norms encourage intergroup interaction and the reduction of prejudice, and the individuals are given the opportunity to get to know each other well. Classes with students from a number of cultures offer the opportunity to employ this strategy through assignments in which pairs of students from different cultures must work on an intercultural assignment as a joint project across the course of a semester and in which they are required to spend considerable time together. This approach should also be expected to have a beneficial effect on reducing stereotypes and ethnocentrism.

Simulation games such as BaFaBaFa (Shirts, 1977) offer some potential as short-term simulations of intercultural contact. As an exercise this game allows discussion of why people tend to develop lack of respect and prejudice toward members of other cultures as a result of misunderstandings. The game also demonstrates how a limited number of negative encounters can produce negative stereotypes and the fact that our own interpretation of behavior is likely to be based on our own culture.

Related to experiential approaches is the use of student observation. In this approach, students are encouraged to observe interaction in another culture. One means of doing this is through viewing movies from another culture. Even unsubtitled movies may be used, but success with this technique requires careful observation by students and some introduction to communicative differences so that students will have some guidance in what they should be looking for. A useful addition to this assignment is to require that students watch the movie with an informant from the same culture as the movie. An alternative to this technique is to have students observe people from another cultural background in a public place. A more elaborate approach of this technique would require students to write ethnographies. Although useful as a means of learning about cultures, it is not clear that this technique readily would result in reductions in ethnocentrism, prejudice, and stereotyping.

Informational approaches to teaching intercultural communication which address respect for other cultures offer the greatest number of alternatives. One such approach is to discuss ethnocentrism, prejudice, and stereotyping directly. This is an approach taken by some intercultural communication textbooks, for example, Jandt (1995). As indicated by research discussed above, this may very well be the least effective approach in dealing with prejudice. It may also not be effective in dealing with ethnocentrism and stereotyping. Another approach involves emphasizing similarities between another and our own culture even as differences are discussed. Presumably, emphasizing similarities serves to cause another group to be seen as part of one's own ingroup. In dealing with cultures of the Middle East it may be useful to present Islam as a religion with a common deity with Judaism and Christianity, a religion sharing similar values, and sharing a common history. One disadvantage of this approach is that it is useful for cases in which cultures do share significant similarities but not for others. More abstract approaches which attempt to emphasize similarities based on a "common humanity" are likely to be less effective. A third informational approach attempts to develop respect for other cultures based on the enumeration of the achievements of the culture. This approach seems to be based on the notion that exposure to the achievements of a culture are positive traits that will result in positive attitudes toward the culture. For example, Chinese culture might be presented in connection with the achievements of Chinese civilization. This approach is difficult to take with small minority cultures such as the Hmong. Another informational approach is based on exploring different interpretations of behavior. Albert and Adamopoulous' (1976) approach to attribution training in which individuals are given situations in which members of different cultures encounter difficulties in interaction and for which attributions for the behaviors are presented from the differing perspectives of members of different cultures is one such possibility. This technique encourages students to acknowledge that members of other cultures may have very different intentions in behaving in certain ways in specific situations and demonstrates that our own interpretations are likely to be very ethnocentric.

An alternative method is the use of cultural case studies. Merriam defines the case study as "an intensive, holistic description and analysis of a bounded phenomenon such as a program, an institution, a person, a process, or a social unit" (1988, p. 15). Nieto (1992) advocates exposure to cultural case studies as a means of reducing cultural stereotyping.

Yet another possibility is based on teaching concepts in an intercultural communication course. Cushner, McClelland, and Safford (1992) suggest that students should be exposed to a culture-general model of the stages that people go through in intercultural encounters. Students are then encouraged to identify examples of the phenomena described by the model in their own interactions, observations, and readings. In this approach, students are encouraged to identify ethnocentrism, prejudice, and stereotyping among other concepts in their own and others behaviors. This approach may be particularly appealing to intercultural communication instructors because it is an extension of conceptual material taught in most courses. Its application, however, requires that students be given material and exercises in which they can apply these concepts.

Informational approaches which emphasize cognitive sophistication may be the most useful with university students. Walsh (1988) has suggested that critical thinking is incompatible with prejudice. Several of the above approaches are capable of fostering cognitive sophistication. Applied to intercultural communication, this approach would encourage students to look at other cultures from the perspective of the members of the culture and to carefully evaluate claims about another culture.

Of the above teaching strategies, both experiential and informational techniques are likely to be effective with university students. Semester-long cooperative assignments which pair students with those from other cultural backgrounds in working on a common task seem potentially most effective as an application of the experiential approach. Of informational approaches, attribution training, case studies, and the application of the culture-general model seem most promising.

SUMMARY

This chapter advocates that teachers of introductory intercultural communication courses include respect for other cultures and the members of those cultures as a course objective. Semester-long experiential learning in which students learn cooperatively with students from other cultures and a range of informational approaches are proposed as teaching strategies for accomplishing these goals with college students. International students, immigrants, and refugees can be a valuable asset in providing extended contact with members of other cultures.

Because intercultural communication texts tend to give limited attention to ethnocentrism, prejudice, and stereotyping, it is recommended that teachers of these courses add additional materials such as case study readings, exercises which foster attribution training, and encourage students to recognize examples of ethnocentrism, prejudice, and stereotyping as they experience, observe, and read about intercultural contact.

For some teachers of intercultural communication, the recommendation that introductory courses deal with respect for other cultures may seem inappropriate. After all intercultural communication has much to offer in improving intercultural relationships as Albert and Triandis (1991) note by simply giving people better communicative skills in interacting with people from another cultural background. Greater knowledge of cultural differences, particularly in terms of communicative differences, might be expected to produce greater success in intercultural encounters thus leading to more positive attitudes toward members of other cultures and thus their cultures. This approach would seem to be a simple applied extension of the study of intercultural communication as a social science.

For other multicultural scholars (Bhabha, 1994; Giroux, 1988) intercultural communication by taking a definition of culture shared with anthropologists and sociologists ignores the power relations within cultures and the role of culture in imposing the interests of some groups on others. Adding concern for respect for cultures and the members of these cultures is seen as merely introducing cultural relativism or worse enforcing the status quo of those groups within power within our own or other cultures.

However, these critics advocate an approach which is far too political for many scholars in intercultural communication. Indeed, the social and political changes advocated by these scholars may seem to intercultural communication scholars to be culturally ethnocentric in their own way. Reducing the ethnocentrism, prejudice, and stereotyping of students toward other cultures and the members of these cultures is close to a value which we hold in attempting objectivity and minimal bias in our own research work on other cultures. It is likely to contribute to the increased success of our students in interacting with people from other cultures.

As defined in this chapter, respect for other cultures requires consideration of other cultures from a more objective and accurate vantage point. This paired with intercultural communication skills and specific knowledge about other cultures should better serve the primary goal that teachers of intercultural communication hold for their students- to solve problems in intercultural communication and increase positive outcomes in intercultural encounters.

DISCUSSION QUESTIONS

1.   What is an example of a way that another culture is different which causes some people not to have respect for that culture?
2.   As an American student how would you like your culture to be presented to the members of another culture?
3.   Which of the techniques for trying to foster respect for other cultures do you believe would be most effective? Why?
4.   What are some experiences that you have had that have made you more respectful of another culture?
5.   Is it ever appropriate to lack respect for some aspect of another culture? Explain.

REFERENCES

Aboud, F. (1988). *Children and prejudice.* New York: Basil Blackwell.

Adorno, T. W. (1950). *The authoritarian personality.* New York: Harper & Row.

Albert, R. D., & Adamopoulous, J. (1976). An attributional approach to culture learning: The cultural assimilator. *Topics in Culture Learning, 4,* 53-60.

Albert, R. D., & Triandis, H. C. (1991). Intercultural education for multicultural societies: Critical issues. In L. A. Samovar & Richard E. Porter (Eds.), *Intercultural communication: A reader* (6th ed., pp. 411-421). Belmont, CA: Wadsworth.

Allport, G. W. (1954). *The nature of prejudice.* Cambridge, MA: Addison-Wesley.

Ben Ari, R., Kedem, P, & Levi-Warner, N. (1992). Cognitive complexity and intergroup perception and evaluation. *Personality and Individual Differences, 13,* 1291-1298.

Bhabha, H. K. (1994). *The location of culture.* New York: Routledge.

Brislin, R. W. (1991). Prejudice in intercultural communication. In L. A. Samovar & Richard E. Porter (Eds.), *Intercultural communication: A reader* (6th ed., pp. 366-370). Belmont, CA: Wadsworth.

Colby, A., & Kolhberg, L. (1987). *The measurement of moral judgment* (Vol I). New York: Cambridge University Press.

Cushner, K., McClelland, A., & Safford, P. (1992). *Human diversity in education: An integrative approach.* New York: McGraw-Hill.

Day, K. D. (1998). The problem of ethics in intercultural communication. In K. S. Sitaram & M. H. Prosser (Eds.), Civic discourse: *Multiculturalism , cultural diversity and global communication* (pp. 131-142). Norwood, N.J. : Ablex.

Dodd, C. H. (1987). An introduction to intercultural effectiveness skills. In C. H. Dodd & F. F. Montalvo (Eds.), *Multicultural skills for multicultural societies.* Washington, D.C.: SIETAR.

Dodd, C. H. (1991). *Dynamics of intercultural communication* (3rd ed.). Dubuque, IO: William C. Brown.

Giroux, H. (1988). *Teachers as intellectuals.* New York: Bergin & Garvey.

Glover, R. J. (1994). Using moral and epistemological reasoning as predictors of prejudice. *The Journal of Social Psychology, 134,* 633-640.

Gudykunst, W. B., & Kim, Y. Y. (1984). *Communicating with strangers: An approach to intercultural communication.* New York: Random House.

Hamilton, D. L., & Trolier, T. K. (1986). Stereotypes and stereotyping: An overview of the cognitive approach. In J. F. Dovidio & S. L. Gaertner (Eds.), *Prejudice, discrimination, and racism* (pp. 127-163). San Diego, CA: Academic Press.

Hogg, M. A., & Abrams, D. (1988). *Social identification: A social psychology of intergroup relations and group processes.* London: Toutledge & Kegan Paul.

Jandt, F. E. (1995). *Intercultural communication: An introduction.* Thousand Oaks, CA: Sage.

Katz, D. (1960). The functional approach to the study of attitudes. *Public Opinion Quarterly, 24,* 164-204.

Klopf, D. W. (1991). *Intercultural encounters: The fundamentals of intercultural communication* (2nd ed.). Englewood, CO: Morris.

Lustig, M. W., & Koester, J. (1996). *Intercultural competence: Interpersonal communication across cultures.* New York: Harper Collins.

Lynch, J. (1987). *Prejudice reduction and the schools.* New York: Nichols Publishing Company.

Merriam, S. B. (1988). *Case study research in education: A qualitative approach.* San Francisco: Josey-Bass.

Nieto, S. (1992). *Affirming diversity: The sociopolitical context of multicultural education.* White Plains, N.Y.: Longman.

Pate, G. S. (1989). Reducing prejudice in the schools. *Multicultural Leader, 2,* 1-3.

Perry, W. G., Jr. (1968). *Forms of intellectual and ethical development in the college years: A scheme.* New York: Harcourt Brace Jovanovich College Publishers.

Pettigrew, T. F. (1981). The mental health impact. In B. P. Bowser & R. G. Hunt (Eds.), *Impacts of racism on white americans* (pp. 97-118). Beverly Hills, CA: Sage.

Ruhly, S. (1976). *Orientations to intercultural communication.* Chicago: Science Research Associates.

Samovar, L. A., & Porter, R. E. (1991). *Communication between cultures.* Belmont, CA: Wadsworth.

Shirts, G. F. (1977). *BAFABAFA: A crosscultural simulation.* Del Mar, CA: SIMILE II.

Tajfel, H. (1969). Cognitive aspects of prejudice. *Journal of Social Issues, 23,* 79-97.

Turner, J. C. (1985). Social categorization and the self-concept: A social-cognitive theory of group behavior. In E. J. Lawler (Ed.), *Advances in group processes* (vol. 2, pp. 77-122). Greenwich, CT: JAI Press.

Walsh, D. (1988). Critical thinking to reduce prejudice. *Social Education, 52,* 280-282.

Wilder, D. A. (1986). Social categorization: Implications for creation and reduction of intergroup bias. In L. Berkowitz (Ed.), *Advances in experimental social psychology* (vol. 19, pp. 291-355). San Diego, CA: Academic Press.

11

SPEECH ANXIETY AMONG INTERNATIONAL STUDENTS

Laurie Wilfred Hodge
Bergen Community College

INTRODUCTION

Many Americans experience great fear when anticipating or delivering a public speech. This fear may manifest itself in a myriad of symptoms: "butterflies in the stomach," weak and trembling knees, shortness of breath, dry mouth, headaches, blurred vision, or a feeling of impending doom. The fear of public speaking has consistently ranked high among Americans' greatest fears, surpassing such phobias as snakes, heights, and elevators (Daly, 1991, p. 11). Jerry Seinfeld, star of the popular situation comedy, *Seinfeld* noted that "delivering a speech is ranked first on the list of things Americans fear most. Death was ranked second... Conclusion?...If these people were to attend a funeral, they would prefer to be in the casket rather than deliver the eulogy." (1996).

This chapter will (1) review the literature concerning the causes of communication apprehension (CA) among native English speakers and international students; (2) advance the interpersonal communication—first approach to the basic speech-communication course as the preferred pedagogical procedure for enhancing oral communication skills and reducing speech anxiety (SA) among international students; and (3) report results of the PRPSA Pre/Post Questionnaire, which was administered to international students in a college level speech course.

CONCEPTUAL GROUNDING

Causes of Communication Anxiety Among Native English Speakers

I view communication apprehension and speech anxiety as existing on a continuum. The former is "a fear or anxiety an individual feels about orally communicating" (Daly, 1991; McCroskey, 1977), and the latter "refers to those situations when an individual reports he or she is afraid to deliver a speech" (Ayers & Hopf, 1993). Both are dimensions of the general fear of communicating orally. Although the causes of this fear are under-represented in the research literature, Daly delineates five explanations that may account for the development of this malady. Heredity, as one of the causes of CA is strongly supported by research on fraternal and identical twins, twins raised apart, and adopted children (1991, p. 5). A history of negative responses and reinforcement may also contribute to the development of CA. Daly (1991) notes that, "One's history of reinforcement and punishment related to the act of communicating may also play a central role in the development of communication apprehension" (p. 5). Under these circumstances, silence may be rewarded, and speaking may incur punishment.

The absence of a consistent level of reward and positive reinforcement may be a cause of CA. "The unpredictability of others' responses to a person's communication attempts leads him or her to become apprehensive about communicating" (Daly, 1991, p. 5). McCroskey (1984) describes this as *learned helplessness and learned responsiveness* (p. 26). The fulfillment of expectations is crucial to this conception. Inappropriate responses regarding specific behavior could erode trust and confidence. Helplessness and eventually CA evolve in the absence of the positive reinforcement of expectations. "Learned helplessness and learned negative expectations are the foundational components of CA" (McCroskey, 1984, p. 29). CA can also develop if effective communication skills are not acquired at an early age. Daly (1991) reports that "children who are not provided with the opportunity to garner good communication skills early in life are more likely to be apprehensive than those who receive a wealth of early experience in communication."

To what extent does the unavailability of good communication models during childhood contribute to the development of CA? It appears that CA could develop if children do not have the opportunity to emulate good communicators. This is understandable, since children who were exposed to good communication models tend to be less apprehensive communicators. When withdrawn youngsters were exposed to films showing their peers engaging in appropriate social-interactive activities, their level of withdrawal was significantly reduced (Daly, 1991, p. 6). Effective communication skills cannot be acquired in a vacuum.

Recently, Motley (1988, 1995) and Motley and Molloy (1994) have noted another cause of CA, especially in the public speaking context. They hypothesize that a cognitive orientation emphasizing performance, instead of an orientation that stresses communication is a primary cause of public speaking anxiety. Motley and Molloy (1994) envision a continuum:

> At one end is what has been called "performance orientation," which defines the primary objective of a speech as making a positive aesthetic impression on the audience, especially via flawless delivery. At the other end is a "communication orientation," which views the primary objective as sharing information with the audience.

Causes of Communication and Speech Anxieity Among International Students

The causes of CA and SA among native English speakers noted above—a) heredity, b) a history of negative responses and reinforcement, c) inconsistent levels of rewards and positive reinforcement, d) the lack of opportunity to acquire good communication skills in childhood, e) the absence of good communication models during childhood, and f) an emphasis on performance in the public speaking situation—are also potential causes of SA among international students. It is necessary to acknowledge additional factors which could contribute to SA among international students. Of paramount concern here are the differences between their first culture and the host culture.

If we agree that "second language learning is often second culture learning" (Brown, 1987), then we must consider the impact of acculturation on (second language) L2 acquisition. Although many international students may have studied English in their first culture, they still need to acquire linguistic strategies in order to use American English effectively within the context of American culture if they are studying in that culture. Of course, this is predicated on the assumption that they intend to reside for a period in the United States and maintain contact with native English speakers.

Acculturation, the process of adjusting to a new culture, could be a difficult, painful process. Oberg (1960) notes that the newcomers may experience a myriad of emotional states during their early attempts to adjust to the new culture: strain, a sense of loss and feelings of deprivation, rejection, confusion, surprise, anxiety, disgust, indignation, and feelings of impotence. These emotional states are anxiety-inducing and may adversely affect international students' ability to develop functional interpersonal communication competence and public speaking skills in the host culture.

According to Kim (1987), "...*host communication competence refers to an immigrant's overall capacity to decode and encode messages effectively in interacting with the host environment.*" It encompasses three interrelated dimensions: cognitive, affective, and behavioral. The cognitive dimension refers mainly to the immigrants acquisition of the host language, verbal and nonverbal modes of expression, and rules of interaction. Motivational coorientation, emotional/aesthetic coorientation and attitude toward the host culture constitute the affective dimension, and the behavioral dimension includes the ability to speak, listen, follow interactional rules, and manage relationships.

While I do not contend that all international students suffer with debilitating SA, cultural discomfort and the ongoing struggle to adapt to the host environment may constrain the development of host communication competence, thereby initiating SA. This scenario mitigates the development of L2 interpersonal communication and presentation skills. Furthermore, not only must students develop strategies to cope with culture shock and adaptation, but must also contend with the continuing process of L2 acquisition. In a cross-cultural analysis of studies concerning "willingness to communicate," McCroskey and Richmond (1990) note that: "For most of the countries, public speaking drew the least willingness…" This evidence further compounds the international student's struggle to facilitate adaptation, acquire host communication competence, and develop presentation skills.

APPROACHES TO TREATING APPREHENSIVE COMMUNICATORS

With the exception of Motley's communication orientation model (COM), the comprehensive list of treatments discussed in Glaser (1981), Allen, Hunter, and Donohue, (1989), and Foss (1982) have not changed significantly. In addition to indicating different types of instruments used in colleges and Universitates, Foss (1981) presents a glossary of approaches to treatment categorized as follows: "1) approaches derived from learning theory; 2) approaches that assume a skills-training orientation; 3) an approach which assumes the appropriateness of the communication fundamentals class as the traditional means of dealing with communication apprehension." However, the categories suggested by Watson and Dodd (1984) are more appropriate: cognitive modification (CM), systematic desensitization (SD), and skills training through education.

These approaches are well represented in the research literature: CM—rational emotive therapy (Ayers & Hopf, 1993; Ellis, 1963; Watson & Dodd, 1984), CM—cognitive restructuring (Ayers & Hopf, 1993; Ellis, 1963; Frenouw & Scott, 1979), SD (Allen, Hunter, & Donohue, 1989; Ayers & Hopf, 1993; Friedrich & Goss, 1984; McCroskey, Ralph, & Barrick, 1970; Paul, 1966; Wolpe, 1958), and rhetoritherapy—skills training through education (Ayers & Hopf, 1993; Kelly, 1989; Kelly, Duran, & Stewart, 1990; Phillips, 1977). A recent approach, COM (Motley, 1988, 1995; Motley & Molloy, 1994) could embellish rhetoritherapy. Motley (1995) criticizes performance orientation motivation (POM) and suggests the advantage of COM:

A useful analogy, and only a very slight exaggeration, is to say that the anxious speaker tends to view the speech much as one would view the gymnastic, diving, or ice skating performances of the Olympic competitions we have seen on television. A group of judges score the performance, each rendering a personal verdict based on how skillfully various tiny parts of the performance were executed. Minor mistakes mean lost points, major mistakes can ruin the entire effort, and even a flawless performance may not be appreciated by a biased judge (p. 50).

With proper planning and an emphasis on communication orientation, "...anxiety tends to subside when a speech is viewed as more similar to normal communication than to performance" (Motley, 1995, p. 72).

Each of these approaches has some merit and warrants consideration. However, higher success rates can be achieved with a combination of approaches (Ayers and Hopf, 1993, 1990; Allen, Hunter, & Donohue, 1989). It is also evident that the order of application could affect results (Ayers & Hopf, 1993). The COM approach, augmented by the interpersonal communication–first instructional format, represents the primary strategy utilized in SIS III.

TREATMENT OF SA—INTERNATIONAL STUDENTS

Research literature addressing this issue is practically non-existent. Except for a few studies which attempted to assess CA levels in countries outside the United States, the majority of the studies available were conducted to assess native English speakers' CA on the college and university levels (Klopf, 1984). Of the approaches noted above, Motley's (1995) COM approach, combined with the interpersonal communication–first instructional format, may be most conducive to reducing SA among international students.

THE COURSE–BACKGROUND AND THEORETICAL FRAMEWORK

Since this chapter discusses the speech anxiety of students in the Speech for International Students Level III (SIS III) course, it is necessary to specify the nature of the course. "SIS III is designed for students for whom English is not a native language. The course seeks to expand students' listening skills, language comprehension, and speech fluency and to develop their confidence in the speaking of English" (Bergen Community College, 1994–1995, p. 127). This course also seeks to enhance students' knowledge of American culture.

I incorporate the interpersonal communicationn–first hybrid approach to the basic speech course in SIS III. Comeaux and Neer (1995) note that, unlike the public speaking-first hybrid format which initiates speech training by requiring formal speeches early in the semester, the interpersonal communication–first hybrid approach focuses on interpersonal communication activities first, in order to gradually develop students' confidence and skills prior to requiring a formal speech.

In their research, Comeaux and Neer (1995) set out to determine the pedagogical soundness of the hybrid approach. They hypothesized that: 1) high communication apprehensives will report lower anxiety levels when administered the interpersonal-first format; 2) high communication apprehensives will report higher oral performance scores when administered the interpersonal-first format of instruction; 3) high communication apprehensives will each rate the course as improving their skill level when administered the interpersonal-first format of instruction.

Results show that students enrolled in the interpersonal–first sections reported lower levels of state anxiety (public speaking anxiety) regardless of the CA level when they first enrolled. Hypothesis two was not fully supported in that higher performance scores were reported only in panel discussions, not during individual speeches. High communication apprehensives earned higher grades when the panel discussion preceded the informative speech. Hypothesis three was not supported, since CA level only affected course ratings, not instructional format.

Although this empirical attempt to validate the pedagogical soundness of the interpersonal communication-first format was not fully realized, speech theorists have been advocating its adoption. Pearson and West (1991) note that "...the hybrid course averts students' fears..Students are gentled into public speaking after participating in interpersonal activities, diadic exchanges, informational interviews, personal conversations, and small group discussions." However, Seiler and McKurkin, (1989) observe that there is insufficient empirical data to warrant the design and implementation of a hybrid format.

This debate not withstanding, the interpersonal—first hybrid format offers many advantages to international students: 1) It permits them to be inconspicuous during the early stages of the course, when their SA would be at its apex. (Conspicuousness is a major contributor to state CA, see Rubin, Palmgreen, and Sypher, 1994, pp. 340-341); 2) International students have the opportunity to participate in group activities which most likely reflect their cultural orientation; 3) It affords the opportunity to build confidence and enhance cultural awareness in a co-operative learning context; 4) Content is emphasized, not evaluation; 5) Students are involved in authentic communication situations; 6) Phonological issues can be addressed in the context of authentic situations, not through the use of oral drills; and 7) It could be instrumental in establishing the foundation for the COM approach, which emphasizes content over performance and delivery.

As noted above, international students' SA is compounded by the ongoing process of L2 acquisition. Hence, it is paramount for the instructor to create a positive, trustworthy, and motivating classroom atmosphere. A threatening, highly judgmental, and abusive decorum would stifle students' creativity and willingness to communicate. In order to protect and amplify self-esteem and cultural identity, tolerance of cultural differences must also be established and encouraged.

The classroom must be student–centered, not teacher–centered. Scarcella (1990, p. 127) notes that: "Teachers in multicultural classrooms frequently lament their students' inability to communicate effectively because of limited English proficiency. Unfortunately, these same teachers often fail to encourage interaction in their classrooms." The teacher must be a facilitator, not a dictator. Cummins (1989) provides guidelines for classroom decorum which would be conducive to students' use of language in interactions.

The instructional pedagogy for the SIS Level III course is well represented in the text, *Speaking Solutions: Interaction, Presentation, Listening, and Pronunciation Skills* by Candace Matthews (1994). The interactive activities in the text involve learners in practicing skills that they can apply to real-life situations. With exercises ranging from "Getting Acquainted" to "Solving a Problem," this text is the epitome of the interpersonal communication–first approach. This format, reinforced by an instructor who encourages communication rather than performance, should simultaneously develop L2 learners' oral proficiency and reduce speech anxiety.

RESEARCH QUESTIONS

A plethora of studies address SA among native English speakers, but there is no research pertinent to international students' SA using L2. Since there is no research upon which to establish hypotheses, the following questions are posed: 1) Do students in a Speech for International Students course on the community college level experience high SA, especially at the beginning of the course? 2) Could the basic hybrid course utilizing the interpersonal communication-first hybrid approach and an emphasis on content, rather than performance, serve to reduce SA among international students? 3) Is there a correlation between the number of years international students have studied English and their scores on the PRPSA Pretest? and 4) Will international students who frequently interact with native English speakers exhibit lower levels of speech anxiety on the PRPSA Pretest?

RESEARCH METHOD

Instrument

The primary assessment tool was the Personal Report of Public Speaking Abilities PRPSA questionnaire (McCroskey, 1970; Richmond & McCroskey, 1992). It provides a variety of anxiety stimuli related specifically to public speaking (Byers & Weber, 1995), and it has repeatedly demonstrated high reliability and validity with three separate internal reliability measures of .94 and test-retest of .84 over a ten-day period (McCroskey, 1970; Richmond & McCroskey, 1992). PRPSA is a 34 item Likert-type questionnaire on which students may report one of five responses to each item, the score of 102 represents the theoretical neutral position and scores may range from 34 to 170.

As suggested by Byers and Weber (1995), scores should be interpreted in the following manner: 1) Scores between 34 and 84 indicate that few public situations will produce anxiety; 2) Scores between 85 and 92 indicate a moderately low level of anxiety; 3) Moderate SA will be experienced by those who have scores between 93 and 100; 4) Scores in the 111-119 range represent a moderately high level of anxiety;and 5) Those from 120-170 exhibit a very high level of anxiety about public speaking.

Participants

The participants were 20 international students enrolled in two Level III sections of Speech for International Students at Bergen Community College in Northern New Jersey. This course is one component of the American Language Program, which also encompasses reading, writing, and grammar. Collectively, students had spent an average of three years studying English in their first country and in the United States, and they represented 11 countries: Poland, Russia, Columbia, Korea, El Salvador, China, India, Ecuador, The Dominican Republic, Macedonia, and Taiwan.

Procedure

The PRPSA was administered during the first and last week of the semester, and pre-test and post-test scores were analyzed for change. The data were also ana-lyzed to determine if any correlation exists between students' PRPSA pre-scores and a) the number of years studying English and b) frequency of contact with native English Speakers.

RESULTS AND DISCUSSION

Extensive statistical analysis was not completed, due to the small sample (N = 20). The PRPSA pre-test results show that 55 percent of the students experienced high to very high SA early in the course, and comparisons of individual pre/post-test scores clearly indicate a reduction in speech anxiety, with the greatest individ-ual difference of 71 points. Actually, 85 percent of the students reported a reduction in SA. There appears to be no distinct correlation between high/low SA scores and the number of years studying English or frequency of contact with native English speakers. Since a significant number of native English speakers suffer with SA, it is evident that high oral proficiency does not ensure low SA. While frequent contact with native English speakers is paramount to acquiring knowledge of American culture and interpersonal communication strategies, it may not be instrumental in reducing SA among international students.

SUMMARY

This paper discussed the causes of CA–SA among native English speakers and international students, presented the advantages of the interpersonal communication–first hybrid format and the COM approach to SA reduction, and reported the results of four research questions. Additional research is needed to explore the causes of SA among international students and the efficacy of various treatments. Speech communication and ESL teachers can play a major role in developing students' self-confidence and preparing them to assume leadership positions in the community. Since most of these students will remain in the United States, they should possess the necessary oral communication skills to function in American society, a society which often rewards assertiveness and eloquence.

DISCUSSION QUESTIONS

1. What are the causes of speech anxiety among international students? Cite causes in addition to those discussed here.
2. What programs or activities would you develop in order to facilitate international students' adjustment to American culture?
3. Besides the Personal Report of Public Speaking Abilities Questionnaire, what other types of research could be used to assess international students' CA–SA?
4. If you were to interview an international student on this subject, what questions would you ask?
5. What social, political and/or economic circumstances enhance or curtail international students' adaptation to American Culture?

REFERENCES

Allen, M., Hunter, J.E. & Donohue, W.A. (1989). Meta-analysis of self-report data on the effectiveness of public speaking anxiety treatment techniques. *Communication Education. 38*, 54-75.

Ayers, J. & Hopf, T.S. (1990). *Coping with public speaking anxiety: An examination of various combinations of systematic desensitization, skills training, and visualization.* Unpublished manuscript. Washington State University.

Ayers, J. & Hopf, T.S. (1993). *Coping with public speaking anxiety.* Norwood, NJ: Ablex Publishing Company.

Bergen Community College (1994-1995). *Bergen Community College Catalog,* p. 127.

Brown, H. D. (1987). Sociocultural Factors in Teaching Language Minority Students. In H. D. Brown, *Principles of language learning and teaching* (pp. 122-145). Englewood Cliffs, NJ: Prentice Hall, Inc. .

Byers, P.Y. & Weber, C.S. (1995). The timing of speech anxiety reduction treatments in the public speaking classroom. *Southern Communication Journal. 60,* 246-256.

Comeaux, P. & Neer, M. (1995). A comparison of two formats in the basic hybrid course on oral and test performance. *The Southern Communication Journal, 60.*

Cummins, J. (1989).*Empowering language minority students.* Sacramento, CA. California Association for Bilingual Education.

Daly, J. (1991). Understanding communication: An introduction for language educators. In Horwitz, E.K. & Young, D.J. *Language anxiety: From theory and research to classroom Implications.* Englewood Cliffs, NJ. Prentice Hall.

Daly, J.A. & McCroskey, J.C. (Eds.) (1984). *Avoiding communication: Shyness, reticence, and communication apprehension.* Beverly Hills. CA. Sage Publications.

Ellis, A. (1963). *Reason and emotion in psychotherapy.* New York, NY. Lyle Stuart. In Frenouw, W.J. & Scott, M.D. (1979). Cognitive restructuring: An alternative method for the treatment of communication apprehension. *Communication Education.* 28, May 1979.

Foss, K. (1982). Communication apprehension: Resources for the instructor. *Communication Education. 31,* 195-203.

Frenouw, W.J. & Scott, M.D. (1979). Cognitive restructuring: An alternative method for the treatment of communication apprehension. *Communication Education 28.*

Friedrich, G. & Goss, B. (1984). Systematic desensitization. In Daly, J.A. & McCroskey, J.C. (Eds.). *Avoiding communication: Shyness, reticence, and communication apprehension.* Beverly Hills. CA. Sage Publications.

Glaser, S.R. (1981). Oral communication apprehension and avoidance: The current status of treatment research. *Communication Education, 30,* 321-341.

Kelly, L. (1989). Implementing a skills program for reticent communicators. *Communication Education, 38,* 85-101.

Kelly, L., Duran, R.L., & Stewart, J. (1990). Rhetoritherapy revisited: A test of its effectiveness as a treatment for communication problems. *Communication Education. 39.*

Kim, Y.Y. (1987). Facilitating immigrant adaptation: The role of communication. In Albrecht, T.L., Adelman, M.B. & Associates. *Communicating social support.* Beverly Hills, CA. Sage Publication.

Klopf, D.W. (1984). Cross-cultural apprehension research: A summary of pacific basin studies. In Daly, J.A. & McCroskey, J.C. *Avoiding communication: Shyness, reticence, and communication apprehension.* Beverly Hills. CA. Sage Publications.

McCroskey, J.C. (1970). Measures of communication bound anxiety. *Speech Monographs, 37,* 269-277.

McCroskey, J.C. (1972). The Implementation of a large-scale program of systematic desensitization for communication apprehension. *Speech Teacher, 21,* 255-264.

McCroskey, J.C.(1977). Oral communication apprehension: A summary of recent theory and research. *Human Communication Research. 4,* 78-96.

McCroskey, J.C. (1978). Validity of the PRCA as an index of oral communication apprehension. *Communication Monographs, 45*, 192-203.

McCroskey, J.C. (1984). The communication apprehension perspective. In Daly, J.A. & McCroskey, J.C., (Eds.). *Avoiding communication: Shyness, reticence, and communication apprehension* (pp. 13-38). Beverly Hills. CA. Sage Publications.

McCroskey, J.C., Ralph, D.C. & Barrick, J.E. (1970). The effect of systematic desensitization on speech anxiety. *Speech Teacher, 19*, 32-36.

Matthews, C. (1994). *Speaking solutions: Interactions, presentations, listening, and pronunciation.* Englewood Cliffs, NJ. Prentice Hall Regents.

Motley, M.T. (1988). Taking the terror out of talk. *Psychology Today, 22* (1) 46-49.

Motley, M.T. (1995). *Overcoming your fear of public speaking—A proven method.* New York, NY. McGraw-Hill, Inc.

Motley, M.T. & Molloy, J.L. (1994). An efficacy test of a new therapy ("communication-orientation motivation") for public speaking anxiety. *Journal of Applied Communication Research 22*, 48-58.

Oberg, K. (1960). Culture shock: Adjustment to new culture environment. *Practical Anthropology.* 7, 182-197. In Gundykunst, W.B. & Kim, Y.Y. Eds. (1992). *Readings on communicating with strangers* (pp. 182-197). New York, NY. McGraw-Hill, Inc.

Paul, G. (1966). *Insight vs. desensitization in psychotherapy: An experiment in anxiety reduction.* Stanford. Stanford University Press.

Pearson, J. & West, R. (1991). The introductory communication course: The hybrid approach. In Hugenberg, L. (Ed.). *Basic Communication Course Annual: III.* (pp.16-34). Boston, MA. American Press.

Phillips, G.M. (1977). Rhetoritherapy vs. the medical model: dealing with reticence. *Communication Education. 26*, 34-43.

Richmond, V.P. & McCroskey, J.C. (1992). *Communication: Apprehension, avoidance and effectiveness.* Scottsdale, Arizona. Gorsuch Scarisbrick, Publishers.

Rubin, R.B., Palmgreen, P., & Sypher, H.E. (1994). *Communication research measures: A sourcebook.* New York, NY. The Guilford Press.

Scarcella, R. (1990). *Teaching language minority students in the multicultural classroom.* Englewood Cliffs, NJ. Prentice-Hall Regents.

Seiler, W.J. & McKurkin, D. (1989). What we know about the basic course: What has research told us? In Hugenberg, L. (Ed.). *Basic communication course annual: I.* (pp. 28-42). Boston, MA. American Press.

Seinfeld J. (Executive Producer). (1996, January, 10). *Seinfeld.* New York, NY. WPIX Television.

Watson, K.W. & Dodd, C.H. (1984). Alleviating communication apprehension through rational emotive therapy: A comparative evaluation. *Communication education, 33.*

Wolpe, J. (1958). *Psychotherapy by reciprocal inhibition.* Palo Alto, CA. Stanford University Press.

12

LATINOS/LATINAS IN THE UNITED STATES: DIVERSITY, CULTURAL PATTERNS, AND MISCONCEPTIONS

Rosita D. Albert
University of Minnesota

Los Angeles is the second largest Spanish-Speaking city in the world (which elicits surprise); that there are presently 25 million Hispanics in the United States (the blunt numbers begin to raise some eyebrows); and that by the middle of the next century, almost half of the US population will be Spanish speaking (it is this figure that causes the students to sit up straight in their small wooden desks and start to gape). ("The living power of language," cited in Lustig & Koester, 1996, p.11)

As this quote indicates, Latinos/Latinas (Latinos/as) in the United States are a large and growing group. Unfortunately, they have been largely invisible. Many people do not realize that by the end of this century Latinos/as will be the largest minority in the United States, and in the next century they will constitute a large proportion of the U.S. population. Few know what Latinos/as value, or what their cultural traditions and patterns are. Thus, along with stereotypes and misconceptions, reinforced by the negative portrayals of Latinos/as in the media, there is a large amount of ignorance about them.

It is not widely known that the United States is currently the fifth largest Spanish speaking country in the world (Reddy, 1990). Given a population in Latin

America of 448,076 million in 1990 (Collier, Skidmore & Blakemore, 1992) and the rapidly increasing numbers of Latinos/as in the U.S., knowledge of their cultural patterns will become ever more important. In order for non-Latinos/as to interact effectively with Latinos/as, it is important that they learn about the background and experiences of Latinos/as, some of their culture specific patterns, and some characteristics of Latino/a cultures (the plural is used to emphasize the multiplicity of Latino/a traditions) which may differ from those found in other cultures, and, particularly, Anglo-American culture. This chapter gives a brief overview of these themes and of differences which may affect communication between Latinos/as and non-Latinos/as.

TERMINOLOGY

There are many terms that members of this group use to designate themselves. Although the census bureau and academic researchers have usually referred to this group as "Hispanic," many members of the group prefer the designator "Latino/a." "Hispanic" is perceived by some as an imposed term which emphasizes connections with Spain—they prefer the designator "Latino/a" because it clearly identifies them with their Latin American origins. Immigrants may prefer to be referred by their country of origin, such as Mexicans, Colombians, or Guatemalans. Some Mexican origin individuals born in the United States. may refer to themselves as "Chicanos;" others, as "Mexican Americans." The term Chicano, believed to be derived from the Aztec word for Mexicano (Mirandé, 1987), was adopted by participants in the Chicano movement of the 1960s, a national political and social movement (Menchaca, 1993). It tends to be preferred by some younger U.S. born university educated people (Padilla, 1995). As Padilla' (1995) states, "The really important issue... has to do with acknowledging that the ethnic and social group identity that the person uses is important in understanding the experience and worldview of the person" (p. xv). I will generally use Latino/a or the terms used by the authors that are cited. Latinos/as usually refer to members of mainstream American culture as "Anglo-Americans," and I will follow this custom here—while many non Hispanic individuals may not feel that they are "Anglos," as many observers have noted, mainstream American culture has basically been Anglo, white, and middle class.

DEMOGRAPHIC CHARACTERISTICS

Who are the Latinos/as? Many non-Latinos think that Latinos/as are mostly new arrivals, often illegal aliens, but while many are immigrants, not all of them are. The reality is much more complex. Latinos/as have lived in areas of the present United States probably since the 1500s. One of the least known facts is that some

Latinos/as in the United States are descendants of Jews who fled from the Spanish inquisition (one third of Spanish Jews fled, one third converted to save their lives, and the remaining third perished). Many of these Latinos/as don't themselves know of this origin, since over the centuries families outwardly converted to Christianity and eventually lost their Jewish traditions.

The Latino population has increased greatly during the last thirty years, to over 22 million in 1990 (Ortiz, 1995). It is expected to increase by 33 percent during the present decade (Hayes-Bautista, Schink, & Chapa, 1988). In California, the immigration of Latinos/as during the last decade has been at the highest level since 1920, and by the year 2030 the Latino/a population may reach 45 percent of the state (Hayes-Bautista et al. 1988; Ortiz, 1995).

Some people may have the misconception that Latinos/as all have similar backgrounds. Others feel that Latino/a groups are all so different that one cannot consider them together. Neither view does justice to the diversity and the commonalities found among Latinos/as.

Based on 1992 census data, approximately 64 percent of Latinos/as are of Mexican origin, 11 percent of Puerto Rican origin, 4.7 percent of Cuban origin, 14 percent from several Spanish speaking Central and South American nations, and 6.3 percent are categorized as other Hispanic (Garcia, 1993, Ortiz, 1995).

Latinos/Latinas of Mexican Origin

This is the largest group of Latinos/as in the United States. Some of its members were already residing in the southwestern United States when their territory was taken over by the United States from Mexico in 1848 following the Spanish American War. Many have immigrated from Mexico since the early 1900s (Ortiz, 1995). Historically the immigrants were poor, from rural areas, and came to work as migrant workers in agriculture. More recently, the Mexican origin population has migrated to urban areas. Although the foreign born constitute a smaller proportion of the Mexican-origin population than of other Latino/a groups, a substantial percentage of Mexican immigrants, 28.5 percent, immigrated during the last five years and settled in the Southwest (Ortiz, 1995).

Puerto Ricans

The Puerto Ricans have come to the cities of the Northeastern United States in large numbers since the 1940s, with the largest migrations taking place in the 1950s and early 1960s. Approximately 50 percent of the Puerto Ricans living in the continental United States were born in Puerto Rico, an island which is a Commonwealth of the United States. Although Puerto Ricans are United States citizens, they speak Spanish and their culture is closer to other Latin American cultures than to that of the United States. They have been disadvantaged in contrast to other Latino/a groups (Ortiz, 1986, 1995).

Cubans

For the most part, Cubans came to the United States during the last years of the 1950s and 1960s when Fidel Castro came to power. They settled predominantly in Florida. Most early Cubans were professionals and entrepreneurs, and were granted refugee status and resettlement assistance by the U.S. government. This population is older and relatively well off economically. Another group of Cubans, called "Marielitos," who arrived in the early 1980s, was of lower socio-economic status and has not fared as well (Ortiz, 1995).

Other Latinos/as

Other Latinos/as have arrived from Guatemala, El Salvador, and other countries, often fleeing war, natural disasters, or difficult economic conditions in their countries. These groups have not received assistance or support from government sources. Many of these Latinos/as are refugees and have suffered isolation, poverty, discrimination, unemployment, lack of services, and have experienced a great deal of stress (Dorrington, 1995).

With the exception of Cubans, Latinos/as have generally been disadvantaged in education, labor force status, occupational status, and earnings. Their families tend to be younger and have more children, and many are immigrants who are struggling to adjust to a foreign language and a new culture (Ortiz, 1995). Consequently, stress is usually high for Latinos/as. At the same time, research in California has shown that they have high labor force participation, low welfare utilization, strong families, strong health indicators, strong educational improvement, and a strong sense of citizenship, and as such do not conform to the urban underclass model, which is one of low labor force participation, high welfare dependency, high family disintegration and health pathology (Hayes-Bautista, Hurtado, Valdez & Hernández, 1992).

OTHER IMPORTANT CHARACTERISTICS OF LATINO/LATINA POPULATIONS IN THE UNITED STATES

Some characteristics which are important for understanding Latinos/as in the United States are discussed below.

Minority Status

As a minority, they face structural conditions in the United States which may affect their patterns of behavior. Included in these are residential segregation, living in areas where there is inner city violence, being for the most part poor, facing discrimination, and having less access to services. Many authors have argued that

Latino/a subordination is not a function of their values, but of the system in which they live (Baca-Zinn, 1995). This is important to keep in mind. In addition, Latinos/as are sometimes treated in the social science literature as if they are similar to the other large U.S. minority, the African American minority. Despite some similarities, they differ from this minority in important respects: greater heterogeneity of the population, differential segregation of different Latino/a groups, the meaning of race, the importance of immigration, and the role played by language (Massey, Zambrana & Bell, 1995).

Race

Latinos/as are racially heterogeneous and include people of European, African, Amerindian, and Asian ancestry, and mixtures thereof (Baca-Zinn, 1995; Massey, 1993). As such, they do not fit into the generally dichotomous thinking about race in terms of black and white (Collins, 1990 cited in Massey, Zambrana & Bell, 1995). In Latin American cultures, race has generally been viewed as a continuum. Massey, Zambrana and Bell (1995) state: "Although color prejudice exists in Latin America, it is more subtle and more intertwined with social class, and does not follow a well-defined color line" (p. 194). For example, 75 percent of Puerto Ricans in the island felt that color had no effect on educational and economic opportunities, and 85 percent felt it did not affect the respect they were accorded (Tumin & Feldman, 1969). In the U.S. mainland, Baca-Zinn (1995) suggests that racial inequalities are powerful shapers of family life by giving some families greater access to resources and rewards, while denying them to others. Montalvo (1987; personal communication, May 14, 1995) has proposed that color is a crucial variable overlooked by researchers and has called for greater attention to this factor in studies of Latino/a acculturation in the United States.

Immigration

The experience of coming to another country with language, customs, values, and laws that are different from those of their country of origin has had a profound effect on Latinos/as who immigrate and on their communities. Many face great risks to come to the United States, while others put up with terrible working conditions to avoid deportation. Some leave their families in their country of origin and suffer isolation and separation. Yet, it is worth noting that Latinos/as contribute more to American society in work and taxes than they use in services. In this brief overview, I cannot do justice to the experiences and consequences that follow from immigration. As we consider Latino/a cultural patterns in the next section, some of the major cultural differences that the immigrants have faced with will become evident.

Language

Latinos/as are generally proud of speaking Spanish and of their culture, and want to keep both. For them, there is no contradiction between this and civic participation in the United States, which they also value. When asked what aspects of Mexican/Latino culture and traditions they felt were most important to preserve, a random sample of Latinos/as in California cited the Spanish language most frequently. Speaking Spanish is part of their social identity. (Hurtado, Hayes-Bautista, Valdez, & Hernández, 1992) Yet, Latino/a children have been punished for speaking Spanish in schools (see Anzaldúa, 1995 for an example). Given that many of these children speak Spanish at home and learn English in school, bilingual education, in which some instruction is provided in Spanish and the rest in English, has been very important for Latinos/as. The majority of them overwhelmingly support it, and studies support its effectiveness. Anzaldúa (1995) points out that even though by the end of this century Spanish speakers will be the largest minority group in the United States, non-Latino/a students are encouraged to study French because it is considered more "cultured." By learning to speak Spanish, non-Latinos/as would be better able to communicate with Latinos/as and may, in the process, learn something about their culture.

Religion and Health

The majority of Latinos/as are Catholic. Religion plays an important role in their cultures. In most Latin American countries, Catholicism has been mixed with religious and ritual elements from African and Native American origins. Thus, Mexican Americans (Ortiz de Montellano, 1992) and other Latinos/as use folk remedies along with traditional medicine. To the surprise of many, a recent Gallup poll in California found that Latinos/as smoke and drink less, and protect their health better than Anglo-Americans in the state (Hayes-Bautista et. al, 1992).

Ethnic Identity

Latinos/as have a strong sense of ethnic identity. Even those who do not speak Spanish and who are very acculturated have positive feelings and ties to their ethnic group. Based on a review of the literature, Phiney (1995) concluded that strong ethnic identity of Latinos/as is related to high self esteem when accompanied by a positive orientation towards the mainstream culture. Thus, contrary to what some might suppose, a strong ethnic identity does not imply a negative orientation towards mainstream culture.

Heterogeneity and Variability

Besides heterogeneity in country of origin, race, and other factors, there is great variability in the levels of acculturation of Latinos/as—from newly arrived immigrants from Mexico and several other countries, who only speak Spanish, to third, fourth generation (and beyond) Americans who are highly acculturated and fluent in English. They also span all social classes and levels of education. Given this great diversity, generalizations are bound to oversimplify a complex picture. In the next section, when I identify some Latino/a cultural patterns, the reader should think of these as patterns that are likely to be more common among Latinos/as than other patterns. This does not imply that other patterns do not exist among these cultural groups: individuals and subgroups may vary a great deal from the cultural norm. In fact, there is often a large range of variation among Latinos/as, and more traditional patterns may coexist with non traditional patterns. For some patterns there is very little research. Whenever possible, I will cite patterns which have been documented by research, and when possible, cite the specific group studied. In this overview, the focus will be in patterns that are likely to differ from Anglo-American patterns. The aim is to be illustrative, not comprehensive. It is important to keep in mind that behaviors and values are not static; they change as a function of the environment and of people's experiences. Consequently, some of these patterns are already changing. The reader should consider these patterns as provisional characterizations, and should look for additional evidence, based on Latino/a worldviews and frameworks (see for example Ramírez, 1983) and social science data that confirm them, reject them, or call for their modification. Ideally, this is only a first step. Much more research needs to be done to document the patterns fully and specify their variations among Latino/a groups of different origins, acculturation levels, and classes.

CULTURAL PATTERNS

In 1996 I proposed a model of intercultural preparation for interacting with people from another culture that makes the learner aware of both culture specific and of relevant crosscultural *patterns of perceptions* (modes of interpreting the world), *cognitions* (modes of thought) and *behaviors* (modes of action) (Albert, 1996). The *culture specific or emic patterns* (Berry, 1980) provide information which is particular to the target culture (the culture the trainee is learning about), while the *crosscultural patterns,* known as *etic patterns*, permit the learner to see how the target culture is similar to or different from other cultures. In addition, I proposed that it is important to be aware of *communication patterns* in the target culture which might be different from those in one's own culture. Based on extensive empirical research on Latino-Anglo interactions, I (1992) have developed an instrument known as an Intercultural Sensitizer or ICS (Albert, 1983a, 1986b,

1995; Cushner & Landis, 1995) . This ICS is designed to help non-Latinos/as make attributions or interpretations to situations which are similar to those made by Latinos/as. In this way, non-Latinos/as can inductively learn about Latino/Latina patterns. Below, a complementary approach to understanding Latino/a patterns, based on research and conceptualizations by many authors, is presented.

Emic Latino Patterns

Latinos/as and Latin Americans share an overarching cultural orientation which I (1996) labeled the "interpersonal orientation." This orientation has the following important components which have emerged from research with Latinos/as:

Respect and dignity

Respect and dignity have been shown to be extremely important for Latinos/as, especially respect for one's elders. Triandis, Marín, Lisansky, and Betancourt (1984) found that in judgments about "respect" made by Hispanic and non-Hispanic Navy recruits, all scales showed significant differences between Hispanics and non-Hispanics. It is important to note that Hispanics perceived criticism or insults as denoting a lack of respect (Díaz Royo, 1974; Tumin & Feldman, 1971).

Loyalty

Loyalty was found by Triandis, Marín and colleagues, 1984, to have definitive meaning for Hispanics, but not for non-Hispanics. Loyalty was seen by Hispanics to include such actions as being "honest," "friendly," "doing what the person wanted done," "defend," "respect the person," "respect the culture of," and "value the language of the other person."

Simpatía

A person who is considered *simpático/a* is "perceived to be open, warm, interested in others, exhibits positive behaviors towards others, is in tune with the wishes and feelings of others, and is enthusiastic." (Albert, 1996, p. 333). This is a personal quality found to be very important for Cubans (Alum & Manteiga, 1977), Mexican Americans (Burma, 1970), Puerto Ricans (Landy, 1959), and, very likely, other Latinos/as.

Cooperativeness

Cooperativeness has been found in many studies of Hispanics (Triandis, Marín, Lisansky & Betancourt, 1984). A fair amount of research has demonstrated greater cooperativeness among Mexican children than among Anglo-American children (e.g. Kagan & Madsen, 1971). The results for Mexican American children and adults are somewhat mixed. While a number of studies found more cooperation between Mexican American than between Anglo-American children and adults, some found no differences between the two cultural groups and some found differences only when cooperation is adaptive (see Albert, 1996 for additional citations).

Avoidance of criticism and of negative behaviors

Latinos/as of Mexican and of Puerto Rican origin have been found to avoid direct criticism (Madsen, 1973), to express a concern with not offending someone (Albert, 1992), to avoid questioning another's' beliefs or actions directly, to avoid and deemphasize negative behaviors, and to expect more positive behaviors (Triandis, Marín et al., 1984). In fact, one observer (Wagenheim, 1972), noted that disrespectful behavior such as arguments, fights and direct confrontation is likely to be interpreted as an assault on the dignity of the other person. Hispanics are more likely to start any criticism by complimenting the other person (Triandis, Marín et al., 1984). Yet, in a recent study, Ferdman and Cortes (1992) found that Hispanic managers in their sample tended to deal with conflict "openly, directly and immediately," but to work to maintain control over their anger.

Personalistic attention and individuality

Observations and my own research (Albert, 1992) suggest that Latinos/as expect and prefer personalized attention, rather than being treated in an impersonal way that would apply to anybody. Individuality, rather than individualism, is valued. In a review of the social science literature, Lisansky states:

> The literature provides a remarkably consistent description of Hispanic emphasis on individuality, an individuality which is fundamentally different from individualism. It is an individuality which recognizes the essential worthiness and uniqueness of each individual. Dignity and self-respect are not necessarily connected to social-economic status, occupation and accomplishments. As one writer commented, it is more an "individualism of being." (1981, p. 75)

Of course, as is true for individuals from other non-dominant cultures, Latinos/as in the United States are very sensitive to being treated in a discriminatory way because of their ethnicity, color, national origin, or language, and have suffered a long history of discrimination (For vivid examples see Anzaldúa, 1995; Menchaca, 1993; Mirandé, 1987; and Ramirez, 1988).

Latino Patterns in Etic or Cross-cultural Dimensions

Familism

There is a substantial body of evidence that Latinos/as from all origins are deeply committed to their families. At all levels of acculturation, they express a desire to live close to their families and perceive a high level of family support (Keefe & Padilla, 1987; Sabogal, Marín & Otero-Sabogal, 1987). Those who are more acculturated tend not to use family members as exclusive role models and have less need to be the only source of material and emotional support to members of their extended family (Rogler & Cooney, 1991). Yet, contrary to common expectations, the evidence suggests that familism seems to increase rather than decrease with each generation living in the United States (Keefe & Padilla, 1987; Ramirez & Arce, 1981). Even the most acculturated are more familistic than Anglo Americans in attitudes and behaviors (Hurtado, 1995). While Anglo Americans do not consider it necessary to live close to relatives and have face to face contact with them, Mexican Americans do (Keefe, 1984).

For most Latinos/as, the family includes not only parents and their children, but also grandparents, aunts and uncles, nieces and nephews, and godparents. The system of *compadrazco* is common: parents invite other adults in the community to become godparents to their children. Godparents have a special responsibility to help their godchildren's children, so this system extends family like connections to others who now help the children throughout their life. Latino/a families living in households with three generations are common, and grandparents contribute to the household with services such as child care (Hurtado, 1995).

This familism is a component of a more general orientation which has been labeled *collectivism* by Hofstede (1980, 1991), Triandis (1995) and others. Based on research with Hispanics, Marín and Triandis (1985) claim that they tend to be more *allocentric* than *idiocentric*, meaning that they pay more attention to the needs, viewpoints, values, and goals of others than to their own individual needs, goals and values. Children are trained to be sensitive to the needs of others and to value harmony in interpersonal relations. This is so different from the predominant individualistic Anglo American pattern that it might be difficult for some Anglo-Americans to grasp fully.

High power distance

Power distance is defined as "the extent to which the less powerful members of institutions and organizations within a country expect and accept that power is distributed unequally" (Hofstede, 1991, p. 28). Latin American and Hispanic cultures were found to be higher in power distance than mainstream American culture. Triandis, Marín and colleagues (1984) found Hispanics had higher means in estimates regarding the behaviors "obey" and "disciplines" than non-Hispanics. They state "among Hispanics in some roles the superordination pattern overcomes the simpatía pattern" (p. 1371). In my own research, Latino/a students tended to select attributions reflecting a higher power distance between teachers and students, and to blame students rather than teachers in stimulus episodes presented to them (Albert, 1983b, 1986a, 1992). Yet, Ferdman and Cortes (1992) reported that Hispanic managers in the United States preferred a participatory, open-door leadership style, were willing to challenge their superiors, and did not like close supervision. (For possible reasons for this discrepancy, see Albert, 1996.)

Status and class differences tend to be greater in Latin American countries than in the United States, and higher status persons are treated with more deference in Latin American cultures.

Gender roles

It is commonly known that there is greater role differentiation amongLatinos/as than among Anglo-Americans. Yet even here there are misconceptions. Although the word "machismo" comes from Spanish, the concept of machismo has very different meanings in the two cultures. Guilbault states: "The Hispanic *macho* is manly, responsible, hardworking, a man in charge, a patriarch. A man who expresses strength through silence...The American *macho* is a chauvinist, a brute, uncouth, selfish, loud, abrasive, capable of inflicting pain, and sexually promiscuous" (1992, p. 34). For Latinos/as, the concept of machismo also includes defending the family honor. Some authors feel that machismo is pervasive among Hispanics, and plays a central in traditional culture; others think it is less ingrained; another group argues that machismo was critical in traditional culture but is on the decline because of acculturation in the United States, modernity, and economic advancement (Casas, Wagenheim, Banchero & Mendoza-Romero, 1994).

Females were traditionally encouraged to be submissive (Lisansky, 1981). They had greater influence in the home, but also, among Puerto Ricans, in public affairs (Fitzpatrick, 1971). Yet a recent survey of a representative sample of Latinos/as in California (Hurtado et. al, 1992) found that first, second and third generation Latinos/as supported womens' right to make decisions about important aspects of their lives, and did not share the stereotypical views of a dominant husband and a submissive wife. Baca-Zinn (1995) argues that instead of representing outmoded cultural forms, Mexican family lifestyles reflect adaptation responses to social and economic conditions. She notes that contrary to stereotyped views, there is great heterogeneity.

Some aspects of traditionalism may persist among some Latinos/as, even though many women now work. For example, some wives from different Latin American countries who were interviewers in my research project had to ask their husbands' permission to drive to a neighboring town, even though they worked. In a more traditional family, female children and young adults may be more protected. Thus, a traditional Latino father may be more reluctant to allow his daughter to go to college in a distant city. Gender roles are changing among Latinos/as. Herrera and Del Campo (1995) reported that working class Mexican American women want their husbands' role to include household and child-care responsibilities. There are more female heads of household, and there are now Latino/a gay and lesbian groups.

Shame

The sense of shame seems more pronounced in Latin American cultures than in mainstream American culture (Albert, 1996). As in other collectivistic cultures,

Latinos/as tend to employ shame as a means of social control. In my research, I found that Latino/a students were much more likely to make attributions or interpretations of shame when explaining the behavior of Latinos/as in stimulus stories than were Anglo-American students (Albert, 1986a, 1992).

Time orientation

Latinos/as have traditionally been considered present oriented (Kluckhohn & Strodtbeck, 1961), while Anglo-Americans have been considered future oriented. Latinos/as have also had a lot of interest in their history and their past, and this contrasts with the Anglo-American's relatively a-historical orientation. As I (1996) have indicated, time orientation, like other variables, is partly a function of social class, with lower classes tending to be generally more present oriented. Perhaps more significant for those interacting with Latinos/as, they tend to be polychronic (Hall, 1984) in their orientation towards time use, that is they focus more on relationships and less on schedules than Anglo-Americans. This has many implications. For example, Latinos/as tend to value relationships above promptness, so if a friend needs help they might be late for some appointments. While Anglo Americans generally view time in discreet episodes, Latinos/as generally have a more fluid conception of time. This fundamentally different view may be the cause of the stereotype of Latinos/as always being late. A Latino once said "Who says Latinos are always late? I am never late—whenever I arrive is the correct time!" When I told this story in class, my Anglo-American students felt that this Latino was either joking or was being somewhat arrogant. In the real situation, he was doing neither; he was merely illustrating that, in contrast to the United States, where business is conducted by the clock, among Latinos/as business is only conducted when the relevant persons arrive.

The "Being" orientation

While Anglo-Americans were identified by Kluckhohn and Strodtbeck (1961) as having a "Doing" orientation, Latinos/as were seen as having a "Being" orientation. This means that Latinos/as can just enjoy just being with friends, talking, living in the moment, without always feeling that they "have to do" something. This does *not* mean that they do not work hard—in fact, many work extremely hard, at two or even three jobs, to support their families. In fact, it has been shown that in California, they have higher rates of participation in the labor force than any other group, including Anglo-Americans (Hayes-Bautista et al., 1992). But work may be viewed differently by Latinos/as, not as an end in itself, but as a means for providing for their families. There is some evidence for this notion from research done in Mexico (Diaz-Guerrero & Szalay, 1991). I have heard a number of Latinos/as say to Anglo Americans: "You live to work, while we work to live!" The stereotype which some non-Latinos hold of Latinos/as as "lazy" may be the result of incorrectly applying Anglo-American patterns to Latinos/as. At the same time, we now hear Anglo-Americans being urged to have "more balance," to "smell the flowers," and so on, that is to adopt some of the being orientation (Albert, 1996).

Music and dancing play a big role in Latino/a cultures, and are examples of the Being and Present orientations. An important social occasion is the dance, which occurs frequently, sometimes weekly, among most, if not all, Latino/a groups. Although each region of Latin America has different music and dances, Latinos/as from different origins enjoy listening to music and dancing. Folk music often recounts history and serves to preserve cultural knowledge. Speaking for Chicanos in the Texas/Mexico borderland, Anzaldúa said "These folk musicians and folk songs are our chief cultural mythmakers, and they made our hard lives seem bearable" (1995, p. 159).

The Dionysian or expressive tendency

Latinos/Latinas can be considered Dionysian, that is, very expressive of their emotions. They are perceived to speak louder and more than Anglo-Americans (Albert & Nelson, 1993). They also report feeling more satisfaction in communicating with Anglo-Americans when both they and the Anglo person can express emotions freely (Hecht, Ribeau, & Sedano, 1990).

Flexibility

I find that Latinos/as tend to be flexible not only in terms of schedules and plans, as one would expect from their polychronic orientation, but also in terms of interpersonal relations, especially when dealing with others of equal or higher status, and with rules in organizations and bureaucracies. Research by Ferdman and Cortes (1992) and a review by Lisansky (1981) corroborate this view.

COMMUNICATION PATTERNS

Orientation Towards Language Use

As we have seen, there is strong attachment to the Spanish language, which is seen an important component of the culture, but this does not mean that Latinos/as do not want to speak English—the overwhelming majority value speaking both. In California, 95 percent want children to learn to read and write in both Spanish and English (Hurtado et al., 1992). Latin Americans are known for their pride in language and eloquence, for their poetry, and for the their world-class writers, several of whom have received the Nobel Prize in Literature. There is a burgeoning of Latino/a poetry and literature in the United States which at times mixes Spanish and English, as Chicanos often do when they speak to other Chicanos.

Politeness and Conversational Rules

In a study of conversational rules, Mexican Americans mentioned politeness, cultural prescriptions and relational climate as important. In conversations with Anglo-Americans, they sometimes felt that their cultural identity was threatened by negative stereotypes (Collier, 1988). In another study, Hecht and colleagues (1990) found that there were seven relational themes that related to communication satisfaction for Mexican Americans: acceptance, expressing emotions, absence of negative stereotypes, holistic and integrative worldview, self-expression, relational solidarity, and behaving rationally.

High Context Communication

Latino/a cultures tend to be *high context* (Hall, 1976). This means that as a general rule Latinos/as may not be as explicit in their verbal communication as Anglo-Americans, especially if they have to say "no" to a request, or ask for a favor. I have indicated that for Latin Americans, "The meaning of messages they send and received are often conveyed by gestures and other nonverbal signals, by the rank and position of those speaking and by reading between the lines" (Albert, 1996, p. 343). Murillo (1976) states that Mexican Americans are likely to use indirect and elaborate expressions in order to maintain harmonious social relations. Face-to-face communication is likely to be preferred by Latinos/as. Thus, Anglo-Americans communicating with them may have to pay more attention to context and to non verbal factors, and to spend more effort listening and deciphering messages.

High Contact Communication

High contact communication is evident in use of eye contact, gestures, proxemic patterns and haptics or tactility. Latinos/as' use of eye contact usually depends on the status and gender of the people involved. In contrast to the Anglo-American pattern, Latino/a children tend to avert their eyes to show respect for the teacher (Albert, 1992). Colleagues and I have observed that Latin Americans tend to stare longer at strangers than Anglo-Americans, and this is not seen as a problem. Women tend not stare at men, however, unless they want to show interest in them.

Coming from more expressive cultures, Latinos/as are more likely to use gestures to call and greet people, and to express feelings. It is widely noted that they are likely to use closer interpersonal distances than Anglo-Americans. Hall (1959) claimed that the close distance that Latin Americans use may evoke very negative reactions on the part of North Americans. At the same time, he noted that because of proxemic differences, Latin Americans may incorrectly perceive North Americans as cold, distant and unfriendly.

Latinos/as are more likely to touch people when they talk or greet others than Anglo-Americans. In my research, Anglo-American teachers thought that the teachers in the stimulus episodes they read were uncomfortable with the fact that Latino/Latina students would touch their arm (Albert & Triandis, 1979). Ferdman and Cortes (1992) found that Hispanic managers felt it was important to touch people, both literally and figuratively. Of course touch may depend on status, and context,. A study done in Latin America (Shuter, 1976) found differences in both proxemics and tactility among Costa Ricans, Panamanians, and Colombians, with higher contact found among Costa Ricans, and the highest among female dyads.

In conclusion, Latinos/as in the United States exhibit great diversity, yet tend to share some important characteristics and to exhibit some emic and etic cultural patterns, and some communication patterns, which are important for non-Latinos to understand. My hope is that this overview has begun to delineate important areas for increasing our society's understanding of Latinos/as in the United States, and that this will lead to more culturally sensitive research on Latino/a perspectives.

DISCUSSION QUESTIONS

1. Have your views of Latinos/as changed after reading this chapter? How?
2. What Latino/a cultural patterns appeal to you and why?
3. What in this chapter was most surprising to you and why?
4. What cultural patterns are likely to cause the greatest difficulty in communication between Latinos/as and non-Latinos/as? How can these difficulties be overcome?
5. What can non-Latinos/as learn from Latinos/as?

REFERENCES

Albert, R. D. (1983a). The Intercultural sensitizer or culture assimilator: A cognitive approach. In D. Landis & R. Brislin (Eds.), *Handbook of intercultural training: Vol. II. Issues in training methodology* (pp. 186-217). New York: Pergamon Press.

Albert, R. D. (1983b). Mexican-American children in educational settings: Research on children's and teacher's perceptions of behavior. In E. Garcia (Ed.), *The Mexican American child: language, cognition and social development.* (pp. 183-194). Tempe, AZ: Arizona State University.

Albert, R. D. (1986a). Communication and attributional differences between Hispanics and Anglo Americans. *International Journal of Intercultural Relations, X,* 41-59.

Albert, R. D. (1986b). Conceptual framework for the development and evaluation of cross-cultural orientation programs. *International Journal of Intercultural Relations, 2,* 197-213.

Albert, R. D. (1992). *Communicating across cultures.* Unpublished manuscript.

Albert, R. D. (1995). The intercultural sensitizer or culture assimilator as a crosscultural training method. In S. Fowler & M. Mumford (Eds.), *The intercultural sourcebook* (pp. 157-167). Yarmouth, ME: Intercultural Press.

Albert, R. D. (1996). A framework and model for understanding Latin American and Latino/Hispanic cultural patterns. In D. Landis & R. S. Bhagat (Eds.), *Handbook of intercultural training*. Thousand Oaks, CA: Sage.

Albert, R., & Nelson, G. (1993). Hispanic-Anglo differences in attributions to paralinguistic behavior. *International Journal of Intercultural Relations, 17,* 19-40.

Albert, R. D., & Triandis, H. C. (1979). Cross-cultural training: A theoretical framework and some observations. In H. Trueba & C. Barnett-Mizrahi (Eds.), *Bilingual multicultural education and the professional: From theory to practice.* (pp. 181-194). Rowley, MA.: Newbury House.

Alum, R. A., & Manteiga, F. P. (1977). Cuban and American values: A synoptic comparison. In *Hispanic subcultural values: Similarities and differences* (pp. 184-202). Mosaic (ERIC ED 144466).

Anzaldúa, G. (1995). How to tame a wild tongue. In R. Holeton (Ed.), *Encountering cultures* (pp. 152-162). Englewood Cliffs, NJ: Prentice Hall.

Baca-Zinn, M. (1995). Social science theorizing for Latino families. In R. E. Zambrana (Ed.), *Understanding Latino families* (pp. 177-189). Thousand Oaks, CA: Sage.

Berry, J. (1980). Introduction to methodology. In H. Triandis & J. Berry (Eds.), *Handbook of cross-cultural psychology* (pp. 1-28). Boston, Mass: Allyn and Bacon, Inc.

Burma, J. H. (1970). A comparison of the Mexican-American subculture with the Oscar Lewis culture of poverty model. In J. H. Burma (Ed.), *Mexican-Americans in the United States: A reader* (pp. 17-38). Cambridge, MA: Shenkman.

Casas, J. M., Wagenheim, B. R., Banchero, R., & Mendoza-Romero, J. (1994). Hispanic masculinity: Myth or psychological schema meriting clinical consideration? *Hispanic Journal of Behavioral Sciences,* 16 , 315-331.

Collier, M. J. (1988). A comparison of conversations among and between domestic culture groups: How intra- and intercultural competencies vary. *Communication Quarterly, 36,* 122-144.

Collier, S., Skidmore, T. E., & Blakemore, H. (Eds.). (1992). *Cambridge encyclopedia of Latin America and the Caribbean* (2nd ed.). Cambridge, UK: Cambridge University Press.

Cushner, K., & Landis, D. (1995). The intercultural sensitizer. In D. L. &. R. S. Bhagat (Eds.), *Handbook of intercultural training* (2nd ed., pp. 185-202). Thousand Oaks, CA: Sage.

Diaz-Guerrero, R., & Szalay, L. B. (1991). *Understanding Mexicans and Americans: Cultural perspectives in conflict.* New York: Plenum Press.

Díaz-Royo, A. T. (1974) *The enculturation process of Puerto Rican highland children.* Doctoral Dissertation, University of Michigan.

Dorrington, C. (1995). Central American refugees in Los Angeles: Adjustment of children and families. In R. E. Zambrana (Ed.), *Understanding Latino families.* (pp. 107-129). Thousand Oaks, CA: Sage.

Ferdman, B. M., & Cortes, A. C. (1992). Culture and identity among Hispanic managers in an Anglo business. In S. Knouse, P. Rosenfeld, & A. Culbertson (Eds.), *Hispanics in the workplace* (pp. 246-276). Newbury Park: CA: Sage.

Fitzpatrick, J. P. (1971). *Puerto Rican Americans :The meaning of migration to the mainland.* Englewood Cliffs, N.J.: Prentice-Hall.

Garcia, J. M. (1993). The Hispanic population in the United States: March 1992. In *U.S. Bureau of the Census, Current population reports*, P20-465V Washington, DC: Government Printing Office.

Guilbault, R. del C. (1992). Americanization is tough on "macho". In R. Holeton (Ed.), *Encountering cultures* (pp. 34-36). Englewood Cliffs, NJ: Prentice Hall.

Hall, E. T. (1959). *The silent language*. Garden City, New York: Doubleday & Company.

Hall, E. T. (1976). *Beyond culture*. Garden City, N.Y.: Anchor Press/Doubleday.

Hall, E.T. (1984). *The dance of life*. Garden City, NY: Anchor Press/Doubleday.

Hayes-Bautista, D. E., Schink, W. O., & Chapa, J. (1988). *The burden of support*. Stanford, CA: Stanford University Press.

Hayes-Bautista, D. E., Hurtado, A., Valdez, R. B., & Hernández, C. H. (1992). *No longer a minority: Latinos and social policy in California*. In Los Angeles, CA: Chicano Studies Center, University of California, Los Angeles.

Hecht, M. L., Ribeau, S., & Sedano, M. V. (1990). A Mexican American perspective on interethnic communication. *International Journal of Intercultural Relations, 14*, 31-55.

Herrera, R. S., & DelCampo, R. L. (1995). Beyond the superwoman syndrome: Work satisfaction and family functioning among working-class, Mexican American women. *Hispanic Journal of Behavioral Sciences, 17*, 49-60.

Hofstede, G. (1980). *Culture's consequences*. Beverly Hills, CA: Sage.

Hofstede, G. (1991). *Cultures and organizations: Software of the mind*. London, UK: McGraw-Hill.

Hurtado, A., Hayes-Bautista, D. E., Valdez, R. B., & Hernández, A. C. R. (Ed.). (1992). *Redefining California: Latino social engagement in a multicultural society*. Los Angeles, CA: UCLA Chicano Studies Research Center.

Hurtado, A. (1995). Variations, combinations, and evolutions: Latino families in the United States. In R. E. Zambrana (Ed.), *Understanding Latino families* (pp. 40-61). Thousand Oaks, CA: Sage.

Kagan, S., & Madsen, M. C. (1971). Cooperation and competition of Mexican, Mexican-American, and Anglo-American children of two ages under four instructional sets. *Developmental Psychology, 5*, 32-39.

Keefe, S. E. (1984). Real and ideal extended families among Mexican Americans and Anglo-Americans: On the meaning of close family ties. *Human Organization, 43*, 65-70.

Keefe, S. E. &. Padilla, A. M. (1987). *Chicano ethnicity*. Albuquerque, NM: University of New Mexico Press.

Kluckhohn, R., & Strodtbeck, F. (1961). *Variations in value orientations*. New York, NY: Harper & Row.

Landy, D. (1959). *Tropical childhood: cultural transmission and learning in a rural Puerto Rican village*. Chapel Hill: University of North Carolina Press.

Lisansky, J. (1981). *Interpersonal relations among Hispanics in the United States: A content analysis of the social science literature* (Technical Report No. 3). Department of Psychology, University of Illinois.

Lustig, M. W. &. Koester, J. (1996). *Intercultural competence*. (2nd. ed.) New York, NY: Harper Collins.

Madsen, W. (1973). *Mexican Americans of South Texas* (2nd ed.). New York: Holt, Rinehart & Winston.

Marín, G., & Triandis, H. C. (1985). Allocentrism as an important characteristic of the behavior of Latin Americans and Hispanics. In R. Diaz-Guerrero (Ed.), *Cross-cultural and national studies of social psychology* (pp. 85-114). Amsterdam, North Holland: Elsevier Science Publishers B.V.

Massey, D. S. (1993). Latino poverty research: An agenda for the 1990s. Social Science Research Council Newsletter. *Items, 47,* 7-11.

Massey, D. S., Zambrana, R. E., & Bell, S. A. (1995). Contemporary issues in Latino families. In R. E. Zambrana (Ed.), *Understanding Latino families* (pp. 190-204). Thousand Oaks, CA: Sage.

Menchaca, M. (1993). Chicano Indianism: An historical account of racial repression in the United States. *American Ethnologist, 20,* 583-603.

Mirandé, A. (1987). *Gringo justice.* Notre Dame, IN: University of Notre Dame Press.

Montalvo, F. F. (1987). *Skin color and Latinos: The origins and contemporary patterns of ethnoracial ambiguity among Mexican Americans and Puerto Ricans.* San Antonio, TX: Our Lady of the Lake University, Worden School of Social Service.

Murillo, N. (1976). The Mexican American family. In C. A. Hernández, M. J. Haug, & N. N. Wagner (Eds.), *Chicanos: Social and psychological perspectives* (pp. 15-25). St. Louis, MO: C. V. Mosby.

Ortiz, V. (1986). Changes in the characteristics of Puerto Rican migrants from 1955 to 1980. *International Migration Review, 20,* 612-628.

Ortiz, V. (1995). The diversity of Latino families. In R. E. Zambrana (Ed.), *Understanding Latino families* (pp. 18-39). Thousand Oaks, CA: Sage.

Ortiz de Montellano, B. O. (1989). *Syncretism in Mexican and Mexican-American folk medicine.* In 1992 Lecture Series College Park, MD: University of Maryland.

Padilla, A. M. (1995). Introduction to Hispanic psychology. In A. M. Padilla (Ed.), *Hispanic psychology : critical issues in theory and research* (pp. xi-xxi). Thousand Oaks, CA: Sage.

Phinney, J. S. (1995). Ethnic identity and self-esteem: A review and integration. In A. M. Padilla (Ed.), *Hispanic Psychology* (pp. 57-70). Thousand Oaks, CA: Sage.

Ramirez, O. & Arce, C. (1981). The contemporary Chicano family: An empirically based review. In J. A. Barron (Ed.), *Explorations in Chicano psychology* (pp. 3-28). New York: Praeger.

Ramirez, A. (1988). Racism towards Hispanics: The culturally monolithic society. In P. A. Katz & D. A. Taylor (Eds.), *Eliminating racism: Profiles in controversy* (pp. 137-158). New York: Plenum.

Ramírez, M. III (1983). *Psychology of the Americas: Mestizo perspectives on personality and mental health.* New York, NY: Pergamon Press.

Reddy, M. (Ed.). (1990). *Statistical record of Hispanic Americans.* Detroit, MI: Gale Research.

Rogler, L. H., & Cooney, R. (1991). Puerto Rican families in New York City: Intergenerational processes. *Marriage and Family Review, 16,* 331-349.

Sabogal, F. M., & Otero-Sabogal, R. (1987). Hispanic familism and acculturation: What changes and what doesn't? *Hispanic Journal of Behavioral Sciences, 9,* 397-412.

Shuter, R. (1976). Proxemics and tactility in Latin America. *Journal of Communication, 26,* 46-52.

Triandis, H. C., Marín, G., Lisansky, J., & Betancourt, H. (1984). Simpatía as a cultural script of Hispanics. *Journal of Personality and Social Psychology, 47,* 1363-1375.

Triandis, H. C. (1995). *Individualism and collectivism*. Boulder, CO: Westview.

Tumin, M. M., & Feldman, A. (1969). Social class and skin color in Puerto Rico. In M. M. Tumin (Ed.), *Comparative perspectives on race relations* (pp. 197-214). Boston, MA: Little, Brown.

Tumin, M. M., & Feldman, A. (1971). *Social class and social change in Puerto Rico*. Indianapolis, IN: Bobbs-Merrill.

Wagenheim, K. (1972). *Puerto Rico: A profile*. New York: Praeger.

13

CRITICAL DISCOURSE ANALYSIS: RACISM AND THE ETHOS OF EQUALITY

Ray T. Donahue
Nagoya Gakuin University

INTRODUCTION

Since passage of the Civil Rights Act, Americans have somewhat wishfully believed that racial equality and sameness have emerged between us (DeMott, 1996). Yet when the issue of racial equality does surface, we quickly become polarized: "Eighty percent of African Americans believe [that] they do not share equal opportunity with whites; almost 70 percent of whites think that African Americans are fine and who share the same opportunity.... We have a different set of referential experiences" (Rice, 1995). This difference, however, is veiled by a "media industry [that] is devoted to the idea of showing us blacks and whites in situations in which they not only behave the same but they have roughly speaking the same advantages and above all they...get along perfectly" (DeMott, 1996). With society under such fantastic belief, it is little wonder that some individuals in cross-cultural training find discussion of such concepts as prejudice and stereotypes distasteful (e.g., Brislin, 1981). More pointedly, I believe that individuals have been encouraged by the ideology (ethos) of equality to believe falsely that they are personally beyond prejudice or racism.

To deal with such problems in training, this paper attempts:

1. To demonstrate how ideology can lead to misperception in cross-cultural observations;

2. To explain, in part, the difference in perception between the races; and
3. To address the self-deception about being beyond prejudice or racism.

To do so, Alexis de Tocqueville's cross-cultural classic *Democracy in America* is taken up for study. This Frenchman's study is a venerated classic referenced in various works dealing with the anthropological, political, or sociological aspects of the United States. However, in some ways, ideology may be operative in American translations of the original and Tocqueville's own cross-cultural observations.

Ideology, in the anthropological sense, refers to a set of social or cultural beliefs (Goodman, 1992) that has achieved the "status of common sense" for its adherents (Fairclough, 1995). The question is not whether we are all equal (socially). Clearly not, as a "large number of acknowledged experts on human affairs have concluded that equality can never be achieved, even in theory; and these experts include righteous people who are just as sentimentally attached to the ideal as are other modern disciples of equality" (Beck, 1978, p. v). Rather the present concern is how the ideology may underlie the perceptual differences between the races concerning "racism" and equality. By identifying ideology, if operative, we may come a step closer to bridging our racial differences (and inequalities?).

TOCQUEVILLE TRANSLATED: TRACES OF IDEOLOGY?

Tocqueville[1] (originally published in 1835) had this to say in *Democracy in America:* "nothing struck me more forcibly [about the United States] than the general equality of condition among the people" (1963, p. 3). In his book, "a consistent theme emerges that America is different from other countries because it was founded on a revolutionary idea that all men are created equal" (PBS, 1995). Presidents and pundits alike refer to him often. Recently, President Bill Clinton did when discussing "the great strength of America" in his State of the Union Address (1-24-95), and Newt Gingrich, the Republican Speaker of the House of Representatives, hailed Tocqueville's book as a "must reading" for the astute leader today (PBS, 1995). This common thread of reference across the American political spectrum suggests a shared cultural belief—ideology, in this case.

Tocqueville was greatly impressed by *l'égalité des conditions* in the United States. American and British translations, however, differ in how *conditions* is rendered (see Table 1). American translations appear to have made *conditions* into a noncountable or mass noun—*condition*. By so doing, the American version may have in effect enlarged the original meaning. A parallel difference exists, for example, with the pair *communications* and *communication*—the latter being broader in meaning. The American version appears to extend the scope of meaning from particular *circumstances* to a *state of being*. Further corroboration comes from another difference in translation from the same passage. The American ver-

TABLE 1
Difference in translations

French *conditions* →	British *conditions* Reeve (1835) Lawrence–Mayer (1966)	American *condition* Bowen–Bradley (1945, 1963)

Note: The French was taken from Tocqueville (1981) and is assumed identical to the original edition. For the "two-person" texts, the translator precedes that of the editor. Nationalities of the individuals have been surmised by this author from the sources available to him. Reeve's was the first translation into English and became the basis of Bowen's later translation in 1862 and subsequently retranslated by Bradley (Bradley, 1945).

sion specifies that the equality of condition was among the *people*, a detail absent from both the original French and the British translations. This difference may be telling because Tocqueville "was devoted to a treatment of the political and governmental *system* of the United States," (Nicholas, 1961, p. 4; emphasis added); rather than social conditions per se.

The nationality of the translators might have bearing on the matter. One could suggest that the American translators were influenced by an American ethos of equality, and thus, tend to overstate Tocqueville's observations. This possibility brings one into the realm of language, culture, and thought. Further "invitations" into that realm will emerge as this study proceeds. By acknowledging this possibility, it may encourage a needed critical stance in observing and interpreting culture. In this vein, discussion turns to further evidence of Tocqueville's restricted meaning of equality—the historical.

TOCQUEVILLE'S RESTRICTED MEANING: LINGUISTIC DETERMINISM?

Relevant here is the classic liberal view of equality, a precursor of the modern Western version and conceived by Tocqueville's time, the details for which this section owes much to Bell (1978). "Classic liberalism defined equality as equality before the law" (Bell, 1978, p. 260). Individuals were to be treated equally under the law regardless of status or privilege. This restriction to political right is in marked contrast to modern liberalism, which conceives of equality as encompassing social right in regard to opportunity and sometimes even outcome.

The definition of equality in classic liberalism can be best seen reflected in the fact that equality and legality are cognate with one another in French, Tocqueville's native language:

French	English
égalité	equality
légalité	legality

Even more striking is the following contrast between English and French when a grammatical article modifies *equality:*

French	English
l'égalité	the equality

Note the closeness of form in French between *légalité* (legality) and *l'égalité* (the equality), the term Tocqueville actually used. Because the orthography and phonology of these words are nearly identical in French, they are probably much harder to distinguish than in English. And, in fact, Tocqueville was found to have confused the terms of equality, democracy, and free institutions (Schleifer, 1980). One, therefore, can perceive possible linguistic determinism by which language could influence conceptualization: For a French speaker, equality might have been restricted to treatment in a court of law without concern for a wider scope socially. Equality might have become unduly restricted to the political sphere at the expense of the social. Whether valid or not, this proposal pertains solely to Tocqueville. For French speakers in general, the question is beyond present scope of this paper.

As a result, Tocqueville seemed cognizant of just one of several possible dimensions of the term. Those dimensions being *equality of conditions, equality of means*, and *equality of outcomes* (Bell, 1978). Equality of conditions refers to mainly political rights: "equalities of public liberties. These include equality before the law, equality of movement in public places, the principle of one man, one vote." (Bell, 1978, p. 262). In some sense, Tocqueville's view of equality appears narrowly conceived in that he was primarily concerned with the organizational structures—the political—of the United States. Consequently, from a restricted focus, an apparent consequence emerges for Tocqueville's thoughts on American racial minorities. This consideration of Tocqueville relates particularly to the challenge of making cross-cultural observations.

TOCQUEVILLE'S OBSERVATION OF RACIAL MINORITIES

According to Zeitlin:

> There is perhaps no better evidence of Tocqueville's humanistic outlook than his rejection of racism in the chapters on the blacks and the Indians2 of the United States....None of the dehumanizing consequences of slavery escaped Tocqueville's notice.... Similarly, the tragic disorders European tyranny had caused among the Indians did not escape Tocqueville. (1971, p. 26-27)

To the contrary, both Fuchs (1990) and Pole (1978) suggest otherwise: "[One] looked in vain in Tocqueville's discussions...for any mention of nationality influences or what would later be called ethnicity" (Fuchs, 1990, p. 19-20); and that Tocqueville gives little mention of "the inequalities of condition and opportunity" (Pole, 1978, p. 338). To the extent that he does comment on African Americans and Native Americans, he only does so in passing. Consider how Tocqueville seems to begrudgingly broach the very topic that Zeitlin praises him for:

> I have now finished the main task....I could stop here, but perhaps the reader would feel that I had not satisfied his [or her] expectations. There are other things in America besides an immense and complete democracy....In the course of this work I have been led to mention the [American Indians] and the [blacks]....These topics are like tangents to my subject being American, but not democratic, and my main business has been to describe democracy. So at first I had to leave them on one side, but now at the end I must return to them. (Tocqueville, 1966, p. 316)

American Inequalities

Though Tocqueville did reject racist theories such as Gobineau's in letters and other forums, one still might expect his most forceful rejection upon direct witness of slavery and other ill-treatment of non-whites in America at the time. That many forms of inequality were present in America at Tocqueville's time appears certain. Consider a few of the economic, social, and racial inequalitites:

- [F]rom its beginning the United States has been a society of unequals. In 1774, for example, among those few Philadelphians affluent enough to pay taxes, 10 percent owned fully 89 percent of the taxable property. (Tesconi & Hurwitz, 1974, p. 12)
- During [the 1800s] egalitarian values lost ground to individualistic ones. Not only was inequality acceptable, it was preferred. (Stacz, 1981, p. 11)
- Even though state legislation abolished slavery in 1827 in New York, its constitution still helped maintain a stigma [of slavery] for African Americans by requiring blacks to have property before they could vote, a requirement dropped for whites. (New York State Bar Association, 1991, p. 8)[3]
- The worst defect of the colonial court system was that it did not provide access to all...and excluded African Americans and Native Americans, and limited the role of women. (New York State Bar Association, 1991, p. 6)
- Many students of intergroup relations believe that two separate and unequal societies, one white and one black, has existed in the US ever since the country's beginning. (Slawson, 1979)

One, therefore, might find Tocqueville's words on American equality regretable given that the sufferings inflicted upon blacks include "forced immigration, slavery, imposed illiteracy, deliberate suppression of cultural folkways, lynchings, Black Codes, Jim Crow, ghettoization with what some might consider genocide in mind, and much more" (Kraft, 1977; quoted by Livingston, 1979, p. 242). (Though Black Codes and Jim Crow were institutionalized after Tocqueville's time, they still grew out of a history stretching back to his era and before.) And of course this does not mention whole Indian nations that were brutally annihilated by the American westward movement.

Even Zeitlin (1971) must admit that Tocqueville had limits of compassion. It seems that his opinion on racism changed when the shoe was on the other foot—in this case, France's. Before a body of the French government, he had this to say: "it is evident that we should not create for [the emancipated black in the French colonies] a domain, where he can easily live by laboring for himself alone" (Drescher, 1968, p. 180; quoted by Zeitlin, 1971, p. 29). "Thus," concludes Zeitlin, "French colonial interests took precedence over equality and freedom" in Tocqueville's thinking at the time.

Social Evolutionism

Such ambivalence was not unusual. For example, many libertarians in early America held contradictory feelings: "In the period before the American revolution (1775-1783) there were few whites who opposed slavery even though many of them demanded freedom from English rule" (New York State Bar Association, 1991, p. 6). Such contradictions, no doubt, were strengthened by social evolutionism, the idea that non-whites held a lower position on a cultural hierarchy headed by those of European extraction (Cheater, 1986). This idea, an early precursor of Social Darwinism, was well rooted by Tocqueville's day:

> it is important to note that evolutionary schemas pertaining to *society*...were floated long before *The Origin of Species* was published in 1859. [Social evolutionism] perhaps date[s] back to the eighteenth-century French social philosophers such as Montesquieu, Condorcet, and Rousseau, rather than to Darwin's ideas.(Cheater, 1986, p. 1-2)

Some of the greatest of minds were not immune to such views as evidenced by this passage written by Thomas Jefferson to a friend in 1824:

> Let a philosophic observer commence a journey from the savages of the Rocky Mountains, eastwardly towards our sea-coast. These he would observe in the earliest stages of association, living under no law but that of nature, subsisting and covering themselves with the flesh and skins of wild beasts. He would next find those on our frontiers in the pastoral stage raising domestic animals to supply the defects of hunting. Then succeed our own semi-barbarous citizens, the pioneers of the advance of civilization, and so in his progress he would meet the gradual shades of improving man until he would reach his, as yet, most improved state in our seaport towns. This, in fact, is to a survey, in time, of the progress of man from the infancy of creation to the present day. (Quoted in Pearce, 1965, p. 155)[4]

Here, Jefferson clearly draws a progression of developmental stages from American Indians at the base to white Europeans at the pinnacle. Considering the medium and Jefferson's old age at the time, such indiscretions might be forgiven. Similarly, the private diary of Malinowski, a father of modern anthropology, revealed that humans do have their frailties.

However, the matter becomes more serious, if social evolutionism is made a basis upon which social science stands. This pertains especially to Tocqueville because nothing could be more antithetical to equality than social evolutionism. Thus, I believe that Tocqueville's study can serve as an object lesson in cross-cultural observation.

Rationalizing Racial Oppression

Although Tocqueville acknowledges racial oppression, he also seems to rationalize it away and even finds a kind of redemption for the white majority. His related observations are collected and preceded by my interpreted summary:

1. **A Cultural Hierarchy:** *The white (European) race is superior to the non-white:*

   Among these widely different people, the first that attracts attention, and the first in enlightenment, power, and happiness, is the white man, the European, man par excellence; below him come the [black] and the [Indian]....Seeing what happens in the world, might one not say that the European is to men of other races what man is to the animals? (Tocqueville, 1966, p. 317)

2. **White Man's Burden:** *Non-whites, seen inferior, are undisciplined, plea-sure-seekers, irresponsible, and are unfit to lead independent lives. Thus, they become the white man's burden. (Native Americans are an exception in that Tocqueville considers them too independent but still burdensome all the same):*

   The [black] has no family; for him a woman is no more than the passing companion of his pleasures, and from their birth his sons are his equals....[He has a] disposition of the soul that makes men insensible to extreme misery [and may even give them a] depraved taste for the cause of their afflictions[.] Plunged in this abyss of wretchedness, the [black] hardly notices his ill fortune...[T]he habit of servitude has given him the thoughts and ambitions of a slave; he admires his tyrants even more than he hates them and finds his joy and pride in a servile imitation of his oppressors. (p. 317)

   Devoid both of wants and of pleasures, useless to himself, his first notions of existence teach him that he is the property of another who has an interest in preserving his life; he sees that care for his own fate has not devolved on him....The Indian lives on the extreme edge of freedom. He delights in this barbarous independence and would rather die than sacrifice any part of it. Civilization has little hold on such a man. (pp. 318-319)

3. **Inferior Traits of the Oppressed:** *Though slavery of the [black] and decimation of the Indian were sins of the white majority, these acts were encouraged by the natural traits of [black] mindlessness and submissiveness, and Indian ignorance:*

[T]he very use of thought seems to [the black] an unprofitable gift of Providence, and he peacefully enjoys all the privileges of his humiliation. If he becomes free, he often feels independence as a heavier burden than slavery itself, for his life has taught him to submit to everything, except to the dictates of reason; and when reason becomes his only guide, he cannot hear its voice.... [With the Indian's] undisciplined courage against our tactics, and the spontaneous instincts of his nature against our profound designs, he fails in the unequal contest. (pp. 318-320)

4. **A Shift in Responsibility:** *Sinful acts against these unfortunates could not really be helped because the victims were simply disposed to be insensitive and, in fact, may have been part of God's will:*

Should I call it a blessing of God, or a last malediction of His anger, this disposition of the soul that makes men insensible to extreme misery and often even gives them a sort of depraved taste for the cause of their afflictions? Plunged in this abyss of wretchedness, the [black] hardly notices his ill fortune. (p. 317)

5. **White Redemption:** *In the end, the white majority must not have been so bad because blacks wish to be part of that society. In the case of Native Americans, they are too savage to expect any treatment other than that received:*

The [black] makes a thousand fruitless efforts to insinuate himself into a society that repulses him; he adapts himself to his oppressors' tastes, adopting their opinions and hoping by imitation to join their community...[As for the Indian] the pretended nobility of his origin fills the whole imagination of the Indian. He lives and dies amid these proud dreams. (p. 319)

The [black] would like to mingle with the European and cannot. The Indian might to some extent succeed in that, but he scorns to attempt it. The servility of the former delivers him over into slavery; the pride of the latter leads him to death. (p. 320)

After an apparent exoneration of white guilt, Tocqueville later seems to paint an idyllic scene between the races with a story about an Indian woman caretaker of a white child with a black woman in tow (1966, p. 320). This story seems to further exonerate white guilt by showing that the oppressors are actually superior to the oppressed and can even become an object of great affection. Interwoven through the tale is the theme of cultural hierarchy or evolutionary development.

After describing the beauty of the Indian costume as compared with that of the black person's tattered attire and thereby suggesting hierarchical ranks between them, Tocqueville relates how these two women lavished attention upon the white child, casting the child as their object of love. He then subordinates these two adults to the child: "the little [white child]...showed by her slightest movements a sense of superiority which contrasted strangely with her weakness and her age, as if she received the attentions of her companions with a sort of condescension" (1966, p. 320). He then reiterates the "predominance" of whites over other races with a reference to other similar cases, while casting this predominance in "a bond of affection unit[ing] oppressors and oppressed, and nature bringing them close together" (p. 320). In other words, the white oppressors are not really so bad after all.

These rationalizations hardly qualify Tocqueville as a humanist. Yet there are those like Zeitlin who claim the opposite. My analysis, if valid, suggests a needed criticalness. For Tocqueville's ambivalence in addressing ethnic and racial issues, his social evolutionism, and his final half-hearted treatment of the issues show how an observer may be confined by his conceptualizations, if not also by personal values. What other areas did Tocqueville choose to ignore? Possibly swayed by social evolutionism once, he may have been affected again in unknown ways when he reported on other aspects of American society.

Slaves and other aliens lack citizenship and rights for equality. For that reason, one might be tempted to exclude them from a study of equality. However, such people are likely to be of a non-mainstream class, if not outright castes. Because "one class presupposes other classes" (Hofstede, 1980, p. 96), African Americans and Native Americans ought to have received more attention, especially if considering equality. Racial minorities, though mentioned by Tocqueville, were really not considered in regard to equality. Rather, the question of equality for Tocqueville was reserved for white males (Rae, 1981).

CLASSLESS SOCIETY

What is fascinating in all this is how some translations, like Bowen-Bradley's, appear to embellish Tocqueville's meaning of equality and overextend its scope. The danger is substituting the classic liberal meaning of equality with its contemporary significance. The unwary might then conclude that social equality is an inherent national trait of the United States. One possible result is a cultural myth that Americans have a classless society (Sirevåg, 1991). For example, despite their strong sense of individualism, nearly all Americans consider themselves middle class (Francese, 1995; Sirevåg, 1991). Peter Francese, president of American Demographics, Inc., states that:

> In random sample surveys taken over long periods of time, 95 percent of Americans say, "I'm middle class." Almost no one admits to being upper class or not middle class. People—Americans—want to be middle class. (Francese, 1995)

It is unknown how strongly these respondents believe that they are, indeed, members of the middle class. Nevertheless, the apparent overwhelming desire to appear to be in the middle class suggests a common cultural mindset, perhaps ideological.

The Case of the Three Country Clubs

The ideological beliefs of an equal, classless society can cause confusion. I, for one, remember feeling that way as a child in school. On the one hand, we heard about the Founding Fathers, Tocqueville, "all men are created equal," and so on. On the other hand, I was aware of several private country clubs in and out of my community that admitted members on the reputed basis of race, religion, and other social criteria. If referring to these clubs as A, B, and C, country club A was located the deepest into the suburbs away from the nearby big city; B, the next furthest away; and C, the closest to the city. C, in fact, was on the boundary line. Club A was known to be WASPish and excluded Jews; B was Jewish; and C, an apparent mixture.

The same rank order coincided with the perceived exquisiteness and quality of its golf course, with A being the apex. Presumably, property values followed in the same order. For example, C, despite its close proximity to the city and its increased vulnerability to vandalism, was not, at that time, fenced in, unlike the other two. In a way, the absent fence was also symbolic, for C was the least exclusive of the three clubs. In sum, the three country clubs could be ranked according to perceived property values and golfing challenge, the best of which reputedly permitted only those of WASP background; the least exquisite club was also the least exclusive.

The Other Side of the Tracks

A similar socioeconomic contrast was also readily apparent to me anytime I used the suburban train into the city, for there existed the proverbial railroad tracks: On one side the serene suburbs lie; on the other, the urban sprawl. Consequently, I perceived socioeconomic differences nearly daily in contrast to the ideology of equality heard in school and elsewhere. What makes America special is not the state but the process of equality—the striving toward equality for a multicultural society. Yet the language of the ideology would lead us to believe that we've already arrived.

Because researchers are products of their culture, they are likely to be influenced by cultural ideology. Ideology may consist of unanalyzed assumptions and, if invalid, could have important consequences for theory and research. For example, a researcher, less sensitive to the nuances of social inequity, could erroneously assume that Tocqueville's "equality" was identical to its contemporary meaning, resulting in treating a *prescriptive* term as if it were *descriptive*. American social equality would then become overstated, thus jeopardizing comparative research in some way. The belief in American equality as unique is such a central American thought (PBS, 1995), that the perception of various social phenomena is likely to be affected. For stratification is part and parcel of society. The issue of equality could therefore have innumerable implications. Tocqueville's reporting on racial minorities stands as a case in point.

AN APPLICATION TO CROSS-CULTURAL TRAINING

An American Contradiction

Today, the United States "has become the most economically stratified" society within the industrialized world (Bradsher, 1995),[5] yet as noted above, as many as 95 percent of Americans see themselves as "middle-class." How is this cultural contradiction explained?

Perhaps by ideological myth—the ethos of equality, in this case. This ethos is more ideal than real, for the United States was never quite the land of equality popularly believed. Politicians like to appeal to the theme of equality as uniquely American, but the term does not appear in the original Constitution nor in the Bill of Rights, and only emerged in the former by amendment—the fourteenth and fifteenth (Bell, 1978)—nearly four decades after Tocqueville's departure. This fact surprises even some historians.

Dealing with Denial

Just as the American ethos can lead to exaggerating equality as in some interpretations of Tocqueville, conversely, it also might likely lead to personal denial of prejudice and racism. Such denial is not uncommon and can present a problem to the cross-cultural trainer. The training situation, purposes, or both might not permit direct intervention (confrontation). What is the trainer to do? One approach is to present the preceding analysis to suggest that equality in America may be far more an ideal than popularly believed in mainstream society. This point is then followed by enlarging the common definitions for prejudice and racism.

According to Bethlehem:

> ...we are all prejudiced, since not even by the most liberal definition of the terms, can any of us be said to have subjected many of our opinions to "adequate test" etc. Life is too short for us to find out or check everything for ourselves. (1985, p. 3)

This view appears more realistic when one considers the unconscious mind, which by definition is beyond an individual's control. Each moment we receive massive amounts of sensory data, far too numerous for our attention. To think that we are completely free of prejudice or racism is to ignore this and other basic facts of perception.

In defining racism, I purposely broaden it to mean simply a racial preference. Despite the unsavoriness of racism, this new definition has merit, I believe. First, *prejudice* and *racism* are commonly used synonymously (Brislin, 1986). Second, individuals tend to define racism in ways that exclude themselves. Although blacks and whites define racism differently (Lichtenberg, 1992), their definitions similarly place racism outside of themselves. Blacks see racism as a characteristic of whites and manifested institutionally; whites, conversely, see it as a personal defect of the stereotypical white supremacist (Lichtenberg, 1992). Both definitions misplace racism exclusively with whites.

Of course, the onus for change ought to be with whites given the litany of horrors suffered by African Americans since first brought to these shores. However, two wrongs do not make a right. To exempt anyone because of skin color would be hypocritical, given that the underlying principle of civil rights is equality.

Third, in line with my definition of racism above, the sociologist Henri Tajfel and others provide a wealth of data that shows:

> Group membership [e.g., nation, race, and various forms of respectability] per se breeds favoritism...[such that] people...discriminate in favor of members of their own group when allocating resources,...serv[ing] to generate inequalities between those who stand inside and outside the circle of belonging. (Hamilton & Sanders, 1992, p. 209).

Similarly, Gaertner's (1973) study found that white, self-proclaimed liberals were six times more likely to hang up on callers on the telephone if they had sounded "black" than if they had sounded "white." To favor one's own ingroup proves no evil; for it may simply be wired into the human species as a matter of survival. However, such preferences may prove baneful in our ever increasing globally interdependent world. And precisely for this reason, cross-cultural/intercultural studies ought to play a significant role.

Lastly, there is again the matter of the unconscious mind, which casts doubt that anyone can be sure of being pure of racism, even given a standard definition, such as the viewing of one's own race as superior (Schaefer, 1993). After all we are products of a racist society—a society that favors one particular racial group over another. Even after (forced) busing and anti-discrimination laws in housing, our society is hardly integrated. How many people are socially involved, outside of school or work relationships, with members of another race? Being separated by race is so extensive, how can anyone think that that has had no effect on their psychological or cognitive makeup?

If still unconvinced, one has only to consider "redlining," a banking practice still in force today, which overly restricts money from being loaned in depressed areas. This practice is found to favor white borrowers over minorities, even when incomes are the same (ABC News, 1995). I became aware of this practice several years ago by a chance encounter with an African American who reported being victimized by this practice. He, an employee of a car rental company, was driving me crosstown to my car. Having returned home after a period abroad, I asked him about racial relations in general. My curiosity startled him, but he kindly obliged me in telling me his perspective. He spoke in an even tone without noticeable bitterness about how he tried to move from his inner city home to a "better neighborhood." He first went to a bank downtown and was told to "go to a bank in his own neighborhood." He followed this advice but found his local bank had little funds available. It seemed tragic that this individual, who appeared conscientious in his work, was literally fenced out of "living the good life."

Admittedly, my story rests on suppositions. I had not seen this person's credit history nor his financial statements. Further, I assumed that he was truthful and his perceptions were correct. I assumed, as well, that banks could or would operate in a racially motivated way. This story impacted me because it is likely that some subjectivity enters into a bank officer's decision making. Given the social psychological findings that individuals tend to favor their ingroup for resource allocation, one does not need much further imagination. My intuitions were then reinforced by the news report that offered documented evidence in support.

Finally, one other point needs to be mentioned here. My broadening the definitions of prejudice and racism to the effect that "we've all got it," intends no way to minimize past sufferings from racist atrocities nor to reduce the seriousness of the matter. This broadening in meaning, to the contrary, is far more beneficial than the personal denials that often occur. Such denials often come from confusing thought or feeling with action: The former does not necessarily translate into the latter.

By recognizing these primordial racial preferences, we may better redirect energy from denial toward acceptance and ultimate control of discrimination. That these primordial preferences are natural does not make them good. Nor does it make them evil, either. But they do give us a greater burden collectively than ever before. Yet, everyone can benefit by refining their communication skills. Why not do it for racial harmony, too?

CONCLUSION

Democracy in America is highly esteemed by scholars and political leaders alike. A central theme of that book is the uniqueness of the United States for its equality. Contemporaries, however, may be more inclined to distinguish two levels of equality: prescriptive and descriptive. In Tocqueville's case, he seemed to address the prescriptive equality for white males, based on his almost exclusive attention to political and legal structures.

Underscoring this focus on the political structure was the discovery of possible linguistic determinism. Interestingly, a close orthographic and phonological correspondence was shown between *legality* and *equality* in French, the latter, a term Tocqueville confused with terms of political structure in his own writing. Thus linguistic determinism may have acted, in small part, to encourage his apparent restricted sense of equality. These findings are corroborated by Bell's (1978) historical distinction of the term and by Tocqueville's purpose.

The significance of this study is that it highlights the need to distinguish for whom equality is meant. Even if "for all men," a feminist might be quick to point out the potential sexism, for suffrage was not achieved until early in this century. Therefore, if genders were unequal before the law, then other social differences were probably present as well. And, indeed, various evidence was shown to make that point. In short, equality in early America was most reserved for a select group. This appears true if present cases of social inequality are any indication. Thus the problem of idealizing American equality and its history becomes more apparent.

Tocqueville's restricted sense of equality appeared evident with his study of racial minorities. He appeared to mention these minorities as an afterthought. In the end, he seemed motivated by social evolutionism and a need to exonerate the white majority. If so, then his other findings would be made questionable. Recognizing this may help indicate how cultural worldview can affect our perceptions of other peoples and cultures. One then might be more disposed into rethinking prejudice and racism. That rethinking is necessary because blacks and whites define racism in ways that exempt themselves. Because they also happen to define the term differently, hardly can they be expected to agree on matters of race. Hence, a redefining of terms is necessary. Given the gulf that presently separates the races, interculturalists have the opportunity and responsibility to make the attempts to bridge it. Without such attempts the racial time bomb will continue to tick.

DISCUSSION QUESTIONS

1. How does an anthropological sense of *ideology* differ from its common, everyday use? Why is ideology (ethos) important to examine from the view of cross-cultural studies?

2. How did language possibly affect Tocqueville's view of American equality and ultimately his observation of American racial minorities?

3. Is the racial divide in America solely the responsibility of one particular racial group? Why or why not? Are the type of responsibilities similar or dif-

ferent between the white majority and racial minorities? What will happen if whites no longer hold a numerical majority of the population?

4. How does the ethos of equality necessitate redefining *prejudice* and *racism*? Or does it?

5. What potential effect would these proposed redefinitions of terms have on Affirmative Action or like programs?

NOTES

[1] Some writers render *Tocqueville* as *de Tocqueville*; however, my choice follows that of his translators, his publisher Garnier-Flammarion, and other specialists.

[2] The terms American Indian, Indian, and Native American are used interchangeably herein for the indigenous people of North America.

[3] I thank Bruce Abrams for providing this reference.

[4] I thank Gregory Trifonovitch for pointing this out and providing this quote and citation, as well.

[5] Although technological change or liberal immigration policies may be partly responsible, the fact still remains that the United States is highly stratified. Moreover, Barlett and Steele (1992), Pulitzer Prize-winning journalists, offer a compelling account why: Tax and fiscal policies have allowed a massive shift in wealth to take place in favor of the rich, resulting in a "dismantling of the middle class."

REFERENCES

ABC News. (1995, April 10). *Nightline.*

Barlett, D. L. & Steele, J. B. (1992). *America: What went wrong?* Kansas City, MO.: Andrews & McMeel.

Beck, B. (1978). Foreword. In M. Lewis, *The culture of inequality.* Amherst, MA: University of Massachusetts.

Bell, D. (1978). *The cultural contradictions of capitalism.* New York: Basic Books.

Bethlehem, D. W. (1985). *A social psychology of prejudice.* London: Croom Helm.

Bradley, P. (1945). A note to the reader. In A. de Tocqueville, *Democracy in America* (vol. 1). P. Bradley (Ed.). F. Bowen (Trans.). New York: Vintage Books.

Bradsher, K. (1995, April 19). U.S. gap in riches widens. *Asahi Evening News*, pp. 1-2.

Brislin, R. W. (1981). *Cross cultural encounters.* New York: Pergamon Press.

Brislin, R. W. (1986). Prejudice and intergroup communication. In W. B. Gudykunst (Ed.), *Intergroup communication.* London: Edward Arnold.

Cheater, A. P. (1986). *Social anthropology: An alternative introduction.* Zimbabwe: Mambo Press.

DeMott, B. (1996, January 15). Interviewed on *The News Hour.* PBS.

Drescher, S. (1968) *Dilemmas of democracy.* Pittsburgh, PA: University of Pittsburgh Press.

Fairclough, N. (1995). *Critical discourse analysis.* London & New York: Longman.

Francese, P. (1995, January 17). Interview with P. Solman. *The MacNeill/Lehrer News Hour*. PBS.

Fuchs, L. H. (1990). *The American kaleidoscope*. Hanover, NH: University Press of New England.

Gaertner, S. (1973). Helping behavior and racial discrimination among liberals and conservatives. *Journal of Personality and Social Psychology 25*: 335-341.

Goodman, R. (1992). Ideology and practice in Japan: Towards a theoretical approach. In R. Goodman & K. Refsing (Eds.), *Ideology and practice in modern Japan*. London & New York: Routledge.

Hamilton, V. L. & Sanders, J. (1992). *Everyday justice*. New Haven and London: Yale University Press.

Hofstede, G. (1980). *Culture's consequences*. Beverly Hills, CA: Sage.

Lichtenberg, J. (1992). Racism in the head, racism in the world. *Philosophy and Public Policy 12*, 3-5.

Livingston, J. C. (1979). *Fair game? Inequality and affirmative action*. San Francisco, CA: W. H. Freeman & Company.

New York State Bar Association. (1991). *A brief history of the New York State Supreme Court*. Albany, NY: Author.

Nicholas, H. G. (1961). Introduction. In A. de Tocqueville, *De la démocratie en Amérique*. H. G. Nicholas (Ed.). London: Macmillan.

PBS. (1995, January 26). *The MacNeill/Lehrer News Hour*. PBS.

Pearce, R. H. (1965). *The savages of America: A study of the Indian and the idea of civilization*. Baltimore: The John Hopkins University Press.

Pole, J. R. (1978). *The pursuit of equality in American history*. Berkeley, CA: University of California Press.

Rae, D. (1981). *Equalities*. Cambridge, MA: Harvard University Press.

Rice, C. (1995, March 12). Interview with D. Brinkley. *This Week*. ABC News.

Schaefer, R. T. (1993). *Racial and ethnic groups* (5th ed.). New York: Harper Collins College Publishers.

Schleifer, J. T. (1980). *The making of Tocqueville's Democracy in America*. Chapel Hill, NC: The University of North Carolina Press.

Sirevåg, T. (1991). *American patterns*. A. Iwasaki (Ed.). Tokyo: Seibido.

Slawson, J. (1979). *Unequal Americans*. Westport, CT: Greenwood Press.

Stacz, C. (1981). *The American nightmare*. New York: Schocken.

Tesconi, C. A., Jr. & Hurwitz, E., Jr. (1974). *Education for whom?* New York: Harper & Row.

Tocqueville, A. de. (1835). *Democracy in America* (vol. 1). H. Reeve (Trans.). London: Saunders & Otley.

Tocqueville, A. de. (1945/1963). *Democracy in America* (vol. 1). P. Bradley (Ed.). F. Bowen (Trans.). New York: Vintage.

Tocqueville, A. de. (1966/1988). *Democracy in America* (vol. 1). J. P. Mayer (Ed.). G. Lawrence (Trans.). New York: Perennial Library.

Tocqueville, A. de. (1981). *De la démocratie en Amérique*. Paris: Garnier-Flammarion.

Zeitlin, I. M. (1971). *Liberty, equality, and revolution in Alexis de Tocqueville*. Boston, MA: Little Brown & Company.

14

THE BLACK PROFESSIONAL: AN ANALYSIS OF THE COMMUNICATIVE STRATEGIES USED IN CROSS-RACE MENTORING

Kathy W. Brooks
Shippensburg University

INTRODUCTION

Culture consists of the rules and expectations that come into play when two human beings interact (Thiederman, 1991). The increase of minorities integrating the work force has resulted in a dramatic effect on the demographics and the culture of the work place. Consequently, the communication techniques one once thought of as universally acceptable are no longer universally applicable. Clearly, if we are to capitalize on the creativity and energy that a diverse workforce can supply, there is much to be learned from the cultural differences that have rendered so many of our notions of effective management obsolete.

One communication phenomenon that has gained a great deal of recognition in recent years for its role in the establishment of successful careers is the concept of mentoring. Researchers have investigated how the mentor-protégé relationship between members of an organization, or profession , helps the organization reach its goals while simultaneously facilitating the career and personal development of both parties (Kram, 1985). This chapter will first define the mentor-protégé relationship, then discuss some critical issues in the development of cross-race relationships, and, finally, examine the communicative strategies employed in these mentor-protégé alliances.

THE MENTOR-PROTÉGÉ RELATIONSHIP DEFINED

It was not until the mid 1970s that mentoring began to appear in the organizational behavior literature (Parsloe, 1992; Short & Seeger, 1984). Derived from Greek mythology, the word mentor denoted the wise and trusted counselor to whom Odysseus entrusted the education of his son, Telemachus (Bushardt, Fretwell, & Holdnak, 1991). The term is operationally defined in several ways, although most researchers cite common characteristics: a mentor is someone who takes a protégé and teaches him or her the basic job, shows the person how to cope with the environment by giving psychosocial support, acts as a model for career behavior, helps participants develop and maintain self-esteem and professional identity, and encourages progress (Kram, 1985; Short & Seeger, 1984; Thomas, 1993). The formation of a mentor-protégé relationship is important to maintain an awareness of important changes within the organization, to be able to carry out duties more effectively, and to become knowledgeable of new career opportunities as they develop.

It is important to note the distinctions from closely related terms, such as a sponsor, which Short and Seeger (1984, p. 4) describe as "someone who possesses the power to bring about job enrichment, promotion, or other goals sought for career advancement." Another interrelated concept is that of a coach, which Parsloe (1992) describes as anyone in an organization with a special expertise (technical or otherwise) or with supervisory or management responsibility who could tutor, train, give hints, or prime a subordinate person with facts. Parsloe makes a critical distinction in terminology, namely, that mentoring is concerned with "the longer term acquisition and application of skills in developing careers by a form of counseling and advising" (p. 73).

Current research is unclear as to the process by which the mentor relationship is established. Preliminary data suggest that the environment—both internal, i.e., within the mentor and protégé individually and between them as a dyad, and external, i.e.. within their shared social environment,—strongly influences 1) whether an mentor-protégé will form and, if it does, 2) how comprehensive, mutual, powerful and complementary it will be, 3) how long it will last, and 4) what combination of career and psychosocial functions it will support (Carden, 1990, p. 283).

While linked to the overt process of career development and mobility, mentoring is grounded in the psychodynamics of identification (Thomas, 1993). Carden (1990) notes that some researchers have suggested that mentors and protégés attract one another because of actual or perceived similarities in personality or background. This theory is consistent with previous literature on mentoring, which generally posits the notion that people choose to mentor protégés who are most like them (White, 1990). By identifying with each other, individuals come to know themselves, to discover themselves through their relationship with others. Carden (1990) describes support relationships along three dimensions: 1) level of emotional involvement, 2) level of identification, and 3) mentor's power, or the degree to which the relationship can effect concrete career advantages for the protégé. It has been argued that effective mentors are self-appointed (Short & Seeger, 1984). The mentor sees parts of him or herself in the subordinate, and the subordinate wants to become like the mentor, to take up his or her voice, manner of dress, and way of thinking (Thomas, 1989). Mentors who wish to attract protégés usually provide strong examples in terms of productivity, excellence, and concern for people, in addition to having wide knowledge of the organization and industry. A protégé can often attract a mentor by modeling him or herself after the chosen person, holding informal talk sessions, becoming visible, and displaying initiative towards formulating a relationship with the mentor (Short & Seeger, 1984). Mentors and their protégés experience a significant level of intimacy and emotional attachment in these relationships, which often exhibit dynamics similar to those in parent-offspring or older-younger sibling relationships (Thomas, 1993).

Protégés are described as typically people under the age of 35 and early in their careers, whereas mentors are seniors, ideally half a generation older than the protégé, and in mid or late career (Short & Seeger, 1984; Thomas, 1993). Kram (1985) points out that it is a misconception that the primary beneficiary in a mentor relationship is the junior person. Mid-career employees are the recipients of several benefits namely, receiving technical and psychological support from loyal subordinates, being recognized by peers and superiors for effectively developing talent, and receiving internal satisfaction from passing on wisdom.

Although mentoring is usually viewed as a type of informal communication, many organizations are nevertheless establishing formalized mentor-protégé programs. Most of the research gathered in this area has focused on the relationship rather than on such programs. The remainder of this chapter reflects the primary focus.

CRITICAL ISSUES IN CROSS-RACE MENTOR RELATIONSHIPS

A survey of 1,200 leading corporate executives revealed that two-thirds of those surveyed had a mentor and that those who did earned more money at a younger age and were happier with their career progress than those who did not (Short & Seeger, 1984). Other research has shown that developmental relationships are important for both Black and white managers (Thomas, 1993). Cox and Nkomo (1986) discovered a positive correlation between being a protégé and upward mobility among Black managers in the company they studied. White (1990), in a study conducted with black women managers from a variety of corporate environments, identified two primary determinants for the black women's success in the corporate culture—one that focuses on strategies and the other on skills. It comes as no surprise that one of the strategies indicated is mentoring. White draws the comparison that white women often set up informal gatherings, such as cocktail parties, for mentoring, whereas black women generally socialize and network through black associations or black colleagues.

The study of race relations in organizations is in an embryonic state compared with that of developmental relationships. How racial dynamics influence cross-race mentor relationships has not been well examined; however existing research suggests that a racial difference does have an impact (Thomas, 1993). Thomas (1990) notes that with few exceptions, most of the research on mentor-protégé relationships has focused on all white populations; when racial minorities have been a part of the study population, little attention had been given to the influence of race on the dynamics of such relationships. Scholars have found that race is an important variable in determining income and occupational attainment, yet again, little research has attempted to compare the experiences of blacks and whites in gaining opportunities and resources found to influence career attainment and experience. Recent studies have also shown that race may significantly influence an individual's adult and career development experiences (Thomas, 1990).

White (1990) reiterates the idea that white women and white men are more likely to network with each other than with blacks or other ethnic minorities. As discussed earlier, people choose to mentor protégés who are most like them. Subsequently, senior management, which is heavily comprised of white males, is unlikely to have among its ranks many individuals who would be willing to mentor to black women (White, 1990).

While the literature on work-centered mentor-protégé relationships has expanded considerably over the last decade, as previously noted, little of it has focused on the experiences of racial minorities (Thomas, 1990). However, that has not hindered some researchers from forming hypotheses about minority experiences in this regard. Much of this pondering has led to the conclusion that minorities do not find mentor relationships in predominantly white organizations. However, research that had been done on black experiences in mentoring suggests that this may be an incorrect generalization.

Ford and Wells (1985) found that 51 percent of the 80 black public administrators and executives they surveyed identified mentor relationships. Thomas (1990) noted in a study of black female administrators that 82 percent reported having mentors. Another researcher, in a study of middle-class black men who worked in predominantly white corporations in the Midwest, found that 51 percent identified at least one mentor (Thomas, 1990). In the first two studies, the majority of the black respondents had black mentors, whereas the majority of black respondents in the last study reported having white mentors. While these examples challenge the popular, anecdotal opinion that suggests that blacks do not establish mentor relationships in predominantly white corporations, it does not speak to the issue of the nature of the cross-race mentor relationship. As the discussion that follows shows, having a cross-race mentor relationships does not automatically correlate to professional or personal satisfaction with that relationship.

In a study of Black managers, those who had white mentors early in their careers were more dissatisfied with their advancement than those who had Black mentors (Thomas, 1993). Thomas found that a racial difference was often an obstacle for white mentors in identifying positively with their Black protégés. By contrast, race served as a positive source of identification in same-race developmental relationships for both Blacks and whites. These results suggest that, to understand the role of mentoring in minority careers, we must look beyond the broad generalizations to the complexities associated with these relationships.

The combination of gender and race is another area that can interfere with Blacks and whites identifying with each other and, thus, forming mentor-protégé relationships (Thomas, 1989). Thomas explains that just as a superior and subordinate can enact the unconsciously experienced dynamics of a parent-child relationship, Blacks and whites can also enact the history of race relations, with all of the challenges associated with it, as they interact in mentoring relationships. Cultural differences, as well as office politics, work against black women forming strong bonds with white males (White, 1990). Scholars of race relations agree that the history of slavery and its chronic aftershocks undergird this schism. There has been a long-standing history of sexual overtones stemming from the slave ideology of the white male as the conqueror and the black female as concubine. Thus, from slavery's beginnings, racial dynamics have been inextricably tied to gender relationships. This taboo that stems from the creation of a liaison between a white man and an Black woman links wider cultural processes to organizational reality, while simultaneously operating to suppress this linkage.

Taboos operate on two levels. They forbid action, and they also forbid reflecting on what is forbidden. The sexual taboo of the white male and the black female, thus, becomes the source of an experiential underground (Thomas, 1989)—a set of experiences rarely acknowledged yet often unconsciously enacted—which ultimately shapes the relationships between Blacks and whites in significant ways. As an injunction not to notice what is forbidden, a taboo operates out of awareness. Thus enters the challenge in discussing taboo issues. The apprehension is not embedded in the idea that a person will perform the act, but rather that he or she will violate the unconsciously accepted mandate to ignore what she or he is ignoring.

The core anxiety of most relationships—the dread of what cannot be predicted—is filled out by the culture of racism. People will either experience or suppress the irrational at work when relating to others. Working in and through these relationships, people serve their conscious, as well as their unconscious, purposes. Shaped by broader social and cultural processes, these relationships reflect the ongoing tension between the rational and irrational levels of experience. However, both mentors and protégés lose out when, unable to identify with each other, they fail to connect emotionally (Thomas, 1989). The unfortunate result is that by stifling the potential developmental relationship, Blacks and Whites not only protect themselves from jointly confronting the anxieties and paradoxes of their alliances, but they also limit their impact and significance.

Finally, a lack of interpersonal skills can interfere with building supportive relationships that provide mentoring functions, even when attitudes and assumptions are positive (Kram, 1985). *The Dictionary of Occupational Titles* classifies mentoring as a highly complex people-related skill, involving comprehensive concern for life-adjustment behavior (Carden, 1990). Combine this element with a previously identified racial tension, and the problem becomes seemingly insurmountable. Skills in active listening, communication, building trust and empathy, and managing conflict and competition are essential to these developmental alliances. Often mentor relationships are curtailed or avoided precisely because individuals do not have the skill to manage them effectively.

COMMUNICATIVE STRATEGIES EMPLOYED IN CROSS-RACE RELATIONSHIPS

Communication offers a valuable method of understanding the mentoring process (Short & Seeger, 1984). In the United States, feelings of racial identity powerfully shape unconscious fantasies and fears. Therefore, one must question how a mentor establishes identification with a protégé of a different race. Thomas (1990) found that the dynamics of cross-racial mentor relationships are influenced by the racial awareness of both parties. He subsequently developed a model that focused on the link between strategies for managing racial difference and type of relationship that develops (Thomas, 1993). According to Thomas, people's racial perspectives predispose them to prefer one of two methods for handling racial difference. Either the direct engagement or denial and suppression strategy— assuming that they are open to forming a cross-race mentor-protégé relationship in the first place. This leads the communication scholar to focus on what type of messages are employed to activate these strategies.

One of Thomas's findings indicated that the strategy chosen was always consistent with the preference of the senior party, regardless of the race and gender of the mentor and the protégé. This is consistent with Asante's and Atwater's (1986) conclusions that the rhetorical condition is embedded in and influenced by the culture of the hierarchical group. Many studies on the subject of mentoring rely solely on retrospective accounts from the protégés perspective (Carden, 1990). Thomas (1993) indicated that in denial and suppression relationships, where either one or both parties choose not to communicate openly about the issue of race, some mentors may have set the tone by suggesting that race is insignificant to them. Mentors described protégés who raised the issue as "having a chip on their shoulder" or made comments such as, "You have a great future in this company as long as you don't start to view race as the source of any of your problems" (Thomas, 1993, p. 191). Gibbons (1993) admonishes White mentors to acknowledge that their protégé is Black, Hispanic, Native American, or Asian American from the start. According to Gibbons, the worst thing to do is to pretend that race is not an issue at all. Unfortunately, many White mentors would rather "bury their head in the sand" and lay claim to the proverbial "color blind" myth than have to open a dialogue concerning racial issues. These examples typify one pervasive rhetorical message that suggests that race is not a topic to be addressed nor that it is of great concern to the mentor.

In direct-engagement relationships, where either the mentor or the protégé openly discussed the race-related aspects of their relationship, again the senior person was consistently the first to instigate a sensitive discussion of race (Thomas, 1993). However, most of the pairs reported that the cross-race dynamics were viewed as a strength of the relationship (Kaplan, 1994). The communicative message in this scenario suggests that if people are comfortable with themselves and, in turn, with their racial identity as an integral part of themselves, then the racial differences within the relationship can be viewed not as a threat, but rather as something to embrace. This attitude is not only necessarily for an individual's self-worth, but it has very practical consequences as well. Racial awareness can influence a White mentor's ability to help his or her Black protégé be promoted in systems in which subtle racism exists.

Thomas (1990) identified two parallel systems of developmental relationships for Blacks. One is defined by the culture of the organization and the other by the need, both developmental and organizational, for Blacks to form relationships with one another. Thomas found that same-race relationships provided more psychosocial support (e.g. emotional support) than did cross-race relationships for both Blacks and Whites. Based on Thomas' findings, I would conclude that that phenomenon is attributable to the inherent link of racial identity. Not only is the ethnic link void in cross-race relationships, but often, it becomes a hindrance to the progression of the relationship for some of the reasons previously discussed.

Several authors have noted the importance White male managers appear to place on feeling socially comfortable with the people with whom they decide to work and promote. If same-race relationships are major sources of psychosocial support, then Blacks who do not have access to such relationships may have very unbalanced work lives or social development, which will result in problems later in their careers (Thomas, 1990). The difficulty in developing the psychosocial aspect of cross-racial mentor relationships most likely contributes to and is caused by the lack of comfort that White and Black managers feel with each other. The long term result may be that Black managers and, for similar reasons, women managers are not given difficult and important assignments of the type that lead to high visibility and advancement because those assignments imply greater risk to the mentor.

The question is: are we promoting a system with the power to enhance knowledge, emotional stability, creativity, opportunity, and overall increased morale and productivity in organizations? Or are we sanctioning an elitist patron system that excludes the socially different and maintains the status quo by cloning managers and administrators and replicating exploitive hierarchical systems? If the former is true, then how can we harness the power of mentoring to maximize its positive impact on individuals and the organization? However, if the latter is the case, then what compensatory actions do we take to open organizational, academic, and professional systems to new directions, and furthermore, how do we provide restitution to those who feel excluded from or exploited in mentor-protégé relationships? I suggest that both alternatives contain some element of trut,; thus the dilemma presented is one of capturing the benefits of mentoring while guarding against its potential pitfalls.

IMPLICATIONS FOR FURTHER RESEARCH

Studying the mentor in contemporary organizations is a critical area for further research for the speech communication field (Short & Seeger, 1984). Organizations would do well to support Blacks in their efforts to build supportive developmental relationships with both Whites and other Blacks. Not surprisingly, recent studies in relational demography suggest that increasing racial and gender diversity in work groups is correlated with reduced commitment and satisfaction among Whites and men (Thomas, 1993). Consequently, scholars should focus their research on positive cross-race relationships, coupled with identifying and studying instances of heterogeneous work units that do not fit this negative prototype.

Such an inquiry could enlighten us as to the cognitive, behavioral, and communication patterns associated with the effective management of diversity and how to intervene to optimize these conditions. Without such research, organizations may be left with the idea that diversity is a detriment to the work environment and, consequently, to their members. Longitudinal studies that follow individuals through periods of stability and transition are also needed (Kram, 1985). However, future research on mentoring must include individuals from populations that have largely been ignored, namely racial and ethnic minority group members.

The mentor-protégé relationship has considerable positive and negative potential. It can serve to include or to exclude, to provide opportunities or to oppress, to encourage creative expression or to maintain the status quo. Without further research and application of the findings, however, the potential for mentoring to serve the best interests of organizations and their members cannot be fully realized.

DISCUSSION QUESTIONS

1. The chapter mentions several issues that may be barriers to obtaining a mentor of a different race. Can you identify any others? What are some strategies that could help eliminate those barriers?

2. If you were to develop a mentoring program for an organization that is comprised of a culturally diverse workforce, what criteria would you use to form the pairs? would you consider race as a criterion? Why or why not?

3. What are the salient characteristics you look for in a mentor? How could a person's race or gender affect these characteristics?

4. Which statement better reflects your feelings: "A person's race really doesn't have anything to do with who he or she is inside." or "A person's race is not something that can be ignored, it is a part of who he or she is."

5. Is it beneficial for researchers to study cross-race relationships? What is a useful schematic and structural framework for examining cross-race mentor relationships?

REFERENCES

Asante, M. K., & Atwater, D. F. (1986). The rhetorical condition as symbolic structure in discourse. *Communication Quarterly, 34*,170-177.

Bushardt, S. C., Fretwell, C., & Holdnak, B. J. (1991). The mentor-protégé relationship: A biological perspective. *Human Relations, 44*, 619-639.

Carden, A. D. (1990). Mentoring and adult career development: The evolution of a theory. *The Counseling Psychologist,18*, 275- 299.

Cox, T., & Nkomo, S. (1986). Differential performance appraisal criteria: A field study of black and white mangers. *Group and Organizational Studies*, 11,101-119.

Ford, D. L., & Wells, L. (1985). Upward mobility factors among black public administrators: The role of mentors. *Centerboard: Journal of the Center for Human Relations, 3*, 33-48.

Gibbons, A. (1993). White men can mentor: Help for the majority. *Science, 262*, 1130-1134.

Kaplan, E. (1994). Confronting the issue of race in developmental relationships: Does open discussion enhance or suppress the mentor-protégé bond? *Academy of Management Executive, 8*, 79-80.

Kram, K. E. (1985). *Mentoring at work: Developmental relationships in organizational life*. Glenview, IL: Scott, Foresman and Company.

Parsloe, E. (1992). *Coaching, mentoring, and assessing: A practical guide to developing competence*. London: Kogan Page.

Short, B. & Seeger, M. (1984). *Mentoring and organizational communication: A review of the research*. Paper presented at the Annual Meeting of the Central States Speech Association, Chicago, IL.

Thiederman, S. (1991). *Bridging cultural barriers for corporate success: How to manage the multicultural work force*. Lexington, MA.: Lexington Books.

Thomas, D. A. (1989). Mentoring and irrationality: The role of racial taboos. *Human Resource Management, 28,* 279-290.

Thomas, D. A. (1990). The impact of race on managers' experiences of developmental relationships (mentoring and sponsorship): An intra-organizational study. *Journal of Organizational Behavior, 11,* 479-492.

Thomas, D. A. (1993). Racial dynamics in cross-race developmental relationships. *Administrative Science Quarterly, 38,* 169-194.

White, Y. S. (1990). Understanding the black woman manager's interaction with the corporate culture. *The Western Journal of Black Studies, 14,* 182-186.

15

AFRICAN-AMERICAN DISCOURSES ON PROBLEMATIC RELATIONS WITH WHITES

Richard Buttny
Syracuse University

Princess L. Williams
Clemson University

INTRODUCTION

W.E.B. DuBois's assessment, "The problem of the 20th Century is the problem of the color line," remains as true today at the end of the Century as it was at the beginning. Racial division continues to be the main North American domestic problem and there seems to be no solution in sight for racial healing. Many have called for honest conversations across racial and ethnic lines. This project may be seen as a small step in this direction. Given the fact that African-American voices have been largely absent from studies of communication, this chapter attempts to examine the discourses that some African-American students use in discussing their relations with White people on a university campus.

The idea for this project arose from a prior study on talking race on campus (Buttny, 1997). We found that the most frequently quoted portion by African-American participants who viewed the documentary, *Racism 101*, was a segment in which an African-American student claims that he does not care if he is liked by Whites, but demands respect. The demand for respect seems to capture a powerful current in contemporary African-American thought. In examining discourses of respect, clearly we are looking at subjective interpretations of interracial contact. But given that interracial contact is all too often problematic (Collier, 1996; Kochman, 1981), making for dissatisfying communication (Hecht, Ribeau, & Alberts, 1989; Martin, Hecht & Larkey, 1994) and difficult dialogues (Houston, 1994; Orbe, 1994), suggests that we need to examine persons' sense-making and evaluative devices. The forming of interpersonal relations has long been advocated as a way to overcome racial barriers and repudiate negative stereotypes (Hewstone & Brown, 1986). However, such interracial relations are at times strained over "race matters" (Frankenberg, 1993; West, 1994). Describing African-American discourses of problematic features of relations with Whites will allow us to become more aware of some of the barriers to multicultural communication.

PROCEDURES

To investigate African-American discourses of intergroup relations with Whites, we conducted interviews with African-American participants as well as used discourse analysis from the transcripts drawn up from a prior study on talking race on campus. From these two data sources, various problematic features of interpersonal relations with Whites are examined. Focus-group interviews were conducted with 20 African-American participants, 13 females and 7 males. Participants included university students and adult members of the community. Volunteers were solicited by a snowball sampling procedure. The session began by showing a video segment from *Racism 101* in which an African-American student calls for the need for respect. Participants were asked to discuss the significance of respect in relations with Whites. Interviews ranged in length from 30 minutes to over an hour. The focus groups were audiotaped. These tapes were listened to repeatedly and transcribed.

RESULTS

Respect and Interpersonal Relations with Whites

The idea of respect is a multifaceted notion for African-Americans. For over four centuries, Blacks have been judged by White standards of beauty, culture and learning. To be accepted, many downplayed their African features and rejected their cultural heritage. With the development of the Black Power movement and "Black is beautiful," many African-Americans developed an ethnic pride. They demanded respect from Whites. While the history of the idea of respect has yet to be written, our concern here is with how African-American participants discursively use respect as an account to make sense of their relations with Whites.

The following transcript reveals some problematic features of interpersonal relations with Whites.

Transcript One

 1 A: And it's also like we have to earn respect with White people,
 2   for example I would be in situations where they would say
 3   she's not like other Black people,
 4   once they get to know you okay you're cool but you're not like the rest,
 5   and it's like no I am,
 6   so it's like we have to earn respect with them whereas they just kind of get it
 7 B: Especially here, when you get to know White people,
 8   I know my freshman year I lived in Davis Hall and it was nothing but White people
         ((*skip one line*))
 9   and we were all friends, it really wasn't a problem
10   but one night we were talking about something
11   and they were like you're not Black,
12   I was like I am Black, I look Black my parents are Black
         ((*skip two lines*))
13   they were just like oh you're not Black
14 D: It's funny that B brought that up because kind of the same thing happened to me
12   my Freshman year because I lived in Henderson and it was mostly White and
13   upper-classmen, and we were watching a movie one time
14   and I forgot exactly what happened- I think it was Juice
15   they were talking about how the characters in the movie was typical Blacks
16   and they looked at me and said you're not like that D, you're all right with us,
17   they didn't put me in that class because I had earned their respect.
18   It's like what you was saying before it's like earning respect with them
19   and if you don't earn their respect then they all group you together,
20   they don't have respect for you

Some of the narratives in the focus groups arose in story rounds—one story leads to another story in kind. Three discursive positions are apparent from this transcript: African-Americans need to earn respect while Whites can just assume it, African-Americans are respected by Whites with whom they are friends, and Whites differentiate their African-American friends from other African-Americans.

The position that African-Americans need to earn respect from Whites was found throughout the focus-group interviews. It fits within the broader theme of the asymmetry of how African-Americans and Whites are treated in society. Whites' presumption of receiving respect in society is taken for granted, while African-Americans, and other minorities, have to prove they are worthy of it, reflects what has been called "White privilege" (McIntosh, 1989). Many Whites do not realize that they have privileges from society that just by virtue of their skin color African-Americans do not (Hacker, 1992). To borrow a distinction from linguistics, respect is unmarked for Whites, but marked for minorities.

A theme evident in the story round is that Whites do respect their African-American friends but they distinguish them from other African-Americans because they are "not like the rest" (line 4). The presumption here ascribed to

Whites is that their African-American friend is an exception to the rule: African-Americans as a group are stigmatized but their particular African-American friend is different—does not posses the negative qualities associated with the group. This rationalizing phenomenon of befriending an out-group member, while holding on to negative stereotypes about the group, is one reason why inter-group contact alone is not sufficient to alleviate racism.

It is informative to see how the teller in the narratives in transcript one describes the White friends' problematic actions. The Whites' utterances are hearably presented as patronizing and are explicitly rejected by the first two narrators. Being differentiated from other African-Americans is framed as a cost of associating with Whites. This seems to be a dilemma for African-Americans: They want respect from Whites, but not at the price of sacrificing their Black identity.

Another version of this dilemma in relations with Whites is seen in the following narrative.

Transcript Two

```
 1  C:  My parents told me like, once I went to an all White school
 2      it's about less than five percent Black,
 3      they were like you're different, I'm like how so,
 4      I mean, like, I wasn't like boisterous and loud or anything,
 5      I didn't express myself like that that's why they I guess they felt like that.
 6      Like at my job I used to work at a consultant firm
 7      and I was the only Black person there
 8      and when the O.J.Simpson verdict came out they were surprised
 9      that I was like well it was a correct verdict
10      because the prosecution didn't prove their case
11      and they were like- they didn't talk to me after that.
12      These were people I talked to everyday after that
13      they were like Hum she's like them she's really Black,
14      I mean that's how it appeared to me, that was kind of funny you know
15  E:  It's kind of like there are acceptable Negroes and hum once you get to a certain
16      point they can you know- proven yourself from being different from the rest of
17      them so therefore they can accept you that sort of thing and then they respect you
```

In the opening short narrative, C recounts how her parents told her she was "different" from the Whites she went to school with. Recall that the prior story round involved Whites telling their African-American friends that they were different from other African-Americans. The importance of social identity issues for African-Americans vis-à-vis Whites is reflected in these narratives.

Looking at the second narrative in the above transcript, we see a complication arise when C's White work colleagues no longer talk to her after she defends the O.J. Simpson verdict. The polarizing effects of race brought out by the O.J. verdict enter their relationship. C frames the significance of the events as the change in her relationship with her White work friends in that she perceives them as seeing her as "really Black" (line 13). This realization of difference can be heard as connecting back to her parents' advice.

Relations with Whites can be troublesome because of matters of race and social identity. This is implicated by E's ironic evaluation of C's narrative, "there are acceptable Negroes" (line 15). The contrast between the ascriptions, "really Black" and "acceptable Negroes," indicates issues about power and accommodation. In short, African-Americans are "acceptable" to Whites if they are not "too Black" in their identification and actions.

These African-American participants do feel they receive respect from their White friends and acquaintances, but, as it were, with strings attached. One is perceived as being different than other African-Americans and one cannot be too ethnically identified to maintain amiable relations with Whites.

Accounting for Social Distance

Another kind of discourse that some African-American participants drew on to explain problematic relations was a kind of duplicity some Whites use in their dealings with them. The following transcript captures an instance of this duplicity.

Transcript Three
A: there's White people in our class who say that
        when they're with their White friends they don't talk to Black people
        when they're alone they'll go up and talk to Black people

Here A draws on the direct speech of what "White people in our class...say" as support for this description of White behavior. The duplicity lies in the difference of behavior depending on whether the White person is alone or with other Whites.

This theme of social distance as a consequence of White duplicity is seen again in the following transcript. Whites are portrayed in this narrative as keeping relations with African-Americans "at an arm's length," as refusing to engage in ordinary codes of friendship, dating, and sociability.

Transcript Four
1   B: I went to a predominately White school I had White friends in school
2   but was I ever invited over to their house?
3   A: That's true
4   B: Or you know my friend Johnny was cool with your parents
5   because he was on the basketball team
6   but let him date your daughter then it was a whole different subject
7   you couldn't even see Johnny any more
8   you know that kind of thing,
9   you know Blacks are okay to be friendly with

In this transcript, B is conversing with two friends; at lines 4-5 she switches footings to address an absent White high school friend (as indicated by "your parents"). B, then, switches footings again to address her White friend's mother, "but let him date *your daughter*" (lines 6-7, emphasis added). It is not clear whether these are direct quotes from a prior conversation or what could/should have been said to confront these White people. My hunch is that it is the latter. Here the speaker's discourse confronts absent others who display White duplicity. B switches footings again to quote a prototypical White, hypocritical position on race relations (line 9). Such prototypical quotes serve to evoke a familiar type of White racist discourse even though a non-racist view is verbally avowed.

B marks this portrayal as typical of Whites by the post-positioned idiomatic evaluation, "you know that kind of thing" (line 8). This comment serves to frame the preceding portrayal as what African-Americans have come to expect from Whites.

Another account for social distance involves so-called voluntary segregation on college campuses (Asante & Al-Seen, 1984; Pinderhughes, 1989). In the following transcript, A raises the voluntary segregation topic by asking B of her reactions to a White person being at an "African-American event."

Transcript Five

```
 1  A:  if you walk into a party and it's filled with Black people and you see
 2      this one White person what is like your first thought like
 3  B:  My first thought it's happened a few times I really don't think nothin' I don't
 4      think nothin' because I know a few White kids I guess so to speak they act Black
 5  A:  Yeah
 6  B:  so when I see a White person I don't think
 7      dang they're the only White person in here
 8      but the people I'm with they be like yo you see that
 9      White person they know they wrong for comin' in here
10  A:  Uh hum
11  B:  That's the reaction of everybody else but nine times out of ten I really don't even
12      notice them or don't really pay attention to the people in the party I mean it's
13      just I don't react to a White person at all
14  A:  See that's like you're one of the few exceptions to the rule because most people
15      like you say like yo what is it unless they know that he's like a quote unquote
16      Black White person
17  B:  Um huh
18  A:  then it's like what are you doing here? and who invited him or who did he come
19      with or you know its like when you get here that's like a stereotype that's placed in
20      you before you even see a White person
```

Here, B contrasts her reaction to seeing a White at an African-American party ("I really don't think nothin'") to other African-Americans (who notice and are critical). She dramatizes their reactions by a direct quote of her group of friends and their criticizing the White for coming to the party (lines 8-9).

A readily confirms B's portrayal. Later, A herself animates a prototypical African-American reaction to the White by a similar kind of summary quote disparaging the White for coming to the party (lines 18-19). The very fact that A raises this question plus her post-positioned evaluation, "that like a stereotype..." (lines 19-20), can be heard to explain as well as criticize African-American student reactions.

Another case of self-reflection on the social construction of in-group and out-group boundaries is seen in the following. Here C formulates the problem of voluntary segregation and addresses absent African-American critics (see arrow).

Transcript Six

C: I think that's a problem that we have as a group of people
        on this campus we separate ourselves from each other and
==>   I don't agree with you that I'm an Uncle Tom if I do something differently
        then it's wrong and they always has to be right and I think a lot of kids up
        still here are growing and that they fail to understand the bottom line and
        they dealing with the surface stuff

So African-American participants are critical of in-group members as well as of Whites for the strained interracial relations.

A portrait of Whites as fearful or displaying a lack of strength vis-à-vis African-Americans is seen in the following narrative involving professor and students.

Transcript Seven

1   B: Like one time I had a political science class and the professor was talking about
2   racism and stuff and like there was only three Blacks in the whole class of like
3   thirty people? And after the class he wanted to talk to us and he was like
4   that he was scared to talk because we were Black and he didn't want us to feel
5   uncomfortable and all this kind of stuff because they were going to be talking
6   about Blacks and everything but he didn't feel comfortable in discussing it
7   because he didn't know how we would take it and all this kind of stuff
8   and it was just weird

The White professor is portrayed through a summary quote as "scared to talk" about racism because of the African-American students in a class. B reconstructs the episode by noting that there were only three African-Americans in a class of thirty, so why should a White professor be "scared?" Also, the asymmetrical membership categories, "professor-student," further render this episode as problematic. The implication here is that the African-American students are singled out as a reason to avoid discussion of racism. B assesses this reported exchange as "just weird."

Another case of everyday racism on campus is offered through a description of a White coach manipulating African-American athletes. An apocryphal quotation is used to epitomize the speaker's response to the coach (see arrows).

Transcript Eight

B: I experienced those attitudes being an athlete you know our coach
        was real racist and stuff and that was one of the reasons that I left
        that school because yes they were paying for my education but
==>   you de-humanizing me wasn't worth me not getting my education when you
==>   tell me you don't care about it=all you care is what I can do for you on the court.
        Most coaches, I don't wanna name any names but, (.) hhh I mean they manipulate
        you mentally ((skip two lines)) you know they play a lot of mind games with you

So narratives of relations with various kinds of White authorities on campus are portrayed in a critical light.

SUMMARY

The good news from this study is that there are narratives of interpersonal relations, but these are sometimes strained by careless remarks and stereotypical comments made by Whites. African-Americans reported that they received respect from their White friends and acquaintances, but these relationships were not without complications. They saw Whites as ascribing that they were different from other African-Americans which was seen as problematic for Black identity. African-Americans seem aware of the fact of "White privilege," but it seems few Whites realize this asymmetry of power. Awareness of respect concerns could contribute to making for more satisfying interracial contact.

Despite these accounts of interracial relations and friendships, overall there was a portrait of social distance between African-Americans and Whites on campus. The African-Americans' ascription of White duplicity in dealings with them is interesting in that, we speculate, few Whites would recognize this. From an African-American viewpoint, Whites draw on a discourse of equality and commonality, while at same time, keeping relations with African-Americans at an arm's length. In other words, Whites are not seen as genuine or trustworthy.

There seems to be the expectation among White students that in the social sphere African-Americans will accommodate to them, but African-Americans seem less willing to make such unilateral accommodations. So the resulting absence of intergroup contact works to perpetuate the voluntary segregation in social life on campus.

DISCUSSION QUESTIONS

1. Why do African-Americans have to earn respect and Whites automatically receive respect?
2. What seems to be the asymmetry between Whites and African-American relations?
3. What do the authors mean by "White duplicity"?
4. What are the implications of Whites treating and perceiving their Black friends to be different and "not like the rest" of African-Americans?
5. How can Whites and African-Americans improve racial relations?

REFERENCES

Asante, M. K., & Al-Seen, N. (1984). Social interaction of Black and White college students: A research report. *Journal of Black Studies, 14*, 507-516.

Buttny, R. (1997). Reported speech in talking race on campus. *Human Communication Research, 31*, 45-58.

Collier, M. J. (1996). Communication competence problematics in ethnic friendships. *Communication Monographs, 63*, 314-336.

Frankenberg, R. (1993). *White women, race matters: The social construction of whiteness.* Minneapolis, MN: University of Minnesota Press.

Hacker, A. (1992). *Two nations: Black and White, separate, hostile, unequal.* New York: Ballantine Books.

Hecht, M. L., Ribeau, S., & Alberts, J. K. (1989). An Afro-American perspective on interethnic communication. *Communication Monographs, 56*, 385-410.

Hewstone, M., & Brown, R. (1986). Contact is not enough: An intergroup perspective on the 'contact hypothesis'. In M.Hewstone & R. Brown (Eds.), *Contact and conflict in intergroup encounters* (pp. 1-44). London: Basil Blackwell.

Houston, M. (1994). When Black women talk with White women: Why dialogues are difficult. In A.Gonzalez, M. Houston, & V. Chen (Eds.), *Our voices: Essays in culture, ethnicity, and communication* (pp.133-139). Los Angeles: Roxbury.

Kochman, T. (1981). *Black and White styles in conflict.* Chicago. IL: University of Chicago Press.

Martin, J. N., Hecht, M. L., & Larkey, L. K. (1994). Conversational improvement strategies for interethnic communication: African-American and European American perspectives. *Communication Monographs, 61*, 236-255.

McIntosh, P. (1989, July/August). White privilege: Unpacking the invisible knapsack. *Peace and Freedom*, 10-12

Orbe, M. P. (1994). "Remember, it's always Whites' ball": Descriptions of African American male communication. *Communication Quarterly, 42*, 287-300.

Pinderhughes, E. (1989). *Understanding race, ethnicity, and power.* New York: The Free Press.

Racism 101 (1988). Transcript. *Frontline #612*: PBS, WGBH Educational Foundation.

West, C. (1994). *Race matters.* New York: Vintage Books.

16

TURN-TAKING AND THE EXTENDED PAUSE: A STUDY OF INTERPERSONAL COMMUNICATION STYLES ACROSS GENERATIONS ON THE WARM SPRINGS INDIAN RESERVATION

G. Scott McLean
The Thomas Jefferson School

For a stranger entering an alien society, a knowledge of when *not* to speak may be as basic to the production of culturally acceptable behavior as a knowledge of what to say." (Basso, 1970, p. 303)

INTRODUCTION

Individuals often consciously prepare for cultural differences when encountering a new environment. One common preparation has been in the classroom setting, where students and teachers review past literature indicating the established importance of silence in Native American speech. Past research and documentation of silence may not be representative of middle-aged and younger Tribal members' speech styles as those of elders.

This study features six recorded conversations with twenty-four community members of Warm Springs, from ages 15 to 94. Across discussions, a pattern emerges which has cultural significance, particularly to the outsider attempting to communicate with members of the Warm Springs community. Turn-taking (Sacks, Schegloff, & Jefferson, 1974) in "mainstream" studied conversation has, in their analyzed conversations, a moderate incidence of overlap and relatively short transition relevance places (TRPs). In studied Warm Springs conversation, TRPs are substantially longer the older the participant. In younger participants TRPs are shorter, and overlaps more common. This trend indicates silence has significant importance when communicating with elders in the traditional manner.

BACKGROUND

Conversation "is an interactional activity exhibiting stable, orderly properties that are the analyzable achievements of the conversants (Zimmerman, 1988, p. 406)," and "that familiar predominant kind of talk in which two or more participants freely alternate in speaking (Levinson, 1983, p. 284)." Conversational analysis is "a set of qualitative procedures based on detailed observation to capture discernable features of conversational exchange, (Zimmerman, 1988, p. 406)," and rests on "repeated listenings to …recordings of natural talk (Sacks, Schegloff, & Jefferson, 1974; Zimmerman, 1988, p. 406)." On reservations, conversation styles have been studied for many years, noting both non-verbal and verbal aspects, as well as situation, context, position, rank, and sex of the participants.

In conversation, we play by rules (Sacks, Schegloff, & Jefferson, 1974). If members of the conversation are playing by different rules and expectations, frustrations and mis-communication can more easily occur. "For a stranger to communicate appropriately with the members of an unfamiliar society it is not enough that he learn to formulate messages intelligibly. Something else is needed: a knowledge of what kinds of codes, channels, and expressions to use in what kinds of situations and to what kinds of people—as Hymes (1964) termed it, an "ethnography of communication (Basso, 1970, p. 303)." If one wishes to enter into conversation in an established system, or cultural climate in this study, one must first understand the rules and be able to apply them.

Rules play a part but cannot account for all of the dynamics of intercultural communication. Gudykundst (1987) details when groups of people who are not familiar or known come together, the individual members of each group treat members of the other group as members, not individuals. It is important to recognize the importance of insuring all members of the conversation are part of the ingroup, rather than communicating with strangers (Gudykundst, 1985; Gudykundst & Kim, 1984). In this study, all members of the conversation are Warm Springs Tribal members, members of the same ingroup, often by direct family relation, district and tribal affiliation, or peer group. This study reflects this familiarity and examines the practiced style of speech in the same population ingroup, or tribe, and its relation to age. Hymes (1967) asserted the native speaker's knowledge of message construction as socially acceptable cannot be separated from "sociocultural knowledge about the situational or contextual appropriateness of an utterance. Communicative competence, then refers to the ability of a member of a given culture to use language in a socially appropriate manner" (Philips, 1983, p. 58; Goodenough, 1976). As members of the following groups are members of a culture, their knowledge and messages cannot be separated into categories of socially acceptable message construction given the context and intuitions about the sociocultural appropriate manner of their turn. This distinction becomes both interesting and problematic when examining the instances where messages are spoken in an inappropriate way of taking a turn and tensions result.

Susan Urston Philips (1983), in *The Invisible Culture: Communication in Classroom and Community on the Warm Springs Indian Reservation*, notes "there is almost no interruption of one speaker by another in Warm Springs talk. ... Rarely do two people begin to talk at the same time. The pause between the talk of two different speakers is typically longer than in Anglo conversation" (Philips, 1983, p. 58). Longer pauses, almost no overlap, and rare simultaneous talking are aspects of traditional Native American speech.

Silence has increased as a topic of study, particularly in intercultural aspects of the field of communication science. The 1990 text entitled *Cultural Communication and Intercultural Contact* features the work of Keith A. Basso (1970) and Charles A. Braithwaite (1981) on silence in Native American speech. Basso quoted an anonymous source as stating "it is not the case that a man who is silent says nothing." Basso (1970, p. 301) states "anyone who has read about American Indians has probably encountered statements which impute to them a strong predilection for keeping silent" and continues with "an adequate ethnography of communication should not confine itself exclusively to the analysis of choice with verbal repertoires. It should also...specify those conditions under which members of the society regularly decide to refrain from verbal behavior altogether" (Basso, 1970). Basso (1970, p. 301) specifically points to the need for studying silence in communication both when people talk and when they do not. Braithwaite (1981, p. 319), in his master's thesis, counters Basso's assertion by stating "to formulate descriptive theory of orality is not enough," and follows with "silence is interesting to study in its own right," declaring that silence, as another "important symbolic resource" can be viewed the same way talk is viewed. Braithwaite (1981, p. 319) continues with address to Basso's assertion about silence across cultures as broad, and asserts while "rules" may be similar, their application varies greatly. Tom Bruneau is widely recognized as a pioneer in the study of silence as communication (Harrison, 1981), examining silence in both Eastern and Western traditions (Bruneau & Ishii, 1988), silence as an aspect of subjective time, social interaction, and personal identity (Bruneau, 1995), and has long argued that "resistance to the consideration of time in the study of communication is reflective of assumptive neglect" (Bruneau, 1995, p. 121; Bruneau, 1974, 1980, 1985, 1988, 1989, 1990).

From these divergent perspectives, it can observed that silence is important, in terms of context and in and of itself as an aspect of conversation. Therefore, this Warm Springs study focuses on the silence in the transitions, from a conversational analysis perspective, noting where conversation ends and silence begins, across generations.

WARM SPRINGS

The research on which this paper is based was conducted from 1994 to 1995 in the central community of Warm Springs on the Warm Springs Reservation in Central Oregon (an out growth of a Robert Wood Johnson Foundation project). Warm Springs residents participate in a relatively stable economy, with a base foundation in wood products from a Tribal-owned and operated mill. A new gambling operation at the renowned destination resort village Kah-Nee-Ta promises to provide additional revenue streams and further diversify the economy. Unemployment and lack of adequate housing are serious problems. The Warm Springs Reservation encompasses 655,000 acres and a total Tribal enrollment of 3525 (WS Vital Statistics, 1994), representing the Warm Springs (Simnasho District), Wasco (Agency District), and Northern Paiute (Seekseequa District) Tribes. Major families within the Warm Springs, Wasco, and Northern Paiute Tribes form the interpersonal and political force within the governing body, a nine-member Tribal Council.

The Robert Wood Johnson Foundation joined in a partnership with the Confederated Tribes of the Warm Springs Reservation of Oregon to reduce substance use and abuse in December of 1993. The needs assessment phase included a behavioral risk factor survey, community meetings, focus groups, and interpersonal interviews. The conversations in this study were collected as the recorded focus groups.

RECORDED FOCUS GROUPS

According to (Levinson, 1983), conversation, in order to be representative, must be natural. This necessity, however, is weighed against practicality (Button & Lee, 1987). Button and Lee suggest making the participants comfortable, in a neutral setting, and insure that the recorder does not feature prominently in the room. The groups came together in a single location for six separate sessions across three days on the main campus of the reservation, a room often used for native (Sahaptin, Wasco, Warm Springs) languages classes and other community events. The room was well lighted and comfortable. In addition to the participants, a reel

TABLE 1
Transcript Symbols

Type	Symbol	Use/Example
Overlapping utterances	[ ]	When one person speaks while another already is.
		[huh?]
Intervals of no speech	( )	When one person just stops speaking (0.5) then starts again (*in seconds, tenths and hundredths*) or at the transition between turns.
Intonation	.	Denotes a fall in intonation OOhhh.
	,	Denotes a continutation in intonation O'Okay
	?	Denotes a rise in intonation Okay?
Sound	:	Denotes an extended sound O:Okay
Inhalation	.h	Denotes a discernable in-breath
Stress	_	Denotes a stress on a letter or syllable
Length of Turn	LT 0:00:00	Denotes length of turn in minutes, seconds, tenths and hundredths of seconds

to reel recorder, its operator, and the study coordinator were present, but not prominent. There were no interruptions. Focus group participants gave consent (or parental consent) to be recorded, and with permission, each session was produced as a thirty minute radio program, broadcast on the pubic Tribal radio station. Participants were asked three questions at the beginning of the discussion: 1) What do you see in our community today?, 2) What can our community do to reduce alcohol and drug abuse? and 3) What can individual community members do to reduce alcohol and drug abuse?

Transitions, extended pauses, and overlaps will be featured, however, due to the length of the conversations, only brief, selected lines of conversation will be used to detail the speech actions. Turns are identified by their order in the conversation and participant. (For an explanation of the symbols used in the transcripts, see Table 1.)

This transcript symbol code used in conversational analysis was developed primarily by Gail Jefferson (Button & Lee, 1987). The code is more detailed and encompassing of speech traits than shown here. Appropriate code markers are detailed as the are pertinant to the conversation actions in this study.

Session One
Participant A: 78 year old female elder
Participant B: 94 year old female elder
Participant C: 62 year old female elder

Out of 28:57 minutes of recorded conversation, there were eight turns, four extended mid-turn pauses, and one incidence of overlap. The longest turn relevance place or extended pause was 17.29, and the shortest was 4.62.

6   A: Ok. <u>Ok</u>. <u>D</u>uring the <u>sum:mer</u> time, <u>Wh</u>en they'r:e home from <u>schoo</u>:l time …
LT 2:23:95

.1   A: We got to <u>something</u> for our <u>children</u> (17.29) Hhh. that 's al:l. I <u>think</u>
someone…

In turn 6, A takes a 17.29 second extended mid-turn pause without interruption before beginning again.

8   A: I, <u>I</u> think it <u>w</u>ould be <u>better</u>: if it was a <u>little</u> bit <u>earlier</u> …

.1   A: e<u>s</u>pecially on a <u>scho:ol night</u> when <u>they</u> should be <u>home</u> in
    C: [oh, I know] (laughter)
    A: <u>bed</u> resting (laughter)LT 0:28:49

A selected to speak after 4.62 seconds in turn 8. The single incident of overlap, where one person spoke while another was already speaking, occured at A8.1, where C indicated her agreement. Laughter expressed a common understanding. Speaker A retained her turn.

Session Two
Participant A: 40 year old male
Participant B: 62 year old male elder
Participant C: 71 year old male elder
Participant D: 64 year old female elder

Out of 64:09 minutes of recorded conversation, there were 17 turns, nine extended mid-turn pauses, and two incidences of overlap. The longest turn relevance place or extended pause was 15.52, and the shortest was 1.14.

10   C: I'll <u>take</u> your word for it, ahh? I don't know much about <u>acupuncture</u>
and ah and ah I don't know about ah I see tha<u>t</u>, ahh for whatever reason kindofa a
hard sell here at home. LT 0:14:13

11   D: [AHHHH]   HHhhhhh you guys <u>just</u> don't <u>wan</u>:nna be
<u>out</u>ttofa job (laughter) (1.14) LT 0:03:87

2.73 seconds pass between D9 and C10, with C responding again to the topic. D re-asserts herself with emphasis as he concludes his turn, speaking, and everyone again laughs.

14   B: I believe <u>th</u>at ahh (2.93) where a <u>family</u>, a w<u>hole</u> family gets involved in
the <u>recovery</u> of one person the whole family is
recovering …

.1   B: and ahh <u>this</u> ahh happened to me (6.69)
    B: I've been <u>abusing</u> alcohol for the <u>g</u>ood part of <u>thirty</u> years before I
decided I'd had enough …

.2   B: <u>it</u> ju<u>st</u> says th<u>at</u> we both had different needs (4.33)
    B: When (2.71) I com<u>pleted</u> thirty days here in this treatment center …

.3   B: the abuse of other drugs is also in this same category (5.57)
       B: These are the thoughts I thought I would like to leave ...
       LT 9:59:10
       B: once you can 'ply to something you can succeed (15.52)

B14 features three extended mid-turn pauses, the first for 6.69 seconds. The second is 4.33 seconds, and the final, 5.57 seconds. At the conclusion of B14, 15.52 seconds pass before A self-selects again.

Session Three
Participant A: 54 year old male
Participant B: 28 year old male
Participant C: 56 year old male

Out of 33:52 minutes of recorded conversation, there were 20 turns, one extended mid-turn pause, and one incidence of overlap. The longest turn relevance place or extended pause was 6.43, and the shortest was 1.86.

18   A: Well, y'kow yuh got Fear, I, I been clean and sober for a little over,
       si::, six years ....
       LT 3:32:31
       I got over it after we started this, y'know this whole thing right here:n' I forgot
       what good I'raised, so (5.42) I want pass it on, okay:.(2.13)
19   B: [thud*]   [hhhhH:::H, (1.86) uhh] (hh.) UMMMmmm,
       W,W,WHh:at what I was going to say before was that um, y'know, when he says
       fear...
          LT 2:54:08
       B: you can be nice and healthy (6.43)
20   C: Yeah k'now Ittt takes:, y'know the body, when I drank ...
       LT 3:24:06

In the excerpt, C takes four extended pauses, and B speaks after a 7.43 second pause. In A 18, A is speaking about a very important topic to A, the fear associated with going dry after years of alcoholism. Near the conclusion of his turn, which may have been a premature conclusion, B drops his left arm from supporting his chin to the table top, making a moderately loud noise, his non-verbal communication expressing impatience. This noise is associated with a 5.42 second pause, followed by A explicitly indicating he was giving up the turn. B overlaps while B is concluding and takes an in-breath. B then self-selects after a short turn relevance place of 2.13 seconds, and again recycles his former topic, not referring to A's comments. B concludes and a 6.43 second pause passes before C self-selects. This session raises a problematic issue: when does one become an elder? The average mortality age on the reservation for men and women is 44. With this lower than average mortality age, those older than 44 might be considered reaching elderhood. While there is no agreed upon age, 60 seems to be the general consensus in Warm Springs.

Session Four
Participant A: 57 year old female
Participant B: 35 year old female
Participant C: 40 year old female
Participant D: 31 year old female
Participant E: 49 year old female

Session four featured five adults in conversation for 44 minutes, 6 seconds, with 20 minutes, 46 seconds examined. There were 11 turns, three extended mid-turn pauses, and three incidences of overlap. The longest turn relevance place or extended pause was 16.10, and the shortest was 1.37.

4   A: It real:l:y starts in the <u>home</u> doesn't it? LT 0:21:93
     C: [oh it does]
     A: you know, like <u>you</u> said, we're role
     models, <u>we're</u> the ones who pass down the values and standards to our children, and
     that's <u>hard</u> <u>work</u>, isn't it? whether its drinking or using drugs, <u>What</u>'s the
     C: [oh it IS]
     D: [cough]
     A: least interest <u>you</u> <u>have</u> is in raising your <u>kids</u> n' being a<u>ware</u> of where
     they are and what they're doin', more wo<u>rk</u>
5   C: [right more work]   <u>IT's</u> our life. <u>LEt's</u> drop them off so
     we can go do our own thing, <u>GOsh</u> that is so selfish its like in your single life
     …
     C: that is really <u>selfish</u> (4.74) LT 0:33:85
6   E: <u>YOu</u> know, as a child growing up in the com<u>mun</u>ity I <u>remember</u> …
     LT 3:01:06
     E: it takes alottta <u>lotta</u> <u>work</u> and support (.96) love. (1.37)
7   A: That's good because your right it starts in the home …
     LT 0:35:47

In turn 4, A references C's topic, indicating agreement, and C overlaps with approval. A retains the turn, and C again overlaps, indicating agreement. A continues speaking and in turn 5, C takes over and continues with the topic. At the conclusion of C5, 4.74 seconds pass before E self-selects. E concludes and A, in turn 7, initiates a turn after a 1.37 second pause.

Session Five
Participant A: 43 year old female
Participant B: 43 year old male
Participant C: 45 year old female
Participant D: 43 year old female

Out of 29:41 minutes of recorded conversation, there were 18 turns, three extended mid-turn pauses, and one incidence of overlap. The longest turn relevance place or extended pause was 9.33, and the shortest was 1.67.

16   C: I guess I could, d'uhhh, probably relate to <u>tha:</u>at …
.1   C: I don't know <u>what</u>, wh't exactly I am <u>teaching</u> them (3.69)
      but I do, do:o <u>accept</u> them (3.87) I gues:s, I gues how I learned to look at
      life is th't you have to appreciate it everyday …
      LT 8:12:23
      C: I'dd <u>like</u> to see morn' <u>more</u> <u>people</u> become that wayy. (4.73)
17   A: So I'm sitting here thinking. what <u>would</u> <u>have</u> <u>happened</u> …
      TLT 0:59:56
      A: It's not gonna wo<u>rk</u> any more (4.56)

The conversation proceeds throughout the duration without major speech actions. Transitional relevance places are much shorter. In turn 14, D concludes and after a 3.83 second pause, A initiates a turn. C self-selects in turn 16 preceeded by a 4.73 second pause. In A16.1 there are two extended mid-turn pauses. The first comes at the end of a sentence and thought, lasting 3.69 seconds. A starts again, modifying his earlier statement, and pauses for 3.87 seconds. A starts again further explaining his original thought. A starts turn 17 after a 4.73 second pause.

Session Six
Participant A: 17 year old female
Participant B: 16 year old female
Participant C: 15 year old female
Participant D: 17 year old female
Participant E: 17 year old male

Out of 10:14 minutes of recorded conversation, there were 71 turns, three extended mid-turn pauses, and 17 incidence of overlap. In the first 1:40 alone, there were 29 turns. The longest turn relevance place or extended pause was 4.99, and the shortest was 0.49.

1   A: I'm (name) (1.83) <u>Soph</u>omore in high school LT 0:05:99
2   B: [UNH Uhhhhh]
3   A: [oh.]
4   C: [ehhhh
      hhhhhs]
5   B: ehhhhhs <u>I</u> wuz just lying I <u>know</u> you are LT0:01:53
6   D: [OKKK] so uhh what do you see in terms of alcohol
      and drug abuse in our community today? (1.52) LT 0:04:62
7   A: I think there's too <u>**MUCH OF IT**</u> It's <u>DUmb</u> and <u>PPay</u>, nnn <u>NNunow</u> I think that
      they should just try and get rid of it 'cause I don't do stuff like that (1.79) LT 0:10:53

In turn 1, A introduces herself, B interrupts with an overlap, questioning her student status. A briefly speaks, and C overlaps with a common Warm Springs slang word "ehhhs," which means "just kidding" and acts like the word "not." In turn 5, B indicates she was kidding, and D overlaps, interrupting, and takes over the turn. She recycles the topic of the conversation. In turn 7, after a 1.52 second pause, A responds.

8   D: Wellll, what do you think the community can dooo about it? (1.01)
    LT 0:02:69
9   A: I DUNNNunow Try an quit I gues:s I Dunnnunuow (1.98)
    LT 0:04:33
10 D: What about an individual, what can and individual do to reduce drug abuse, substance abuse (.84) What can we do to help them (.76) LT 0:04:40
11 A: [MEEE?]
12 A: HHHunh (1.28) In a way try to help someone else by trying to keep them away and try to doing stuff with the people, Uhnm like going aout and doing stuff without drugs and alcohol an trying to help ummm (.86) LT 0:15:54
13 D: Is there anyhting else ya wanna say about alcohol and drug abuse in our community like what's up here in Warm SPrings err, like (1.82) 0:17:87
14 A: Hmmn. I think everyone should just try and quit it but itss probably pretty hard for dem to dat but ssince I don't do that i would n't know how it could go through trying to come out of it (2.29) LT 0:12:88
15 D: It's a problem? (1.04) LT 0:01:62
16 A: YEAH I THink ITS a REally big problem around here. LT 0:02:76

D begins turn eight by recycling the topic, and A responds after a 1.01 second pause.

A quickly concludes, and D recycles the topic. A briefly overlaps in turn 11, inquiring to whom the question is directed. A then intiates a turn after a 1.28 second pause. D recycles the topic in turn 13, and A responds after a 1.82 second turn. D then asks a follow up question after 2.29 seconds of pause, and after a 1.04 second pause at the conclusion of turn 16.

SUMMARY

In session one, each of the elders speaks at a slow pace. Pauses are long, ranging from 4.62 to 17.29. The sole instance of overlap is detailed, and the main speaker retains the turn. In session two, TRPs are long, ranging from 15.52 to 1.14, with the older participants showing longer TRPs before and after their turns. TRPs are shorter in session three than sessions one or two, ranging from 6.43 to 1.86. Session four features pauses between speakers ranging from 16.10, after speaker A, the eldest person in the conversation, to 1.37. The majority of pauses are much shorter than in sessions one, two, or three.

In session two, the youngest participant takes over a turn. In session four, a younger participant overtakes an older participant's turn after repeated attempts. Braithwaite (1981) asserts "silence as a communicative action is associated with social situations in which there is a known and unequal distribution of power among focal participants" (Braithwaite, 1981, p. 322). The instances of interruption, overlap, and overtaking a turn in session two and four do not support a traditional recognition and deference to the elder in the conversation.

Session five proceeds with pause lengths ranging from 9.33 to 1.67. No overlap occurs. Session six is marketedly different that those preceeding. There is a high degree of overlap, with pause length from 4.99 to 0.49. There is much less concern for space in terms of turn length. Warm Springs slang and more emphatic speech are characteristics of this conversation. Session six participants are closely age grouped and members of the same school system.

ACCULTURATION

One imporant factor in intergenerational speech style differences is the process of acculturation. After the turn of the century, the Federal administrative policy wherein Native Americans "might be absorbed into the prevailing civilization or be fitted to live in the presence of that civilization" (Meriam, 1928, p. 92). was widely supported. George Peter Murdock (1949) detailed the social organization of the Tenino, a region of the Wishram or Wasco, known for its importance as a crossroads of trade among groups, noting the long series of exchanges, and the importance of ceremony, speaking, and status. The pre-contact Columbia River Basin groups such as the Tenino, Sahaptin-speaking people, the Lutuamian-speaking Klamath, to the southeast the Shoshonean-speaking Northern Paiute, the Umatilla, a Sahaptin-speaking group closely linked to the Teninos, the Klikitat and two Chinookan speaking groups, the Wascocs on the southbank of the Columbia River near the Dalles and the Wishram on the north bank in Washington intermingled in trade, in celebration, in language, and in marriage (Murdock, 1949).

Tribes were later grouped by geography rather than culture, further intermingling tribes and languages (Murdock, 1949). Leslie Spier and Edward Sapir (1939) noted in a study of the Wishram group, later called Wasco, that one obstacle to learning about the ethnographic and linguistic tradtions in the Columbia Basin group was the shortage in numbers and the loss of native culture among the few survivors, and the unwillingness on the part of some informants.

World War II saw a great migration of Native Americans from reservations to military service and travel. Returning veterans soon found the Bureau of Indian Affairs exerting pressure on parents to send their children to dormitory schools, often far from home, where English was the dominant language (McNickle, D'Arcy, & Pfrommer, 1964) A Warm Springs elder stated in the recorded discussions that Warm Springs Tribal members who attended boarding schools were forbidden to speak their native languages, and severely punished if they were discovered doing so. Contributing to this effort to assimilate at the time was the distinct likelihood that tribal status would be terminated.[1]

Dr. Sol Tax, supported by Emil Schwarhaupt Foundation, noted "for years Indians have been more or less isolated from the mainstream of American life. The movement of Indians to urban centers ... now proves an unparalleled opportunity to interpret the city to all American Indians. The rapidly growing number of reservation Indians who come the city and stay a few months for always and learn of life here may well turn out to be to be the first really important channel of communication between Indian communities and the general American society (Tax, 1956; Tjerandsen, 1980, p. 52)." The very channel of communication Tax details may have contributed to the deterioration of an existing channel across native generations.

CONCLUSION

In session one, the shortest turn relevance place length is 4.62. In session six, the longest turn relevance place is 4.99. In sessions two and four, an elder speaker is overlapped and their turn taken over by a younger speaker. Closely age grouped conversations have closely grouped turn relevance pause lengths. Elders allow for more space between turns, between other elders and younger members, while young participants allow less time to pass after an elder or peer concludes before speaking. Extended pauses are taken by elders usually without challenge.

When to speak and when to be silent are as yet unresolved issues and it appears that the multi-generational participants also share in this dilemma. Participants range in experience as well as age. As a child, the oldest participant interacted with her grandparents who were they themselves children at the signing of the Treaty which formed the Reservation in 1855. The youngest have not known a day without television. If the elders are to pass on traditional values and culture, effective intergenerational communication needs to occur. As in sessions two and four, if an elder is interrupted, the perceived rudeness will pre-empt them from taking another turn and the information will not be passed along. What a mid-turn extended pause is to an elder may be interpreted as a long transitional relevance place by a younger member. A better understanding of intergenerational speech style differences among all participants in the conversation may improve its tone and quality.

There is a need to replicate this study in both Warm Springs and other native nations. For now, it serves to highlight the trend away from silence, towards shorter pauses and increased overlap, in Warm Springs conversations.

ACKNOWLEDGEMENTS

My thanks to the late Pierson Mitchell, Warm Springs elder, Harry Millstein, for access to the Warm Springs Culture and Heritage Department's historical archives, Tom Bruneau, Radford University, for his encouragement, and Bob Nofsinger, Washington State University, for his introduction to the study of conversation. This study was a direct outgrowth of The Robert Wood Johnson Foundation sponored *Healthy Nations* program.

DISCUSSION QUESTIONS

1. How could you extend this study with a qualitative methodology?
2. How could you extend this study with a quantitative methodology?
3. What are the strengths of this study? The weaknesses?
4. What additional research in this field of study has been represented in recent literature?
5. How does this study relate to other studies on similar topics, in similar cultural groups, or with similar methodologies?

NOTES

[1] The Eisenhower adminstration processed legislation to terminate tribal status which had disastrous effects on many tribes, most notably the Menominee and the Klamath tribes. Nixon called for a reversal of the policy in 1971, and the Commissioner of Indian Affairs "announced abandonment of the relocation policy in favor of development on or near reservations, with greater control of programs in the hands of the Indians themselves" (Tjerandsen, 1980, p. 71).

REFERENCES

Basso, K. A. (1970). To Give up on words: Silence in Western Apache culture. In D. Carbaugh (Ed). *Cultural communication and intercultural contact* (pp. 301-318). Hillsdale, NJ: Laurence Erlbaum.

Button, G., & Lee, J. R. E., (Eds.) (1987). *Talk and social organisation* (pp. 9-18). Avon,England: Multilingual Matters Ltd.

Braithwaite, C. A. (1981). Communicative silence: A cross-cultural study of Basso's hypothesis. In D. Carbaugh (Ed). *Cultural communication and intercultural contact* (pp. 319-334). Hillsdale, NJ: Laurence Erlbaum

Bruneau, T. (1974). Time and nonverbal communication. *Journal of Popular Culture, 8,* 658-666.

Bruneau, T. (1980). Chronemics and the verbal-nonverbal interface. In M.R. Key (Ed.), *The relationship of verbal and nonverbal communication* (pp.101-117). The Hague: Mouton.

Bruneau, T. (1985). Silencing and stilling processes: The creative and temporal bases of signs. *Semiotica, 56,* 279-290.

Bruneau, T. (1988). Personal time and self-identity. In P. Reale (Ed.), *Time and identity* (pp. 102-115). Milano: F. Angeli.

Bruneau, T. (1989). The deep structure of intrapersonal processes. In C. Roberts and K. Watson (Eds.) *Interpersonal communication processes: Original essays* (pp. 69-86). Scottsdale, AZ: Gorsuch Scarsbrick.

Bruneau, T. (1990). Chronemics: The study of time in human interaction. In J. DeVito & M. Hecht (Eds.), *The nonverbal reader* (pp. 301-311). Prospect Heights, Ill.: Waveland Press.

Bruneau, T. (1995). Subjective time, social interaction, and personal identity. In H. B. Mokros (Ed.), *Interaction and identity: Information and behavior* (vol. 6, pp. 119-145). New Brunswick, NJ: Transaction Publishers.

Bruneau, T. & Ishii, S. (1988). Communicative silence: East and West. *World Communication, 17,* 1-33.

Goodenough, W. (1976) Multi-culturalism as normal human experience. In M.Gibson, (Ed.) *Anthropological perspectives on mulit-cultural education, Anthropology and Education Quarterly VII,* 4-7.

Gudykundst, W. (1987). Cross cultural comparisions. In C.R. Berger & S.H. Chaffee Eds. *Handbook of communication science* (pp. 818-847). Newbury Park, CA: Sage.

Gudykundst, W. (1985). Normative power and conflict potential in intergroup relationships. In W. Gudykunst, L. Stewart, & S. Ting-Toomey (Eds.), *Communication, culture, and organizational processes.* Newbury Park, CA: Sage

Gudykundst, W., & Kim, Y. Y. (1984). *Communicating with strangers.* Reading, MA: Addison-Wesley

Harrison, R. P. (1981). *The cartoon: Communication to the quick.* Beverly Hills: Sage

Hymes, D. (1967). On Communicative competence, Manuscript. Referenced in S.U. Philips (1983). *The invisible culture: Communication in classroom and community on the Warm Springs Indian Reservation* (pp. 58-61). Prospect Heights, IL: Waveland Press.

Levinson, S. (1983). *Pragmatics.* Cambridge: Cabridge University Press.

McNickle, D., D'Arcy, M., & Pfrommer, V. G. (1964). Dinetxa: A community experience. In C. Tjerandsen *Education for citizenship: A foundation's experience* (p. 16). Santa Cruz, CA: Emil Schwarhaupt Foundation, Inc.

Meriam, Lewis, and Associates. (1928). The Problem of Indian administration. In D. McNickle (Ed.) *Native American tribalism: Indian survivals and renewals* New York: Columbia University Press

Murdock, G. P. (1949). Social organization of the Tenino. *Miscellanea P. Rivet, Octogenario Dicata* (pp. 298-315). From the archives of the Culture and Heritage Department of the Confederated Tribes of the Warm Springs Reservation of Orgeon.

Philips, S. U. (1983). *The invisible culture: Communication in classroom and community on the Warm Springs Indian Reservation* (pp. 58-61). Chicago, IL: Waveland Press.

Sacks, H., Schegloff, E. A., & Jefferson, G. (1974) A simplest systematics for the organisation of turn-taking for conversation. *Language, 50,* 696-735.

Spier, L. & Sapir, E. (1939) "Wishram ethnography." *University of Washington Publications in Anthropology* (vol. 3, pp.151-300) From the archives of the Culture and Heritage Department of the Confederated Tribes of the Warm Springs Reservation of Orgeon

Tjerandsen, C. (1980). *Education for citizenship: A foundation's experience.* Santa Cruz, CA: Emil Schwarhaupt Foundation, Inc.

Tax, S. (1956). The Schwarhaupt Foundation Tama Indian Program, report of activities 1955-56. In C. Tjerandsen *Education for citizenship: A foundation's experience.* Santa Cruz, CA: Emil Schwarhaupt Foundation, Inc.

Zimmerman, D. H. (1988). On conversation: The conversation analytic perspective. *Communication Yearbook II* (pp. 406-432). Newbury Park: Sage.

17

THE NATURE AND CULTURE OF CONFLICT— THE INDIAN CASE: SOME COMMUNICATION IMPLICATIONS

Closepet N. Ramesh, Ph.D.
Truman State University

In the natural world, the world of plants and animals, conflict takes the form of the struggle for survival. Food and space, for animals and plants respectively, are scarce resources, and each species and every individual animal and plant is subject to the laws and vagaries of nature; the food chain is well-established, and it seems that every animal has imprinted in its being the knowledge of what it can eat, what can pose danger to it, and what it can pose danger to. Conflict, in the form of survival needs, is thus "natural" to the non-human world: it just is—it cannot be chosen, nor can it be rejected. But human beings, while part of the natural world, seem saddled with conflicting ideas of conflict. We wish to escape conflict, we sometimes deliberately seek conflict, we are unsure of the nature of the outcome of conflict, we have strategies to deal with conflict, and we imagine what it would mean to live without conflict. Liberating and burdensome at the same time, the human mind and the human spirit are constantly warring with themselves and with other minds and spirits, and constantly seeking reconciliation. This paradoxical pursuit is a strange and unique phenomenon in the human world, and this paper clearly should not be expected to resolve the paradox!

Instead, it has the limited purpose of seeking to describe and explain conflict in a particular (and yet large) context, and propose ways of productive conflict interaction in that context.

Before taking the step of describing and explaining the nature and culture of conflict in the Indian context, it is necessary to first define conflict. Most scholars now agree that conflict not only is about the pursuit of incompatible goals by people or groups, but it is also the *perception* of incompatible goals, and the *interdependence* of the two or more people or groups in conflict. So, for example, Hocker and Wilmot (1985), define conflict as the interaction of interdependent people who perceive incompatible goals and interference from each other in achieving those goals. Elaborating on this definition, Folger, Poole, and Stutman (1993) point out that the most important feature of conflict is *interaction*. Without interaction, conflict is not present and cannot be sustained. The focus on interaction, or behaviors, will enable us to understand and manage conflict better. The next feature of conflict is the *perception* of conflict by interactants. Perception or beliefs or interpretations of incompatible goals play an important role in conflict. However, Folger and co-workers caution that this does not mean that goals are always conscious, and that people can and do act without a clear sense of their goals and interests. Perception, of course, is mostly shaped by *communication* or the lack or impropriety of it.

People's interactions are shaped or influenced by their *interdependence*. Without interdependence there is little or no consequence (And if we believe in an interconnected world, then we cannot not be interdependent!). Interdependence means that the conflicting parties can potentially hinder or help each other. Thus, "conflicts are always characterized by a mixture of incentives to cooperate and to compete" (Folger, Poole, & Stutman, 1993, p. 5).

The arenas of conflict range from the interpersonal to group to intergroup conflict. Interpersonal conflict is between two or a small number of people; group conflict involves a larger number of people who are members of a larger unit; and intergroup conflict involves "two or more large groups of people who represent some political or ideological stance or who are members of cultural, community, action, or neighborhood groups" (Folger, Poole, & Stutman, 1993, p. 7).

These arenas of conflict are characterized by different types of interdependence, but whatever the nature of interdependence, we have to remember that interaction is key to conflicts. Also, conflicts can be productive or destructive. Coser (1956) distinguished between realistic and non realistic conflicts, describing realistic conflicts as those based on disagreements over the means to an end or the ends themselves, and unrealistic conflicts as expressions of aggression aimed at defeating or hurting the other. Folger and colleagues (1993) point out that productive conflicts depend upon flexibility of the parties, and destructive conflicts are characterized by the inflexibility of parties. In productive conflicts there is an expectation or belief that all parties can attain important goals; whereas destructive conflict is based on a win-lose premise.

A survey of conflict studies done by communication scholars shows that studies so far have been done mostly using American and British subjects (Folger, Poole, & Stutman, 1993). They, along with others (Avruch, Black, & Scimecca, 1991; Krauss, Rohlen, & Steinhoff, 1984; Miller & Bersoff, 1992; Ross, 1993), acknowledge that conflict styles differ among groups and among cultures, and that it may prove difficult to use information and knowledge gathered in one society to effectively analyze conflict situations in another society. (It is interesting to note that the term *conflict* doesn't even appear in the index of the *Handbook of International and Intercultural Communication* published in 1989.) Deutsch (1973) also notes that conflict resolution will be strongly influenced by the context within which the conflict occurs. Ross (1993) and Avruch and Black (1991) argue that the culture of conflict—a society's norms, practices, and institutions—affects what people fight about, the culturally approved ways of pursuing goals in disputes, the institutional support or resources that shape the process or course of conflicts, and the outcomes of those conflicts. Ross (1993) also points out that there is great variation from society to society in both the amount of conflict and the responses to conflict. Viewing conflict as cultural behavior will help explain why disputes over seemingly similar issues can and are dealt with differently in different societies. Avruch (1991) concludes that the most important perspective on conflict and conflict resolution is the necessity to place them "in a larger sociocultural context and not isolate them from the encompassing worlds-of-meaning in which, in ongoing ways, they remain embedded. In particular, attention must be paid to the native's understandings of human nature and personhood (self and others)—and affect—as the starting points of our enquiries" (p.15).

THE CASE FOR STUDYING INDIA

India is the second most populous country in the world with about 900 million people (estimated 1994 figures). About 28 percent of the population live in urban areas, and the rest in about 75,000 villages. In terms of ethnic diversity, 72 percent are Indo-Aryan, 25 percent Dravidian, and three percent Mongoloid. Sixteen major languages, and many hundred dialects spoken by a diverse population—83 percent Hindu, 11 percent Muslim, three percent Christian, two percent Sikh, and the remaining one percent made up of Parsis, Jains, Jews, and others—make this a truly polyglot country (USNWR, 1993). Having gained independence in 1947 after about 150 years of British rule, this, the largest democracatic country in the world, confronts its own set of problems of order and conflict.[1] The study of conflict (its nature, genesis, and consequences) and conflict resolution in the Indian context is rather scattered and not well organized. Other than the surfeit of articles in popular media, there are only a few scholarly attempts at studying conflict. The authors, many of them political scientists, focus more on a socio-structural explanation of conflict than on the cross-cultural, social-psychological, and communication perspectives needed to bear on their theses.[2] The small number of books on the subject, while welcome adumbrations, are by historians and journalists who have their own selective and somewhat restricted perspectives.[3] However, all of these works constitute a rich resource base for those interested in understanding the culture and nature of conflict in India, and contribute to the scholarship in that area. For the purposes of this paper, the argument can be made that intercultural communication scholars have neglected an important area of research and that lacuna needs to be filled. In this paper therefore I will provide a theoretical perspective for explaining and understanding conflict, summarize the literature on conflict phenomena in India under the theoretical rubric laid down, discuss a few communication implications, and conclude with some suggestions for appropriate communication strategies for conflict resolution in that context.

THEORETICAL PERSPECTIVES—CULTURE OF CONFLICT

I will draw upon two theoretical perspectives to provide both a convenient and an easy handle for understanding conflict in the Indian context. The two theories are the socio-structural conflict theory (SSCT) and the psycho-cultural conflict theory (PCCT). For an understanding of the two, I mostly rely on Ross' (1993) work.[1]

SSCT does not seek to explain individual conflict incidents; instead, it focuses on forces or structures that make a society more or less prone than another to particular levels and forms of conflict and violence. As Ross puts it, "the organization of the society determines which outcome is most likely" (p. 35). SSCT has two goals. First, "it uses the structure of society to understand who is likely to initiate conflict with whom…" and on such factors as "how, where, and with whom people spend their time and share common resources." Second, "social structure offers an explanation of how conflicts, once started, develop. The relationship between the original disputants and the extent to which it reinforces other societal divisions determine whether or not a dispute is likely to escalate… and… how different groups are likely to be aligned" (p. 35). Ross points out that the usefulness of SSCT lies in the clear way it portrays group interests and the actions groups take to pursue them. However, there are some problems with the theory. For example, it posits that there could be alternative bases for conflict. It would be more useful if it could specify which interests would be more crucial in which situations. Also, it does not explain the relationship between individuals and groups, the role of consciousness in group action, and how potential conflicts are translated into action (Ross, p. 47). The limitations of the theory can be bridged with support from PCCT.

PCCT accounts for conflict behavior in terms of motives for action rooted in culturally shaped images and beliefs of the external world. The term psycho-cultural refers to psychological processes whose patterns and content are pervasive within a culture. One of the examples that Ross gives of such patterns is the shared norms regarding disciplining disobedient children. Another is the primordial nature of culturally shared targets of ethnic hostility. These psycho-cultural dispositions are culturally shared response tendencies acquired through mechanisms that are spelled out in psycho-dynamic and social learning theories. Dispositions are "fundamental orientations vis-a-vis the self and others and include culturally learned and approved methods for dealing with others both within and outside one's community" (Ross, 1993, p. 51). The interpretations shared by community members enable them to act, relieve them of anxiety and ambiguity, and infuse actions with intense social and political meanings. As can be expected, these interpretations are also the source of cognitive and perceptual distortions.

PCCT, Ross argues, provides a strong challenge to the anti-psychological view of conflict. It does so by addressing the problem of "intensity" of some conflicts, by viewing society as more than the family writ large (as it was for Freud), and by making us aware of the importance of understanding how intra-personal and cultural frameworks, not just objective conditions, shape social action. Pointing out that humans are predisposed to establish social bonds from birth and that strong ties to others have important adaptive significance, Ross argues that an individual's external experiences thus provide the raw material for constructing the person's internal world, which in turn fuels action. In terms of conflict interaction then we not only need to identify who the allies and enemies are, but how they can be expected to behave.

Identifying psycho-cultural dispositions related to conflict and violence therefore requires the specifications of mechanisms linking early learning to personality formation and adult behavior. Making specific hypotheses, Ross submits that a) harsh socialization makes it difficult to establish bonds with others later in life, and is likely to be associated with low levels of trust in social relations and exaggerated emphasis on social (or political) attachments as a compensatory mechanism; b) open expression of affection toward children, greater emphasis on values such as trust, honesty, and generosity, and closer father-child ties encourage individuals to develop social skills needed to resolve conflicts without violence; and c) a good deal of aggressive action is compensatory behavior arising out of male gender-identity confusion, and so in cultures in which male gender-identity conflict is common, disputes escalate rapidly and resolving them is difficult as long as individuals continue to see the outcomes as related to identity issues and self-worth.

THE NATURE AND CULTURE OF CONFLICT IN INDIA— A SUMMARY AND AN ANALYSIS

Like any other old culture, Indian society has experienced a myriad of conflicts, many local, quite a few regional, and a fair number societal. History books take us through a number of them, and tell us whether the conflicts were based on religious, communal, ethnic, racial, or other grounds. A country's history influences its present postures and predilections. Embree (1990) writes that "the truly astonishing factor in Indian civilization is the endurance and persistence of its style and patterns," and indicts Hinduism's encapsulation of other religions as neither "toleration, absorption, nor synthesis." He is thus rather pessimistic of the outcome of conflict and violence in India which he argues are neither "senseless and random" but "a way of changing things." While Embree has long studied India, and his analyses are rather carefully drawn, India (like many other non-western societies) has been saddled with a variety of cultural stereotypes. These stereotypes are then used simplistically to explain the problems that confront the nation (Moog, 1993). Some of the stereotypes are now being challenged through some interesting empirical work (see Moog, 1993; Chibber, Misra, & Sisson, 1992; Price, 1993). However, to understand the "culture" of conflict in India we need both some structural and some psycho-cultural perspectives. Also, we need to keep in mind the interpersonal and inter-group levels of conflict. First, let me deal with the inter-group level of conflict.

Major and rather persistent inter-group conflict in modern India is usually based on separatist nationalism (for example, the Punjab and Kashmir conflicts), religion based (mostly Hindu-Muslim clashes), caste based (a variety of higher caste atrocities committed most often in the northern states of Uttar Pradesh and Bihar, and the southern state of Andhra Pradesh; this is not to deny that such conflicts don't occur in other states), and more rarely language based (for example, the anti-Hindi riots in Tamil Nadu in the 1960s and 1970s).[4] Most recent analyses of the Indian situation has focused on one incident—the destruction of the Babri Mosque on December 6, 1992 in the town of Ayodhya. This town in the state of Uttar Pradesh in Northern India was the target of militant Hindus who claimed that the mosque built by Babur, the first Mughal emperor, in the sixteenth century was built on the ground on which stood a Hindu temple for Rama.[5] The destruction of the mosque by a mob that was politically organized by militant Hindus was followed by communal violence and riots across the country in which more than two thousand people died, the majority of them Muslims (Sen, 1993). The Bharatiya Janata Party (BJP) and its affiliated organizations, including the Shiv Sena (a regional political party in the state of Maharashtra) which were mostly responsible for fueling the destruction of the mosque have gone on to demand an official end to Indian secularism. A variety of commentators have thus focused their analyses of conflict based on the Ayodhya incident in particular, and Hindu-Muslim division in general. These are perceptive analyses. However, the contexts for their analyses are sometimes restricted to the immediate, and sometimes only to the religious dimension. To understand the nature and culture of conflict in India, it is imperative that we cast our net wider to include the disjunctures in life brought about by the process of modernization. Modernization implies not just changing our exterior world but acknowledging the profound changes it brings about in our inner world. To understand these changes (and here the PCCT angle will work well) we need to understand how the life of ordinary Indians have changed in terms of domestic patterns of tradition, ritual, child-rearing, and so on.

First, let me explain the Ayodhya incident from a social structural conflict theory perspective. From a SSCT perspective we need to look at the structure of society to understand who is likely to initiate conflict with whom. And to understand the structure of Indian society we need some historical background. Singh (1990) posits that India may be seen to have gone through three major transformations historically: 1) "from lineage-based, primitive political systems to the origin of the state in the post-Vedic period and on the tribal peripheries of Brahmanical, Indo-Islamic, and Indo-British civilizations throughout Indian history;" 2) "from regional kingdoms to sub-continental imperial states dotting the entire historical landscape, beginning at least with the Maurya empire in Magadha in the fourth to second centuries B.C. (sic) and culminating in the British colonial state in the nineteenth and twentieth centuries;" and 3) "from empire to nation-state following the British withdrawal in 1947" (p. 809). Within these transformations is contained two competing world views: the society-centered and state-centered conceptions of a political system (Singh, 1990; see also Gurumurthy, 1994). These competing ideologies can be found to have a long historical tradition.

The society-centered view originated in the Rig Vedic times (ca. 1500-1200 B.C.E.), and was essentially a pre-state lineage system based on uni-lineal kinship differentiated by age, family and household production, and through the exchange of gifts and tributes ritually. The society-centered polity survived the emergence of monarchical and republican states in the post-Vedic period until overwhelmed by the Mauryan state centered in the capital of Pataliputra.[6] After the decline of the Mauryan empire, the society-centered polity re-emerged and was reinforced by the rise of feudalism during the Gupta regime.[7] Singh (1990) says that the normative archetype for such a polity can be found in the *Dharmashastras* (law books) that outline the classical Hindu conception of political order in which "the state was expected to protect rather than supersede the caste, guild, and feudal autonomies of a society based on the idealized *varnashrama dharma*."[8] The Cholas (tenth and eleventh centuries) and the Vijayanagara kingdom (fourteenth to sixteenth centuries) in South India also displayed a political order in which society and state coexisted in a symbiotic relationship, though Vijayanagara, at the height of its glory, was probably the only Hindu warring state (Singh, 1990). The medieval Muslim kingdoms and the British colonial state belong to the strong state tradition.

Singh posits that similar competing ideologies can be found in modern Indian political thought. Religious communalists, proponents of economic free enterprise, and Gandhian communitarians, for example, are all essentially for a society-centered conception of political order (though, as can be surmised, for different reasons). The statist tradition, on the other hand, is supported by Nehruvian developmentalists, and secular and communal nationalists (also for different reasons, and thus making strange bedfellows). These competing ideologies, and the perceptions of opportunities and dangers within such systems of governance, fuel and sustain some of the major inter-group conflicts. Given the present global order made up of nation states, what chance is there for India to be other than a nation state? And what does a nation state imply for those contending parties with competing ideologies?

When the British left, India was partitioned into India and Pakistan. Pakistan chose to be an Islamic Republic, whereas India chose to be a secular democratic republic. Secularism, Sen (1993) points out, is part of a comprehensive idea—that India is an integrally pluralist country, made up of different religious beliefs, distinct language groups, divergent social practices, etc. But this idea of secularism is both too broad and undifferentiated in the Indian context. Varshney (1993) distinguishes between three different types of nationalism in India: a secular nationalism, a Hindu nationalism, and two separatist nationalisms in the state of Punjab and Kashmir. Hindu nationalism, he argues, is a reaction to the two other nationalisms. Madan (1987), and Nandy (1988) argue that secularism is intrinsically unsuited to India though they too "do not sufficiently differentiate varieties of secularism" (Varshney, 1993, p. 228). Separatist nationalisms (Kashmir, Punjab) have threatened the integrity of India as a nation state. The other two nationalisms, while committed to India's territorial integrity, are seeking to pursue it in different ways. For separatists, Kashmir and Punjab are different nations, while Indian nationalists claim that Kashmiris and Punjabis are ethnic groups, not nations. Secular nationalists seek to preserve the geographical unity of India, and include all ethnic and religious groups in its definition of a nation. They consider giving security to the various groups as integral to nation building. For Hindu nationalists, however, Hinduism is the source of India's identity, and it alone can provide national cohesiveness. Non-Hindu groups can become a part of India only through assimilation, they argue (see Gurumurthy, 1994). They point out that Parsis and Jews have become part of the nation's mainstream. Christianity, with the departure of the British, has lost its political edge. Thus, Muslims are the principal adversaries of the Hindu nationalists. They do not want to exclude Muslims from India, but to become part of India, Muslims must agree to four things: 1) accept the centrality of Hinduism to Indian civilization; 2) acknowledge Hindu figures such as Rama (or Ram, as the North Indians prefer to pronounce the name) as civilizational heroes, not just as religious figures; 3) acknowledge that Muslim rulers destroyed many pillars of Hindu civilization, especially Hindu temples; and 4) make no claims to special privileges, such as the maintenance of religious personal laws (see Varshney, 1993, for further elaboration).

Hindu nationalists provide their own rationale for why they want *Hindutva* (or political Hinduism). Gurumurthy (1994), one of their prominent intellectuals, argues that in India society and individuals were the pivots around which the polity revolved, and that the state was merely a residuary concept. This enabled the people to develop a variety of institutions and accept diversity of thought and practice. Whereas, the Semitic tradition of the West, with its centralizing tendencies, invested the state with supreme power. He goes on to develop this premise to claim that that was how India survived—not as a state but as a society—from onslaughts by foreign invaders. He then posits that whereas the Christian West evolved dynamically from a theocratic state to a secular state, then to a democracy which is giving way to a commercial and technological state, Islam is a story of "1500 years of unmitigated stagnation" (p. 51) because anyone who attempted to start a variant of the faith, or argue about its tenets were severely dealt with. The encounter between the "inclusive" Hinduism and the "exclusive" Islam in India has left behind an "unassimilated Islamic society," he claims. The Hindu nationalist movement, he suggests, is the Indian contribution for a review of the "conservative and extremist Islamic attitudes towards non-Islamic faiths and societies" (p. 52), and that secular nationalists are beating up on Hindu nationalists only to garner Muslim votes. The Indian problem cannot be divorced from the international Islamic politics and the world's reaction to it, he suggests.

From a SSCT point of view we can see how different positions in the social structure produce different interests among individuals. It would direct our attention to forces which make the Indian society more or less prone to violence and conflict. It is especially useful in explaining the particular targets of aggressive actions, and why one target is chosen over another. Thus, for example, forces that increase group cohesion (Hindu nationalism) and limit conflict (for example, intragroup Hindu conflict, or conflict between Hindus and Christians) may also make aggression against an outgroup (for example, Muslims) more likely. Secular nationalists perceive only Hindu nationalists as the catalysts of violence and conflict. They ignore pan-Islamic and international Islamic forces and their influence on the Indian, especially Indian-Muslim polity. They have also been hesitant to take on separatist nationalists, targeting their criticisms mostly on the corrupt, communal, opportunist politics of mainstream political parties and the government at the Centre. Separatist nationalists, in turn, have sought support for their cause both in terms of *materiel* and ideology from outside (for example, from Pakistan, expatriate Sikhs, international forums, and some anti-Indian Republican politicians in the U.S., and conservative politicians in the U.K.). Hindu nationalists focus their energies on opposing Muslims. Meanwhile, opportunist politicians of all ilks, in the garb of secularism and nationalism cater to vote banks, which in turn become both outgroups and targets of violence and discrimination.[9] This focus on Hindu-Muslim structural forces should not blind us to various other forces and groups that coalesce to produce common interests. In a very interesting study, Chibber and colleagues (1992) provide evidence that conflict and the "problem of order" in India today is perceived more as a national, less as a state, and not really as a local-level phenomenon. The study points out that many Indians perceive the major public problems to be economic and infrastructural, and that the "problem of order" is most pronounced in the perceptions of upper class, urban, alienated, and forward caste members.

Hindu nationalists complain that secularism in India is pseudo-secularism, a term that the BJP leader Advani uses to describe what he thinks is an excessive appeasement of minorities in India.[11] While minorities are represented fairly well in the upper layers of Indian bureaucracy and politics, as well as cultural layers (see Varshney, 1993), Muslims and many of the Scheduled Caste and Scheduled Tribes are among the poorest and least educated communities in the country. But Sikhs, for example, are among the most well-to-do and educated sections of the population. Varshney (1993) argues that when principled secularism (like the kind Nehru practiced) was replaced by unprincipled secularism (embodied in the politics of Indira Gandhi and Rajiv Gandhi, and now filtered down and assimilated into every level of Indian politics), India's secular project began to unravel. An interesting and useful study from a SSCT perspective would be to list oppositional forces in the country. Such a list, with a description of the historical, political, and economic reasons for such oppositions would enable us to understand the dynamics of present day conflict and violence, and help us choose carefully strategies to minimize such conflicts.

Psycho-culturally, we can see the construction, or attempts at construction of a new Hindu identity. Kakar (1994) says there are a few well-marked steps in the construction of this identity: first, there is a marking of the boundary of the Hindu community by hailing selected gods[10] and heroes, and offering them up as ego ideals to be shared by community members and for bringing about group cohesion; second, the marking of boundaries is followed by invoking actual or perceived events of shared loss (for example, the supposed destruction of the temple in Ayodhya by Babur); third, the addressing of perceived threats from inimical forces, and how those forces should be defeated; and fourth, the idealizing of the ingroup and the demonizing or scape-goating of the outgroup. The demonizing of the outgroup is a reflection of the ingroup's anxiety about its own identity. Thus, the Hindu self-image—that of a tolerant, compassionate group—exposes what it fears about itself—"the specific Hindu shame and fear of being cowardly and impotent to change the material or social conditions of his life" (Kakar, 1994, p. 45). This vulnerable self then has to be shored up through forceful action so that the group becomes more cohesive. This follows Ross' (1993) PCCT in that psycho-cultural explanations enable us to understand conflict or cooperation in terms of shared, deep-seated fears or threats to identity. Kakar says that a sense of superiority is invoked by all groups to serve the purpose of increasing group cohesion, and thus the enhancement of self-esteem of its members. The problem though is when this narcissism becomes deviant. Kakar believes that though there is no "standard" against which to measure such narcissistic deviance, "a group wherein all individual judgement is suspended and reality-testing severely disturbed, may legitimately be regarded as pathological" (p. 46). Kakar argues that the group pride that *Hindutva* forces engender has made it possible for them to provide an alternative vision of India's future to the ones offered by the modernists (for example, secular nationalists) and the traditionalists (for example, neo-Gandhians). While modernists are votaries of the modernization project and don't consider the importance of cultural authenticity, the traditionalists reject the modernity project solely on the basis of cultural authenticity. Kakar claims that Hindu nationalists have reformulated the modernity project in "a way that its instrumentalities are adopted but its norms and values are contested. The pivotal issue for them is not whether to accept global techno-science and the economic institutions and forms of modernity, but the impact such acceptance will have on the project to salvage Hindu culture and identity—as defined by them" (p. 46).

This Hindu culture and identity sought to be carved out by Hindu nationalists who, as Kakar points out, seek to conserve only certain aspects of the Hindu past by silencing contrary interpretations is authoritarian by nature. Nandy (1980) provides a perceptive analysis of the Hindu authoritarian personality. The authoritarian is basically a sadomasochistic character, who is a sadist with regard to the targets of his destructiveness and a masochist when it comes to authority figures. Such a person is the product of a repressive family and disciplinarian parents. There are variations of this basic personality. For example, instead of identifying with parental authorities, the person may rebel against them and generalize the rebellion to all authority, rational or irrational, democratic or not. This is in brief the portrait of the authoritarian (see Nandy, for a fine summary of the authoritarian personality). Nandy argues that what technology and science did to the West and to creating authoritarian/fascist tendencies among the marginalized, political and social change is now doing to India. An expanding sector of marginalized and incompletely socialized people on the one hand, and those searching for order, security, and meaning on the other constitute the authoritarian tendency in India. Such people have the conviction that an internally consistent, unambiguous, ethical system is necessary for social progress and moral growth. This is in fact the very anti-thesis of the Indian worldview which stresses "ideological flexibility and structural rigidity."

Nandy says that the Indian fascist is a lonely man compared to his Western counterpart, and that he handles his loneliness by idealizing his loneliness and isolation as indicators of his moral superiority and piety. While he may stress duties and obligations, it is not so much to establish group identity as much as to give meaning to his "unreal world where neither the aggressor nor the victim is real and where suffering does not have the concreteness of a real-life event" (p. 106). A number of studies of the Indian personality show that the individual lives in his inner world less with a feared father than with a powerful, aggressive and unreliable mother. He doubts his mother's nurturance, and sees his father as a co-victim of his castrating mother. Thus, the mother serves the Indian as his ultimate model of authority, and this identification with the mother makes him a passive aggressive feminine character identifying with the ideology of "mother, motherland and mother-tongue." The Hindu concept of "Maya" (the unreality of the outer world) may then enable him to rationalize his own withdrawal from the world and the cynicism he develops in response to his distrust of his mother's nurturance. Ending up not making emotional investments in the outer world, he is the obverse of Indian spiritualism, Nandy argues.

Kakar (1981), in a seminal work, explores the Hindu self and world image. The traditional Hindu way of life provides an individual a certain patterned way of living which is a kind of template that enables them to absorb and accept the uncertainties and the ebb and flow of life. This Hindu way of life, whether consciously acknowledged or not, has influenced the Hindu's thinking, perceiving and experiencing.[1] The themes of *moksha* (self-realization, salvation, and the overcoming of the distinction between subject and object), *dharma* (law, moral duty, or conformity with the truth of things, the principle underlying social relations), and *karma* (namely, individual action and individual fate affected and influenced by each other through the endless cycle of birth, growth, and death, and how right action would intervene in this process) are the three essential ideas that influences and controls the Hindu's life and spiritualism. Kakar explores Indian spiritualism through the developmental significance of Hindu infancy and childhood, and how they influence Indian identity formation. He builds the psycho-social foundations of the Indian inner world using anthropological evidence, clinical data, mythology and folklore, and concludes that there are no insurmountable psychological obstacles for the traditional Indian identity to evolve in a manner that it maintains its historical continuity while integrating with a changing environment. He, however, cautions that there may be some individuals who would make determined efforts to restore an earlier and imagined "idyllic" state, and there would be still others who may regress and react with a depressive mode of apathy, resignation, and withdrawal.

For most Indians, social change has been gradual and the disjunctures brought about by modernization bearable. They therefore continue to remain "traditional" in the sense that their identity, their inner world is made up of the maternal cosmos of infancy and early childhood, Kakar claims. The economic is still subordinate to the religious, and so the spiritual quest is dominant over the material. However, with the kind of pressures being brought about by an increasingly interdependent, commercial, and technological world Indians are under great pressure to abandon their "cultural emphasis on the emotional, aesthetic and instinctual qualities of life, on the primary group relationships and on the communal sharing of responsibility for individual lives" (Kakar, 1981, p. 185). How Indians have reacted to such changes are now grist for our analytical mills. The Ayodhya incident and the events following it are one indicator of the effect of such environmental pressures. Kakar had predicted that these changes might trigger violence on inconsequential pretexts, as "individuals react with narcissistic rage to the attack on the idealized parental image incorporated and elaborated in traditional norms and cultural values" (p. 186). Following the regressive phase would be a phase in which people would frantically search for leadership, and submit uncritically to charismatic leaders without regard for their political ideology. That happened (and we still have residues of it) during the 1980s when Indira Gandhi, and her sons at the Centre, and various cult leaders like Bhindranwale in Punjab held sway over the masses, and the country was in the throes of the worst sort of confusion and conflict, and it seemed to some observers that Hindu culture could be caught up in too many internal contradictions, and that the Indian nation state could face the kind of Balkanization now being witnessed in the former Yugoslavia, or the kind of fundamentalist reaction against governments in Algeria, Egypt, and elsewhere.

In terms of interpersonal conflict, the Hindu way of life imposes certain strictures that may force individuals to deny conflict and to suppress it. Roland (1988) says that the profound social and psychological changes brought about by modernity influences the individual in three areas: decision making, child rearing, and institutional structures. The demand for greater autonomy and independent decision making by modern institutions of individuals has led to the experiencing of increased strain and anxiety by adult urban men. Such anxiety and strain is especially experienced after the death of a parent on whom they had depended for decisions. In the area of child rearing, conflict is generated when parents give ambivalent and conflicting signals to their children for greater freedom and autonomy on the one hand, and expecting them to be deferent and obedient on the other. Thus mother-in-law/daughter-in-law conflicts are common to almost every Hindu household, and innumerable films have story plots revolving around this theme. These conflicts, especially in joint-family households, have serious and tragic consequences with the kind of alignment of forces that are doomed for failure.[14] When women, because of the kind of sexual taboos in joint family households, channel their erotic feelings toward their sons, they increase the anxiety feelings in the sons who then develop a fear of women, mature love, and sexuality. The male child's identity with the mother leads to his supporting his mother in her battles with her daughter-in-law. The loss of control over her husband and her children leads the woman to extend a provocative sexual presence toward her sons, which leads to another vicious cycle (see Kakar, 1981; Barnouw, 1985).

Modern institutional structures borrowing western management practices seek to inculcate autonomy and individuality in its members but ignore the needs of the individual's familial self. Thus inefficiency, shirking of responsibility, delay, and passing the buck have become the hallmark of Indian organizations, especially government organizations.

Indians also exhibit a need to deny any issues of dissension where issues of conflict are to be discussed. Disagreement and conflict are usually swept under the rug, and agreements are made when there are no real agreements. Anger is contained, swallowed, or denied (Roland, 1988). The internalized structures in the Indian conscience thus severely inhibit the direct and open expression, and sometimes even awareness, ambivalence, anger, annoyance, and hostility, Roland points out. The emphasis on harmony and emotional connectedness at all costs lead to the expression of annoyance and anger nonverbally and indirectly, occasionally building up to an outburst.

COMMUNICATION IMPLICATIONS

Dealing with inter-group conflict is a complex endeavor, and it takes the both the shrewd and the wise leader/s to deal with the problem strategically. For secular nationalists to make their case, it is imperative that they recognize (not just implicitly) the real and significant pan-Islamic influence on Indian politics and polity. To train their rhetorical guns only on Hindu nationalists is a sure way to alienate those moderate or undecided and mostly new middle class Hindus who seem to be committed to both nationalism and to the idea of a developed, techno-logical, modern Indian state. Hindu nationalists, who pay lip-service to the idea of pluralism and accommodation, and who have allowed the rise of fascist forces through the use of religious and sectarian symbolism and by acts of rampant and egregious violence, should understand that they are resorting to the classic, unpro-ductive conflict resolution strategy of win-lose. Not only that, they should realize that the large majority of lower caste Hindus will never support the kind of Hindu nationalism based on a crass version of higher caste religious and political values. The overt and overuse of religious symbols and metaphors will weaken and undermine the Hindu nationalists' quest for a strong, modern Indian state.

Nandy suggests that the way to curb authoritarianism in India is by building new institutions on the basis of its old traditions, by monitoring change and growth in society so that they don't destroy the basic dignity and self-esteem of the individual, by openly debating social choices, and by creating institutions that promote political leadership that don't take advantage of the latent tendency towards passive obedience and mindless aggression.

Implications for interpersonal communication and the resolution of conflict are discussed by Roland (1988). He says it is essential to take into account how resis-tance, transference, and counter-transference are influenced by the social and cul-tural factors that shape familial and individual relationships. Since heirarchical relationships are the norm—either in the family or institutional structures—indi-viduals are usually hesitant to express their thoughts and feelings, especially those of anger and hurt. Feelings are expressed only when there is some trust that the other will be receptive and confidentiality will be kept. Thus, for example, in terms of mother-in-law and daughter-in-law problems, the daughter-in-law usu-ally spends some time anguishing over and dealing with the acts of hurt and dis-regard by her in-laws. Gaining the trust of her husband and especially of her mother-in-law is fraught with anxiety. But once a relationship is established it is also more rewarding. As Roland puts it, "Indian relationships and communication are often overwhelmingly governed by varying subtle balances between the intense, emotional intimacy needs and wishes of the qualitative mode and the deeply internalized expectations of superior and subordinate in the structural hier-archy," and in the "daughter-in-law/mother-in-law relationship, structural hierar-chical expectations of deference and subordination strongly predominate over emotional intimacy in the early years of a young woman's marriage" (p. 221).

Because of the imbalance in hierarchical relationships, Indian communication, especially relating to conflict, have to be studied both at the verbal and nonverbal levels. The verbal communication is usually dictated by considerations of hierarchy and is therefore frequently indirect, implicit, and ambiguous, whereas the nonverbal communication can be either more positive or negative. Roland gives numerous examples from case studies to support his point. He also describes some of the nonverbal communication in conflict situations. These include: suddenly stopping talking; leaving the room; not eating the next meal while conveying that you are feeling fine; or simply walking around looking unhappy. These indirect expressions of hurt and anger are meant to shame the other person into realizing what s/he has done. Gandhi's tactic of going on fasts or *satyagraha* can be seen as coping with British acts of violence or Indian acts that he didn't concur with. Roland concludes that the acute sensitivity of most Indians to the moods and emotional states of the other, and therefore to the development of conscience, is due to close familial interdependence, whereas the American superego, for example, is trained for eventual autonomous adaptation in extrafamilial relationships.

In changing times, and under the influence of sweeping technological and social forces, the Indian (man) exhibits enormous identity conflicts, which in turn could influence his politics. We can see here how the interpersonal and social/ political coalesce, and thus strategies to reduce conflict and violence in India should take into account these familial factors. But as the Chinese say, where there is danger there is also opportunity. These kinds of identity issues provide Indian men opportunities for better integration into "an expanding self" (Roland, 1988, p. 332). Modernization and Westernization are making the Indian more individualistic. Roland believes that this movement will not lead to the kind of individualism that prevails in the West, but instead will be incorporated in a broader "familialism." This change, in the process of happening, can and will also generate considerable conflict.

What are the ways in which such conflict can be managed and directed toward productive ends? Sen (1993) points out that the lack of education, especially in the more nationalistic North, has contributed to the lumpenization of politics and to increasing violence and regressive nationalism. Varshney (1993) believes that the re-instituting of secular nationalistic ideals as espoused and practiced by Nehru would stem the tide toward disintegration and crass nationalism. Nandy (1980) says India has gone through a period of self-searching, and that Indian politics and society organized around Hindu culture, and not around an authoritative center, have different functional links with various groups and elements of Hindu tradition, and supports these groups and elements dispersing therefore the centers and play of power. And since the most respected from of power is power over self, according to the Hindu ideal, Indian power politics is recognized as amoral statecraft. Nandy says that the tradition in India is to alter the dominant culture from within, and so any abuses of power will be recognized from within and acted upon. I think all three commentators have valid points to make, and none is anti-thetical to the other.[15]

For the resolution of interpersonal conflicts one has to understand the nature and role of the Hindu familial system, and how it reinforces certain recurring patterns of behavior. The changes through modernization have chipped away at the joint family system and therefore at the pathology of conflict in such families.[16]

CONCLUSION

This paper makes the argument that the study of conflict in a variety of cultural contexts is woefully inadequate, and such studies are necessary to understand the nature and culture of conflict, and to design particular strategies for the resolution of those conflicts. Under the rubric of a socio-structural and psycho-cultural conflict theory it is argued that the roots and causes of inter-group and interpersonal conflict in India are varied, and some communication implications are drawn that should enable students of India and of intercultural communication to do some interesting work. Given the large context of India and Hindu culture, this paper should be considered a first, and rather imprecise template upon which to base future studies. However, I also believe that it gives students and scholars who are unfamiliar with the territory some important landmarks, and directs them to works and ideas that should prove fruitful if their interests are kindled.

NOTES

[1] The problem of order and conflict gets a lot of play in the media, and there have also been some scholarly concern. For example, the *Far Eastern Economic Review* (September 9, 1993) carried an article titled "The Coming Indian Crack-up." Another article in the same journal was titled "In Timeless India Time is Running Out." The *Asian Survey* (December 1992) had an article titled "India Adrift: The Search for Moorings in a New World Order," and the *World Press Review* (March 1994) contained an article with this headline, "How India Can Survive." For more such listings of articles with such dire titles see Chibber et al., "Order and the Indian Electorate: For Whom Does Shiva Dance?" *Asian Survey* (July 1992).

[2] For example, Chibber, Misra, and Sisson (July 1992) "Order and the Indian Electorate: For Whom Does Shiva Dance" in *Asian Survey*; Singh (August 1990) "The Crisis of the Indian State: From Quiet Developmentalism to Noisy Democracy" in *Asian Survey*; Mathur (April 1992) "The State and the Use of Coercive Power in India" in *Asian Survey*; Varshney (Summer 1993) "Contested Meanings: India's National Identity, Hindu Nationalism, and the Politics of Anxiety" in *Daedalus*; Price (May 1993) "Democracy and Ethnic Conflict in India: Precolonial Legacies in Tamil Nadu" in *Asian Survey*; and Moog (December 1993) "Indian Litigiousness and the Litigation Explosion: Challenging the Legend" in *Asian Survey* are all political scientists working and writing in the U.S. or in India.

[3] Embree (1990), a historian, has written *Utopias in Conflict: Religion and Nationalism in Modern India*; Bonner (1990), a journalist, is the author of *Averting the Apocalypse: Social Movements in India Today*; Nanda (1991), a scientist and Gandhian, is the author of *Conflicts and Coexistence: India*; the one author who brings a communication and conflict resolution perspective (Weber, 1991) in his book *Conflict Resolution and Gandhian Ethics* focuses less on the Indian context than on a general/global context. Two books, of much older vintage but which provide some fine analyses of the complexity of the conflict contexts in India are *Group Prejudices in India: A Symposium* (Nanavati & Vakil, 1951/1970), and Harrison's (1960) *India: The Most Dangerous Decades*.

[4] See Nanda (1991) for a comprehensive list of conflict situations and contexts in India.

[5] Sen (1993) points out that in certain parts of India (especially in the North and in the West) Rama is identified with divinity, but elsewhere (for example, in West Bengal) Rama is mainly the hero of the epic *Ramayana*, rather than God incarnate.

[6] Chandragupta, who is said to have met Alexander, assembled a force and seized the kingdom of Magadha. The accession of Chandragupta may be dated in 322 or 325 B.C.E. The family name Maurya is supposed to be derived from Mura, the mother of Chandragupta. The line of his successors down to about 184 B.C.E. is spoken of as the Mauryan empire or dynasty (Smith, 1972).

[7] Chandragupta I in 319-320 established the Gupta era to commemorate his coronation. The Gupta period, especially the fifth century, is regarded as the golden age of Northern India. The Gupta period lasted till about 650 (Smith, 1972).

[8] Social system of Hindus based on a partition into four classes and four stages of life.

[9] See Varshney (1993) and Sen (1993) for a more elaborate description of the influence of socio-structural forces.

[10] See Sen (1993) for an interesting and perceptive commentary on the choosing of Rama (or Ram) as the Hindu ideal/God, and how such a selection is biased and does not reflect regional differences.

[11] Muslims, Sikhs, Christians, and Buddhists were added to the Scheduled Castes and Tribes list, and together they now constitute 37 per cent of India's electorate. Compounding the problem and the confusion is the rush by a variety of castes and sub-castes to be included in what has been termed "Backward Classes List." So, in states like Karnataka and Tamil Nadu more than 80 percent of the population are listed as SC/ST or Backward classes. This has allowed politicians to play the game of "reservation"—reserving seats in medical and engineering colleges, and in government for these groups. For further elaboration on this topic, see Weiner's (1989) *The Indian Paradox*.

[12] See Sen (1993) for an interesting and perceptive commentary on the choosing of Rama (or Ram) as the Hindu ideal/God and how such a selection is biased and does not reflect regional differences.

[13] For an articulate and easy to follow summary of the Hindu way of life, see Kakar (1981), especially Chapter II.

[14] See Kakar (1981) especially chapters III and IV, Nandy (1980) chapters I and II, and Roland (1988) for fine discussions on child rearing and familial relationships and conflicts arising from them, as well as the nature and course of conflict resolution.

[15] I recognize this as rather a fairly simple generalization. The three commentators provide different and fairly lengthy analyses of their positions, and I recommend the curious reader the original texts.

[16]For specific recommendations on dealing with interpersonal conflict, from a Gandhian point of view, see Weber (1991), especially chapter III.

REFERENCES

Avruch, K. (1991). Introduction: Culture and conflict resolution. In K. Avruch, P.W. Black, & J.A. Scimecca (Eds.) *Conflict resolution: Cross-cultural perspectives* (pp. 1-17). New York: Greenwood Press.

Avruch, K., & Black, P.W. (1991). The culture question and conflict resolution. *Peace and Change, 16,* 22-45.

Avruch, K., Black, P.W., & Scimecca, J.A. (1991). *Conflict resolution: Cross-cultural perspectives.* New York: Greenwood Press.

Barnouw, V. (1985). *Culture and personality.* Homewood, IL: The Dorsey Press.

Bonner, A. (1990). *Averting the apocalypse: Social movements in India today.* Durham, NC: Duke University Press.

Chibber, P.K., Misra, S., & Sisson, R. (1992). Order and the Indian electorate: For whom does Shiva dance? *Asian Survey, 32,* 606-616.

Coser, L. (1956). *The functions of conflict.* New York: Free Press.

Deutsch, M. (1973). *The resolution of conflict.* New Haven: Yale University Press.

Embree, A.T. (1990). *Utopias in conflict: Religion and nationalism in modern India.* Berkeley: University of California Press.

Folger, J.P., Poole, M.S., & Stutman, R.K. (1993). *Working through conflict: Strategies for relationships, groups, and organizations.* New York: Harper Collins.

Gurumurthy, S. (1994). Semitic monotheism: The root of intolerance in India. *New Perspectives Quarterly, 11,* 47-53.

Harrison, S.S. (1960). *India: The most dangerous decades.* Princeton: Princeton University Press.

Hocker, J.L., & Wilmot, W.W. (1985). *Interpersonal conflict.* Dubuque, IA: Wm.C. Brown Publishers.

Kakar, S. (1981). *The inner world: A psycho-analytic study of childhood and society in India.* Delhi: Oxford University Press.

Kakar, S. (1994). The new Hindu identity: A profile. *New Perspectives Quarterly, 11,* 45-47.

Krauss, E.S., Rohlen, T.P., & Steinhoff, P.G. (Eds.) (1984). *Conflict in Japan.* Honolulu: University of Hawaii Press.

Madan, T.N. (1987). Secularism in its place. *The Journal of Asian Studies, 46*(4), 747-759.

Miller, J.G., & Bersoff, D.M. (1992). Culture and moral judgment: How are conflicts between justice and interpersonal responsibilities resolved? *Journal of Personality and Social Psychology, 62,* 541-554.

Moog, R. (1993). Indian litiguousness and the litigation explosion. *Asian Survey, 33,*1136-1150.

Nanavati, M.B., & Vakil, C.N. (Eds.) (1970/1951). *Group prejudices in India: A symposium.* Westport, CT: Greenwood Press.

Nanda, J.N. (1991). *Conflicts and co-existence: India.* New Delhi: Concept Publishing Co.

Nandy, A. (1980). *At the edge of psychology: Essays in politics and culture.* Delhi: Oxford University Press.

Nandy, A. (1988). The politics of secularism and the recovery of religious tolerance. *Alternatives, 13:3.*

Price, P. (1993). Democracy and ethnic conflict in India: Precolonial legacies in Tamil Nadu. *Asian Survey, 33,* 493-506.

Roland, A. (1988). *In search of self in India and Japan: Toward a cross-cultural psychology.* Princeton, NJ: Princeton University Press.

Ross, M.H. (1993). *The culture of conflict: Interpretations and interests in comparative perspective.* New Haven: Yale University Press.

Sen, A. (1993). The threats to secular India. *The New York Review of Books, 40:7,* 26-32.

Singh, M.P. (1990). The crisis of the Indian state: From quiet developmentalism to noisy democracy. *Asian Survey, 30:8,* 809-819.

Smith, V.A. (1972). *The Oxford student's history of India.* Delhi: Oxford University Press.

U.S. News and World Report (1994). *New world of nations: Today's almanac.*

Varshney, A. (1993). Contested meanings: India's national identity, Hindu nationalism, and the politics of anxiety. *Daedalus, 122,* 227-261.

SECTION III OVERVIEW: COMPARATIVE STUDIES OF CULTURE AND COMMUNICATION

Several early texts published during the past 30 years have pointed out how basic values can be used to distinguish the many cultures of the world. These basic values are internal—hidden in a milieu of beliefs, expectations and customs. These values may be difficult to isolate, but they do influence behaviors which can be observed and even measured by applying appropriate research techniques. Based on the values that have been discussed in the earlier publications, we may even develop scales to measure the influence of values in business and education. Many scholars have done just that.

The chapters included in this section report studies that were designed to demonstrate how cultural values of participating instructors as well as students in intercultural classes affect teaching and learning in the classroom settings. Teaching in such settings become learning experiences for the instructors, too.

In her chapter, "Hofstede's Intercultural Dimensions and the Decision Making Process: Americans and Malaysians in a Cooperative Setting," Wilhelm explains the role of cultural values in decision making process even in the classroom situation. In a study that included Malaysian and American instructors, she applied the scale of Hofstede's intercultural dimensions, and found that values of the participants do influence decision making in the classroom.

Ognanova explains another dimension of learning in the classroom situation. In her chapter, "Educators Crossing Cultures: Evaluation of Past Work and Guidelines for the Future," she shows how teaching and consulting abroad is in itself a learning experience to an instructor. Such learning may help the instructor better understand different cultural groups within his/her own country. This conclusion is based upon a study done in East Central Europe involving American educators and local teachers, students and enterpreneurs.

Ekachai, Hinchcliff-Pelias, and Greer present yet another view of how teaching intercultural Communication helps not only the instructors of the course, but also the students in the course better understand their own cultures. These interactions also help the interactors better perceive their own communication competence in intercultural settings.

Many milestone studies of stereotypes were done by social scientists several decades ago. Old research findings about how stereotypes influence communication may not be accurate especially in intercultural situations today. Young-Ok Yum found the evidence of this phenomenon in a study she conducted. In her chapter, "The Communication Stereotypes of Whites and Asians in the White Dominated Classroom," she reports changing stereotypes in such a classroom. As the author mentions, applying theories of stereotyping to intercultural communication is relatively new in scholarly research. Perceived and attributed stereotypes of students of other cultures by American students indicated a deviance from traditional stereotyping of those students by American students. Actual participation and observation in intercultural classes changed the interactors' attributes of others.

Speech is an essential area of study especially in democracies. However, speech and rhetoric have not been an area of study in higher education in Asian countries whose cultures belong to the so called responsibility oriented value system. The tradition in these cultures does not encourage argument and debate especially when disagreeing with authority figures such as parents and teachers. However, with the advent of modernity in the traditional societies of Asia, speech and communication have become important academic disciplines there. Heisey explains how the academic area of public speaking is currently being taught in the Peoples Republic of China (PRC). The Chinese language is among the oldest in the world and Chinese culture is greatly influenced by the Confucian and Taoist schools of philosophy. Speech and rhetoric have emerged as a new and major discipline in recent years in Chinese institutions of higher education. Text book writing and curriculum development include integrating ancient Chinese philosophy and modern communication theories. The development of rhetorical theory is also linked to modernization and economic development in the PRC.

18

INTERCULTURAL RELATIONSHIPS ACROSS GENDER: A LOOK AT THE COMMUNICATIVE PARALLELS THAT CHARACTERIZE INTERCULTURAL AND CROSS-GENDER RELATIONS

Roberta Bell Ross
Pennsylvania State University

Sandra L. Faulkner
Pennsylvania State University

INTRODUCTION

People have always been intrigued with and confused by the relationships between men and women. Significant amounts of research aim to explain the differences that often plague male/female relationships and the conflict those differences can cause (Barna, 1994; Gilligan, 1982; Pearson, 1985; Tannen, 1990). A fundamental purpose for studying gender and communication is to discover explanations that will help men and women (who seek explanations) have healthier relationships with each other. A conceptual framework that has been effective for examining the misunderstandings between men and women is a cross-cultural approach. A close examination of cross-sex communication reveals many parallels to the dynamics of cross-cultural behavior. Hence, the difficulties encountered in cross-cultural communication and cross-sex communication are in many ways "two examples of the same larger phenomenon: cultural difference and miscommunication" (Maltz & Borker, 1982, p. 51).

What is it that makes one culture different from another? If one were to do a cross-cultural analysis, he or she would probably investigate areas such as the culture's language, rituals, dress, traditions, values, interests, etc. in hopes of developing a greater understanding of the culture itself. The intercultural framework has been used to study the communication between men and women (Maltz & Borker, 1982; Tannen, 1990). Gender research suggests that although women and men may have grown up in the same culture, within that culture the way in which they were "gendered;" that is, taught to speak, behave, and value certain qualities deemed appropriate for their gender over those appropriate for the "other" gender, socialized them into two separate worlds (Maltz & Borker, 1982; Tannen, 1990).

Approaching gender communication from a cross-cultural perspective is a relatively new area of research and is advantageous for a number of reasons. People from various countries, cultures and subcultures are having to share the world more closely (via the global marketplace, immigration, etc.), which means they are meeting and forming relationships, and often marriages, together. This rise in "heterocultural"communication brings with it unique properties worth examining.

Looking at the parallels between cross-gender and intercultural communication is useful because they share a similar purpose: to understand differences and minimize miscommunication. It is ironic, however, that in our quest to understand differences we find a paradox of similarity in both intercultural and gender research. As with intercultural speakers, the assumption of similarity can cause men and women to bypass each other in conversation. Barna (1994) claims that at the root of the misunderstandings between men and women lies the fact that "many of us naively assume there are sufficient similarities among peoples of the world to enable us to successfully exchange information and /or feelings, solve problems of mutual concern, cement business relationships, or just make the kind of impression we wish to make" (p. 322). Focusing too much on similarities, therefore, can be misleading. For instance, although Darwin's theory of the universality of facial expressions may be true, it is the cultural upbringing that determines "whether or not the emotion will be displayed or suppressed, as well as on what occasions and to what degree" (Barna, 1994, p. 323). Carroll (1987) illuminates the similarity/difference issue that often plagues intercultural and cross-sex communication:

On the one hand, since we know more about the world (thanks to anthropology, travel, cinema, television, tourism, immigration, wars of independence, and ethnic and civil rights movements), we are aware of differences, and we fight for the right to maintain these differences. On the other hand, the (justified) fear of racism and its hideous consequences incites us to maintain forcefully that we are all the same, universal human beings. We constantly fall into the trap of wanting to reconcile these two truths; we are caught between the desire to deny differences (we are all human) and the desire to emphasize them (the right to be different) (p. 2).

Tannen (1990) has come across this conflict in her work. She states that some people "become angry at the mere suggestion that women and men are different...some men hear any statement about men and women, coming from a woman, as an accusation...some women fear, with justification, that any observation of gender differences will be heard as implying that it is women who are different" (p. 14). Another objection that arises is the denial that there are subcultural differences among men and women because of the frequency in which men and women interact (Maltz & Borker, 1982). In general, however, scholars suggest that we keep in mind that we are more alike as human beings than different as men and women (Tannen, 1990) or as cultures (Carroll, 1987) and "knowledge of the similarities and differences involved allows the actor in such situations to exert some measure of control over his or her communication behavior and thus become more effective in establishing, maintaining, and terminating interpersonal relationships" (Cushman & Cahn, 1986, p. 331).

Another reason for taking a cross-cultural approach to studying gender differences is that it helps clarify some of the nature/nurture issues frequently associated with gender. Men and women *are* different (Tannen, 1990), but which differences can be attributed to nature and which to nurture? Examining the behavior of males and females across culture, therefore, may reveal information that supports or rejects notions that differences are largely due to biological or cultural factors.

Finally, an awareness and appreciation for the differences between women and men can lift "the burden of individual pathology" (Tannen, 1990, p. 17). Many of the problems that occur between cultures are typically attributed to personality clashes or are interpreted through stereotypical filters (Maltz & Borker, 1982). Rather than considering conflict as a problem in the communication, differences are typically considered deficiencies. "We know we are unique individuals, but we tend to see others as representatives of groups...this useful ability to see patterns of similarity has unfortunate consequences" (Tannen, 1990, p. 15).

Therefore, when women and men become dissatisfied or confused with the relationship and can't work things out they tend to blame each other as the problem. Misunderstandings are often attributed to the gender or to the culture of the individual rather than the individual him/herself. Thus, a cross-cultural approach helps to clarify the causes for the misunderstanding without accusing the other or the relationship of being wrong.

COMMUNICATION VARIABLES ACROSS CULTURE AND GENDER

There are many communicative parallels that characterize gender and intercultural research. The following draws from a number of works to explore the areas of language, conversational style, nonverbal communication, relational roles, and worldview. In addition, the implications for intercultural and cross-sex communication competence will be discussed.

Language

In her discussion of intercultural communication, Asuncion-Lande (1990) states that "language is the most obvious and most enduring difficulty in intercultural communication" (p. 213). Ironically, language is probably the least obvious difficulty between men and women of the same culture because there is an assumption that the same language is being spoken. For instance, if an American who speaks only English is attempting a conversation with a Argentinean who speaks only Spanish, no one will dispute that there is a language barrier between the two interlocutors. Between a man and a woman who both speak English, however, the gender differences within their shared language often goes unnoticed. Research has revealed, however, that beginning at an early age, boys and girls have been found to demonstrate different ways of conversing with their same-sex peers. Conversations among boys reveals a language of status and independence where winning and losing are emphasized, while conversations among girls reveals a language of support and intimacy where agreement and the cultivation of relationships are emphasized (Tannen, 1990; Wood, 1994).

There are a number of ways in which the differences in the language of men and women parallel language differences across cultures. One difference is demonstrated by the vocabularies of members of a particular culture or gender. As the language of a culture develops within its own context and comes to reflect it, the words that men and women, or interculturals use reveal that which is salient or of general interest to their gender or culture. Interdisciplinary scholar Kenneth Burke explained "how a system of language can make people emphasize certain features of the world that are highlighted by their language, while failing to notice other features that the language does not mention" (Bate, 1988, p. 78). "Thus, the native Eskimo speaker, who has many words for snow, may notice nuances concerning snow that would escape a native English speaker's attention" (DeVito, 1991, p. 438). In gender communication research, women have been found to use words of support and affiliation (Tannen, 1990) and demonstrate a greater vocabulary for color variations (Pearson, 1985) and men have been found to choose words of sports and combat and demonstrate a greater vocabulary for male (Cameron, 1992) and female body parts, and sexual intercourse (Pearson, 1985).

Another concern with language in intercultural and gender communication is when people assume that, because they understand the language, they will understand what is being *communicated*. In cross-cultural communication, fluency in a foreign language does not insure understanding of meaning. "In some cultures, it is polite to refuse the first or second offer of refreshment. Many foreign guests have gone hungry because their U.S. host or hostess never presented the third offer—another case of "no" meaning "yes" (Barna, 1994, p. 326). Men and women face the same dilemma. Men have been known to attest that when a women says she doesn't want a gift for her birthday it does not mean that she does not want a gift for her birthday, but that she is leaving the opportunity open for the person to be spontaneously generous out of his or her own free will. Knowledge of the language, or linguistic competence, therefore, is inadequate for resolving these misunderstandings.

Conversational Style

Conversation style differences are found in both gender and intercultural communication research (Maltz & Borker, 1982; Pearson, 1985; Tannen, 1990; Wood, 1994). Men and women have been viewed as being of different "gender cultures" (Collier, 1994) who speak different "genderlects" (Tannen, 1990). Carroll (1987) draws a distinction between Americans and French that Tannen (1990) describes as commonly found between American men and women. Carroll (1987) reports that even Americans with an excellent fluency in French will find engaging in French conversation frustrating because they do not understand the cultural conversational style. For the French, frequent interruptions are a sign of spontaneity, enthusiasm and connection between friends. It is this animated style that binds and stimulates the French. "Long, uninterrupted responses, attentively listened to, are reserved, by French people, for so-called serious conversations, which are out of place at a party" (Carroll, 1987, p. 36). Serious conversants isolate themselves from the rest of the room, which, if carried on too long, will appear rude to the French. Carroll (1987) claims that Americans, on the other hand, feel most at ease under these more serious conditions because it is a closer resemblance to their own conversational style.

Tannen (1990) discovered two conversational styles that frequently contribute to communication conflicts and/or misunderstanding—high involvement and high considerate styles. The "high involvement" style refers to those that talk along and interrupt in the conversation to show connection, support, and participation. The "high considerate" style, however, refers to those that expect and wait for a pause that indicates it is their turn to speak. This dynamic is particularly problematic when a high involvement and a high considerate engage in conversation. The high considerate keeps waiting for the pause, but the high involvement person, thinking the high considerate has nothing to say because he or she does not chime in, keeps talking.

Tannen (1990) suggests that these two distinctions can be gender *or* culturally related. This claim is supported by the work of Carroll (1987) who's description of the conversational style of the French parallels the high involvement style discussed by Tannen (1990). He claims that Americans accuse the French of being rude because they interrupt all the time, and the French accuse Americans of being boring conversationalists because they don't engage themselves in the conversation. Therefore, depending on whether the style of interruption is gender-based or culture-based, the same behavior may be perceived as rude and dominant behavior or as a sign of support, caring, and sharing. The point is that, in order to accurately interpret ones communication, it is essential to understand the speaker's intentions.

Gender and cross-cultural research indicates that many problems that develop between people of different "speech cultures" are due to a lack of understanding the speaker's intent. "Conversation...progresses in large part because of shared assumptions about what is going on" (Maltz & Borker, 1982, p. 54). Carroll (1987) illustrates this phenomenon in his discussion of the differences between the conversational styles of American friends and French friends. He claims that Americans stand by their friends and show agreement during disputes and/or debates to express their loyalty to each other and to demonstrate the strength and degree of closeness of the relationship to others. French friends demonstrate the qualities of support and loyalty in their relationships as well, but do so by playing the devil's advocate when disputing, thereby demonstrating that the relationship can withstand conflict and disagreement. As a result, Americans often describe the French as fighting all the time and the French are often suspicious of Americans because they do not. The point is, that if an American and French become friends, the American would take the French's behavior as being disloyal and the French would take the American's behavior as indicative of someone who does not believe that the relationship is strong because he/she never challenges it. If both continue to operate on these shared assumptions, they will never be able to effectively communicate their feelings of loyalty and support. In addition, if an understanding for each other's *intent* is not reached, this misunderstanding may spiral into a very destructive relationship.

One conversational characteristic that is commonly a source of misunderstanding is the use of intonation. In cross-cultural communication, the structural intonation can change the entire meaning of words. For example, Indian waitresses use a falling intonation when offering food to customers. Although both Indians and Americans consider the act of asking a polite behavior, Americans ask questions with a rising intonation. This difference rendered the offer with a falling intonation rude and inappropriate to the American customer (Maltz & Borker, 1982). In gender communication, the differences of men and women intonation carry messages of their own and those meanings are subject to change depending on the gender of the speaker. Women who upspeak (end sentences with a rising intonation), use tag questions (end statements with a question), hedges, and qualifiers are often viewed as less credible than men who use them (Bate, 1988; Pearson, 1985).

Nonverbal Communication

Understanding the nonverbal messages of others is an essential component of communicative competence and can be as challenging and confusing as understanding verbal messages. As with verbal interaction, people learn the rules for nonverbal interaction. Violation of these rules can produce a number of unintended meanings. Even seemingly simple forms of nonverbal communication, such as the hand gesture, can be a source of misunderstanding because the same gesture often carries different meanings across culture (Parker Pen Company, 1990). For example, in the United States, the "thumbs up" gesture symbolizes agreement, however in most middle eastern countries the same gesture is considered highly offensive.

The same dilemma is found with facial expressions. Different cultures may use the same facial expressions, such as smiling, however the way in which we interpret and react to them is often much different. "Smiling is one type of facial expression that may be used for a variety of different purposes" (Pearson, 1985). Barna (1994) demonstrates the dangers of misunderstandings between men and women of different cultures in her report of the various ways foreigners have responded to the smiles of Americans. A Japanese student misinterpreted the smiles of American girls, thinking that they were interested in him because if a stranger smiles to another in Japan, especially a male to a female, he would be perceived as a sexual maniac or a very impolite person (Barna, 1994). A similar situation that occurred between an American woman and a foreign man is described below.

> I was waiting for my husband on a downtown corner when a man with a baby and two young children approached. Judging by small quirks of fashion he had not been in the U.S. long. I have a baby about the same age and in appreciation of his family and obvious involvement as a father I smiled at him. Immediately I realized I did the wrong thing as he stopped, looked me over from head to toe and said, "Are you waiting for me? You meet me later?" Apparently I had acted as a prostitute would in his country (Barna, 1994, p. 339).

Other nonverbal qualities that are subject to cultural influence are the use of space and touch. A person's use of personal space, or proxemics, and touching behavior with others are largely attributed to cultural learning (Asuncion-Lande, 1990; Bate, 1988). Often one culture will be offended by another's "inappropriate" use of space or touching behavior, despite that there is no objectively "correct" physical distance or touching behavior between people (Watzlawick, 1976). Research suggests that American women and men touch more in opposite-sex pairs than do same-sex pairs (DeVito, 1991; Rosenfeld, Kartus, & Ray, 1976). In support of the notion that touching behaviors are culturally learned and gender-specific, DeVito (1990) reports that in the Middle East same-sex touching in public is very common. For example, men seen walking with their arms around each is a common practice—one that "would cause many raised eyebrows in the United States" (p. 177).

As with verbal communication, gender differences in nonverbal communication intended to reinforce the roles prescribed by the culture. Tannen (1990) provides an excellent example of the influence gender role expectations have on nonverbal expression. She describes a scene from the movie *The Accidental Tourist*:

> The hero, Macon, appears, disheveled and distraught, at the home of Muriel, a woman who has shown a romantic interest in him. Macon tells Muriel the dreadful story of his son's death, and confesses that he has been unable to recover from it. Touched by his confession, Muriel leads Macon to bed, to comfort him for his devastating loss. In bed, Macon lies on his back and lifts his arm to place it around Muriel, who snuggles against him. In choreographing this scene, the director apparently felt that the demands of convention, which require the man to take the physical position of protector and comforter, were stronger than the demands of the immediate scene in which Muriel is comforting Macon (p. 286).

This example not only illustrates how influential the expectations that people have with regard to nonverbal behavior can be, but perhaps more importantly, speaks to larger concerns surrounding the issue of relational role expectations.

Relational Roles

"Role relationships provide insights into the ways a culture maintains social order and control among its members...[and] are organized according to age, sex, social status, kinship, power, wealth, knowledge, and experience" (Asuncion-Lande, 1990, p. 215). When cultures come together, role expectations not fulfilled in cross-cultural communication can turn a positively intended message into a hostile one. For example, eye contact among Americans is considered a friendly way of showing sincerity no matter the status of the individuals involved. Within the Navajo culture, however, direct eye contact—especially between speakers of different status—is considered an act of aggression. Thus, the failure to meet the others' expectations for the nonverbal behavior of eye contact may violate more significant rules for relational roles.

The violation of behavioral expectations for men and women in a heterocultural setting can be equally disharmonious. Watzlawick (1976), in his discussion of the punctuation of events, describes how confusing a heterocultural communication contact can be when relational roles are misunderstood. He describes the differences in the courtship patterns of a U.S. soldier and a British woman during the last years of World War II.

> Both American soldiers and British girls accused one another of being sexually brash. Investigation of this curious double charge brought to light an interesting punctuation problem. In both cultures, courtship behavior from the first eye contact to the ultimate consummation went through approximately thirty steps, but the sequence of these steps was different. Kissing, for instance, comes relatively early in the North American pattern (occupying, let us say, step 5) and relatively late in the English pattern (at step 25, let us assume), where it is considered highly erotic behavior. So when the U.S. soldier somehow felt that the time was right for a harmless kiss, not only did the girl feel cheated out of twenty steps of what for her would have been proper behavior on his part, she also felt she had to make a quick decision: break off the relationship and run, or get ready for intercourse. If she chose the latter, the soldier was confronted with behavior that according to his cultural rules could only be called shameless at this early stage of the relationship (p. 63).

Understanding the behavioral expectations for a particular gender or culture is important, however, our cultural and gender identities extend far beyond the roles we perform. The way in which we perceive ourselves and the world is shaped by our membership to a particular culture and gender.

Worldview

Worldview "is considered to be one of the most important cognitive mechanisms influencing communication" (Asuncion-Lande, 1990, p. 214). It represents the personal view of the individual or group as socialized from his or her culture—reflecting values, beliefs, and attitudes (Asuncion-Lande, 1990; Dodd, 1987). A person's worldview, which is largely influenced by culture, becomes a filter for interpreting all incoming messages and expressing all outgoing messages. When cultures of differing worldviews come together in conversation, there is a greater potential for misunderstandings. For example, a person from a culture that emphasizes controlling the environment would tend to perceive the world much differently than someone from a culture that strives to live in harmony with the environment. This difference is significant because it encompasses how an individual will think, perceive, make decisions, and communicate with others. The greater the polarization of the views between people, the greater the basis for them to experience misunderstandings, conflict, and disagreement.

Similarly, men and women tend to have their own belief systems that characterize their gender. For example, Bate (1988) mentions what Anne Wilson Schaef calls, in her book *Women's Reality,* the White Male System (WMS) in which "white males dominate and define what is going on" (Bate, 1988, p. 36). She suggests that the central beliefs of this system emphasize innate male superiority, the ability to be completely objective, etc. In the WMS, self and work are the focus of one's life. Within the Female System of beliefs, human relationships are central to life and knowledge. Again, these different sets of belief systems are significant because they influence the way the sexes talk, think and make decisions in their lives (Gilligan, 1982; Bate, 1988).

Although gender research suggests that the male perspective is often treated as the norm, and the women's as deviating from that norm (Tannen, 1990), the general tendency for men and women to judge the other gender according to their own standards of "normal" behavior remains (Maltz & Borker, 1982). In essence, the sexes, like interculturals, are ethnocentric, and therefore, see their "world-view" as central to all others. That is, they demonstrate "the tendency to evaluate the values, beliefs, and behaviors of one's own culture as being more positive, logical, and natural than those of other cultures" (DeVito, 1991, p. 429). This bias can create a subtle, but profound communication barrier between people of different cultures and genders.

A cross-cultural approach attempts to overcome the ethnocentric barrier. It attempts to do with men and women what anthropologists aim for with people from different cultures. It is "a means of perceiving as "normal" things which initially seem "bizarre" or "strange" among people of a culture different from one's own" (Carroll, 1987, p. 2). Therefore, to take on the task of understanding the other, one must be prepared to accept behaviors that initially seem shocking, strange, or inappropriate, and imagine how the same behavior can be "normal." Tannen says that by recognizing and understanding our differences we can "banish mutual mystification and blame" (1990, p. 48).

CROSS-CULTURAL AND CROSS-SEX COMPETENCE

"No person can communicate as a free agent" (Asuncion-Lande, 1990, p. 223). "As soon as there is contact with another culture [or sex] (and this will always be the case), there is potential for conflict" (Carroll, 1987, p. 3). One who lacks knowledge of the rules and customs of the society cannot communicate effectively in it (DeVito, 1991). To achieve intercultural and cross-gender competence, one must avoid the trap of right or wrong thinking. Paul Watzlawick (1976) provides an excellent foundation for thinking about intercultural communication:

> Communication creates what we call reality. At first this may seem a most peculiar statement, for surely reality is what it is, and communication is merely a way of expressing or explaining it. Not at all…our everyday, traditional ideas of reality are delusions which we spend substantial part of our daily lives shoring up, even at the

considerable risk of trying to force facts to fit our definition of reality instead of vice versa. And the most dangerous delusion of all is that there is only one reality. What there are, in fact, are many different versions of reality, some of which are contradictory, but all of which are the results of communication and not reflections of eternal, objective truths (p. xi).

People tend to defend their "culture" or "gender" as they do their version of reality—as superior to all others, or the correct way. There are many "real" perspectives that take place between interculturals, the sexes, and heteroculturals. Few people are helped by being told that what they do is all wrong (Tannen, 1990). Besides, "there may be little wrong with what people are doing, even if they are winding up in arguments. The problem may be that each partner is operating within a different system" (Tannen, 1990, p. 297).

It is important to remember that everyone behaves in the way which is natural to him or her while assuming that this *is* the natural way. However, to become more effective communicators across gender and culture, Asuncion-Lande (1990) makes several recommendations, such as becoming self-aware of one's own cultural and gender behavior, being open-minded, and flexible. An awareness of one's cultural assumptions helps to overcome barriers to effective communication as well (Barna, 1985; Asuncion-Lande, 1990). Moreover, an extended level of awareness can expand the choice of cultural influence and personal values (Cushman & Cahn, 1986). In cross-gender communication this could mean the adoption of a communication style that satisfies both partners of a couple, or simply an appreciation for the style of the other.

Understanding that others may have a different concept of reality is an important step toward reaching understanding. However, what happens when we *do* become aware of our cultural assumptions and reach a level of understanding of each others differences? Uncertainty reduction theory tells us that the potential for problems and misunderstanding is at its height in the beginning of the relationship because there the least amount of information to reduce uncertainty. Carroll (1987), however, says that when we get to know each other at a deeper level the differences really come out. He suggests that the greatest potential harms to cross-cultural relationships are those of an intimate nature.

We can illustrate this perspective further in an analysis of relationship conflicts. The more we get to know another, the more we learn to appreciate in the other and feel connected to the other. However, the more we learn of the other, the more differences can be detected, and therefore, the more reasons for leaving the other.

Despite these difficulties, Carroll (1987) emphasizes how important it is to avoid trying to psycho-analyze the other or attempt to get at the deep-seated reasons for why a people are the way they are. Rather, he suggests we try to understand the system of communication by which meaning is created in their culture or gender.

DISCUSSION QUESTIONS

1. How does examining gender communication across culture provide insight into questions of nature versus nurture in studying gender differences in general?
2. The authors looked at communication parallels that characterized intercultural and cross-gender relations in the areas of language, conversational style, nonverbal communication, relational roles, and world view. Can you think of other areas in which there may be similar parallels?
3. What does the author mean when she says "a cross-cultural approach helps clarify the causes for misunderstanding without accusing each other of being wrong?"
4. Explain the notion that "people assume that, because they understand the language, they will understand the communication."
5. Since contact between people of different cultures and genders is on the increase, how would you suggest that a person set about trying to communicate effectively with someone from a different culture who is also of the opposite sex?

REFERENCES

Asuncion-Lande, N. C. (1990). Intercultural communication. In G. L. Dahnke, & G. W. Clatterbuck (Eds.), *Human communication: Theory and research* (pp. 208-225). Belmont, CA: Wadsworth Publishing Company.

Barna, L. M. (1994). Stumbling blocks in intercultural communication. In L. Samovar & R. Porter (Eds.), *Intercultural communication: A reader* (7th ed., pp. 337-346). Belmont, CA: Wadsworth Publishing Company.

Bate, B. (1988). *Communication and the sexes.* New York: Harper and Row Publishers.

Cameron, D. (1992). Naming of parts: Gender, culture, and terms for the penis among American college students. *American Speech, 67,* 367-382.

Carroll, R. (1987). *Cultural misunderstandings: The French-American experience.* Chicago: The University of Chicago Press.

Collier, M. J. (1994). Cultural identity and intercultural communication. In L. Samovar & R. Porter (Eds.), *Intercultural communication: A reader* (7th ed., pp. 36-45). Belmont, CA: Wadsworth Publishing Company.

Cushman, D. P., & Cahn, D. D. (1986). Cross-Cultural relationships and interpersonal communication. In Stewart, J. (Ed.), *Bridges not walls: A book about interpersonal communication,* (4th ed.) New York: Random House.

DeVito, J. A. (1991). *Human communication: The basic course,* (5th ed.). New York: HarperCollins Publishers.

Dodd, C. H. (1987). *Dynamics of intercultural communication.* Dubuque, IA: Wm. C. Brown.

Gilligan, C. (1982). *In a different voice.* Cambridge, MA: Harvard University Press.

Maltz, D. N., & Borker, R. A. (1982). A cultural approach to male-female miscommunication. In Gumperz, J. (Ed.), *Language and social identity* (pp. 146-216). Cambridge: Cambridge University Press.

Parker Pen Company (1990). In R. E. Axtell (Ed.) *Do's and taboos around the world: A guide to international behavior* (2nd ed.) New York: John Wiley & Sons, Inc.

Pearson, J. (1985). *Gender and communication.* Dubuque, Iowa: Wm. C. Brown Publishers.

Rosenfeld, L., Kartus, S., & Ray, C. (1976). Body accessibility revisited. *Journal of Communication, 26*, 27-30.

Tannen, D. (1990). *You just don't understand: Women and men in conversation.* New York: Ballantine Books.

Watzlawick, P. (1976). *How real is real? Confusion, disinformation, communication.* New York: Vintage Books.

Wood, J. T. (1994). Gender, communication, and culture. In L. Samovar & R. Porter (Eds.), *Intercultural communication: A reader* (7th ed., pp. 155-165). Belmont, CA: Wadsworth Publishing Company.

19

HOFSTEDE'S INTERCULTURAL DIMENSIONS AND THE DECISION-MAKING PROCESS: AMERICANS AND MALAYSIANS IN A COOPERATIVE UNIVERSITY SETTING

Kim Hughes Wilhelm
Southern Illinois University at Carbondale

INTRODUCTION

The purpose of this chapter is to relate Hofstede's (1984) findings that "no management activity can be culture-free" (p. 81) to the decision-making and communicative processes of Malaysian and American instructors when implementing a new English as a Second Language program in Malaysia. Intercultural communication and value differences were identified which sometimes affected the success with which colleagues were able to interact and problem-solve together. These differences related, as well, to Hofstede's 1984 findings which describe 50 countries according to their relative emphases at the societal level on four dimensions:

- Social differentiation by gender   →   MASCULINITY–FEMININITY
- Desire for certainty   →   UNCERTAINTY AVOIDANCE
- Acceptance of unequal power distribution →   POWER DISTANCE
- Interdependence between individuals   →   INDIVIDUALISM–COLLECTIVISM

Hofstede studied employees of 67 countries, all of whom worked for the same multinational business enterprise, controlling for occupation. Participants responded to 32 value statements which were collected by psychologists within the company's subsidiaries. The 50 largest subsidiaries were included in Hofstede's 1984 rankings.

When comparing only Malaysia and the United States, we find they rank similarly on the two dimensions of "uncertainty avoidance" and "masculinity." However, they are widely divergent regarding "power distance" and "individualism." Figure 1 in Appendix A provides a comparison of Malaysia and the United States on Hofstede's dimensions. The dimensions are discussed in more detail in the section which follows by first defining each and offering descriptors, then relating the dimensions to decision and communication differences noted in teacher interactions.

MASCULINITY VERSUS FEMININITY

This dimension relates to the degree to which a society emphasizes competitiveness over solidarity and equity over equality. Societies with a high degree of social differentiation by gender, termed by Hofstede "masculine" societies, value performance, feel that competitiveness is good and that the strong should win. High achievers are rewarded and work is made more challenging in order to stimulate a worker. People in these societies (e.g. Japan, Austria) typically have higher ambitions concerning "making a career" than people in more "feminine" societies (e.g. Switzerland, Norway).

In feminine societies, solidarity is considered good and there is an emphasis on helping the weak and reward according to need. Hostede used the term "welfare" society when describing a feminine society. The stress is on relationships and, to stimulate a worker in this society, social units in the work setting may be developed.

The United States rated 36th of 50 countries (the 62nd percentile) on this dimension, indicating a stronger orientation toward masculinity than Malaysia, which rated 26-27, exactly midway between a performance-oriented versus welfare-oriented society. Table 1 in Appendix B provides a summary of descriptors related to the masculinity dimension.

STRONG VERSUS WEAK UNCERTAINTY AVOIDANCE

Societies which are concerned about controlling the future and "the extent to which behavior should follow fixed rules" (Hofstede, 1984, p. 92) are strong in uncertainty avoidance. This type of society (e.g. Greece, Portugal) desires conformity and certainty. Rigid codes of behavior and belief are imposed and may help to maintain emotional equilibrium. Law and order are "important symbols" in these societies, which are intolerant of deviants. Ritualization of words, dress, and actions "satisfy deep emotional needs" in these societies. Meetings, reports, etc. may serve ritual ends as much as decision-making ends. There is often a strong belief in fate.

Societies with weak uncertainty avoidance (e.g. Singapore, Jamaica) tend to believe in luck as a factor and that a person can positively influence his or her own future. Strategic planning and preventive maintenance are more popular in these societies. There is also less top-down management for short- and medium-term planning. There tends to be less emphasis on punctuality and precision and, while there are unwritten rules of conduct, they are considered to be mostly for convenience and can be broken. Practice counts more than principles. In weak uncertainty avoidance societies it is easier to get people to relax and life tends to be less hurried. However, perhaps due to less overt societal stress, it is less acceptable to express emotions in this type of society.

Both Malaysia and the United States are weak in uncertainty avoidance, with Malaysia a bit weaker (Malaysian rated eighth of 50 and the United States eleventh of 50). Descriptors associated with uncertainty avoidance are provided in Table 2, Appendix B.

LARGE VERSUS SMALL POWER DISTANCE

Hofstede defined power distance as "the extent to which the members of a society accept that power in institutions and organizations is distributed unequally" (1984, p. 83). Societies which accept that power is distributed unequally, or "large" power distance societies (e.g. Malaysia, Panama, Guatemala), are more accepting of hierarchical order. An individual's status is often ascribed on the basis of a subordinate's respect for the superior's power and authority, which are commonly linked to ancestry and wealth. Rulers are less likely to consult with their citizens.

In the work setting, a superior is expected to make and pass down decisions, acting in a "paternalistic" role. Similar to a good mother or father, the superior has a great deal of power and control, but is expected to be benevolent and to not abuse his or her power. Unfortunately, if the superior does abuse his power, grievance channels are generally missing. A subordinate who complains about his superior would be putting himself at risk and showing disrespect. More indirect communication channels (e.g. use of a third person as a "go-between" or withdrawal of a favor) are used to express complaints or reprimands, thereby preserving "face."

In a stratified, hierarchical society, expectations of the individual emphasize obedience and conformity. According to Hofstede (1984, p. 90), respect and loyalty are considered "supreme virtues" in a large power distance society. Individuals are expected to honor parents and teachers throughout their lifetimes. Students show respect by never openly disagreeing with teachers, treating them always as highly respected "sources of wisdom." Exam success is considered very important as it is viewed as "an entry certificate to a higher status group (ascription)."

On the other hand, in a small power distance society, one which promotes power equalization, differences in power are associated with power abuse and there is typically a system of checks and balances in place to guard against such abuse. In other words, there are usually channels by which subordinates can complain about superiors with protection against reprisal. The small power distance society, Hofstede explains, "demands justification for power inequalities" (1984, 83) and is more relaxed hierarchically. In this society, rulers are more likely to consult with citizens. In the work setting, open, two-way communication, directness, and relative independence of subordinate to superior are expected so that the two can "act as genuine negotiation partners" (p. 91). Individual status in the small power distance society is based on personal merit. Success in achievement, with corresponding credentials, indicates that the individual has proven his or her mastery of a subject or skill. Countries which were most oriented toward small power distance in Hofstede's study were Austria and Israel. Table 3, Appendix B, provides descriptors used by Hofstede when describing large versus small power distance societies, with Malaysia rating highest of all countries ranked in orientation to large power distance. Conversely, the United States was 16th of 50, indicating an orientation toward small power distance.

INDIVIDUALISM VERSUS COLLECTIVISM

Hofstede concluded that less economically developed countries versus more economically developed countries ranged at opposite ends of the continuum when considering the degree to which their societies valued collectivism or individualism. Hofstede defined this dimension as "the degree of interdependence a society maintains among individuals" (1984, p. 83). According to Hofstede, collectivist societies (e.g. Guatemala, Ecuador) emphasize loyalty to the clan or "in-group," with a focus on "WE." There is a tightly knit and ordered social framework, with importance placed on proper form so as to avoid loss of "face." Group interests dominate and self-effacement is common. Harmony is sought and conflict suppressed, with indirect communication strategies employed. In these societies, the group watches out for the individual and it is common to have extended family involved together in business ventures. Business and private life are integrated, with relationships having priority over task accomplishment. Employment relationships have a moral component and are typically long-term, with loyalty and benevolence expected on the part of employee and employer.

In contrast, societies which are individualistic in orientation (e.g. the United States, Australia) emphasize independence, a focus on "I." Self interest dominates and self-promotion is common. The social framework is more loosely knit and employee/employer relationships are viewed as being more equal. Business relationships are maintained only as long as there is mutual advantage so are often calculative in nature. Tasks take priority over relationships and there is a separation of business and private life. Loyalty and responsibility are to the immediate family but, even so, individuals are expected to take care of themselves. Direct communication is valued, with disagreements expressed more openly in an attempt to resolve conflicts expeditiously.

As shown in Figure 1, Malaysians and Americans were found by Hofstede to have divergent trends when comparing the degree to which their societies maintain interdependence between individuals. Malaysia ranked 17th on the "individualism" index scale, toward the collectivist side of the continuum. The United States, on the other hand, was most oriented toward individualism of all the countries measured, ranking last out of 50. Table 4 (see Appendix B) provides a sample of descriptors used by Hofstede when discussing collectivist versus individualist societies.

MALAYSIAN/AMERICAN TEACHER DIFFERENCES RELATED TO THE POWER DISTANCE DIMENSION

Societal orientations toward interdependence and power seemed to influence the effectiveness with which Malaysian and American teachers were able to make decisions and to communicate together during 15 months of field testing and evaluating a new curricular model. Of the 12 instructors involved, four were American and eight Malaysian (ethnically mixed with three Caucasian Americans, one African American, three Indian Malaysians, two Bumiputra Malaysians, and two Chinese Malaysians). The curriculum developer was an American and the director a Malaysian. The developer worked closely with an American coordinator and a Malaysian teacher liaison during the implementation and evaluation stages. She was on-site two to three days a week and during weekly teacher meetings. Immediately following the teacher meetings, the developer, coordinator, and liaison met for debriefing. As an outcome of those meetings and listening to audio tapes of two major curriculum meetings held 10 weeks apart, cultural differences were identified which seemed to reflect differences in communication patterns between the Americans and Malaysians (Wilhelm & Pereira, 1993).

Power distance seemed to influence teachers' views of themselves as instructional decision-makers or "experts." Malaysian teachers seemed more uncomfortable with "bottom-up" decision making, with some saying, "it's not my place" or "you're the expert" when asked to problem solve with management. In meetings, Malaysian teachers were much more reticent than American teachers, often giving opinions only when called upon directly. Criticisms, usually offered only when solicited, were stated using tentative language and were paired with praise. It was considered impolite and disrespectful to criticize the curriculum with the developer present. This linguistic and social behavior seemed to reflect an attitude that "You are what you produce. The plan and the person are one and the same." It also reflected a discomfort with a management style that differed from the "top-down" style typical in Malaysian educational settings.

For those teachers who had taught in Malaysian settings, the curriculum had always been imposed by the Ministry of Education, with little control over texts, materials, or methods. Many teachers expressed the desire that the curriculum developer "just tell me what to do" with great detail provided. Conversely, managers wanted the teachers to act as instructional decision-makers and to take ownership of the curriculum, but it became clear that many of the Malaysian teachers were uncomfortable when asked to function in these roles. The majority of Malaysian teachers preferred to have management be responsible for decision-making.

Subsequently, it was difficult to institute a "bottom-up" communication flow. A problem with the curriculum was often perceived of as the individual teacher's own problem, seeming to reflect a fear that teaching skills were inadequate (rather than that the curriculum needed revision). This was most obvious when trying to get the teachers to respond to the scheduling of instructional content. Teachers felt bound to keep up with the schedule, for example, despite repeated reminders that some activities and chapters may require additional time and the schedule may need to be adjusted. There seemed to be a need to conform individual behavior to the group schedule, rather than to work together to revise the schedule so that it better reflected what individual teachers were able to accomplish.

This need for detail and a "set" program of instruction also surfaced in the classroom setting and in teachers' perceptions of themselves as content experts. The teachers were asked to teach English through Earth Science content which included video documentaries and rather scientific concepts (e.g. tectonic plates, ocean floor rifts, hypotheses regarding the age of the Earth). The focus was on teaching critical thinking and problem-solving skills to better enable students to learn how to study and remember information for academic purposes. American teachers and the younger Malaysian teachers seemed comfortable with this teaching/learning style and were able to set up group activities and take the role of "facilitator" of instruction, orchestrating the classroom to create a learner-centered environment. The majority of Malaysian teachers, however, were very uncomfortable with this teaching context, feeling they were losing "face" by not conducting a teacher-centered class. They expressed the fear that the students would report back to their parents that they were being asked to "learn on their own." This is consistent with an orientation in strong power distance societies toward the teacher as the source of wisdom and reflects a more traditional, teacher-centered system of education.

There was also an emphasis on formal testing and a great fear that students would not know the answers to the test. Teachers wanted to know test questions and answers well in advance of the testing date so that they could prepare the students to answer correctly. This was a big problem, since the tests were designed to assess the students' abilities to apply language and study skills. Malaysian teachers routinely expressed the fear that poor performance by their students on the final exam would result in poor teaching evaluations or even dismissal by management. It was obvious that they felt a lack of power and control in the employment situation. While managers made no attempt to compare test outcomes by teacher, the Malaysian teachers themselves made comparisons and sought out managers to explain final exam results.

It was meant for exams to be a learning experience for students, so time was built into the schedule for individual debriefing over exams with students. After scoring, teachers were expected to meet individually with students to go through the exam, discuss progress in the course, and identify individual strengths and weaknesses. Only the American teachers conducted these debriefing sessions. The American teachers, in general, seemed to be more concerned with student progress over time, with student motivation and recognition of their learning needs, and with daily attendance and participation. The Malaysian teachers were seemingly more influenced with student performance on exams (especially the final) and were less concerned about daily participation, weekly quizzes, or homework scores. These findings are consistent with Hofstede's descriptions of the roles of exams in strong versus weak power distance societies.

On an interpersonal level, problems with individuals were dealt with using a paternalistic management style and third party "go-betweens." For example, if a group member was being difficult, confrontational, or incompetent, the Malaysian strategy was to "Let it be... give it time." The prevailing attitude seemed to be that people would (hopefully) come to their senses on their own, without anybody having to embarrass them by pointing out the problem. It was considered the duty of their closest friend/colleague to point out the problem to them in private. If that didn't work, it then became the supervisor's responsibility to work with the difficult person in order to solve the problem. (Intervention by the supervisor meant loss of face for the employee, however, so it was desirable to resolve the problem through friends.) Praise, solidarity, and status were expressed very indirectly, through special invitations, small gifts, or inclusion within a higher status group. Similarly, reprimands or problems were also expressed indirectly, typically through questioning (e.g. "Aren't you quite hot wearing blue jeans?" which really meant "Blue jeans are not considered acceptable dress for a teacher."). Other ways to indirectly express disapproval included the omission of favors or avoidance which let everyone know that the person had been (temporarily) excluded from the status group.

It took the American teachers quite a long time to catch on to these indirect hints as to inappropriate behavior. Even if they did catch on that something was wrong, the American was more likely to directly confront in order to clarify or discuss the problem (which typically resulted in the Malaysian denying that a problem existed). The Malaysians were very forgiving of these social blunders and, as a consequence, many Americans were generally insensitive or uninformed as to the mistakes they were making. Americans who were most successful at fitting into Malaysian society learned to decode the indirect language and to go through friends/colleagues to clarify problems and to get advice as to how to apologize or "fix" the blunder. Table 5 in Appendix C provides a summary of differences between the teacher groups which relate to power distance differences at the societal level.

MALAYSIAN/AMERICAN TEACHER DIFFERENCES RELATED TO INDIVIDUALISM VERSUS COLLECTIVISM

In the Malaysian setting, differences along the dimension of individualism versus collectivism were evidenced in the teachers' preparation for and personal role in meetings, how the decision-making process was conducted, and the teachers' willingness to share classroom materials and methods. The American meeting style used by the curriculum developer was to distribute the meeting agenda and venue ahead of time so that everyone would come to the meeting on time, with materials in hand, having considered and come to a stance on the issues under discussion. At the close of the meeting, it was expected that the issue would be resolved, a decision reached, or a plan of action agreed upon. Individuals were expected to present and support their personal opinions as a means to discuss the issue and reach a decision. The American view of a meeting seemed to be "Come to the meeting ready to hear everyone's point of view, discuss and decide. Then we can get on with it," with an expectation that all members will freely and openly offer their opinions, stay on task, and negotiate together a plan of action to be implemented after the meeting. Decision-making in U.S. society is often according to majority rule, with those in the minority expected to "agree to disagree" and at least try out the plan to see how it works. In this way, the plan can be implemented more quickly.

The Malaysian style was quite different, reflecting a view of meetings as social, interactive opportunities with colleagues (refreshments and socializing usually held before or after the meeting). Malaysian teachers were less likely to view themselves as participants in the meeting, often taking the view that meetings were conducted so that management could announce decisions. (Meetings were to be endured, not participated in.) It was common for Malaysian teachers to arrive late or unprepared with materials needed for the meeting. At first, some teachers made other appointments during the meeting times, asking that others just "tell me what they said." There seemed to be a perception that meetings (held Friday mornings, when everyone was supposed to be working) were cutting into the teachers' "free time." This behavior was confusing to the Americans, who viewed meetings as a time for individuals to share their ideas and express opinions openly.

Malaysians seemed to view meetings as initiating events in the decision-making process or cycle. At the meeting, issues were identified and management's positions made known. After the meeting, friends met to discuss the issues and to express opinions privately. Once it was fairly clear what the main opinions were, delegates or "friendly surrogates" went to managers to inform, negotiate, and then report back to the group. This process continued until the entire group had reached consensus, at which time another meeting was often called in which the decision was passed "down" from management. This style reflected a view that "You should take time and make sure that everyone agrees. That way you ensure that everyone will implement the decision whole-heartedly."

There were times when a decision or policy was stated as having been resolved, but it later became clear that the decision was still up for discussion. If strong disagreements occurred during a curriculum meeting, it was common for Malaysian teachers to talk privately with their friend/colleague (sitting next to them) at such length that the meeting virtually stopped until everyone was ready to pay attention again. To find out what the disagreement were, however, it was usually necessary to meet more socially to clarify and compare views. If it became clear that the decision was actually still an unresolved issue, friendly surrogates were typically sent to managers to reopen the issue and begin negotiation toward a solution. Most of the decision-making process, therefore, took place outside of the meeting context, with the follow-up meeting providing a forum whereby decisions which had already been agreed upon by all members of the group were publicly announced by management. It was considered desirable to take the time to make a good decision and to ensure that everyone was in agreement. Inability to quickly reach consensus did not cause as much stress and frustration as it normally would in an American context.

While extremely time-consuming, an important benefit of this decision-making and communication style was that the people who felt most comfortable interpersonally were the ones put into the roles of negotiators, with positive interpersonal relationships maintained throughout the process. The importance of friendship was overtly recognized and there was an expectation that business colleagues would draw upon their personal relationships as a means to further business endeavors. It was unusual to have a business relationship with someone who was not your friend or known to you through introduction by a friend. Business commonly took place in a context of mutual trust and a recognition of ongoing commitment to one another. There was a long-term view and awareness that providing a good business deal to a friend would ensure not only the friend's business, but also the friend's recommendation and subsequent business of others.

An overriding concern within personal and business relationships was the desire to preserve dignity or "face" among group members. Protection of face meant not openly criticizing others, their plans, or their policies. The result of this value was a reluctance on the part of Malaysian teachers to provide constructive criticisms of the new curriculum plan, especially in meetings. As mentioned earlier, this was a problem since, from the American developer's point of view, the purpose of the meetings was to conduct formative evaluation of the new curriculum prototype so as to identify problems and improve the model. Teachers were asked, for example, to compare the amount of content they were able to comfortably complete that week, to discuss testing and instructional needs, and to identify problems so that the curriculum and schedule could be adjusted accordingly. American teachers volunteered criticisms freely, solicited opinions from others, and were active in working with managers to decide upon changes. Malaysian teachers were very reluctant to criticize the curriculum, seeming to feel that "the plan and the person are one and the same." For the Malaysian teachers, it was impossible to criticize the plan without implying that the person was at fault. Respect for the individual, a recognition of the time and effort put into developing the plan, and a reluctance to hurt the developer's feelings impinged upon their ability to offer helpful criticisms. The prevailing attitude was "everything is personal."

The Americans were also surprised at the Malaysian teachers' reluctance to share instructional materials in a common file. The Malaysian teachers felt very strongly that impromptu, public sharing of classroom stories, methods, or materials was a form of "showing off." It was only considered acceptable to offer ideas and materials when explicitly asked by a close friend/colleague. The American teachers' attitude, conversely, was that "If you have something that worked well in class, it's your duty to share it with others."

An anonymous system of materials' sharing was developed to help deal with this self-effacement issue. In addition, the teachers themselves initiated an extra teachers' meeting at the beginning of each week during which they took turns presenting (in friend/colleague pairs) their instructional ideas and plans for the upcoming week of instruction. Having a scheduled time to present ideas made it clear to everyone that they had been asked to perform in that leadership role, gave everyone ample preparation time, and allowed them to self-select instructional content and methods to share with the group. Table 6 in Appendix C provides a summary of teacher values which seemed to be influenced by collectivist versus individualist orientations. These values also influenced decision-making and communication effectiveness between the teacher groups.

ORAL VERSUS WRITTEN LANGUAGE

Hofstede chose to focus on culture from a cognitivist point of view, indicating that culture is an outcome of the "collective programming of the mind," with "patterns of thinking" transferred, for example, from parents to their children (1984, p. 82). The link between culture and cognition is thereby recognized, but the role of language not fully discussed. Possible areas warranting further research are the extent to which a society transmits information through written versus verbal communications and the effects of media communication preferences on intercultural communication.

It seemed that American teachers were more literate-based than Malaysians, who seemed more "oral-aural based." For the Malaysian teachers, what was "real" (what could be believed) was what they heard. American teachers, on the other hand, needed to see it in writing before it could be believed. An example from Malaysia was the day the national soccer team won the Southeast Asian championships and we heard that a holiday had been declared and classes canceled for the afternoon. This rumor went around the halls at about 11 a.m. and the Malaysian teachers were gone by noon. The American teachers, however, had received no written notification and remained on site until after 1:30 p.m., when no students showed up to their classes. Nobody ever did receive confirmation of any official sort that classes were canceled; what was heard through the grapevine was "real." Differing perception of communication importance on the basis of language medium (written vs. verbal) occurred regularly. Malaysian teachers were more likely to discount written communications and American teachers more likely to discount verbal communications. This has great implications for contexts in which written-based societies typically communicate via memo, E-mail, or reports, while oral-based societies rely on verbal messages and may require verbal confirmation or ignore written communications. Cultural conflicts and misunderstandings can easily result when one communicator believes verbal messages and the other believes written messages.

Educators should also be aware of the media by which they transmit important information. Malaysian (and other students from more "orally-based" societies) often ask for verbal confirmation of information already provided on a syllabus or handout. It may very well be that these students read the information but couldn't consider the message "real" until it had been heard. Not only do instructors need to be aware of the need to supply verbal confirmation, but they should also teach skills which can help students from oral-based cultures succeed in more written-oriented societies.

CONCLUSION

Hofstede stated that "Effectiveness within a given culture, and judged according to the values of that culture, asks for management skills adapted to the local culture" (1984, p. 98). Similarly, effectiveness in inter-cultural communications requires that communicators be aware of differences in decision-making processes and communication purposes. Within the Malaysian context, Americans needed to understand that meetings were not decision-making events, but rather decision-initiating events. In addition, the importance of friendship and the roles of friendly surrogates had to be understood so that negotiation and consensus-reaching processes could be carried out smoothly. Americans needed to be aware of stress and seek methods to alleviate it when soliciting open, direct communications and constructive criticisms. They also needed to learn communication techniques and forms of behavior which enhanced and protected others' dignity or "face." Similarly, the Americans needed to learn how to listen to indirect communications in order to sort out the true message. Lastly, the importance of the medium of communication (oral versus written) needed to be considered along with the effects on communication and management effectiveness in verbal versus written-based cultures. It is hoped that these concepts and examples will be of use to managers, educators, and students as they communicate and interact interculturally.

DISCUSSION QUESTIONS

1. Decide, from the descriptors provided in Table 3 of large versus small power distance societies, which would be most problematic or require the most attention for someone interacting cross-culturally in your profession. Explain and support your choices while discussing implications.

2. Consider then discuss both positive and negative outcomes of a collectivist-oriented society. Do the same for an individualist-oriented society. Provide evidence and examples, drawing from personal, academic, and professional contexts.

3. Observe and analyze a decision being made in your society. Document and be ready to describe a) the steps/stages of the decision-making process and b) the point at which a real decision has been reached. Share your results and be ready to describe both positive and negative aspects of the process you observed.

4. Consider the concept of "preservation of "face" and describe at least three ways in which face is preserved or enhanced within teacher interactions described in this chapter. How is 'face' preserved or enhanced in your culture? Discuss while providing concrete examples.

5. Everyone is influenced by culture, including the writer of this chapter. What evidence can you find of the author's cultural orientation? What, in your opinion, are the most valuable lessons to be learned from this chapter?

APPENDIX A

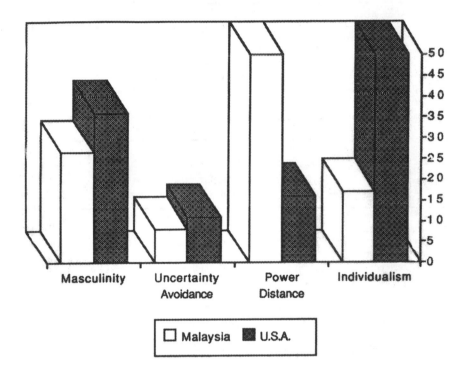

FIGURE 1. Comparison of Malaysia and the United States on Hofstede's Four Societal Dimensions

APPENDIX B: HOFSTEDE DESCRIPTORS
OF SOCIETAL DIMENSIONS

TABLE 1.
Masculine versus Feminine Societal Descriptors

Masculine	Feminine
■ Competitiveness is good; the hero is the high achiever.	■ Solidarity is good; rewards are according to need.
■ The strong should win; performance is stressed.	■ Help the weak; relationships are stressed.
■ Stimulate workers through challenging work.	■ Stimulate workers through social units.

TABLE 2.
Strong versus Weak Uncertainty Avoidance Descriptors

Strong Uncertainty Avoidance	Weak Uncertainty Avoidance
■ Desire for "law & order," an emphasis on certainty & conformity.	■ Tolerant of ambiguity and prepared to change the rules.
■ Intolerant of deviants.	■ Practice counts more than principles.
■ Maintain rigid codes of belief and behavior.	■ More relaxed; less hurried.
■ Feel a need to control the future.	■ Time runs one way. The future is unknown.
■ Expression of emotions.	■ Hiding of emotions.
■ Ritualization of words, dress, actions.	■ Unwritten rules of conduct, but mostly for convenience.

TABLE 3.
Large versus Small Power Distance Societal Descriptors

Large Power Distance-oriented	Small Power Distance-oriented
■ Accepting of unequal power distribution and hierarchical order.	■ Striving for equal power distribution; more relaxed hierarchically.
■ Individual status based on perceived power and authority.	■ Individual status based on personal merit.
■ "Paternalistic" management.	■ Superior/subordinate as "genuine negotiation partners."
■ Indirect communication (use of "go-betweens").	■ Direct, two-way communication.
■ Parents/teachers as "sources of wisdom."	■ Success in achievement due to individual's mastery of a subject.
■ Exams as an entry certificate to a higher status group.	■ Exams as a means to prove mastery.

TABLE 4.
Collectivist versus Individualist Societal Descriptors

Collectivist-oriented	Individualist-oriented
■ Emphasis on interdependence - We	■ Emphasis on independence - I
■ Tightly knit (ordered) social framework.	■ Loosely knit (equal) social framework.
■ Group interests dominate; self-effacement.	■ Self interest dominates; self-promotion.
■ Relationships have priority over the task.	■ Tasks may have priority over relationships.
■ Employment relationships have a moral component (loyalty).	■ Business relationships are calculative (mutual advantage).
■ Integration of business and private life.	■ Separation of business and private life.
■ Maintenance of harmony; conflict suppression.	■ Conflict resolution; disagreement expressed openly.
■ Conform to proper forms; avoid loss of face.	■ Emphasize equality and informality; openness is a virtue.
■ Indirect communication.	■ Direct communication.

APPENDIX C: MALAYSIAN/AMERICAN DECISION-MAKING AND COMMUNICATION DIFFERENCES

TABLE 5.
Difference Related to Large versus Small Power Distance

Malaysian Teachers	American Teachers
■ "Another meeting with the boss." Meetings seen as information-sharing from the top-down & for identification of issues to be considered.	■ "I'm glad you brought that up. In my opinion...." Meetings are for open discussion and collaboration.
■ "You're the expert; you decide and let me know." Top-down management.	■ "We're all experts; let's decide together what to do." Bottom-up management.
■ "Teachers transmit knowledge and, as content experts, must have all the answers." Teacher-centered classrooms.	■ "Teachers model how to learn. You should be able to show students how to find the answer." Learner-centered classrooms.
■ "If you're a good teacher, your students will get good grades on the exam." Teachers are responsible for their students' learning.	■ "Good teachers sometimes have unmotivated students." Students have to take responsibility for their own learning.
■ "Teach to the test." Focus on mastery of (often memorized) content. Focus on product.	■ "Can you work this problem?" Focus on extended and applied learning. Focus on process and progress.
■ "Good morning, Professor." More formal classroom style. Rigid codes of behavior exist between management, teachers and students.	■ "Call me Bob." Informal style and more equal social interactions are acceptable between students/teachers and managers/teachers.
■ "You're friends... you could tell her." Protection and enhancement of "face." Use of friendly surrogates to point out problems or difficulties.	■ "If you don't like it, just let me know." Expectation of direct, two-way communication and explicit discussion of unhappiness between individuals.

Note: Based on Wilhelm & Pereira (1993).

TABLE 6.
Differences Related to Collectivism versus Individualism

Malaysian Teachers	American Teachers
■ "Some people think this... but we don't have to decide right now." Private negotiation until all members reach consensus. If everyone agrees, there is more chance of success.	■ "Here's the agenda. We hope to get this decided as soon as possible." Public discussion of personal opinion. Majority rules. Eagerness to get started.
■ "Everything is personal." You show respect for someone's work by not criticizing it. It's better to be less than frank than to hurt someone's feelings. Focus on keeping friends as colleagues.	■ "Don't take it personally, but...." Work is divorced from personalities. You show respect for that person's work by helping to improve it. Focus on tasks.
■ "If you take more time, you will make a better decision."	■ "The sooner the decision is made, the better."
■ "Don't show off." It's only OK to offer ideas or materials when asked. Don't imply that you know more than your colleagues.	■ "If you have something that worked well, your duty is to share it with others."

REFERENCES

Hofstede, G. (1984). Cultural dimensions in management and planning. *Asia Pacific Journal of Management, 2,* 81-99.

Wilhelm, K. H. & Pereira, M. (1993). *Instructional problems/solutions and cross-cultural issues arising from the implementation of an EAP course in Malaysia.* Presented at RELC (Regional Language Centre) Conference on Language for Specific Purposes, Southeast Asian Ministers of Education Organization, Singapore.

20

EDUCATORS CROSSING CULTURES: EVALUATION OF PAST WORK AND GUIDELINES FOR THE FUTURE

Ekaterina Ognianova
Southwest Texas State University

INTRODUCTION

Since the fall of communism in 1989, North American educators have been involved in a number of technical assistance programs, sharing their expertise in a free market society with professionals, educators, and students throughout East-Central Europe.[1] This chapter examines the work of 25 North American educators who participated in 38 programs providing technical assistance in applied fields throughout East-Central Europe from 1991 to 1995. The first objective was to distill from the educators' experiences insights that would inform future training and consulting programs with the participation of Western educators and East-Central European professionals. The second objective was to find in the literature on intercultural communication solutions to some of the problems experienced by the 25 North American educators. The third objective was to propose a checklist of practical guidelines that would help make the most of continuing exchanges in East-Central Europe and could be applied to intercultural technical assistance programs in general.

This chapter starts with the assumption that foreign aid in the form of educational and training exchanges is beneficial to both sides. The vast literature on intercultural education, even as early as the late 1960s/early 1970s, suggests and includes evidence that cultural exchanges are mutually useful. For example, Mead (1968) stressed the potential for an educator to gain special insights during the process of teaching in a different culture. Field experiments, in which U.S. teachers participated in seminars abroad, showed that their experiences led to better understanding of the diverse ethnic groups and their cultures within the United States (Leestma, 1973).

In the context of East-Central Europe, for citizens of the post-communist countries the transfer of knowledge can bring some of the ideals of a stable market economy, democratic laws, and free and responsible media that are viewed as a cornerstone to a healthy democracy (Gray, 1995). For the North American educators, visiting the emerging democracies offers an opportunity to critically evaluate their own culture (Palmer, Cartford, de Vargas, Trueman, & Reyes, 1980).

The chapter addresses the following research questions: How do North American educators teach in intercultural settings? What, if anything do they need to do differently when they teach in such settings? How does a visiting professor juggle being a tourist with the obligation to do the best job possible in an international setting with a different language, culture, and etiquette? What should future exchange programs with East-Central Europe stress or change?

THEORETICAL FRAMEWORK AND LITERATURE REVIEW

The topic of teaching and doing consulting work in the evolving European democracies can be analyzed in several theoretical frameworks. On first sight, it might seem appropriate to apply the early communication and national development paradigm, placing attempts to rebuild the East-Central European institutions in the tradition of communication's powerful effects on a country's development (Lerner, 1958; Lerner & Schramm, 1967; Lerner & Nelson, 1977; Pye, 1963, 1966; Schramm, 1964; Schramm & Lerner, 1976; Rogers & Svenning, 1969). However, East-Central Europe differs from the traditionally-called "Third World" in three critical aspects: high literacy rate, availability of cultural resources, and—most relevant to the technical assistance programs—lack of commercial enterprise for at least 50 years (Ognianova, 1996). Therefore, the development communication framework is not the most appropriate for analyzing the effectiveness of technical assistance programs in post-communist countries.

Another possible framework is the diffusion of innovations theory viewing the visiting educators as potential change agents and the local professionals, participating in the foreign-sponsored training, as early adopters of innovations (Rogers, 1983; Rogers & Shoemaker, 1971). A study that uses this framework, however, faces the impossible task of establishing a cause-and-effect relationship of Western influence and East-Central European adoption of knowledge, habits, and mindset. It is doubtful that the take-off of Western ideas in East-Central Europe has a direct association with the West-sponsored training sessions. Other circumstances from within the country, such as the changes in the economic, social and political system, are more likely to have impacted the transition to a pluralistic democracy and an open market.

A more appropriate framework, especially in terms of suggesting guidelines to future exchanges, is the literature on intercultural communication. There are two trends in the study of intercultural communication. First, it is considered an extension of communication in general, with the same variables as in intracultural communication (Gudykunst, 1983). This trend applies to intercultural communication basic concepts of the act and structure of communication, such as Laswell's formula, Shannon and Weaver's mathematical model, the study of codes in general, and theories of mass communication (c.f. Casmir, 1978; Prosser, 1973; 1978a, b; Sitaram & Cogdell, 1976; Wiseman & Koester, 1993). Second, intercultural communication research extensively explores issues of cultural identification, interaction between groups with diverse cultural norms and values, communication competence, and adjustment to different cultural settings (Smith, 1966). In this trend, the first two concepts focus on cultural differences or variability (Grove, 1976), while the latter two stress similarities, which make it possible to communicate across cultures (Prosser, 1978a, c). We now look briefly at some specific suggestions from that literature. Because of the applied nature of the study described here, we focus only on applied research that can be used in developing practical guidelines for future technical assistance programs.

One of the first steps toward a successful intercultural interaction is awareness of possible differences in the "other culture." An international business communication course in Eastern Michigan University outlined several factors that are most likely to change across cultures. They included: language, environment, technology, social organization, way of placing things in context, concept of authority, nonverbal communication, and concept of time (Victor, 1987). Similarly, Talbott (1990) identified 36 obstacles to adjustment to foreign cultures based on the experiences of Glenville State (West Virginia) College participants in exchanges with Western Europe. The main obstacles included communications, differences in the measurement system, and personal inconveniences. Transportation, food, money transactions and customs/immigration ranked as lesser obstacles.

A next step, of course, is overcoming those differences. The literature on intercultural communication and intercultural education suggests several practical guidelines for acquiring intercultural communication competence. It is worth noting Sarbaugh's (1988, p. 126) questions that, ideally, are to be considered when preparing to work interculturally. These questions include:

1. What must one do to get along?
2. What must one not do?
3. What ought one to do?
4. What ought one not do?
5. What is one allowed to do?
6. What are the sanctions for not following the cultural rules?
7. How do persons in this culture view themselves and the world around them?
8. What verbal and non-verbal codes are more critical to know?
9. How direct and open are people in their communication with one another? How does this differ, if at all, for strangers?

This list of questions may be helpful to North American educators preparing to teach and consult in East-Central Europe.

Finally, the literature on intercultural communication and intercultural education includes recommendations to exchange programs. Stone (1975) outlined elements that exchange programs should contain, including adequate orientation before leaving and access to competent guidance abroad. Martin (1963) advised journalism Fulbright lecturers on how to deal with potential frustrations during their teaching abroad, e.g. not to get involved in local politics. He recommended to avoid attempts for promoting the educators' own values and simply transplanting their country's press (in the context of this chapter, it could be economic, legal, agricultural, etc.) system. To "go to your [host] country with an open mind" was Clayton's (1963, p. 119) suggestion, too. That does not mean not to prepare. The educator's advice will be most helpful when it is geared to the local needs, so these needs must be known in advance, Clayton argued.

In terms of selecting people for intercultural exchanges, the intercultural communication/education literature emphasizes the personal qualities of the educators. The criteria for Peace Corps applicants provide a useful example of selection and preparation for intercultural technical assistance programs. Besides the need to do a particular job and the strength to serve for the required time period, Peace Corps volunteers are required to know their own culture and heritage, be sensitive to people of different cultures, and (not always followed) use the language of the host country (Scanlon & Shields, 1968). We now turn to our study that attempted to integrate suggestions from the literature with insights from North American educators' personal experiences.

THE STUDY

The study described in this chapter relies on intensive semi-structured interviews. Although the results can hardly be generalized, this method offers flexibility and an opportunity to establish a rapport with the interviewees (Wimmer & Dominick, 1997, p. 100). The method is especially relevant to the objectives of the study, which require distilling the personal insights of the educators and the nuances of their experiences.

The interviews were conducted with a convenience sample narrowed to North American educators with teaching and consulting experience in applied and professional fields in East-Central Europe. The interviewees represented a variety of U.S. institutions: the American Bar Association, Indiana University, Oklahoma State University, Norfolk State University, University of Minnesota, and the University of Missouri. The interviewees had taught and consulted in the following countries: Bosnia-Herzegovina, Bulgaria, the Czech republic, Estonia, Georgia, Hungary, Kazakhstan, Latvia, Lithuania, Macedonia, Poland, Romania, Russia, Slovakia, and the Ukraine.

Of the 25 participants, 20 were men and 5 were women. In this study, women (20 percent) are actually over-represented slightly, compared to some of the programs for technical assistance. For example, in the programs of Volunteers in Overseas Cooperative Assistance (VOCA) and Citizens Democracy Corps (CDC) only approximately 10 percent of the volunteer advisors/consultants are women (Hughel, J., VOCA Regional Recruitment Director, personal communication, June 6, 1995; Schiager, J., CDC program officer, personal communication, June 6, 1995).

Eighteen educators were interviewed in person, three by phone. The in-person and phone interviews lasted about an hour. Four educators were reached via the Internet; two of them at the time were teaching in Bulgaria and the Czech republic respectively. The interviewees were asked, on average, 21 questions regarding their preparation for teaching abroad, what they taught, and what they would recommend to North American educators going to teach in East-Central Europe in the future. Each interview sought to identify aspects of cultural variability, such as language, etiquette, customs in interpersonal communication, reception of and attitudes toward foreigners, traditional type of relationships between teachers and students, and among professionals in the country's institutions. Finally, interviewees were asked for their suggestions on how these potential hindrances to intercultural exchanges can be overcome in future programs.

Overview of the Programs

On average, the 38 training and consulting programs, in which the interviewees participated, lasted from one day to a week, eight to ten hours a day, to a year in the case of the Fulbright professorship. Topics of the training and consulting programs included: business (management, marketing, finance, industrial relations); agriculture (farm management, farm tourism, dairy product processing, meat processing); journalism (management, reporting, advertising); coaching judges on handling a courtroom and lawyers on setting up private practices; institution building in business and public administration; and working with teachers and mental health specialists on counseling children with post-traumatic stress disorder. The material presented by North American educators in management, business, economics, and advertising was new to the East-Central European participants, due to their lack of free market experience.

Selection of Educators

Most of the educators were chosen or approved to participate in technical assistance programs in East-Central Europe by their North American colleagues. For example, four of the interviewees had volunteered to participate in consulting programs in East-Central Europe. The main criterion for selection was the educators' expertise in particular areas and/or experience with professional workshops in the United States and abroad. In addition, three educators were selected under the rigorous competition for a Fulbright professorship/scholarship. An exception to the majority selected by North Americans was a journalism professor who was invited by Bulgarian photojournalists to organize a photojournalism seminar there.

The level of teaching and consulting experience varied widely among the interviewees. Some had extensive experience with professional workshops both in the U.S. and abroad. Some had lived in other countries, knew at least one foreign language and had undergone the adjustment to a different culture. Others did not have that advantage, but were eager to offer their expertise to the emerging European democracies.

Preparation

Preparation varied from "hundreds of hours" to "very little time," depending on prior knowledge about the country and the problems to be addressed, the role of the educators in the training programs (e.g., teaching, consulting, and/or organizing a workshop), and the scope and length of the programs. Some educators studied the history and the language of the country they were about to visit and read about current developments in their fields of expertise. Others concentrated on preparing their teaching/consulting materials. For two management professors, it was a challenge alone to condense semester-long human resource management classes into one-month courses. A professor in meat processing spent a week converting American meat product recipes into the metric system.

The organizers of the programs sometimes provided briefing material as well as formal classes and orientation sessions. For example, VOCA arranged briefings both in the United States and the host country and supplied each volunteer with an individual folder, containing an outline of the consulting assignment; geographic, historic, and economic information about the country; an introduction to the country's cultural norms; and practical traveling hints. Before leaving, some of the educators met at least one person from the host country and that meeting served as an orientation session, sometimes formally resembling one, with slide presentations and verbal explanations.

However, even the orientation sessions and briefings were not enough preparation, interviewees said. For the longer programs, six of the participants suggested that the educators make a preliminary visit—up to two weeks—to the country as part of their preparation. The visit would help educators understand the environment and the people, and most of all, assess their needs so the training could be specifically tailored to them. This suggestion is not unreasonable because most of the participants knew very little about the country in which they were expected to teach and consult. Prior knowledge was limited to "a little" history and, at best, general awareness of recent events acquired from the media. In many cases, the interviewees admitted they had needed to consult a map to locate the host-to-be country.

Cultural Variability

Once in the countries, the American educators faced several cultural challenges, such as the combination of: 1) the foreign culture, 2) different social role schemas, and 3) the still-present heritage of Communism. In Bulgaria, for example, a public administration professor faced a "culture of silence" where people slowly opened up to ask questions (R. Baker, personal communication, June 1, 1995). Throughout the East-Central European countries, there was a still-living communist tradition that said, "unless something is specifically permitted, it is forbidden." (L. Scanlan, personal communication, December 3, 1993). In Russia, Ukraine and Kazakhstan, an animal sciences professor encountered reminders of the past regime that indirectly and directly affected his work. He was puzzled when he noticed that, in general, people did not smile in public. But if you constantly face the bureaucracy of government officials you learn not to smile, he was told. He also discovered the need to frame questions differently from the way local government officials did. When he inquired about the yield of crops in Kazakhstan, his hosts responded with the unrealistically big figure required by the state. Such misleading information, of course, would only hinder his efforts to help modernize the dairy industry there. Moreover, certain words took on different meanings due to their previous use in the communist centralized economy. The word *cooperative* had a negative connotation for the East-Central Europeans because of the forced collective farming during communism (B. Steevens, personal communication, June 2 and 7, 1995).

The educators also had to struggle with their own illusions and cultural background. When a San Francisco attorney volunteered for the Central and East European Law Initiative in 1993, she expected to find in the region the enthusiasm for a democratic reform that marked the fall of the Berlin Wall. Instead, she met disillusioned people, exhausted by economic hardships and political uncertainty (M. N. Pepys, personal communication, June 17 1994). Some of the educators assumed, from their own previous lack of knowledge about the region, that people there were ignorant about the West or did not understand the ideas of democracy. In the longer programs, the educators realized that what East-Central Europeans needed was not the ABCs of democracy but experience with it.

In addition, most educators lacked the patience for post-communist life where things that would take minutes in the United States require more time or become impossible. In the Balkan countries, for example, placing a phone call can take several hours because of outdated equipment. Buying an airplane ticket can also be a time-consuming ordeal that is better arranged by the hosts. This mixture of old habits and inaccurate expectations, on the part of both the East-Central Europeans and the North Americans, caused frustrations among the educators. But it also taught the educators to be patient and helped them understand the daily lives of their hosts/trainees.

Local Participation

The participants in the educational and consulting programs varied from new entrepreneurs, students, teachers, to experienced and beginning judges, lawyers, and journalists, to academics with long careers who had switched to the new discipline of business. The numbers varied with each program, from less than five to 200. The interviewees agreed that participants appeared eager to learn and convert into their own needs the message brought by the North American educators. "They absorb like a sponge," a management professor said of his Romanian colleagues (R. Penfield, personal communication, June 1, 1995). All programs encouraged participants to ask questions. After overcoming initial shyness, the participants wanted to know "why, how, what do you mean" (Penfield, personal communication). Some of the training sessions turned into discussions rather than lectures from the visitors.

At least in one case, however, a program was inappropriately scheduled at a time when the locals in need of training could not attend. The visiting educator suspected the polite hosts had randomly rounded up people for an audience.

Most workshops had out-of-class time in their schedules. Informal receptions helped the faculty and students establish a rapport. In some week-long programs, faculty and participants shared accommodations. In the longer programs, the hosts regularly invited the educators to their homes, to picnics, family dinners, tours, and events of the local culture. The process of knowledge transfer continued outside of the classroom.

Teaching Through Interpreters

Most of the programs used consecutive interpreting. Some programs depended on interpreters; in others the participants understood English but few spoke it. Most interviewees agreed that teaching through interpreters was a hindrance. It slowed the educators down, allowing them to deliver half of the material they would teach in English in the same time. Some nuances of the language and direct interaction with the audience were inevitably lost in translation.

Even so, two participants expressed a favorable view of using interpreters. Consecutive interpretation, they said, gives speakers time to collect their thoughts, choose words carefully, and reflect on the audience's reactions and understanding. Because of that, one interviewee argued, the speakers could make up for some of the time lost in translation. She recommended that interpreters stand beside the speakers so they do not forget to slow down. A psychologist advised educators to get to know their interpreters. All interviewees suggested that educators avoid long sentences and idioms, enunciate slowly and carefully, and are prepared to repeat and rephrase. They recommended visual examples instead of verbal descriptions.

In most programs, interpreters were reliable, especially if they specialized in the field in which the knowledge was transferred. Yet, something is always lost in translation, most interviewees said. One exchange program found a solution to the problem by bringing the Romanian trainees to the United States to help them learn English.

Access to Teaching Resources and Introducing Technology

Availability of instructional facilities varied from one country to another and, within a country, from one city to another. Some interviewees shared their frustrations with technology that was available but not usable due to power outage or insufficient voltage. In some countries there was a shortage of paper. A marketing professor brought an overhead projector to Romania and washed the transparencies to use them again. Photographs were an animal sciences professor's best teaching aid.

Others found in the host countries everything they used at home: overhead, slide, and video projectors; copy machines; personal computers; laser printers. An agricultural economics professor brought his own equipment with him. It allowed him to modify his lectures according to the audience's needs, which had not been clear in advance. He also spent time in the computer lab of the host institute, demonstrating applications to students on their machines.

Participants agreed that East Central Europeans accepted new technology without reservations, mostly with a great deal of curiosity. New equipment was introduced usually in longer programs, when participants had time to familiarize themselves with it. But it is important to consider if and how the participants' self-esteem may be affected when they are introduced to technology they cannot afford to have. Perhaps that is why some of the exchange programs include a budget for the purchase of technology.

Program Evaluation and Effectiveness

Only 5 of the 25 interviewees were aware of the results of formal evaluations conducted by the program organizers after the training.[2] Although VOCA evaluates
each of its consulting programs, one of the three VOCA consultants received
feedback about his visit. Most of the journalism faculty who taught in East-Central Europe in the early 1990s lacked feedback. "To this day... I don't know what
I did wrong, other than what my own feelings tell me. I tried to watch people carefully but it was difficult to tell—these people are so polite they probably would
not have told us except in an anonymous evaluation, " said an interviewee who
taught at a 1991 media management workshop in Poland (P. Hoddinott, personal
communication, November 17, 1993). The trainees' hesitation to openly and critically evaluate the performance of their North American teachers became evident
in other fields. An agricultural economics professor shared his frustration after
hosting Bulgarian academics in his university in 1993. "I didn't know whether I
was speaking beneath them or over them," he said (P. Warnken, personal communication, June 7, 1995). Because it is not polite to criticize guests or hosts in the
East-Central European cultures, an anonymous evaluation is the only way for
educators to get a sincere feedback about their work.

Feedback can also be obtained in *informal* conversations with the participants
and the sponsors. Seeing how the local media have covered the training program
is another way. But perhaps the best option is continuing contacts with the hosts
after the training. Such contacts reveal exactly what parts of the training, if any,
the participants have implemented in their own work.

In this respect, results have been encouraging. After the first year of training by
a Midwestern university business faculty, a Romanian university created two new
courses in management and marketing, along with textbooks for them. The recommendations of a food sciences and human nutrition professor to a meat processing plant in Ukraine were strictly followed and it became a market success (D.
Naumann, personal communication, June 2, 1995). In a different context, the war
in Bosnia-Herzegovina, a psychologist from a Midwestern university was also
able to see the fruit of her work. She told the story of a child who had lost his family while running to a refugee camp in Sarajevo. In the camp, he was placed in a
special classroom for students with post-traumatic stress disorder. When he was
announced a math champion, the psychologist felt the same gratification as the
child's teachers in Sarajevo who had participated in her training. For many of the
educators, the practical use of their knowledge represents the best evaluation and
the most accurate measure of a program's effectiveness.

Going Back

The majority of the interviewees said they would go back to the region for more
technical assistance programs. Several explained that they "believed in what they

were doing," citing the ideals of freedom and democracy as their reasons. One, however, cautioned against such "lofty goals" (Warnken, personal communication). "I just like to open up people's eyes to new ideas. That's what teachers do," he said. Others said they enjoyed being involved in a country's efforts to betterment. "You feel good about going back to a place where people are fighting hard to improve," said a management professor who later went back to Romania for a semester (Penfield, personal communication). Another group said they had a wonderful time, praising the people and the beauty of the lands. Finally, some interviewees said they would go back because they would know better what to do next time.

Most importantly, the interviewees stressed how much they had learned and grown personally because of their intercultural teaching or consulting experiences. Two of the educators said specifically that their lives had become richer with their East-Central European experiences (Pepys, personal communication; Steevens, personal communication). Another, participant, a journalism professor who had taught in Jamaica, two Caribbean Islands, India, Tunisia, and Hungary, and said he would go back "in a minute" explained: "Every time I go to these places—they may not have enough material resources...—but I learn more than I ever teach." (D. Moen, personal communication, November 16, 1993).

CONCLUSIONS AND PRACTICAL RECOMMENDATIONS

One of the critical conclusions of this chapter is that cultural differences can be overcome, especially if the educators are educated in advance. Careful preparation both about the country and the needs of the program participants, an open mind, and sensitivity would almost certainly decrease the "noise" that cultural differences cause in intercultural training. First, the benefit for the host country would be greater if the task is clearly tailored to the needs of the participants, negotiated with them, and constantly redefined in light of the fast changes in the region. Second, the educators would learn themselves and have a more rewarding experience if they are given the time and resources to prepare in advance. We now look at specific changes that could improve North American exchanges with East-Central Europe.

The Role of North American Educators in East-Central Europe

North American educators should continue their involvement in East-Central Europe—with certain changes. The recommendations for the educators' future role can be summarized in two points: (1) selective use of short-term programs, and (2) engagement in longer term commitments with the goal to turn the education of East-Central European professionals over to East-Central European educators.

1. *Short-term training sessions* can be useful—for consulting, trouble-shooting, and solving specific business problems. The training has to be practical and use technology readily available in East-Central Europe
2. *Long-term commitments* are more useful. It is more realistic to train a group of people who will later train their fellow country people in their native language and culture. For the North American educators this will ultimately mean stepping aside from their leading role, but remaining "on call" for consultation and moral support. When the East-Central Europeans acquire the necessary competence to work in a free market economy, the educational exchanges will provide greater opportunities for collaboration in research.

Here are specific suggestions for longer-term training:

1. Provide M.A. and Ph.D. fellowships in North American universities for East-Central European educators and professionals who want to teach.
2. Send North American educators to East-Central European universities for at least a semester, preferably a year, to teach and consult on curriculum development.
3. Send North American graduate students to East-Central Europe for a semester, preferably a year, to do research or work on professional projects, and be available to assist professionals, academics, and students there.
4. Bring young professionals from East-Central Europe to the United States for internships in institutions of their choice.
5. Send North American educators to extended, on-site visits of East-Central European institutions—for observation and coaching. Pair every visitor with a local professional who can serve as interpreter, guide to the culture, and mediator between the trainees and the visiting educator.
6. Involve East-Central European professionals, academics, and students in all activities of North American and international professional and academic organizations.

Guidelines for Educators Participating in Intercultural Technical Assistance Programs

Before leaving:

- Get input from the participants about what they need. Ask what their specific questions might be and request from them cases to analyze in advance.
- Learn as much as you can about the country. Study its geography, history, culture, and people: where they are technologically, their unspoken cultural rules, and what to expect as visitor, teacher, consultant.
- Review the metric system.

- Try to learn a few words, greetings, numbers and prepare your business cards, itinerary, biography, handouts/overhead transparencies, or slide shows in the language of the country you will be visiting. This will show your respect for the hosts.

In the country:

- Reserve the beginning of the training program for making contacts and getting to know the participants. Be curious, ask questions, and listen.
- Respect people. Don't ever look down upon them for what they do not have. Be tactful not to offend them with anything you say or do. But maintain a balance: try not to fall in the extreme of apologizing all the time.
- Attempt to find a common ground and establish a rapport with the participants. (For example, talk about your families and jobs, show family pictures.)
- Even if you find a bleak situation in the host country, look for positive things to say. If your students are at a professional level that would be considered good in your own country, tell them so.
- Present the way you do your job at home not as the only way to do it but rather as one of many ways that work.
- Avoid promoting yourself or the institution you represent.
- Remember that you are dealing with sophisticated, bright, well-educated professional people.
- Accept it when they do not agree with your points of view. It is for them to decide whether and how much of what you have to offer will be useful to them.
- Prepare to get into big discussions about things you have taken for granted at home.
- Seek formal and informal evaluations. For best feedback, arrange for an anonymous evaluation at the end of the training/consulting.
- Be flexible. Your plan A will not always be appropriate, plan B will often fail, and you will need to have plans C, D and E.

Upon return:

- Follow up on the promises you have made.
- Keep in touch with your hosts to find out the true, long-term impact of your visit.

SUMMARY

This chapter examined technical assistance programs offered by North American educators to East-Central European professionals in the first five years after the fall of communism. The main objective was to learn from past experiences and offer suggestions for improvement of future programs. The researcher conducted intensive semi-structured interviews with 25 North American educators who participated in 38 programs providing technical assistance in applied fields throughout East-Central Europe. Based on the interviews and a review of applied literature in intercultural communication, the chapter suggested practical guidelines for future exchanges in East-Central Europe and for intercultural training in general.

DISCUSSION QUESTIONS

1. What are the purposes and goals of intercultural technical assistance programs? The benefit for a country in need of specific training is fairly clear. But what is the benefit for the people who provide that training and the country they represent?

2. Technical assistance programs are generally offered by Western, more developed countries to countries that are technologically less developed and cannot fully utilize their resources. How can a technical assistance program avoid actually playing the role of or the appearance of being a tool for cultural imperialism?

3. What would you add to the list of guidelines for educators participating in intercultural technical assistance programs that concluded this chapter?

4. Imagine that you are a world-class North American specialist in your field. You have just received a call with an invitation to join educators and consultants in a technical assistance program abroad. You have agreed to do it. What would you do next?

5. Find an international student or a group of international students in your school. Spend a week with them, joining them for meals and social gatherings. Keep a journal, recording your daily conversations and experiences with them. At the end of the week, write a three-page essay about what you think you learned from this experiment.

NOTES

[1] Throughout this chapter, the term East-Central Europe is used for convenience and shortness, but it includes the former Soviet republics.

[2] The task of one interviewee, an economics professor who has published a book on institution-building, was specifically to evaluate a technical assistance project.

REFERENCES

Casmir, F. L. (Ed.) (1978). *Intercultural and international communication*. Washington, D.C.: University Press of America.

Clayton, C. (1963). A challenging and rewarding experience—some ground rules. *Journalism Educator, 18*, 117-119.

Gray, R. (1995, May 31). US group gives civics lessons in former East Bloc: Program offers on-line access to democracy. *USA Today*, p. 5A.

Grove, C. L. (1976). *Communications across cultures*. Washington, D.C.: National Education Association.

Gudykunst, W. B. (Ed.) (1983). *Intercultural communication theory: Current perspectives*. Beverly Hills, CA: Sage.

Leestma, R. (1973 Ethnocentrism and intercultural education. *International Education, 2*, 11- 16.

Lerner, D. (1958). *The passing of traditional society: Modernizing the Middle East*. New York: The Free Press.

Lerner, D., & Schramm, W. (Eds.) (1967). *Communication and change in the developing countries*. Honolulu, HI: East-West Center Press.

Lerner, D., & Nelson, L. M. (Eds.) (1977). *Communication research--A half-century approach*. Honolulu, HI: The University Press of Hawaii.

Martin, L. J. (1963). What a Fulbright professor should stress in journalism programs abroad. *Journalism Educator, 18*, 115-117.

Mead, M. (1968). Education and the problem of transfer in developing societies. In D. G. Scanlon and J. J. Shields (Eds.), *Problems and prospects in international education* (pp. 130-43). New York: Teachers College.

Ognianova, E. (1996, August). *The transitional media system of post-communist Bulgaria*. Paper presented at the annual meeting of the Association for Education in Journalism and Mass Communication, Anaheim, CA.

Palmer, W. R., Cartford, P. F., de Vargas, D. E., Trueman, B. A., & Reyes, L. (1980). The overseas teaching experience. *International Education, 10*, 31-38.

Prosser, M. H. (Ed.) (1973). *Intercommunication among nations and peoples*. New York: Harper & Row.

Prosser, M. H. (1978a). *The cultural dialogue: An introduction to intercultural communication*. Boston: Houghton Mifflin.

Prosser, M. H. (1978b). Basic concepts and models of intercultural communication. In M.H. Prosser (Ed.), *USIA intercultural communication course: 1977 proceedings* (pp. 34-38). Washington, D.C.: International Communication Agency.

Prosser, M. H. (1978c). USIA 1977 intercultural communication course: An introduction. In M.H. Prosser (Ed.), *USIA intercultural communication course: 1977 proceedings* (pp. 1-9). Washington, D.C.: International Communication Agency.

Pye, L. W. (Ed.) (1963). *Communications and political development*. Princeton, NJ: Princeton University Press.

Pye, L. W. (1966). *Aspects of political development: An analytic study*. Boston: Little Brown.

Rogers, E. M. (1983). *Diffusion of innovations* (3rd ed.). New York: Macmillan.

Rogers, E. M., & Svenning, L. (1969). *Modernization among peasants: The impact of communication*. New York: Holt, Rinehart & Winston.

Rogers, E. M., & Shoemaker, F. (1971). *Communication of innovations*. New York: Macmillan.

Sarbaugh, L. E. (1988). *Intercultural communication* . New Brunswick, N.J.: Transaction.

Scanlon, D. G., & Shields, J. J. (Eds.) (1968). *Problems and prospects in international education*. New York: Teachers College.

Schramm, W. (1964). *Mass media and national development: The role of information in the developing countries*. Stanford, CA: Stanford University Press.

Schramm, W., & Lerner, D. (Eds.) (1976). *Communication and social change: The last ten years--and the next*. Honolulu, HI: The University Press of Hawaii.

Sitaram, K. S., & Cogdell, R. T. (1976). *Foundations of intercultural communication*. Columbus, OH: Charles E. Merrill.

Smith, A. (Ed.) (1966). *Communication and culture*. New York: Holt, Rinehart & Winston.

Stone, F. A. (1975). World-minded learning. *International Education, 5*, 7-19.

Talbott, I. D. (1990). Obstacles to host country adjustment in an international travel/study program. *International Education, 20*, 32-38.

Victor, D. A. (1987). Teaching cross-cultural conflict management skills. *Language and communication for world business and the professions*. [On line]. Conference proceedings. Abstract from an ERIC File.

Wimmer, R. D., & Dominick, J. (1997). *Mass media research: An introduction* (5th ed.). Belmont, CA: Wadsworth.

Wiseman, R. L., & Koester, J. (Eds.) (1993). *Intercultural communication competence*. Newbury Park, CA: Sage.

21

ARTIFACTS OF INTERCULTURAL COMMUNICATION BETWEEN U.S. AND INTERNATIONAL UNIVERSITY STUDENTS

Daradirek Ekachai
Southern Illinois University at Carbondale

Mary Hinchcliff-Pelias
Southern Illinois University at Carbondale

Norman S. Greer
Eastern Illinois University

According to recent U.S. Department of Education figures cited in the *Chronicle of Higher Education*, there are currently over 450,000 international students enrolled in institutions of higher education in the United States. These students comprise about three percent of the total population of students currently seeking degrees at colleges and universities throughout the United States. (*Chronicle*, 1994). Many of these international students have extensive experience interacting with persons from cultures other than their own. However, a substantial number of these international students may have quite limited previous interactions with individuals from the United States. Once in residence at their U.S. colleges and universities, international students' day to day living experiences require increased interactions, and thus, increased intercultural communication.

Although U.S. students likely have some exposure to subcultures (or better termed co-cultures) within their own culture (Kuh & Whitt, 1988), they also may enter their institutions of higher learning with limited experience in interacting with individuals from other countries and other cultures. Therefore, when these two populations (i.e., international students and U.S. students) do interact, and intercultural communication transpires, the interactants may have disparate skills, experiences, needs, and outcome expectations for the intercultural encounter.

It is an interest in what transpires in these intercultural encounters between U.S. and international students, and an interest in examining what outcomes (or artifacts) of these interactions remain after those encounters, that provided the impetus for the study reported in this chapter. Specifically, the study was interested in collecting self-reported information (i.e., scales, narrative accounts) from U.S. and international students regarding their personal encounters with one another in the university environment. To this end, the following series of questions informed this study: What are the typical products or results of intercultural communication interactions between U.S. and international students? Are these interactions resplendent with appreciation and understanding and acceptance of an other's world view? Or do they resonate with uncertainty and anxiety and solipsism? How are these encounters characterized by the interactants? Are the interactants reflective about their intercultural encounters? Do they perceive themselves as competent in this particular interpersonal context? Do they perceived themselves as changed, and/or as agents of change? Do they desire further intercultural interactions as a result of these experiences? These questions are but a few that might be asked related to communication interactions between university students who are persons from different cultures. However, insights gained from addressing these few simple questions may add to our continuously developing understanding of intercultural communication.

INTERCULTURAL COMMUNICATION

Intercultural communication involves communication between people from disparate cultures. Given the increased mobility of the world's citizenry, burgeoning transnational business dealings, intensified multicultural political, economic, educational, and social interdependency, and rapid advancement in information transmission, contact between people of dissimilar cultural backgrounds is becoming more and more commonplace. Indeed, given the increased interactions between persons of differing cultures (and co-cultures), it is likely that there are few communication interactions that are *not* intercultural in some way.

Study of intercultural communication allows us to develop knowledge, appreciation, and skills appropriate for communicating in a multicultural world. Dodd tells us that intercultural communication involves skills that "facilitate relationships, break down barriers, and create foundations for new visions" (1995, p. 20). Enhanced intercultural consciousness nurtures informed, inclusive, reflective and ultimately, more responsible citizenry.

Intercultural communication is not a new phenomenon. Indeed, as Samovar and Porter remind us, "it has existed as long as people from different cultures have been encountering one another" (1994, p.1). Nor is intercultural communication a new area for research and pedagogy. Pioneer intercultural communication scholar and teacher K.S. Sitaram taught a course entitled "Introduction to Intercultural Communication" at the University of Hawaii as early as *1968* (Sitaram, 1995). Moreover, classic texts including Condon & Yousef's *An Introduction to Intercultural Communication* (1975), Sitaram and Cogdell's *Foundations of Intercultural Communication* (1976), Samovar and Porter's *Intercultural Communication: A Reader* (1976), and Prosser's *The Cultural Dialogue: An Introduction to Intercultural Communication* (1978) either have reached or are closely approaching their twentieth year publication anniversaries.

Most recently, increased systematic study of intercultural communication is evidenced by the growing number of conference papers, scholarly journal articles, and available texts dedicated to the subject. Increased instructional focus also supports this trend. The number of courses in intercultural communication offered at U.S. colleges and universities has expanded steadily over a number of years. Beebe and Biggers (1986) found a 44 percent increase over a six-year time span in the number of institutions of higher education offering introductory courses in intercultural communication.

Approaches to Intercultural Communication

Sitaram (1995) points out that there are multiple ways of approaching intercultural communication, including behavioristic, humanistic, and what he terms a "moderate" approach that combines the best features of the two aforementioned approaches. He encourages continued study of intercultural because of a "dire need for the study and practice of the discipline" (p. 8). Sitaram goes so far as to state in answer to the question, who should study intercultural communication?: *"Every person in the world should study intercultural communication"* (emphasis added) (p.7). He includes individuals (e.g., students, university professors, journalists, mass communicators, businesspersons) as well as organizations (e.g., officials with UNESCO, Equal Employment Opportunity, Immigration and Naturalization) in his list of those who need intercultural study.

In her discussion of intercultural pedagogy, Ting-Toomey (1992) advocates an identity-based interaction approach to intercultural communication. From this perspective Ting-Toomey conceptualizes intercultural communication in the following manner: "...a transactional, symbolic interactive process whereby individuals from two or more cultures attribute and negotiate meanings in this give-and-take process" (p. 159). Consequently, from this perspective, a primary function of intercultural communication is the negotiation and support of identity (i.e., group and self) for self and the other in the communication interaction. Ting-Toomey's approach, as well as Broome's (1986) contextual approach for teaching intercultural communication, allows for both cultural–general and cultural–specific focus for understanding the intercultural communication process.

Gudykunst (1991) and Gudykunst and Kim (1992) approach intercultural communication from the perspective of communicating with "strangers." As such, the communication encounter is characterized by interacting with someone perceived as "different" from the communicator. This difference can be based on culture, gender, ethnicity, age, or other group memberships. This perceived dissimilarity is often a stumbling block for effective intercultural interactions. As Dodd tells us, "all too often, experts find messages and relationships halted, because one or both people in the relationship are not sure how to respond to a person who is perceived as dissimilar " (Dodd, 1995, p. 4). Samovar and Porter (1994) also see perceptions of cultural dissimilarity as potentially problematic in intercultural communication encounters. They state, "intercultural communication can best be understood as cultural diversity in the perception of social objects and events. A central tenet of this position is that minor communication problems are often exaggerated by perceptual diversity (p. 19).

Increased Demand for Knowledge

The increased number of students enrolling in intercultural communication courses offered at U.S. colleges and universities no doubt reflects increased interest and needs in the larger population. Brislin and his associates (1986) affirm that a steadily increasing number of people will likely have extensive intercultural interactions at some point in their lives. Thus, the need for continued development of knowledge regarding intercultural communication is paramount. Increased intercultural communication knowledge can enhance our ability to identify and analyze the influence of culture on communication behaviors. Concomitantly, this allows us to develop understanding and appreciation of differences between people, world views, customs, thought, and language.

STUDY PURPOSE

The research reported in this study adds to existing knowledge of intercultural communication through systematic study. This study examined personal characterizations of intercultural communication interactions between U.S. and international students attending a large U.S. university. The overriding purpose of the study was to explore potential differences between U.S. students' and international students' accounts of their intercultural communication experiences. This information should provide a more detailed picture than presently exists of this important and timely interpersonal context.

The following research questions were posed for this study:

1. In what ways do U.S. students characterize their intercultural encounters with international students?
2. In what ways do international students characterize their intercultural encounters with U.S. students?
3. Are there differences in the characterizations of intercultural encounters between U.S. students and international students?

METHOD

Participants and Procedures

Ninety undergraduate and graduate students (37 males, 53 females, 53 U.S. students, and 37 international students) enrolled at a large public midwestern university participated in the study. The institution was ranked 10th among U.S. institutions of higher education in international student enrollment in 1994. The participating international students for this study were from China, Japan, Korea, India, Israel, India, Malaysia, Russia, Spain, Taiwan, and Thailand. All of the students participating in the study (U.S. and international) completed a self-administered questionnaire that was designed to measure how often they have experienced intergroup anxiety and uncertainty (Gudykunst, 1991, p. 15). The questionnaire also asked them to rate their own intercultural communication, whether they have changed in any way as a result of their intercultural interactions, and whether they are likely to seek out future intercultural encounters. The students were also asked to write a description of their recent intercultural interactions.

Data Analysis

The data from the first part of the questionnaire were analyzed statistically, using Chi Square tests, in order to determine differences between the U.S. students and International students along the dimensions examined in the study (e.g., experience of anxiety, likelihood of seeking out further intercultural interactions, etc.). The narrative descriptions of the students' intercultural encounters were content analyzed. Additionally, statistical analysis (again, Chi Square tests) were conducted to discern differences in narrative content between the U.S. students and

International students. For the content analysis, six thematic categories were examined: (1) context of communication, (2) evaluation of the communication, (3) learning from communication, (4) presence of emotional content of the narratives, (5) response or action taken based on the communication, and (6) assumed responsibility of the communication.

FINDINGS

Questionnaire Results

The majority of both U.S. and international students rated their intercultural encounters as good and very good (62 percent U.S., 54 percent international) and they were both likely to seek out further intercultural interactions (79 percent U.S., 69 percent international). The statistically analysis showed no differences between the U.S. and international students regarding their anxiety and uncertainty, although two variables (that they were stressed and concerned during the encounter) approached the significance level.

The majority of both groups reported that they were sometimes anxious when the two groups communicated with each other, (49 percent U.S., 57 percent international), sometimes frustrated (47 percent U.S., 49 percent international), never or almost never insecure (72 percent U.S., 60 percent international), sometimes uncertain how to behave (49 percent U.S., 51 percent international), never or almost never indecisive (53 percent U.S., 56 percent international), sometimes unable to predict the other's behavior (53 percent U.S., 66 percent international, and sometimes unable to understand the other (62 percent U.S., 69 percent international).

Although the international students seemed to be more likely than the U.S. students to be "sometimes under stress" (42 percent versus 29 percent), and they were "sometimes concerned" (53 percent versus 28 percent) when they were interacting with persons from the United States, the difference between the international students and the U.S. students was not statistically significant

Regarding whether they have changed as a result of their intercultural communication, the difference between the two groups was statistically significant. The U.S. students were more likely than the international students (89 percent U.S., 69 percent international) to report that they have changed in some way.

Content Analysis Results

Context of communication

Thirty-five percent of the contexts of the narrative accounts were non-university related socials (e.g., at parties, bars) and 25 percent were class related (communication happened in class or in a group project). Other contexts in which intercultural interactions occurred include university related meetings (13 percent), on university grounds such as library, student union (7 percent), and other (19 percent, travel, work, unspecified).

Direction of narratives

The majority of the narratives (42 percent) depicted their encounters as positive, 29 percent neutral, 12 percent negative, and 17 percent mixed. There was no differences between the U.S. and international students in their evaluation of the encounters.

Samples of positive encounters (from international students) include the following:

> An American friend of mine was helping me put a software on my computer this afternoon. He and I are what he considers "good friends." We laugh at the same things and have a lot of things in common.

* * *

> My language exchange partner called me last night. He had trouble with his chairperson in his major about his internship for summer term. He was very disappointed and depressed. I tried to be positive to him and tried to cheer him up. ... I do not know how Americans usually cheer their friends up, so I followed my own cultural communication style. Anyway, he became fine a little bit in the end and it made me happy because he is my friend.

Samples of positive encounters (from U.S. students) include the following:

> My most recent interaction with a person from another country was this week when I had a brief conversation with a young woman from India. As in previous contacts, our interaction was warm, humorous, and openly friendly. We discussed a project on which she had asked my input. We also discussed her new living quarters and her roommate. Because this interaction was so warm and open, I almost forgot to select it as an interaction with a person from another country; it is a non-salient issue.

* * *

> A former student of mine and I were having a conversation at the Student Center. Tomoko is from Japan and we often talk about how our cultures are different. ... We "gossiped" for over two hours and had a lot of fun. I find that I am now very comfortable telling when I don't understand her. I used to be uncomfortable, but I took Tomoko's lead. She asks for clarification, so I do too. This leads to a lot of laughter, some embarrassment, and a closer friendship.

Learning from encounter

Although the majority of the narratives did not contain references to learning from the encounter, the descriptions written by the international students appeared to contain fewer references regarding learning new information from the communication.

Samples of narratives (from U.S. students) which make references to learning include:

I have recently been in a small group project with a student from Japan. We (the group) spent many hours together completing the project. During a break I asked him his views on the dropping of the atomic bombs during World War II. I learned that he felt bad for the people, but did not hold a grudge and was not mad. It was a good learning experience.

* * *

I recently interacted with a female from Malaysia. The interaction, though it was brief, told me a lot about her culture. It was interesting to chat with her. I discovered that in her country, women don't have much of a voice. In fact, they are expected to live for their husbands. She was timid and very soft-spoken.

* * *

This individual is an international student from Greece. During class we were discussing the significance of gender inclusive language. After class, the individual approached me and commented that the Greek language does not account for male or female characteristics. I found this statement curious so I asked him to clarify. He simply stated that they don't have a way to distinguish between positions in society held by women and men. For example, he noted that there is no comparable term in the Greek language for Congresswoman. I found the conversation very interesting and I felt as if I learned as much about my own culture as I did about his.

Narratives containing emotion

Of the 90 narratives, 49 (54 percent) contained some emotional states during the encounter. Further analysis found that those narratives clustered around four themes, ranked in order: (1) positive emotion (happy, pleased, interested), (2) anxiety (anxious, frustrated, concerned, stress), (3) uncertainty (not confident, indecisive, confused), and (4) negative emotion (angry, upset).

Thirty-one percent of the emotional accounts contained references that attributed language barriers as a cause of the anxiety, uncertainty and negative emotion. Other causes attributed to those emotions were cultural differences (20 percent), individual differences (10 percent), communication incompetence of self (6 percent), and communication incompetence of the other (8 percent). Some examples of various emotions follow:

Positive emotion:
I've met many Americans, most are very nice to me, some are nice, only a few of them are not nice. The recent interaction with an American, who is my classmate, made me so happy and more confident to see other Americans. He came to talk to me about the party last night at a professor's house. I feel free with no worries or any concerns. Perhaps it is because of his cordial personality that makes me so confident and willing to have a chat with him and some other Americans.

* * *

Anxiety:
Last week an international student from one of my classes called me for clarification on an assignment that was due the next day. She is from Taiwan. After I explained the instructions of the assignment, she seemed to still be unsure as to what the directions were. I found myself getting frustrated with her. I felt like I couldn't make things any clearer. ... I thought I was merely repeating myself. Despite the frustration I was feeling, I felt guilty for getting impatient.

* * *

Presently I am working as a graduate assistant for a professor. He is the person from the U.S. whom I interact at least 3-4 times a week. We don't have much problems understanding each other in terms of language. However, we have different working habits due to different cultures. Sometimes this can be frustrating when we do not fully understand and appreciate each other's working manners.

* * *

Uncertainty:
I was working in a group with an Asian girl. She was confused about the topic and need some help. My main problem was the language. I couldn't understand what the question was. Her English is not that good and she didn't know what words to use.

Response/Change after intercultural interaction

Only 11 percent (10 out of 90) of the students' narratives made references to any response or action taken based on their intercultural communication interactions. Of those reported, 70 percent were positive actions or responses.

Some examples (from U.S. students):

The interaction which I've encountered was very brief. While we were interacting, I felt comfortable. After my interaction with this individual, our communication has dispelled some of the stereotypical ideas which I had formed.

* * *

My last roommate was from Taiwan. He was here studying for a business degree. When I first met him he knew a little English and one day I was asked to explain what "riding shotgun" meant. I had known what it meant in my head but was not able to describe very easily what I meant in the amount of English he knew. After talking with another friend I now had a better idea of how to explain it and was able to successfully explain to him what it meant. I am proud to say my roommate now comprehends and speaks English as well as most Americans.

* * *

Recently I passed a young woman I at first perceived to be Afro-American. First it is unusual for me to pass anyone walking around here (I'm 48). So as I passed I asked if she was feeling OK (joking) and explain that she was the only person I've passed since being on campus and thought she might not be up to "par" for her age. As she turned, I noticed the red dot between her eyes and realized she was Indian or whatever. I have talked with this nationality in past, but this young girl had no accent, did not appear or sound as if she carried any of the cultural identity of her people. We had a pleasant chat about things in general as we walked. Of course I would attempt that regardless. Point being actually my perception was wrong twice within 60 seconds. And we interacted enough for my view to change considerably.

Assumed responsibility of communication

Almost one-fourth of the descriptions (22 percent) contained references to the assumed responsibility of the effectiveness or failure of the intercultural communication. Of these, the two groups attributed almost equally as to who would be given the credit for the effective communication or who was to blame for the unsuccessful encounter. Both international and U.S. students gave credit to either themselves or both conversation partners when they had a successful communication and both also blamed either themselves or both partners when their intercultural communication failed.

Some examples of narratives:

Americans' address is explicit and clear. Yet it seemed to be low patient to listen to others' feelings and reaction. Americans seem not to take the responsibility of other's reaction or feeling. In my culture, we will use more polite tone and indirect intent in the beginning of the conversation. We will always worry about other's feeling or afraid of hurting them by direct address. For saving face I would avoid talking with some Americans who always assert themselves without considering others' feeling. Also, I need to talk logically in the conversation. Otherwise, Americans cannot follow what I want to say. Their thinking style is linear and logical. My thinking style is "spiral." So, I need to adapt my thinking style and avoid ambiguity.

* * *

Our department secretary was on vacation and I had to fill in for her. We have a lot of Asian students and on this occasion this student was asking for directions to a room in the Communication Building.

* * *

The only problem was I had a great difficulty understanding what he was saying. Instead of listening, I found myself trying to tell him what he was telling me. This conversation went on for a while until I said, "Okay, let's try this again," and this time I did listen.

* * *

I was working in a group project with three international students.The interactions were productive and "normal" except that I need to listen more attentively because English is their second language.

CONCLUSION

This study extends existing knowledge of intercultural communication by examining personal accounts of intercultural interactions between U.S. and international students. The questions posed at the beginning of this chapter bear restatement in this section. In brief, we asked, what are the typical products or results of intercultural communication interactions between U.S. and international students? We also asked how intercultural encounters are characterized by U.S. and international students. Additionally, we wanted to know if these intercultural interactants perceived themselves as competent in this particular interpersonal context, and if they perceived themselves as changed, and/or as agents of change. Of particular concern was to determine if U.S. and international students were interested in pursuing further intercultural interactions as a result of their past intercultural experiences. The results of the study suggest that a product of intercultural encounters is that both U.S. and international students experienced some degree of stress, anxiety, uncertainty, and frustration related to their intercultural interactions. Both groups reported these experiences to a similar degree; thus, there is no significant difference related to these affective products or artifacts of their encounters. However, the two groups did differ in their acknowledgment of changed perceptions of other cultures as a result of their intercultural interactions. The U.S. students reported more often having learned new information about another culture than did the international students.

It is especially important to note that the majority of both international and U.S. students rate their intercultural encounters as either good or very good. Moreover, in response to the question of whether they were likely to seek out further inter-cultural interactions, we found that both U.S. and international students viewed this as a desirable communication option. Thus, despite some negative affective experiences (e.g., frustration and uncertainty) the international and U.S. students were interested in continued intercultural encounters.

This study provides a foundation for future studies of intercultural interactions between U.S. and international students, specifically in the area of examining links between individuals' previous knowledge of other cultures and contexts. This represents the continuation of a lengthy process to gain insight into the com-plex process of intercultural communication. Future research in this area must continue to explore the intricate communication systems negotiated, employed and characterized by individuals interacting with individuals from other cultures.

DISCUSSION QUESTIONS

1. According to the information presented in this chapter, what are some of the factors that account for the increased need for intercultural communication today?
2. This chapter states that "it is likely that there are few communication interac-tions that are *not* intercultural in some way." Do you agree with this state-ment? Explain how and why this statement is or is not true.
3. The study reported in this chapter found that U.S. students reported that they learned new information about another culture as a result of their intercultural interactions more often than did international students. How might this find-ing be explained?
4. After reading about the study reported in this chapter, how would you char-acterize the intercultural interactions reported by the U.S. and international students? Were the experiences positive or negative or both? Explain.
5. K.S. Sitaram states that "every person in the world should study intercultural communication." Do you agree or disagree with this statement? Are there any individuals for whom intercultural study is particularly important? Identify and explain.

REFERENCES

Beebe, S. A., & Biggers, T. (1986) The status of the introductory intercultural communica-tion course. *Communication Education, 35,* 56-60.

Broome, B. J. (1986). A context-based framework for teaching intercultural communica-tion. *Communication Education, 35,* 296-306.

Chronicle of Higher Education (1994, September 1). *Almanac Issue.*

Condon, J. C., & Yousef, F. (1975). *An introduction to intercultural communication* . Indianapolis, IN: Bobbs-Merrill.

Dodd, C. H. (1995). *Dynamics of intercultural communication.* (4th ed.). Madison, WI: Brown & Benchmark.

Gudykunst, W. B.(1991). *Bridging differences: Effective intergroup communication.* Newbury Park, CA: Sage.

Gudykunst, W. B., & Kim, Y. Y. (1992). *Communicating with strangers: An approach to intercultural communication.* (2nd ed.). New York: McGraw-Hill.

Holsti, O. (1969). *Content analysis for social sciences and humanities.* Reading, MA: Addison-Wesley.

Kuh, G. D., & Whitt, E. J. (1988). *The invisible tapestry: Culture in American colleges and universities.* ASHE-ERIC Higher Education Report No. 1. Washington, D.C.: Association for the Study of Higher Education.

Prosser, M. H. (1978). *The cultural dialogue: An introduction to intercultural communication.* Boston, MA: Houghton Mifflin.

Samovar, L. A., & Porter, R. E. (1976). *Intercultural communication: A reader.* Belmont, CA: Wadsworth.

Samovar, L. A., & Porter, R. E. (1994). *Intercultural communication: A reader* (7th ed.). Belmont, CA: Wadsworth.

Sitaram, K. S. (1995). *Culture and communication: A world view.* New York: McGraw-Hill.

Sitaram, K. S., & Cogdell, T.T. (1976). *Foundations of intercultural communication.* Columbus, OH: Charles Merrill.

Ting-Toomey, S. (1992). Intercultural Communication. In Lederman, L. C., (Ed.), *Communication Pedagogy*, (pp. 157-171). Norwood, NJ: Ablex.

22

THE COMMUNICATION STEREOTYPES OF WHITES AND ASIANS IN THE WHITE-DOMINANT CLASSROOM

Young-ok Yum
Pennsylvania State University

INTRODUCTION

Racial-ethnic stereotypes have been studied largely by social psychologists who have looked for sets of general attributes or traits that are seen as characteristics of a certain racial-ethnic outgroup, as distinguished from ingroup. For example, Katz and Braly (1933) examined stereotypes held by one hundred White college students, using a checklist of traits, and found that White students characterized Blacks as *superstitious*, *lazy*, *happy-go-lucky*, *ignorant*, *musical*, *ostentatious*, *very religious*, *stupid*, *physically dirty*, *naive*, *naive*, *slovenly*, and *unreliable*. With these general traits and stereotypes, however, it is not certain what communication behavior individuals specifically display in social interaction in specific settings. This chapter presents a study that examined communication stereotypes held by college students. First, the definitions and functions of stereotypes will be presented. Second, three research hypotheses grounded in two prominent theoretical approaches of stereotypes (i.e., attribution theory and schema theory) will be presented. Next, relevant methods of this study will be described, followed by presentation of results and discussion.

STEREOTYPES

The definitions of stereotypes are various. Lippmann (1922) views stereotypes as oversimplifications and incorrect, illogically-derived, and rigid generalizations about categories of people. Katz and Braly (1933) also view stereotypes negatively as the set of attributes agreed on as typical of the group but conforming very little to actual behaviors or facts. According to Campbell (1971), stereotypes are inferior judgmental processes that can distort the real picture of outgroup behavior and exaggerate intergroup differences. However, Bodenhausen and Wyer (1985) see some validity in stereotypes and explain that "the standard processing strategies of human cognitive system can successfully account for stereotyping phenomena" (p. 267). Bodenhausen and Wyer further state that stereotypes result from "the need for coherence, simplicity, and predictability in the face of an inherently complex social environment" (p. 195). Thus, in summary, stereotypes are generalizable attributes assigned to a group. They are not always incorrect or illogical overgeneralizations, but often this is the case. Many definitions of stereotypes are innately related to the functions of stereotypes in actual interactions. As implied by the incongruent definitions of stereotypes, the function of stereotypes is also controversial.

According to Ogawa (1971), stereotypes are "relatively simple, generally rigid cognitions of social groups" that function to "blind" the individual from neutral and informed judgment about outgroups based on race, ethnicity, age, sex, or social class. On the contrary, Smith and Bond (1993) view stereotypes as efficient tools in social interactions because they "allow those who hold them to reduce uncertainty about what members of other groups are likely to want, to believe, and to do in social interactions" (p. 169). In the same vein, Hamilton and Troiler (1986) maintain that stereotypes facilitate interaction by reducing the need to attend to and process individual information about the other. Boski (1988) also states that stereotyping is "the first step in the process of cognitive/evaluative differentiation, but then it evolves along divergent lines" as interaction and individual information about outgroups increase. In other words, stereotypes are used to increase individual information about groups and build group schemata (Taylor & Crocker, 1981). Thus, stereotypes can help to evaluate outgroups fairly and adequately. In the service of building valid and effective group schemata, the accuracy of stereotypes and generalized group information is as important as its quantity.

A schema is a mental structure of accumulated observations and evaluations based on an individual's personal characteristics, as well as preconceived group characteristics. The schema perspective (Hewstone, 1988) takes an interpersonal (not a group) level of analysis and relates an observed behavior in a particular context to the schema in the observer's head to increase the accuracy of stereotypes. Thus, given the explanations of schema theory, information on specific behavior in interpersonal interactions (i.e., communication stereotypes) appears to be useful to reduce uncertainty about outgroups in initial interactions and smooth interracial or interethnic communication to a degree. According to Ogawa (1971), communication stereotypes are directly concerned with "a specific behavior in a specific situation" and thus will help build accurate schemata about the target outgroup.

Communication stereotype studies are few in the literature. Ogawa (1971) examined small group communication stereotypes of Blacks held by Whites by using Katz and Braly's (1933) checklist that was adapted to communication-specific traits. Communication-specific traits concerned typical communication behavior of Blacks, Mexican Americans, and Japanese Americans in a discussion situation. These attributes had been generated by 35 college students prior to the actual administration of the checklist. As a result, the top 12 typical communicative behaviors of each group were identified which reflected group differences clearly. The top 5 traits assigned to each group were as follows: Blacks are *argumentative*, *emotional*, *aggressive*, *critical*, and *sensitive*; Mexican Americans are *emotional*, *argumentative*, *sensitive*, *straightforward*, and *talkative*; and Japanese Americans are *intelligent*, *courteous*, *industrious*, *quiet*, and *soft-spoken*. According to Ogawa, one interesting finding is that Whites perceived Japanese Americans in the most stereotypical way and thus the traits selected for Japanese Americans converged on a few terms.

While Ogawa (1971) examined only Whites' perceptions of other groups, Rich (1974) examined communication stereotypes of Whites held by Blacks. Blacks saw Whites as *evasive*, *critical*, *conservative*, *ignorant*, *boastful*, *aggressive*, *arrogant*, *ostentatious*, *concealing*, *emotional*, *individualistic*, and *nonmilitant*. Rich interpreted that these findings were a reflection of distrust and hostility between Blacks and Whites that influence selective perception and reinforce negative views. In Ogawa (1971), as listed above, Blacks were seen by Whites as argumentative, emotional, aggressive, critical, and sensitive. Rich's (1974) findings interestingly contrast Ogawa's (1971) in that Rich's respondents apparently perceived Whites negatively, whereas Ogawa's respondents were not particularly negative. Leonard and Locke (1993) suggested that the discrepancy is related to the fact that the participants in the two studies were quite different: Ogawa's sample was students at UCLA, while Rich's was ghetto residents.

To test this hypothesis, Leonard and Locke (1993) administered a variation of Katz and Braly's checklist to Black and White college students who attended either a White-dominant (93 percent) or Black-dominant (99 percent) school. Non-communicative descriptors (e.g., *conservative* and *imitative*) were replaced by communicative terms (e.g., *supportive* and *articulate*). The analysis of results revealed that Blacks (as well as Whites) perceived the other group negatively and "threateningly" regardless of socioeconomic class, age, geographical location, and education. Blacks most frequently assigned to Whites traits such as *demanding*, *manipulative*, *rude*, *critical*, *aggressive*, and *arrogant*, whereas Whites perceived Blacks as *loud*, *ostentatious*, *aggressive*, *active*, and *boastful*. Of the twelve attributes selected by both groups, Whites perceived six of the attributes assigned to Blacks as threatening, whereas Blacks perceived ten of Whites' stereotypical behaviors as threatening to themselves. Naturally, both groups perceive interracial interaction between Blacks and Whites as potentially threatening, which will block or interfere with genuine and pleasant communication between members of the two groups.

Considering the existing literature on communication stereotypes, a few general conclusions can be drawn. First, future research using inductive data collection methods is warranted to reduce researcher bias and reflect the perspectives of respondents more accurately. Imposing a limited list of attributes as has been done in much of the existing research may have served as cues and constraints that affected respondents' judgment and sense of freedom of choice. Observations in a natural or laboratory setting, or free thought-listing methods may be better.

Second, neither the validity nor accuracy of the stereotypes found in previous studies has been checked. According to Iwao and Triandis (1993), stereotypes need to reach a certain level of validity to ensure their usefulness as group schema. The validity of stereotypes can be checked by identifying the degree of agreement between stereotypes held by the target group (self-stereotypes) and stereotypes held by outgroups (other-stereotypes), the degree of convergence across several stereotypes of the target, and the degree of convergence between empirically-identified stereotypes and other-stereotypes found in several different samples.

Third, although White, Black, and Mexican Americans are distinctive "racioethnic" groups, groups from outside the United States need to be examined. In particular, Evangelauf (1990) reports that Asian-international student enrollment in the U.S. universities has skyrocketed during the recent past years and comprises 60 percent of the total foreign student enrollment. In addition, Asians are generally perceived as most distinct in communication behavior compared to the U.S. culture and easily stereotyped in a few convergent terms (Ogawa, 1971). Thus, in relation to specific communication behavior, it is expected that White or Black American teachers, as well as Asian students, in the U.S. classroom, may encounter embarrassing moments due to their differences. Education and communication researchers have provided sufficient evidence that cultural differences in communication style influence student learning. Awareness of accurate communication stereotypes will reduce uncertainty and increase effective communication and, as a consequence, teaching and learning in the classroom. In the next section, relevant hypotheses will be posited, following brief description of the two theories that explain how stereotypes are formed and play out in intergroup interactions (i.e., ethnocentric attribution theory and schema theory).

RESEARCH HYPOTHESES

First, according to ethnocentric attribution theory (Ben-Ari, Schwarzwald, & Horiner-Levi, 1994), individuals attribute their negative behavior to external/situational factors and their positive behavior to internal/dispositional factors. For instance, an individual is likely to attribute his or her low classroom participation to class climate or other external factors, whereas he or she is likely to attribute low participation by an outgroup member to his or her lack of competence or other internal factors. Ben-Ari and colleagues (1994) found that individuals tend to attribute negative ingroup behavior to external/situational factors, whereas they are likely to attribute negative outgroup behavior to internal/dispositional factors. Low classroom participation is considered as negative behavior, whereas high participation is viewed as positive. In addition, according to schema theory predictions, Whites tend to hold stereotypes about Asian communication style. For example, according to Ogawa (1971) and Maykovich (1972), Whites tended to view Japanese Americans most stereotypically as *quite, soft-spoken,* and *reserved,* whereas they were seen as *outspoken* and *self-expressive* commonly by themselves as well as by others. Naturally, Asians are expected to behave differently from Whites in classroom situations. Thus, the first two hypotheses are proposed:

H1:   Whites tend to attribute low participation by Asians to internal/dispositional factors and low participation by themselves to external/situational factors.

H2:   Whites are likely to view Asians as the least active participants in the classroom and themselves as the most active participants.

Although the predictions made based on ethnocentric attribution theory and schema theory are still prevalent, younger generations (i.e., college students, versus older adults) prefer or are likely to base their judgments on personal observation or exposure to individual outgroup members rather than on traditional stereotypes. For instance, Maykovich (1972) found that college students tend to evaluate outgroup members objectively. Specifically, Maykovich meant that younger generations are more likely to be objective and evaluate outgroup members' behavior individually rather than categorically because they have been taught to evaluate objects critically and are still in the active process of inquiry about the world and people around them. Thus, the third hypothesis is posited:

H3:   Young White college students are reluctant to make generalizations about Asian communication behavior based on preexisting stereotypes.

To test these hypotheses, I examined classroom communication stereotypes that are commonly held by Whites of themselves and others and the attributions or causes of those stereotypes (e.g., "Japanese are less active *because they are shy*"). Although the initial purpose of the study was to identify classroom communication stereotypes in a racio-ethnically diverse classroom and to compare self- and other-stereotypes across groups, the White sample outnumbered other groups overwhelmingly. As a result, I will focus primarily on Whites' perceptions of their own and outgroup communication behavior.

METHOD

Participants

The participants were 127 undergraduate students (110 Whites, 17 Asians) enrolled in 6 sections of an introductory speech communication course and 1 section of an advanced speech communication course at The Pennsylvania State University. Initially, 142 questionnaires were collected; however, 15 were discarded for a lack of information provided. Of 110 Whites, 57 were males and 53 were females. Of 17 Asians, 8 were females and 9 were males; 12 were East Asians and 5 were South Asians.

Instrument

The questionnaire contained 5 open-ended questions on communication stereotypes and attributions. Five 7-point-Likert-type questions were used to measure the level of class participation, comfort in the process of communication, and satisfaction with the communication outcome after whole-class or small group discussions are over. The questionnaire contained four demographic items concerning *race*, *nationality/ethnicity*, *sex*, and *age*. Two additional items were addressed specifically to international students regarding their *English fluency level* and *length of stay in the U.S.*

The 5 open-ended items were as follows:

- What factors affect your participation (self-participation) in class? (This question was only given to low-participating students who had indicated their participation level as below 4 in a preceding question)
- Who is the most actively participating race in the classroom and what are the reasons for this?
- Who is the most actively participating nationality/ethnicity in class and what are the reasons for it? Who is the least actively participating group and what are the reasons for this?
- What factors affect self-participation?

The reliability of the Likert-type-scale items was 7.17 (Kuder-Richardson Formula 21). The results of the Likert-type questions are not reported in the present paper.

RESULTS

To the first question on the factors affecting low self-participation in the class discussion, Whites responded that they participate less for a variety of reasons: *shy, no significant contributions, prefer listening, not interested, uncomfortable, afraid of looking stupid, don't know the answer, etc.* Twenty-four percent of Whites felt that they participate relatively less in the whole class and 36 percent felt they participated relatively less in small group discussions. Fifty percent of Whites viewed themselves as active participants in the whole class, and 58 percent in a small group. Fewer people were moderate participants in a small group than in the whole class (6 percent versus 26 percent). Thus, it seems that people tend to participate more in small group discussions than in the whole class. Overall, respondents tended to attribute their low participation to internal factors (e.g., *shy, prefer listening, don't know the answer*).

In response to the question regarding the most actively participating race, Whites selected themselves as the most active participants (69 percent). However, a number of respondents (22 percent) reported that "race has nothing to do with classroom participation" (*no group difference*). Sixty-five percent attributed active participation of Whites to their *majority status in the class*. Some attributed active participation to *individual differences, extroversion,* and *language fluency* (6 percent respectively). About 5 percent of the participants confessed that they did not have any experience in multicultural settings. Interestingly, a great majority of the respondents (78 percent) attributed their active participation to external factors (e.g., majority status in the class, language fluency, cultural learning). Only one student attributed Whites' most active participation to an internal factor, *being smart.* Another respondent uniquely indicated that ethnic minorities are the most active participants because of *social input in boosting the confidence level of minorities.* This suggests that positive outgroup behavior was attributed to an external factor.

In response to the question on the most actively participating nationality or ethnicity, Whites selected themselves most frequently (69 percent) and attributed it to their *majority status in the class* (50 percent), *fluency in English* (16 percent), *familiarity with social conventions* (13 percent), and *social learning* (5 percent). Sixteen percent reported *no group differences* and approximately 6 percent, respectively, either indicated that they did not know which ethnicity was the most active participants or were not able to answer because they could not tell the nationality or ethnicity of the target (2 percent). Positive ingroup behavior was attributed to external factors (86 percent) (e.g., majority status, language fluency, familiarity, social learning). One student responded that Asians are most active because they are *self-confident* (internal factor), while another reported that Asians were active because they seemed always asking questions. Interestingly, two respondents indicated that Whites participated most actively because they are *smart* or *intelligent* (internal factors).

In response to the question on the least actively participating nationality and ethnicity, 29 percent selected Asians: Most of them selected specifically East Asians (11 percent) or South Asians (11 percent), but others used generic terms (e.g., "Asians" or "Orientals"). Approximately 5 percent selected "any international students." Twenty-three percent responded that there were *no group differences.* Twelve percent selected Native Americans as the least active participants. Apparently, Asians are seen as the least active participants, mostly because of their language barriers (27 percent) and minority status (27 percent). Some students (16 percent) were not able to respond because they had no, or insufficient, exposure to multicultural groups. The negative behavior of minorities (low participation) was usually attributed to external factors such as *language barrier, minority status, not comfortable, not prepared, intimidated, sociocultural learning (69 percent).* Interestingly, low participation by Blacks was perceived by one student as a result of their "laid-back" attitude (internal factor). About 7 percent reported that *individual differences* caused low participation, making no reference to group differences. Nobody selected Whites as the least active participants.

DISCUSSION

Hypothesis 1 was not supported for whites. The respondents did not evaluate themselves and others differentially. The analysis revealed that Whites attributed their own negative behavior equally to external and internal factors, and negative outgroup behavior was attributed more to external factors. Hypothesis 2 was confirmed. Whites selected themselves as the most actively participating race and people from the U.S. as the most actively participating national group. In addition, Whites typically selected Asians as the least participating ethnic group in the classroom as predicted. This finding tentatively supports what was found by Ogawa (1971) and Maykovich (1974) that Japanese Americans are *quiet, soft-spoken,* and *reserved.* Hypothesis 3, that college students will be less likely to use stereotypes and will attempt to judge outgroup behavior on an individual basis, was moderately confirmed. A considerable number of respondents seemed to "resent" being forced to generalize participation level solely based on a certain racio-ethnicity. *No group differences* and *individual differences* were relatively frequent responses across questions.

Although these findings warrant more research on classroom communication stereotypes to confirm their validities, the results in this sample of Whites do not confirm the attribution hypothesis (Ben-Ari et al., 1994). It was confirmed in the Asian group. Asian participants believed that they were the least active participants and attributed their low participation to external factors (e.g., *language barrier, minority status),* whereas they consistently attributed the active participation of Whites (positive behavior) to external factors.

It is not clear why the attribution hypothesis was not confirmed in this sample and, further, why Whites in this study were judging Asians objectively and with a relatively unbiased attitude. Perhaps they were rather conscious of egalitarian beliefs, relatively unprejudiced, and able to avoid bolstering negative stereotypes in evaluating outgroup behavior (Devine, 1989). Another possible interpretation is that Whites' seemingly unbiased evaluations may be due to their lack of interest in racial or ethnic issues. In addition, younger generations are familiar with politically correct ideas and have been taught to use them in situations where they are forced to judge outgroups, regardless of their personal attitudes. Thus, they may be afraid of the social ramifications and legal and moral concerns associated with racially or ethnically inappropriate remarks.

Although the majority of students tended to use fewer stereotypes and based their judgments on idiosyncrasies, there is some evidence that ethnocentric attitudes of the dominant group do still exist. A few White respondents attributed their positive behavior to internal/dispositional factors (e.g., *smart, intelligent*). These students probably attributed the negative behavior of minorities to a lack of intelligence and cognitive ability. Interestingly, minorities appear as ethnocentric as (or more ethnocentric than) the dominant group in this study. While Whites attributed their negative and positive behavior inconsistently to either internal or external factors, the Asian sample in this study consistently attributed their negative behavior to external factors. Simplistic comparison and generalization, however, should be avoided because the Asian sample is significantly smaller than the White sample.

Majority or *minority status* seems to make a difference in a group member's communication behavior in the classroom. For example, Whites were consistently perceived to participate more actively because they were in the majority, whereas Asians or any other minorities tended to participate less because they were in the minority. *Majority status* may indeed help individuals feel confident of themselves and comfortable with classroom participation. On the other hand, individuals in the minority may not actually participate less but are perceived to participate less because there are significantly fewer of them in the class. In addition, not all individuals in the majority are active participants in the classroom. Minorities, however, who are confounded with *language barrier* and the resulting discomfort and lack of confidence, seem to perceive themselves as participating less than Whites who happen to be native speakers of the language spoken in the classroom. *Language barrier* and *minority status* were the most frequently cited reasons for the low participation of minority students. Whites also cited their *language fluency* very frequently as the reason for their most active participation. Kirchmeyer and Cohen's (1992) laboratory study remotely supports this finding in that ethnic minorities participated considerably less than did majorities in decision making processes, due to their minority status. Kirchmeyer and Cohen further reported that the increasing use of constructive conflict resulted in an increase in the contribution level of ethnic minorities in ethnically heterogeneous groups.

Apart from racio-ethnic identity (e.g., minority or majority status), Kirchmeyer (1993) found that personal characteristics also accounted for variances in the contribution levels of minority and majority group members. The personal variables in Kirchmeyer's study were *communication competence, masculinity-femininity, motivation,* and *group attachment.* These personal variables served as a better predictor of contribution than did *minority status* alone. For example, low communication competence and low masculinity were associated with minority status and with low contribution. Especially noteworthy were minorities' report of considerable communication difficulties in the university setting. Also, communication competence or difficulty was found to make the greatest difference between minority and majority responses.

In this study, both Whites and Asians reported that *language barriers* are the greatest barriers to classroom participation. *Fear of making mistakes* and *looking stupid* also applied (even to a greater extent) to Asians and Whites. *Age* was also reported to affect participation level. A White female who reported that she was older than anybody in the class said that she participates less because she has different values and attitudes from the rest of the class, with respect to her age (and religion). Thus, it appears that cross-cultural stereotype studies should caution the significance of intergroup differences and not emphasize them at the expense of individual differences.

A few limitations and implications of the study warrant discussion. First, the size of the Asian sample was too small for comparing and verifying their observations sufficiently. Regardless, the self-perceptions of the Asians in this sample, and the reasons that they reported for their lack of classroom participation, indicate a strong convergence between Asians' self-perceptions and the stereotypes of Asians held by Whites. For example, both Asians and Whites see Asians as less actively participating. In addition, both Asians and Whites attribute their low participation to *language barrier.* One piece of supporting evidence that external factors (e.g., *language barriers)* are better explanations for low participation of Asians is that the Asian sample overall reported that they participated more actively in the classroom in their first language ($M = 5.118$) than did their White counterparts ($M = 4.673$). Still, direct comparison should be avoided. These results, furthermore, support Iwao and Triandis's (1993) finding that the younger generation of Japanese differ greatly from the older generation who were the stimuli for the "typical Japanese" image held by Westerners. Iwao and Triandis concluded that cultural differences between Japan and America have been overly exaggerated.

Second, the adequacy of White sample also seems problematic. Sixteen percent of the White respondents indicated that they had no or insufficient exposure to ethnic outgroups in class and thus found it hard to judge outgroup behaviors.

Another implication of this study is that the tactics teachers use to manage the class is an important factor that will impact student participation and other communication behaviors. One respondent in this study reported explicitly that types of classroom activities make a difference in her participation level. Teachers are the very group of individuals who have to build accurate cultural schemata and facilitate classroom interaction in order to make actual learning occur. Teachers do have a great control over external/situational variables that will affect classroom participation. Similarly, according to Haslett and Ogilvie (1996), leaders can give negative feedback in a non-offensive and non-face-threatening way, for example, by "sandwiching" it between positive feedback, to create active participation.

In addition, teachers have to attempt to see individual differences, beyond cultural differences, to meet student needs and expectations related to learning. Any student from any kind of background (e.g., a shy boy from a White middle-class family) can be a minority. The homogeneity-heterogeneity dimension of group composition involves a variety of components, such as personality traits, sex, race, and conceptual systems (Shaw, 1981). A racio-ethnically homogeneous classroom can be extremely heterogeneous for many different reasons. Specifically, students in an apparently homogeneous class may exhibit incongruent communication behaviors across situations, even within the context of the same class. Given these individual differences and situational variations, I conclude that the best way to examine classroom communication behavior of students is to disregard group stereotypes and base one's judgment on individual observations and experience in a given context.

SUMMARY

This chapter has presented a study that examined the communication stereotypes of Whites and Asians in the college classroom. As predicted, Whites perceived Asians as low participants in classroom discussions. Contrary to the ethnocentric attribution hypothesis, Whites largely attributed Asians' low participation to external causes (language barriers and minority status). In addition, young college students were less prejudiced and used fewer fixed stereotypes than their older counterparts. Another interesting finding is that Asian students in the U.S. classroom perceive themselves as more active participants in their first language relative to Whites in their first language. Further, individual difference variables (e.g., age, confidence) seem to influence communication behavior in relation to group differences. Thus, the study suggests that teachers can make a difference in Asian and White students' class participation behavior by employing a variety of teaching strategies to encourage and motivate students to participate more in the classroom.

DISCUSSION QUESTIONS

1. Discuss the definitions of stereotypes. Do you believe that stereotypes typically have negative connotations? Specify the reasons.

2.   Discuss the communication stereotypes of diverse ethnic groups you have encountered thus far. Explain on what basis those stereotypes have been created and how these stereotypes affect your interaction with a member of a particular group about which you hold those stereotypes.

3.   Do you agree with the findings of communication stereotypes about Whites and Asians in this study? Specify the reasons you agree or disagree with specific stereotypes. Also, compare the self-stereotypes and other-stereotypes of your own group. Do self-stereotypes generally agree to other-stereotypes? Give specific examples of the agreements and disagreements.

4.   Describe communication stereotypes of different racial or ethnic groups in other domains of behavior such as verbal/non-verbal communication behavior (e.g., immediacy or proximity, humor, hand gestures).

5.   Discuss the limitations of the study presented in this chapter. What would you do to improve the quality of this study?

REFERENCES

Ben-Ari, R., Schwarzwald, J., & Horiner-Levi, E. (1994). The effects of prevalent social stereotypes on intergroup attribution. *Journal of Cross-cultural Psychology, 25*, 489-500.

Bodenhausen, V. G., & Wyer, S. Jr. (1985). Effects of stereotypes on decision making and information-processing strategies. *Journal of Personality and Social Psychology, 48*, 267-282.

Boski, P. (1988). Cross-cultural studies of person perception: Effects of ingroup/outgroup membership and ethnic schemata. *Journal of Cross-cultural Psychology, 19*, 287-328.

Campbell, A. (1971). *White attitudes toward Black people*. Ann Arbor, MI: Institute for Social Research.

Devine, P. G. (1989). Stereotypes and prejudice: Their automatic and controlled components. *Journal of Personality and Social Psychology, 56*, 5-18.

Evangelauf, J. (April, 1990). 1988 enrollments of all racial groups hit record levels. *The Chronicle of Higher Education*, pp. A1, A37.

Hamilton, D. L., & Troiler, T. K. (1986). Stereotypes and stereotyping: An overview of the cognitive approach. In J. F. Dovidio & S. L. Gaertner (Eds.), *Prejudice, discrimination, and racism* (pp. 127-163). Orlando, FL: Academic Press.

Haslett, B., & Ogilvie, J. R. (1996). Feedback processes in task groups. In R. S. Cathcart, L. A. Samovar, & L. D. Henman (Eds.), *Small group communication: Theory and practice* (pp. 254-267). Madison, WI: Brown & Benchmark.

Hewstone, M. (1988). Attributional bases of intergroup conflict. In W. Stroebe, A. W. Kruglanski, D. Bar-Tal, & M. Hewstone (Eds.), *The social psychology of intergroup conflict*. Berlin: Springer-Verlag.

Iwao, S., & Triandis, H. C. (1993). Validity of auto- and heterostereotypes among Japanese and American students. *Journal of Cross-cultural Psychology, 24*, 428-444.

Katz, D., & Braly, K. (1933). Racial stereotypes of one hundred college students. *Journal of Abnormal Social Psychology, 28*, 280-290.

Kirchmeyer, C., & Cohen, A. (1992). Multicultural groups: Their performance and reactions with constructive conflict. *Group & Organization Management, 17*, 153-170.

Kirchmeyer, C. (1993). Multicultural task groups: An account of the low contribution level of minorities. *Small Group Research, 24*, 127-148.

Leonard, R., & Locke, D. C. (1993). Communication stereotypes: Is interracial communication possible? *Journal of Black Studies, 23*, 332-343.

Lippmann, W. (1922). *Public opinion.* New York: Harcourt Brace.

Maykovich, M. K. (1972). Stereotypes and racial images-white, black and yellow. *Human Relations, 25*, 101-120.

Ogawa, D. M. (1971). Small-group communication stereotypes of Black Americans. *Journal of Black Studies, 1*, 273-281.

Rich, A. L. (1974). *Interracial communication.* New York: Harper & Row.

Shaw, M. (1981). Group composition. In M. Shaw, *Group dynamics: The psychology of small group behavior* (3rd ed., pp. 210-261). New York: McGraw-Hill.

Smith, P. B., & Bond, M. H. (1993). The characteristics of cross-cultural interaction. In P. B. Smith & M. H. Bond, *Social psychology across cultures* (pp. 163-190). Boston: Allyn and Bacon.

Taylor, S. E., & Crocker, J. (1981). Schematic bases of social information processing. In E. T. Higgins, C. P. Herman, & M. P. Zanna (Eds.), *Social cognition: The Ontario symposium* (vol. 1, pp. 89-134). Hillsdale, NJ: Lawrence Erlbaum.

23

A COMPARATIVE ANALYSIS OF RHETORICAL THEORY IN CHINA AND THE UNITED STATES

D. Ray Heisey
Kent State University

INTRODUCTION

In 1993 I was invited to present a paper in Haikou, the southern-most city in China, on cultural characteristics of communication pattens in China. I was invited back the next year to Beijing to present another paper on rhetorical characteristics of the modernization process in China. At that conference was a professor who expressed great interest in my paper because she was a professor of rhetoric and dean of the Chinese Language Department in the International Relations Institute. She gave me a copy of her book on Chinese rhetoric which resulted in extended conversations through my interpreter.

As result of this and other connections I have learned of the public speaking interest that exists in China. It is a phenomenon that is making considerable impact in that country. This provides the motivation for the present exploratory paper.

A good example of this public interest is the publication of a popular monthly magazine called *Speech and Oral Discourse* that is read by 980,000 readers, according to its editor, Shang Shou Yi, vice chair of the Jilin Teachers Institute (personal communication, December 8, 1994). He is professor of rhetoric and public speech at the Institute. The readers are mostly young people and come from many careers in the government, military, agriculture, factories, as well as students. There are ten editors from different areas of the country who are professors, professional writers, and military officers. Let me quote from a letter he sent to me recently. He wrote:

> Public speech ... has developed rapidly with the deepening implementation reform and the open-door policy. Realizing its influence in our daily life, more and more people are interested in public speech and currently recognize that it is an important measure of communication by people in different fields. (personal communication, December 8, 1994)

A copy of the issue that was sent to me includes the following articles and topics: Conversation skills, social interaction, the art of speaking, skills of debating, oral communication between teachers and students, public relations, criticism of famous speeches, oral discourse and the professions, and fortune and misfortune brought by language.

These articles and features are prepared for young people, especially, to meet a need in society, according to Shang. Since public speaking is still not taught in the schools and universities, Shang points to his magazine's success, now going on 10 years, as evidence that people want to improve their ability to speak in public.

On the back cover of the magazine are advertisements for buying books on speech making and tapes of debates. For example, the Speech and Oral Discourse Publishing House in Jilin City publishes, in addition to the magazine, a book of 400 speeches of famous politicians, educators, and public figures from China's history. The book focuses on the debate strategies used by these speakers. The title is, *The Treasure Chest of Ancient Chinese Debating Strategies*. The Readers Service Department, learning from marketing tactics, sells tapes of the International Debating Contests held since 1993 in China. It also has made available a book collection of the best articles on speech from the magazine's 10 years of monthly publication.

According to my Chinese students, television in China includes speech and debating contests for college-age students. Each country in Southeast Asia has its own debate team and is sponsored by the Central TV Station of China or the Singapore Broadcasting Bureau, for example. In mainland China the different universities also sponsor debate competition on TV, judged by professors of different disciplines and other prestigious persons. Public speaking activity is on the rise and much interest exists on university campuses.

My own contacts in Beijing have resulted in invitations from the international politics departments at People's University and Peking University for my department to supply professors for teaching courses in speech communication within their curricula. We have already begun these exchange programs.

There are other scholars who have been invited to China from our discipline. The interest is growing. Conferences on intercultural communication have been held in Harbin (1995) and Beijing (1996). The important fact is that not only are Chinese educators expressing an interest in American rhetorical and communication theory, but a number of Chinese books have come out by Chinese authors on public speech.

A SELECTED THEORY TEXT IN THE UNITED STATES

Since readers of this volume are familiar with the nature of public speaking and communication theory as taught in the United States, I will not spend much time reviewing this. For comparative purposes of this chapter, however, I have chosen the James McCroskey text, *An Introduction to Rhetorical Communication* (1993), as the sample American theory text to use for two reasons. First, it is the one used at my university and I think is one of the best. Second, it provides a very clear organization of the material, including the importance of the classical background. A brief overview of the text's contents and its philosophical orientation will be sufficient. This shows the sequence of the topics covered and relative weight of importance devoted to the various components.

Part One, on getting started, is about 50 pages. It gives attention to the rhetorical tradition in ancient times, contemporary models, the goals of rhetorical training, and the normal problem of stage fright as an up-front way of dealing with the biggest problem students face at the beginning. Part Two, on basic theory, is 85 pages, and covers theory of attitude formation, the dimensions of ethos, persuasive argument, and nonverbal messages. Part Three, about 130 pages—the largest part of the text—deals with message preparation and presentation. This includes the standard theory on audience analysis, the nature of informative messages, the classical concepts of invention, topoi, disposition, style, and delivery. Part Four, about 30 pages, covers the ethics of communication and persuasion, and societal implications for a free society. An appendix provides five model speeches for study and analysis.

The theories included in the McCroskey text might vary from one text to another, but by and large, any public speaking text used in the United States. would be similar in most aspects of the theory covered. There would be a section on the speaker, the audience, message preparation and message presentation. This format is after 200 years of giving attention to the role of speech training in higher education in America. Of course, the relative importance of such training and of theory components varies from one part of the country to another, as it would from institution to institution. The philosophical orientation of the Western approach is that speech, or oral discourse, differs from written discourse in scope, range, function, and effect. Though the word, rhetoric, has been variously defined in the West throughout different periods of time, it is being reclaimed in many places by the English departments. Even in speech communication departments, rhetoric now includes not only public speech but media contexts, which obviously allows in the printed page, as well. The disciplinary lines are getting more blurred and more interdisciplinary research and teaching are being done. This is partly due to intercultural and international communication studies.

SELECTED THEORY TEXTS IN CHINA

To begin to compare speech communication theory with that of other countries causes numerous problems. Not all countries have an open society or a government that respects free speech. Not many countries include speech or communication within the curricula of their institutions, especially in non-Western countries.

On the other hand, when one hears that a country usually not associated with the value or practice of free speech, such as China, finds itself with a growing popular movement for speech training, one takes notice. This is especially true when serious scholars are doing research, holding seminars and international conferences to explore theories of rhetoric, and are publishing scholarly books as well as textbooks on rhetoric.

I turn now to books that were made available to me in my recent trips. These are published in Chinese and have been translated into English by my student, Changjun Yi. I do not consider these definitive translations but at this point working first drafts for the purpose of getting the concepts and topics into the public arena for discussion.

The first one is the rhetoric text by Professor Wu Jiazheng that I mentioned before, titled, *The Rhetorical Art of the Modern Chinese Language*, published by Beijing Normal University in 1992. In her preface she presents the reason and the purpose for writing this book. Social changes that come from opening up from previous isolation require a kind of profound public mentality that demands research into rhetoric because language is a reflection of thought, and the interaction and wider communication among science, commerce, trade, and public relations have penetrated every corner of daily life, thus urgently cultivating the growth of rhetorical art.

An overview chapter comments on the rhetorical aspects of the modern Chinese language and reviews the conditions of cultivation, changes, characteristics, the trend of research, and existing problems. As people want to obtain more and more new information and knowledge, and objectivity, with the development of people's daily language intercourse, and activities of science, commerce and trading, the rhetorical art becomes a most necessary medium.

In the rhetorical aspects of Chinese, there are two conspicuous developments: the utilization of new words which reflect the new situation and new problems of Chinese modern society. The language of literary works of the new period must not be ignored because authors are pursuing new rhetorical forms to create the distinctive style and lasting appeal of the works by enlarging the range of using a single word as a sentence, sentences without punctuation, and changing the utilization of old rhetorical methods.

The modern rhetorical art emphasizes the appeal, interior or hidden meaning and the eloquence of rhetoric, and has features of the harmony of simplicity and complexity, theory and practice, elegance and commonality. The chapter stresses that rhetoric as the study of the effect of language expression should not be limited to the study of "elements of native language," but should involve many other related aspects of the practical and theoretical use of modern language. The connection of rhetoric and other disciplines is one of the important topics for researchers.

Existing problems in the study of rhetoric include the transmission of information when obstructed by obscure and vague language, because of the excessive pursuit of novelty and dimness of writing without considering needs of the theme, plots and circumstances; the principles and methods of rhetorical research on the Chinese language; the ambiguity of Chinese language; the transmission of the potential information with the surface meaning; and the influences coming from language use in Hong Kong and Taiwan.

The application chapter includes a discussion of modern rhetorical art in titles of articles, books, documents, programs; "extended utilization" of modern professional and specialized words; informal comments on the rhetoric of modern commercial advertising; the rhetorical features of scientific language forms; the utilization of substantive sentences without the subject and predicate forms; and the rhetoric of modern song lyrics.

The next chapter explores the new orientation of rhetoric, including the kinds of new rhetoric and the new uses of old rhetoric. This orientation also includes the regular form and irregular form of punctuation rhetoric and the shapes of Chinese characters and their rhetorical use. Characters express feelings by adding or deleting parts of a character, by using the appearance of a character, or the fonts of characters or the arrangement and positioning of characters. Further aspects include nonverbal signals and their rhetorical art and gestures and public relations along with new words and new proverbs. Comments on the analysis of rhetorical effect include adaptability and casualness as a problem in rhetorical analysis and losing the spirit of language in rhetorical analysis.

The chapter on oral language stresses three necessary personal abilities in oral rhetoric: Capturing the audience's interest in line with one's goals, adapting decisively and intelligently to unexpected audience responses, and communicating hidden meanings indirectly. The characteristics of oral rhetoric are: Colorful language that is friendly and commonly understood, reinforcement of meaning by nonverbal communication, and assistance from metalanguage and vocalics. Common techniques used in oral rhetoric are effective humor and ambiguity. The conclusion of the book is that, compared with written rhetoric, oral rhetoric has broader application, is more flexible and adaptable, and requires more language and personal resources.

Wu's book shows signs of an emerging academic discipline in contrast to a Western discipline that has been evolving over centuries. This is the first difference I see in comparing her text to the McCroskey text. She makes much of the changes that are occurring in language and rhetorical use in Chinese society, thus warranting more research and more training. She reviews the changes, the problems faced, the new trends, and the conditions necessary for cultivating rhetorical theory. There is little reference to classical sources in China, such as the writings of Confucius, Mencius, and Hsiin Tzu, which could have provided much theoretical and a uniquely Chinese perspective. My view is that as Chinese researchers continue to do research on rhetoric in China, going back to such sources will be a natural next step. There is also little consciousness if any, of Western sources as well, in the exploring and building of rhetorical theory.

The second difference between the Western and Eastern approach to rhetorical theory, based on these selected texts, is that the Chinese approach is more clearly an integrated approach that combines the written and oral dimensions. It reminds one of Hugh Blair's approach in the Scottish school of the 18th century where his *Lectures on Rhetoric and Belles Letters* (1862) became the standard for use in educational circles.

Wu, for example, uses prolific examples from literature in her discussion of rhetorical principles. Her chapters on application and exploration seem to emphasize all forms of writing and persuasive communication, including advertising. She does use the Aristotelian method of observing how rhetoric is practiced by people in their daily lives and then describing for her students and others what these practices are. In this sense, she is descriptive rather than prescriptive.

The integration of written and oral rhetoric does provide the motivation, however, for the third difference. Instead of the entire book focusing on oral discourse as the McCroskey book does, it instead calls attention to the distinctive nature of oral discourse by providing a designated chapter to its nature, characteristics and techniques. In this way, it does not encompass the breadth or depth of coverage of oral discourse that the Western text does.

But this again, in my opinion, is evidence that the discipline is still emerging in China. Scholars are focusing on the oral dimension now because oral theory has been integrated with written theory and that may not be serving the needs of society. As 1 have indicated, Wu's motivation for writing such a text is that the opening up of society is causing people to realize that they need to be trained to communicate in public.

The fourth difference I wish to note between the Western and Eastern texts is that the Eastern text is much more conscious of the unique rhetorical aspects of the Chinese linguistic form and structure than the Western text is of the English language. She focuses on such elements as Chinese characters and punctuation and how their placement, combinations, and arrangements can have persuasive effect. This again refers to the visual or printed form of language, but it does disclose an interest in the uniqueness of the Chinese language.

The other aspect of the uniqueness of Chinese that does focus on the oral rhetoric and the cultural environment in which it is used is the special emphasis given to Chinese ambiguity and indirectness. Wu believes this is one of the most rhetorical and unique dimensions of the Chinese language. The Chinese people delight in (and are very experienced in) communicating subtle meanings and below-the-surface interpretations of characters and concepts. This is a characteristic of social interaction as well, symbolized by the face-saving practice and the use of a mediator or third party to communicate a message. Wu explores the relationships between ambiguous rhetoric and the traditional way of thinking, its social characteristics, its psychological bases, its form of presentation, and its various applications.

The final difference is the role of rhetoric in society. McCroskey, and most Western texts, give considerable attention to the role rhetoric plays in the social and political life of the country. Democracy depends upon informed and articulate citizens. The Wu text makes much of the social and economic conditions that make public speech necessary now in China, but, understandably, there is no mention of the role of rhetoric in political life. Her indirect reference is to "the public mentality" and the need to know how to communicate in this age of reform. This is a reference to the changes coming, including perhaps even political changes.

In short, I see here a text that is pointing in several directions that show hopeful signs of an emerging discipline in rhetorical and communication study in China.

Wu has written other works, called "A Discussion of Rhetorical Ambiguity in the Chinese Language" (1988) and "An Exploration into the Ambiguous Rhetoric of the Contemporary Chinese Language," a paper presented at the 7th annual conference of the Chinese Rhetoric Association in Haikou in December 1994. Wu cites a number of other texts in her book that deserve mention. One that she believes has been especially influential in "opening up a new page in rhetorical research" is Wu Shi Wen's *Discussion and Analysis of Rhetoric* (1932). In the preface of this book, the author acknowledges that research in rhetoric is still weak and is waiting for people to explore such fundamental questions as, the definition and range of rhetoric, how to reflect the internal structure through clear formulas, how to make the classification of rhetoric more reasonable, how to distinguish between rhetoric and nonrhetoric, and what is the theoretical basis of rhetoric?

Another book Wu cites is more recent. *The Origin and Development of Rhetoric* by Professor Chen Wang Dao published in 1976 by the Shanghai People's Publishing House, describes 38 kinds of rhetoric.

In her text, Wu claims that because of changes in society and the Cultural Revolution, the research of rhetoric was depressed for a time. After the end of the Cultural Revolution in 1976, the Chen book on the origin of rhetoric was published and two years later, in 1978, research in rhetoric was revived and further developed, resulting in the establishment in 1980 of the State Rhetoric Committee in Wuhan. This committee organized a group of experts working in the field of rhetorical education and research. Since then, multidimensional work has been started. According to Wu, a professional association of rhetoric professors meets annually for conferences.

Another book by Chen that professor Wu refers to is *Rhetoric: A Collection of Essays*, (1985). One of Chen's contributions, according to Wu, is the new emphasis on the meaning of rhetoric as that ability to adapt language to the speaker's purpose and to the creation of an appropriate "emotional environment." She believes that more emphasis should be placed on these dimensions of rhetorical art.

Research in Chinese rhetoric has been advanced also by Jan Young Xiang's *New Rhetoric* and Lu Jian Xiang's *The Application of Rhetoric*. Mr. Lu advances four basic principles, according to Wu. They are: (1) pay attention to the internal characteristics of rhetoric, (2) be adaptive to the external relationships that will influence the application of rhetoric, (3) follow the logical rules of rhetoric, and (4) create a rhetorical effect with appropriate modification of traditional forms with a style and spirit from contemporary changes in language use.

Other books Wu mentions that would interest rhetorical scholars are: *The Dictionary of Rhetoric*, edited by Wang De Chen in 1987; *The New Version of the Theory of Rhetoric* by Zheng Yi Shou and Lin Chenzhang; *The Rhetoric of Public Relations* (1989), by Wu Shiwen and Tang Songbo; and *The Dictionary of Chinese New Words* (1986), by Ming Jia Yi.

The second major book, other than Wu's, that I wish to present is *The Theory of Public Speaking* (Liu, 1992) published by the Public Speech Research Committee of Shanghai. Different chapters are written by different authors. I now also include a translated version of the chapter contents. Chapter 1 is on the theory of speech (pp. 1-35), including characteristics, meaning, elements, clarification, history and the research of the theory. Chapter 2 deals with speech writing (pp. 36-66), including title, material selection, structure, language, and the rhetoric of speech writing. Chapter 3 covers the artistic method of making the speech (pp. 67-88), such as humor, philosophy, expression of feeling, suspense, and others. Chapter 4 is on the language of the speech (pp. 89-120), its characteristics, basic skills, and developed skills. Chapter 5 is on the nonverbal language of the speech (pp. 121-13 8), including the functions and application principles of nonverbal language; facial, hand, and gesture expressions; appearance and garments. Chapter 6 (pp. 139-158) is about speech psychology and its significance; psychology of the speaker and audience. Chapter 7 (159-197) deals with specialized speech and its application; conference speaking; scientific speaking; speech competition. Chapter 8 (pp. 198-226) covers debating and its skill, and Chapter 9 includes (pp. 226-248) the structure and methods of impromptu speech. Chapter 10 (pp. 249-277) deals with talking and its art, and Chapter 11 covers the appreciation and criticism of speeches (pp. 278-294). An appendix includes the criticism of famous speech texts.

This text is edited by Liu DeQiang, Chairman of the Public Speech Research Committee of Shanghai and teacher of public speech in the Party School of the Shanghai City Communist Party Committee.

Liu's approach is to provide in the first chapter a definition of speech and a rationale for its study. His definition is that public speech "is the practical social activity in which the speaker systematically develops his idea on a selected topic to an audience primarily through the medium of oral language and assisted by nonverbal communication" (1992, p. 1).

Liu's rationale for studying speech includes three observations. First, speech is an important way to promote and inspire. This has special significance at a time when economic reform and more openness are being advocated by the government. Liu believes that "many practical social problems need new answers from the leaders," so "speech is a very important measure to promote the policies of our Party, and to lead people to execute them" (1992, pp. 5, 6).

Second, Liu suggests that speech is very critical in the teaching of knowledge and in the development of scientific theories (1992, p. 6). He quotes a book on teaching to say, "Teacher's quality of language, to a very high degree, decides the effectiveness of the students' brain work in the class" (p. 6). Good speech work by the teacher can assist understanding by its "simplicity and explicitness," can assist in gaining attention and acceptance by its "mildness," can assist in deepening one's impression by its "vividness," and can assist in "making students' thinking more active and creative" by its inspiration (p. 6).

Third, speech, according to Liu, is one of the important ways to achieve successful management. He believes that the new leaders needed in China will be more inspiring, full of enthusiasm, and be able to obtain respect and trust from their workers if they know how to be persuasive through the use of good reasons and real emotions (Liu, 1992, p. 6).

Fourth, speech is the basic skill of social intercourse as people use language to exchange ideas and communicate information. This is all the more important in an open society in an age of information explosion. Liu concludes by reminding his readers of a proverb, "Good economic relationships will be based only on good human relationships" and effective communication is the means in social interaction of improving friendships among people and relationships among countries" (p. 7). Like Wu's book, this text connects speech training to economic reform, not to political participation. The book emphasizes the different contexts of speech activity, much like Western texts. Also, like Western texts, there is a section on speech criticism and the inclusion of famous speeches. This text does focus more on speech, as such, than the Wu text which seems to be more research oriented. The Liu text is more skills oriented than Wu's and thus is more applied than theoretical.

SUMMARY OBSERVATIONS ON
RHETORICAL THEORY IN CHINA

Based on my annual visit to China over the past six years, the conferences I have attended in China, the numerous books that I have been introduced to, especially the two reviewed here, the scholars I have met in China, and the university departments that I have visited in Beijing, I have prepared 10 observations that I believe can serve as points of inquiry for continued research on the topic of rhetorical theory in China. Since the Chinese scholars themselves are making a link between rhetorical theory and practice with the economic reform in the country, the time is ready for American scholars and Chinese scholars to develop ways to cooperate in this research and training endeavor.

My observations on the conditions and nature of contemporary rhetorical theory in China are as follows:

1. There is a renewed scholarly interest in China in rhetorical theory and training.
2. There is an increasing popular interest in the improvement of public speaking ability.
3. The rationale for renewed interest and improvement is both theoretical and pragmatic. Research into the nature and role of oral and written language and the practical use of effective communication in a changing economy rather than in a participatory government contribute to the significance of speech study.
4. There is a raised consciousness about the unique conditions, characteristics, and applications of the Chinese language in both its verbal and nonverbal forms as they function rhetorically in society.
5. There is a heightened awareness of the impact of oral rhetoric in persuasion as compared to that of written rhetoric. The variety of contexts in which the speaking dimension is primary poses new challenges for scholars and practitioners.
6. There is growing interest in the historical and cultural dimensions of rhetorical theory in China as well as in Western rhetorical theory.
7. The Chinese concept of rhetoric is comprehensive in its philosophical and linguistic bases and in its application to specific contexts.
8. Rhetorical concepts that are at the forefront of exploration are the unique role of language meaning and ambiguity in persuasion, the central role of the audience and the speaker's adaptation to it, and the development of appropriate rhetorical models that reflect function, structure, and method.
9. Just as Western scholars are indebted to Socrates, Plato, and Aristotle as classical sources of rhetorical theory, Chinese scholars can look to Confucius, Mencius, and Hsiin Tzu as sources of classical Eastern rhetorical theory. This observation is not based on the texts reviewed here but on my knowledge of other resources, one of which I cite in my conclusion.
10. The evidence of mutual interest by Eastern and Western rhetorical theorists in each other's theories, perspectives, and methodologies is gaining ground and should be encouraged by cooperative efforts of scholars and funding agencies. First-hand experiences in teaching and in research would help bring about this cooperation.

CONCLUSION

This chapter has been an exploratory study comparing a typical Western theory text from the United States to selected rhetorical theory texts in China with much work yet to do in examining more in depth the books included in this paper. Complete translation of these and additional texts needs to be done and also investigation as to where and how these texts are actually used in schools, institutes, and universities within China.

There is one other limitation and suggestion for further research that is suggested by this chapter. A preliminary examination reveals no reference to classical sources, but I did not yet go through these texts fully (because the translations are not complete) to determine all their sources and references either with respect to Western concepts and authors or classical Chinese concepts and authors. The potential for exploring classical Chinese concepts is real indeed. I refer to Xing Lu and David Frank's article in *Western Journal of Communication* (1993). These authors state in their "On the Study of Ancient Chinese Rhetoric/Bian" that "The ancient Chinese had "senses" of rhetoric (Scott, 1973) and that these senses of rhetoric reveal a tradition of speech and argumentation that should be recaptured by historians of rhetoric" (p. 445). They refer to other work on Chinese rhetoric by Garrett (1983, 1991, 1993), Jensen (1987, 1992), and Kincaid (1987) in which a comparison is made between the rhetorical theories of Confucius and Aristotle. These are excellent beginnings that will no doubt inspire other critics to examine Chinese rhetorical theories both ancient and modern.

To cite further evidence for the claim that there is real potential for exploring classical Chinese rhetoric, I would like to conclude with describing what I consider to be a very important book that exemplifies the kind of research that ought to be done in Chinese rhetorical theory if contemporary theory is to be well informed by classical theory. It is *Ethical Argumentation: A Study in Hsiin Tzu's Moral Epistemology*, by A. S. Cua, published by the University of Hawaii Press in 1985. In this work, Cua attempts to reconstruct Hsiin Tzu's (320-235 B.C.) concept of argumentation by offering not a structure, but a profile of argumentation. It is one that includes: "(1) the desirable qualities or attitudes of the participants, (2) the standards of competence, (3) phases of discourse, and (4) diagnosis of ills that beset the participants and corresponding remedial measures" (p. 7). He defines argumentation as "a reason-giving activity engaged in for the exposition and defense of value-claims or normative proposals" (p. 5). For him, argumentation is "not a chain of demonstrative reasoning" (p. 94) but "a circular process" (p. 94) that is "subject to further questioning and reconsideration in light of its import to other situations which are not now in question" (p. 94). This conception from a philosopher who was a student of Mencius who was a student of Confucius is quite similar to that of Chaim Perelman (Perelman & Olbrechts-Tyteca, 1969), where he claims that the speaker and listeners must be in essential agreement about facts, values, and assumptions if the process of "adherence of minds" is to be successful.

Hsiin Tzu believes that the dynamic and cooperative nature of the argumentation process is its essence. He says there are four phases to such discourse that may be disrupted or challenged at any time by the participants:

> When the actualities referred to by our terms are not understood, one must fix their references (*ming*). When the fixing of references is not understood, one must secure concurrence in linguistic understanding (*ch'i*). When one fails to secure this concurrence, one must resort to explanation (*shiro*). When such an explanation fails, one must embark upon a course of justification (*pien*). (cheng-ming, L521) (Cua, 1985, p. 43)

First, the essential attitude of one engaged in argumentation is the willingness to keep engaged in this process of seeking understanding, not to become contentious and, second, the essential requirement is to demonstrate competence in discrimination (Cua, 1985, p. 15), in "conceptual clarity and coherence" (p. 38), and in "goal articulation and implementation" (p. 37). The phases of discourse cited above, this attitude and this competence of the participants all lead to *tao* as Hsiin Tzu's "ethical vision of human excellence" (p. 160). *Tao* is "the ultimate ethical standard for speech, thought, and action" (p. 160) because "*tao* is manifested in *jen* or benevolent affection (I-ping, L328, D168, W69) in fitting and appropriate ways as determined by *li* (ritual rules) and *i* (sense of what is right)" (p. 161). He distinguishes between "li" and "i," according Cua, calling "li" "rule-dependent" and calling *i* "situation dependent" (p. 162). The important consideration is that *jen*, *li*, and *i* are interconnected in the fulfillment of good and right conduct in human communicative behavior. In the sense that this is a cooperative process between the speaker and the addressed party one is reminded of Aristotle's concept of the enthymeme where the argument is jointly or cooperatively constructed by the speaker and the audience on matters that are worthy of deliberation. Hsiin Tzu's concept of argumentation as "a cooperative enterprise" complying with "the rules of civility" makes it an ethical "art of accommodation" (p. 11). It is a public speech activity.

By exploring Hsiin Tzu's concept of ethical argumentation, which is clearly a rhetorical concept, Cua enables us to see whether there are or are not elements of classical Chinese rhetorical theory in contemporary rhetorical constructions. Much more research needs to be done by scholars on both sides of the Pacific.

DISCUSSION QUESTIONS

1. Discuss the similarities between Chinese and Western rhetorical theory.
2. Discuss the differences between Chinese and Western rhetorical theory.

3. What might be some cultural dimensions that help account for these differences?
4. Discuss ways in which Western and Chinese teachers and scholars can collaborate and discuss the pitfalls to avoid in these collaborations.
5. Do you think rhetoric is a universal concept or a cultural one? Why?

REFERENCES

Blair, Hugh. (1862). *Lectures on rhetoric and Belles Letters.* Philadelphia: T. Ellwood Zell, 1862.

Chen Wang Dao.(1976). *The origin and development of rhetoric.* Shanghai: Shanghai People's Publishing House. (Changjun Yi, Trans.) Cited in Wu Jiazheng, 1992.

Chen Wang Dao.(1985). *Rhetoric: A collection of essays* (vol.3). Fu Jian: Fu Jian Publishing House. (Changjun Yi, Trans.) Cited in Wu Jiazheng, 1992.

Cua, A. S. (1985). *Ethical argumentation: A study in Hsiin Tzu's moral epistemology.* Honolulu: University of Hawaii Press.

Garrett, M. (1983). *The "Mo-Tzu" and the "Lu-Shih Ch'un'ch'in:" A case study of classical Chinese theory and practice of argument.* Diss. University of California, Berkeley.

Garrett, M. (1991). Asian challenge. In S.K. Foss, K.A. Foss, & R. Trapp (Eds.), *Contemporary perspectives on rhetoric* (2nd ed.). Prospect Heights, IL: Waveland.

Garrett, M. (1993). *Pathos* reconsidered from the perspective of classical Chinese rhetorical theories. *The Quarterly Journal of Speech, 79,* 11-39.

Jan Young Xiang. (n.d.). *New rhetoric.* (Changjun Yi, Trans.) Cited in Wu Jiazheng, 1992.

Jensen, J.V. (1987). Rhetorical emphasis of Taoism. *Rhetorica, 5,* 219-229.

Jensen, J.V. (1992). Ancient eastern and western regions as guides for contemporary communication ethics. In J.A. Jaska (Ed.), *Conference Proceedings of the Second National Communication Ethics Conference.* June 11-14 (pp. 58-67). Western Michigan University.

Kincaid, D.L. (1987). Communication east and west: Points of departure. In D.L. Kincaid (Ed.), *Communication theory: Eastern and western perspectives* (pp. 331-340). London: Academic Press.

Liu DeQiang. (Ed.)(1992). *The theory of public speaking.* Shanghai: Public Speech Research Committee of Shanghai. (Changjun Yi, Trans.)

Liu Meiseng. (n.d.). *Management oral discourse.* (Changjun Yi, Trans.) Cited in Wu Jiazheng, 1992.

Lu Jian Xiang. (n.d.). *The application of rhetoric.* (Changjun Yi, Trans.) Cited in Wu Jiazheng, 1992.

Lu, X., & Frank, D.A.(1993). On the study of ancient Chinese rhetoric/bian. *Western Journal of Communication, 57,* 445-463.

McCroskey, J.(1993). *An introduction to rhetorical communication.* Englewood Cliffs, NJ: Prentice Hall.

Ming Jia Yi. (1986). *The dictionary of Chinese new words.* (Changjun Yi, Trans.) Cited in Wu Jiazheng, 1992.

Perelman, C., & Olbrechts-Tyteca, L. (1969). *The new rhetoric: A treatise on argumentation.* London: University of Notre Dame Press.

Scott, R. (1973). On not defining "Rhetoric." *Philosophy and Rhetroic, 6,* 81-96.

The treasure chest of ancient Chinese debating strategies. (n.d.). Jilin: Speech and Oral Discourse Publishing House. (Changjun Yi, Trans.)

Wang De Chen. (1987). *The dictionary of rhetoric.* (Changjun Yi, Trans.) Cited in Wu Jiazheng, 1992.

Wu Jiazheng. (1988). A discussion of rhetorical ambiguity in the Chinese language. Cited in wu Jiazheng, 1992. (Changjun Yi, Trans.).

Wu Jiazheng. (1992). *The rhetorical art of the modern Chinese language.* Beijing: Beijing Normal University. (Changjun Yi, Trans.)

Wu Jiazheng. (1994). *An exploration into the ambiguous rhetoric of the contemporary Chinese language.* Paper presented at the Chinese Rhetoric Association, Haikou. (Changjun Yi, Trans.).

Wu Shi Wen. (1932). *Discussion and analysis of rhetoric.* (Changjun Yi, Trans.) Cited in Wu Jiazheng, 1992.

Wu Shi Wen & Tang Songbo. (1989). *The rhetoric of public relations.* (Changjun Yi, Trans.) Cited in Wu Jiazheng, 1992.

Zheng Yi Son & Lin Chen Zhang. (n.d.). *The new version of the theory of rhetoric.* (Changjun Yi, Trans.) Cited in Wu Jiazheng, 1992.

SECTION IV OVERVIEW: MULTICULTURAL AND MULTINATIONAL ORGANIZATIONS

An area of application of intercultural Communication theories to practical situation is the range of multicultural and multinational organizations. These organizations consist of commercial, educational and governmental institutions. The leaders of such organizations should be educated and trained in multicultural communication including the basic values of individuality and responsibility cultures. Emphasizing one's own basic values even in multicultural situations can cause breakdowns in business, education, and government. The chapters in this section point out how ignoring the values of the others result in unproductive intercultural communication.

In the chapter, "Women's Rights as Human Rights in the United Nations: Three Perspectives," Monfils analyses the communication that took place at the much publicized Fourth World Women's Conference of 1995 in the Peoples Republic of China. The powerful speech presented by The U.S. First Lady Hillary Rodom Clinton at the conference was a conference highlight. The emphasis of her speech was that human rights are women's rights, too. Her discussion of the 12 critical areas of women's rights made a great impact on the conferees, Monfils argues. The very presence of the American First Lady added tremendous prestige to the meeting in the Peoples Republic of China.

In the chapter, "The AID Communication Seminars as a Factor in The Development of Intercultural Communication Study, 1958-1978," Ellingsworth explains how the discipline of communication developed as a behavioral science in the 1950s at the University of Illinois (Urbana-Champaign), Michigan State University, and other universities. Cross-cultural communication was a part of this discipline. Then, intercultural communication was developed as a new discipline in many universities. In order to emphasize the importance of this area, a new division was established at International Communication Association. An interesting project at that time was a training program in communication sponsored by the United States Agency for International Development (U.S.AID). These U.S.AID seminars served as guidelines for the participants in developing future programs in cross cultural communication. This chapter is important since these seminars have not received much publicity, yet they still exist in the memories of the participants and had an impact on the development of intercultural communication as a field of study.

In his chapter, "The Global Economic Societies and the Polycultural Teams," Gehani points out that multinational business organizations, as well as global economy, and their interactions are multicultural in nature. Presenting several case studies, Gehani explains the need for learning the theories and skills of multicultural communication by employees of large multinational corporations.

Another view of multicultural corporations is the chapter, "Can We Talk? A Guide for the Twentieth Century CEO Managing in a Multicultural Environment," by Brooks. She explains why executives in multinational corporations should have communication competence. Message interpretation, tolerance of communication ambiguity, understanding of non verbal codes, and decision making in heterogeneous groups are some of the topics in which the executives should be proficient. These are necessary in corporate cultures, Brooks says.

Neuman discusses the unique communication patterns in a small organization known as microculture. In his chapter, "Jumping Off the Bridge: Rites of Passage and Other Indicators of Organizational Culture," he says that a small organization is a microculture with its own values and vocabulary. He found that a small restaurant, which is a landmark in the state of Maine, U.S.A, is such a microculture and during each tourist season the restaurant's clients will experience this unique culture.

24

WOMEN'S RIGHTS AS HUMAN RIGHTS IN THE UNITED NATIONS: THREE PERSPECTIVES

Barbara S. Monfils
University of Wisconsin at Whitewater

INTRODUCTION

Without progress in the situation of women, there can be no true social development. Human rights are not worthy of the name if they exclude the female half of humanity. The struggle for women's equality is part of the struggle for all human beings, and all societies. (Boutros Boutros-Ghalli, 1996).

These words, by the then-Secretary General of the United Nations were found on a home page on the United Nations' World Wide Web Site in mid-1996. Although the message, "women's rights are human rights," has been often heard, this line of thinking represents an evolution in the activities of the U.N. in regard to the rights of women over the U.N.'s 50 years of existence. This chapter compares and contrasts three views on the status and conditions of women: *Preparations for the Fourth World Conference on Women: Action for Equality, Development, and Peace: Review and Appraisal of the Implementation of the Nairobi Forward-Looking Strategies for the Advancement of Women*, (1995); *Platform for Action* adopted at the U.N.'s 1995 Fourth World Conference on Women in Beijing (1995), and Hillary Rodham Clinton's speech at the Fourth World Conference on Women (1995).[1] Each of these three perspectives is significant. The first document mentioned, *Preparations*, provides an assessment of the ways in which and the extent to which the status of women's issues has changed since the 1985 Nairobi conference. It also provides a convenient ending point in the 50-year scope of U.N. policies on women's issues. The *Platform for Action* sets forth specific critical areas of concern, as well as strategic objectives and actions, in 12 specific areas. Finally, Clinton's speech is significant not only because of her position as First Lady of the United States when she delivered the address, but also because of the world-wide coverage her speech received. A comparison and contrast of these three perspectives will thus provide three perspectives of U.N.-related views on women's issues.

BACKGROUND INFORMATION

According to U.N. documents, the affirmation of equal rights for men and women were stated since its inception. The Preamble to the U.N. Charter, for instance, specifically stated its faith in: "...fundamental human rights, in the dignity and worth of the human person, in the equal rights of men and women and of nations large and small" (Charter of the United Nations. [On Line]. Available: http://www.umn.edu/humanrts/instree/preamble.htm). The main body for women's issues in the U.N. is the 45 member Commission on the Status of Women, CSW, established by UNESCO in 1946. Both the CSW and CEDAW, or the Convention on the Elimination of All Forms of Discrimination against Women, to be discussed subsequently, fall within the Division for the Advancement of Women (DAW) of the Department of Policy Coordination and Sustainable Development.

Early U.N. conferences on women reflected concerns that women were facing in the 1950s and early 1960s. These included the 1952 Convention on the Political Rights of Women, the 1956 Convention of Recovery Abroad of Maintenance, the 1957 Convention on the Nationality of Married Women, and the 1962 Convention on Consent to Marriage. By the 1970s, however, the emphasis of U.N.-sponsored women's conferences had shifted to a more global or macroscopic perspective. The U.N. proclaimed 1975 as International Women's Year, and sponsored a conference on this theme in Mexico City. This conference was followed by conferences in Copenhagen, Denmark, in 1980, Nairobi, Kenya, in 1985, and Beijing, China, in 1995. In addition to these four World Conferences on Women, three other U.N.-sponsored conferences are also noteworthy. CEDAW, or the Convention on the Elimination of All Forms of Discrimination against Women, was adopted in 1979 by the U.N. General Assembly and entered into force on September 3, 1981. Its provisions included a preamble and 30 articles which codified discrimination against women and called for ending all forms of discrimination against women. As of 1996, 139 nations had ratified or acceded to this Convention. The second conference was the 1993 World Conference on Human Rights, held in Vienna, Austria. Participants at this conference not only reaffirmed women's rights as human rights, but also called for establishing a Special Rapporteur on Violence against Women to monitor and draw attention to such abuses when they occurred. The third conference, The U.N. Third Population and Development Conference, held in Cairo in 1993, linked global development to the need for a more equitable distribution of policy changes, including the empowerment of women (Chen, Fitzgerald, & Bates, 1995; Heschel, 1995).

Thus, from the beginning, the U.N. Charter has affirmed the belief in equal rights, and has established organizational representation, conferences, and themes promoting women's rights and women's issues. The linking of human rights with women's rights, initially through CEDAW in 1979 and reaffirmed by the Vienna and Cairo conferences in 1993, provided evidence of the U.N.'s concerns on these two issues. From this perspective, then, the U.N. may be viewed as being at the forefront of women's issues through its linkage with women's rights as human rights.

PREPARATIONS FOR THE FOURTH CONFERENCE ON WOMEN

Although the U.N. has taken courageous stands on some women's issues, such as reproductive rights, an examination of the document, *Preparations for the Fourth World Conference on Women: Action for Equality, Development, and Peace: Review and Appraisal of the Implementation of the Nairobi Forward-Looking Strategies for the Advancement of Women,* (1995) presents a mixed picture. This document was written shortly before the 1995 Beijing conference.

The "Overview of the Global Economic and Social Framework" portion of the document highlighted both benefits and losses in women's issues in the 10 years since the Nairobi conference. Among the positive elements cited were changes in development policy and the recognition of women as active influences in economic activity, rather than solely as being affected by them. However, competing claims on economic resources, political agendas by powerful groups in many nations, and changes in the world economy have, in many cases, slowed or nullified gains that women have made in recent times, according to this document.

The document cited three specific trends that have significantly impacted women's issues in the world since 1985. These included the adjustments that countries made to their national economies as a result of worldwide economic recessions, the rapid rise of technology, and the trend to globalization and economic interdependence. According to this document, women in Latin America and the Caribbean and in sub-Saharan Africa have suffered the most from economic restructuring, and women in the former USSR and Eastern Europe, in particular, have endured difficult conditions while the economies of these nations have adjusted from controlled- to free-market status. Furthermore, even in nations and regional areas in which substantial progress has been made, gains either are expected to slow or to be reversed in the next few years.

A second set of issues related to women addressed the consequences of economic conditions on the employment of women and the active participation of women in the workforce. First, the move to greater accountability-based methods in assessing employee productivity has resulted in problems for women in particular. Since women are more likely to be in service-related occupations in which "objective" means for assessing productivity are more difficult to do measure, the report concluded that women's "wage bargaining power" has actually lessened in some instances. Secondly, the rise in part-time employment in the last 10 years, an important economic trend, has often been equated with fewer (if any) benefits and lower salaries. Thus, women, who are significantly more likely than men to be employed part-time, have been doubly harmed by this trend. The combination of low wages and scarcity of benefits, in turn, has meant that growing numbers of children have not had adequate access to education, nutrition, or health care. Finally, the report noted that even though economic growth in some parts of the world has resulted in larger numbers of women entering the workplace, the participation of women in organized labor activities, including unions, have not been occurring with any regularity. Thus, women's advancement opportunities have been limited in this aspect as well.

The "Other Factors" section of the *Preparations* document likewise cited disturbing trends. This section focused on the issue of the feminization of poverty, world-wide, and its effect on women. In this document, poverty was reaffirmed as a primary factor in problems facing women. Similarly, the ten-year change on focus in development from "economic growth-oriented" to "human-centered" issues was noted for having resulted in gains for women. Again, however, many negative factors cited in the report have minimized the gains. Negative factors cited in the report contained economic, political, and social dimensions. Economic development of nations or regions has not always resulted in the redistribution of resources to women. In some nations, political practices have sought to disenfranchise women or to deter their participation in political activities. Socially, the report noted that attempts to eradicate poverty have slowed since the 1980s, while at the same time, the number of urban residents in poverty has swelled. The report identified specific groups of women who have especially suffered during the last ten years, particularly refugees and displaced women, elderly women, and indigenous women. Added to these factors have been the increase in the worldwide divorce rate and the lack of gender-specific programs to alleviate poverty, thereby exacerbating the difficulties for millions of women throughout the world.

PLATFORM FOR ACTION

The *Platform for Action,* adopted at the 1995 Beijing conference, both expanded on topics discussed in the *Forward-Looking Document* of the Nairobi conference, and highlighted additional critical areas of concern. In the "Beijing Declaration," at the beginning of the Platform, the authors acknowledged that the Beijing Conference was occurring during the 50th year of the U.N., recognized that some progress has been made, and also identified poverty as a major reason why some changes have not taken place. Commitments to equal rights, the empowerment of women, and women's rights as human rights were clearly stated. The 12 "Critical Areas of Concern" were then listed: women and poverty; education and the training of women; women and health; violence against women; women and armed conflict; women and the economy; women in power and decision-making; institutional mechanisms for the advancement of women; human rights of women; women and the media; women and the environment; and the girl child. Following the listing of the 12 areas, each concern was discussed in a problem/solution format. In each area, specific recommendations were made for eliminating the barriers faced by women. The Overview of the "Strategic Objectives and Actions" statements concluded with the recognition of additional barriers faced by refugees and displaced women, as well as harms to women by environmental factors, disease, and violence.

A comparison of the 1995 *Platform* with the *Preparations* document showed great similarity regarding the issue of women and poverty. The Platform continued the perspective that economic policies must be human-centered if significant numbers of women are to break out of the cycle of poverty. Although the issue of poverty did not receive overwhelming emphasis in the *Platform*, its placement as the first issue lent credence to the alleviation of poverty among women as a major goal in achieving equality world-wide. In addition, several other issues, including education and training of women, women and the economy, women and decision-making, and institutional mechanisms for the advancement of women, referred back to recommendations made in this section of the *Platform.*

Environmental issues also received similar coverage in both documents. Both documents used the eradication of poverty and human-centered economic growth as important factors influencing environmental concerns, and both identified the roles of women as caretakers and educators in having a great impact on the world's ecological balance. Moreover, both reports cited women as being often the most negatively-impacted by environmental pollution, both at home and on the job.

One major difference between the issues cited in *Preparations* and the *Platform* was the attention given to violence against women in the latter document. Indeed, violence against women was discussed as a separate category in the *Platform.* Moreover, the *Platform* expanded the definition of violence to include forced sexual practices, including sterilization or abortion. Finally, the Platform devoted a specific section to violence suffered by women in armed conflict situations Thus, the attention given to actions to protect women from violent acts by family members and by their own Governments contained an emphasis not found in the *Preparations* document.

Similarly, women and health received more attention in the 1995 *Platform*. Although the Holy See delegates expressed reservations about this section, it was a critical issue in the final draft. The inclusion of health rights as women's rights—including the rights to their own bodies, reproductive freedom, and access to information for informed choices—represented a significant step in the evolution of the U.N. perspective on women's rights (Women's Conference in Beijing, 1995).

Although the *Preparations* document discussed the importance of technology, the *Platform* did not identify technology as an area *per se*; instead, attention was focused on the media. In this section, emphasis was given to empowering women in mass media industries as the primary means of bringing about change. Noting that women, in general, lacked either the training or the access to communications media, the *Platform* writers argued that if women were given greater access and greater training, media portrayals of men and women would be less gender-biased. Additionally, messages that exploited women and children would be less likely to be presented, and the media could be used to promote campaigns to make all persons more aware of women's rights.

The final two areas, human rights of women, and the girl child, were specific to the *Platform*. As discussed previously, the inclusion of human rights of women as a separate critical area of concern in the *Platform* was both noteworthy and clear. This section of the *Platform* began with the following paragraphs:

> 210. Human rights and fundamental freedoms are the birthright of all human beings; their protection and promotion is the first responsibility of Governments. 211. The World conference on Human Rights reaffirmed the solemn commitment of all States to fulfill their obligations to promote universal respect for, and observance and protection of, all human rights and fundamental freedoms for all, in accordance with the Charter of the United Nations, other instruments relating to human rights, and international law. The universal nature of these rights and freedoms is beyond question.

The *Platform* specifically mentioned the rights of women and girl children two paragraphs later: Governments were then assigned the tasks of educating all persons on women's rights as human rights, on enforcing laws and provisions to ensure and protect the rights of women, and of monitoring violations so that women would not fear retribution when seeking redress for actions that violated their human rights. Similar admonitions were given on protecting the rights of female children in "The Girl Child" section of the *Platform*. This section listed nine strategic objectives: eliminating all forms of discrimination against girl children; eliminating negative cultural attitudes and cultural practices against girls;

promoting awareness of the rights and needs of girls; eliminating discrimination in educational and/or training; eliminating discrimination in health and nutritional policies and practices; eliminating practices that result in economic exploitation of girls; eliminating violence against girl children; promoting awareness of girl childrens' participation in social, political, economic life; and strengthening the role of girl children within the family. Thus, even though the *Preparations* document reviewed the "Forward Looking Strategies" of the Nairobi conference, the emphasis placed on the issue of women's rights as human rights and the inclusion of the rights of the girl child served to advance these issues in the *Platform*.

HILLARY RODHAM CLINTON'S SPEECH
TO THE DELEGATES

When Hillary Rodham Clinton addressed the delegates at the Beijing Conference on September 5, 1995, her audience was far greater than the 1500 participants who were able to gain entrance into the auditorium in which she delivered her speech. In fact, worldwide attention was focused on China, especially since some had questioned whether or not she should attend the Conference (e.g., Casey & George, 1995; Women in China, 1995). Having returned from Beijing the previous day, I was personally aware of the international controversy surrounding her upcoming speech. An analysis of her speech affirms Clinton's view, as stated in her title: "Women's Rights are Human Rights" (1995). This analysis focuses on Clinton's speech as an example of narrative communication. In her speech, Clinton wove a tapestry of examples and personal experiences to construct a story about women's lives that, when analyzed,coincided with the major issues that were to emerge in the *Platform for Action*.

In developing the narrative paradigm of communication criticism, Fischer (1987) argued that storytelling is among the earliest forms of communication humans learn. The dimensions that made for good stories when we were children continue to make for "good stories," even as adults. As such, narration is inherently rhetorical (Hollihan & Baaske, 1994). The narrative paradigm has been used to study societal and cultural practices, conflict, spiritual conversion, political rhetoric, organizational communication, and journalism (Hollihan & Riley, 1987; Mullins, 1994). Through a combination of narrative probability, or how well the parts of a story fit together, and narrative fidelity, or the extent to which a story "rings true" with what else is known, the story becomes a measure of "truth" for both storyteller and listener. Hollihan and Baaske noted that stories "...not only come to reflect our reality, they actually become our sense of what is real" (1994, p. 15). Through an application of Hollihan and Baaske's components of argumentative narration, including characters, scene, events, and context, to Clinton's speech to the delegates at the Women's Conference in Beijing, the "story" that

Clinton told to delegates about women's rights as human rights can be more clearly understood.

In her speech, Clinton used a combination of characters, scene, events, and context to tell her story. The characters in Clinton's story were primarily, though not exclusively, women. She began by noting that the delegates at the Conference had come together, just as women throughout the world come together, "every day in every country" (Clinton, 1995, p. 738). She told about her own experiences in meeting mothers, parents, women, and health care providers throughout the world, all of whom expressed their concerns about issues relating to women and children. Clinton, as narrator, then continued her story from two perspectives. First, as a woman, she wished to speak on behalf of all of the women who were unable to speak for themselves at this Conference.

Secondly, as an American, she represented American women at the Conference. She also assured delegates that the actions taken as a result of the Conference would be felt by women throughout the world. In Clinton's speech, the scene was two-fold. The specific scene was Beijing, the site of the Conference. However, Clinton also used the conference site as a microcosm for the sites in which women meet daily, including "fields," "factories," "village markets," "supermarkets," "living rooms," and "boardrooms." She continued: "Whether it is while playing with our children in the park, or washing clothes in a river, or taking a break at the office water cooler, we come together and talk about our aspirations and concerns. And time and again, our talk turns to our children and our families" (Clinton, 1995, p. 739).

Similarly, Clinton's discussion of events was multidimensional. In the beginning of the speech, she identified the Conference as being a joyous event:

> This is truly a celebration—a celebration of the contributions women make in every aspect of life; in the home, on the job, in their communities, as mothers, wives, sisters, daughters, learners, workers, citizens and leaders" (Clinton, 1995, p. 739).

She also developed the theme of the Conference as a learning event: "It is conferences like this that compel governments and people everywhere to listen, look and face the world's most pressing problems" (Clinton, 1995, p. 739), she said. She then described the many events in women's lives that have contributed to their status as less-than-equal participants in world events. By pointing out how women have not been receiving equitable treatment, she provided a rationale for change.

In this context, she revealed the central theme of her "story." Early in her speech, she reminded delegates that the conditions of women have a direct bearing on family and world conditions: "What we are learning around the world is that, if women are healthy and educated, their families will flourish. If women are free from violence, their families will flourish. If women have a chance to work and earn as full and equal partners in society, their families will flourish. And when families flourish, communities and nations will flourish" (Clinton, 1995, p. 738).

Cautioning delegates that there is no single way in which women should act, she argued for respecting the choices that different women will make. She then argued that women will not receive their full share of dignity until, as she said, "their human rights are respected and protected" (Clinton, 1995, p. 739). She referred to the Vienna conference to develop the theme that many of the conditions suffered by women are violations of human rights. Calling for an end to silence, she continued: "It is time for us to say here in Beijing, and the world to hear, that it is no longer acceptable to discuss women's rights as separate from human rights" (Clinton, 1995, p. 739). Repeating that the silence must be broken, she began a litany of specific human rights violations:

- It is a violation of human rights when babies are denied food, or drowned, or suffocated, or their spines broken, simply because they are born girls.
- It is a violation of human rights when women and girls are sold into the slavery of prostitution.
- It is a violation of human rights when women are doused with gasoline, set on fire and burned to death because their marriage dowries are deemed too small.
- It is a violation of human rights when individual women are raped in their own communities and when thousands of women are subjected to rape as a tactic or prize of war.
- It is a violation of human rights when a leading cause of death worldwide among women ages 14 to 44 is the violence they are subjected to in their own homes.
- It is a violation of human rights when young girls are brutalized by the painful and degrading practice of genital mutilation.
- It is a violation of human rights when women are denied the right to plan their own families, and that includes being forced to have abortions or being sterilized against their will.
- If there is one message that echoes forth from this conference, it is that human rights are women's rights...And women's rights are human rights. (Clinton, 1995, p. 739)

In developing this theme, she provided a moral to be learned. As she neared the conclusion of her speech, she reminded delegates that taking action to improve women's rights would result in the betterment of everyone in the human family: By telling her "story" to the delegates, Clinton articulated compelling reasons as to why women's rights must be viewed as human rights, and why specific actions should be taken to improve women's rights as human beings. Although there is no way to know for certain the impact that Clinton's speech had on Conference delegates, the emergent Platform for Action includes many of Clinton's themes in its 12 critical areas. Much of the reaction to her speech in the United

States was positive (e.g., Fox, 1995; CNNa, 1995; CNN, 1995b; "Clinton's Unwavering Words," 1995). The official Chinese press, however, did not acknowledge her remarks for two days, and then dismissed many of her statements ("China Brushes off Negative Remarks at Conference," 1995).

SUMMARY

This comparison and contrast of three perspectives on women's rights thus reveals significant similarities and differences. In the 10 years between the Nairobi and Beijing conferences, advances have been made in the greater acceptance of a human-centered approach to women and national development, in the recognition of the importance of women in environmental concerns, and in the identification of the deleterious effects of armed conflict on women. Furthermore, the eradication of poverty as an issue central to the betterment of women, rather than as an after-effect of the status of women, is stated and reaffirmed, as is the recognition of the worldwide growth of the feminization of poverty.

A greater number of critical issues are cited in the 1995 *Platform for Action*. These include expanding the definition of violence against women, reproductive rights as health issues, the importance of media access, and the human rights of women and girl children.

Since inception, the U.N. Charter, organizational structure, designation of the International Women's Year, and sponsorship of women's conferences all attest to the U.N.'s interest in women's issues. The evolution of the theme of women's rights as human rights extends the scope of women's issues to fundamental human concerns. The success of this theme in advancing women's rights throughout the world will certainly be a major "benchmark" by which U.N. activities related to women's rights will be judged in the years to come.

DISCUSSION QUESTIONS

1. What were the major similarities and differences in how the U.N. delegates viewed women's rights before and after the 1995 conference in Beijing, China?
2. In what ways has the U.N. demonstrated its commitment to women's rights and women's issues?
3. What economic changes have influenced the status of women since the 1985 U.N. Women's Conference in Kenya?
4. What changes have been made to the definition of violence against women in the 1995 *Platform for Action*, and why are these significant?
5. How did Hillary Clinton use storytelling techniques to advance her theme of women's rights as human rights in her speech to the 1995 Women's Conference in Beijing?

NOTE

[1] Acknowledgement is made of the role of the U.N. in making these documents available for reproduction and dissemination, including electronc access. Because I accessed the documents electronically, I did not attempt to assign page numbers to sections of the *Preparations* and *Platform for Action* documents.

REFERENCES

Casey, R. P. & George, R. P.(1995). Just don't go. *National Review, 47,* 40-42.

Chen, L .C., Fitzgerald, W. M., & Bates, L. (1995). Women, politics, and global management. *Environment, 37,* 4-9.

China Brushes off Negative Remarks at Conference. (1995, September 7). [Radio Transcript]. National Public Radio Morning Edition, Program #1689. Online. Available: Periodical Abstracts. [1977, May 21].

Clinton, H. R. (1995). Women's' rights are human rights. *Vital Speeches of the Day, 61,* 738-740.

Clinton's unwavering words. (1995, September 7). *New York Times,* p. A24.

First lady takes on the Chinese. (1995b, September 9). [Television Transcript, D Bonoir, M. Shields, R. Novak]. CNN Inside Politics. Online: 1702 words. Available: Reed Elsevier/LEXIS/NEXIS Academic Universe Web. [1998: August 20].

First lady's unwavering words win her play of the week. (1995a, September 8). [Television Transcript, H. Clinton, D. Thomas, W. Clinton, W. Schneider]. CNN Inside Politics. Online: 647 words. Available: Reed Elsevier/LEXIS/NEXIS Academic Universe Web. [1998, August 20].

Fischer, W. (1987). *Human communication as narration.* Columbia: University of South Carolina Press.

Fox, T. (1995). HRC was right to go. *National Catholic Reporter, 31,* 2.

Heschel, S. (1995). Feminists gain at the Cairo Population Conference. *Dissent, 42,* 15-18.

Hollihan, T. A. & Baaske, K. T. (1994). *Arguments and arguing;The products and process of human decision making.* New York: St. Martin's Press.

Hollihan, T. & Riley, P. (1987). The rhetorical power of a compelling story: A critique of a 'Toughlove' parental support group. *Communication Quarterly, 35,* 13-25.

Mullins, D. (1994). AIDS advocacy and awareness: The perceptions of afflicted and non-afflicted celebrities as reflected in personal accounts. Paper Presented at the 1994 Convention of the Speech Communication Association, New Orleans, La.

The Official Report of the FWCW containing the Beijing Declaration and Platform for Action. [On-line], Available: http://www.umn.cdu/humanıts/instree/preamble.htm

Preparations for the Fourth World Conference on Women: Action for equality, development, and peace: Review and appraisal of the implementation of the Nairobi forward-looking strategies for the advancement of women. [On-line], Available: http://www.un.org/fwcw/plat.html.

Signy, H. & Adam, W. (1995). Beijing women's summit. *World Press Review, 4,* pp. 4-5.

Women's conference in Beijing adopts positive language (1995, September 11). All Things Considered. Program Number 1967.

25

THE AID COMMUNICATION SEMINARS AS A FACTOR IN THE DEVELOPMENT OF INTERCULTURAL COMMUNICATION STUDY, 1958-1978

Huber W. Ellingsworth
University of Tulsa

INTRODUCTION

New themes and programs of study are introduced into the curricula of U.S. universities in a number of ways. Some come about through the divergence of interest and methodology in existing fields, as in the case of Philosophy and Psychology and also English and Speech early in the century. Some change occurs through new syntheses of a body of existing knowledge—"An Idea Whose Time Has Come." Urban Studies, Oceanography, and Environmental Studies are examples. Communication study was also such an occurrence. Later, attention was given to a special focus which came to be called "Intercultural Communication."

THE BEGINNINGS OF COMMUNICATION STUDY

In order to understand the creation of Intercultural Communication scholarship, one must first be aware of how its larger context—the behavioral study of human communication—came about. The most coherent account of this is found in "Human Communication as a Field of Behavioral Science," a document originally titled "A Memo to Jack Hilgard and His Committee." The paper is undated, but its content places the writing as around 1965. Hilgard headed an American Psychological Association committee on the study of human communication. He was aware of the remarkable rise and development of the social-behavioral study of Communication in the 1940s, 1950s and 1960s and asked Schramm for a formal explanation. Schramm did this by first tracing the research and theory of Harold Laswell, Paul Lazarsfeld, Kurt Lewin and Robert Merton and then citing the establishment of research centers at Columbia University, Yale University, The University of Illinois, The University of Wisconsin, Michigan State University, Stanford University, and the Annenberg School of Communications (Schramm, 1989).

The Beginnings at the University of Illinois

Schramm had been a contemporary of the developments which laid the base for establishing the first graduate program in social-behavioral communication at the University of Illinois in 1952. This program bespoke the multidisciplinary approach which would characterized the field as it developed. Since there was no existing department sufficiently interdisciplinary to sponsor the new program, it was created and administered initially by a University-wide Committee, which included: Schramm (Communication Research), Fred Siebert (Journalism), Charles Osgood (Psychology), O. Herbert Mowrer (Psychology), and Joseph Casagrande (Anthropology). Later the program was based in the Communication Research Institute.

The Beginnings at Michigan State University

Among the first recipients of the new doctorate were David Berlo and Hideya Kumata. Both joined the new College of Communication being formed at Michigan State University. By 1958, a graduate department and a research center were in place. A doctoral program in communication was begun. Additional faculty members at the beginning were Paul Deutschmann, Huber Ellingsworth, Malcolm MacLean and Gerald Miller. By 1960, there was a full complement of doctoral students from the United States, Colombia, Chile, Brazil, Costa Rica, Cuba, India, Pakistan and the Philippines. Students came from the fields of agriculture, anthropology, broadcasting, English, journalism, business administration, psychology, sociology, and speech. No undergraduate discipline was seen as a particular prerequisite for entrance. Students were expected to know, or to learn, quantitative research methods at a sophisticated level.

MICHIGAN STATE UNIVERSITY
AND INTERNATIONAL PROGRAMS

During this same decade (1950-60) Michigan State University was becoming a major overseas contractor with the International Cooperation Administration (later U.S. Agency for International Development and referred to hereafter as "AID"), plus the Ford Foundation, the Food and Agriculture Organization of the UN, the Rockefeller Brothers Foundation and the Kellogg Foundation. Training, development, consultation, and research were being operated by MSU in Afghanistan, Brazil, Chile, Costa Rica, India, Jamaica, Thailand and Viet Nam, and negotiations were under way for establishing a new land-grant-style university in Enugu, Nigeria. In 1960, Kumata taught a graduate seminar at MSU which was probably the first academic instruction ever offered in Cross-cultural Communication (the term "intercultural" came later).

One of the programs at MSU was the National Project in Agricultural Communication (NPAC). NPAC had begun in 1953 under Stanley Andrews, a former Director of the Point IV (Marshall Plan) Program. It was charged with providing training and resources in the diffusion of information about agriculture and home economics and was financed by the Kellogg Foundation.

NPAC offered three levels of training: Basic Communication, Written Communication, and Visual Communication. They were staffed by NPAC personnel and other specialists at sites including Kingston, Jamaica, East Lansing, Atlanta, Baton Rouge and Oakland, California. These were intensive, one and two week programs for state-level administrators of agricultural extension programs. Since the state personnel were then expected to conduct county-level programs, there was a strong "train the trainer" component.

The training was highly participatory and the Basic program included exercises and case studies designed to demonstrate and test theories of learning, message design, social and cultural variables, visual and auditory perception, group and community leadership. The Written and Visual programs were participatory and production-oriented, drawing upon the theories in the Basic program. There was a close liaison between NPAC and the College of Communication from the beginning, both shared personnel and ideas. Francis Burns provided a vital link between the programs. Innovative new approaches to training were developed, stressing maximum participation and interaction between staff and trainees. The NPAC trainees were homogeneous groups with common educational backgrounds and a shared range of professional problems.

In the summer of 1957, AID began sending agricultural trainee participants to NPAC Basic programs. The response was sufficiently positive to encourage the agriculture training officials to urge AID that such training developed for AID participants from all specialties.

BEGINNINGS OF THE AID COMMUNICATION SEMINARS

The Role of the NPAC in the Development of the AID Seminars

In 1957, NPAC Director Andrews was approached by representatives of AID with a request for assistance. This request was referred to the MSU College of Communication, which had been formed in 1956 under the leadership of Dean Gordon Sabine. With the end of the Marshall Plan, which had initially been about economic and industrial rebuilding of Europe, US State Department officials in the early 1950s saw the need for the United States to expand and extend the concept of foreign aid world-wide. Some aspects would continue to involve major economic development and the construction of infrastructure, but an equally important need would be for more and better middle-management technicians and professionals from less-developed countries in Latin America, Africa and Asia, many newly independent or in the process. The ICA (known after 1962 as AID) was established as an agency of the State Department to administer most aspects of foreign aid. A Training Division was created to identify training needs, locate potential trainees, recruit them, plan in-service internships and training activities in the United States lasting about one year, and return them to their countries. Unites States Operations Missions (USOM) were established as rapidly as possible in countries where bi-lateral agreements for such aid had been negotiated. Initially there were 16 participating countries, a number which had expanded to over 90 by 1962.

The primary goal was to update the managers' skills, introduce them to new technologies and in general to motivate them to be more effective agents of change and modernization. Since world-wide treaties had standardized air traffic protocols for international flights, one of the earliest training priorities was for air traffic controllers.

In 1958, AID was sponsoring about 5000 trainees (officially known as participants), a number which would expand to about 12,000 by 1961. By 1957, more than a thousand such sojourners had come to the United States, completed their training and returned home (Ellingsworth, 1981).

Two things were evident in the early years. One was that the goal of training in new ideas, practices and technologies was succeeding even better than could have been expected. Participants generally were reported as well-motivated and eager to learn things that would upgrade their future performance and were highly positive about most aspects of American culture.

The second, alarming aspect of the experience was that many participants had over-adapted to U.S. culture and methodology. On their return home they were impatient in demanding that American-style technology and procedures be adopted, and that change be undertaken quickly. Complaints were received at USOMs that the specialists, often in desperately short supply within the emerging country, had been rendered more competent, but less functional by the training. It appeared that the classic U-curve of Adjustment which had been expanded by John and Jeanne Gullahorn into a "double-U" model was being dramatically demonstrated (Gullahorn & Gullahorn, 1963). AID officials sought some means by which participants could be "de-briefed" and psychologically prepared for their return home.

Creation of the AID Seminars

Having seen that the NPAC model of communication training appeared to be efficient and effective, AID requested that MSU develop a similar program for their participants. The response was affirmative and the effort got underway in 1957. A development group was formed at MSU with thirty-two representatives from audio-visual instruction, communication research, communication skills, agriculture, education, journalism, political science, anthropology, speech, NPAC and the MSU Brazil and Viet Nam projects. Because of the urgency perceived by AID, the group was allocated only four months to outline and detail the program sufficiently to conduct a pilot seminar in June, 1958. The planning sub-groups confronted a variety of problems, some of which would be faced a decade or more later in attempts to develop intercultural communication as a field of academic study and research.

Seven major issues emerged and were decided upon during the course of the meetings:

1. What should be the general objectives?
    The objectives agreed upon by representatives of AID and MSU were:
    A. Improvement of the participant's understanding of the factors to be taken into account in becoming a responsible and effective change agent.
    B. Development of the participant's sensitivity to problems in re-establishing contact with family, friends, and work associates.
2. Would the seminars be "culture-specific" or "culture-general?"

While there was considerable interest in programs that would deal specifically with problems of facilitating change and development in a particular country or region, this alternative was quickly pushed aside by practical considerations. The agency programming schedule could seldom provide homogeneous national groups of participants. Other problems involved content and staffing. There were not bodies of information sufficiently synthesized for use in dealing with communication and change country-by-country. Nor could the group visualize how to staff such programs. There were already 16 USOM's sending participants and expansion plans were well underway.

The only alternative was to structure the program around general theories of communication, change and adaptation and press the participant to supply culture-specific details appropriate to their own circumstances. This was attempted in practice by presenting the generalities and discussing actual culture-specific case studies supplied by AID, plus conferences to discuss participants' plans for change and assist them in developing a plan of action based on the themes of the Seminar.

3.   Would the training be instructive or facilitative?

Training at that time was usually conceived in the United States as a focused, specific body of ideas, and/or skills to be taught and mastered. It was clear from the beginning that such an approach could not be functional. Not only was there the country diversity previously mentioned, but the participant groups would be randomly composed of trainees in agriculture, education, public health, public administration, business, labor, industry and transportation. No set of instructions about communication techniques for change would fit these overlapping cultural and technical diversities. In addition, one of the two main objectives concerned successful re-entry of the returned participant into the social system and work group. While there was some anecdotal data on this, sojourner re-entry had in 1957 not yet generated much research or theory.

The content would need to be facilitative in nature, presenting urgent challenges and questions to the participants and then encouraging them to think through responses appropriate to their home environments. This reinforced the earlier decision to call the program a Communication Seminar, rather than a training program.

4.   Would the program be original in concept or adapted from the NPAC basic program?

While desirous of outlining a program with maximum fit to participant needs, the group soon acknowledged that available time and resources would require building upon the NPAC program, which had been carefully constructed, tested in use and employed in one off-shore setting in Jamaica. The content of materials and techniques was examined for items which might prove so culture-bound as to enigmatic or inappropriate for the variety of technical specialists—e.g., heavy reliance on agricultural examples and illustrations. Emphasis on how to develop and use audio-visual material was scaled down, and materials to be used by staff were modified for the new group. AID training officers who attended some of the sessions agreed to supply anecdotal materials from a range of field experiences. The analysis of the decision-making process was changed to reflect traditional, hierarchic societies. Treatment of the roles of religion and family life in the change process was considered for inclusion. The major themes selected to give structure to the week were designated as communication models, learning theory, perception, the psychology of rumor, organizational structure, cultural change, a social-action construct and problems of reentry.

Operational matters were also considered. One was the placement of the communication seminars within the participants' year-long sojourn. It was agreed that the ideal time would be the final week of the program, just before the participant went to Washington D.C. for pre-departure formalities. AID representatives concurred that this would be the most functional for travel planning and would find the participants in a state of heightened anticipation and anxiety at the prospects of returning home.

The preferred site for the program was seen as an isolated setting within a few hours of Washington D.C. by chartered bus. The goal was to locate pleasant rural surroundings with meeting rooms on the site, limit distractions and provide food service suitable for a wide range of dietary preferences. A lodge in a state park was regarded as ideal (such a facility was found at Cacapon State Park in West Virginia). Staffing and staff preparation were also discussed and this matter was assigned to those who would later manage and conduct the program.

Culture and Change

Questions were raised during the discussion which might in 1996 fall under the rubric of "cultural sensitivity" or "political correctness." The U.S. government was committed to the central goal of checking the spread of Communist ideology by military means, but more comprehensively, by helping less-developed and newly-independent countries improve nutrition, health, education, productivity and transportation. Inevitably this meant adopting some Western values for modernization, industrialization and change and weakening some of the values of traditional societies. Should academics, who were conventionally liberal, take part in a program devoted to accelerating change and modernization at the risk of weakening or destroying traditional values?

While acknowledging the sensitivity of this issue, most of the planners did not see the matter as a major impediment to proceeding. There was general agreement that the participants should be encouraged to think of themselves as "Change Agents." In the Seminar as it developed, this matter emerged as the theme of a half-day session called "Culture and Change." The participants were asked what they wanted to take home with them from the United States as well as to identify what they would not want to introduce from the United States. They were then challenged to perceive that many of their desired changes would have culturally undesirable or imponderable side effects as part of the package. For example, almost everyone admired U.S. efficiency and the use of technology for data processing but had not recognized that back home this would mean unemployment for masses of clerks who were presently doing these functions by hand. Many initially believed that modernity could be infused without tearing the fabric of traditional culture. After sometimes heated discussion within the planning group, this matter would be intentionally left unresolved. Many staff members and some participants would later regard this intense session on culture and change as the high point of the seminar week.

THE AID-MSU SEMINARS AS AN INSTITUTION

In mid-March, the Development Group turned their recommendations over to David K. Berlo, who had been appointed as the first Director of the AID Communication Seminars. Berlo chose a staff, conducted a "dry-run" on campus, and in June the first seminar (designed "pilot") took place on schedule with 30 participants. Based on its apparent success, AID and MSU then negotiated a contract for 14 seminars beginning in August, 1958. The program was to be contracted on an annual basis, with no implication of longer-term commitment. It could not have been possible then to imagine that the seminars would continue basically the same for 20 years, involve some 20,000 participants from 100 countries and utilize as weekly staff about 500 faculty members from more than 20 academic fields in 60 U.S. and Canadian colleges and universities, plus others from government agencies and private corporations. I replaced Berlo as Director after the first year of operation.

In addition to their unanticipated longevity, the seminars demonstrated a remarkable continuity of form and content. Repeated evaluations disclosed a high level of satisfaction by participants, staff and AID sponsors. There was strong support for keeping things much as they had begun. As trainees became more cosmopolitan and modernization appeared less threatening, somewhat more attention was given to effectiveness of communicating new ideas and less to problems of re-entry. The basic approach of the seminar concept—challenging questions for which the participants would need to seek answers—remained until the end. In its final years the program was operated under private contract by several staff "alumni" from the MSU operation, but with a recognizable format from the past.

PROCESS AND OUTCOMES OF THE AID-MSU SEMINARS

One of the elusive challenges which persisted through the many years of the seminars was how to assess and measure their outcomes. While the structure was durable, every seminar was in several senses unique. During nearly 500 repetitions under MSU sponsorship, there were perhaps no more than half a dozen with identical training staffs and, of course, none in which the participant group was repeated. A dozen different sites were employed. Participant nationality and training specialty varied randomly. About half the weekly staff, usually numbering four or five, came from MSU and the balance from the Universities of Illinois, Wisconsin, Oklahoma, Iowa, Penn State, Florida, Michigan, Miami (Ohio), Oregon and many other places. Most staffers were strangers to one another, especially in the early years, and came from more than 25 different academic disciplines. Narrowly construed, the seminars could only be evaluated a week at a time, but that would serve no longer-range purpose. What is knowable (or at least known) about the process and outcomes of the seminars can be understood from the perspectives of the three groups—participants, AID sponsors and staff—whose lives it affected.

Participant Response to the Seminars

It was to be expected that the main focus of the seminar evaluation would be on participant acceptance and understanding of the seminars at the site and on what happened to them after return home. An immediate concern was whether the participants, with a wide range of English-language competence, cognitively understood what was happening and whether they perceived it as relevant. The staff was reluctant to undertake direct evaluation, believing that this would interfere with the dynamic of the week and trusting that participants would provide sincere feedback, whatever their feelings. Since trainees met with the AID officials in Washington D.C. for exit interviews just before departure, the seminars were added to that agenda and copies of responses were sent to MSU. These comments were generally very favorable.

As a check for cognitive understanding, during 1962 the participants were asked to write a "Letter to A Friend" who was hypothetically scheduled to attend later and had written, asking for an explanation of what went on at the seminars. These descriptions were content-analyzed and revealed a high level of convergence with what the staffs thought was happening.

An unanticipated anecdotal evaluation occurred later, when I and several other alumni staff members engaged in other projects ran across returned AID trainees in their work environments in Latin America, the Philippines and Malaysia. Upon learning that the visitor had been connected with the Seminars, the returnee would often point to his framed certificate of completion and group picture from the seminar and produce his seminar notebook. This was usually followed by inquiry about the well-being of favorite staff members from the week, and often led to pleasant social evenings.

In 1960, AID undertook a "world-wide evaluation" of the entire Agency training operation and included two questions for trainees about the Seminars. Responses produced a positive recall of the experience.

There were other short-term attempts at evaluation—one devised by this author. I announced to a particular seminar that in one year each attendee would receive a letter asking some questions about how things were going and if anything in the Seminar had proved useful in his work. About half of the 43 participants returned the questionnaire and wrote personal letters indicating that the cautionary aspects of the Seminar (not to move too fast) were especially valid and had proved useful in introducing change. (Ellingsworth & Welden, 1968).

The number and variety of efforts to check on participant responses was indicative of the continuing concern by Seminar management and staff about effectively reaching the participants. The anxiety proved unfounded. In all forms, evaluation of participant response was rewarding and reinforcing.

Client Response to the Seminars

The Seminars came about because AID requested that MSU undertake the program. This fact defined the relationship between client and contractor throughout the years of operation. The AID Training Division was an active partner in providing requested information and cooperation but did not attempt to interfere with operating decisions. For their part, the MSU managers maintained close contact with their Washington D.C. sponsors. MSU felt particularly gratified in 1961 when AID included the Seminars as a line item in the AID budget and asked us to provide testimony for budget hearings. Earlier funding had been from "left-over" AID appropriations and on several occasions left me uncertain as to whether I could meet our fiscal commitments for staff, facilities and expenses the following week. Happily, these anxieties always proved groundless.

Evaluation of Participant Performance

Participants were often told that the "Final Examinations" of the training experience and the Seminars would be after the sojourn, when their effectiveness as change agents would be tested daily. At MSU, there was increasing interest in this matter, partially because of the institutional commitment to overseas operations. Paul Deutschman (then Director of the MSU Communication Research Center), Huber Ellingsworth (Director of the AID Communication Seminars) and John McNelly (Doctoral candidate in development communication) received funding from the Ford Foundation in 1961 to conduct a research project involving returned trainees in Central and South America.

This was not to be an evaluation of the Seminars, but a more comprehensive examination of the concept Communication and the Change Agent. With the help of AID, the investigators identified 150 trainees from 11 countries in central and South America who had attended the seminars and had been back home for at least a year. Investigators would interview respondents in their work environments and would ask each to nominate for interview a "counterpart" who had about the same rank and responsibility but had not been on an AID training sojourn. The investigators spent several months designing and testing a two-hour interview schedule which would generate quantitative data throughout, including a semantic-differential scale. After pretesting, which included Spanish-speaking students at MSU, a final version in Spanish was completed. All interviewing was to be done in Spanish except for a Portuguese version which was used in Brazil by a graduate student from that country.

The resulting book is too detailed to be summarized here but some relevant findings were that the returned trainees were positively distinguishable from their stay-at-home counterparts in the range of their communication behavior and their attitudes and activities in introducing changes. An unanticipated bonus was that 16 returned trainees, who had not attended the seminars, were added in the field as replacements for unavailable trainees from the original list. This made possible a three-group comparison (Seminar participants, non-seminar trainees and counterparts) which placed the non-seminar trainees as less active and effective than Seminar attendees and above their counterparts in communication and change activity. (Deutschmann, Ellingsworth & McNelly, 1968). So on the basis of quantifiable data, one is entitled to conclude that the goals of AID training were being met (at least in Latin America) and that the Seminars could generate positive effects.

Effects of the Seminars on the Seminar Staff

There have been no systematic studies of how those who conducted the seminars may have been affected by their experiences. This information now exists in the recollections of staff members and in anecdotal descriptions of memorable events which alumni share when they encounter one another. I assert that for a substantial number of people these experiences were profound and that they changed outlooks, careers and lives. They challenged jaded professors to rethink what they taught and how they taught it, whatever their academic fields. For those who had traveled little and had not experienced the need for much adaptation to cultural differences (initially I would have been high on such a list) this concentrated exposure to a multicultural environment was a crash course in the World.

The seminars quickly developed a mystique perhaps unparalleled in academia. The combination of a comfortable reimbursement, a flight to Washington D.C., a trip to a comfortable lodge in a beautiful mountain setting, first-time experience with teaching in the presence of peers, an exotic group of students with a wide range of English proficiency, the schedule of presentations, involvement activities and small-group discussions, a day-and-night work schedule with little time for sleep and a program orchestrated to build toward tension and emotional climax in the last day all interacted to provide a week with remarkable impact on staff members. We quickly discovered that two seminar weeks in a row were the most that most that some staffers could manage. As Berlo put it 15 years later, "I was first pleased though dismayed to hear self and colleagues respond to the question 'what do you teach at an AID Communication Seminar?' by saying that such a seminar could not be described, it had to be experienced. After all, communication is a process, without beginning, and or boundaries." (Berlo, 1977).

So staff members went home exhausted and enthralled, to the routines they had left. We sometimes contemplated a staff debriefing to help them with readjustment, as we had presumably been doing for the participants. Others attempted to increase the use of questioning, class discussion and case studies. At least two left tenured positions and set themselves up as training consultants. Still others urged campus colleagues to join them in interdisciplinary team teaching. Some even undertook to learn their students' names. The true innovators often annoyed their colleagues and surprised their students. A few worked for reorganizing the semester into three-week intervals during which the students would take only one course at a time. Some such innovations were abandoned because they could not be inserted into an existing instructional stream. Others violated the norms and standards of the larger institution. But faculty who took the time to study their own behavior and energize their students became true agents of educational change. They were also able to enrich their teaching with references to cultural difference, world problems and the processes of communication and change.

CONCLUSION

The purpose of this chapter has been to define and document our experiences in creating an operational approach to intercultural communication. Ideally this whole process would have been accompanied by ongoing research and publication of the experience. But very little information survives except in the memories of those who were involved. As with most action programs, research priorities are pushed aside by the demands of operation. Beyond that, there are special constraints imposed by the nature of this program. We quickly realized that there was no way to offer solutions for the multiplicity of communication problems faced by our multicultural population of change agents. We tried instead to create an intense format within which the participants could hardly avoid seeking culturally-appropriate solutions. Such an environment did not allow for intrusive, data-based investigation. In addition, there were frequent change in management, both because of the unanticipated burn-out rate and by the desire of the founders to move on to new projects. And as previously noted, the staff was widely scattered geographically and by discipline, discouraging collaborative research possibilities. Field investigation of trainees (both before and after the sojourn) was very expensive and had to be funded by external grants. This could only be done in countries and regions where the investigators had language competence. So today the interested reader can find only a very small body of literature, most of it cited in this chapter.

Meanwhile on U.S. campuses there was a rising interest in cross-cultural communication and by the 1970s, some instruction was being offered, usually in departments of Speech Communication. The International Communication Association formed a division on the subject in 1970, followed later by other academic associations in communication. Course offerings were expanded to minors, majors and even a few Masters degree programs, but the AID tradition and this formal instruction did not intersect much. Seminar staff alumni had come to see intercultural communication as a comprehensive, pervasive point of view toward the world; the academic developers followed a more traditional pattern of establishing courses, curricula and small-scale graduate research. I had some misgivings about this latter development and wrote in 1977 that it was an unfortunate conceptualization of the idea and that intercultural communication was too vital a concern to be encapsulated as its own field of study, rather than being diffused into every course and research design conducted in the name of human communication (Ellingsworth, 1977). This view was not widely accepted on campuses. The resulting debate did little to alter the development of such instruction. Nevertheless the validity of the process approach was not challenged and might attract more support now than it did two decades ago.

DISCUSSION QUESTIONS

1. How did the idea of studying human communication as a field of behavioral science come about? Which two universities were first to establish degree program?
2. How did Michigan State University become involved in creating the AID Communication Seminars?
3. In what ways did the seminars appear to affect the participants?
4. How were the staff members affected by their participation in the seminars?
5. How did the seminars influence the development of academic study of intercultural communiction? Why?

REFERENCES

Berlo, D. K. (1977). Communication as process: review and commentary. In R. Budd (Ed.), *Communication Yearbook I*. Rutgers, NJ: Transaction Books.

Deutschman, P., Ellingsworth, H. W. & McNelly, J. T. (1968). *Communication and change in Latin America: Introducing new technologies*. New York, NY: Praeger.

Ellingsworth, H. W. (1977). In R. Budd (Ed.), *CommunicationYearbook* I. Rutgers, NJ: Transaction Books.

Ellingsworth, H. W. (1981). In N. Asuncion-Lande and E. Pascascio (Eds.), *Building bridges across cultures*. Manila: Solidaridad Press.

Ellingsworth, H. W. & Welden, T. (1986). *A mail interview of participants in AID communication seminar #219*. Paper presented at the annual meeting of the Speech Communication Association, Chicago, IL.

Gullahorn, J. T. & Gullahorn, J. E. (1963). An extension of the U-Curve hypothesis, *Journal of Social Issues*, 19, 33-47.

Schramm, W. (1989). In S. S. King (Ed.), *Human communication as a field of study: selected contemporary views*. Albany, NY: Albany State University Press.

26

THE GLOBAL ECONOMIC SOCIETY AND THE POLYCULTURAL TEAMS

R. Ray Gehani
The University of Akron

INTRODUCTION

In this chapter, we will explore the implications of the irreversible process of globalization of economies and multicultural interface, in the increasingly diverse U.S. work-groups. We will consider the performance of work-groups, teams and organizations operating in a global economic society. Our objective is to develop a clear understanding and a new multicultural construct for diverse work-groups producing superior performance.

THE AGE OF GLOBAL ECONOMIC SOCIETY

The Globalization Twister

The end of the Cold War in the early 1990s ushered in intense new economic forces of change. They redefined the power distribution among the nation states, markets and the civil society. The national governments lost some of the autonomy they had earlier, whereas the business firms and other economic institutions picked some of the slack thus generated (Mathews, 1997, p. 50). This storm of globalization increasingly engulfed most of what we humans did around the world. Almost every economic or socio-cultural event taking place in one part of the world became only a few nano-seconds away from the events at the other end of the world. Whether the local politicians and national governments in Russia or China, France or Japan liked it or not.

Globalization of Business Work-Groups

The new global linkages, facilitated by the fast emerging tele-communication technologies, drastically changed the way business firms must conduct their businesses. The global technological connections intimately tied the different product markets, financial markets, and the business organizations in unique new ways. A banking scandal in the Far East affected the financial markets and work-groups throughout the world.

This global interdependence was not all that new. In the 1970s, the devastating effect of the two oil shocks helped the Japanese firms quickly jump into America to produce more fuel-efficient automobiles side by side with the American Big Three automakers. Further back in the past, in the 18th century the policies of the East India Company and economic fluctuations in its tea-trade in South Asia had a profound effect on the events and work-groups working in the Boston Harbor, leading to the birth of a new business leader in the New World.

WORK-GROUP GLOBALIZATION: A GOOD NEWS OR A BAD NEWS?

Given below are some examples of how economic globalization affects different work-groups in the U.S. business organizations. Typically, economic globalization causes apprehensions in some, and jubilation in other work-groups. The difference in our response is best explained by how well prepared our work-group or business organization is for multicultural globalizing.

Globalizing is like Swimming

A business firm's participation in the new global economy is very similar to the act of a person jumping into a swimming pool. In the case of the swimming activity, if the person is fit and knows how to swim, then the swimming activity can produce great pleasure. A good swimmer may even compete in tough competitive events such as at Olympics and win awards and recognition. On the other hand, if the person has never taken any swimming lessons, swimming in the deep end is likely to cause great anxiety. Even when other swimmers may seem like having a great time in the water. We know that with persistent effort and some guidance we all can learn to swim and enjoy it as well.

The participation of a business firm in a global economy works the same way (Gehani, 1995b). Globalization can produce enormous apprehensions in some work-groups, and great jubilation and excitement in others. Let us next consider a few real-life case studies illustrating the proverbial "good news–bad news" dilemma associated with globalization of national economies.

Globalization Causing Apprehensions

Case-study #1: Rockefeller Christmas Tree

During the 1980s, the business firm that owned the Rockefeller Center in Manhattan, a landmark in the heart of New York city, was having severe financial difficulties. They sought help from many financial institutions in the United States. Yet no one came forward. They also approached some international investors. The management of the landmark building was offered a financial rescue by Mitsubishi Real Estate Corporation of Japan. This helped the managers of the city landmark pay for maintaining its glory and grandeur, but this involvement by a foreign investor also caused some cultural anxiety among the residents of New York city. The New Yorkers were afraid that the new Japanese owners of the building would not pay for the New York tradition of lighting the Rockefeller Center Christmas Tree. Or that the Japanese investors would not let them and their kids skate in its ice-skating rink during the year-end holiday season. There was also an uproar among many proud American businesses, who expressed their concern that the global investors (particularly from non-European cultures) were acquiring too many U.S. business assets and cultural landmarks (Tolchin, 1990).

Case Study #2: Franco-American-Spanish Jeep Production

Not so long ago, the Chrysler Corporation, the smallest of the Big Three auto makers in the United States, got into a joint venture with Renault of France. Their strategy was to manufacture Junior Jeeps in Spain. The plant was planned to be located in Valladolid, Spain, about 100 miles north of Madrid (New York Times, 1990). Within few months, and as soon as the two global corporations sat down to plan for the joint venture, complications developed due to differences in perceptions. They were unable to resolve their differences, and the joint venture as well as the dreams of hundreds of new jobs for Spanish workers and brighter economic futures for the French and American partners ended.

The Good News of America's Global Successes

The global successes by the U.S. corporations are unfortunately not as widely reported as the occasional anxiety-provoking business actions by foreign investors in the United States. When the trade of goods and services are combined, the U.S. has the largest net trade surplus in the world (Gehani, 1991). In 1991, the United States exported $580 billion worth of goods and services to other world markets. The U.S. exports have accounted for a very large part of the $5.7 trillion American economy, and about 20 percent of the profits of American corporations (O'Reilly, 1992). Each $1 billion of revenue generated abroad by a U.S. corporation was equivalent to maintaining or creating tens of thousands of jobs in the United States. Exports have generated or paid for one in every six American manufacturing jobs, which are the better paying jobs. According to the chief economist at the World Bank, the American workers in export-driven industries made 12 percent more than what an average American worker earned. These significant foreign revenues have kept the U.S. standard of living one of the highest in the world.

Contrary to the popular opinion in America, the imports from other global markets also play a strategic role in America's global competitiveness and high standards of living. For a business firm to become a world-class exporter, very often the firm must also access and use the best world-class suppliers. Freedom to import goods from anywhere in the global markets has given American consumers more choices at reasonable prices, and thereby a very high standard of living.

Global Direct Investments

Globalization also involves free flow of foreign direct investments around the world-wide. The case studies mentioned earlier included the Japanese investments in Rockefeller Center. Similar foreign direct investments, beside causing apprehensions and anxiety in the minds of some Americans, had some positive effects. They poured in large amounts of new investment dollars, generated new tax revenues, added new jobs for Americans, and stimulated further export growth (Czinkota, Ronkainen, & Mofett, 1994, p. 3).

What is also often less known is that many American businesses have similarly acquired and invested trillions of dollars in their global operations in foreign countries. The sales revenues generated from these international investments are about three times the exports from the United States. In 1990 these foreign revenues amounted to $1.48 trillion, a fairly large part of American economy (O'Reilly, 1992).

Table 1 and Table 2 in the Appendix show the global sales outside the United States for the largest U.S. multinational corporations in 1994 (Forbes, 1994). The share of U.S. businesses from sales abroad ranged from 77.3 percent in Exxon's $97.8 billion sales, to 28.0 percent in General Motors's $138.2 billion sales. A total of $316.8 billion in global revenue, amounted to 48.9 percent of these top ten companies' total sales. Other American companies, such as Coca Cola earned 67 percent of its $13.9 billion revenue in 1993 from sales in global markets. In the same year, Gillette brought in 67.5 percent of its $5.4 billion total revenue from abroad, and McDonald's collected 46.9 percent of its $7.4 billion sales from global markets.

In this increasingly inter-dependent economic world, the successful and progressive business firms must pursue innovative and new ways of ensuring their survival and success. Working together with people of other cultures is an important requirement in this pursuit. The high performance polycultural teams proposed in this chapter offer one effective path to success in increasingly global economic world. Kodak's creative use of polycultural team for technological pioneering in a highly globalized photographic industry is discussed below.

Case Study #3: Eastman Kodak's Advanced Photo System Team

On April 22, 1996, five photographic business rivals from different parts of the world, including Eastman Kodak, Fuji-Photo, Canon, Nikon and Minolta, after working together for ten years, introduced a revolutionary new Advanced Photographic System (APS) technology. APS radically changed the format of films and cameras for photographers world-wide (Gchani, 1996). Kodak's Chief Executive Officer George Fisher called the APS technology 'monumental,' and with as much strategic significance as George Eastman's pioneering commercialization of *Brownie* camera in the year 1900. A major difference between the two Kodak endeavors was that *Brownie* camera was developed by Kodak alone, whereas *Advantix* cameras were developed by high performing polycultural teams consisting of members from Kodak's global competitors. The polycultural global cooperation had become a business necessity for all of them.

The APS technology was shared with over forty other licensers including other global rivals such as Agfa in Germany and 3M in the United States. Based on APS technology Eastman Kodak team set a target to sell over two million Advantix cameras within a few months before the end of 1996, which it easily met. In a matter of few months the five developing companies and forty licensers developed and offered more than ninety models of new cameras to millions of very eagerly awaiting photographers. The polycultural APS team had revitalized an otherwise maturing photographic industry.

TYPES OF MULTICULTURAL DIVERSITY

Multicultural diversity in work-groups comes in different forms and shapes (Prosser, 1985, 153). Two major relevant forms are discussed below.

National Multicultural Diversity in Work-Groups

Even without the added effects of globalization, the work-groups in the United States are becoming increasingly multicultural. The U.S. Bureau of the Census statistics in 1994 made it very clear that there is an increasing ethnic diversity in the U.S. population. Therefore, U.S. business organizations must learn to work with more heterogeneous work-groups than what they have ever done before. At the same time, and as illustrated earlier, increasingly larger number of American organizations are dependent on their revenues and operations in global markets. Their bottom-line profits and top-line revenues depend on selling to customers, or working with employees, with different cultural backgrounds. Furthermore, to nurture flexibility and creative responsiveness, more and more U.S. organizations are increasingly resorting to the use of cross-functional and inter-disciplinary teams. This forces more social interactions and influences between people in work-groups with different skills, educational knowledge, attitudes, value systems and other cultural attributes.

Global Multicultural Diversity

The anxiety caused by multicultural diversity is often further amplified in global multicultural work-groups with members from different nationalities and cultures. In increasingly larger number of global organizations, such multicultural work-groups must perform at their best to win the global competition. In global multicultural work-groups, some apprehensions arise from members' feelings about certain past historical events such as wars or invasions. (Gehani, 1993; Gehani, 1995a; Gehani, 1995c). Other apprehensions arise from members' lack of knowledge about people from other cultures. Members of global work-groups often are ignorant of the different national characteristics or decision making styles in people from different parts of the world (Fisher, 1980).

For example, the Japanese workers and managers value harmony in their work-groups. To them formal settings in negotiations are merely of ceremonial value. Any open disagreement in these ceremonies is frowned upon. Therefore much of the bargaining among the Japanese work-groups is smoothed out ahead of time. American work-groups, on the other hand consider negotiations as problem-solving exercises. These encounters are used as opportunities for personal showmanship. It is therefore not surprising that during the United States–Japan trade negotiations, the two groups of people often clash in unproductive ways (Gehani, 1992, 1995c). Such lack of knowledge about other global cultures can deepen misunderstandings and mistrust in future social interactions between people with diverse multicultural background.

MULTICULTURAL DIVERSITY AND WORK-GROUP PERFORMANCE

Organizational researchers have discovered that the multicultural diversity of a work-group influences its performance in a non-linear manner. Multicultural diversity may act either as a threatening exogenous force, or as a source of creativity and endogenous strength. For a homogeneous work-group lacking experience or skills in working with multicultural diversity, any introduction of such diversity may be perceived as a threat to the harmony of the work-group. Higher multicultural diversity in a work-group sometimes results in lower group integration (O'Reilly, Caldwell & Barnett, 1989). This may manifest in higher turnover and dissatisfaction among work-group members (Jackson et al., 1991; Wagner, Pfeffer, & O'Reilly, 1984). On the other hand, other work-groups with more open minds and better multicultural skills, often welcome the introduction of multicultural diversity as an opportunity for more enlightening interactions. With diversity they can consider a larger range of possibilities, and develop their capability to resolve ill-defined strategic issues in the Age of Global Economy (See Hoffman & Maier, 1961; McLeod & Lobel, 1992; Watson, Kumar & Michaelsen, 1993).

TRUST AS THE KEY TO SUPERIOR
WORK-GROUP PERFORMANCE

Many constructive practices that make significant differences in the performance of work-groups are related to trust in the work-group. In a diverse multicultural work-group, trust acts as the invisible reinforcing glue that marginalizes the destructive effects of diversity, and synergizes the strengths of multicultural members (Fukuyama, 1995). Trust turns a low performing multicultural work-group into a high performing polycultural team. In the high performing polycultural teams, the diverse cultures of different team members are intimately woven together by trust in a polymeric chain. Due to this mutual trust, the diverse members of polycultural teams feel free to perform at their best, and produce superior performance for their team.

An important clue to the significance of trust-building interactions in performance of work-groups came from the fact that the homogenous and heterogeneous groups perform differently as more time elapses. In the earlier phases, homogenous groups produce more and perform better than the homogeneous work-groups. Over time, such work-groups may develop a "groupthink" stagnation. On the other hand, as time elapses heterogeneous work-groups score on productivity as well as creativity either equal or higher than the homogeneous groups.

Trust Building Team Interactions: Turning Salad Bowls into Gumbo Stew

Left alone, the high entropy in multicultural work-groups due to underlying differences in conscious and unconscious perceptual influences of members, can cause serious difficulties in coordinating the efforts of diverse members. The different work-group members act independently without much interactions, as in a salad bowl However, the organizations that focus on developing trust-building social interactions between members, channel this high entropy energy due to heterogeneity, into a synergistic fission energy between members with superior team performance. This is sort of like the Gumbo stew, where the diverse ingredients and the different Cajun spices reinforce each other to produce its superior taste. The different ingredients do not stand out in a Gumbo stew like they do in a salad bowl.

Some successes with diversity and pluralism programs in companies such as Eastman Kodak, Xerox and Monsanto, suggest that people with diverse cultural backgrounds can perform well when trust-building social interactions are nurtured by higher managements. In these excellent organizations, managements make it very clear that such trust-building cooperation between members is expected and valued by the organization (Gehani, 1993a). Research has indicated that social interactions involved in the process of earning higher education, and urbanization, also help people become more accepting and trusting of multi-cultural work relationships (Tuch, 1987).

Polycultural teams have the bonding of minds due to mutually satisfying trust-building interactions (See Gehani, 1987, for team harmony in the case of Japanese work-groups). The diverse team members are therefore ready to set aside their differences, and weave their efforts and passions to resolve common problems facing their team. The desire and ability of members to produce superior performance together is an important distinguishing feature between multicultural work-groups and the polycultural teams.

Three Sources of Trust-building Team Interactions

The trust between diverse members of a polycultural team is built on the cumulative experiences of a series of mutually satisfying team interactions in the past and present. Trust-building is based on the clear understanding of a set of commonly shared social expectations (Zucker, 1986, 54). These expectations emerge from three sources described below.

Trustworthy inter-personal perceptions

As discussed earlier, trust-building involves dyadic relationships and social influences between trustworthy persons of multicultural backgrounds. A trustworthy manager is presumed to proactively promote excellence, and reward competence in the subordinates—irrespective of their cultural backgrounds. Their shared trustworthy perceptions lead to higher congruence of trust-building expectations.

In the case of members of highly dissimilar cultures, such congruence must be carefully nurtured and constantly developed by managers with power. To do so team members must learn that people from different cultures have significant differences in their work-related values and inter-personal relationships. Such major differences in global multicultural teams have been mapped on four dimensions (Hofstede, 1980).

These dimensions are: (1) *Power distance*, the extent to which less powerful members accept unequal distribution of power; (2) *Collectivism vs. individualism*, based on the roles and responsibilities of individuals and their propensity or preference to work alone or together; (3) *Uncertainty Avoidance*, the degree to which different people feel threatened by uncertain and ambiguous situations, and how they try to avoid such situations; and (4) *Masculinity/Femininity*, based on whether the dominant values in a culture are power, money and material goods, or they are caring for others and quality of life.

With the sudden economic growth in the Asia-Pacific region, a fifth dimension called *Confucian Dynamism*, was developed and added to the above four dimensions to explain the same (Hofstede & Bond, 1988). The booming economic growth in Asia-Pacific was linked to their people's acceptance of selected Confucian teachings, such as persistence, thrift, acceptance of social statuses and personal shame.

Trust-building processes used

Trust-building in polycultural teams depends on access to a historical record of past trust-building operations of the same or similar teams. These recorded events help build more trust among diverse members. An American lawyer or a journalist is likely to be confided in because in the past he was permitted to keep the words of his clients or sources as confidential. Eye-witnesses come forward in America because the judicial system has protected an individual from incriminating herself or himself in a court of law.

Multicultural work-groups go through four stages in evolving to a high performing polycultural team. These stages are (1) *Recognition stage,* where a work-group is formed by diverse members introducing themselves and recognizing each other's cultural differences; (2) *Roaring stage,* where different members compete for power positions in the group, in an open manner; (3) *Registering stage,* where members arrive at an agreement on certain basic group norms, and register their approval explicitly; and finally (4) *Result Producing stage,* when members with diverse backgrounds get down to the task of working together and producing results for the polycultural team as a whole.

Team's institutionalization of trust-based frameworks

Continuous trust-building is based on formal mechanisms and institutionalization of team processes that guarantee trustworthy behavior and performance by all members, and their successive generations. Many societies have institutionalized professional ethics codes for accountants, lobbyists, and lawyers. A person in a police uniform is trusted to protect the citizens, and maintain law and order for all. In the absence of trust-building institutions, a nagging question that repeatedly emerges in multicultural work-groups is: who guarantees the actions and policies of the guarantors themselves? Only a continual, open, and critical public scrutiny of actions of team members with more power, keeps them away from non-trustworthy temptations. Such institutionalization is critical to motivate all team members to give their best.

CONCLUSION

In conclusion, this chapter investigated the impact of globalization and diversity on multicultural work-groups and polycultural teams. The differences in their performances were attributed to the dyadic interpersonal perceptual influences and social interactions. We developed two models, the Salad Bowl Model for multicultural work-groups, and the Gumbo Stew Model for high performing polycultural teams. With trust-building social interactions, organizations can face global competition better.

DISCUSSION QUESTIONS

1. What is unique about the Global Economic Society?
2. How are the forces of globalization changing the work-place?
3. What are the different forms of multicultural diversity in the Age of Global economies?
4. What is the key difference between a low performing multicultural work-group and a high performing polycultural team?
5. What are the different sources of trust in polycultural teams?

APPENDIX

TABLE 1.
Share of Global Assets for U.S .Multinationals
(In billions of 1993 U.S. dollars)

Rank	US company	Total sales	Global sales	Total assets	Global assets
2	Exxon	111.2	87.7	84.1	47.4
3	IBM	64.1	17.0	81.1	44.1
4	General Motors	133.6	28.6	167.6	36.9
5	General Electric	60.5	11.2	251.5	31.6
7	Ford	108.9	36.0	198.9	30.9
12	Mobil	63.5	42.5	40.7	23.1
24	Du Pont	37.1	16.8	27.1	16.4
26	Philip Morris	65.1	22.5	51.2	15.6
34	Chevron	36.2	10.2	34.7	12.6
36	Dow Chemical	18.1	8.8	24.6	11.5

Source: Adapted from *Financial World*, March 11. 1996. "Free Trade."

TABLE 2.
Share of Global Revenue for Top 10 Large U.S. Multinationals
(In billions of U.S. dollars)

Rank	U.S. corporation	Total	Global	Percent global
1	Exxon	$ 97.8 B	75.6 B	77.3%
2	General Motors	138.2	38.7	28.0
3	Mobil	57.0	38.5	67.5
4	IBM	62.7	37.0	59.0
5	Ford Motor	108.5	32.9	30.3
6	Texaco	45.3	24.2	53.5
7	Citicorp	32.1	20.7	64.5
8	E.I. DuPont	32.6	16.8	51.4
9	Chevron	40.3	16.6	41.1
10	Procter & Gamble	30.4	5.8	52.1
	Total	$644.9 B	$ 316.8 B	48.9%

Source: Adapted from Forbes 1994. (*Forbes,* 1994).

REFERENCES

Czinkota, M. R., Ronkainen, I. A., & Moffett, M. H. (1994). *International business* (3rd ed.). Fort Worth: The Dryden Press.

Fisher, G. (1980). *International negotiation: A cross-cultural perspective.* Yarmouth, ME: Intercultural Press.

Forbes. (1994, July 18). Getting the welcome carpet: The largest multinationals, 276-277.

Fukuyama, F. (1995). *Trust.* New York: Free Press/Simon & Schuster.

Gehani, R. R. (1987). The invisible side of Japanese management. *Management Review,* 14, 9.

Gehani, R. R. (1991, February 25). US still No. 1 in trade. *Democrat & Chronicle,* p. 9A

Gehani, R. R. (1992, September 25). US-Japan relations rooted in past. *Rochester Business Journal,* p. 7.

Gehani, R. R. (1993, February 26). Globalization changes manager's role. *Rochester Business Journal,* p. 7.

Gehani, R. R. (1993a, October 12). How would George (Fisher) do it? *Democrat & Chronicle,* p. 9A.

Gehani, R. R. (1995a, February 24). Global market opportunities beckon. *Rochester Business Journal,* p. 18.

Gehani, R. R. (1995b, February 24). To remain competitive Japan needs new leaders. *Rochester Business Journal,* p. 20.

Gehani, R. R. (1995c, June 23). Arm-twisting Japan unlikely to pay off. *Rochester Business Journal,* p. 7.

Gehani, R. R. (1996, December 31), Science for bad or good? *Democrat & Chronicle,* p. 9A.

Hoffman, L. R., & Maier, N. R. F. (1961). Quality and acceptance of problem solutions by members of homogeneous and heterogeneous group. *Journal of Abnormal & Social Psychology, 62,* p. 401-407.

Hofstede, G. (1980*). Culture's consequences: International dimensions in work-related values.* Beverly Hills, CA: Sage Publications.

Hofstede, G. & Bond, M. H. (1988). Confucius and economic growth: new trends in culture's consequences. *Organizational Dynamics, 16,* 4-21.

Jackson, S. E., Brett, J. F., Sessa, V. I., Cooper, D. M., Julin, J. A., & Pyronnin, K. (1991). Some differences make a difference: Individual dissimilarity and group heterogeneity as correlates of recruitment, promotions, and turnover. *Journal of Applied Psychology, 76,* 675-689.

Mathews, J. T. (1997). Power shift. *Foreign Affairs, 76,* 50-66.

McLeod, P. L., & Lobel, S. A. (1992). The effects of ethnic diversity in idea generation in small groups, *Academy of Management Best paper Proceedings,* 227-231.

New York Times. (1990, June 13). Chrysler-Renault project is ended, p. D1.

O'Reilly, B. (1992, October 19). How to keep exports on a roll. *Fortune,* 68-72.

O'Reilly, C. A., Caldwell, D. F., & Barnett, W. P. (1989). Work group demography, social integration, and turnover. *Administrative Science Quarterly, 34,* 21-37.

Prosser, M. H. (1985). *The cultural dialogue.* Washington D.C.: Sietar.

Tolchin, M. (1990, June 13). Foreign investors hold $2 trillion in U.S. in '89, *New York Times,* p. D1.

Tuch, S. A. (1987). Urbanism, region, and tolerance revisited: The case of racial prejudice. *American Sociological Review, 52,* 504-510.

Wagner, G. W., Pfeffer, J., & O'Reilly, C. A., (1984). Organizational demography and turnover in top-management groups. *Administrative Science Quarterly, 29,* 74-92.

Watson, W. E., Kumar, K., & Michaelsen, L. K. (1993). Cultural diversity's impact on interaction process and performance: Comparing homogeneous and diverse task groups. *Academy of Management Journal, 36,* 590-602.

Zucker, L. G. (1986). Production of trust: Institutional sources of economic structure, 1840-1920. In B. M. Staw & L. L. Cummings (Eds.), *Research in organizational behavior,* (vol. 8, pp. 53-111). Greenwich, CT: JAI Press.

27

CAN WE TALK?: A GUIDE FOR THE TWENTY-FIRST CENTURY CEO MANAGING IN A MULTICULTURAL ENVIRONMENT

Kathy W. Brooks
Shippensburg University

INTRODUCTION

Several major work force-related trends highlight the magnitude of intercultural factors that are causing a tremendous impact on the work forces in organizations in the 1990s. In most organizations, the representation of culture groups in the overall work population, and especially in the most powerful positions, is highly skewed in favor of Caucasian males. However, current demographics reported by *Work force 2000* document that organizations in many nations of the world are becoming increasingly more diverse long such dimensions as gender, race, and nationality (Blank & Slipp, 1994; Swanger, 1994; Thomas, 1991). It has been projected that from the years 1985 to 2000, minorities, women, and immigrants will compose 85 percent of the *growth* in the work a force. The demographics are changing in other areas as well: within 25 years, one out of every four workers will be age 55 or older (Blank & Slipp, 1994; Fernandez, 1991). Of the 43 million people with disabilities in this country, many will seek equal opportunity in employment, encouraged by the Americans with Disabilities Act of 1990 (Blank & Slipp, 1994). Consequently, a greater realization by CEOs of the potential of a more culturally diverse work force will be more crucial in the next decade if corporations intend on remaining economically viable.In addition to these demographic trends, organizations are placing an increased emphasis on global marketing and multinational business operations. The competitive global market sets new rules for survival. It is well known that understanding the effects of culture on human behavior is crucial to the business success of multinational companies. The key to the United States' successful competition in the new global marketplace will be the diversity of its people (Fernandez, 1991; Thomas, 1991). Organizations may gain a competitive advantage from the insights of employees from various cultural backgrounds who can assist organizations in understanding culture effects on purchasing decisions, and in mapping strategies to respond to them.

In this chapter, I will discuss four critical areas in understanding cultural diversity that any CEO must have a working knowledge of in order to minimize (or possibly thwart) communication problems relative to the cultural differences within an organization. The assertions advanced emerge from a wide range of academic research in diverse areas, and as such, a rationale for each inclusion is offered. *

COMMUNICATIVE COMPETENCE

The first area in which a CEO would need to be aware of in order to better understand cultural differences in an organization deals with what Hymes labels "communicative competence" (as cited by O'Keefe & Delia, 1990). It is imperative that a CEO understand what it means to be communicatively competent in an intercultural setting, and develop strategies to enhance this skill.

Communicative competence has less to do with second-language acquisition, but rather is more closely associated with knowledge of linguistic variation, knowledge of the structure of speaking situations, and a commonality of experience for successful message interpretation. Senior executives need to realize that communication involves the interpretation of both verbal and nonverbal messages through a shared meaning. Asuncion-Lande (1990) suggests that the way in which we communicate, inclusive of the symbols we use, and our interpretations of messages are all prescribed by our culture. Interpretation of a message is an act by the interpreter, not an attribute of the object interpreted (Pearce & Foss, 1990). Consequently, one ought not assume in cross-cultural contexts that there is a default shared meaning for any given message. As cultures vary, the manner, form and style of communication also differ (Asuncion-Lande, 1990). In addition, one cannot simply assert that they are effectively communicating merely through the acknowledgment of sending codes because the use of codes does not take into account the cultural and perceptual considerations that are associated with communication.

For example, an American manager may give instructions for completion of an assignment to an Asian employee. At the end of the discussion, the American manager questions whether the information was acknowledged, to which the Asian employee responds with an affirmative "yes." The American manager's referent for the code "yes" is interpreted as the message having been received and understood. However, the Asian employee's referent includes acknowledgment that the information was received, however, it may not necessarily include a positive acknowledgment of understanding of said message. Thus language reflects the way of life and view of reality shared by members of a culture (O'Keefe & Delia, 1990). When people employ different codes, miscommunications and misunderstandings occur (O'Keefe & Delia, 1990).

The elements of the code have no inherent meaning, rather it is when we attach the significance to the code that there is meaning. O'Keefe and Delia (1990) assert the notion that "the human world is a world that is defined and organized through symbolic communication among individuals" (p. 24). The key point CEOs need to understand is that the symbolic communication is intrinsically intertwined with cultural orientation. While the need to develop culturally diverse linguistic competencies may seem burdensome to some executives, Asuncion-Lande (1990) reports that one of the skills necessary for effective intercultural communication includes a tolerance for ambiguous communication behavior. Cross-cultural relationships are facilitated by the communication system. Therefore a necessary condition for cross-cultural communication flow is that members of different cultures share an understanding of the cultural variables that influence encoding and decoding rules (Asuncion-Lande, 1990; O'Keefe & Delia, 1990). These rules are derivations of cultural characteristics. Shared understanding can be acquired through a learning process in which the participants develop a common understanding of each other's encoding and decoding rules (O'Keefe & Delia, 1990). The communication system facilitates the sharing of cultural values by the participants which in turn, strengthens the corporate culture and increases employees' commitment to corporate goals and shared values (Erez & Earley, 1993).

INDIVIDUAL RECOMMENDATIONS

It has been suggested that a full understanding of the influence of cultural diversity on organizations should give analysis at the individual level, the group level, and the organizational or systematic level (Cobbs, 1994; Cox, 1993; Morrison, Ruderman & Hughes-James, 1993), with which this author would agree. In response to this query, I have chosen to examine the individual-level factors of nonverbal cues; the group factors of homogeneity, cohesiveness, and organizational effectiveness; and the organizational context factors of the organizational environment.

In discussing the individual factors, the second idea I believe CEOs need to be aware of in an effort to minimize potential communication problems is the notion that the nonverbal codes of diverse cultures can be as disparate as the cultures themselves. Because nonverbal codes are unconscious acts, they are more prone to misinterpretations and are less conducive to corrective influences (Asuncion-Lande, 1990). CEOs need to recognize that nonverbal communication is as susceptible to cultural influence as verbal communication. Consequently, the same level of evaluation (from a shared reality) needs to be applied when encoding and decoding nonverbal messages. For example, the use of silence in American culture is symbolic of apprehension, especially if it is prolonged. However, in the Indian culture, silence can be an indication of intense, pleasurable, or meditative communication (Asuncion-Lande, 1990).

It is especially critical to give attention to the possible intercultural influences on nonverbal cues because in many situations, the nonverbal cues are more likely to receive credence than verbal messages (Knapp, 1990). The rationale for this is that adults perceive nonverbal cues as more honest because they are more difficult to invent, they seem to be more spontaneous, and they are less apt to be manipulated (Knapp, 1990).

Another area CEOs should be aware of in relating nonverbal cues to cultural differences is the variance of adaptability at perceiving nonverbal cues. Knapp (1990) reported that women are considered to be more skilled at correctly decoding negative nonverbal cues than men. One possible explanation for this phenomenon is that generally speaking, females are often reared to more attentive to others (Knapp, 1990). This understanding could conceivably have potential impact on a CEOs placement decisions within the hierarchy of an organization.

LaBarre (as cited by Knapp, 1990) found that much of our nonverbal behavior is learned. Consequently, as is the case with verbal messages, nonverbal messages are subject to cultural influences, which could lead to people from different cultural backgrounds reacting differently to the same stimuli. Asuncion-Lande (1990) suggests that it is important to avoid making generalizations about other cultures unless one is thoroughly familiar with them. I would further suggest that CEOs take head to this advice, especially in assigning meaning to a person of a diverse culture's nonverbal cues, which is probably an area of communication that we know least about.

GROUP RECOMMENDATIONS

The next level of analysis explores the impact of intercultural factors on organizations by examining group-related factors. The third idea a CEO should understand is how group composition, in terms of cultural diversity, impacts on the overall effectiveness of the group within an organization. There is a body of research (Cox, 1993) that suggest that heterogeneous groups (as defined by the extent to which the members of a group have similar or dissimilar personal characteristics, such as gender or racial background, Shaw & Gouran, 1990) in organizations have performance advantages over homogeneous groups. Standing somewhat in contrast to this perspective is the argument that increasing diversity in work groups may lead to certain dysfunctional outcomes such as miscommunications and lower team cohesiveness (Cox, 1993). This school of thought would seem to suggest that diversity results in lower organizational performance.

Advocates of the former argument have also suggested that heterogeneity in work teams promotes creativity and innovation. There are several streams of research that tend to support this relationship. Kanter's (as cited by Cox, 1993) early studies of innovation in organizations revealed that the most innovative companies deliberately established heterogeneous teams. In addition, Kanter noted that companies high on innovation had done a better job than most in the eradication of racism, sexism, and classism in the work environment and also tended to employ more women and minority men than less innovative companies (Cox, 1993). This research suggests that if persons from different sociocultural backgrounds tend to hold different attitudes and perspectives on issues, then that diversity should increase team creativity and innovation.

These early findings have been confirmed in later studies on the effects of heterogeneity on group decision quality (Cox, 1993). In addition, the same conclusion is indirectly indicated by the research on Janis's well-known groupthink phenomenon (Shaw & Gouran, 1990). Most of the examples cited, such as the Challenger space-shuttle disaster, portray decision processes that are affected by groupthink that were, at the very least, lacking in critical analysis. Because group cohesiveness is directly related to the degree of homogeneity (Cox, 1993), and because groupthink only occurs in highly cohesive groups, the presence of cultural diversity in groups should reduce the probability of groupthink. In addition, I would assert that because diverse groups have a broader and richer base of experience from which to approach a problem or decision, critical analysis in decision groups is enhanced by member diversity.

The conclusion that group cohesiveness is reduced by a more culturally diverse group is largely based on the idea of interpersonal attraction; people are more highly attracted to, and feel more comfortable with, group members who are like themselves (Miller, 1990; Shaw & Gouran, 1990). Another theoretical explanation of the effects of homogeneity on cohesiveness in groups can explained by social comparison theory (Cox, 1993). This theory holds that people tend to seek homogeneity in groups in order to facilitate social comparisons, which they rely on to conduct self-evaluations. Since such comparisons are more reliable when the comparison person is viewed as similar, heterogeneity may be avoided because it makes valid social comparisons more difficult.

The bottom line issue of the importance of the relationship between heterogeneity and cohesiveness for the CEO rests on whether or not cohesiveness affects the performance of groups. Shaw and Gouran (1990) suggest that "most groups initially experience uncertainty and require time for orientation, experience a stage of conflict regarding personal and authority relations among group members, resolve these conflicts, and eventually reach a productive state in which members work toward achieving group goals" (pp. 128-129). It is imperative that a CEO recognize that all of these stages may be intensified by the additional component of a group composite that is culturally diverse. One research study (Cox, 1993) relayed that culturally heterogeneous groups reported a less pleasant atmosphere and experienced greater communication difficulties than the culturally homogeneous groups. It should be emphasized, however, that research has not shown that cohesiveness improves the work performance of groups (Cox, 1993). The largest-scale study of the relationship between the cohesiveness and productivity of groups revealed that highly cohesive groups are just as likely to have lower productivity as they are to be more productive (Cox, 1993). As noted earlier, the groupthink phenomenon illustrates that excessive cohesiveness and preoccupation with preserving it can lead to highly ineffective task performance. Schachter (as cited by Shaw & Gouran, 1990) found that cohesiveness promotes an expressed intolerance for deviant opinions, even when such opinions held the potential for constructive value.

There can be little question that communication differences related to culture may become the source of misunderstandings and ultimately lower work group effectiveness. This would then in turn impact on the overall effectiveness of the organization as a whole. Once the existence of these differences is acknowledged, an immediate action step for the CEO would be to educate and train organizational members on cross-cultural differences so as to minimize any negative effects. From this discussion, it is obvious that it is critical for any CEO to understand the potential consequences of culturally diverse work groups on the organization's overall effectiveness in an effort to maximize the positive attributes and minimize the negative ones.

ORGANIZATIONAL RECOMMENDATIONS

The fourth area in which I would recommend that a CEO who is attempting to minimize problems in communication relating to cultural differences become familiar with concerns understanding the relationship between the organizational environment and cultural diversity.

The more contemporary organizational theories are contingency theories, which purport the idea that rather than assume that there is one optimal way to organize, it is more advantageous to identify and understand the relationship between an organization and its environment (Jablin, 1990). One area of the organizational environment that a CEO should focus on because of its direct implications for cultural diversity is its flexibility.

First, there is some evidence that members of minority groups tend to have especially flexible cognitive structures (Cox, 1993). For example, research has shown that women tend to have a higher tolerance for ambiguity than men. Tolerance for ambiguity, in turn, has been linked to a number of factors related to flexibility, such as cognitive complexity and the ability to excel in performing ambiguous tasks. In addition, a series of studies on bilingual and monolingual subpopulations from several different nations of the world have shown that bilinguals have higher levels of divergent thinking and cognitive flexibility than monolinguals (Cox, 1993). Since the incidence of bilingualism is much greater among minority culture groups (especially racio-ethnic or non-native nationality groups) than among majority group members, I find it reasonable to assert that cognitive flexibility is increased by the inclusion of minority groups in organizations.

Second, I suggest that changes to the organizational culture will impact on the management of other areas as well. For example, as policies and procedures governing how business is conducted are broadened to allow for the influence of cultural diversity, the corporate culture should become more accommodating of uncertainty and more adaptable to change. Also, the tolerance for alternative points of view that is fostered by the increasingly diverse work force should lead to more openness to new ideas in general. Globalization is forcing major companies from many nations to give more attention to cultural-difference effects upon its employees. Very often employers have to interact outside their local environment and with unfamiliar players. Often this results in increases in both the level of ambiguity and risk, and consequently there is a growing need to learn about the characteristics of new people and to adjust to them. This is an extension of the theory of uncertainty reduction (Asuncion-Lande, 1990; Miller, 1990) which states that whenever we encounter a stranger, our primary concern is to increase our ability to predict our behavior and the behavior of the other person.

Finally, the notion that people prefer to resist change for the sake of resisting change is unfounded (Burgoon & Miller, 1990). If CEOs are successful in overcoming the resistance to change in the especially challenging area of managing a more culturally diverse work force, they should be well positioned to deal with resistance to other types of organization change.

CONCLUSION

In conclusion, Asuncion Lande (1990) asserts that culture provides the context for communication to take place, however, communication is what allows a culture to develop, maintain, and perpetuate itself. The implication for organizations is that effective communication relies on the congruence between cultural values and the communication system. In this essay, I have suggested four areas of a

knowledge base CEOs should maintain in order to minimize potential communication misunderstandings stemming from cultural differences that may occur
within the organization.

In my final analysis, I believe that culture shapes the communication system in
organizations, and reciprocally, the system enhances the organizational culture by
facilitating the communication of shared values.

REFERENCES

Asuncion-Lande, N. C. (1990). Intercultural communication. In G. L. Dahnke & G. W.
Clatterbuck (Eds.), *Human communication: Theory and research* (pp. 209-225).
Belmont, CA: Wadsworth.

Blank, R. & Slipp, S. (1994). *Voices of diversity*. New York: Amacom.

Burgoon, M. & Miller, M. D. (1990). Communication and influence. In G. L. Dahnke & G.
W. Clatterbuck (Eds.), *Human communication: Theory and research* (pp. 229-258).
Belmont, CA: Wadsworth.

Cobbs, P. M. (1994). The challenge and opportunities of diversity. In E. Y. Cross, J. H.
Katz, F. A. Miller & E. W. Seashore (Eds.), *The promise of diversity* (pp. 25 - 31).
Burr Ridge, IL: Irwin.

Cox, T. (1993). *Cultural diversity in organizations: Theory, research and practice*. San
Francisco, CA: Berrett-Koehler.

Erez, M. and Earley, P. C. (1993). *Culture, self-identity, and work*. New York: Oxford University Press.

Fernandez, J. P. (1991). *Managing a diverse workforce*. Lexington, MS: Lexington Books.

Jablin, F. M. (1990). Organizational communication. In G. L. Dahnke & G. W. Clatterbuck
(Eds.), *Human communication: Theory and research* (pp. 157-181). Belmont, CA:
Wadsworth.

Knapp, M. L. (1990). Nonverbal communication. In G. L. Dahnke & G. W. Clatterbuck
(Eds.), *Human communication: Theory and research* (pp. 50-69). Belmont, CA:
Wadsworth.

Miller, G. R. (1990). Interpersonal communication. In G. L. Dahnke & G. W. Clatterbuck
(Eds.), *Human communication; Theory and research* (pp. 91-122). Belmont, CA:
Wadsworth.

Morrison, A. M., Ruderman, M. N., & Hughes-James, M. (1993). *Making diversity happen*. Greensboro, NC: Center for Creative Leadership.

O'Keefe, B. J., & Delia, J. G. (1990). Language and communication. In G. L. Dahnke & G.
W. Clatterbuck (Eds.), *Human communication: Theory and research* (pp. 23-49).
Belmont, CA: Wadsworth.

Pearce, W. B., & Foss, K. A. (1990). The historical context of communication as a science.
In G. L. Dahnke & G. W. Clatterbuck (Eds.), *Human communication: Theory and
research* (pp. 1-19). Belmont, CA: Wadsworth.

Shaw, M. E. & Gouran, D. S. (1990). Group dynamics and communication. In G. L.
Dahnke & G. W. Clatterbuck (Eds.), *Human communication: Theory and research*
(pp. 123-155). Belmont, CA: Wadsworth.

Swanger, C. C. (1994). Perspectives on the history on amelioration oppression and supporting diversity in United States organizations. In E. Y. Cross, J. H. Katz, F. A. Miller & E. W. Seashore (Eds.), *The promise of diversity* (pp. 3 - 21). Burr Ridge, IL.: Irwin.

Thomas, R. R. (1991). *Beyond race and gender.* New York: American Management Association.

28

JUMPING OFF THE BRIDGE: RITES OF PASSAGE AND OTHER INDICATORS OF ORGANIZATIONAL CULTURE

David R. Neumann
Rochester Institute of Technology

INTRODUCTION

There are many areas of society that can benefit from an increased understanding of intercultural communication—from both macro and micro perspectives. The paradigms and other psychological and sociological structures that govern the way people perceive, interact, and create meanings play roles in many contexts of daily experience. Understanding others' views can help aid increased understanding and empathy and may result in healthier relationships whether intrapersonal, interpersonal, or in the organization.

"Two limbos, a trecter, steambag, toss, votis, g-bread, two cups, a limbo, and a line to the sheer!" "OK, the rent-a-cops gone. Time to jump!" "I've got a pregnant one, gotta throw her back. Into the cove with you. Swim away, you're free, but see you next year I hope." Are the statements made in the context of a fanatical cult or a bizarre culture? Upon become immersed in this culture, the preceding statements make perfect sense and the idioms and rituals create communication efficiency and tight social bonding.

Cultures and communication can be studied from macro perspectives by examining differences and similarities between cultures separated by mountain ranges, deserts, oceans, and forests. They can also be examined in micro perspectives by studying cultures defined by boulevards, institutional walls, and organizations' parameters. This chapter examines culture from a micro perspective. It is less an examination of intercultural communication and more a study of corporate or organizational culture. Nonetheless, it is the focus on the cultural paradigms that add to our understanding of organizations. The culture under examination in this chapter is that of a small seasonal restaurant in a tourist costal town in southern Maine. Using this restaurant as a frame of reference and basis for examples, this chapter will discuss the conceptualization of culture as applied to organizations and present examples of cultural indicators.

THE ORGANIZATION

Between early September and May, Ogunquit, Maine is a quiet New England town with the population of under one thousand people. During the summer months, Ogunquit services tourists mainly from Boston and Montreal but also from throughout the United States and many other countries. During the height of the tourist season, the population increases to as many as twenty thousand people including residents, summer employees, and tourists. The shops and restaurants of Ogunquit hire summer help to service the tourists. So, the culture of the restaurant under investigation is one that does not operate throughout the year. The employees, except the managers and owners, only work with one another for three month during the summer.

The restaurant is called "Barnacle Billy's." Its owner, Billy Tower, opened the business 30 years ago. Over the past three decades, Barnacle Billy's has enjoyed heathy growth and has garnished a strong reputation among Oqunquit tourists and residents alike. A large part of the success of Barnacle Billy's is due to the employees who cook the lobsters, steam the clams, and prepare and serve other items. Most of the employees are between 16 and 24 years old; a majority are college or high school students who find Barnacle Billy's to be gainful summer employment. It is not uncommon for an employee to work for five or six consecutive summers. Often, siblings or relatives of an employee are hired . The kitchen is in open view to the customers so the cooks not only have to perform their culinary duties but also need to practice customer service and be aware of projecting the proper image. There are many areas of this restaurant that are rich in culture and suitable for analysis.

ORGANIZATIONAL CULTURE

Culture has been defined as a "relatively enduring, interdependent symbolic system of values, beliefs, and assumptions evolving from and imperfectly shared by interacting organizational members that allow them to explain, coordinate and evaluate behavior and to ascribe common meanings to stimuli encountered in an organizational context" (Schall, 1983, p. 557). It is in this definition that one finds several reasons why culture analysis is fruitful for studying organizations. Values and beliefs may be more powerful in guiding employee motivation than salary, benefits, and other hygiene factors (Herzberg, 1966). Culture from this perspective can have very pragmatic applications. This definition also considers the inevitable change in symbolic interaction that coincides with the human communication process. Human communication is an "imperfect" system flawed (or blessed, depending on your perspective) with many opportunities for incongruity of perceptions. It becomes evident by examining organizational culture that the myths, stories, and legends with a culture change over time. Part of this change is due to the "imperfection" of interpersonal and other communication contexts.

Anthropologist Clifford Geertz defines culture as the spun web of social significance that is created via human communication (Packanowsky & O'Donnell-Trujillo, 1982). His metaphor of a spider web is especially fruitful for examining how culture is created and communicated. As a spider depends on its web to trap its prey and other tasks related to its survival, employees of an organization rely, perhaps unconsciously, on the culture to survive in the organization. One cannot become an effective member of an organization without understanding the subtle and often complex practices that can only be discovered through experience. Understanding the culture allows employees to solve problems, create relationships, understand norms and realize how they are evaluated by the hierarchy—realizations that often differ from published corporate policies.

Another interpretation of the spider web metaphor focuses on the interdependent and symbiotic relationship between communication and culture. Just as the spider cannot exit without its web and the web cannot be spun without the spider to spin it, culture can not exit without communication and communication has no meaning without a cultural framework for interpretation. Complexities of communication can be quite expansive in a complex organization rich with culture. Through experiences and acute perceptions, one can come to understand the culture or the "web of social significance."

A final interpretation of the metaphor can be drawn from the visual image of a spider web. One sees strands in the web similar to a sociogram or network map. These strands can be seen as symbolic of repeated patterns of communication. To become a significant part of an organization's culture, the communication or event must be repeated over time. While this may not be true for certain major events (i.e. corporate mergers, layoffs, catastrophes, etc.), it is true for the more subtle aspects of a corporate culture. An organization's vernacular, rituals, stories, and other communication that are diffused throughout the organization need to be repeated over time. This repetition is like the strands of the spider web. The spider can move about over the strands of the web with ease, just as the employee who knows the strands of the corporate culture can move about the organization more easily. Through repeated interactions, organizational members come to understand much more about the organization, the employees, the values, rituals, norms and other components of symbolically created realities. Repeated interactions increase predictability and add confirmation to social knowledge.

This view of organizational culture is radically frin more traditional approaches. Traditionally, organizational communication focused on the scientific paradigm of cause and effect. Questions about productivity, morale, absenteeism, and the like were the genesis of the field. The systems theory perspective also prevails in many studies of organizational communication.

Breaking away from the systemic, linear, and mechanistic implications of systems theory, an organizational culture view allows the investigator to examine histories, values, and beliefs of an organization from an interpretive perspective (Packanowsky & O'Donnell-Trujillo, 1982, 1984; Smircich, 1981; Smircich & Calas, 1987). One of the goals of the culture perspective is to uncover how organizations create social realities in which people communicate (Hawes, 1979). These social realities of organizational cultures and climates are extremely complex (Jablin, 1980). There are many interacting forces which allow for the "web of significance" (Packanowsky & O'Donnell-Trujillo, 1982, p. 123) to be spun. The systems theory approach of nonsummativity has been applied to this perspective (James & Jones, 1974) whereby the total significance of the organization may be interpreted only when the forces act as a collectivity. It is the human mind that "creates order to the environment" (Schneider & Bartlett, 1970, p. 510) by interpreting this collectivity of information.

CULTURAL INDICATORS

In a seminal article, Packanowsky and O'Donnell-Trujillo (1982) discuss the differences between the cultural and traditional approaches to organizational communication. They also discuss Geertz's spider web metaphor and lastly supply a non-exhaustive set of indicators which focus on organization sense-making. These cultural indicators are communication events existing within the spun web of significance of the organization. The remainder of this chapter will discuss these indicators using Barnacle Billy's as a context to draw examples from. In several instances, research into intrapersonal communication will be discussed where relevant. This is less of a case study and more of an investigation into Packanowsky and O'Donnell-Trujillo's cultural indicators. The indicators to be examined are relevant constructs, facts, vocabulary, metaphors, stories and myths, rituals, and rites of passage.

Relevant Constructs

According to Packanowsky and O'Donnell-Trujillo, relevant constructs help to give structure to the experiences of employees. Without the proper contextual framework, objects, individuals, and processes would have little meaning. Through experiences in the organization these constructs begin to have shared meanings between people. The constructs help employees to create meaning and are, in turn, created by interaction

One relevant construct of Barnacle Billy's is the architecture and interiors design of the restaurant. Different areas of the restaurant where food and drinks are prepared are referred to as "bays." Front bay is where lobster and clams are cooked. Middle bay is where salads and grill items are prepared. Back bay is where drinks and ice cream are prepared. The dish room, located two steps below the bays, is called "the bilge." These terms are metaphorically appropriate as they refer to the various parts of a ship. The bilge is the bottom of a boat that, through the forces of gravity, house various waste products. While the names of the restaurant's parts resemble a ship, they also reflect the hierarchy of the restaurant. A typical employee will start out working in the bilge, and then move up to rear, middle, then front bay.

There are many other relevant constructs that can be discussed. But the architecture in and of itself is a good indicator of how Barnacle Billy's is tied into its sea coast location and reflects the hierarchy of the organization.

Facts

"Each organizational culture has its system of facts which members use to explain how and why the organization operates the way it does" (Pacanowsky & O'Donnell-Trujillo, 1982, p. 124). These facts are actually relevant constructs used to create "social knowledge." It is though repeated interaction that this social knowledge becomes fact. Facts are used to explain how things operate, predict outcomes, and justify action and attitudes. An individual may use "facts" as an explanatory tool to justify his or her own social status in the organization. "I am being picked on by other employees because I am 'the new guy'" may be a statement of fact used by someone to describe his or her own status.

Barnacle Billy employees are only working there three months out of the year. Yet they know a lot of work has to be done during the off season. One cultural fact is that management cleans the entire restaurant, stores equipment, and then leaves for the Caribbean for the winter. Actually the winters are much less leisurely for the management than these facts assert.

Vocabulary

"Another distinguishing feature of any organizational culture is the particular vocabulary used by its members" (Pacanowsky & O'Donnell-Trijillo, 1982, p.

125). Internally, we engage in internal dialogues (Weaver, Neumann, Cotrell, & Weiss, 1988), self-talk (Ellis, 1962), or conversations with ourselves (Mead, 1934). The vocabulary we use about ourselves has a strong impact of our perceptions of ourselves an our environment.

In Barnacle Billy's, idiosyncratic vernacular serves several purposes. First it makes for more efficient communication. While indecipherable to the outsider, an experienced member of the organization can understand the following statement: "A deuces, a trecter, steambag, two dry dotis, g-bread, two cups, a limbo, and a line to the sheer!" Translated, this order consists of a two pound lobster, a one and three quarter pound lobster, an order of steamed clams, two tossed salads with salad dressing on the side, and garlic bread as the main course. Also two cups of clam chowder, a glass of lemonade, and a cola should be given to the customer immediately.

However, language has much more powerful implications to the employee than sheer pragmatic communication. Barnacle Billy's is an open kitchen that allow the cooks little privacy from the customers. Special codified language allow employees to communicate in secrecy while being observed. Language in this sense is a tool used by employees to separate themselves from the customer. Vernacular is also created to draw attention to specific customers.

Language can also decrease boredom on the job. Repetitive tasks can be invigorated by using new language to describe the task. It adds an element of creativity and individuality to the job. Employees constantly change the vernacular. While some language has kept constant over the decades, some changes. Employees often try to introduce new jargon, perhaps from a need for creativity, power, or status. Without knowing the vocabulary, one cannot function in the restaurant.

Metaphors

"Useful displays of organizational culture related to vocabulary are the metaphors used by organizational members" (Pacanowsky & O'Donnell-Trujillo, 1982, p. 125). Several researchers have examined how linguistic analyses can give the communication researcher insight into the hidden world of intimate private relationships as well. There has also been significant attention paid to gender-based differences and language use in relationships. Sillars, Weisberg, Burggraf, and Wilson (1987) performed content analyses on married couples' conversations and correlated their marital type (i.e., traditional and separate) with relationship satisfaction and conversational themes. They discussed how "individualistic themes may signal and reinforce relational trouble, impersonal themes circumvent emotional issues concerning blame, equity, and personality. Communal themes, on the other hand, emphasize the interdependence and shared identity of the couple" (p. 499). Owen (1982) also discussed different themes associated with couples.

Within these themes, metaphors abound and can prove to be fertile in understanding relationship descriptions and expectations. The focus on metaphor in the communication field has undergone considerable evolution. From a persuasive technique and continuing to a central focus of constructivism, metaphors have been applied to most facets of our field—from intrapersonal communication to organizational communication. The organizational culture approach utilizes metaphor analysis to develop a view of organizational and social reality (Packanowsky & O'Donnell-Trujillo, 1982). By uncovering the metaphors that employees use to describe their organization, one can develop a fuller picture of the nuances and idiosyncracies of the work environment. Metaphors as symbolic interaction help us to understand and come to a more full view of the organization. Using ideas from psycholinguistics and sociolinguistics help us to understand how people really view the organization. Metaphors reflect attitudes and values that underlie employees' views of organization. One can speculate about the underlying meanings of the following metaphors used to describe an organization: "mom and pop shop," "pressure cooker," "team," "sweatshop," "rats in a maze," "low security prison." Metaphors that reoccur by Barnacle Billy employees include the following: "family," "a three-ring circus," "nut house," "magic."

Stories

Stories and legends are communicated within an organization. They serve to create continuity between generations, as folklore, and put the organization into historical context. "These legends weave an historical texture into the organization, a texture which members come to recognize and re-shape in their continual narration" (Packanowsky & O'Donnell-Trujillo, 1982, p. 126). Just as we pass stories of our personal experiences to others, we communicate them to ourselves. We rely on our experiences to shape our interpretation of the present and expectation of the future, and to direct our actions. We are often "guilty" of re-shaping our past experience and personal stories when we pass them to others, and when we recall them for personal purposes. Our stories become less detailed, more dramatic in these details, and are filled in with what our perceptions tell us should be there (Allport & Postman, 1945). Nonetheless, both organizations and individuals rely on stories for sense-making purposes.

Again, stories are a way of communicating history, values, and morals of an organization and over time they change to reflect theoriginal story and values as well as incorporated current values and experiences. Stories often center around archetypal dichotomies such as success and failure, heroes and villains, radicalism and status quo, rules and rebellion.

One prominent story is about the genesis of the idea for Barnacle Billy's. Legend has it that Billy, a high school dropout, was sitting on the rocks on the coast of Maine talking to his friend about restaurant idea. The images in this story are very rustic and play on the image of the rugged New Englander and the Horatio Alger myth that with a good idea, drive and hard work, anyone can go from rags to riches.

Another common story is about a strong winter storm that almost swept the restaurant out to sea. It is a story of heroism and ingenuity. When the sea rose and threatened to rip to building out of its foundation, the managers cut holes in the floor of the dining room with axes and chain saws to let the room fill up with water, hence relieving pressure and saving the restaurant from being swept out to sea. This story, in all of its embellishments, communicates a brave act of heroism and the value of ingenuity and resoucefullness.

Rituals

Rituals can be viewed as symbolic activities that are repeated over time that signify something important about the organization. They can indicate levels of connection between the culture and its external environment and can elevate the importance of a common activity. Ritualistic communication and behavior are often time exaggerated and their langauge is embellished with hyperbole.

It is illegal to trap a lobster bearing eggs on the bottom of her tail. Lobster cooks quickly check the bottom of each lobsters' tail before cooking them. It is immediately apparent when a pregnant lobster is found. Upon this discovery, the lobster cook takes the lobster and walks through the dining room area of the restaurant announcing the find: "I've got a pregnant one, gotta throw her back. Into the cove with you. Swim away, you're free, but see you next year I hope." The lobster it thrown back into the cove amidst the cheers of patrons.

Rites of Passage

Finally, rites of passage are various actions that help employees to define their level of belonging within an organization. These rites of passage can be formalized rituals or informal subtle initiations that are not sanctioned, authorized, or approved by the formal hierarchy. They can often be underground in their execution in that a subgroup of employees who are initiated by others then initiate subsequent employees. Psychological torment, where older more experienced employees will verbally abuse, tease, kid, or pull pranks on underlings, is a common rite of passage at Barnacle Billy's. It is a method of testing new employees' resilience. Part of the work ethic communicated by this abuse is that one needs to be able to stand the fire to stay in the kitchen. It also serves to cleanse oneself of being previously initiated: "once tormented now a tormenter," said one employee. This rite of passage is a clear example of a continuous cycle in the culture of the organization.

While there are many other rites of passage at Barnacle Billy's, perhaps the most powerful and enduring is referred to as "bridge jumping." "OK, the rent-a-cops gone. Time to jump!" Bridge jumping is a long standing tradition that goes back almost thirty years. It is illegal and the seasonal police often patrol the areas. In exciting, daring, and dangerous display, employees jump off of a twenty five foot bridge into the ocean below. One must jump when the tide is right; if the tide is too low a person will hit bottom onto rocks and razor-sharp barnacles. If he or she jumps the current is wrong, the individual can be pulled towards the sea. So one would be foolish to jump with out the guidance of more experienced people. Being invited to bridge jump is a right of passage. Not everyone is invited to jump and not everyone who is invited will jump. But this activity, like many others at Barnacle Billy's communicate a lot about the organization and help employees to make sense of their surroundings.

There are other cultural indicators and methods of examining sense-making in social collectivities (Hawes, 1979). But Packanowksy and O'Donnell-Trujillo's (1982) list proves fruitful and interesting in this investigation.

CONCLUSION

Culture can be examined from a variety of perspectives. Clifford Geetrz's conceptualization of culture lends itself well to examining cultural communication from a grand macro perspective as well as more precise macro perspectives. Using Geetrz's ideas and applying Packanowsky and O'Donnell-Trujillo's cultural indicators, this chapter supplied a brief examination of the organizational culture of a small restaurant on the coast of Maine. The indicators examined included relevant constructs, facts, vocabulary, metaphors, stories and myths, rituals, and rites of passage. While not on a grand scope of intercultural communication, this examination from a micro-perspective can aid in understanding of communication within cultures.

DISCUSSION QUESTIONS

1. What metaphor, besides the spider web, would provide us with understanding culture?
2. How do you think the diffusion of a culture differs based upon the size of an organization?
3. Which cultural indicators can best be used by management to motivate employees?
4. How do organizational cultures change? Can a CEO create predictable changes in an organization's culture?
5. What methodologies are best suited to help a researcher understand the culture of an organization?

REFERENCES

Allport G. W., & Postman, L. J. (1945). The basic psychology of rumor. *Transactions of the New York Academy of Sciences, 2*, 61-81.

Ellis, A. (1962). *Reason and emotion in psychotherapy*. NY: Stuart.

Hawes, L. C. (1979). *On characterizing organizations' cultures*. Paper presented at the Purdue Lecture Series on Theoretical Perspectives in Organizational Communication, Purdue, IN.

Herzberg, F. (1966). *Work and the nature of man*. Cleveland: World.

Jablin, F. M. (1980). Organizational communication theory and research: An overview of communication climate and network research. In D. Nimmo (Ed.), *Communication Yearbook 4*, (pp. 327-347). New Brunswick, NJ: Transaction.

James, L. R., & Jones, A. P. (1974). Organizational climates: A review of theory and research. *Psychological Bulletin, 81*, 1096-1112.

Mead, G. H. (1934). *Mind, self and society*. Chicago: University of Chicago Press.

Owen, W. F. (1982). Interpretive themes in relational communication. *Quarterly Journal of Speech, 70*, 274-287.

Owen, W. F. (1990). Delimiting relationship metaphors. *Communication Studies, 41*, 35-53.

Packanowsky, M. E., & O'Donnell-Trujillo, N. (1982). Communication and organizational cultures. *Western Journal of Speech Communication, 46*, 115-130.

Packanowsky, M. E., & O'Donnell-Trujillo, N. (1984). Organizational communication as cultural performance. *Communication Monographs, 50*, 126-147.

Schall, M. S. (1983). A communication-rules approach to organization culture. *Administration Science Quarterly, 28*, 557-581.

Schneider, B., & Bartlett, C. (1970). Individual differences and organizational climate II: Measurement of organizational climate by multitrait multirater matrix. *Personnel Psychology, 23*, 493-512.

Sillars, A. L., Weisberg, J., Burggraf, C. S. & Wilson, E. A. (1987). Content themes in marital conversation. *Human Communication Research, 13*, 495-528.

Smircich, L. (1981). The concept of culture and organizational analysis. Paper presented at the SCA/ICA Conference on Interpretive Approaches to Organizational Communication, Alta, UT.

Smircich, L. & Calas, M. B. (1987). Organizational culture: A critical analysis. In F. M. Jablin, L. L. Putnam, K. H. Roberts, & L. W. Porter (Eds.), *Handbook of organizational communication: An interdisciplinary perspective* (pp. 228-263). Newbury Park, CA: Sage.

Weaver, R. L. II, Neumann, D. S., Cotrell, H. W., & Weiss, P. E. (1988). Imaging as an aid in understanding and practicing public speaking. *Texas Journal of Speech Communication, 13*, 37-47.

SECTION V OVERVIEW: MULTICULTURALISM, CULTURAL DIVERSITY, AND HEALTH

Another area in which intercultural communication theories can applied is the health care profession. Personal experiences of medical professionals, as well as research studies have shown that cultural values do affect results in health care. In her chapter, "Multicultural Issues in Health Communication." Kunimoto explains how health care services in the United States today have become multicultural in nature. With the example of health care in the state of Hawaii, United States, she points out how the professionals in such services can function better—if they have multicultural communication skills. Cultural values do motivate patients, and an understanding of these values would help physicians treat their patients better. Kunimoto explains how Hawaiian cultural values, such as extended family (Ohana), harmony (Lokahi), and cooperation (Kokua) play an important role in perception of illness and motivation to get better.

The chapter, "The Process of Bridging Global Multiculturalism, Communication, and Disability," explains why both people of color and disabled persons consider themselves as a different culture since their needs, values, and goals in life are different from those of others in society. Communication with and within this group is complex and multicultural. The author, Olubodun explains this special and complex culture, its history, legal status and communication patterns.

In their chapter, "Deaf Culture, Pluralism, and the Field of Communication," Campbell and Friend explain another dimension of intercultural communication, communicating with the hearing disabled using American sign language (ASL). If a society wants to be truly pluralistic, the authors argue, deaf culture should be a part such a society. By definition "deaf" is a culture by itself since it has its own language and its own value system. The members of this culture have their own common values and goals.

An area of importance in health care profession is the lack of minority nurses. In the chapter, "Why Minorities Aren't Choosing Nursing Careers: Intercultural

Communication, Recruitment, and Minority Underrepresentation in Nursing," Askew shows how minority nurses are the link between the health care providers and minority patients. Recruiting minority nurses is in itself a task in multicultural communication. A study done in six schools consisting of 425 women and 218 men as respondents showed that the attributed status, illness-orientedness, and other related factors influenced minority persons in going into or avoiding the nursing profession as a career option.

29

MULTICULTURAL ISSUES IN HEALTH COMMUNICATION

Elizabeth N. Kunimoto
University of Hawaii

INTRODUCTION

I was an advocate for my mother and father-in-law until they died—within months of each other. This experience propelled me into the area of *health communication*. I am a licensed psychologist, and I prefer to focus on the prevention of psychopathology through the teaching of the theory and practice of multicultural communication proficiency in my communication classes.

In, *Effective Communication in Multicultural Health Care Settings,* Kreps and I proposed a Wellness Model that I adapted from George Albee's Primary Prevention of Psychopathology (Kreps & Kunimoto, 1994). The Wellness Model is represented by a fraction, with the numerator comprised of stress factors and the denominator comprised of coping factors. This fraction provides a visual aid to demonstrate that the larger the value of the coping factors, the smaller the stress factors. The model indicates that stress factors impact your immune system, causing pathologies ranging from mental illness to tooth decay. Stress can affect the pH balance of your saliva and cause tooth decay. Stress from the innability to deal with the changes in a job situation can contribute to burnout.

A most valuable coping skill is *multicultural communication proficiency* because this skill will enable you to communicate effectively with many cultural groups, enabling you to access information (cognitive), experience as well as affect attitudinal changes (affective), and acquire skills and behavioral change (psychomotor), thereby decreasing stress factors. Multicultural communication proficiency is positively correlated with health and negatively correlated with illness (Kreps & Kunimoto, 1994).

In this chapter I will discuss how diversity in cultural perspectives impact issues in health communication, such as informed consent, pain management, treatment of terminal illness, and communication between medical professionals (doctors, nurses, and social workers) and patients and their families. I will be including perspectives from health professionals and clients from the continental United States, Asia and the Pacific Islands, especially Hawaii.

INFORMED CONSENT

The ideal patient-physician model in the United States is one in which the physician educates the patient about health care resources and makes the final decision with the patient (Balint & Shelton, 1996). The nature of the relationship has changed from a paternalistic one to one of cooperation between equals. I would like to present two examples concerning informed consent in the United States: (1) in which a cancer patient was informed by the doctor about the protocol he was using, and (2) in which a cancer patient was told to undergo chemotherapy over alternative methods but was not informed about some of the side-effects and dangers of the experimental drug.

The first patient was a young Asian American man who had graduated from a prestigious university in the West with a degree in mathematics. He was diagnosed as having testicular cancer, a form of cancer striking young men in their late teens to mid-thirties, particularly young professionals in the "fast lane." The oncologist who treated him had tears in his eyes when he presented the diagnosis and outlined the treatment for the young man. He described the possible side effects, such as hearing loss and hair loss. Because the protocol was aggressive and harsh, the young man's mother had suggested alternative therapies, such as *reiki* (healing by touch), herbal teas, and meditation. Her son had a worldview that trusted data more than Deity, and he refused to go along with his mother's tearful entreaties. He decided to follow, instead, the path of chemotherapy.

Today, fifteen years after his treatment with the experimental drugs, he has been pronounced cured. The drugs are now a part of standard treatment for testicular cancer, and the remission rate for this form of cancer is greater than 95 percent. This story had a happy ending, or more accurately, a happy beginning. He is still in the fast lane, swims with corporate sharks and dolphins in international waters, and although he has won many honors, he was proudest when his life-saving partner, his doctor, was named one of the outstanding oncologists in the nation (Kreps & Kunimoto, 1994). And he was able to say to his mother, "Aren't you glad that I didn't listen to you then? If I had those therapies you suggested instead of chemotherapy I might not be here today." His mother has reperceived her view of alternative therapies. She looks upon them as complementary therapies and would go to the doctor for antibiotics or a stitch-in-time if she feels she needs them.

The other cancer patient is a Euro-American female program analyst, a former nurse, who underwent a radical mastectomy for breast cancer. After her surgery, six cancerous nodes were discovered in her lungs. Rather than undergoing surgery again or chemotherapy, she chose to attend a National Holistic Nurses Alliance Conference in Colorado, where she learned about alternative medicine. When she returned to Hawaii, X-rays showed that the nodes had disappeared. Her oncologist then had her undergo a CAT-scan, and they showed two minute nodes which were undetected by the X-rays. The doctor urged her to undergo chemotherapy with an experimental drug. This doctor was an Asian doctor who exercised paternalism. To the dismay of her friends, this patient decided to undergo treatment with this drug not once but twice. Each time she became extremely weak, experiencing heart failure. At least two of her friends were concerned that their relatives who had undergone chemotherapy with this particular experimental drug had died.

After the second protocol, her doctor wanted her to have a third and fourth treatment. However, after experiencing another heart failure, she said, "No more!" The drug weakened her, and a year later when she underwent hip replacement surgery, her doctor told her that she also needed to undergo an angioplasty because of clogged valves. However, she changed doctors and found a board-certified cardiologist who gave her an angiogram and assured her that her valves were normal and that she could control her heart palpitations with medication. He also informed her that the side effects from the first experimental drug that caused burning pain in her legs can be taken care of in time. Today she is in better spirits than she has been for the last five years, and much of the improvement has been derived from the trusting relationship she and her doctor have developed through the communication process of informed consent.

Physicians in Japan usually take great care to fully inform families of the patient's prognosis and consult with them much more than with the patients themselves about treatment decisions. Although this is slowly changing, Japanese doctors still exercise the tradition of *benign paternalism*, taking charge of the patient's well-being rather than forming a partnership in recovery with the patient. The average stay in Japanese hospitals is forty-five days. Several years ago, my aunt in Hiroshima was hit by a cyclist and was in a coma for several months. Yet when I saw her a year later she was fully recovered, energetic, lucid, agile, and was able to travel to several cities with me. She explained that her doctor gave her an experimental drug that helped her to be alert but that he informed her that he would not be able to give it to her any more after a certain date, because it failed to meet the criteria for approval. A year after she stopped taking the drug, however, she was still alert and was grateful to the doctor for taking the initiative— and risk—in giving her the experimental drug.

PAIN MANAGEMENT

Culture is a potent force in shaping beliefs, behavior, and meaning about pain. The literature supports the idea that pain does not have the same debilitating effect in the Eastern cultures as it does in the Western cultures (Kodiath & Kodiath, 1992). In the qualitative research based on grounded theory, there was a significant difference in the degree of pain experienced by members of each culture, which was related to available resources. The most significant finding was that the report of pain was not proportional to the quality of life and meaning found in this pain experience for each patient.

Empowerment of the patient through respect for cultural diversity can aid in the management of stress factors that amplify pain (Walding, 1991). A children's hospital in Hawaii recently reported that a Pacific Islander was attached to a cultural artifact and insisted on having it in the operating room. (Many of the young children who come to this hospital for surgery need to be motivated to keep their spirits up and to participate in the rehabilitation program.) Because the medical staff understood the value of the artifact toward his motivation, they went along with it. They sterilized it and allowed him to keep it with him in the operating room until the anesthetic took effect. And the staff made certain that it was available to him in the recovery room.

The Asian American cancer patient I mentioned earlier was acutely aware of the mistakes made in hospitals, and he monitored what the nurses and aides did whenever he was conscious. He also tried not to complain and call his nurses too frequently, because he felt that he didn't want to be known as a whiner whose signal they would ignore when he really needed them. So he indicated that he was saving his requests for moments that he considered to be urgent. During chemotherapy, his Euro-American wife stayed with him and made certain that the nurses inserted hypodermic needles into the appropriate arm. His oncologist expressed his surprise when he made his rounds and found his patient to be barely conscious but his wife who was hidden under the blanket to be alert, assertive, and ready to be his advocate. Fortunately, this doctor recognized this as an important partnership in facilitating the recovery of his patient.

Early last year you may have read about a Japanese tourist in Hawaii who was sent to a hospital in a cab by a hotel employee, when an ambulance would have been more appropriate, and subsequently, died in the emergency room. There was a great deal of criticism because an ambulance had not been called. A conjecture was that the patient was a member of a culture where *gaman* (endurance or *noblesse oblige*) was a value that was reinforced and therefore he downplayed the severity of his pain or symptoms.

One out of every four deaths in Japan is due to cancer (Takeda & Uki, 1994). The national government has disseminated information on cancer pain relief, especially morphine preparations. However, the annual consumption per capita is still much smaller than that in other developed countries.

TREATMENT OF TERMINAL ILLNESS

Rather than the more "popular" diseases under the category of terminal illness, such as cancer, I would like to share some examples that concern members of the "sandwich generation," including myself. We are so-called because we are sandwiched between the caring of our own children and our aged parents. As I mentioned, I was their advocate until my mother- and father-in-law died within months of each other five years ago. Mother was 83-years-old, and my father-in-law was 96. Mother was healthy and ambulatory, but she was experiencing dementia for the last three years of her life. She lived with me for five years, and my father-in-law lived with his daughter for five years. Although Mother became forgetful and was lost once, she was lucid enough to tell me on several occasions to place her in a care home when it became too much for me to care for her. Through practicing intercultural communication, "talking story," and interacting with health care professionals, I found an ideal place for Mother. It was an assisted-living home run by a Filipina LPN, who treated her like family. She was highly recommended by professionals, and to this day, long after Mother has died, we are still in touch.

Mother was ambulatory and really kept the home's family members on their toes, and so I brought her to my home on Sundays and also paid for respite care for the caregivers by enrolling her in a Day Health Program for adults. Three times a week she was driven there in a Mercedes by the caregiver's husband, who was a successful businessman. The caregiver and her family members, who all participated in the care of their three patients, exemplified *aloha*, *lokahi*, *ohana*, and *kokua*. Whenever I had a deadline to meet at the University, she refused to let me bring Mother home with me, saying that she would like me to have time for myself and that Mother would be in better hands in her home. Mother died peacefully in her adopted home, and to this day the family has prayers said for her.

My father-in-law was in another assisted-living home, also run by a Filipino family who practiced all those four values. We brought him home every Sunday with my mother, and they were good company for each other. After Mother died in June, my father-in-law became despondent. He began to stop eating at the home. He was hospitalized when he developed pneumonia. He told us that he had lived long enough (96 years), and although he seemed strong enough to live to reach 100, he was adamant about not going on. He was a World War I veteran who was receiving a small pension every month along with his social security. When he was in his late eighties, he gave up his pension, saying that the U.S. government needed it more than he did.

His doctor was sensitive to Dad's cultural values, that he wanted to die a clean death, and he did not prescribe forced feeding. He would be taking water intravenously, and meals would be served regularly. However, he never ate a bite of his meals or snacks, and the nurses recorded this, and he was peaceful and happy, chatting with his children all over the world on the cellular phone and saying his goodbyes. His hospital roommate was a pitiable contrast. He was forcefed regularly through a tube, even though he was unconscious, and he would groan and moan frequently. One evening my husband noticed that his father was no longer passing urine, and so he called the priest and had a bedside service while Dad was still lucid. He had a beautiful smile on his face as he slept, and he died early the next morning. His relatives in japan called it *rippa na shini kata* or "a splendid way of dying."

I'd like to mention other examples of the sandwich generation who were long-distance advocates. Three sisters lived in Connecticut, Arizona, and Texas, and their parents lived in Hawaii in a retirement home. One of the sisters flew to Hawaii to visit their parents and found that the mother was distraught because her husband was experiencing symptoms of Alzheimer's Disease.

A hospital social worker who was proficient in multicultural communication referred her to a self-help group, Alzheimer's Disease and Related Disorders Association, for support and to the hospital's adult day care for respite for the mother. Today the sisters are in touch with the support team and their mother by telephone and e-mail as well as occasional visits. I call it the rainbow connection.

The Sociology Department of the University of Hawaii conducted a survey of 100 caregivers of Alzheimer's patients (Wegner, 1990). A by-product of the survey which did not interest the investigators—but which interested me and the nurse who did the survey—was this: Although they were often on the edge of burnout, the caregivers noticed that their self-esteem was higher after a period of care-giving. They had become proficient in multicultural communication. They had learned to communicate effectively with a wide range of health care professionals—doctors, nurses, social workers, pharmacists, insurance providers, and adult day care workers. They often had to confront bureaucracy as well as ask for help from family members, friends, and the community. They learned how to accept and to communicate love. They learned how to forgive siblings who would not help. Most of all, they learned to forgive themselves for not meeting their own expectations of serving their parents.

A policeman who was concerned about his rapidly deteriorating mother came to a meeting of the Alzheimer's Disease and Related Disorders Association, accompanied by his partner who wanted to support him. The partner was a young man whose grandmother, an Alzheimer's patient, was being cared for by his mother. Because his aunts and uncles did not want to get involved, he and his siblings occasionally gave their parents respite by taking care of the grandmother and sending them on a trip to the Neighbor Islands.

COMMUNICATION BETWEEN PROFESSIONALS
AND PATIENTS AND THEIR FAMILIES

The James A. Burns School of Medicine includes values of the Hawaiian culture in their problem-based learning tutorial teams (Little & Else, 1995). Because PBL requires small group interaction and stresses group learning, sharing, problem solving and consensus development, Native Hawaiians are not only well suited but actually flourish in the environment. Four basic Hawaiian values, *aloha*, `*ohana*, *lokahi* and *kokua*, have been proposed as instrumental in preparing Native Hawaiians to excel in PBL.

- *Aloha* has a myriad of positive meanings which can be divided into two sub-groups. The first group of meanings deals with *aloha* as the term for love, affection, compassion and kindness for one another. The second is used as a warm greeting or salutation (Pukui & Elbert, 1986). Both are meaningful in a PBL environment.
- `*Ohana* stresses the importance of family, extended family or friends who are regarded with affection. Members of `*ohana* do not have to be blood relatives. Within the `*ohana* there are feelings of unity, shared love, shared responsibility, and shared material goods. A predominant social characteristic of native Hawaiians is a tendency to see oneself in relationship with others as a contributing group member (Braun, 1995).
- *Lokahi* stresses harmony, unity and the ability to work together to solve problems. It is the way to live in unity or at peace with oneself, the family, the gods, and the land (Braun, 1995). Thus, it is important to native Hawaiians to live in harmony with others, to be respectful of the natural environment, and to acknowledge that spirits and gods are an integral part of nature.
- *Kokua* refers to mutual help and cooperation, which contributes to group unity by fostering cooperation, interdependence, and reciprocity (Braun, 1995). The focus is on the group rather than on the self. Processes seen as benefiting others are more acceptable than those that lead to personal gain.

Throughout this chapter, I have emphasized the importance of multicultural communication proficiency. This skill requires *perceptual flexibility*. We know that perception calls for our interpretation of raw sensory data through observation, inference, and judgment, and that perception is an active, voluntary process that is within our control to a great extent.

Perceptual flexibility is a valuable skill which contributes to multicultural communication proficiency. It calls for making tentative rather than permanent judgments, looking at contextual cues, understanding cultural differences, and respecting diversity. Developing this skill impacts our immune system, because it enables us to look at things objectively and less defensively, thus reducing the stress factors that contribute to psychopathology. It enables us to go beyond stereotypes and the impersonal toward what is unique, more personal, and more humane (Kreps & Kunimoto, 1994).

Because perception is an active, learned, voluntary process, we can also experience the transformational power of *reperception*. Reperception can help to reshape relationships, reconfigure worldviews, impact our immune systems, empower one another, create a positive Pygmalion, a positive Galatea, and create a healing relationship.

Multicultural communication proficiency enhances the healing relationships between caregivers and patients. It empowers the caregiver as well as the patient.

SUMMARY

Diversity in cultural perspectives impact issues in health communication, such as informed consent, pain management, treatment of terminal illness, and communication between medical professionals (doctors, nurses, and social workers) and patients and their families. Multicultural communication proficiency enables effective communication with many diverse groups in achieving the objectives of information gain (cognitive), attitude change and/or reinforcement (affective), and skill acquisition or behavioral change (psychomotor). Perceptual flexibility is a valuable skill which contributes to multicultural communication proficiency.

DISCUSSION QUESTIONS

1. Identify at least three issues in health communication impacted by diversity in cultural perspectives.
2. Describe the Wellness Model and why multicultural communication proficiency is one of the most valuable coping factors that reduce stress.
3. Give an example of how cultural values affect management of pain.
4. Select a Hawaiian value that would be appropriate for use in the training of future doctors.
5. Explain why perceptual flexibility is a valuable skill for health care professionals for both health care professionals and patients.

REFERENCES

Balint, J. & Shelton, W. (1996). Regaining the initiative, Forging a new model of the patient-physician relationship. *Journal of the American Medical Association, 275*, 887-92.

Braun, K. L., Cook, M. A., & Tsark, J. U. (1995). High mortality rates in native Hawaiians. *Hawaii Medical Journal.* 54, 723-729.

Kodiath, M. F. & Kodiath, A. (1992). A comparative study of patients with chronic pain in India and the United States. *Clinical Nursing Research 1*, 278-91.

Kreps, G. & Kunimoto, E. (1994). *Effective communication in multicultural health care settings.* Thousand Oaks, California: Sage Publications.

Little, D. & Else, I. (1995). *Native Hawaiian culture across the curriculum at the John A. Burns School of Medicine.* Paper presented at the national Conference on Cultural

Competence and women's Health Curricula in Medical Education, Washington, D.C.

Pukui, M.K. & Elbert, S.H. (1986). High mortality rates in native Hawaiians. *Hawaiian dictionary*. Honolulu, Hawaii: University of Hawaii Press.

Takeda, F. & Uki, J. (1994) Recent progress in cancer pain manaagement and palliative care in Japan. *Annals of Academy of Medicine in Singapore. 23*, 296-299.

Walding, M. F. (1991). Pain, anxiety and powerlessness. *Journal of Advanced Nursing, 16*, 388-397.

Wegner, E. (1990). *Assessment of 100 caregivers of Alzheimer's patients*. Paper presented at the Hawaii Psychologists' Conference, Honolulu, Hawaii.

30

THE PROCESS OF BRIDGING GLOBAL MULTICULTURALISM, COMMUNICATION, AND DISABILITY

William Olubodun
Rochester Institute of Technology

INTRODUCTION

Diversity and disability are like catalystic agents and when both are present in one individual, there is a myriad of difficult circumstances. There is a unique need to promote and understand global multicultural communication as well as to encourage the inclusion of students of color who have disabilities as a facet of diversity. The absence of meaningful fora on higher education and disability may continue to impede progress towards social egalitarianism, integration, and real learning for all people with disabilities. Meaningful and conscientous social discourse on disability issues will help bridge the artificial chasm that has historically served to divide and subjugate (rather than unify and strengthen) inculcatory activities— including access and retention. Our educational systems, including planning and administration, have historically assumed that most learners are of average learning faculties, with the expectation that every individual comes to the learning theater with perfect physical and mental capacity for learning. For those who do not meet this expectation of imagined perfection, or who have different abilities, or whose learning styles do not meet the traditional expectations, there is an oppressor/oppressed circumstance which Paulo Freire identifies in his book *Pedagogy of the Oppressed* (1994).

A person of color is defined as any non-white individual. Disability is defined, using the Americans with Disabilities Act of 1990 definition: "any mental or physical impairment, which substantially limits one or more major life activities, person with a history/record of such impairment, or a person that can be regarded as having such an impairment."

PHILOSOPHY

The following philosophy represents my personal thoughts and reflections. References will be made to the work of others where appropriate. Any similarity this section has to another person's or group's work is simply a meeting of the minds.

Education per se is a tool by which an individual is equipped to cope with life's various challenges and to prepare for learning on a higher plane. In much of this preparation where disabilities and minority status are impinged, there are circumstances of contradictions and intricacies. The intricacies are further complicated as education has become interwoven with survival in a capitalist society. For people with disabilities in general, and people of color with disabilities in particular, education has also become synonymous with the only avenue for being "somebody" in a world that rewards only the fittest. In this regard, the fittest are those whose faculties are held intact by an imaginary benevolent god, and are without manifested disability.

Disability is communicated as a blemish to this group of contestants, and therefore those with disabilities are not expected to enter the race. As contestants in the daily struggle to be somebody, and to be part of the humanistic exisitent, the intricacies create rather insurmontable obstacles in the path leading to successful emancipation. This class of contestants is constantly measured by a tipped scale of designed perfection, and therefore, their efforts are less rewarded, as they are often subjugated by the realities of their less-than-conceptually-perfect faculties.

In such a state, education becomes a navigational compass that is not an end in itself. Rather, it is a constant, painful reminder to those who are aware of their disabilities as well as a combination of the double effect of ethnicity and different needs for full inclusion and participation in the race of life and learning. Thus, their less-than-perfect faculties in an environment where perfection is enshrined as the core of the universal operational rule become an artificial barrier and a tool of oppression.

Such a system operates to subjugate those who have neither acquired the skills and/or tools to navigate, nor have fully comprehended the socio-political structures used to ascribe roles, expectations, status, and positions. If the ideology of education is in the interests of social justice, knowledge, and the application of that knowledge to better one's prospect of a successful life using the capitalist cat-alytic concession, how does it benefit a society when disability becomes an auto-matic stamp of disapproval? For persons so afflicted, living in a society becomes a constant test of will. It is definitely a constant test of will when a person of color with disability decides to attend college or university or to engage in modern employment opportunities in institutions of higher learning, which have histori-cally been mono-cultural, mono-linguistic, and Anglo-Saxon in orientation.

A casual look around many college campuses will attest to this. How many per-sons of ethnic background who also have profound disabilities are tenured faculty members? How many graduate students are on your campus who have disabilities and are ethnic minorities? From Freire's ontological and axiological points of view, disability manifestation ought not to prevent an individual from being fully human. I want to relate this "being fully human" as the freedom to be, to experi-ence, and to benefit from education and available opportunities. For people with disabilities, service delivery of every type from medical/health maintenance to activities of daily living, including shopping, has hitherto been provided by peo-ple with less personal knowledge of the various disabilities or the degree of phys-ical and emotional pain that the person with disabilities suffers. Service delivery provision where the provider does not possess the direct experience either through training or personal history, always provides the potential for marginalization.

ORGANIZATIONS OF PEOPLE WITH DISABILITIES

There have been several major emancipatory activities by people with disabilities in the past two decades in the United States which have improved communication and understanding across culture and communities. A deep examination of these activities closely resembles those stages stated by Freire and which marginalized/oppressed people must experience in an attempt to affirm individuality and humanization.

One of the first of such organizing activities was the establishment of various national organizations catering to independent living , legal and other issues gen-erally affecting people with disabilities. Examples of these organizations include various state associations of the deaf or the blind, or councils on independent liv-ing. Some organizations are local; others are regional; and others are nationwide. One thing in common is the provision of certain services otherwise unavailable or inaccessible to their members. Inaccessibility occurs when service delivery is in a building that persons using wheelchairs cannot enter, or discussion/instruction is presented orally without the benefit augmentation like a sign language interpreter, or instructors or service providers without such skills. Inclusion of people of color in those movements continues to be much more the act of "after thought," espe-cially when diversity issues are raised by governmental or funding agencies. As Freire (1994) said, "almost always, during the initial stage of the struggle, the oppressed, instead of striving for liberation, tend themselves to become oppressors, or 'sub-oppressors.,'...during the initial stage of their struggle the oppressed find in the oppressor their model of 'manhood '" (pp. 27-28).

The organizations that started as grassroots movement evolved gradually very similarly to elite groups of middle-class white friends. The initial grassroot ideals upon which the organizations were founded were inadvertently discarded as the organizations strove to maintain their new elite status. This seeming abandonement of fundimental principles can only be perceived as a betrayal of the struggle, especially by members of the movement whose issues are yet to be recognized or adequately addressed within organizational parameters. Thus, those organizations continue to grope for viable internal unity that will portray a cohesive force. Unity can be achieved only when the "humanity" of all members of the struggle is recognized, respected, and embraced by all.

Many of the organizations were effective in numerous ways, especially by collaborative efforts that resulted in various accessibility and inclusion legislations. An example of such legislation is the Americans With Disabilities Act (ADA) of 1990. There was a collective and collaborative force from all disability groups during the negotiation and "dialogue" that went into ADA enactment. However the participation of people of color with disabilities remained very low, even after decades of the movement. The perception of powerlesness led people of color from the initial disability movement to begin building their own alliance. For example, the Black Deaf Advocates (NBDA) was established when it was perceived that the National Association of the Deaf (NAD) was yet to put issues affecting black members of the deaf community in the proper order. The Deaf Hispanic community has established a similar organization with similar principles to those of the NBDA. Thus in many instances, when people of color with disabilities who are members of the disability organizations perceive shifts in organizational paradigms, they tend to separate and form new entities with a similar ideology to that of the first group, but which cater to the cultural affiliation.

In this context, the real oppressed, who are doubly affected by first level of oppression, begin the process of emancipation. The move by the new group at first was strongly resisted by initial organizational members. When a group of people with disabilities is united by a common denominator, which is oppression based on disability experience or conditions, there remains a divisor of minority status within the group. This perception has caused prejudice and discomfort among members. The above conditions agree with Freire's argument when he wrote that "in order for the oppressed to be able to wage the struggle for their liberation, they must perceive the reality of oppression not as a closed world from which there is no exit, but as limiting situation which they can transform (Freire, 1994, p. 31)."

In our daily quest for improved communication and human interactions as educators or in which ever relationship we are presented with, communication must embrace the inherent diversity of all people. Diversity in ethnicity, linguistics, phonetics, abilities, opinions, beliefs, and stature is a facet of the human condition which must be brought to the center of our consciousness when we communicate. When we fail just a little at this task, we are disaffirming the humanity of all people. Race-based discrimination and prejudice have been some of the most volatile issues in the American political landscape. They span all facets of life. However, when race is combined with the presence of one or more disabling conditions, whether visible or otherwise, the resulting human condition is unimaginably difficult. The issues that people of color with disabilities have had to face in education, economics, housing, and even in purchasing services have historically been far less than flattering.

The disability movement rejects the notion that professionals necessarily know best. The past two decades have witnessed a radical movement to change this historical service paradigm. The radical movement has built self affirmation on the principle that the person with disability knows best and must be allowed to make informed choices and decisions. According to this affirmation of being fully human, information is needed first and foremost, and a decision is arrived at with full participation of the person with disability. This self affirmation has led to another journey towards a real consciousness which began to open channels of communication and led to dialogue between the disability community and the rest of the society. The dialogue established this way has provided wide awareness and cognizance of the various disabling conditions and the potential human resources. Federal laws were enacted to protect people with disabilities as a social class. An example is the Civil Rights Act of 1964.

EDUCATION: THE CONTRADICTION

With the new social awareness, came another liberatory movement which suggests that people with disabilities are best able to manage programs designed to serve their disability community. This new movement elevated participants of the initial disability movement. The new status created a better opportunity to dialogue and to determine collaboratively the needs for appropriate pedagogical preparation in the forms of higher education as tools and a precondition for effective dialogue became apparent. Prior to the 1970s, educational opportunities for people of color who had disabilities were limited, except as noted earlier. Thus, at the initial stage of the movement, there was a lack of trained persons of color with disabilities for positions of responsibilities in the rehabilitation services. Stated simply, positions of responsibility managing disability related services requiring higher education degrees became yet another artificial barrier. It was artificial because the reasons advanced, while not without merits, did not consider decades of marginalization.

Thus, the artificial barrier created a significant stumbling block and mistrust. Mistrust basically occurs when people of color with disabilities are told that they lack the skills or education to assume positions of responsibilities. An example is the Gallaudet University's experience in 1988 when the students took to the street in protest of the Board of Trustee's appointment of a new president for the university who was neither deaf nor able to communicate with the students in sign language. During the Gallaudet University uprising, there was mistrust among the deaf community and the professionals engaged in the education of the deaf. The former president of the Board of Trustees stated that deaf people were not ready to manage their own affairs. At that time, there were also many other professionals in the fireld of deafness who believed in that assertion. Members of the deaf community disagreed, and the trusting relationship faltered. "Trust is established by dialogue. Should trust flounder, it will be seen that the preconditions for dialogue were lacking. False love, false humility, and feeble faith in others cannot create trust. To glorify democracy and to silence the people is a farce; to discourse on humanism and to negate people is a lie" (Freire, 1994, p. 72).

We have witnessed political administrations and higher education community discourse on models of educational reform. The models must invariably tie educational reform in its entirety to pedagogical unification, where the end result is an expectation that is neither in reality nor in practice. Theoretically they subscribe to the notion of improved productivity and in the global order of competitiveness, that values the fittest and the brightest. Productivity is measured by capitalistic conscientization, which is a feeder to the labor market that in turn satisfies the established order of economic expectation. Thus, in terms of pedagogical reforms, there has not been much attention given to the needs of learners with disabilities in higher education.

Reforms most often discussed have emphasized the concept of inclusion. A closer look at the concept itself reveals that there are different interpretations for different disenfranchised groups to gain more widespread inclusion in the promises of education, and thus a part of the American dream. For example, people of color clamor for an egalitarian "big picture," and the middle and upper classes wish for "utopian pedagogy," while the poor class emphasizes just a "window of opportunity." In these continua, where should one put the need of learners with disabilities? For that matter, where do learners of color with disabilities claim their rightful place in all of these debates?

People with disabilities thus began to voice disaffection over service delivery and the rather paternalistic view notably of medical communities and institutions of higher education, which assumed that disabilities are anomalies to be remedied by medication and institutional confinement. Segregation and isolation were the primary means of service delivery; educational opportunities were limited to vocational programs and sheltered workshops where earnings were typically a fraction of the minimum wage. Various research was conducted largely in a sociological realm, rather than exploring pedagogical and intellectual insights into disabilities. That research emphasized the person with disabilities as the object of research, not an active participant in the quest for information and knowledge. The person with disability had virtually no input in those service delivery systems; only the professionals were thought to "know what is best for him/her."

It was not until the late 1970s and early 1980s that higher education became an option for people with disabilities, due largely to the requirements of section 504 of the Rehabilitation Act of 1974. That law stipulates that any organization receiving federal funding cannot discriminate against a qualified applicant by reason of his or her handicap. Institutions of higher education of that era prided themselves more in the architectural form of their major buildings, rather than their accessibility to all segments of society. Lack of access to these buildings was a major barrier that people with disabilities encountered in their initial efforts to obtain higher education. In the same period, the United States was coming to the crossroads of affirmative action and enforcement of the Civil Rights Act of 1964. So, for people of color with disabilities, there was the attitudinal barrier; the disability manifestations further compounded and complicated the experience.

At that time, the "age of enlightenment" was just coming to the disability communities. However, for the members of that community who are people of color, access to the necessary information that allows full dialogue and participation in the process of emancipation did not begin until much later. Thus, we have the condition of self depreciation. While the deaf and hard-of-hearing communities had earlier access to higher education through Gallaudet University (then a Liberal Arts college), it was unusual to find a person of color on the Gallaudet campus, which is located at the center of governmental activities in Washington, D.C. The consciousness of people of color who are deaf or hard-of-hearing was not raised then, nor were such people exposed to the transformational information by which they could be empowered to participate in the emancipation process. "Real consciousness implies the impossibility of perceiving the "untested feasibility" which lies beyond the limit-situations. But whereas the untested feasibility cannot be achieved at the level of "real [or present] consciousness," it can be realized through "testing action "which reveals its hitherto unperceived viability" (Freire, 1994, p. 94).

Such removal from the early emancipation process is certainly an oppressor/oppressed situation for people of color with disabilities. The new arrival (person of color with disability) neither possesses nor is aware of the differential cultural values, community subjectivism, and norms on a predominantly white campus. The new arrival sees his or her defined roles and responsibilities in academic terms, but unwritten and subtle and deftly crafted into the roles and responsibilities is that of cultural/disabilities/gender expert. Whatever his/her discipline, and regardless of his/her actual knowledge area or expertise, s/he is expected to be well versed and articulated in the affairs of his/her race and disability as well as to be a renowned leader in the racially congregated residential community. For example, most invariably few people of color with disabilities serve on various minority caucuses, and affirmative action advisory committees. Such covert expectations serve only to subjugate, and actually fail rather than educate and alert the learning community to the global responsibilities of inclusiveness and to needs for cultural and disability access.

As race divides the United States, so does disability, but for people of color with disabilities there are several levels of separation from society. The first separation is race. Race-based separation may be taken for granted, as it is almost the norm in this society, but the same division is also apparent within the disability community itself. Therefore, the effects of alienation and mistrust cannot be over-emphasized. To become an educated disabled person of color is surmountable only through sacrifices. This chapter explores the historical facts of participation in higher learning by people of color with disabilities. For the few people of color with disabilities in academia or in high positions in government, the recurring echo is isolation in their respective fields. The lack of role models to serve as mentors, as the youth of color with disabilities aspire to achieve their personal, professional, and academic goals, was frequently mentioned as one of the factors contributing to the problems of insufficient literature on this subject.

There is virtually no information on people of color with disabilities as a group or as participants in higher educational opportunities. The search has been no easy task. Not only in the United States, but across the world, disability education and rehabilitative services tend to be least in an array of national educational and social development plans. Mazurek and Winzer, (1994) in *Comparative Studies in Special Education* conducted a survey of disability services among selected countries of the world. Most of the countries surveyed are said to have one or another kind of elaborate development plans, but special education is rarely a high priority in them. This is not to say that the countries lack interest in the issue, but the lack of a high priority for special education illustrates the marginalization of anything or anyone who is different.

HISTORICAL PERSPECTIVES ON DISABILITY, DISABILITY EDUCATION, AND REHABILITATION

The United States has a long history of considering the needs of the disabled for education and access. Special education programs and disability access legislations have minimized, to some extent, the social stigma surrounding individuals with disabilities. And to some extent, the efforts of special educators and legislators' initiatives have minimized the effects of stigmatization and marginalization experienced by those with disabilities. Marginalization is reduced as society's social awakening continues and more people recognize that those with disabilities have abilities that extend far beyond the limitations posed by their disabling conditions. Much work has been done on the educational, psychological, psycho-social, and sociological implications of disabilities in general. For example, Wright, in *Physical Disability: A Psycho-social Approach*, (1983) documented and discussed the various disability issues ranging from circumscribing the problem, status position, self esteem, succumbing and coping, mourning, societal sources of attitudes, and other pertinent issues. Likewise, Mazurek and Winzer, (1994) in *Comparative Studies in Special Education*, a largely comparative work on special education around the world, documented the understanding and approaches to special educational programs in 26 countries, including Canada, Japan, the United States, and England. Much research has also been done with education and communication needs of the deaf. For example, Martin (1994) edited a comprehensive research work on the subjects of deafness and deaf youth. However, in none of the above works was there mention of the higher education participation that specifically addressed diabled people of color in higher education.

Similarly, a lot of work has been done on retention and recruitment of students of color, including practical applications, models and guides to make such aggressive recruitment and retention strategies effective. All these works discussed the emotional, psychological, physical, and intellectual growth of minority youth at predominantly white institutions of higher education. Yet, none of these works mention even the possibility of the presence of minority students with disabilities on those campuses. Thus, while we have done much to remove barriers and raise awareness about persons with disabilities and about persons of color, we have failed completely to address the needs of people of color with disabilities.

POSTMODERN IDENTITY AND POLITICS OF DISABILITY

For people of color with disabilities, post-modern identity politics can best be described as the renaissance of the civil rights struggle. It has begun to evolve as a struggle for recognition and the right to participate in issues that affect our lives. These issues are not limited to education alone but also include the need for cultural recognition and expression. This is the need to emphasize that one's disability manifestations do not make one less a person of cultural difference. There is a need to recognize that disabilities and culture are separate issues and that treating or recognizing disability manifestations ought not to overshadow the person within.

It was this recognition of the values and roles culture plays in the mindset of decision makers that prompted US Congressman Major Owens in 1994 to call the first national conference to study the chronic problems in special education of overrepresentation of children of color and under-representation of people of color in decision making roles. The conference drew together, for the first time, 400 people of color who were working with children and adults of color with disabilities, but there were few representatives from academia.

The historical perspectives discussed above suggest that people of color with disabilities continue to be underrepresented at various institutions of higher education. It does appear, however, that less attention has been focused on this group as a necessary component of the learning community. A search through back issues of *The Journal of Blacks in Higher Education*, which is supposedly prominent reading among the country's elite black academicians, reveals no mention of disabled members of this class in higher education. This virtual reality makes one wonder whether people of color can be classified as a new group within academe in search of an identity that is whole, new, and distinct when, although they are a part of the whole, they are yet not fully, completely members.

Giroux and McLaren (1994) in *Between Borders: Pedagogy and the Politics of Cultural Studies*, condemned the left wing social critics for their attempts to organize and be recognized within the cultural and social milieu. Giroux and McLaren stated that in such left wing views, attempts on the part of various social groups to combat racism, homophobia, or sexism are overtly determined by psychological concerns with self-identity, self-esteem, and anomie (p. 34). He illustrated this point by quoting Philipson (1991). Identity politics, Philipson maintained, "inevitably redirects our attention away from the fact that, apart from a tiny group at the top of the class hierarchy, alienation, a sense of not being recognized for who one is, and feelings of impotence and failure affect us all-certainly to different degrees and with different repercussions...[I]dentity politics is not sufficiently radical to speak to this distress, to get at the root sources of our alienation and individually experienced lack of social recognition."

This view of identity politics is part of the social and institutional barriers to potential opportunities to identify persons of color with disabilities in academia. Documentation is needed, at least in light of the new era disability identity politics that has been rejected by Philipson. Even though identity politics is not at the core of why it was impossible to identify persons of color with disabilities in higher education, views such as those espoused by Philipson make one wonder whether, without an active identity politics across academic campuses, the "silenced voices" are ever to be heard. It has been claimed, although without validation, that there are no less than 40 million people with disabilities (excluding disabled war veterans) who form the core of radical disability movements in this country. But identity politics, according to Giroux, "covers a complex and diverse terrain of theoretical positions of discourses concerned with questions of subjectivity, culture, difference, and struggle" (p. 34). Giroux further suggested that the issue of identity politics needs to be engaged more dialectically where critical perspectives on identity politics should be seen as fundamental to any discourse of social movement that believes in the radical renewal of democratic society.

Disability politics has been on the rise ever since the first person in a wheelchair attended the University of California at Berkeley. That admission set the stage for the proliferation of Independent Living Centers across the country where people with disabilities receive non-traditional instruction and hands-on experience in the areas of advocacy, self advocacy, and living independently in individual chosen residential arrangements. However, like Maslow's hierarchy of needs, those training centers have traditionally focused almost exclusively on the immediate survival approach. It has been suggested that the most popular areas of employment for persons with disabilities are in those centers and with state rehabilitation agencies. Only a handful of persons with disabilities attempt to break the mold. Once they do, of those interviewed, many became outcasts within the company of persons with whom they would normally feel kinship because of disability manifestations. Accordingly, people of color with disabilities have not been very active in the core front-line of disability rights, education, and advocacy. As a philosophy, mainstreaming (fashionably/ politically correctly known as inclusion) serves only a socio-political purpose without a clear definition of how it should apply or be practiced where an individual's unique, compelling, accessibility and socialization opportunities or needs are concerned.

In preparing to write this chapter, I was frustrated by the virtual lack of information on as I searched for previous works on this subject; there was almost none. I interviewed ten individuals with disabilities via telephone to gain insight into their experience in academe. Only one interviewee holds a doctoral degree, is blind, and African American. There are only three other African Americans holding doctoral degrees; all three are deaf including one woman and two men. There are also three Hispanic men and one Asian man, but among these interviewees there is no other woman of color with disability holding such higher education credentials. All holders of doctoral degrees are employed in higher education or education of the deaf. The rest of the interviewees are master's degree holders. (See Table 1.)

It was discovered that compared with other disability groups, deaf and hard-of-hearing groups boast the highest percentage of individuals with higher education credentials, whether white or of color. This higher accomplishment is attributed to the presence of Gallaudet University and the National Technical Institute for the Deaf at the Rochester Institute of Technology. These institutions of higher learn-

TABLE 1.
Employment of People of Color With Disabilities

Race	Gender	Disability	Degree	Job type
Hispanic	M	Deaf	Ph.D	Education
Hispanic	M	Deaf	MS	Service
Asian	M	Deaf	MA	Service
Black	F	Blind	Ph.D	Education
Asian	M	M	MbA	Business
Black	M	Deaf	Ph.D	Education
Black	M	Deaf	Ph.D	Education
Black	F	M	Ph.D	Education
Black	M	M	MA	Service
Black	M	Blind	Ph.D	Education

Note: $n = 10$

ing for the deaf, together with the Tsukuba College of Technology in Japan, are the only such institutions in the world today. The interviewees were questioned as to what constitutes reasonable access, or, if they had not yet experienced the need for such access in higher education, what they envisioned to be an ideal situation. They were also asked how many people of color they knew with any form of physical, mental, or auditory disability and if any were employees or students in higher education.

The most interesting finding in my interviews was the constancy with which the absence of role models and the proper access to information were mentioned. Another key finding was the lack of access to peripheral learning in academia to enable them to satisfy their hunger. The redundant theme was that there is presently little or no incentive for them or the youth they knew, to aim to achieve education beyond the baccalaureate level. Interviewees who were deaf felt alienated from the rest of the campus community because of inadequate interpreter service. Those with physical disabilities—who need services such as assistance with activities of daily living and body management functions, or guide dogs in the classroom—cited teachers' discomfort with them in class. They also found that their classmates tend to be more sensitive, positive, and respectful when teachers' attitudes were at least accommodating. Those who were blind mentioned that they have difficulty with academic tasks, and the readers assigned to them sometimes did not comprehend the subject matter. Each of the interviewees felt alienated by racial tensions coupled with the presence of disability.

Hannah, writing in *The Second Handbook of Minority Students Services*, (Taylor, 1990) traced the historical experiences of minority students in predominantly white higher education institutions in the early 1970s when many colleges and universities initiated a variety of programs to identify, motivate, prepare, recruit, enroll, retain, and graduate non-white students at the graduate and professional levels. He further stated that the proportion of non-whites in virtually all disciplines, including health care and law, has always been less than that of non-whites in the general population. He attributes this to unequal educational opportunities, including a relative lack of access to education in the professions and under-preparedness in secondary education for those professions. As a result, "there is a gross under-representation of non-white professionals among the number of practicing professionals in America" (Taylor, 1990, p. 85). The same situation applies to people of color with disabilities. They are virtually unrepresented in higher education professions because they lack access to the means of attaining the necessary credentials to teach at the college level or to participate in the other professions identified by Hannah.

For a person of color with a disability, the above factors have a doubly negative impact. While the historically negative view of persons of color has been interwoven into fabric of the American world view, the disability manifestation has become another negative factor contributing to an overwhelming and negatively stereotypical social perception. This somewhat reaffirms the conservative view of funding of public higher education that the conservatives' definition of the primacy of schooling is to serve as the guardian of Western civilization. Under this view, the pedagogy is "unencumbered by the messy concerns of equity, social justice, or the need to educate a critical citizenry." Indeed, people of color who have disabilities are members of the critical citizenry, but in a conservative sense, the affirmation of their individuality and membership in the society is marginalized to the extent that, rhetoric aside, only a minimal educational opportunity is made available to them.

This phenomenon is not limited to the United States but is widespread across the world. In an edited work on international comparative special education, *Comparative Studies in Special Education*, (1994), Mazurek and Winzer explained that in the functionalist view, special education is inevitably related to a society's social, political, economic, and even religious structures and its attitudes and values are fashioned by the prevailing culture, government, religion, and economic conditions. They also stated that education generally tends to reflect the political and legal foundations on which a society is built. If the foregoing is true, then Americans and others as a people should improve their perceptions of disabling conditions at least in order that the traumatic effects of stigma attached to disabilities might function less as agents of self defeat for people of color experiencing those conditions.

Other views of special education that emerged from Mazurek and Winzer's work are that the care and training of persons with disabilities is a function of social attitudes toward the disability, which, in my opinion, mirrors social imperatives regarding equality and justice. They argue that the education and care of exceptional individuals, and the way in which a society responds to the problems of deviance and disability, reflect the general cultural attitudes concerning the obligations of a society to its individual citizens. Therefore, it is not surprising, to note the magnitude of political and social debates over the needs of people with disabilities in this country and the various proposed formulas for addressing those needs. Former President Bush gained popularity among the 40 million American people with disabilities by signing the Americans with Disabilities Act of 1990. President Clinton was said to have actually benefited politically at the polls by ensuring that people with disabilities were actively involved with his 1992 presidential campaign. Each of the politicians and policy decision makers having a stake in the way social progress is measured have historically devoted their energy to adopting careful policies that treat people with disabilities or exceptionalities in ways that provide the appearance of moving away from the status quo, whatever that may be.

Generally, policy formulations tend to direct education and training of people with exceptionalities to follow certain conservative design. Perhaps it is part of such design that has grossly contributed to the gap between the quality and level of access to higher education and the presence of membership in the elite genre of notable academicians and thinkers of our day. Policy makers seem to believe that the best way to educate deaf learners is to integrate them with their peers who are without hearing loss. Of course, this may actually have some merit, especially when one considers the myriad social interactions which define an individual in the community and/or even within the family structure. However, the concept of inclusion, mainstreaming, and equal access needs to be refined, especially attitudes and societal perceptions of disabilities, so that the whole issue and concept do not become just so much camouflage.

Recent American administrations and several state governments in the United States have begun to view special education as an appropriate mobilization of human capital. For example, we are witnessing for the first time significant numbers of people with physical disabilities as presidential appointees. Kate Steldman is a hard-of-hearing woman who has directed the National Institute for Disability Rehabilitation Research (NIDRR); Judith Heumann, a Hispanic woman with physical disability has been the Assistant Secretary of the Office of Special Education and Rehabilitative Services (OSERS), and some of her high officials have also been people with disabilities. This new development seems to support Mazurek and Winzer's (1994) notion that the central tenet of education for people with disabilities is that usefulness determines a person's value to society.

Winzer and Mazurek (1994) and DeJong (1978) explained this concept further by stating that such usefulness places emphasis on the training and socializing function of schooling and on the value added to an individual's productivity skills, and therefore, to his or her social value. This assumption in our present educational sociology, philosophy, and theory, seems to lead to the other view suggested by Winzer and Mazurek. In this view, they stated that "the provision of equal access to educational and rehabilitation services to all people, exceptionality notwithstanding, is an integral component of civil rights that disallows discrimination on any grounds (p. xxx)."

Institutions of higher education seem to be cautiously embracing this view, at least in light of the ADA and other federal and/or in some instances state access and accommodation laws. While there seems to be a general willingness to provide equitable access and accommodation in principle and practice, it seems as if the process will only continue gradually to unfold, be refined and perfected, so that the ideal services and access provision are manifested, acknowledged, and implemented on the basis of the above views that an individual human resource should be well developed and integrated fully into society's mainstream. For this to happen, institutions of higher learning must put on the leadership mantle in designing viable and workable pragmatic accessibility and accommodation.

Although special education as a conscientious movement in the United States is not a new phenomenon, it has been somewhat more of a trickle-down social service for people of color with disabilities. That is: recruitment, retention, and quality of instruction are not on the same level as general education. For example, it took Gallaudet University more than 50 years to admit its first African-American or Hispanic-American student. Therefore, it is not surprising to note that there is virtually no documentation on this issue upon which an adequate literature review of pertinent historical and pedagogical trends could be conducted. Since the advent of the gender revolution in the United States, educational processes and procedures for attaining positions of power and responsibility have taken on a monetary, value-based culture of their own. Learning is no longer for the sake of acquiring knowledge, but instead for the necessary tools for sustenance. Thus the process has become an individualized and personal-goal-oriented, rather than a community-oriented enterprise. Alienation for the sake of personal satisfaction through education has thus been complemented by shifts in social order. Liberal education in a conservative society produces an ideological scheme of educational reforms that attempts to provide avenues for all persons to acquire this needed tool of being educated; quality is of little significance.

Although the issue of affirmative action in the United States is becoming quite muddy, it is still imperative that institutions of higher learning begin aggressive recruitment and retention of students, faculty, and more multicultural staff members with disabilities. Faculty in higher education are faced with the attainment of upward mobility based on votes of their peers. There can be no peers for the few pioneers, especially people like those interviewed for this chapter. Thus, there is first the quest for knowledge and the battle for access to that knowledge. Once attained, there is yet another competition for the same advantages: higher wages, promotion, position attainment, and academic tenure, in a market place dominated by continous strategic planning and managed attrition. Institutions of higher learning can lead the way by providing the same opportunities to people of color with disabilities as are extended to everyone else in all areas of participation in the academic enterprise.

This is not going to be an easy task given historical institutional neglect and legal sanctions aimed at preserving pervasive marginalization. Federal and state rehabilitation agencies need to design a real reform in approaches to advance participation of people of color with disabilities in higher education rather than the current state of dependency on authority figures seen in the rehabilitation professionals.

We need an informed dialogue to design a viable pedagogical structure that will increase visibility, productivity, and total inclusion of all learners with disability and will destroy the negative pre-conceptions and stereotypical notions that doubly jeopardize people of color with disabilities who aspire to full participation in the enterprise of higher education. Such a dialogue must be real, unambiguous, meaningful, and purposeful. This is because "true dialogue cannot exist unless the dialoguers engage in critical thinking " (Freire,1994, p. 73). This critical thinking must occur not apart from, or only within, the community of people of color with disability; rather, there is the need for open fora, where real and actual dialogue can happen. It must happen in an atmosphere of collegiality, trust, and beliefs in the rightful place of learners of color with disabilities among the managers and policy makers of higher education.

One example is the often voiced statement that qualified people of color cannot be found to fill positions of responsibility. However, to find the people, we must actually look for them; we must leave our ivory towers and journey to a place where these individuals can be found. We can utilize a network of contacts to locate, recruit, and engage our talents and intelligence. Every possibility needs to be investigated with the correct approach and attitude.

Following such a dialogue, policy, institutional, and attitudinal barriers—along with the pervasive paternalistic opinions of the efforts of learners of color with disabilities—might begin to disappear. The ownership of such pedagogical transformations can, therefore, be claimed by every citizen, particularly those who have come together in the theater of dialogue where the transformations were begun. It shall no longer be "inclusion for them;" but rather a personal challenge to institutions of higher education actively to cultivate, recruit, enroll, and graduate more people of color with disabilities. With this transformation, there shall be "meaningful human aspirations, motives, and objectives" (Freire, 1994, p. 88). When this happens, or while the transformation is taking place, we can all investigate together without "antidialogical" characteristics in our motives and actions. There will be no need to preserve the status quo, and thereby preserve domination, as the latter will have become meaningless.

In closing, I want to again return to Freire, who said, "[I]f we consider society as a being, it is obvious that only a society which is a being for itself can develop. Societies which are dual, reflex, invaded, and dependent on the metropolitan society cannot develop because they are alienated; their political, economic, and cultural decision-making power is located outside themselves, in the invader society" (Freire, 1994, p. 142)." This statement perfectly describes the current state of affairs of people of color with disabilities, especially those of us aspiring to attain higher education. There is most invariably a duality in our association and interaction with people. As people of color with disabilities, our relationships with the larger disability community is eroded by color, while within our cultural identities, the association is demarcated by disabilities manifestation. Mandated assimilation cannot produce trust, but breeds irritation and further alienates. "Can't you get out of that chair and walk? Why can't you understand me without an interpreter? Why do I have to speak slowly for you to understand me?" These are some of the question with which we are barraged on a daily basis, which in turn are a denial by forces of domination of our individuality and our being fully human. The questions are innocent themselves, but indeed they serve to subjugate and further negate self affirmation.

Together, we can change this picture of forced isolation of people of color with disabilities in higher education. One way is to engage in organizing and investigating actively without preconceptions and with a willingness to restructure higher education as the "practice of freedom—as opposed to education as the practice of domination " (Freire, 1994, p. 62).

As a further reference, you might wish to consider the U.S. Department of Education's Summary of Existing Legislation Affecting Persons with Disabilities. A publication of the U.S. Department of Education, Office of Special Education and Rehabilitative Services Clearinghouse on Handicapped, Washington, DC. Publication #E-88-22014.

DISCUSSION QUESTIONS

1. What are the major issues contributing to effective participation of people of color with disabilities in higher education?
2. What have you observed in your institution regarding accessibility?
3. What are or should be the roles of federal governments in the issue of higher education opportunity for people of color with disabilities?
4. Attitudinal barriers remain the most salient barrier of all. What can you do personally to change attitudinal barrier in your institution?
5. Do you agree with Freire's philosophy regarding oppression and how does that philosophy relate to people of color with disabilities?

REFERENCES

DeJong, G. (1979). Independent living: From social movement to analytic paradigm *Archives of Physical Medicine and Rehabilitation, 60,* 435-446.

Freire, P. (1994). *Pedagogy of the oppressed* (Newly revised 20th-Anniversary Edition). New York: Seabury Press.

Giroux, H.A. (1992). *Border crossing: Cultural workers and the politics of education.* New York: Routledge.

Giroux, H.A. & McLaren, P. (Eds.), (1989). *Critical pedagogy, the state, and cultural struggle.* Albany, NY: State University of New York Press.

Giroux, H. & McLaren, P. (1994) *Between borders: Pedagogy and the politics of cultural studies.* New York, NY: Ruthledge.

Hannah, Howard-Hamilton, Stikes, Young, Special Service for Professional Students. (1990). In Taylor, C.A., (Ed.) *The Second Handbook of Minority Student Services.* Madison, WI: Praxis Publications.

Martin, D.S. (1995). *Proceedings from the International Symposium on Cognition, Education, and Deafness* held at Gallaudet College, June 1984. Washington, D.C. Gallaudet College Press.

Mazurek, K. & Winzer, M.A. (Eds.) (1994) *Comparative studies in special education.* Washington DC: Gallaudet University Press.

National Center for Law and Deafness. (1992). *Legal rights—The guide for deaf and hard of hearing people.* Washington, D.C: National Center for Law and Deafness, Gallaudet University Press.

Philipson (1991), "What is the Big I.D.? The Politics of the Authentic Self," *Tikkun Magazine, 6,* (6) 51-55.

Taylor, C.A., (Ed.) (1990). *The second handbook of minority student services.* Madison, WI: Praxis Publications, Inc.

U.S. Department of Education. *Summary of existing legislation affecting persons with disabilities.* Publication of the U.S. Department of Education, Office of Special Education and Rehabilitative Services Clearinghouse on Handicapped, Washington, DC. Publication #E-88-22014.

Winzer, M.A. (1993). *The history of special education: From isolation to integration.* Washington, D.C.: Gallaudet University Press.

Winzer, M.A. & Mazurek, K. (Eds.) (1994). *Comparative studies in special education.* Washington, D.C.: Gallaudet University Press.

Wright, M. (1983). *Physical disability: A psycho-social approach.* Washington, D.C.: Gallaudet University Press.

31

DEAF CULTURE, PLURALISM AND THE FIELD OF COMMUNICATION

Cindy Campbell
Rachel Friend
Syracuse University

INTRODUCTION

Deaf culture has existed as a subculture within America for many years. Based on a long recorded history of over 200 years, American Sign Language is the only "natural" language Deaf people use to communicate within their culture. Throughout history and up to the present time, most hearing people regard Deaf people as disabled. Contrary to this belief, Deaf people view themselves as a culture and as bearers of linguistic values which make them a discourse community. These contradictory beliefs have created problems with how Deaf culture is viewed as a subject of academic inquiry.

For example, within the field of Communication, little research has been done on ASL as a cultural pattern of communication. Virtually, all communication theories have been developed out of studies of hearing cultures where, at best, they offer narrow interpretations of communication and applications to Deaf culture. However, a fairly innovative concept within the communication field is pluralism, which provides a viable rationale for the study of different language cultures or communities. Despite being a subculture, Deaf culture is excluded from these pluralistic works of communication scholars.

The concept of pluralism explained in this paper seeks to expand the scope and flexibility of the communication discipline to open the possibility of including the study of Deaf culture in the communication field. In addition, it will open the prospect of developing new, or altering prior theories of communication to enhance our understanding of this cultural foundation of communication.

CONTENTION OF PLURALISM

Communication scholars have developed an array of theories to account for the diversity of language and its acquisition. Each theory posits distinct outlooks to view the phenomena of communication—within its broad scope. Overall, the field of communication studies is increasingly advancing to new theoretical bounds. One such innovative approach is to enhance the idea and concept of pluralism as a distinct perspective, by which the general society and its sub-groups' communicative techniques can be understood, inclusive of its shared diversity.

Many disciplines, such as Philosophy, Feminist Studies, and Communication may call upon the necessity of pluralism to explore the differences among people within one societal boundary, where social interpretation allows altered and varied conceptions of reality. One may ask, "What is pluralism and what is this need to employ it based on?" Pluralism itself, is a fairly new concept, which idealizes the abundance of diversity among people. Walter Watson, defines diversity among people in his article entitled, "Types of Pluralism" by stating:

> We are all different centers of experience. There is diversity both in ourselves and in what we encounter. *Except for identical twins our initial endowments are different, and we experience the world from different locations in space and time. We grow up within different familial and cultural traditions* (Italics added) (Watson, p. 351).

To view the definitive qualities and usages of pluralism within the communication field, we must overview other fields and their use of pluralistic concepts in order to integrate them into communication research. The necessity of doing so lies within the brief history of the communication field. The history itself indicates that the field of communication is fairly young and still growing.

The communication field itself is in the process of expanding. The emergence of distinctions, including types of language acquisition, communicative processes and social construction of language introduce a pluralistic outlook to view these and other phenomena. In order to use pluralism in any study, the understanding of this concept is critical because it provides a direction of understanding towards communication research. Thus, some foundational definitions of pluralism will be posited; followed by the relationship of these definitive properties to communication; and last, a historical outlook on the political and social purposes involved in utilizing this viewpoint.

One way to conceptualize or define the idea of pluralism is within a notion of plausibility. As Eugene Garver states in his article entitled, "Why Pluralism Now?...one could equally well note the existence of a desire for uniqueness and individuality at the root of today's pluralism. We both want the scope of Us to expand until it is universal, and we want to maintain the borders between Us and Them" (Garver, 1985, p. 398). One aspect of plausibility regarding this pluralistic outlook is to have this concept of the generalizable whole—yet, with sub-cultures depicting the specific differences—which open the prospect of considering definitive aspects of each specific group. Known examples of these sub-cultures are African-Americans, Feminists, and political parties, such as the Democrats or Republicans; along with a lesser known group, Deaf. People are diverse in thought, action and communication due these differences in cultural backgrounds. At the same time, Americans function as one primary culture, by which there are generalizable shared experiences. This madates a need for researchers and theorists to view the similarities and differences across and among sub-cultures, leading to plausible—but different—accounts of communication grounded in different cultural perspectives.

Another considered accent of pluralism within historical boundaries and language is the use of accounts. Many would agree, when communicating about historical accounts, that something has occurred in the past yet the account which one may offer can differ significantly from another person's regarding the same experience temporally. The hierarchy of meaning, depicted by Pearce, Cronen and Harris within their theory of "The Coordinated Management of Meaning", posits this distinction. The hierarchy is flexible, allowing one to view an account as a definitive part of the cultural boundaries, while the other person may view the account in regard to the conversants' relationship (Cronen, Pearce, & Harris, 1982, p. 71). Thus, meanings are context-dependent because people "assign different meanings to certain key messages" (Cronen, Pearce, & Harris, p. 68). This concept of pluralism is characterized as a type of historical pluralism, which operates within a field of plausibility where difference is not viewed as a conflict or error. This sense of pluralism and plausibility are related to communication and language, but referenced by its foundation within a historical discipline. The correlation of this form of pluralism and communication is most notable due to the differing perceptions, one relates when speaking of historical accounts. This too, occurs during all types of accounts regarding relational experiences. Quite basically, pluralism is the use of multiple interpretations of a culture and the use of those differing interpretations to make a more comprehensible and workable meaning of experience for more than just one section of the culture.

Pluralism is not an avenue to posit the value that each thought is equal to another and to speak of those thoughts as related; but rather, it is a form of theorizing which allows multiple routes for the attainment of knowledge. It is analogous to viewing life experiences through many different "colored glasses" simultaneously, instead of using one view to encompass all people. With the advent of voice and power of many different sub-cultures within American society, one universal outlook for formulating and reviewing theory can no longer suffice.

One notable philosophy of a language theorist who uses the tenets of pluralism is Ludwig Wittgenstein. His theory of language is called the Game Theory, whereby the metaphor of "language games" depicts what occurs when people communicate. Language games reflect a socially constructed reality, whereby meaning is regulated and altered by the involved actors. Therefore, each person has the ability to perceive the communication act her own way, along with creating meaning among the actors, in consideration of the entirety of the group and act which has been committed.

People generally are of differing experiences, with individual interpretations of the society they inhabit. It is provincial and discriminatory to provide only one viewpoint of interpretation, rather than evaluating many positions or methodologies of worth. Thus, a pluralist outlook is necessary in communication theory. The communication field is encouraged to encompass the concept of pluralism to account for the many purposes of language use.

One such cultural distinction that has had little recognition within the field is Deaf culture. For 30 years, research has shown that Deaf use their own language, American Sign Language. Thus, the communicative value of American Sign Language as a part of pluralism must be included when theorizing and researching within communication disciplines.

MYTHS AND HISTORICAL CONTEXT
OF AMERICAN SIGN LANGUAGE

With evidence, history indicates that Deaf people have their own language— American Sign Language which has been fundamental in creating a Deaf culture over time. To the Deaf community, with the help of scholarly studies, American Sign Language currently operates as an official language. From a historical point of view, American Sign Language still struggles to deserve its recognition as a natural language rooted in development among Deaf people for more than 200 years. This struggle originates from misconceptions about American Sign Language as a form of gesture. Many still think that American Sign Language is "bad English," "broken English," or "short English." Up to to a certain point, the falsification of a few myths associated with American Sign Language needs to be addressed, due to the belief in these falsehoods that has been ongoing for many years.

First, American Sign Language is a unique language with its own grammatical rules and syntax, just like other languages (Baker & Cokely, 1986; Moore & Levitan, 1993; Padden & Humphries, 1988). Second, people still assume that once they know English, they can learn American Sign Language easily because American Sign Language uses the "English" system.

This assumption must be nullified before learning American Sign Language, because the linguistic studies show that American Sign Language has its own creation of lexicons and complicated grammatical rules, which owe English nothing. Conceptually, the comparison of similarities of two foreign languages, such as Spanish and Hebrew, is an impossible task. This principle is similarly applicable for American Sign Language and English.

The third myth, which we often heard from my former students, is the assumption that they would become fluent in signing American Sign Language just after one semester of learning. Unfortunately for these students, American Sign Language is unique and at the same time very complicated because of the use of different body parts which blend together simultaneously, while at the same time, specific meanings within the grammatical structure are organized. Often, hearing people find themselves very awkward in using their body parts to sign. Time is of the essence for them to learn and get used to this "foreign" language.

To become fluent in American Sign Language, depending on the motivation, attitude, and open mindedness of the learner, will take about two full years. Some experienced interpreters that I have worked with express their opinions differently. They believe that they always are in a constant process of learning American Sign Language. At this point, we agree with them because one main characteristic for any language is that it cannot be static or it will diminish on its own. Changes are a very crucial part in the process of using a language based on the evolution of environment, technology, lifestyles, etc. (Daniels, 1985). If the desire is great for a quick road to achievement as an expert in American Sign Language, one can fully immerse oneself within Deaf culture.

Naturally, a hearing person can expect many struggles when she/he attempts to immerse fully. However, hearing people need to understand the underlying rules, in terms of when to socialize with Deaf people because Deaf culture is a sheltered community which Deaf people protect and share by the use of their common language. This is another complex part of Deaf culture that will be detailed later.

So far this chapter has offered a clarification of the misconceptions about American Sign Language as a form of English and has shown its value as a natural language. In the article, "The Relationship of Deaf Studies and Deaf Identity," B. Kannapell sums the above points by stating:

1. American Sign Language is not just an instrument for communication among Deaf people. American Sign Language is also a symbol of social or group identity, an emblem (badge) of group membership and solidarity among Deaf people.

2. American Sign Language is simultaneously a store or a repository of cultural knowledge, a symbol of social identity, and medium of interaction among Deaf culture (Gumperz quoted in Kannapell, p. 4)

Simply, American Sign language is a unique language that is used in the Deaf community.

Next, a common question regarding American Sign Language might be asked, "Where does it come (originate) from?" The historical aspects indicate that American Sign Language originates from two parts of an evolutionary process. The first part of evolutionary process is called "Old" American Sign Language, which began as a blend of French Sign Language and signs used before the 1700s. Historical evidence states that a large number of Deaf people residing on Martha's Vineyard Island had a knowledge of signs during the early 1700s. An anthropological study shows that for two centuries the deaf population ballooned (Groce, 1985, p. 4). Evidence strongly suggests that the large number of Deaf persons living on Martha's Vineyard for two centuries used signs to communicate.

The dwindling numbers of deaf persons on the island was caused by the introduction of a new "opportunity"—special education. In 1817, the American Asylum for the Deaf and Dumb, the first school for the deaf in United States, was established at Hartford, Connecticut. The original sign language from Martha's Vineyard Island was employed by that Deaf school. Another facet in the development of Old American Sign Language was Old French Sign Language. This started in 1816 which was the important journey for Thomas Hopkins Gallaudet. An unexpected encounter occurred between Thomas Hopkins Gallaudet and a nine year old girl, Alice Cogswell at Hartford, Connecticut.

He observed her as she did not socialize with her peers. Alice's father informed Gallaudet that she was deaf (Williams, 1983, p. 6). He and Dr. Cogswell (Alice's father) expressed their concerns of establishing a deaf school for Alice and other deaf children. They gathered support from the citizens and raised some funds. At first, Thomas Gallaudet agreed to study the techniques used there to educate deaf children in England. He met Mr. John Braidwood who founded an oral school, however, to be brief with history, Gallaudet rejected his proposition as it required him to serve as an apprentice for a few years and was not allowed to share the information with others. In London, Thomas Gallaudet met Abbe Sicard, the head adminstator of Paris Institution for the Deaf and he was invited to stay there to learn about the teaching methods.

In 1816, Gallaudet went and studied there;however, he had limited funds and was running out of time. Gallaudet needed more time to learn, so to make things easier, he invited Clerc. Clerc agreed—he was underpaid and was eager for a change, too. On a ship called Martha Augusta where Clerc and Gallaudet began their long journey and at the same time both were busy educating each other as it was told in the book, "Deaf Heritage:"

> Clerc knew little English, and so he spent much of his time on the crossing learning the language from Gallaudet. In return, he taught Gallaudet the language of signs. He kept a diary of the trip, which lasted 52 days because of frequent calms and head-

winds. Clerc recorded the events of each day, and then Gallaudet corrected his English. (Gannon, 1981, p. XXI)

When they arrived in the United States, they committed themselves to traveling and giving numerous presentations to obtain support and funds to open their first Deaf school.

One year later on April 15, 1817, the Connecticut Asylum for the Deaf and Dumb was founded as the first Deaf school in America and opened its doors to educate deaf children. The initiation of Old French Sign Language was developed and merged with the signs used before the 1700s which created the old (original) American Sign Language. The reflection of the history is necessary in understanding of how it was developed here in United States.

The next common question is "Who uses American Sign Language and how do they learn American Sign Language?" First, the statistics currently show that ten percent of Deaf children are from Deaf parents. The remaining 90 percent of deaf children are from hearing parents. This will bring about an interesting communication dynamic— how 10 percent of Deaf children from Deaf parents hold their powerful instrument and influence in creating the Deaf culture. Before going into the details, the definition of a deaf residential school is necessary because it is different from regular hearing schools. First, the school has classrooms for educational purposes, residence (dorms) for Deaf students who live far from the school, and many extracurricular activities for the students to participate after the formal education school. The environment school really gives the sense of "home" for Deaf students because it provides them with "24 hours" of barrier free communication, while developing and creating the closest bonds due to seeing each other everyday. Deaf school plays an important role for the language transmission which generates the development of Deaf culture within the environment. Ten percent of Deaf children from Deaf families have the primary responsibility for creating this cultured environment because they have their language model from their parents. Not only that, but imagine how powerful this transformation of other Deaf children is for them to become the "cultural" children. Deaf schools are the primary source for development of Deaf culture.

Deaf culture maintains its survival through many tribulations. An example of this is how a motion was made at the Milan Conference (1880) that forced the change of communication methods in Deaf schools in America—by utilizing an introduction of Oralism. The oral method was almost completely instilled as the primary communication mode at deaf education schools started in America in the 1880s. Sign Language at that time was prohibited to use in the classroom and in the dorms. Deaf children were starved to communicate freely. They found some ways to continue signing under the tables, or signing small so they would not be caught by teachers or supervisors. The subsistence of signing underground did not affect the survival of American Sign Language through this adversarial period. Oralism only existed in Deaf education for about 90 years until the discovery was made and paved a clear path for American Sign Language to be expanded and used openly among Deaf members.

American Sign Language was not recognized as a language until William Stokoe's research in the 1960s. He argued that American Sign Language does have the linguistic requirements to function as a language. For the next 30 years, the research in this area proliferated and confirmed the validity of Stokoe's claim that American Sign Language operates as a language.

With the assistance of Stokoe, Deaf people use the research to justify their rights of using American Sign Language. This became a rhetorical movement inclusive at different levels—social, political and economic. The most important movement to be remembered that changed many points of view toward Deaf culture was the Gallaudet protest. It occurred in March 1988 regarding the decision in selecting a president candidate. The selection at first was announced and shocked Deaf students. A hearing candidate, Dr. Zinser, was selected over two Deaf candidates. The students decided to have a peaceful protest that led to the close of campus for a week. Their four demands were outlined: 1) Select a Deaf president 2) Ask Spilman to resign as the Board chairperson 3) The board members should have 51 percent of deaf members representing 4) There will be no reprisal actions against the students (Gannon, 1989). Interestingly, the four demands were successfully met (Gannon, 1989). Currently, Dr. I King Jordan is president of Gallaudet University. Every year in March, the students celebrate the special occasion to remember and remind themselves that they have rights to live equally.

Not only this big change but many small changes are happening in our lives. More states passed legislations to recognize American Sign Language as a foreign language. This is what promotes universities and colleges to add an optional course for the students to meet the linguistic requirements. Another distinction is the American Disability Act (ADA), a law that was passed focusing on the accessibility for people with disabilities. That law provides more rights for Deaf people to obtain interpreters at different places, though, this had led to a crisis—a shortage of interpreters. Therefore, a solution is made by implementing more interpreting programs at different universities to train hearing people in becoming professional interpreters. This also enhances a privilege for Deaf teachers to obtain employment.

There are many significant changes that promote the strengths in preserving American Sign Language and Deaf culture. The question has been raised whether or not Deaf culture should be a part of the communication field. To reflect the concept of pluralism, it indicates that American Sign Language operates as a valuable language which contains significant rhetorical tools to create a "cohesive" culture. By utilizing the tenets of American Sign Language and its communicative values within the field, the phenomena of communication will not only be explored but expanded to new horizon. Thus, pluralism is used as a rationale to investigate these objectives.

"PATHOLOGICAL" VERSUS CULTURAL VIEWS

Even though the Deaf community is a subculture in America, the remaining gap between hearing and Deaf culture still continues based on prevailing attitudes. The view from hearing culture stems from the historical ideological system, perceiving Deaf people as inferior citizens of their culture. This needs to be redefined in order to recognize how the linguistic values in Deaf community actually perform a crucial role in maintaining the shared, common cultural truisms, values, and goals as a culture. Charlotte Baker and Dennis Cokely develop two different categories, clinical-pathological and cultural views (1986).

The first view is clinical-pathological, considers the behaviors and values of the hearing majority as the "standard" or "norm" and then focuses on how deaf people deviate from that norm (Baker & Cokely, p. 55). This clinical-pathological outlook reflects the attitude of the hearing majority and shows that they still perceive Deaf people as disabled because they are not able to "function" as equal citizens based on their inability to hear. It is their belief that Deaf people should be "helped" in becoming normal citizens.

The cultural view is the second category which describes that people recognize the differences based on the language, experiences and values of a particular group of people (Baker & Cokely, 1986, p. 54). Deaf people who are members of Deaf culture tend to hold this view. Baker and Cokely expand the cultural view, to encompass Deaf people who share a common means of communication (signs) which provide the basis for group cohesion and identity, as well as a group of persons who share a common language (American Sign Language) and a common culture (Padden & Markowicz, 1976).

With these descriptions of two different views, the hearing majority often exercise the first view (clinical pathological) toward the Deaf community. This chapter introduces this attitudinal concept for the hearing majority to raise their consciousness, and enable them to become sensitive toward Deaf culture by critically reevaluating the old view. The non-members of Deaf culture need to understand the *cultural* view, in order to recognize the cultural differences and acknowledge that Deaf people are an independent subcultural group. Hearing scholars in the communication field should also adopt the cultural view, in order to work with the Deaf community, and of utmost importance, introduce Deaf culture into the context of pluralism.

SENSITIZATION TOWARD DEAF CULTURE

The Deaf community is separated from the hearing population for a very good reason. During the 1977 National Symposium on Sign Language Research and Teaching, Barbara Kannapell disclosed a justification of why Deaf people show their hesitation in using American Sign Language with hearing people:

It is important to understand that American Sign Language is the only thing we have that belongs to Deaf people completely. It is the only thing that has grown out of the Deaf group. Maybe we are afraid to share our language with hearing people. Maybe our group identity will disappear once hearing people know ASL. Also, will hearing people dominate Deaf people more than before if they learn ASL?" (Kannapell quoted in Baker & Cokely, 1986, p. 59)

To expand on Kannapell's statement, history indicates that ASL was almost wiped out by oralism. Most older Deaf people experienced the oppression from oralism; therefore, they became conservative in using ASL because of their fear of ASL being taken away by hearing people.

Before introducing Deaf culture into the communication field, there are some guidelines for communication scholars to follow to become familiar with the Deaf before working with them. Having intensive linguistic knowledge in American Sign Language is critical in the process of studying Deaf culture. Dell Hymes's assertion verifies this point. He states that language is the basic structure to a science of "man" because it provides a link between the biological and sociocultural levels (Hymes, 1968, p. 99). Furthermore, Hymes asserts that: a general theory of the interaction of language and social life must encompass the multiple relations between linguistic means and social meaning (p. 39). Therefore, the first requirement is to have interested communication scholars establish their competency to communicate on an advanced level with American Sign Language.

Language is a social institution. In her article Joyce Hertzler states:

Language as a social system ...is a constructed, even though not planned, human institution. It is learned by the members of the community, firmly established in their communicative behavior, and involved in most of their other social behavior. (Hertzler, 1965, p. 73)

Communication scholars, not only need the ability to communicate, but also they need to learn and acknowledge the cultural practices (identity, values, and traditions) of Deaf culture, which becomes the second guideline to get familiarized with Deaf culture.

American Sign Language is accepted as a research tool to study and expand many disciplines to provide in-depth knowledge of Deaf culture. This provides an opportunity for many Deaf people to study and advance their academic degree. The strongly recommended third guideline is to have communication scholars work with Deaf scholars since they have intensive primary knowledge, and they are more "accessible" to work with. In addition, recognition is long overdue in acknowledging the Deaf scholars and their interested works.

Moreover, an important factor involved in working with Deaf scholars is that the hearing scholars must foster the cultural view and respect Deaf culture. Deaf culture has been oppressed for a long time, therefore it becomes a sheltered community with the "Berlin Wall" dividing the hearing and Deaf worlds. To hammer out an ounce of the wall requires an equal amount of respect interchangabely, which becomes the fourth guideline in working with the Deaf community. In return, Deaf people, in a strict sense, are more likely willing to open the door and work with hearing people.

The suggested four guidelines are offered in the hope of having the Deaf community recognized as a true individual culture. To be involved in and work with Deaf culture is demanding and challenging. However, the reward is incredible because it will bring the best out of these two cultures—hearing and Deaf

SUMMARY

In sum, history already indicates that American Sign Language plays an important role in developing Deaf culture. Unfortunately it still continues to be either denied or oppressed by hearing people based on the misconceptions and attitudes. The concept of pluralism was introduced by different definitions which promotes a sense of "cumulative" point where American Sign Language and Deaf culture fit into. Therefore, to study Deaf culture, one must understand its culture thoroughly and follows the guidelines in order to show respect and work with Deaf people.

DISCUSSION QUESTIONS

1. Explain the different perspectives of pluralism.
2. Do the descriptions of pluralism fit an alternative perspective when theorizing about Deaf culture to become a part of communication discipline?
3. How does the concept involved in pluralism aid in the constructing of the communication field?
4. How does Deaf culture play its role of being pluralistic in the communication field?
5. Describe how Deaf culture became an appropriate category that fits to the conception of pluralism.

REFERENCES

Baker, C. & Cokely, D. (1986). *American sign language*. Silver Spring: TJ Publishers, Inc.

Cronen, V. E., Pearce, W. B., & Harris, L. M. (1982). The coordinated management of meaning: A theory of communication. *Human Condition Theory*, 61-89.

Daniels, H. (1985). Nine ideas about language. In V. Clark, P. Eschholz, & A. Rosa (Eds.) *Language: Fourth edition*. (pp. 18-36). New York: St. Martin's Press.

Gannon, J. (1981). *Deaf heritage: A narrative history of deafamerica*. Silver Spring: National Association of the Deaf.

Gannon, J. (1989). *The week the world heard Gallaudet.* Washington D.C.: Gallaudet University Press.

Garver, E. (1985). Why pluralism now? *InternationalPhilosophical Quarterly, 25,* 388-410.

Groce, N. (1985). *Everyone here spoke sign language.* Cambridge: Harvard University Press.

Hertzler, J. (Ed.)(1965). *Language as a social institution. A sociology of language* (pp. 71-97). New York: Random House, Inc.

Hymes, D. (1968). The ethnography of speaking. In J. Fishman, (Ed.) *Readings in the sociology of language* (pp. 99-137). Paris: Mouton & Company Publishers.

Hymes, D. (1972). The model of the interactions of language and social life. In D. Hymes (Ed.) *Directions in sociolinguistics: The ethnography of communication*(pp. 35-65). New York: Holt & Rinehart & Winston, Inc.

Kannapell, B. (1991). *The relationship of deaf studies and deaf identity.* Paper presented at the meeting of the Deaf Studies for Educators Conference, Dallas, TX.

Moore, M. & Levitan, L. (1993). *For hearing people only: second edition.* Rochester: Deaf Life Press.

Padden, C. & Humphries, T. (1988). *Deaf in America: voice from a culture.* Cambridge: Harvard University Press.

Reck, A. J. (1985). An historical sketch of pluralism. *International Philosophical Quarterly, 25,* 367-387.

Van Cleve, J. & Crouch, B. (1989). *A place of their own: Creating the deaf community in America.* Washington DC: Gallaudet University Press.

Watson, W. (1985). Types of Pluralism. *International Philosophical Quarterly, 25,* 350-366.

White, H. (1986). Historical Pluralism. *Critical Inquiry, 12,* 480-493.

Williams, J. (1883). *All About deaf-mutes.* Ann Arbor, MI: University Microfilms.

32

WHY MINORITIES AREN'T CHOOSING NURSING CAREERS: COMMUNICATION, RECRUITMENT, AND MINORITY UNDERREPRESENTATION IN NURSING

Mary Henderson Askew
Meheas Continuing Education Consultants

INTRODUCTION

Ethnoracial minorities have always been underrepresented in professional nursing. Despite legal and social initiatives, open employment, and high starting salaries, numbers remain low. Research on non-choice of nursing careers has been limited, with subjects typically being nurses or nursing students rather than those who have made other choices, and samples either have not included persons of color or been limited to blacks. Thus the profession's ideas about why minorities have often not found nursing an attractive career choice lacked authority. These flaws, coupled with nursing's failure to recruit in a culturally mindful way may have contributed significantly to the problem.

Persons of color are underrepresented in professional nursing when compared with their presence in the population. Their failing to choose nursing careers in greater numbers contributes significantly to that deficiency and impedes fulfillment of nursing's avowed commitment to increase its ethnic diversity. This study was done to learn more about why persons of color may not see nursing as an attractive career option.

My interest in this project grew out of a broader interest in culture and how it influences the decisions people make, and in ways to enhance provision of culturally sensitive and appropriate patient care. I wondered why nursing schools in localities with rich cultural diversity were having difficulty recruiting persons of color, especially in the face of a seemingly insatiable demand for nurses, of a slowing economy—which should have made nursing's typically ready employment and excellent entry salaries especially attractive, and of schools' efforts to remove various academic and financial barriers to their entry. I wondered about cultural influences on such choices and the role of such influences on nursing's minority recruitment difficulties.

LITERATURE REVIEW

Apart from factors inhibiting college entry in the first place, and acceptance into nursing programs in the second, something to do with the career choice process itself seemed the most likely place to look for explanations. I knew of several groups for which religious or cultural prohibitions might be deterring factors but thought the largest contributor would probably be what people knew or believed about nursing.

Several career choice theories confirm that the information and perceptions people have about occupations play important roles in determining what they eventually select (e.g., Ginzberg, 1984; Gottfredson, 1981; Mitchell & Krumboltz, 1990; Super, 1990). However, research on non-choice of nursing among persons of color was scarce, mostly outdated, and/or flawed in one way or another. The older studies often failed even to include persons of color, particularly other that black, and many contemporary researchers failed to describe the ethnic makeup of samples or to examine variables in an ethnic context. Moreover, researchers interested in the "Why not nursing?" question typically looked among "choosers" (the name I adopted for those already having chosen nursing careers) for clues to its lack of appeal as a career choice.

Variables thought to influence people to choose careers in nursing have been deduced from nurses' and nursing students' personality profiles and reported motives for entering the field. Those thought to influence *non-choice* have been extrapolated from those same data and from reasons choosers gave for changing their minds. These variables had not been validated among non-choosers, and especially not among persons of color. Only one study was found which was focused primarily on the minority underrepresentation problem in nursing, which included persons of color other than black, and in which those not interested in nursing were actually asked why they had rejected it. This study was a 1976 survey of high school students' attitudes about nursing as a profession, carried out for the Division of Nursing of the U.S. Public Health Service by Rudov, Wilson, and Trocki (1976). In short, researchers have not been sufficiently interested in the topic; more important, most have been asking the wrong questions of the wrong population.

If people of varied cultural backgrounds differ in what they know and believe about nursing, and these differences could be identified, it should be possible to overcome some of the barriers to their choosing nursing careers by designing recruitment strategies and materials—that is, telling the nursing story—in a more effective and culturally sensitive way. Since 90 percent of U.S. nurses are white non-Hispanics (U.S. Bureau of Health Professions/Moses, 1994), recruitment of persons from other ethnic groups is, almost by definition, an enterprise in intercultural communication.

THE STUDY

Target Population and Research Questions

Although data on whites and men are included for purposes of comparison, this study focuses on ethnic women of color. Because nursing is still considered by many to be a women's profession, and women still constitute the overwhelming majority in the field, I chose to exclude issues related to men's choice of nursing. Because the majority of nurses is white, I chose to look for differences in choice factors among other ethnic groups. In order to avoid feasibility issues for college-going and accessibility of nursing schools, I chose to survey undergraduates in institutions having nursing programs. Two of the study's research questions were: "What influences undergraduate women of color against choosing nursing careers?" and "Do the influences differ on the basis of ethnicity?"

Questionnaire

Although there are a number of career choice theories and models, there is no definitive set of variables shown to influence the selection process, especially not for minority groups. Moreover, career choice researchers have not been particularly concerned with nursing. A 74-item questionnaire (Askew, 1994) was therefore developed around variables emerging from several areas of research. The 48 career choice items were grouped into areas impacting selection processes: academic background and feasibility concerns; occupational information and perceptions; occupation-related experiences; and issues around gender, ethnicity, discrimination, image/status, and salaries. Most items were presented as statements about an aspect of nursing with the students being asked to indicate on a five-point scale from None to Very Strong the level of each item's influence against choosing nursing. Each content area ended with an invitation to write in any other comments.

Reliability and Response Rate

Cronbach's alpha reliability for the instrument was .90; and for all but one of its scales, .74 or higher. Principle components factor analysis confirmed the a priori organization of statements into content groups. Eleven factors accounted for 63.3 percent of the variance.

Response rates were quite good: 77 percent (848) of the 1096 instruments shipped were returned; 82 percent (694) of these had at least one answer to a career choice item, although actually all but 31 were 85 percent or more complete, that is, having no more than 7 of 48 the career choice items unanswered.

Settings and Sample

Six schools participated in the study: Robeson Community College and Pembroke State University in North Carolina; Florida International University in Miami; University of New Mexico at Gallup; City College of New York; and the University of Virginia. All schools except PSU and UVA have minority enrollments of 55 percent or more.

Non-choosers (425 women, 218 men) made up 93 percent of the total sample; of those, 65 percent were persons of color. Ethnicity was self-identified except that black non-Hispanics were subdivided into American and non-American groups based on background information they provided about birth country, native language, and where they completed high school. Women nonchoosers included 134 white non-Hispanics (32 percent), 99 Hispanics (23 percent), 96 Native Americans (23 percent), 61 American blacks (14 percent), 16 non-American blacks (.04 percent), and 13 Asians (.03 percent). Women of color made up 44 percent of all non-choosers and 62 percent of non-chooser women. Non-chooser men included 78 white non-Hispanics, 42 Hispanics, 51 Native Americans, 26 American blacks, 10 Asians, and 9 non-American blacks.

The typical non-chooser woman of color was a middle- to upper-middle-class 24-year-old social sciences or business major with a B-minus high school average. She had a 44 percent chance of lacking a nurse among close family or friends and a 5 percent chance of having been specifically advised against a nursing career by someone, often a nurse, among those friends and relations.

Methodology

In order to determine what influenced these students against choosing nursing careers, a Negative Influence Score (NIS) was derived from the ratio of the number of students answering the question to the number who reported being influenced by that variable (regardless to what degree); variables were then ranked on that score. To identify influences about which students felt strongest, the variables were also ranked on the mean of the Likert values of the responses. Leading deterrents and response patterns for women of color as a whole, white women, men of color, and white men were identified and compared; then women's ethnic groups were compared with each other. Statistical procedures used to determine whether women of color differed significantly on the basis of ethnicity about what influenced them against nursing careers were: (a) Kruskal-Wallis Analysis of Variance by Ranks (KW) to test whether differences in responses among the groups were statistically significant; (b) Tukey's HSD post hoc procedure to identify the significantly different pairs of groups; and (c) multiple discriminant analysis (MDA) to test whether responses could be used to classify participants by ethnic group. Finally, content analysis was carried out on the "Anything else?" items in order to obtain a more subjective picture of the influences and to identify any concerns not covered in the structured part of the questionnaire.

RESULTS

Results are described in terms of the major influences against choosing nursing careers and the differences between groups. Write-in responses relating to ethnic minority groups, the nursing profession, and to nurses themselves are also described.

Influences Against Choosing Nursing

Rank-ordering of NIS scores showed that, regardless of gender or ethnic group, students were most frequently—and most strongly—dissuaded from choosing nursing, not surprisingly, by aspects of illness-oriented, hospital-based practice. Next in order were concerns about image/status and salaries and about getting adequate financial and social return on educational investments. In general, there was a squeamishness about sickness and injury and an aversion to the degree of intimacy and responsibility required in caring for patients coupled with "blue-collar" and "women's work" views of nursing, its perceived low status, and a servant (rather than service) occupational image. In addition, students underestimated nurses' average salaries by about $5000 a year; and on a ten-position list of occupations requiring baccalaureate degrees that had been ranked on the basis of salary one year after graduation, they placed nursing at the bottom, below education, instead of in its actual second-place position, below engineering (U.S. Bureau of Health Professions, 1990).

Students' negative experiences with nurses and concerns about academic discrimination (fairness of financial aid awards, admissions, and grading policies) were generally more influential than work-place prejudice issues (ethnic or gender imbalance in the profession and reservations about caring for, working with, supervising or being supervised by persons not of one's own gender or ethnic group). While beliefs in the existence of both academic and work-place discrimination were fairly widespread, gender-based work-place prejudices were typically more influential than the same items cast in ethnic terms. About 30 percent of the women reported believing they lacked appropriate academic preparation for a nursing program and about 35 percent thought they lacked the math/science abilities they would need in the program or in practice.

The top few influences against choosing nursing are especially important. Consequences to patients of making mistakes, dealing with body fluids, and bathing/feeding were in first or second place for all groups. In the next three places were risk of infection, being around people sick and in pain, the idea that nurses and their work are not appreciated, or the perception that nurses' salaries fail to compensate for required education. These rankings are in line with conventional wisdom about why nursing is rejected as a career choice and they represent a core of resistance with which recruiters must deal, regardless of audience or medium. However, as NIS scores decreased, the groups diverged from one another and subtle patterns emerged which provide useful insights for designing recruiting materials to address concerns of specific groups. For example, among Asian women, the prospect of shift work placed fourth with the remaining five of the top eleven deterrents involving aspects of nursing's occupational image, that is, the perceptions that nursing requires hard physical work, that salaries fail to compensate for required education, that nurses' pay is low compared with other options, that nurses are seen as servants, and that uniforms are required for some jobs. Being able to refute such inaccuracies might persuade these women to take a second look at nursing. For the other women's groups, the idea that nurses and their work are not appreciated was more important than image issues, ranking third for non-American blacks and between fifth and eighth for the others. The idea that nurses have little opportunity to think for themselves ranked tenth for Hispanics, influencing 59 percent, but ranking only twenty-second for Asians (31 percent) and fourteenth and sixteenth for the others. Describing the expanded roles and responsibilities now existing for nurses in many contemporary practice settings might dispel some of their misgivings on this point.

Differences on Influences Among Groups

The KW results showed that excluding men and white women from analysis essentially removed the chief sources of variability in the responses. Post hoc analysis confirmed this: 42 pairs of groups differed significantly from one another on one or more items but only 10 of those pairs were between ethnic minority groups. Items about which women of color differed most among themselves were salary information and concerns about return on educational investment, autonomy, appreciation, risk to personal image from being in an occupation perceived as having low status, ethnic imbalance, bathing/feeding, and wearing uniforms. Hispanics were the group with which the others differed most often and differences between Hispanics and blacks and Native Americans were most pronounced.

The MDA classified only 52 percent of women to the correct ethnic group. Perhaps there were not enough differences among the groups' responses to discriminate among them on that basis or perhaps the instrument was not powerful enough to detect differences that did exist. Of the twelve items which did differentiate the groups (that is, loading at .40 or higher), seven were related to gender/ethnic prejudice (gender/ethnic imbalance in the profession, lack of willingness to care for, work with, and/or supervise/be supervised by persons not of one's gender or ethnic group); two involved non-patient-care aspects of nursing (working with complicated equipment and the prospect of hard physical work); and three involved salary/image issues (salaries not compensating for education, nurses not being appreciated, and nurses being seen as occupying a servant role).

Write-in Responses

Students' answers on the "Is there anything else?" items were generally in expected directions, given current unfortunate stereotypes about nursing and those which members of all ethnic groups have about each other. These comments supported results from the questionnaire's structured section as well as arguments in the literature that career choices are often made on insufficient and/or inaccurate information and on an emotional rather than a rational level, especially when threats to self-image, psychological comfort, and social mobility goals are involved.

The following are examples of comments which demonstrate some of the sources of nursing's recruitment difficulties in general—and in recruiting persons of color in particular—and with which the profession must deal if concerns about nursing as a career choice are to be addressed and nursing's story is to be communicated more effectively.

About ethnic minority groups

Stereotypes about members of ethnic minority groups were evident from cliché responses given by some students of all ethnic groups and both genders as they explained their own decisions not to enter nursing and speculated about those of others. Some students, both white and of color, perceived members of ethnic minority groups as: (a) not well enough prepared academically because of poor-quality education available to them and of high drop-out rates; (b) often coming from homes with fewer advantages and opportunities; (c) less motivated to achieve academically or to attempt difficult programs; (d) lacking role models for professional nursing careers so that young people are not encouraged to believe that nursing is an attainable goal or a career in which they could succeed; (e) desiring upward mobility therefore not considering occupations seen as having low status or as not providing sufficient financial reward or prospects for advancement which, coupled with other stereotypes about nursing, places it outside the zone of acceptable options relative to that goal; (f) not wanting to work in a white-dominated occupation and/or one in which ethnic discrimination is perceived to exist.

About nursing

Other inaccuracies in students' information surfaced as stereotypes about the profession: (a) Nursing education takes longer and costs more than other post-high school options such as commerce or engineering. (b) Length, difficulty, and cost of nursing programs are similar to those for medical education as evidenced by such comments as "for all that time, effort, and expense, I'd rather be a doctor." (c) Nursing is a "take orders" position and nurses are similar to maids or secretaries therefore nursing is not suitable for members of upper social classes and/or not a viable means of achieving social mobility. (d) Nursing work consists chiefly of "routine" and "cleaning" jobs or, conversely, working with the dreadfully sick and injured and is equated with hospitals, shift work, and uniforms and with lack of professional autonomy or practice independence.

About nurses

A clear message was expressed that nurses themselves often contribute to influencing people against careers in the field. In addition to reporting specific advice they received from nurses against choosing nursing careers, students commented negatively about nurses' personalities; about their expressed or acted-out dissatisfactions with the profession, their jobs, and their lives; and about their behaving in uncaring, unkind, and unprofessional ways toward patients. One man said "I don't remember a nurse that I ever dealt with that I really liked." Others described nurses who had cared for them or with whom they had come in contact as "very hateful," "very unfriendly," "uncaring and stupid," "lazy, cold, and indifferent," "callous," "very mean," "nasty and obnoxious" and as "low class, stupid bimbos," to quote a few. Some nurses were seen as "not paying attention to their jobs," as "having an attitude problem," and as "giving a bad image" of nurses or a negative impression of the profession. Some students commented specifically about problematic intercultural communication and attitude problems. Although only 20 students (3 percent) commented in these highly negative ways about their contacts with nurses, the power of the attitudes of a few to influence a great many others against nursing and nurses must not be ignored. This is a communications problem of giant proportions.

Summary of Results

First, most of the statistically significant differences in responses were between women and men and/or between persons of color and whites. Perceptions and concerns of women of color actually differed significantly from those of white women on almost half the variables. Second, women of color were, more often than not, in agreement with each other about what influenced them against careers in nursing, regardless of the ethnic group to which they belonged. Even so, there were some differences which should not be ignored. Both structured and unstructured responses generally confirmed that many non-choosers simply do not find nursing work appealing but also that many continue to reject nursing careers based on incomplete or inaccurate information and outmoded stereotypes about the profession and its practitioners. In addition, personal prejudices and beliefs about the existence of discrimination in nursing education and practice may be playing a more significant role in the rejection of nursing than is typically acknowledged or even recognized.

Many variables obviously exert influences that transcend ethnic differences. Although the number of variables differing significantly on the basis of ethnicity among women of color was small, that the differences exist at all argues against recruiting members of ethnic minorities as though they were a single, homogeneous group.

The study's results support the need to know more about how cultural elements influence career choice in nursing, including how various groups perceive current recruitment activities and career-related media; they also support the need to interpret career choice influences in an ethnocultural context, regardless of the group being approached, and the need to take groups' concerns, communication styles, and cultural traditions into account when planning and carrying out recruitment activities.

RECOMMENDATIONS FOR FURTHER RESEARCH

First, better use needs to be made of career choice and development theories as a resource in examining nurses' occupational behaviors. Second, study samples should include specific ethnic groups and subgroups—especially the smaller ones—and be more diverse in terms of geographic region, age, socioeconomic and educational levels, and career stage. Third, studies should be conducted in a context of cultural sensitivity, especially acknowledging and valuing researchers' and respondants' differences in background, perspectives, and goals. Fourth, qualitative approaches should be used to determine what other questions need to be asked and to probe areas not readily accessed by survey methods, for example, the influence of first-hand contacts with nurses, concerns about image, and discrimination issues. Fifth, designs should include analysis of interactions among the many variables, especially ethnicity and other background characteristics—such as socioeconomic status, academic performance, the presence or absence of nurse role models, and the nature of career advice received—and their influence on choosing or not choosing nursing as a career.

SUMMARY

Results of this study have confirmed that influences on the career choice process are complex and have validated the role of a number of variables previously only assumed to affect non-choice of nursing. They have also highlighted the need to understand more fully how the rich influences arising from ethnocultural background combine with other aspects of personality and environment to influence career choice and how nurses can more effectively communicate an accurate picture of the profession to others.

The American Academy of Nursing's Expert Panel on Culturally Competent Nursing Care (1992, pp. 227-278) has said, "No rationale is needed for planning and implementing culturally sensitive and competent care" but standing in the way are underrepresentation of persons of color among health care professionals and limited knowledge about beliefs, values, experiences, and health care needs of some client populations. Recruiters need to gain a fuller understanding of cultural influences on choice and other career behaviors and use it when marketing nursing, especially if the goal of increasing ethnic diversity in the profession is to be realized. Finally, outworn stereotypes about nursing must be counteracted by effective communication of accurate and up-to-date information, especially in recruiting materials and presentations, and by correction of nurses' behaviors which harm both the profession and its clients and which create the destructive stereotypes that influence the public from which new nurses must come.

DISCUSSION QUESTIONS

1. In what ways do inaccurate stereotypes and other forms of misinformation and/or miscommunication influence the perceptions people form about various career options?
2. How might an individual's cultural background influence his or her choice of a career?
3. In addition to the survey approach used in this study, what other approaches might a researcher use to investigate the reasons behind a specific group's lack of interest in a particular career?

4. Discuss positive and negative ways in which a recruiter's cultural background might influence design of recruitment materials and activities.
5. How might intercultural communication techniques and skills be used to improve career recruitment?

REFERENCES

American Academy of Nursing Expert Panel on Culturally Competent Nursing Care (1992). Culturally competent health care. *Nursing Outlook, 40,* 277-283.

Askew, M. H. (1994). *Influences on nonchoice of nursing careers by women of color.* Doctoral dissertation, University of Virginia. Available through University Microfilms International (Dissertation Services) (300 N Zeeb Rd) Ann Arbor (Michigan 48106).

Ginzberg, E. (1984). Career Development. In D. Brown & L. Brooks (Eds.). *Career choice and development: Applying contemporary theories to practice* (2nd ed., pp. 169-191). San Francisco: Jossey-Bass.

Gottfredson, L. S. (1981). Circumscription and compromise: A developmental theory of occupational aspirations. *Journal of Vocational Behavior, 28,* 545-579.

Mitchell, L. K. & Krumboltz, J. D. (1990). Social learning approach to career decision making: Krumboltz' theory. In D. Brown & L. Brooks (Eds.), *Career choice and development: Applying contemporary theories to practice* (2nd ed., pp. 146-196). San Francisco: Jossey-Bass.

Rudov, M. H., Wilson, M. T., & Trocki, K. F. (1976). *High school seniors' attitudes and concepts of nursing as a profession.* Bethesda, MD: DHEW/PHS/HRA/Division of Nursing (DHEW Pub No (Hra) 76-35).

Super, D. E. (1990). A life-space approach to career development. In D. Brown & L. Brooks (Eds.), *Career choice and development* (2nd ed., pp. 176-261). San Francisco: Jossey-Bass.

United States Bureau of Health Professions (1990). *Seventh report to the President and Congress on the status of health personnel in the United States.* Washington, DC: DHHS/PHS/Health Resources and Services Administration.

United States Bureau of Health Professions, Division of Nursing/Moses. (1994). *The registered nurse population 1992: Findings from the National Sample Survey of Registered Nurses, March 1992.* Washington, DC: DHHS/PHS/Health Resources and Services Administration

EPILOGUE
CIVIC DISCOURSE:
MULTICULTURALISM,
CULTURAL DIVERSITY, AND
THE SHARING OF POWER
IN THE GLOBAL SOCIETY

Michael H. Prosser
Rochester Institute of Technology

Culture and communication have always been linked in the most basic manner possible. It is impossible for us to have one without the other. In human history, very few persons have been considered to be without culture. Culture is always communicated, both to those who are part of the culture, and to the outside world. Neither culture nor communication remain static. While many historical societies have simply called themselves a term related to "the people," when they face outsiders, they have been forced to communicate interculturally. Such communication has often been painful, filled with misunderstandings, and even dangerous.

Ancient societies, depending upon their own cultural attitudes, beliefs, and values, communicated intraculturally and interculturally in very different ways. Contemporary stages of individualistic versus collective societies began to surface early in recorded history. Different cultural logics, and thus different cultural rhetorics, developed in the preChristian Egyptian, Greek, and Roman societies versus those in ancient Eastern societies such as China and India. K.S. Sitaram has identified several of these culturally different logics and rhetorics in the introduction to this book. In ancient Western cultures, the civic discourse of the period called for promoting the speaker's own welfare or that of the audience, with an argumentative, overtly persuasive, highly logical, intensely personal, and individualistic emphasis. This early Western stress on individuality finds its current application in North America and several Western European countries as perhaps their chief cultural value. In contrast, the ancient Eastern traditions prescribed a depersonalized communication event, in which the audience was assured that nothing in the message was original, but developed from a higher authority, or intuitively, and with the intention to create a harmonious, face saving, reciprocal, and dual responsibility of speaker and audience. Varied oral-aural cultures today, including not only Asian but also African and Middle Eastern cultures, have communicative patterns that are far more similar to ancient Eastern societies than either ancient or modern Western societies.

It is not surprising that much of the initiative in current studies of the linkages between communication and culture have developed either among Western communication scholars, and often initially by rhetorical theorists and critics, or among Western anthropologists. Until the last two or three decades, even when studying other cultures, Western communication scholars generated their theories and their rhetorical critiques almost entirely from Western models. In a similar way, the early social change and national development models were Western in their orientation. By the nature of their field, anthropologists had an intense interest in studying specific cultures—often exotic in nature to the Western mind—and in cross cultural comparisons and contrasts, but frequently without factoring communicative components into their theories and analyses. More recently, several anthropologists have seen communication as central to a clear understanding of culture and have recognized that there is a marked difference between the cultural logics and cultural rhetorics of one society versus that of another society, particularly when a culture is either highly individualistic or highly collective in nature.

With the ever increasing development of global villages and global cities throughout the world, it is inherent that more and more intercultural communication will occur across cultural, societal, and national boundaries. Certain societies are extremely homogenous, resulting in very difficult intercultural communication. Others have a great deal of cultural diversity. This diversity does not guarantee that intercultural communication will be easier for its members. Each culture, however, and indeed individual members of each culture, may be very open to new cultural experiences and communication, or very closed to such contacts. The goal of those who believe that cultural diversity has both positive and negative features is to support these positive attributes for each culture, without losing his or her own positive cultural attitudes, beliefs, and values. There is often a backlash against such a view with charges from both the right and left that political correctness demands one perspective against another. It is also not of course useful to argue that one should respect cultural diversity for its own sake, without evaluating its positive or negative thrust. Violations of human rights, for example, in any place, time, or culture are not simply a recognition of cultural diversity, but are genuinely anti-cultural.

Certain individuals in every society seek to remain absolutely monocultural and culturally static. The exponential spread of technology, particularly in a communicative sense, makes it increasingly difficult to remain isolated, and thus unlikely or unnecessary to avoid intercultural communication or contamination as such individuals might wish. Such individuals might not like members of other cultures, but in their neighborhoods, student and work situations, shopping, and even limited travel, it is prudent and reasonable to understand that cultural diversity is more and more the norm. If such intercultural contacts are to have any positive results, tolerance of cultural differences, even if not empathy, is a fundamental principle of life.

Some individuals grow up in multicultural settings; others move into such settings, often against their will, such as the millions of refugees displaced from their own cultures because of natural disasters, harassment, strife, or war. Some actively seek to become multicultural individuals. It is easier to move from being monocultural to bicultural, but essentially it is a modern and rather rare phenomenon to be fully multicultural. Like intercultural communicators and culturally diverse individuals, becoming a multicultural person may have both positive or negative aspects. Being multicultural may mean from a negative perspective that one is culturally schizophrenic, in a state of creative tension, and neither clearly in the boundary of his or her own culture, nor fully a member of other cultures, but always on the boundaries of cultures.

It has been approximately twenty five years since Peter Adler was among the early contemporary writers on the nature of the multicultural person. His perspective remains useful with his statement: that such an individual "approaches, in the attributions we make about him (her), the classical ideal of a person whose lifestyle is one of knowledge and wisdom, integrity and direction, principle and fulfillment." He argues that multicultural persons are those who are transitional, standing between the old and the new, with three distinguishing features: psychoculturally adaptive and thus situational in their relationships to others and with their connections to culture; always undergoing personal transitions, grounded in their own cultures and always in a state of "becoming" or "unbecoming" a part of new cultures; and maintaining indefinite self-boundaries with tolerance for different cultural forms, responsiveness to change, and with identities that are neither fixed nor predictable. (Adler, 1974, pp. 23-40)

More recently, we have come to understand that if we are to live productively in multicultural societies—especially as members of the global society—and thus as global communicators, we must move beyond the negative aspects of crossing cultural boundaries, where authentic power is shared unequally. Power in the most negative sense, when combined with prejudice, leads to such negative "isms" as racism, ethnocentrism, sexism, and ageism, and on a more international scale, colonialism, fascism, and imperialism. On the other hand, power in the best multicultural and culturally diverse sense in the global setting is shared power. We should neither subject others nor be subject to anti-cultural tendencies which stem from the violation of human rights. All people, in all places, and in all times are entitled to the protection of their basic human rights. Sharing power is of course antithetical to many societies, and in many hierarchical organizational settings. As the truly multicultural individuals are rare, transitional, and living on boundaries between the old and the new, between their own cultures and others, and responsive to change, so too are individuals who commit themselves to eliminating or sharply reducing their own potential for prejudice, sharing power with others who have been excluded from power or who have much less power, and becoming fully integrated into the global society.

Kwame Anthony Appiah and Henry Louis Gates, Jr. note in their coedited *The Dictionary of Global Culture:*

> In the year 2,000, half the world's people will be Asian, one-eighth African, and a majority non-Christian. Of the world's twenty largest cities, none will be in Europe or the United States. We are entering a truly global society and can no longer afford to be limited to an understanding of culture that begins and ends in the West.... In the vast process of development of the modern global system, cultures and traditions have mixed and melded to produce in many places—but perhaps above all in the old centers of power, in the United States and Western Europe—new kinds of culture that draw on traditions from all over the planet.... [Both high and low culture] draw on contributions that are an inextricable mixture of elements from Europe, Africa, America, and Asia, and draw also on an endless stream of new ideas.... What we are suggesting, in effect, is that we all participate, albeit from different cultural positions, in a global system of culture. That culture is increasingly less dominated by the West, less Eurocentric, if you like. (Appiah & Gates, 1997, back cover and p. xi)

K.S. Sitaram and I hope that the chapters in *Civic Discourse: Multiculturalism, Cultural Diversity, and Global Communication*, written as they have been by academics both from diverse cultures and disciplines, and from various perspectives related to the title of the book, have increased your interest in the topics of multiculturalism, cultural diversity, and global communication. Additionally, we hope that they have guided you in your own potential movement from monocultural individuals,to multicultural and cultural diverse, and indeed to global communicators.

Paulo Friere's perspective offers a useful goal for all of us: "To be human; fully human and aware, fully human, aware, and alive; to be fully human, aware, alive, and creative; to be fully human, aware, alive, creative, and free." Our goal, thus, is to develop and enhance our abilities to live increasingly multicultural, culturally diverse, and global lives rooted in the creative tension of a new millennium.

REFERENCES:

Adler, P. S. 1974. Beyond cultural identity: Reflections on cultural and multicultural man. In *Topics in Learning*.

Appiah, K. W. & Gates, H. L. Jr. (Eds.). 1997. *The dictionary of global culture*. NY: Quality Paperback Book Club, Knopf.

AUTHOR INDEX

SUBJECT INDEX

ABOUT THE
CONTRIBUTORS

Albert, R. D.
Rosita D. Albert is an Associate Professor in the Department of Speech-Communication at the University of Minnesota, where she leads the pioneering intercultural communication program. A Latina, she does research and consulting on diversity and on intercultural training for multicultural organizations.

Askew, M. H.
Mary Henderson Askew, Ph.D, RN; Maheas Education Consultants, received her PhD from the University of Virginia; her MPH, from the University of North Carolina-Chapel Hill; and her BA, Duke University. She was a member of the U.S. Public Health Service Commissioned Corps, assigned to the Indian Health Service and the Immigration and Naturalization Service.

Asuncion-Lande, N.
Nobleza Asuncion-Lande (Ph.D., Michigan State University), Professor in the Communication Studies Department at the University of Kansas, was an early founder in the field of intercultural communication. She has served as a Fulbright Professor in Singapore and the United Kingdom. Her chapter, "English for Intercultural Communication: Prospects for the Next Century," served as the Keynote Address at the 1996 RIT Conference.

Bing, J. W.
John W. Bing, Ed.D. is President of ITAP International, Inc. John Bing has consulted to companies, the UN, and the American Management Association. He received the International Practitioner of the Year Award from the American Society for Training and Development. His degrees are from Harvard (BA) and the University of Massachusetts (Ed.D.).

Brooks, K.
Kathy Brooks received her B.A. in Modern Languages and Linguistics from the University of Maryland, her Masters from Morgan State University, and her

Ph.D. at The Pennsylvania State University where her concentration was organizational and intercultural communication. She teaches at Shippensburg University. Her chapter, "The Black Professional: An Analysis of the Role of Cross-Race Mentoring," was the Outstanding Student Paper (in absentia) at the 1995 RIT Conference.

Buttny, R.

Richard Buttny is an Associate Professor of Speech Communication at Syracuse University. He has published *Social Accountability in Communication* (Sage, 1993) as well as a number of journal articles. His primary research interests are in conversation analysis and discursive analysis.

Campbell, C.

Cindy Campbell received her Master's degree from the Department of Speech Communication at Syracuse University.

Day, K. D.

Kenneth D. Day is an Associate Professor and Chair in the Department of Communication at the University of the Pacific. His scholarly work includes consideration of ethics for intercultural communication, pragmatics of languages, and the relation of mass media to culture. His chapter, "The Problem of Ethics in Intercultural Communication," was an award winning paper at the 1995 RIT Conference.

Donahue, R. T.

Ray T. Donahue (Ph.D, University of Virginia), Professor of Intercultural Communication in Foreign Studies and Japanese Studies at Nagoya Gakuin University (Japan), has also taught at universities in the United States and China. He has authored *Japanese Non-Linear Discourse Style* (Applied Linguistics Research, 1990), co-authored *Diplomatic Discourse* (with Michael H. Prosser, Ablex, 1997), and authored various articles on discourse analysis and cross-cultural topics.

Ekachai, D.

Daradirek Ekachai, Ph.D., is Assistant Professor of Speech Communication at Southern Illinois University at Carbondale. Her recent research is focused on intercultural communication and public relations. She has published work related to international public relations, mass communications, and intercultural communication.

Ellingsworth, H. W.

Huber Winton Ellingsworth (B.A. Pacific University, 1949; M.A. Washington State University, 1950; Ph.D Florida State University, 1955) is Professor of Communication at the University of Tulsa. Much of his career has been devoted to communication, change and international development. His field experience includes agriculture and family planning projects in Latin America and Southeast Asia.

Friend, R.
Rachel Friend received her Master's degree from the Department of Speech Communication at Syracuse University.

Gehani, R. R.
R. Ray Gehani earned a doctorate in Polymer Engineering from Tokyo University and a Ph.D. in strategic management of technology driven organizations from New York University. He has taught business policy, total quality management, and productions operations in New York City and the Rochester Institute of Technology. He teaches international business and management of technology and operations at the University of Akron.

Greer, N. S.
Norman S. Greer, Ph.D., is Associate Professor of Speech Communication at Eastern Illinois University, Charleston, Illinois. His teaching and research interests include the areas of intercultural communication, business and professional communication, persuasion, and at-risk students. His publications include monographs focused on business communication.

Heisey, D. R.
D. Ray Heisey, Professor and Director Emeritus of the School of Communication at Kent State University, has been involved in intercultural/international communication teaching and research for thirty years. He has taught for varying periods of time in Belgium, Iran where he also served as President of Damavand College, Sweden, Estonia, and most recently at Peking University in Beijing, China. Heisey presented an Award Winning Paper at the 1996 RIT Conference.

Hinchcliff-Pelias, M.
Mary Hinchcliff-Pelias, Ph.D., is Associate Professor of Speech Communication at Southern Illinois University at Carbondale. She is the author of numerous journal articles and monographs related to communication pedagogy. Her research interests include intercultural and multicultural pedagogy, the communication needs of at-risk student populations, and communication anxiety across cultural boundaries.

Hodge, L. W.
Laurie Wilfred Hodge is Associate Professor in Communication at Bergen County Community College in New Jersey. He has a special interest in communication anxiety, and communication for the international student.

Johnson, R.

Ruth Johnson is an Assistant Professor in the Department of Linguistics at Southern Illinois University at Carbondale. Her research interests include investigating ways of teaching intercultural communication in the ESL classroom and understanding student teachers' conceptions of themselves as teachers.

Kunimoto, E. N.

Elizabeth Nakaeda Kunimoto is Associate Professor and Chair of the Department of Communication at the University of Hawaii-Manoa in Honolulu, Hawaii. She and Gary L. Kreps have co-authored *Effective Communication in Multicultural Health Care Settings.* She is a licensed psychologist whose practice is in a classroom rather than a clinical setting, focusing on the prevention of psychopathology through multicultural communication proficiency. Kunimoto's chapter, "Multicultural Issues in Health Communication," served as a Plenary Address at the 1996 RIT Conference.

Lang, E.

Eveline Lang, Associate Professor at the Department of Speech and Theatre Arts at Shippensburg University, Shippensburg, PA, received her M.A. (Sociology) and Ph.D. (Communication) from Ohio University. Her research interests include critical pedagogy, critical perspectives on communication theory and research methods, feminist approaches to the study of human communication, critical perspectives on technology and communication, and research in culture and communication.

McLean, G. S.

Gordon Scott McLean, from Omak, Washington, on the Western edge of the Colville Indian Reservation, directed the Healthy Nations program in Warm Springs, Oregon, and holds a masters in communication from the Edward R. Murrow School of Communication, Washington State University. He is at the Thomas Jefferson School in Concepcion, Chile.

Monfils, B. S.

Barbara S. Monfils earned a B.A. degree in speech communication and a B.S. in computer science. She earned her M.A. and Ph.D. degrees at Indiana University. She has published in regional, national, and international journals. She is Associate Professor of Communication at the University of Wisconsin-Whitewater.

Neumann, D. R.

David R. Neumann (Ph.D. 1987, Bowling Green State University) is an Associate Professor, and former Chair of Professional and Technical Communication at the Rochester Institute of Technology. His areas of research range from organizational culture to mental imagery and visualization. He is also an experienced waiter and lobster cook.

Ognianova, E.
Ekaterina Ognianova, a former journalist from Bulgaria, has participated in and helped organize intercultural journalism programs. She has master's degrees from Sofia University and Indiana University. She wrote this chapter during her doctoral studies in journalism at the University of Missouri-Columbia. She is an Assistant Professor at Southwestern Texas University in Mass Communication.

Olubodun, W.
William Olubodun studied in Nigeria and at Gallaudet University. He has been an Assistant Professor and is the Coordinator of Multicultural Activities at the National Technical Institute for the Deaf at the Rochester Institute of Technology. He is a doctoral student at the University of Nebraska-Lincoln.

Over, W.
William Over, Associate Professor in St. Vincent's College at St. John's University in Jamaica New York, has an extensive background in theatre, language, and philosophy. His book, *Human Rights in the International Public Sphere: Civic Discourse for the 21st Century,* is in progress for the Ablex Series: "Civic Discourse for the Third Millennium."

Ramesh, C.
Closepet Ramesh (Ph.D., Michigan State University) is an Associate Professor of Communication at Truman State University. Before coming to the U.S. he worked as a bank officer, a school teacher, and a copy editor in India. His current research interests include conflict and negotiation studies.

Rodríguez-Rodríguez, A. L.
Aixa L. Rodríguez-Rodríguez is an Assistant Professor of Mass Communication at Quinnipiac College in Hamden, Connecticut. Her area of specialization is Critical and Cultural Studies, with emphasis on Media Studies, Latin American Cultural Studies and Puerto Rican popular music.

Ross, R. B.
Roberta Bell Ross is a doctoral candidate and former instructor in the Speech Communication Department at The Pennslyvania State University. Her research interests include intercultural, interpersonal, and organizational communication.

Varis, T.
Tapio Varis, formerly of the University of Helsinki, is Chair of the Communication Department at the University of Tampere. He is internationally known as an European leader in the study of mass communication as well as distance learning. He served as a Plenary Address speaker at the 1996 RIT Conference and as the Keynoter at the 1997 RIT Conference.

Wilhelm, K. H.

Kim Hughes Wilhelm is an Assistant Professor of Linguistics at Southern Illinois University in Carbondale. She taught four years in Malaysia with the Indiana University Shah Alam Cooperative University Program. Other overseas teaching experience includes The Chinese University of Hong Kong.

Williams, P. L.

Princess L. Williams is a graduate student of Speech Communication at Syracuse University. Her long range interest is to help improve intercultural communication. She received her B.S. in Speech Communication at Syracuse University and plans to pursue a Ph.D. in Speech Communication specializing in the area of intercultural communication.

Yum, Y.

Young-ok Yum is a doctoral candidate in the Department of Speech Communication at The Pennsylvania State University . Her area of focus is interpersonal communication, particularly, relational maintenance behaviors used by romantic couples. She received her Master's degree in Teaching English as a Second Language and is interested in applying interpersonal communication theories to classroom teaching. Her chapter, "The Communication Stereotypes of Whites and Asians in the White-dominated Classroom," was the Student Outstanding Paper at the 1996 RIT Conference.

ABOUT THE EDITORS

K.S. Sitaram (left)
K.S. Sitaram, Professor of Radio-Television at Southern Illinois University at Carbondale, is the coauthor of *Foundations of Intercultural Communication* and author of *Communication and Culture: A World View.* He has had broadcasting experience in India, where he has also been a Fulbright scholar, and has taught in such American universities as the University of Hawaii, University of Utah, and Governor's State University. Sitaram was the founding chair of the Intercultural and Development Communication Division of the International Communication Association.

Michael H. Prosser (right)
Michael H. Prosser, Kern Professor in Communications at the Rochester Institute of Technology (1994-1998) and Professor at the University of Virginia since 1972, has taught in other American and Canadian universities, and was a Fulbright Professor in the University of Swaziland. Prosser founded the Commission leading to the current International and Intercultural Communication Division of the National Communication Association. Editor or author of eight published books, he is series editor for "Civic Discourse for the Third Millennium" being published by Ablex.